From M

Peter Taane

socialist books

From Militant to the Socialist Party

Peter Taaffe

© Socialist Publications 2017

First Edition May 2017

Classification: Peter Taaffe

History/Politics/Economics/Sociology/Current Affairs

ISBN 978-1-870958-75-2

A catalogue record for this book is available
from the British Library

Published by Socialist Books, an imprint of Socialist Publications

Cover Photograph © Christopher Furlong/Getty Images

Printed and bound by CPI Group (UK) Ltd, Croydon, CR0 4YY

Contents

Preface

This book is a sequel to The Rise of Militant, covering the history of Militant, now the Socialist Party, from where that book left off at the end of 1995 to 2007.

Our original intention was to produce one volume covering the period from 1995 until today, 2017. However, once we began to assemble, sift and write about this period it became obvious that it would not be possible to compress the colossal events, and our role in them, into one book.

After all, this period encompassed the after-effects nationally and internationally of the collapse of the Stalinist regimes in Russia, Eastern Europe and elsewhere. This put its stamp on the whole political character of the era which followed. The disintegration of hated Stalinism was also unfortunately accompanied by the dismantling of the planned economies, which had previously been a progressive factor for the world working class in its struggle against rotted capitalism, despite the bureaucratic mismanagement by the privileged elite.

This was shown in the growth rates – which exceeded that of capitalism at a certain stage – and to some extent the raising of the living standards of the mass of the population, from underdeveloped economies to relatively modern societies. This contrasted with the recent miserable growth rates of capitalism and the social ills which flowed from this: unemployment and the widening gap between rich and poor that capitalism shows even in the most 'advanced' economies.

In this sense the planned economies, despite the monstrous incubus of Stalinism, indicated the potential, once freed from the grip of the bureaucratic elite and replaced by workers' democracy, for a democratic socialist planned economy. They were, to some extent, a reference point for the world working class in the struggle against capitalism and provided a powerful example of what was possible through real democratic socialism.

The capitalist ideological offensive which followed – with the help of right-wing trade union and labour leaders – maintained that 'socialism' had been once and for all buried under the rubble of the Berlin Wall. The capitalist media claimed with one voice that the future now belonged to capitalism with the prospect of new economic fireworks cementing its grip. A world boom would create a 'blooming landscape' first of all in Eastern Europe and Russia and then the rest of world, including the neo-colonial countries.

Indeed, in the infamous phrase of Francis Fukuyama, we had arrived at 'the end of history', by which he meant it was impossible to qualitatively and substantially improve on liberal bourgeois democracy that was now almost the eternal fate of humankind. This, in turn, was linked to the perspective of everlasting peace and prosperity. However, that perspective has been shattered.

We describe in this book the retrogressive effects that this had on working-class consciousness and the political outlook of the labour movement. We recognised that we – the Marxists as well as the working class in general – faced an historic defeat but not of the kind experienced in the 1930s. Then, the triumph of fascism through Hitler, Mussolini and Franco led to the destruction of democratic rights, elections, the right to strike, as well as the dismantling of the workers' organisations: parties and unions. The effects of the collapse of Stalinism and with it the planned economies were largely of an ideological character, but at the same time did have a material effect in weakening the organisations of the working class, particularly the unions, whose right-wing leadership accommodated itself to the bosses in a new era of 'partnership' and social peace.

Therefore this posed new tasks for Marxism involving the defence of the past gains of the working class, including the historic aim of the Labour Party for socialism enshrined in Clause IV of the Labour Party constitution and in many of the rulebooks of British trade unions.

This book traces out how this battle unfolded in its different phases leading to the triumph of the Blairite right, changing the Labour Party from a specifically reformist pro-workers party at its base into a 'new' prop of capitalism.

This in turn led to us raising the question of the need for a new mass workers' party, rooted in the unions and the working class. We were the first to raise this but others, like Arthur Scargill and the late Bob Crow, later followed. We detail the kind of battles which were required and are still going on over this key question for the working class.

Other issues that we were forced to deal with, as the reader will see, were over a number of theoretical questions, particularly involving perspectives for the capitalist economy and whether or not a new economic crisis was likely or even possible in the light of the bourgeois claim that a new 'economic paradigm' loomed for their system.

Then there were the related changes in the position of the trade unions and their leaderships compared to the previous period. How could the unions be transformed once more into fighting organisations for the working class and what was our role in this process? What was now the position of 'Militant' itself? Was this still an appropriate banner, would it put off workers from agreeing with our ideas, and was it now necessary to adopt a new name fitted for the period we faced? These issues and many more are dealt with in this book.

The period we cover here resulted in an ideological churning, with splits and divisions manifesting themselves in all parties, both those which based themselves upon the interests of the bourgeoisie, as well as those who claimed to represent the working class.

How we faced up to this new situation – one of the most difficult and therefore challenging for Marxism – we leave the reader to judge.

Acknowledgements

In the same spirit as I wrote at the time of the publication of The Rise of Militant, I acknowledge tremendous help from many comrades and friends, too numerous to mention here. However, the following deserve special acknowledgements for their encouragement, work, criticism and advice. Firstly, Kevin Parslow, who has collaborated with me for many years, for his exacting research and gathering of materials, and famous ability to remember and verify facts. The following comrades have read different drafts of the book: Linda Taaffe, Clare Doyle, Hannah Sell, Tony Saunois, Bob Labi, Alec Thraves, Barbara Clare, Judy Beishon, Manny Thain, Niall Mulholland and others are thanked for the reading and checking of different chapters.

I would also like to thank Ben Robinson for his layout of the book and assistance in the latter stages of gathering and selecting photographs and Sarah Sachs-Eldridge for designing the cover and for progressing the speedy publishing of the book.

I repeat what I said in the previous book in thanking all those comrades who sustained first of all Militant and then the Socialist Party over years. I deeply regret not being able to mention all of them by name. Indeed, I have not been able to mention even all of the main participants in the many struggles to build our party. And the last thanks are to those full-time workers, past and present, who remained firm – in the very difficult period covered here from 1995 to 2007 – in keeping the flame of socialism and Marxism alive, and handing it down to the next generation, and those after them, to continue the struggle until victory and a new socialist society.

Chronology

29 April 1995	Clause IV of the Labour Party Constitution abolished at Special Labour Party Conference following proposals from Tony Blair
Sept 1995 – Feb 1998	Liverpool dockworkers' strike
February 1997	Socialist Party and the Socialist launched
1 May 1997	Labour wins landslide victory in general election and Blair becomes Prime Minister
6 June 1997	General election in the Irish Republic results in Joe Higgins' election as a TD (MP)
31 August 1997	Death of 'Princess' Diana Windsor leads to crisis in monarchy
11 Sept 1997	Referendum in Scotland votes in favour of establishing a Scottish Parliament
18 Sept 1997	Wales Referendum votes in favour of establishing a Welsh Assembly

1997-98	Economic crisis develops in East and South-East Asia due to growth of credit bubbles. Crisis spreads to Brazil and Russia
10 April 1998	Good Friday Agreement signed in Northern Ireland to establish power sharing
1999-2001	Series of anti-capitalist demonstrations rocks governments worldwide, beginning in Seattle and ending with Genoa
2000-02	Bursting of the 'dotcom bubble' in the US, leading to collapse of a string of companies including Enron and WorldCom
1 April 2000	Demonstration of 100,000 Rover workers and supporters against BMW's closure threats and redundancies in Birmingham leads to takeover of firm by Phoenix Consortium, which itself went bust in 2005
4 May 2000	Greater London elections see Ken Livingstone become Mayor as an independent
8-16 Sept 2000	Fuel dispute shakes Blair government
7 Nov 2000	US Presidential election eventually results in a narrow victory for George Bush amidst 'hanging chads' controversy
7 June 2001	Labour wins second consecutive landslide general election victory

11 Sept 2001	Al-Qa'ida attacks four targets in US including the 'Twin Towers' in New York City
October 2001	US and allied forces invade Afghanistan. A swift initial victory and the overthrow of the Taliban government are followed by a long period of occupation and turmoil
1 Dec 2001	Socialist Party leaves Socialist Alliance in protest at refusal to adopt a federal structure. Alliance later disintegrates
11 April 2002	Attempted coup by pro-US right-wing forces in Venezuela is defeated by mass movement of workers and poor and spurs leftward move of Chavez regime
15 February 2003	Mass demonstrations in protest against proposed invasion of Iraq in US, Britain and rest of world
20 March 2003	Invasion of Iraq brings a swift military victory but embroilment in a bloody occupation and turmoil in region for many years
May 2003	Scottish Socialist Party wins 6 seats in Scottish Parliament elections up from 1 in 1999
11 March 2004	Madrid bombings by al-Qa'ida cell raises anger against right-wing government leading to its defeat in general elections
26 Dec 2004	Tsunami wreaks devastation and death around coasts of South and South-East Asia

March 2005	With the threat of a big public sector strike looming, Blair government backs down over pensions' reform
5 May 2005	Labour under Blair wins third consecutive general election but with a much-reduced majority
July 2005	Mass protests against G8 leaders meeting in Edinburgh, Scotland
7 July 2005	Wave of al-Qa'ida bombings in London
August 2005	Hurricane Katrina hits New Orleans and anger rises against Bush administration
27 June 2007	Blair steps down as Labour leader and Prime Minister, and is replaced by Gordon Brown

Introduction

In The Rise of Militant (1995) we dealt with the origins of a small Marxist force and its development into a powerful movement. Militant in its heyday shook the serious representatives of capitalism and the Labour Party hierarchy to the core. This was shown in two mighty mass movements: the struggle of Liverpool City Council between 1983 and 1987, and the anti-poll tax campaign of the late 1980s and early 1990s.

In Liverpool, a colossal movement of working people, involving city-wide general strikes and mass demonstrations, forced Tory Prime Minister Margaret Thatcher to retreat and give significant concessions in 1984.[1] The Liverpool battle seriously wounded Thatcher but she was able to recover after 22 Labour councils which had pledged to oppose Tory attacks on local authorities deserted the field. Liverpool City Council stood alone, with the exception of Lambeth initially. It went down to defeat, ultimately, with the assistance of Neil Kinnock, the then Labour leader who infamously vilified the immortal 47 Liverpool councillors, thereby facilitating the aims of Thatcher. He will be forever associated with defeats for the labour movement. He was the gateman for Tony Blair and the subsequent destruction of the Labour Party as a workers' party at base for a whole historical period.

The poll tax struggle mobilised at its height an estimated 18 million people who refused outright to pay this iniquitous tax. This was Thatcher's flagship but it sank and took the admiral down as well! Thatcher herself was consigned to history and, as she admits in her autobiography, it was the poll tax that achieved this. It remains an incontestable fact that it was not the leadership of the Labour Party – under the perfidious Kinnock – nor the trade union leaders, let alone the noisy left groups on the outskirts of the labour movement, which defeated the poll tax. It was Militant and its supporters who supplied the energy, strategy, tactics and leadership.

This was not achieved without considerable effort and sacrifices. More than 100 people were jailed for non-payment of the poll tax, 34 of them supporters of Militant. Given the scale of the defiance and its outcome, this struggle, like the miners' strike, is forever engraved on the consciousness of representatives of the ruling class. They were determined to extirpate the lessons. Look at the way in which the most well-known leaders of the struggle, such as Tommy Sheridan, were hounded, vilified and ultimately imprisoned – as was the Labour MP and Militant supporter Terry Fields – through a campaign orchestrated by Rupert Murdoch and his newspapers.

Observe also the shameful coverage of the poll tax struggle on a BBC Radio Four programme in 2013. Not a single supporter of Militant was invited onto the programme, or any of the most well-known public figures like Tommy Sheridan, nor even those jailed for their self-sacrificing resistance. It is in this way that official history is written and distorted, not just by the ideologues of the ruling class but also by their shadows within the labour movement. This includes left-wing groups which, it seems, cannot give credit to Militant either in the Liverpool struggle or the poll tax battle.

The Rise of Militant was written precisely to combat such a false view of history and mark the important milestones in our development. We expressed the view at the time, as we do now, that we are not interested in appealing to the summits of the labour movement or tiny unrepresentative groups, but to the working class, particularly its more politically advanced guiding layers. With them we hope to draw out the real lessons of history, not for the sake of it but in order that they, particularly the new generation, can learn the lessons, the better to prepare for the

It remains a striking fact that Th
extensive analysis and account of Mil
forth one serious challenge by our op
to the details supplied. We were th
Trotskyist organisation in Western E
amongst the working class since th
International Left Opposition of the 192

The recent influx of thousands of men ... Labour Party
to fight austerity has produced a new interest in socialist ideas. A
product of this has been a renewed interest in the ideas of Marxism.
One of our old 'foes', Michael Crick, has republished his book, The
March of Militant, and there have been programmes about the
Corbyn phenomena in which we have featured. In one, Crick said
that the thing about Militant was that they were "brilliantly organised, brilliant orators. They plan things, know what they're doing
and they keep at it. They're committed, they put the hours in, they
go to meetings night after night after night and they commit huge
amounts of their own personal income and their lives"![2]

Trawling through the archives our opponents came up with just
one supposed 'damning' statement. In 1989 the headline over an
article I wrote was the 'Red Nineties'.[3] This was undoubtedly a mistake, but the same kind of 'mistake' which Marx, Engels, Lenin and
Trotsky made over perspectives. Karl Marx, for instance, predicted
that the 1848-50 revolution would continue because the economic
crisis would continue. However, when it became clear that the
French economy was recovering, he changed his perspective.
Trotsky predicted when the Spanish revolution broke out in 1931
that the bourgeoisie would not ditch the king. Yet such was the
deep-going character of the revolution, the monarchy was thrown
overboard. Like our latter-day critics, the Stalinists launched a
noisy campaign against Trotsky over his mistaken prognosis. His
rejoinder? "Did you foresee any better?" Of course, they were completely incapable of putting forward any perspective, relying on a
crude, empirical approach.

hen our 'infamous' statement was written, it was
ch way events were likely to develop in Russia and
urope. On the basis of the information in our hands it was
cluded that the youth and working class could succeed in
verthrowing the bureaucratic regimes and move towards setting
up democratic workers' states. An absence of Marxist perspectives
characterises these Marxist groups. They cover over their mistakes.
We use mistakes to educate our ranks on why they have been made
and to learn from them.

The last book dealt largely with the progress of Militant over
three decades. This did not proceed in a seamless manner, with success piled upon success. There were periods of rapid growth in
influence and numbers, but there were also periods when little
progress was possible. The class struggle and its reflection within
the labour movement – the trade unions and particularly the
Labour Party within which Militant operated at that time – did not
always proceed at fever pitch. There were times of slow progress
and even of stagnation which demanded slow and patient work.
Nevertheless, this period was generally marked by an upward curve
of the labour movement and of Militant itself.

By the end of the 1980s, however, this was beginning to come to
an end. A series of defeats of the British working class – the miners'
strike, Liverpool City Council, the victory over the print workers –
had an effect on the political outlook of the broad mass of the working class, above all, of the politically more developed workers. This
was reinforced by developments within the labour movement –
sharply expressed within the Labour Party – with the move towards
the right, including expulsions by the Kinnock leadership. Liverpool
was particularly affected with the expulsion of Derek Hatton, Tony
Mulhearn and many other leading figures who had led the council
struggle. The scale of the defeat was compounded by some political
mistakes in our response to the wave of expulsions.

Militant supporters had been trained in the importance of the
mass organisations, the Labour Party and trade unions. But this,
probably inevitably, assumed a somewhat one-sided character by

most of the leadership as well as in Militant's ranks. Expulsions were to be fought but not to be taken too far in the direction of a split from Labour because they were seen as temporary setbacks. Any attempt to form an alternative pole of attraction outside the Labour Party ran the risk of 'isolation' from its rank and file, and therefore political impotence. Such was the reasoning of those like Ted Grant and Alan Woods who split from Militant in 1992. In reality, the course I advocated in the late 1980s – of setting up a new party, initially in Liverpool at least – held out the best chance of preserving the lessons of the struggle and with it the members and cadres who had engaged in the battle. There is no doubt that, with subsequent developments, some of the 'independent' forces that would have been assembled by such a tactic would have dropped away following the collapse of Stalinism and the ideological counter-revolution that followed in its wake. However, much more influence and support would have been retained, even given the unfavourable climate, than with the self-defeating retreat and acceptance of the expulsion of leading Militant supporters.

It was this issue, first rehearsed in discussions that took place in 1987, which formed one of the aspects of the split in 1992. Those who at least belatedly took to the road of independent work in the 1990s have been relatively successful in retaining a significant force, which is having an impact on the labour movement today. Those like Alan Woods and his followers – Ted Grant passed away in 2006 – have been pushed to the margins with few supporters and even less impact.[4] This picture of the labour movement in retreat in the late 1980s, however, is just one side of what was taking place. During this time the anti-poll tax struggle was in full swing and was developing into a massive social conflict, which resulted in victory and the subsequent expulsion of Thatcher from office.

Nevertheless, the ideological retreat underway – particularly by the tops of the trade unions and Labour Party – was reinforced by the development of neoliberalism. The weakening of the trade unions and with it the supposed partial disintegration of the working class, deindustrialisation and globalisation of production, led to the development of 'post-Fordist' ideas. This was championed in particular by the Eurocommunist wing of the Communist Party gathered around its journal Marxism Today. We combatted these ideas, which were having a politically corrosive effect within the labour movement but the Kinnock leadership leaned heavily on these ideas to push Labour further towards the right and, in the process, marginalised the Labour left. This was enormously reinforced by the collapse of Stalinism between 1989 and 1991.

This represented a historic turning point, a colossal blow ideologically for the left and Marxism in particular. Its effects were not immediately obvious to those who lived through these events, including the Marxists gathered around Militant. As we have explained elsewhere, we had underestimated the degree to which the Stalinist Russian regime had rotted away, particularly in the decade which preceded its overthrow. The period of stagnation under Leonid Brezhnev and his feeble successors demonstrated the incapacity of these regimes to further develop the productive forces. Russian society and the other Stalinist regimes were in a state of atrophy, no longer capable of working within the bureaucratic straitjacket. The only viable alternative was for the working class to rise in a political revolution, overthrow the bureaucracy and establish genuine workers' democracy, which in turn would regenerate the planned economy and open up huge possibilities in all fields. However, the stagnation and decay of Stalinism unfolded against the background of a boom – feeble as it was – in the capitalist economies in the West. If these non-capitalist societies were to break with the planned economy and take the road of capitalism, promises were made that living standards comparable to the best in the West were possible. If not the levels of the US then at least those in West Germany could be attained, argued the capitalist theoreticians: "Blooming landscapes," predicted former German Chancellor Helmut Kohl. We commented: "But via Bangladesh."

Our prognosis was entirely borne out by subsequent events as the planned economy gave way to shock therapy and 'wild capitalism' resulting in a catastrophic collapse of the productive forces.

This was the greatest economic contraction in history, even exceeding the US Great Depression in the 1930s and brought with it all kinds of social horrors. Mass pauperism, the decline in life expectancy, orphans cast out into the streets and left to scavenge for a crust of bread, were conditions which lasted for more than a decade. I witnessed this first-hand on a visit to Moscow, St Petersburg (Leningrad) and Ukraine in 1998 – the results of the 'victory' for the oligarchs and their capitalist international backers!

Nonetheless, we were the first Marxist tendency that understood what had taken place and drew the necessary political lessons. As early as Boris Yeltsin's coup of 1991, we concluded that the pro-bourgeois wing of the Stalinist bureaucracy in the 'Soviet Union' had begun to liquidate the planned economy and was navigating a return to capitalism. The same process subsequently unfolded in most of the countries of Eastern Europe at various speeds depending upon their specific national conditions. Just what political effect this had is indicated by a subsequent comment of the late Cuban leader Fidel Castro: "It is as if the sun has disappeared." Despite Stalinism's monstrous bureaucratic regimes, the existence of the planned economies – the last remaining conquest of the Russian revolution – served as a point of reference for what was possible for the working class and labour movement internationally. Now that had gone and the bourgeoisie worldwide was triumphant, proclaiming through the Wall Street Journal that capitalism had won! The working class – particularly its more politically conscious layer – gradually understood the consequences of this defeat. I remember speaking at a meeting in Birmingham in the early 1990s when a member of the Communist Party, speaking for many who harboured illusions in the political system of Russia and Eastern Europe, started to weep when he recounted that his life had been wasted and now lay in ruins because the "Soviet Union was no more".

Militant supporters did not react in this fashion because of the priceless asset of the political analysis of Stalinism which Trotsky had handed down. We were irreconcilably opposed to Stalinism and wished to see it overthrown. However its replacement by capitalism signified not progress but a terrible regression. It was a defeat and a serious one at that. A sober analysis of what had taken place was therefore necessary if genuine Marxism was to avoid being thrown back. This was not a defeat on the scale of the victory of fascism by Mussolini, Hitler and Franco in the pre-war period. Fascism's victory had meant the crushing of the working class and annihilation of its organisations together with all democratic rights.

This victory of the bourgeoisie allowed it to conduct a ferocious campaign asserting the 'superiority' of capitalism over discredited 'socialism'. The fact that Stalinism was a horrible caricature of genuine democratic socialism – the idea of the planned economy with workers' democracy – counted for little against the propaganda barrage which was unleashed. The ruling class was fortunate that this process coincided with an economic boom – following the recession of the early part of the decade – as this seemed to reinforce their arguments.

If the restoration of capitalism had taken place against today's dire world economic situation – a crisis manifesting in clear depressionary features particularly in southern Europe – then the reaction may have been different. As in previous crises of Stalinism – Hungary 1956, Czechoslovakia 1968 and others – the working class and revolutionary intellectuals could have sought changes in the political superstructure of the societies while maintaining and regenerating the planned economies. This in turn would have thrown up the idea of a return to Lenin's genuine ideas of workers' democracy and socialism, combined with an appeal to the world working class to join them in a new socialist era. All the evidence shows that, initially, Russian leader Mikhail Gorbachev was seeking the 'liberalisation' of the bureaucratic regime from above. As is often the case, however, concessions from the top provoked revolution from below. Because of the dark night of Stalinism over the previous 70 years, no independent organisations of the working class had been able to develop. The pro-bourgeois wing of the bureaucracy quite clearly developed to become a majority in the late 1980s and seized the opportunity to sideline Gorbachev after the coup of 1991 and then, through the figure of Yeltsin, moved to install a brutal pro-capitalist regime.

What followed was the greatest robbery in history, putting in the shade the exploits of US gangsters like Al Capone in the 1930s. The consequences of this theft of state property – in which former Communist Party bureaucrats were in the vanguard – and the creation of obscenely rich oligarchs was played out in the British law courts. Rival oligarchs sued each other over who initially stole state property from whom – property belonging (theoretically at least) collectively to the Russian people. It was as if Bugsy Spiegel and Al Capone had recourse to US law courts to settle gangster issues such as who controls territory and the division of the swag from robberies!

It became clear that if the ideas of Militant were to survive then it would be necessary to face up to this now difficult objective situation. We and our international organisation, the Committee for a Workers' International (CWI), were clear about the scale of the defeat and how much the workers worldwide, particularly the socialist project, had been set back. We were now swimming against the stream and it was entirely different to the situation that we experienced in the 1970s and 1980s. Then we were going with the grain of the workers' movement and, because of our clear analysis and policies, we gained significantly. Now we faced a much more difficult situation, which required a change in tack. Others did not face up clearly to the drastically changed situation.

Those who had departed from our ranks – the supporters of Ted Grant and Alan Woods – were in denial about what had transpired in Eastern Europe and the former Soviet Union. In the early 1990s they still maintained that a capitalist counter-revolution had not yet succeeded! They finally got round to recognise in 1997 what had been evident to us for five to six years, that Russia was now a capitalist regime. This lagging behind events was not an accident. It became an organic part of the method of this increasingly politically conservative organisation, something we witnessed during the political disputes leading to the split in the CWI. It would manifest itself in their approach towards the 'traditional' workers' organisations and many other issues which developed both then and later, as we shall see.

Nor did other left organisations fare any better. The Socialist Workers' Party (SWP) and its international body, the International Socialist Tendency, characterised the collapse of Stalinism not as a defeat but as a 'sideways move'. This flowed from the erroneous analysis of Tony Cliff, the leading SWP figure, that Russia was not a 'degenerated workers' state' but a 'state capitalist' regime. Therefore, nothing fundamental had changed in the transition from 'state capitalism' to a 'normal' capitalist regime. They were among the only people on the planet, from either a bourgeois perspective or from the labour movement, who failed to recognise the huge historic defeat that had taken place. From the tabloid press to the 'learned' journals of capitalism, all were crowing throughout the 1990s that their system had emerged triumphant from the ruins of Stalinism.

Alan Greenspan, Chairman of the US Federal Reserve, later said that capitalism was the best system for "producing and delivering goods and services". The collapse of Stalinism led to ideological turmoil in which mass communist parties disintegrated. Moreover, some Marxist-Trotskyist forces capitulated to the prevailing pessimistic mood. All over the world, labour leaders were accommodating to the ruling class and becoming playthings of the bosses. Never at any time did we fall prey to this. The class struggle went on, as we shall see, in which we sought to intervene. This was not, after all, the first time that the workers' movement and Marxism had experienced setbacks and defeats. The working class had been forced to climb up the ladder of history step by step and sometimes facing huge obstacles. There were periods of big advances but also others when it was difficult to move ahead even by an inch. There were times when the class enemy dynamited the steps previously taken – such as under fascism. Undaunted, the working class rebuilds the steps in which to advance.

The 18th century ideas of socialism and communism – formulated by Babeuf – which were suppressed in the French revolution by the newly victorious bourgeoisie, were kept alive, as Friedrich

Engels pointed out, by a handful of followers "in the back alleys of France". They were later taken up by the emerging French proletariat, then given a scientific basis by Marx and Engels and subsequently embraced by mass parties in Europe in the 19th century. The Bolsheviks in Russia, following the defeat of the 1905-07 revolution, were reduced to a handful. Nevertheless, despite banishment, imprisonment, torture and 'Stolypin's noose' (the hanging of revolutionaries), the Bolsheviks were able once again to engage with the working class following the mass movements which re-emerged in 1912.

While the counter-revolution which followed the collapse of Stalinism did not assume the bloody and repressive form which was deployed by tsarism, it was on a much bigger scale, it was international in its character and was uniform. The Bolsheviks, even at the time of the worst repression, could look internationally and see the advance of the workers' movement in Europe and even the USA, with the success of Eugene Debs in the 1912 presidential elections when he received over 900,000 votes (just under 6%), equal to almost eight million today. Debs also received 913,000 votes (3.4%) in 1920, following women's enfranchisement.

There was no light shining internationally which was able to dispel the bleak political situation confronting Marxism and the workers' movement in the noughties. Not only was there an ideological counter-revolution, but this had very real material consequences in the sharp shift towards the right, particularly at the top of the trade unions and the workers' parties which were rapidly becoming ex-workers' parties. In the factories and workplaces the bosses went on the offensive. All the past gains of the working class began to be challenged: wages, welfare, housing, all were savagely cut. Rather than fighting and promising to cancel out the past defeats – particularly those inflicted by Thatcher and continued by John Major's government – the Labour and trade union leaders acceded to them. The outline of a decisive shift towards the right within the Labour Party became particularly evident as Militant faced up to the events of 1995.

1. End of the Tory government 1995

In 1995 the Tories could not escape electoral nemesis – the legacy of the 1992 European Exchange Rate Mechanism (ERM) disaster – and they were aware of this. The Observer reported from their 1995 conference: "Whenever two or three middle ranking ministers were gathered together the talk was of... what alternative employment they were each going to have in the years AD (after defeat)."[1] Yet Blair and the Labour leadership drove even further towards the right, shamelessly stealing the ideas and garb of Tory Prime Minister Major. The latter, in his evidence to the 2011 Leveson inquiry into press ethics, said he was not surprised that the Sun switched its support to Labour in 1997. He said he used to joke: "I went swimming in the Thames, left my clothes on the bank and when I came back Mr Blair was wearing them."[2]

As is our custom we began 1995 with a brief analysis of what was likely to face us, the working class and the labour movement in the forthcoming year. We wrote: "The Tories ended 1994 with massive splits and three massive defeats – by the signalworkers, over Post Office privatisation and on VAT on fuel."[3] The Scott inquiry into the scandal of arms sales to Saddam Hussein's Iraq was likely to force further ministerial resignations. We speculated that, because of the volatile situation, an early general election could not be ruled out. However, due to the ineptitude of the Labour and trade union leaders, the government staggered on till 1997.

The social and industrial situation in Britain in this

period contrasted with the sharp clashes affecting most European countries, particularly France and Italy. But we predicted that there were bound to be similar conflicts in Britain at a certain stage – 137 disputes had recently taken place within the Post Office alone. Yet it was precisely at this moment that the Labour leadership began the process of abandoning the party's historic aim of socialism, making fervent efforts to try and break the trade union link.

The issue of council cuts was a big issue then as now. Hundreds of thousands of local authority employees were battling to defend their jobs and conditions and to protect vital frontline services. Action by Newcastle teachers and council staff took place in February, while 3,000 people marched through Oxford in protest at the Tory-controlled county council's proposal for cuts. Mass meetings of over 2,000 council workers voted to reject the three-year pay freeze as part of a £20 million cuts package. Emulating what right-wing Labour councillors are doing today, Strathclyde Labour Council leader Robert Gould was challenged by local unions about what his group's political strategy was to solve the council's £107 million underfunding crisis. His comments were worthy of New Labour's response later: "We don't have a political strategy. We are an administration."[4] New Labour councillors merely act as a transmission mechanism for passing on Tory cuts!

However, the lessons of Liverpool's victory over Thatcher's attempts to inflict cuts in 1984 were still fresh in the memories of workers and the labour movement, despite the rapid shift towards the right that was taking place at the summits of the movement. We contrasted the capitulation of the right wing with the idea which formed the basis of the struggle of Liverpool: the adoption of a 'needs budget' to be fought for by mass mobilisations. If anything, the overall position facing councils was far worse in 1995 than it was ten years previously in Liverpool and elsewhere – and even worse in 2017. The Tory government's theft of over £1.5 billion from local council budgets was beginning to provoke rebellion, not seen in many areas since the demonstrations against the poll tax. The threats to teachers alone – it was expected that 10,000 teaching jobs would go – put pressure on even the timid leadership of the National Union of Teachers (NUT) to agree to a day of action the following March. This in turn ratcheted up the pressure on the local government union Unison.

The brewing mass opposition to the Major government widened the split within the Tory party. The economic upswing which British capitalism was experiencing resulted from the unexpected eviction from the ERM and the forced devaluation of sterling on Black Wednesday, 16 September 1992. Even the Tory supporting Daily Telegraph, through its columnist Peregrine Worsthorne, exclaimed: "The feeling of depression that would sink over the country if the Tories won again is inconceivable. I think we're in a bit of a 1945 position when the country's made up its mind that it's time for a change. I think there will be a very, very big swing to Labour next time."[5] The massive groundswell against the Tories had nothing to do with the policies of the Labour leadership. Dissatisfaction with the government stood at 80%, a record high and Major's approval rating plummeted to 15%. But there was no-one else in the Tory leadership capable of doing any better. While there was undoubtedly economic growth, its benefits were spread unevenly as the rich skimmed off the cream from the 'boom' while the real wages of the poorest actually fell.

The general dissatisfaction was reflected in the local elections in England and Wales on 4 May 1995. They were a catastrophe for the Tories. This followed the humiliation in the Scottish local elections with the Tories failing to win control of a single council, becoming the fourth party after Labour, the Scottish National Party (SNP) and the Liberal Democrats. In the elections in England and Wales the Tories received only 25% of the vote, their lowest ever in a national election. In their previous worst local council performance in 1981, the Tories polled 38% in the middle of a recession. In 1990, at the height of the poll tax struggle, they registered just 32%. There was speculation that they were going the way of the Tories in Canada where they had been reduced to just two MPs in the 1993 general election.

Consequently Tory candidates found novel ways to differentiate themselves from the national party. One greeted people with the opening line: "Hello I'm the sad bastard standing as your local Conservative candidate"! This was the only way he could stop the door being immediately slammed in his face. In the Manchester area, one hapless Tory argued on his campaign leaflets that, if a voter was depressed and lonely, they should start thinking what it was like to be a Tory candidate! Yet the elections were not an endorsement of Labour, attracting a very low turnout of only 30%. Disillusioned Tories did not vote but neither did huge numbers of the working class in Labour's traditional heartlands who had suffered cuts at the hands of local Labour councils carrying out the Tory government's programme. At least 20 Labour groups were 'power sharing' with the Liberal Democrats, even though this was prohibited under the party's constitution at that stage. Many Lib Dems ruled out sharing power on a national scale – something which the right wing of Labour was raising even then – because Blair's Labour Party was too right wing for them! On the other hand, psephologist Antony King commented: "The Tories aren't in a hole. They are in an enormous bomb crater. Devastation is all around."[6]

The growing anti-Tory mood was not restricted to elections. In June 1995 riots erupted in the Manningham area of Bradford. They were prompted by racism, police harassment and the searing social issues scarring inner-city areas, in particular unemployment and desperate housing conditions. At the same time local people were adamant these were not 'race riots'. It was certainly not 'anti-white'. The authorities were taken aback because, up to this time, Asian youth were seen as far more placid than young whites or African-Caribbeans. Yet people in Manningham were angry and determined to find a solution to the growing social problems in their area.

Reflecting the pressures from below, a gaping chasm opened up within the Tory Cabinet. Major's description of the Thatcherites – Michael Portillo, Peter Lilley, Michael Howard and John Redwood – as 'bastards' and their heroine, Thatcher, as "the grandmother of all bastards" was widely disseminated. They reciprocated by dismissing Major as a "wimp". Sixty backbench eurosceptics ridiculed him to his face at a meeting in the House of Commons just a few days before he resigned as party leader and stood for re-election. 'Nice guy, but a loser,' was the only 'praise' Major received from the Tory right. Major's gamble that his resignation would force his opponents to shut up rather than put up failed as the right-winger Redwood challenged him. We commented: "British capitalism still ruled over one-quarter of humanity 40 years ago. Its loss of 'Empire', together with its rapid economic decline, has left it as a minor player on the world and European stage. The evident weakness of the Major government... shows the decline of British capitalism."

Even then, almost 30% of the population no longer had an income from a job. Part-time working was taking root. The introduction of new technology should theoretically open up the opportunity, on the basis of the same economic and political system, to cut down the working week. However, more and more workers were becoming industrial helots as the bosses attempted to squeeze more from their labour, thereby increasing profits. Thirty-four million were unemployed in the advanced industrial countries, but more than 800 million were unemployed or underemployed in the capitalist world as a whole. In a prophetic warning we stated: "At the same time the piling up of debt, particularly of government debt, as a consequence of the profligacy of the 1980s, means that the capitalists will have to rein back on public expenditure or risk another inflationary spiral."

The general decay of world capitalism was aggravated in Britain with the frightening collapse of manufacturing industry – then down to less than 20% of GDP and employing just four million workers. We pointed out: "Capitalism will never be able to unify Europe, but the divisions over this issue [would] continue to divide the Tory party whether Major wins or loses... a general election." Heseltine was touted as a successor to Major, and we commented: "Heseltine... with that mixture of ruthless right-wing demagogy and brutal class hatred shown against the miners in October 1992, would do everything, including 'mortgaging the future' in an attempt to at least limit the scale of a Tory defeat."[7]

2. Blair's counter-revolution in the Labour Party 1995

The right-wing leaders of the Labour Party did everything to shore up the government. Tony Blair and David Blunkett openly supported grant-maintained schools, which led to criticism even from right-wingers such as Roy Hattersley. Harriet Harman, Labour's employment spokesperson, disgracefully accepted the Tories' opt outs from European legislation, including paying young workers less. Labour was likely to be returned at the next election but we pointed to Sweden where the biggest left vote in history had been recorded in the previous September's general election. This carried the Social Democrats to power yet generated no activity within the party as widespread opposition developed against the adoption of a savage austerity programme.

Blair adopted the law and order programme of Major, calling at Labour's 1995 conference for 3,000 extra police on the beat, and making the infamous pledge "to be tough on crime and tough on the causes of crime". More importantly, working class living standards had gone back under the Tories because real wages had dropped by at least £50 a week on average compared to 16 years before. In early 1996 we stressed that the official tops of the labour movement had fully embraced capitalism politically and the majority of trade union leaders likewise. Echoing Blair's approach, John Monks, General Secretary of the Trades Union Congress (TUC), commented: "The debate on the centre-left is no longer about socialism versus capitalism. It is about different kinds of capitalism."[1]

Earlier in 1995, we had launched the idea of a new mass party – initially suggesting a new socialist Labour Party. We later conceded that "the yearning for change will probably lead to the Tories' defeat and carry Blair into power. These hopes for change, however, will be cruelly dashed."[2] We expected that out of the splits that would develop in the Labour Party, recruits for a new mass socialist Labour Party would begin to be made. The precondition for such a party would be that it should be democratic, inclusive and not exclusive. Conservative forces on the left jeered – and continue to do so – at our idea of a new mass party of the working class. They point to the fact that this idea has taken hold in the British labour movement but conveniently ignore its traditions: the stubborn way that the masses cling to an old party, hoping against hope that they will be able to change and refashion it in their own interests. Look how long it took for the working class in Britain to disengage from the Liberal Party and raise on its mighty shoulders – particularly from the trade unions – a new party, the Labour Party, formed in 1900. Even then, it took almost 20 years for it to embrace the long-term aim of socialism. Truly an impatient approach bears no fruit within the British labour movement.

The dragging out of the process was also conditioned by the boom – lopsided though it was – during the 1990s and the first part of the new century. Blair in his memoirs boasted: "I won three general elections. Up to then, Labour had never even won two successive full terms. The longest Labour government had lasted six years."[3] The New Labour government lasted 13 years and he puts this down, of course, to his charismatic qualities: "The British people are, at their best, brave, determined and adventurist... That is why I will remain first and foremost not so much a politician of traditional left or right, but a moderniser."[4] Blair was only able to puff himself up in this vainglorious fashion because of the objective situation against which his government came to office.

Unusually, his Labour government was elected with the

economic boom not yet fully exhausted. When the first signs of crisis were manifested in 2001 the massive injection of liquidity by the central banks managed to stave off the crisis. However, this only aggravated those factors – massive debts and the accompanying bubbles – which led to the crash of 2007-08. This, in turn, prepared the downfall of Labour, which would have happened even if Blair had stayed in power rather than the hapless Gordon Brown. Just how alienated Blair had been from the base, the outlook and loyalty of the ranks of the labour movement, was indicated by his revelation: "I voted Labour in 1983. I didn't really think a Labour victory was the best thing for the country, and I was a Labour candidate!"[5] From the beginning, Blair and his like were the real 'entrists' into Labour – in the interests of capitalism!

But credit where credit is due, Blair was unashamed about his origins and his politics: "What sort of leader was I at that point? I had a philosophy that was clearly different from that of the traditional Labour politician. I was middle class, and my politics were in many ways middle class... I didn't want class war."[6] Nevertheless, class war is a fact and Blair throughout his prime ministership was a better representative – more fitted for the times – than the Tories in carrying out class politics in the interest of big business.

From the outset he hated the Labour left, with special venom reserved for Militant. He recounts a journey back from a meeting in the company of Tony Benn: "We talked about Militant. I wanted to know what he thought about this Trotskyist sect that had infiltrated Labour. I was representing the party in the legal case against them and, having studied them and their methods, I knew there was no dealing with them, other than by expelling them. He didn't agree, and I spotted the fundamental weaknesses in this position: he was in love with his role as idealist, as standard-bearer, as the man of principle against the unprincipled careerist MPs."[7] In some ways this sums up what the Labour Party became under Blair – and in contrast to what it could have become if Benn had won the deputy leadership in 1981. Blair was to preside over 13 disastrous years of right-wing Labour government which resulted in a hollowed out organisational shell and almost five million lost general election votes. Benn enjoyed widespread support and affection within the ranks of the labour movement until his death in 2014 and after, despite the fact that he quite wrongly clung to the wreckage of the Labour Party.

The years 1995 and 1996 stand out as the time when the Blair counter-revolution against the Labour Party – previously a workers' party at its base – was carried out. This vindicated the analysis of the majority in Militant during an internal debate which culminated in a minority led by Ted Grant leaving our ranks. Blair was compelled, at first, to disguise his intentions about the change in the constitution – the elimination of Clause IV Part 4, with its aspiration for a socialist society – as merely a 'rephrasing'. But it was quite clear that the aim was to create an entirely new party – a bourgeois radical party along the lines of the Democrats in the US. In his autobiography this is spelt out: "After the 1992 defeat, and without discussing it with anyone, not even Gordon [Brown], I had formed a clear view that if ever I was leader, the constitution should be rewritten and the old commitments to nationalisation and state control should be dumped."[8] Blair, a relatively new member, helped expel the alleged 'entrists' of Militant – who had decades of membership of Labour behind them. I had at least 21 years membership. The dirty work by him and Kinnock succeeded in ridding Labour of Militant. But this was just one of his and the right wing's aims. The rest of the left was subsequently attacked, as we had warned at the time of our expulsion. Indeed, the expulsion of Militant supporters and the heroic Liverpool city councillors represented a key moment in the shift towards the right within the Labour Party. In time this would lead to its demise as a specifically workers' party at its base.

Some of the woolly middle class left – particularly those gathered around the Tribune newspaper – allowed themselves to be persuaded that the attack on Militant was a one-off, that by our 'intemperate tone' and militancy we were partly responsible for the attacks on us. They consistently and completely underestimated Blair and what he represented. Whether Blair was conscious of his role or not is beside the point. The British ruling class, particularly Thatcher, had a long cherished ambition to destroy the basic class character of the Labour Party, determined by its link to the trade unions and its socialist aspirations as envisaged by Clause IV Part 4.

However, whenever the Labour right wing had attempted this in the past, they were defeated. They attacked the left gathered around Aneurin Bevan in the 1950s, even considering at one time his expulsion from the party. They were thwarted by the mass opposition of the rank and file of the party, particularly manifested within the Constituency Labour Parties. In the wake of the German Social Democrats' abandonment of their socialist aims at the Bad Godesberg conference of 1959, the Labour Party leadership of Hugh Gaitskell tried the same thing in Britain. They were met with a brick wall of opposition, particularly from the trade unions, some of whom formally stood politically on the right. Faced with huge opposition the leadership retreated. Similarly, the first attempt at anti-union legislation after the Second World War was defeated. Shamefully, it had been undertaken by the Labour government in 1969, with the alleged left-winger Barbara Castle the main advocate. Ironically, it was Jim Callaghan, by no means on the left but having connections with the trade union leaders, who led the charge in Harold Wilson's Cabinet against the proposed anti-union legislation. If Wilson had not retreated, it is no exaggeration to say that his Cabinet would have faced a split, which could have brought the government down, paving the way for the return of the Tories even earlier.

Blair succeeded where other right-wing attempts at destroying the Labour Party as a voice of working people had failed. He would never have been able to achieve this without the fundamental change in the political situation following the collapse of Stalinism (the effects of which were analysed above). This changed the overall class balance of forces in Britain and internationally, particularly from an ideological point of view. Blair, as a precondition for his success, wanted to distance New Labour from any semblance of the class struggle or socialism. He wished to destroy the trade unions' integration with Labour, in the manner of the Democratic Party in the US. There, the unions give money, claim to have 'influence' over the Democrats but are not affiliated to it.

Blair's autobiography is, from the first page to the last, a hymn of hate against the trade unions combined with laudatory comments about business. He laments: "Where was our business support?... Where were the aspirant people, the ones doing well but who wanted to do better; the ones at the bottom with dreams of the top?"[9] The basic idea upon which the labour movement is founded is the necessity of class solidarity as opposed to petty bourgeois individualism. Blair's philosophy was diametrically opposed to this. It allowed the bosses and their stooges to play off working people against one another, to constantly attempt to buy off shop stewards or corrupt them with petty concessions, such as a supervisory or foreman's job. Blair reveals that he cannot envisage a society without a dominating layer. Of course, special skills would be more rewarded in the first stages of the transition to socialism but any differential in wages and income would be strictly controlled. In the highest stage of socialism the aim would be for complete equality; in Marx's optimistic scenario: "From each according to his abilities, to each according to his needs." Absolutely ruled out would be the huge and growing gulf between bankers, chief executive officers and the like on the one hand and the vast majority of the population on the other. Workers who may be slightly more fortunate than others, having a better lifestyle, particularly if they are class conscious, still see the necessity for class solidarity and struggle leading not just to gains for some but for the idea of 'all boats rising together'. Just what Blair meant by aspiration was subsequently demonstrated when he left office, as he and his family amassed a fortune estimated at £20 million and growing.

Blair was determined to brook no opposition to plans to abandon Clause IV and weaken union influence: "From the very beginning I was determined to be the architect of something revolutionary, transformative and undeniable. I had kept the plan on Clause IV very tight. On the opening weekend of party conference, just before the beginning, I started consultations with other key people."

Recruited to the cause was Jack Straw, "who had written a pamphlet on the subject, and was delighted".[10] Straw had spent many years cultivating a reputation as a 'left'. He had moved towards the right, particularly playing a pernicious role in attacks on Militant supporters who were influential in the struggle of Liverpool City Council. He later buttressed Blair during the Iraq war, swallowing the fairy tale about 'weapons of mass destruction'. It has subsequently been revealed that, while he was Home Secretary, Straw covered up the Hillsborough scandal – when 96 Liverpool football supporters were crushed to death on 15 April 1989. Consequently, he is loathed and held in contempt by the families of the victims, as well as the left inside and outside the Labour Party.

In his autobiography, Straw claims to have suffered for years with depression, even stating explicitly that this was caused by the 'Militant tendency' in the early 1980s! The Liverpool councillors who faced losing their homes and were barred from office for standing up for working class people, workers blacklisted from their occupations and those who saw family members die deserve every support and sympathy to deal with depression and mental illness. Straw, the opportunistic 'Vicar of Bray', has made his career by cynically switching his positions and ideas when it is most advantageous to himself. At the time of the controversy over the elimination of Clause IV Part 4 from Labour's constitution, he brazenly confessed to the Independent: "No longer do we have to worship false gods, utter prayers that have lost all meaning. Instead, for the first time in my political life, ordinary party members have had the confidence to speak openly about how a democratic socialist movement can embrace the market economy with values of justice, fairness and equity; of different forms of capitalism, rejecting the false dichotomy between 'socialism and capitalism.'"[11]

This was a complete rupture with the ideas upon which the Labour Party was based – certainly since 1918 – of breaking from capitalism and initiating a new socialist society. Moreover, it was taking place when capitalism worldwide was incapable of significantly improving the conditions of working class people. The

International Labour Organisation did not have the same touching faith in the 'market' as Straw. It had reported that in 1994 one third of the world's labour force, more than 800 million people, were either unemployed or underemployed. And this while world capitalism – including Britain – was in the midst of a lopsided boom in which the rich were doing very well while living standards of the working class were stagnating.

This was one of the reasons why Labour was ahead in the opinion polls in 1995 – and not the alleged superstar image of Blair. We pointed out: "Blair's successful campaign against Clause IV is on the coat-tails of the capitalists' offensive. He was enormously assisted by the purge against Militant and others on the left." In 1985, at the height of the campaign to expel Militant and dismantle the Liverpool District Labour Party, Tony Benn said that it was not just Liverpool Labour which was being destroyed but the Labour Party itself. We wrote in Militant: "The expulsion of Militant supporters, with the acquiescence of some erstwhile lefts, was a body blow to the left in the Labour Party from which it has never recovered."[12]

We also pointed out that revolts of the working class were inevitable given the incapacity of capitalism to satisfy human needs. The more farsighted representatives of capitalism understand this. It is for this reason that the Clause IV issue had assumed such importance. the Economist, for instance, characterised it as a 'symbol', a legacy of 'Marxism' within the Labour Party which could be seized on by the mass of workers when a revolt takes place. This assumed that Labour remained a party of the working class. Writing in the Financial Times, Ben Pimlott, professor of politics, indicated why Clause IV historically occupied such a key position: "In the 1970s, the left began to present common ownership, once again, as the essence of socialism. In an age of grassroots industrial militancy, it became harder to argue that the inscription on every comrade's membership card was there just for sentimental reasons. Those were remarkable times. It is extraordinary to recall that in 1973 the Labour Party National Executive Committee advanced the plan for the state takeover of 25 leading companies; that the figure of 25 was reached because... if it was not quantified someone might try to duck out of the obligation." He went on to say: "Even this figure of 25 did not satisfy the hard left, which wanted to add a further 250 major monopolies together with the land, banks, finance houses, insurance companies and building societies with minimum compensation... all under democratic workers' control and management."

This learned professor failed to point out what we stressed, "that this later resolution was moved, with considerable support, by Militant delegates at the Labour Party conference in 1973".[13] Blair's right-wing leadership was therefore quite conscious that Clause IV was not just some outdated totem. In conditions of crisis it could become a beacon, a point of reference for radical policies, with the demand for nationalisation of important sections of industry – steel for instance in 2016 – if not for the 250 monopolies that controlled the economy. Today, such is the further concentration and centralisation of capital – a process described by Marx more than 100 years ago – that the number of monopolies which effectively control 75% of the economy is down to 150 or less. The exact figure will not be known until the company books are open to inspection by a system of workers' control and management.

Blair, with the support of the media, pushed relentlessly for the elimination of Clause IV. However, it met resistance from below, with a survey revealing that 60 out of the 62 Constituency Labour Parties (CLPs) that had debated the issue passed resolutions demanding it be unchanged. The leaders of some unions – the Transport & General Workers Union (TGWU), the General, Municipal & Boilermakers (GMB) and Unison – demanded commitments from the Labour leaders that they would renationalise the water industry in exchange for their support. Militant criticised them: "An attempt to stitch up a fudged compromise on such a vital question is a glaring example of 'undemocratic manoeuvres in smoke-filled rooms'. The union leaders should be fighting for the nationalisation of all privatised industries as well as the retention of Clause IV."[14] Blair talked of replacing the 'anachronism' of the clause with a modern expression of 'broad values', like justice, equality and opportunity. Nobody would disagree with such aims but they remained a pipedream in a crisis-ridden capitalist system. The press and the ideologues of capitalism never stopped repeating that 'socialism is dead'. Why then were they and their right-wing allies in the labour movement so ferociously determined to see the removal of Clause IV? They correctly feared that future big social upheavals in Britain – following on the heels of economic crisis – would crystallise mass support around the ideas of socialism if Clause IV remained in Labour's constitution.

Although expelled from the Labour Party, Militant joined with others on the left in the defence of Clause IV. When Labour's Deputy Leader John Prescott visited North Kent for a rally, Militant supporters organised a lobby of the event in defence of the clause: "We received a very good response from most who went in, selling over 20 copies of Militant, although a few of the more sharply dressed wouldn't take the leaflet from socialists like us... We'd bought tickets. In fact one of us had been sent a very nice 'personal' invite from John Prescott... We were about to take our seats when men in red-rimmed glasses and linen suits carrying mobile phones... appeared from nowhere. The stewards were surprisingly keen to speak to us, especially about the contents of our bags. As soon as they confirmed we were the dreadful lefties they suspected, we were surrounded by even more of them who asked us... to leave. Apparently we couldn't stay as we were members of an 'entrist organisation'. A local Labour Party member – a retired trade unionist, active in the movement for over 40 years and not a member of Militant Labour – who was passing, protested. He was told: 'You'd better leave as well'... So desperate were they to see the backs of us that they gave us our ticket money back out of their own pockets! Keep it quiet but we managed to get a bit more money from them than we'd actually paid – it's all going in the Militant Fighting Fund."[15]

As Tony Blair assaulted Clause IV, he also publicly expressed his admiration for the most hated Tory politician of the 20th century, Margaret Thatcher. In an interview with the Sunday Times, when asked whether Thatcher's eleven years in power did some good, he replied: "Yes. Britain needed change at the end of the 1970s." He added: "She was a thoroughly determined person and that is an admirable quality." Thatcher, as the conflicts over the miners, Liverpool and the poll tax demonstrated, was a determined class warrior whose stated aim was "the destruction of socialism". Thus, there was a certain symmetry between her and Blair. He went on: "I believe Mrs Thatcher's emphasis on enterprise was right."[16] We commented: "Perhaps he is referring to the enterprise which saw the gap between rich and poor, and between the highest-paid and the lowest-paid, grow to the widest in 100 years. Thatcher introduced vicious anti-trade union legislation to paralyse the trade unions. Blair confirms in his interview that Labour will not repeal these anti-working class laws."[17] This was borne out when he came to power as he and Brown maintained Thatcher's crippling legislation against the unions throughout the 13 years of New Labour government.

New Labour would not touch the anti-union legislation. This alone should have been sufficient for the unions to dump it and prepare the basis for a new mass party. It was, after all, the anti-union position of the Liberal Party, culminating in the Taff Vale judgement in 1906, which gave a massive impulse to the unions' determination to break away and establish the Labour Party. Blair's belly-crawling to Thatcher contrasted sharply with his arrogant attacks on the unions, still the paymasters of Labour. He warned that the unions would never again have an "arm lock on a Labour government; they would have no more influence over that government than the employers". And he was true to his word from day one in office as he bent the knee to big business and spurned the demands of the working class and poor. In a direct attack on the then TGWU leader Bill Morris, he said: "It would be good if the day before [Labour Party conference, he] was not talking about Labour and the trade unions but about what the unions are doing for their members." The capitalist press hailed Blair's speech as "tough, blunt and courageous". More than any previous Labour leader he was seeking to mollify big business by 'putting the unions in their place', even before coming to power. He was conducting a war, calling for the continual revision of the trade union block vote until it was reduced to only individual union members holding a party card. Instead of completely rejecting Blair's approach, Morris conceded that he was prepared to see the proportion of the block vote as a total at conference cut from 70% to 50%.[18]

Former 'left' ex-leader Kinnock supported Blair's project and willingly joined the gravy train which would follow in its wake. Like Blair, this had enabled Kinnock to mount the golden staircase to increased riches via the European Union (EU) where he was a commissioner 'earning' £1.85m in ten years! At the same time his wife added to the family treasure trove at £70,000 a year as a member of the European Parliament, while his son was also employed within the same institution. Overall, it is estimated that Kinnock was later 'worth' £10 million! Not bad reward for a self-proclaimed 'boyo' from the Welsh valleys, an apostate who is forever associated with using his left-wing credentials in order to stab the miners and Liverpool City Council in the back! The history of the labour movement is littered with right-wing leaders, and former lefts, who took the bosses' shilling and betrayed the working class. Their philosophy is summed up by the cynical comment of one-time Labour MP John McGovern: "I believe in the emancipation of the working class, one by one, commencing with myself."[19]

Yet none went quite as far as Blair in consciously setting out to destroy Labour as a workers' party, making sure that he lined his pockets in the process. In 1994, without consultation with any section of the party apart from his press officer, Alistair Campbell, he renamed the party New Labour. Moreover, he would not tolerate any compromise which would involve downplaying 'New' in the title. He wrote: "New Labour with a capital N was indeed like renaming the party." However, there was some resistance: "As if to underscore how difficult it was all going to be, the next day the party, at the insistence of the unions, passed a resolution reaffirming Clause IV... For me, I was absolutely clear: if the change was rejected, I was off."[20] Blair's blackmail worked in the debate which evolved over the following six months, as one after another the different sections of the party – beginning with the Scottish Labour Party – voted for change.

It had been expected that opposition to the removal of Clause IV would be greater in Scotland because of its militant fighting traditions. Therefore, it was with some surprise that the Scottish Labour Party voted by a larger margin than expected to ditch the clause, with 58% to 42% in favour of 'reforming' Labour's constitution. While the leadership wined and dined, 50 yards down the road supporters of Clause IV heard a passionate speech in its defence by Tony Benn. At the Campaign Group meeting he reminded everyone that hearts and minds are not won by mere sound bites but by debate and argument: "Don't think it was Kinnock who got rid of the poll tax, as opposed to the mass campaign of non-payment, for he was too busy expelling Tommy Sheridan from the party to do anything else."[21]

At Labour's special national conference the atmosphere was muted because the decision to scrap Clause IV was decided well in advance – even the speakers were predetermined. Delegates were forced to fill in speakers' cards, a well-known right-wing device for stitching up debates. Benn, Labour's longest serving MP, tried to speak throughout the debate on this vital issue but shamefully was not called. The right-wing evolution which had even corroded its base was reflected most glaringly in the CLP delegates. At past conferences right-wing union leaders had usually attacked the left-wing constituencies. This time right-wing CLP delegates attacked the unions for their 'irresponsibility' in not backing the elimination of Clause IV. Arthur Scargill, leader of the National Union of Mineworkers (NUM), was slow handclapped as he pointed out that the way the change in the constitution had been undertaken had actually broken the party's constitution, which only allowed rule changes to be made at the annual conference.

Incredibly, 90% of the constituency delegates voted for Blair's abandonment of socialist principles, something that would have been absolutely unheard of in the 1950s and 1960s boom when the rank and file were consistently on the left. But the new breed of 'delegates' – smart suited careerists seeking a shortcut to power and influence – were far removed from worker delegates of the past. Only two out of eleven CLP speakers opposed the dropping of Clause IV. The mood was captured by Garfield Davies of the shop-workers' union USDAW. He concluded that one of the three land-marks in the recent history of the party had been Kinnock's attack on Militant, claiming it saved the party and ensured that the aboli-tion of Clause IV could happen.

In opposition constituency delegates reminded the conference that when the Gang of Four split to form the Social Democratic Party in 1981, they had demanded that Labour should abolish Clause IV, introduce one member one vote and break with the unions. "Doesn't this sound familiar?" asked one. Another "recalled that Labour had won its largest ever parliamentary majority in 1945 by promising and carrying through a programme of public owner-ship of the railways, pits, and creating the National Health Service".

Even in this 'Blairised' conference some opposition was evident from right-wing unions. John Edmonds of the GMB said: "It's no secret that the GMB would have written this new clause differently." Nevertheless, they went along with Blair largely because working people and particularly the unions were desperate for a change of government. They therefore swallowed the argument that 'mod-ernisation' was necessary to get rid of the Tories, even if this meant ditching principles. The vote on the amendment to abandon Clause IV was 65% in favour with 34% against. The unions were split with 38% in favour and almost 32% against, while the CLPs voted in favour with a meagre 3% against! Many delegates were disgusted and walked out of the conference, some of them greeting Militant Labour members outside, including Dave Nellist, the Labour MP for Coventry South East during 1983-92, who had been expelled in 1991 for his socialist beliefs.[22]

Clause IV was rewritten by Blair and Derry Irvine, whose claim to fame was that he was the barrister used by the Labour Party

right wing to expel Militant. An innocuous new clause was adopted where all mention of socialism, the idea of a planned economy
and nationalisation, were expunged. Blair was ecstatic: "Although
we were only a small group of co-conspirators, as time went on we
drew significant numbers of people to us."[23] It should not be forgotten that it was not only Blair but also Brown who was one of
the architects of New Labour. As the author of the Red Book, pro-
fessing "red blooded socialism" in the past, Brown bears joint
responsibility for the party's swing towards the right. His conflict
with Blair was within the New Labour apparatus, a personal
struggle for power.

Blair himself said that the elimination of Clause IV was a "defining moment" for the Labour Party, quite clearly indicating that he
had been successful in changing its class character. However, much
as he would bask in this unique "personal achievement", the reality
was that a similar process had developed worldwide. The shift
towards the right of 'socialist', 'labour' and even 'communist' parties
indicated a wide, deep-going ideological shift. The political wind
was in the sails of all those organisations that positioned themselves
within the framework of capitalism. Alternatively, those who
defended the 'socialist project' were forced to swim against the
stream, not for the first time in history.

Yet few generations of socialists had faced such a daunting task.
For instance, the forces of British Trotskyism faced a similar situation in the period from 1950 to the late 1960s when radicalisation in the trade unions and amongst the youth began to develop.
The long boom, which led to significant rises in the standard of
living of the working class, in turn strengthened the ideas of
reformism within Labour and the trade unions: of incremental
changes which hopefully would lead to the 'gradual' establishment of socialism. This was the dominant view, particularly of the
left wing of the labour movement. In this situation the
Revolutionary Communist Party (RCP) of 1944-49, which at its
height had 500 members, was bound to be thrown back and relatively isolated. It was reduced to a handful of members divided

into three main groups: the Ted Grant group, out of which came Militant; Tony Cliff's group, the current Socialist Workers' Party (swp); and the hooligan sect led by Gerry Healy which became the Workers' Revolutionary Party (wrp).

However, now in a much more difficult situation, Militant and its successor organisation, the Socialist Party, withstood pressures more successfully than the rcp and its counterparts during the post-war boom. Although we suffered a membership decline in the 1990s, aggravated by the splits and divisions that we suffered – touched on in The Rise of Militant and which we will describe later – this was not on the scale of the collapse of the rcp. We retained a significant membership never less than 1,000, a firm base in the trade unions and an important position amongst young people.

Because the wheel of history had been turned back by the ship-wreck of the mass working class parties and, to some extent, the bureaucratisation of the trade unions, we were faced with a funda-mentally new situation. Tasks which were posed in the formative period of the labour movement became relevant again. For instance, it was necessary to defend the basic ideas of socialism, to answer the barrage of anti-socialist propaganda and, above all, to seek to win over those of the new generation who came into conflict with capitalism – as they would, even in a 'boom' period. At the same time, it was crucial to maintain a Marxist perspective and organisa-tion which would be decisive in the long run in constructing a force which could lead the battles of the working class in all its phases, but particularly in the struggle for socialism. We identified these as the 'dual tasks'. A vital part of this – now that the Blair counter-revolution had destroyed the workers' political voice – was to fight for new, broad socialist parties of the working class while maintain-ing the thread of a revolutionary, Marxist perspective and organisation.

3. Blair encourages the Tories 1995

Blair lost no time in continuing his ideological counter-revolution following his victory on Clause IV by changing all policies which did not accord with a pro-capitalist agenda, even if he came into conflict with public opinion. Rail privatisation was opposed not just by the rail unions and the trade union and labour movement as a whole, but by voters. The Sunday Times – controlled by Murdoch – found that only 16% of voters supported rail privatisation. Even 48% of Tory voters were in opposition. Yet the New Labour leaders steadfastly refused to give an unequivocal commitment to renationalisation.

This only served to give confidence to the Major government in pressing ahead with privatisation. They calculated that if they could flog off the railways for £6 billion, this would be earmarked for a pre-election tax bribe. Lines and stations would be shut, with only one station in eight selling tickets to other parts of Britain. Will Hutton, then writing for the Guardian, pointed out that if there was a clear pledge to renationalise the railways, the "top investing institutions would then be faced with a no-win investment decision... because the risks of Labour being elected are so high, the risk would be very high indeed. The flotation might even fail." However, Prescott, a signed up supporter of New Labour, said on BBC Radio: "Our commitment to public ownership will be tempered by the amount the Tories have privatised... Renationalisation, costing £4 billion is not on the agenda." New Labour repeatedly refused to consider renationalisation of privatised industries.

Militant commented: "It is as if [New Labour is] giving the government the green light to rush through as much as possible." Tory government ministers taunted Labour spokespeople about where they would get the money to take the railways back into public ownership. Embroiled as they were in rejecting Clause IV, they could not effectively answer this. We did: "It should not be a question of buying back the railways but renationalising them under workers' control and management without giving the parasites a penny compensation."[1] This represented a certain hardening of our position. Our usual position was to concede compensation, but on the basis of proven need. However, given that the privatisation of the railways had not yet taken place, it was legitimate to warn those who intended to make big gains from the looting of public assets that they would receive no compensation in the event of renationalisation. Small investors would still be compensated, perhaps, particularly those who in ignorance bought shares in privatised industries, but we wished to make clear that the spivs and crooks in the City of London, gambling with public assets, deserved to lose by getting nothing!

Blair, in his autobiography, spelt out in detail how he used his victory on Clause IV to bolster his right-wing agenda: "No return to the old union laws; no renationalisation of privatised utilities; no raising of the top rate of tax; no unilateralism; no abolition of grammar schools... pro-Europe and pro-US... even-handedness between business and labour (employees might have additional individual rights, but not collective ones)."[2] And Blair left nothing to chance. He was determined to push his pro-capitalist counter-revolution through to the end: "Between 1995 and 1997, even after Clause IV, I was in a perpetual motion of reassurance. The more the poll lead went up, the more I did it [shifted policy further to the right]. Members of the Shadow Cabinet would frequently say: Come on, enough, we are miles ahead... I would get hyper-anxious, determined not for a single instant to stop the modernising drive... Day in and day out, with the party's reactionary elements [code for the left and the working class] as my foil, I would prove them wrong with a raft of modernising moves."[3] Blair was making clear to the bourgeoisie that he was no danger to them. In fact, he was the best representative they could possibly have at that stage, leading a nominal 'Labour' Party but with an agenda which was more right wing than at any time in its history.

To emphasise the point he decided to visit Murdoch, the owner of the Sun, in his lair in Australia. It would be more accurate to say that Blair went on a belly-crawling mission to this arch enemy of every worker who had gone on strike – miners, printers, local government workers – and those who come up against the system, such as the victims of the Hillsborough tragedy and their families. Even Blair's advisers were against: "If I had told him I had a friend called Faust and he had cut this really great deal with some bloke called Satan, it couldn't have gone down worse. I also knew Neil Kinnock would hate it and feel, understandably, betrayed... Not to go [to Murdoch] was to say carry on and do your worst, and we knew their worst was very bad indeed. No, you sat down to sup; or not. So we did."[4] This underlined our contention that if you accept the 'market' – capitalism – ultimately you have to accept everything which goes along with it, including the diktats of the likes of Murdoch and his seemingly all-powerful Sun and other media outlets. Blair, followed by Brown and Ed Miliband, could not envisage any course other than bowing the knee to capitalism.

The sense of betrayal felt by workers in particular, as well as the labour movement generally, was summed up in an open letter to Blair which appeared in the Militant. "Ten years ago, Murdoch was planning to smash genuine trade unionism on the four national newspapers he owned. The dispute, which began in January 1986, was more than a struggle for jobs... You may have forgotten the printworkers' campaigns but have you forgotten the strike? If not, then why did you travel halfway around the world to address Murdoch's top bosses?... Did you ever experience the brutality of the police as they attacked the sacked printers? Surely, at least, as a trained barrister, you remember the injunctions against strikers or the court's sequestration of the print unions' funds? So how dare you even consider Murdoch's invitation. Is this part of New Labour's approach?... Are you so naïve to believe, as you say in your speech to Murdoch's chief henchmen and henchwomen, that Murdoch papers were 'anti-establishment'? The national newspapers, including Murdoch's five – he now owns Today – are all an essential part of the propaganda machine of big business. Anyhow, his editors do exactly as they are told. Way back in 1972 Murdoch made it clear how he intervenes in the independence of his editors."[5]

Those who went along with this, who saw no other alternative for fear of further electoral failure, have to accept their responsibility. They did not have the courage to break out of the straitjacket of a right-wing party, appealing to the working class directly. This includes the trade union leaders and what remained of the left in the Labour Party. Before Blair seized the crown the left was already in disarray and decline. Blair was completely aware that some of the left spokespeople of the past, like Dennis Skinner, supported him, imprisoned as he was within a right-wing, pro-capitalist party. Blair wrote: "Dennis was one of my best (if somewhat closet) supporters. He didn't agree with any of my policies, but he liked someone who whacked the Tories. Though I'm not sure he would thank me for saying so, he mellowed and became a nicer person."[6]

Tony Benn was more outspoken in his opposition to Blair but he also refused to take to the open road, to mobilise the massive constituency that was there for an independent party. Moreover, it was not at all true that accommodating to right-wing forces – because that was what Blair was about – was the only road for electoral success in the 1990s. Benn himself faced defeat within the Labour Party at every stage, as he remarks in his diaries, which are very honest even, at times, unflattering to himself. At the Labour Party conference in 1994, after he was knocked off Labour's National Executive Committee (NEC), he wrote: "At the end of conference they played 'The Red Flag' in jazz time and people waved Union Jacks, just like demonstrators for the Queen. Another Mandelson gimmick. Just turns your stomach. There is a semi-fascist element in the Labour Party at the moment, a 'hand over to international capitalism, wave your little Union Jack tendency.'[7] At his last NEC meeting, he quoted left reformist former MP Ian Mikardo: "He'd never known a bird that could fly only on its right wing. People laughed."[8]

He also records a discussion with the 29-year-old David Miliband, already an adviser to Blair, revealing Benn's opposition to the removal of Clause IV. Miliband replies: "I thought you would agree that we need wider objectives," to which Benn said: "It is the de-gutting of the Labour Party... Nothing in the world will ever persuade me to accept a dynamic market economy. I just won't accept it." This conversation reveals the gulf between Miliband – totally shallow and without any real understanding of the labour movement – and someone like Benn who, despite his limitations, did reflect the socialist aspirations of the rank and file of the Labour Party in the past. Benn's parting shot was to relate a discussion he had with a ticket collector on a train: "Mr Benn, I am a right-wing Callaghan-ite Labour man and I don't identify with the new leadership of the Labour Party." He gave some advice to Miliband: "I said to David the answer is that you have to keep Clause IV, and add others, as did Gaitskell."[9]

The Liverpool Militants had shown how it was possible to counter the lies, distortions and misinformation of the capitalist press and media. Following the victory of 1983 the Liverpool media, particularly the local Liverpool Echo, was unremitting in its hostility to the council, carrying all kinds of false information. This even included a story that "the Pope was unhappy" with what was happening! Despite the press barrage, the local Labour Party – under the decisive influence of the ideas of Militant – won election after election. The highest Labour vote for many years in Liverpool Council elections was achieved in 1984. The poll tax struggle illuminated the same lessons. The press and the media – despite the misgivings about Thatcher's policies – gave huge coverage to the propaganda in favour of the poll tax and virtually nothing to its opponents, particularly to the All-Britain Anti-Poll Tax Federation.[10]

Why should socialists be surprised by this? Throughout history, the ruling class has never hesitated to use their control of information to lie through their teeth and seek to destroy anyone who represents the slightest threat to their control over society and the means of production. They will always give support to the right within the labour movement in their struggle to shift the centre of gravity away from the left. The only way to push history forward is for the courageous minority to strike out on a different road, confident that the more advanced layers initially, and eventually the mass of the working class, will embrace an idea and organisation that represents progress for the majority.

With each passing month the Blairisation of New Labour continued unabated. An internal, leaked report for the Labour Party, 'The Unfinished Revolution', indicated that Blair and his supporters were not content just to change policy. They wanted to reconstruct the party from top to bottom in their own image. Appropriately, this report was written by a former adviser to both Neil Kinnock and US Democrat President Bill Clinton. It called for a "unitary command structure leading directly to the party leader", and for "an integrated party sharing the same political integrity". Militant commented: "In plain English, this means Tony Blair and his unelected clique of advisers decide and the rest of the party has no say." Even Deputy Leader Prescott was not given a copy of the document, which set out essentially to create a dictatorial right-wing regime inside Labour. Ironically, it mirrored those Stalinist parties to which the Blairites professed such hostility. Anybody who did not share Blair's ideological commitment to the market, it was now made clear, had no place in the 'modern' Labour Party. All ideas of the past about the Labour Party being a 'broad church' were unceremoniously discarded. One worker remarked: "Our party leader's nickname – Tory Blair – is looking less like a joke."[11]

However, Militant recognised that many Labour Party members and voters reluctantly acceded to the changes as the 'price that had to be paid' for the defeat of the Tories and their replacement by a

New Labour government. They were hoping against hope that, once in power, the New Labour leaders would throw off their conservative shell and come forward with policies which would substantially benefit working people. Traditionally, Labour voters have been fed the myth that the Labour leadership is compelled to play down radical policies in order to get elected. They were really 'wolves in sheep's clothing'. Blair did not remotely accord with this image. He was a sheep in sheep's clothing! Uniquely in the history of Labour, Blair was promising little other than being a better manager than the Tories of 'Great Britain Ltd'.

4. Time for a new party
1995

While Blair had eliminated Clause IV, he had not fully succeeded in formally breaking the link with the trade unions. Any continued connection of the unions with the Labour Party was largely at the top and through the inertia of the bureaucracy, which was incapable of facing up to the new situation. They were neutered as a political force within the Labour Party. Over time the trade union block vote was watered down, reduced from more than 90% to 50% at conference, effectively destroying their collective voice within the party. Thousands of socialists abandoned any prospect of transforming Labour into a vehicle for socialist change. Red Pepper, the radical periodical, estimated at that stage that there were two million people to the left of Labour. Militant commented: "Many of these would support a call to build a mass socialist Labour Party."[1]

Militant Labour, the name we adopted in the early 1990s, had been the first to raise clearly the need for a new party. Our previous perspective – even when we were forced to establish an independent banner – was that this was a temporary tactic. Once the internal balance of forces within the Labour Party changed – which we envisaged would happen under the hammer blows of a worsening economic situation – it would be reflected politically within Labour by strengthening the left. We would then retake our position within a growing left wing. However, this perspective was not borne out for the reasons we have explained and we called for a new party.

A new approach, a new orientation, was necessary if a genuine Marxist force was not to atrophy and disappear. The surprise election of Jeremy Corbyn to the Labour leadership 20 years later has not up to now fundamentally altered this orientation. At the time of writing, Labour is in effect two parties in one, embroiled in a civil war to decide which will win: the left in a new party or the return of the Blairites. However, we never completely wrote off the possibility of the Labour Party changing its character once more. In 2002, we wrote: "Theoretically, Marxism has never discounted that, under the impact of great historic shocks – a serious economic crisis, mass social upheaval – the ex-social democratic parties could move dramatically towards the left. Indeed, when we were forced out of the Labour Party, we worked as an independent organisation but with the perspective that events could later lead to a further shift towards the left in the Labour Party and the beginning of its transformation. Subsequent events, however, falsified this perspective."[2] This is what has happened to Labour since the 2015 general election.

However, earlier debate and discussion within the ranks of Militant Labour convinced the leadership and the overwhelming majority of our members and supporters on the necessity of proclaiming that the Labour Party was now dead as a useful tool of the working class and that it was necessary to take a different road. Labour, we declared, had separated itself from its history and in so doing was not remotely similar to its past. At times the Labour Party was a very effective weapon for workers moving into struggle, particularly in periods of heightened class tension. In the early 1980s, for instance, the Labour Party organised mass demonstrations against unemployment of 150,000 in Liverpool, 100,000 in Glasgow and elsewhere. You could not imagine any New Labour leader sanctioning strikes against the government of the day.

Even the elimination of Clause IV and breaking the links with the trade unions would not be sufficient in itself to put a minus sign against the Labour Party as a workers' party. More decisive was the consciousness and psychology of the working class, or significant sections of it, towards Labour. Then and in subsequent years, young people, many blacks, Asians, the unemployed, single-parent families, as well as conscious socialists, no longer considered the Blairite Labour Party as 'theirs'. Even the Economist estimated that 35% of the electorate supported Clause IV. That was scope enough for a new 'socialist party'. We pointed out that in France the vote for Lutte Ouvrière, a Trotskyist group, of 1.6 million in the first round of the 1995 presidential elections expressed the revulsion felt by many workers and youth at the betrayals of the French Socialist Party. We answered the argument that there was still space for the left within Labour: "The Blair leadership has either blown up, dynamited, or blocked these channels, even for the trade unions."[3] Our hope was that a significant split from the Labour Party would join up with a figure like Arthur Scargill to launch a new initiative, in which we would participate, but in a broader, federal form rather than the centralised bureaucratic structures in place under Blair and Brown.

Arthur Scargill, at the previous Labour conference, had floated the idea of building a new socialist Labour Party. Militant Labour, before the special conference which abandoned Clause IV, was the first "to call for the formation of a new mass socialist party". We explained: "In the past, Militant worked successfully, together with others, in turning the Labour Party towards the working class, as shown in the mass struggles like Liverpool and the poll tax battle. Then, we held out the prospect of the trade unions moving into the Labour Party in the future and transforming it in a socialist direction."[4]

Scargill seemed to agree with us when he declared: "I believe the case for a Socialist Labour Party is now overwhelming." He went on: "The newly-formed Labour Party made clear its aim of abolishing capitalism and establishing a socialist society – an object which many trade unions incorporated into their own rule books." He also berated those who naïvely still believed that Labour could be changed towards the left. Indicating the changes that were taking place over the selection of parliamentary Labour candidates, he said that, in dropping Clause IV, "New Non-Socialist Labour demonstrated its covenant with capitalism by its disgraceful refusal to endorse a first-class socialist, Liz Davies, as a parliamentary candidate. It had no difficulty, however, in embracing into party membership Tory defector Alan Howarth, an MP who voted for the policies and philosophy of Thatcher, including the butchery of health care, education, mining and other basic industries and services."

He argued: "Labour's new rules and constitution can only be described as an unmitigated disaster that make it increasingly difficult, if not impossible, for people within the Labour Party to campaign for socialism – which is no longer constitutionally enshrined as a vision to fight for." Correctly drawing organisational conclusions, Scargill posed the question: "Do we, and others who feel as we do, stay in a party which has been and is being 'politically cleansed'?" He therefore called for the convening of a "special 'Discussion Conference' to which all those committed to founding such a party should be invited with the aim of formulating a constitution and structure for a Socialist Labour Party."[5] Militant enthusiastically endorsed this call: "Working class people need a party that can organise a fightback. The Labour Party cannot play that role. A new socialist party has to be formed. But why wait? Militant Labour will support steps to launch a new mass socialist party."[6]

The idea of a new party found a receptive audience. In fact, this mood was already there amongst advanced workers and the trade unions. However, we warned in the pages of the Militant that, unless the initiative for a new party was carefully prepared, it could fail: "New parties can be compared to an aeroplane on a runway. Properly prepared and organised the 'plane' can take off. Yet history is littered with examples of 'crash landings', parties formed in high hopes which never actually get off the ground."[7]

We particularly stressed that a new party must be broad-based, embracing all genuine forces fighting for a mass socialist alternative in Britain. Crucially, it should be inclusive. Unfortunately, these warnings were not heeded then or subsequently. Where successful initiatives were taken in Europe, such as in Italy with the Communist Refoundation (Partito della Rifondazione Comunista – PRC) and the United Left (Izquierda Unida – IU) in Spain, success was only possible through adopting open forms of organisation and avoiding the bureaucratic structures of the rigid social democratic and Stalinist parties. The development of the PRC bore this out. Coming in the main from the Italian Communist Party (PCI) and its Stalinist tradition, although not perfect it avoided the worst aspects of Stalinist forms of organisation. In the PRC's initial period, when the idea of a new party was in the process of formation, Militant and the CWI recognised that it represented a significant development and an opportunity for the genuine forces of Marxism to play a role.

The development of the PRC took place amidst our intense debate of the early 1990s, which subsequently led to Ted Grant and Alan Woods separating themselves from Militant – after a vote of 93% in favour of the position known as the 'Scottish turn'. The minority argued ferociously in favour of maintaining an orientation towards the 'traditional organisations'. They were so wedded to this idea they discounted even the possibility of developments of small left splits from a big party. This could take place even when a workers' party retained a mass base but a left or revolutionary minority split away to form a small party which could then offer a united front to the larger party.

If such a development should take place in spite of their perspective, they invariably discounted that it could grow into a mass force. In relation to the PRC, they ruled out that it could develop because it represented a minority at the outset. Moreover, it was trade union leaders like Fausto Bertinotti, who had stood on the right in the past, who were identified with the foundation of the PRC. Woods and Grant's perspective was that the mass of workers would still turn towards the PCI despite its continual move rightwards. This actually led to the PCI renaming itself the Democratic Party of the Left (Partito Democratico della Sinistra – PDS). It then subsumed itself into the current bourgeois Democratic Party of Matteo Renzi![8]

Once they had seen that their fetish about the traditional organisations was falsified by the march of events – at least in Italy – they switched tack and, without any explanation to their members, entered the PRC. All the dictums of the past, that when mistakes are made – inevitable even in the best organisations – they should be corrected openly, were conveniently ignored by Grant and Woods. But it is not just a question of adopting the correct tactics – seeking to widen the influence of Marxism by joining with bigger organisations and forces in a principled manner – but how the tactic is carried out in practice, avoiding the pitfalls of sectarianism and opportunism. The organisation led by Grant and Woods adopted a ritualistic repetition of abstract propaganda without any real attempt to forge a broader alliance of the left on a principled basis.

The Mandelites of the United Secretariat of the Fourth International (USFI) within the PRC adapted opportunistically to the leadership of Bertinotti. Others such as Projetto Comunista initially listened to our advice, formed themselves around a newspaper and had a certain effect, even though they were ultra-left in their approach, including at the level of the national leadership of the PRC. The ex-minority of the CWI was reduced to a passive role and did not have a decisive influence. The forces around them during the dissolution of the PRC were no greater than they were when they first participated in its ranks. Compare this to the tremendous success of Militant, a small minority of no more than 40 members from the outset in 1964, which emerged from the experience of the Labour Party work with a huge reputation for mass struggle in Liverpool and the poll tax, three MPs and over 8,000 supporters.

In Britain we drew on the best experiences of new workers' organisations like the PRC. This ran counter to the arguments that Arthur Scargill put forward in relation to the foundation of the Socialist Labour Party (SLP). It will be impossible to capture the imagination and support of the new layers of the working class without drawing on the best democratic features of workers' organisations in Britain and internationally. It is true that there are differences historically in the way that parties have been constructed. Originally, the Labour Party was a federation of tendencies, including important Marxist forces. That federation tended to be undermined by the right through witch-hunts against left figures like Aneurin Bevan, Michael Foot and the Communist Party. But it had now been destroyed by the right-wing coup orchestrated by Blair and Brown. We issued the call for all those who accepted an explicitly socialist agenda to be invited to the discussions to set up a new party: "Appeals should be made to trade unionists to join the party."

We were quite realistic about what could be expected in this field in the first instance: "This would not lead to big affiliations from the trade unions initially, but that would come" in the future. Important layers of trade unionists would join such a party very quickly if it was sufficiently open and democratic. This was the experience of other countries. It is true that many of the older layers disillusioned with the shift towards the right would drop out of activity. We energetically pursued the argument that a refusal to take an initiative quickly would mean that the left would leave the field free to Blair's right-wing Labour Party.[9]

Very soon Scargill's call "generated enthusiasm amongst activists and working-class people in general. This is even before there has been much publicity and debate on the issue," reported Steve Score from the East Midlands. Alec Thraves, a long time stalwart of Militant, also reported that "at a stall in Swansea... two Labour councillors came up to us asking us how to join the new party". Similarly, Tommy Sheridan was approached in Glasgow City Hall by councillors who asked him if he had details of how to join the SLP. After this, Tommy was invited to Barnsley to meet Scargill to discuss the idea of a new party. Dave Nellist stated: "Arthur Scargill could play an enormous role in reactivating thousands of ex-Labour Party members and drawing in new people. I hope a Socialist Labour Party gets formed and I, along with other Militant Labour members, will do all we can to assist."[10] Dave participated in discussions on our behalf with Scargill and his supporters, as I did, on proposals for a new party.

The obstacles to forming a new party were considerable. Many arguments were used against: 'historical inertia', 'the time is not right', 'all attempts in the past failed', 'the Labour Party still has deep roots in the working class'. Scargill replied: "The significance of last month's constitutional changes including the ditching of Clause IV has not been fully appreciated by many left comrades who should know better. They believe it is still possible to reverse the 'setbacks' suffered as a result of Blair's destruction of Clause IV and abandonment of fundamental socialist policies."[11] Not just policy but organisation within the Labour Party was used to exclude the left, as the case of Liz Davies indicated. Scargill's call for a special conference with the aim of formulating a constitution and structure for a Socialist Labour Party – and to which all those committed to founding such a party should be invited – was the answer to those on the left who intended to remain in the Labour Party. We declared: "There are many who are prepared to fight for socialism; millions according to Red Pepper. They were to the left of New Labour even before Blair's counter-revolution."[12]

Militant Labour's creative independent work outside the Labour Party had contributed to this. The Political Studies Association in April 1995 referred to our work in Scotland. It said that our Pollock general election campaign "achieved the finest result of any independent candidate other than an independent MP since 1945".[13] And it was not just in Scotland. In Coventry in May 1995, Dave Nellist took 40% of the vote for Militant Labour and strong votes were also recorded in Liverpool and London. Nearly 60,000 votes for Roger Bannister, a Militant Labour member, in the 1995 Unison general secretary election was also a significant indication of support for us and the left.

However, Scargill's intolerant and sectarian manner was manifested from the beginning. He stated that if an SLP was formed there would be a demand to end "internal wranglings and sectarian arguments".[14] We replied: "Destructive sectarianism has no part in the labour movement. But a new Socialist Labour Party, if it is to attract the new layer, will be one big argument and debate and this will be a good thing. Discussion is necessary if joint action – campaigns, elections, civil disobedience, etc. – against the capitalist enemy is seriously undertaken."[15]

Arthur Scargill could not ignore, we argued, that Militant Labour had ploughed the ground for the launch of a new party. Even the Glasgow Herald stated: "The Scargill document... comes very close to being a blueprint for an existing model. Scottish Militant Labour already has made the struggles its chosen battleground... [and] has had some limited electoral success and has forged its own identity."[16] The same could increasingly be said of Militant Labour in the rest of Britain. This was based on an understanding of political conditions and also timing. For instance, Scottish Militant Labour was launched before the 1992 general election, which brought great advantages to the organisation afterwards. There was a lesson here. Big gains could not be expected in a general election. Workers would be eager to get rid of the Tories and the majority would vote Labour – holding their noses – to keep them out. But a socialist challenge would be an important marker for the future.

Unfortunately, Scargill and his allies did not possess the necessary imagination or openness to seize this moment to establish a relatively small but democratic socialist party. This was despite the fact that more and more sections of the movement were rallying to the call. Even a Labour MEP, Michael Hindley, wrote in the Morning Star, the daily newspaper of the Communist Party of Britain (CPB), which has consistently opposed the formation of a new party: "That door to democratising the Labour Party has been firmly shut and cannot be reopened. The party has been gutted of its democratic accountability."[17] In contrast, others like Dennis Skinner MP, at a meeting of Deptford Labour Party, used "half an hour of fiery rhetoric... [to rail] against Arthur Scargill's proposal for a new Socialist Labour Party". Militant correspondents at the meeting countered the arguments of Skinner, who revealed the poverty of ambition now felt by many considered to be leaders of the party's shrivelled left wing. He said: "Even if we get six pits reopened, and they've closed 170, I'd call that a victory."[18]

In December 1995 Scargill announced that there would be a meeting of specially invited people to consider the rulebook of the new party. This was preceded by an exclusive meeting on 4 November. Just 40 people were selected to discuss and take decisions about the party's structures. Individuals representing important groups and trade unions were present, plus members of the Haldane Society, the Southall Monitoring Project and the Scottish Socialist Movement. Militant Labour was excluded as Scargill was not prepared to accept our affiliation. He said that he would consider alliances with organisations like Militant Labour on concrete issues and discuss arrangements with 'individuals' like Dave Nellist. But on affiliation, the SLP declared: "Why do we need them? There should be no need to belong to another organisation. If I can leave the party I've been a member of for 30 years [Labour] to join this one, why can't everyone else do the same?"[19]

This was an argument that had been rehearsed in private discussions with Militant Labour's leaders previously. For instance, Bob Crow – then the Deputy General Secretary of the Rail Maritime and Transport union (RMT) – met me, as General Secretary of Militant Labour, and Bill Mullins our trade union organiser in London to discuss Militant Labour's approach. He said that Arthur had given up his party, Bob himself had left the CPB, so why couldn't we give up Militant Labour? We gently pointed out that Scargill, like many others, was driven out of the Labour Party in effect. As for the CPB, it was small and ineffective.

These arguments were a sideshow. The real reason why Scargill wished to exclude Militant Labour from the new party was a fear that we would 'take it over' because of our size. This betrayed a singular lack of ambition that the forthcoming SLP would be so small it could be taken over by one organisation, in violation of the general principles of federation upon which we hoped the new party could be formed. At the same time, in the Scottish Socialist Alliance, we were prepared to agree that no single organisation could have representation on leading bodies of more than one third or 40% at most. This would ensure that there could be no 'takeover', either in terms of policy or organisation, by one group. Moreover, there would be the goodwill of all parties to ensure that the project succeeded. Alternatively, it would surely be shipwrecked almost before it began if an intolerant approach was adopted as, unfortunately, the subsequent actions of Scargill proved.

Nevertheless, Scargill pushed ahead with a twelve-page draft constitution and rulebook for the SLP. All three representatives of the Scottish Socialist Forum, including Tommy Sheridan of SML, indicated dissatisfaction with the constitution: "'I'm very enthusiastic about the project but bitterly disappointed with the lack of autonomy for Scotland.' They made clear the developments in Scotland, in advance of those England, had been based on flexible, inclusive structures consciously incorporating existing groups."[20] It was clear that there was no room for this in Scargill's new party.

Proposed restrictions on membership flew in the face of the experiences of the formation of trade union broad lefts. In these bodies members of Militant Labour, the CPB and others worked openly and, most times, constructively together. We pointed out that the restrictions would jeopardise the very future of the SLP. It laid the basis potentially for some expulsions. Even the Labour Party in the 1980s established a register of groups organising within it (although Militant was excluded!). The SLP's proposed rule book sent out disastrous signals of intolerance and top-down control which would be anathema to thousands of potential new members. Some of the best representatives of the broad lefts would not be invited, excluding people like John Macreadie, former left-wing General Secretary-elect of the CPSA civil service union and a member of the TUC General Council.

Scargill's increasingly intolerant approach was at odds with the enthusiastic mood for a new party displayed at meetings throughout the country. In Liverpool 150 people turned up to the first meeting organised by Militant Labour to explore the possibility of setting up a socialist Labour Party. Representatives of the dockers, who were engaged in their own titanic struggle at the time, spoke at the meeting, as did ex-Labour MP Terry Fields. They all expressed great support for the idea. One docker, Terry Teague explained how their dispute had brought about the realisation that a party was needed that represented workers in struggle and stood in opposition to the capitalist system, as typified by the Mersey Docks and Harbour Company. This was especially the case after experiencing the national leadership of the TGWU refusing even to acknowledge their dispute by not sending a national speaker to their last demo. There was tremendous enthusiasm for a new socialist formation. Representatives came from all over Merseyside, particularly Knowsley, Bootle and the Wirral. Even Labour Party members in the pub afterwards said they would come to the next meeting.

5. New party, new forms of organisation
1996

This mood was soon deflated by the signals that came from the small exclusive meeting Arthur Scargill had convened. We warned: "Unless there is a broadening and opening up of this preparatory phase, there is the serious danger of a crash landing halfway along the runway."[1] Most of those present, however, simply endorsed the proposals put before them. This was entirely premature because no real debate had taken place amongst a wider layer who had supported the formation of the SLP. In fact, Scargill's constitution was even more undemocratic than that which prevailed in the Labour Party in the period between the abolition of the bans and proscriptions against the CPB and other left organisations, and the witch-hunt against Militant. It banned any member from supporting other 'political organisations' other than the SLP. This meant a far less democratic structure than the PRC in Italy, the Workers' Party (Partido dos Trabalhadores – PT) in Brazil or the United Left (IU) in Spain. Ironically, one of those present who reportedly supported the constitution was John Hendy QC, who represented several Militant supporters during the witch-hunt.

Scargill took refuge in constitutional measures while ignoring the fact that caucuses, trends and organisations are the reality of political life within the labour movement. He himself was undoubtedly involved in such caucuses, both in the NUM and the Labour Party. Indeed, he had met and caucused on resolutions with Militant supporters, including myself, at Labour Party conferences. Leaks confirmed that Arthur Scargill told Tony Benn about his fears of a takeover by organisations such as Militant. It was an unspoken assumption of many of those who were present that the constitution was precisely designed to keep out one larger organisation: Militant Labour. Some of the speakers supporting Scargill's constitution lavished praise on the campaigns of Tommy Sheridan and Dave Nellist and they were no doubt keen for them to be included on any SLP platform.

At the same time they wanted to ignore Militant Labour's political successes – achieved in many cases through broad campaigns in which we and the SML had worked harmoniously with other organisations and trends. Examples of this included the Campaign Against the Criminal Justice Act, the Campaign Against Domestic Violence, and the Campaign for a Fighting Democratic Unison. We predicted that there would be enormous disappointment at Scargill's approach from the wider layer of activists who were eager to support the formation of the SLP but were implacably opposed to repeating the experiences of the right-wing dominated Labour Party, and felt the need to debate all the issues which were then facing the workers' movement.

Militant Labour and others did not want to repeat the experiences of the Labour Party in a bureaucratic 'Labour Party Mark 2', even if it had the socialist aims of Clause IV. This did not meet the needs of the new situation. The collapse of Stalinism and the ideological crisis of the left that followed called for a far-reaching reappraisal of socialist strategy and forms of organisation. Both in organisation and ideas Scargill proved to be extremely rigid. Thus a golden opportunity to form a small but politically substantial party was lost. This was not immediately obvious, but Scargill's erratic and intolerant behaviour both at the time of the SLP's launch and subsequently alienated many of those who joined the party at its outset and those who were put off from the beginning.

Some of those did not give up on the attempt to regroup the left. Some participated in the ill-fated Socialist Alliance, which we will deal with a little later, and some in the Trade Unionist and Socialist Coalition (TUSC). It is notable that TUSC has been organised on a federal principle, a coalition of left parties and trade unions, the very principle that was rejected by Scargill. Nonetheless, we did not abandon immediately our hope that the SLP – particularly its rank and file – could be persuaded to abandon this narrow approach. With others we made a joint attempt to establish a powerful left point of reference for the millions who were disenfranchised by Labour's move towards the right. We took a positive attitude to the SLP in elections. For instance, in the Hemsworth by-election of early 1996, the SLP received a creditable 1,193 votes, 5.4%. We said at the time that this "vindicated the decision to break with Labour and make a stand for socialism".[2]

We pointed to the fact that in 1991 Lesley Mahmood, standing as the Real Labour candidate in the Walton by-election following the death of Eric Heffer, faced the vilest abuse from our opponents, but won 2,613 votes (6%) coming third and beating the Tories. Moreover, in the 1992 general election Terry Fields, as a Socialist Labour candidate, won 5,952 votes (14.2%), while Dave Nellist, for Independent Labour, got 10,551 (28.9%), and only narrowly missed winning. In addition, Tommy Sheridan, standing in the Pollok constituency under the banner of SML, won 6,287 votes (19.3%) from his prison cell – he had been jailed for leading the anti-poll tax campaign – coming second to Labour. This success was repeated in the European elections when Tommy polled 12,113 votes (7.6%). In the previous May's local elections, SML polled an average of 22.5% in the 19 Glasgow Council seats it contested.

This showed that, despite the intense hatred of the Tory government and the need to get rid of it – which for most of the mass of voters reflected itself in voting for Labour – there was an important constituency for a fighting left-wing party. This was at the time when MPs, including Labour MPs, were pleading poverty and were ready to raid the public purse for a wage increase. Dave Nellist, who had taken the average wage of a worker when he was an MP, along with Terry Fields and Pat Wall, commented: "I think that MPs need a halving of their wages not a doubling, to bring them into the real world of what the majority of ordinary working class families have to live on."[3]

Meanwhile, a number of conferences were organised by Scargill to confirm the SLP. At these meetings Scargill consistently ruled out any concessions to the arguments of those like Militant Labour who, although excluded from the SLP by fiat, fought for the maximisation of the socialist challenge at the general election through left unity. At the SLP's founding conference on 4 May 1996, Scargill claimed that the party already had 1,252 members with another 3,121 wanting to affiliate through trade union branches and regions. This was considerably smaller than the membership of Militant Labour at the time. Nevertheless, Scargill claimed that the SLP stood for "'revolutionary change' and put forward 'revolutionary arguments' against the capitalist system".

The policies put forward by the SLP do not bear out this description. Speakers addressed the conference from the Cuban CP, the PRC and the IU. The political attacks on the Cuban exiles received rapturous applause. However, during a debate somebody criticised the "lack of democracy in Russia, China and Cuba", only to be denounced by an older delegate, to voluminous cheering: "How dare you criticise Cuba." Scargill was to criticise Cuba later after a none too satisfactory holiday on the island! Militant pointed out that the international delegates at the conference had a different form of organisation in their own countries to the bureaucratic structures proposed by Scargill. For instance, the IU described itself as a 'coalition of forces'. Not aware of the details of the SLP party structure, the PRC speaker stated: "Like you, the PRC brings together different groups and individuals." The constitution could not be amended at this meeting – resolutions could be suggested for the following year's conference. However, to change the constitution would require a two thirds majority! Scargill's bureaucratic behaviour was already alienating many. At the SLP launch press conference the political commentator, the late Vincent Hanna pointed out that some Labour MPs were already saying that they would not join

Scargill's party.

During the debate on Northern Ireland Pat Sikorski – previously a member of the Trotskyist United Secretariat of the Fourth International (USFI) – said that they could not comment on or criticise the strategy and tactics of those "fighting the liberation struggle". This implied tacit support for the methods of the IRA. Terry Burns from Cardiff countered that the SLP was a workers' party and correctly argued that its job was to advance the interests of the working class, both Catholic and Protestant.[4]

Militant Labour still adopted a friendly approach. Our Executive Committee wrote once more to the SLP to ask for a discussion around the general election, proposing a joint campaign if possible, or at least an agreement not to stand against one another. This followed reports that the SLP had decided not to have any electoral agreements, especially with Militant Labour! We pointed out that we had had discussions and worked with many groups in the recent past, in many parts of the country, through socialist alliances and forums aiming at unity, and that we should have a united approach in the general election too. Moreover, prominent SLP members told Militant supporters that they were prepared to work with us but only unofficially at this stage because their NEC's attitude (read Arthur Scargill) said they couldn't.

The SLP's sectarian approach was taken to absurd lengths. At a meeting of around 120 people on 19 April 1996 in Swansea the SLP outlined their vision of socialism. Alec Thraves, long-standing full-time worker for Militant in Wales, reported that the SLP "displayed such a vehement opposition to alliances and electoral pacts with other socialist organisations that it took many in the audience aback". Bob Crow, an early adherent to the SLP, and Arthur Scargill, who were the main speakers, insisted that they would contest every seat in the general election if finances permitted. Alec reported: "When asked whether they would stand if it meant splitting the socialist vote, for example in Wales where Wales Militant Labour has received over 20% of the vote in local elections, Scargill's reply was categorical. The SLP would not participate in any socialist forums or alliances, he said, and would not enter into any electoral pacts."[5]

Scargill's stance was not reflected amongst all his members. In a Wales Socialist Forum meeting in Cardiff the following day the SLP were on the platform alongside other socialist organisations stressing a common strategy that could confront New Labour in Wales. Scargill repeated his position when he addressed 200 people at the Nottingham SLP launch saying, even more bluntly, that he opposed any alliances or electoral pacts with other organisations. Tactical voting in elections for other parties was out of the question as well. The analogy he used to justify his opposition to joint work was that you could not play for both Manchester and Newcastle United on the same pitch. Our riposte was: "What Militant Labour proposes is the expansion of the team – 'Socialist United' – for the polling day match!"[6]

This did not, however, stop us from consistently approaching the SLP for common work. For instance, we wrote to the SLP after the Braunstone by-election for Leicester Council, pointing out what good support existed for both Militant Labour and the SLP. Militant Labour got 150 votes (12.5%). Despite numerous attempts to get agreement with the SLP prior to the election, they stood against us but fell well short of our vote. Nevertheless, the two parties notched up nearly 21%. We pointed out: "Jointly, we will boost the results for socialist ideas and policies. We have the opportunity – are you bold enough to take it? We appeal to the [SLP] NEC to agree to meet with us to discuss a joint approach."[7] Thirteen people applied to join our party in the campaign.

The same pattern was demonstrated in the December 1996 parliamentary by-election in Arthur Scargill's own backyard of Barnsley East. On this occasion he was not able to prevent a certain amount of joint work. We did not put up a candidate but supported Ken Capstick former NUM Vice-President. This time the SLP campaign was better organised than before, with four public meetings over three weeks attracting audiences of up to 100. The biggest problem the SLP faced was getting across that they were standing and convincing people supporting them that it would not be a wasted vote, given the close proximity of the general election. On the doorstep many people said they wanted the Tories out and they did not dare do anything else but vote Labour. A lot said they would like a socialist alternative to 'Phoney' Blair. Militant Labour campaigned in one ward, taking responsibility for leafleting in full agreement with the local SLP. We campaigned as Militant Labour with stalls and petition, and were publicly thanked for our efforts. But for the old party political reasons Ken Capstick preferred to suggest we had agreed not to distribute material. This merely satisfied the SLP leadership's preference not to be seen to enter into alliances, although we cooperated very well with its rank and file.

The episode of the SLP and its failure to take off was an important negative political experience for the labour movement, particularly for the left. Although we had been amongst the first organisations internationally – and the first in Britain – to raise the need to form a new mass party, that idea is yet to be realised in Britain, while the working class in other countries have taken this step. In no small measure this is due to the sectarian intransigence of Scargill and his close supporters. By failing to reach out to a broad layer of leftward moving workers, a very favourable opportunity to establish a platform for a new small left party was squandered. Undoubtedly, this acted as a barrier to subsequent efforts to regroup the left on an independent basis. Scargill himself had a huge reputation arising from his leadership of the NUM.

In other countries – for instance, in Germany with the development of Die Linke (The Left party) – a similarly radical figure in Oskar Lafontaine provided the impetus for the formation of the party. Unfortunately, it has not yet developed as a mass alternative to the right-wing Social Democrats. This is due to serious political mistakes by the leadership, including support for the idea of unprincipled coalitions with bourgeois parties. Furthermore, the absence of Lafontaine from Die Linke – due to illness and some political differences with the leadership – also played a role in stalling the party. Nevertheless, it remains an important vehicle for workers who will be compelled to move into action in the future because of the worsening economic situation in Germany. Many could fill out the ranks of Die Linke from below. It is still possible it could move to the left.

A similar development could have taken place in Britain, given a different, more open approach by Arthur Scargill and those who supported him. Instead, it inevitably led to stagnation and disaffection with his intolerant approach and the internal regime he presided over. What could have become a serious left challenge to the right-wing trade union bureaucracy and to a Blairised Labour Party failed. It helped to reinforce all those faint-hearts and sceptics who saw no alternative but to passively sit in an increasingly moribund 'Labour' Party, reduced to merely waiting for it to be transformed in a left direction. Twenty years later they still live in expectation.

The election of Jeremy Corbyn to the leadership of the Labour Party – against all expectations, including his own – has not contradicted this prognosis. It was a spectacular manifestation of the law of unintended consequences. A right-wing Blairite amendment to the party constitution allowing anyone to vote for £3 – less than a pint of beer – facilitated that, primarily from the outside. As we write, the issue of Corbyn's leadership remains unresolved with two parties existing within Labour but the conditions which led us to pose the need for a new party persist. In fact, they became much more urgent following the devastating economic crisis of 2007/08. Ed Miliband's disastrous leadership of the Labour Party and his catastrophic general election defeat of 2015, if anything, led to a further shift to the right in the Parliamentary Labour Party. We were still firmly committed to encourage and take the initiative to regroup the left, as a necessary precondition for laying the foundations for a new mass left party.

6. Militant Labour campaigns 1995-96

Because Militant Labour attempted to continue the socialist traditions upon which the labour movement was built, we experienced some success electorally – for instance, in the European elections in Glasgow in 1994 where we received 7.6% of the vote. An indication of our continued presence as a factor in the working class and the labour movement was that hardly a single social movement took place without the involvement of our organisation, often with our comrades playing a leading role. Internationally, we still forged ahead with the Committee for a Workers' International (CWI), discussing with groups in Africa, including Zaire (now the Democratic Republic of Congo), the Philippines and many other areas of the world with a view to collaborating in the building of worldwide struggles of the working class. This contrasted sharply with the capitulation of the trade union and labour leaders internationally.

One of the key issues on which we concentrated our youth work was in campaigns against racism and fascism, which assumed some importance in the struggle directed at the British National Party (BNP), in which Youth against Racism in Europe (YRE) played an important role. The BNP's headquarters were in Welling, South London, where a mass demonstration had taken place on 16 October 1993. This demo was viciously attacked by the police and 41 marchers were hospitalised as a result of indiscriminate attacks by police officers. Lois Austin, YRE spokesperson, pointed out that the police had been drafted in to protect the fascists at a cost of nearly £1 million. They used indiscriminate violence, as they later admitted. We pointed out: "An internal Metropolitan Police document has just revealed that flawed police tactics caused the riot... This isn't the first time the truth about police tactics has emerged after the event. During the miners' strike at the Battle of Orgreave, police claimed that pickets had attacked them. But after the strike ended, the police were forced to admit they instigated the violence. Again, during the anti-poll tax demonstration at Trafalgar Square, police blamed the marchers for the riot."[1] This is reminiscent of other clashes between demonstrators and police – and the tactics used by the latter – where protection has been given to far-right organisations like the BNP then and, following them, the English Defence League.

Militant Labour sharply differentiated its position from ultra-left organisations in our approach towards the police, or the ranks of the army for that matter. We never adopted blanket opposition to the rank and file of the police or other forces of the state. We have never hesitated to criticise and condemn them when they were used as a battering ram against workers in struggle or against anti-racist demonstrators, as was the case in Welling. At the same time, we are not averse to appealing to the police – supposedly part of the 'citizenry' – to desist from violent actions against those exercising their legitimate democratic right to organise, strike and demonstrate. This becomes particularly important in periods of heightened social tension when the police themselves can come under attack from the government and can therefore be susceptible to pressure from the labour movement.

The 'revelations' by former police officer Peter Francis that undercover officers had infiltrated socialist and campaigning organisations to gain information on their activities came to light in 2010. The police had tried to smear the Stephen Lawrence Campaign and its struggle for justice. Francis himself joined Militant Labour in the first half of the 1990s and was active in the YRE. Hannah Sell and Lois Austin were granted 'core participant' status in the Pitchford

Inquiry into undercover policing because of this, as was Dave Nellist for suspected infiltration while he was an MP.

In Greece police protesting in 2012 against the austerity measures being applied to them, demonstrated in the streets of Athens and clashed violently with the riot police! In this situation, to refuse to fraternise and appeal to the police – because of their past actions against working class people, which we never forget and will criticise – is self-defeating. In Britain the police also came into semi-opposition to the government because of cut-backs. These led to wage restraint while prices rose and the reduction of at least 5,000 police jobs, resulting in intensified pressure on the existing workforce. We demand in such situations the right for the police to be members of a trade union with the right to strike. There have been many occasions when they have actually exercised this right: in 1911 and 1919 in Liverpool and London. Moreover, James Connolly and James Larkin, the great Irish socialist leaders, collaborated with radical elements in the Belfast police and assisted them in the formation of police unions, which led to the police actually coming out on strike.

We also adopted a similar approach towards the army, particularly towards rank and file soldiers, who can be profoundly affected by developments within society. We witnessed this in the Portuguese revolution of 1974 with left-wing radicalisation leading to the formation of the Armed Forces Movement (MFA). Incredibly, this organisation came out for socialism and even for the establishment of a workers' state! Nor have the traditions of the revolution been completely wiped out over 40 years later. This was revealed in demonstrations in Portugal in 2012 and 2014 when different governments attempted to implement vicious austerity and sections of the army demonstrated together with workers.

There was a steady drift away of lefts from the Labour Party – sometimes through expulsions – as Blair consolidated his grip in the run-up to the general election of 1997. Ian Page was a Militant supporter who had represented the Pepys ward on Lewisham Council for Labour since 1990. He had consistently voted against the Labour council's attacks on its own workforce. In June 1995 he was barred from attending the ruling Labour group and then expelled from the party. His crime? Standing up for the working class and for socialism! Ian had criticised the council for cutting the pay and conditions for its direct workers' team and complacently implementing Tory cuts. He commented: "The manifesto I was elected on... didn't include implementing £70 a week wage cuts and the loss of a week's holiday for workers."[2] He subsequently stood as a Militant Labour candidate and was elected as a councillor for many years. Alongside Chris Flood, another elected local councillor of the Socialist Party, they heroically championed the workers of Lewisham.

Three months earlier in the by-election in the Weavers ward of Tower Hamlets, Militant Labour's candidate Hugo Pierre received a creditable 3.7% of the vote in "political conditions unlike anywhere else in Britain".[3] Hugo stood on a programme against the Labour council's cuts and a £5 a week rent rise. The BNP also stood. We had to weigh up whether or not to stand, as this could have risked the BNP capturing the seat and the unfavourable publicity and effect that would engender. However, we calculated that they had no chance of winning. They were polling 20% in neighbouring wards but this time their vote fell below that. Nonetheless, many people who seriously considered supporting Militant Labour voted Labour to make certain the far-right was defeated. This was, in fact, the main appeal of Labour's leaflets as polling day approached. As well as running in the election campaign, Tower Hamlets Militant Labour members worked with Bengali youth to set up the YRE 'whistle alarm system' to deal with the BNP presence. The main national black British newspaper, The Voice, commented: "The BNP are being chased out from the Weavers ward in Tower Hamlets... At the sound of the whistle people band together... It is working, as people are responding to the 'distress call'... Already BNP campaigners have twice been driven away."[4]

In Hillingdon in West London Julia Leonard, who was a councillor, announced her decision to leave the Labour Party after 19 years and join Militant Labour. In her statement to the press Julia stressed that it was New Labour that had changed radically not her own beliefs. In Cardiff, Wales Militant Labour achieved 10% of the vote in a council by-election in the Ely ward, beating the Tories, Liberal Democrats and Plaid Cymru. We saw this local work – digging roots in working class communities – as a vital step towards building a national presence. It is not just in industrial struggles, vital though they are, that a party earns respect from working people. There are the million and one social struggles in which the members of Militant established reputations as amongst the best working class fighters.

Typical of this period was the community action in Waltham Forest where Louise Thompson, chair of the local tenants' federation, played a key role. One day a bailiff appeared on her doorstep. He said he had a warrant for her arrest for not paying the poll tax. Louise refused to open the door and got straight on to other Militant Labour members. Within minutes the landing of their floor in the tower block was full and the bailiff looked decidedly less cocky by the minute! Doors were locked and it was explained to neighbours what was going on. Word spread and it seemed that the whole block was outside Louise's front door! The bailiff was heard to complain that he couldn't wait to get back to his own turf where it was a lot less hassle! It turned out that he only had a court summons to serve and was just trying to put the frighteners on Louise. He had picked on the wrong woman and party!

A series of local struggles – largely unreported by the media – took place at this stage. These often included a slow but clear war of attrition by the capitalists – misnamed 'developers' – to destroy hard-won facilities. These had been built up in the more favourable conditions of the post-war economic upswing. Now, in the lopsided boom from the 1980s into the 1990s, there were attempts to take away these conditions, falsely described as 'modernisation'. Typical was the situation in Southampton, in the past seen as a relatively prosperous southern town. Years later in 2012 a struggle developed over the closure of a swimming pool by the Labour council which was resisted by the local community. They were supported and encouraged by two courageous Labour councillors, who were subsequently banned from the Labour group and expelled. Yet in 1995 Nick Chaffey, who worked full-time for us in Southampton, reported: "Here facilities have gone, one by one, leaving the city resembling a black hole, in particular for young people." He went on to quote Chris from Weston in the city: "With a population of over 200,000 and the hottest summer for over 200 years, Southampton has no swimming pool."[5] After the protests at the vandalising of the city, a swimming pool was actually built. Now that pool has been snatched back and closed by a combination of a crisis-ridden capitalist system and those Labour councillors who adapt to it instead of fighting for the interests of working people.

Militant Labour announced that it was putting up 40 candidates in elections in England and Wales on 4 May 1995. This was in addition to the 30 already standing for Scottish Militant Labour in Scotland's unitary elections on 4 April. Apart from the very successful campaign of Dave Nellist (mentioned below) we did well, considering the proximity of a general election and the overwhelming desire to get rid of the Tories. Militant Labour received an average of 9% in the seats we contested, coming second to Labour in nine seats and third in 16. In Sheffield Park Ward, we won 21.5% of the vote. The candidate was Ken Douglas, later an editor for our paper and now the National Treasurer of the Socialist Party. More significantly, we were "inundated with new members,"[6] reported Hannah Sell, from the Executive Committee of Militant Labour and later Deputy General Secretary of the Socialist Party.

One of the areas in which we concentrated was, of course, Coventry where Dave Nellist was the former Labour MP. The news that Dave was once more prepared to stand, this time in the 1995 local elections but now as a Militant Labour candidate, caused consternation in our opponents' ranks. An article in the Coventry Evening Telegraph was headlined: 'Labour Haunted by the Ghost of Nellist'. According to the article: "'News that the much-threatened attack by hard-left Militants at next year's city council election is now certain to take place' is provoking panic amongst Labour right wingers. 'The fear haunting Labour can be summed up in two words – Dave Nellist.'" It continued: "'It would be a brave person who would bet against his chances of election. Nellist... comes from the Rottweiler school of debaters' and 'would have a field day with some of our more comatose councillors.'" It seemed that the right-wing Labour establishment was asking potential councillors a "novel question at selection meetings. 'What would you do if Militant was to stand against you?'" The reporter stated: "That is the question from hell... Much anger continues to simmer... about the way Nellist was expelled from the Labour Party... Over 11,000 people voted for him when he stood as an independent candidate at the 1992 general election... One thing is certain. If Dave Nellist becomes Councillor Nellist, Coventry's dreary council chamber will be transformed."[7]

By the time of the elections in 1996 Dave's campaign clearly had Labour on the run. They were fighting to gain control in numerous wards but only in Dave's were six Labour MPs and MEPs out campaigning against him on the night before the election. In the event, he came close to victory with 1,420 votes (42%) to Labour's 1,617.

Over 220 people attended Militant Labour's very successful weekend school held at the University of London in July 1995. All the sessions were well attended and provoked lively discussion. These annual schools – designed to educate the new generation, most entering the struggle for the first time – became a regular feature of our work over the next two decades, culminating in the highly successful 'Socialism' weekends that take place today. The timing was also significant because our new monthly magazine, Socialism Today, was launched the same month, edited by Lynn Walsh and Clive Heemskerk. Its predecessor, Militant International Review, was first published in autumn 1969 and played a vital role in theoretically arming the supporters of Militant in the period when reformist ideas dominated the labour and trade union movement. In 1969, as we detailed in the first volume of our history (The Rise of Militant), our membership was small. But Socialism Today set itself a greater task in a sense: producing a monthly journal out-lining the policies and the analysis of Militant Labour, but in greater detail and probing more deeply than is possible within the confines of a weekly paper.

Militant Labour members were undoubtedly disappointed at the failure of the first attempt to establish a broad left party through the SLP, but it did not lead to pessimistic conclusions that 'nothing could be done' until there was a change in the situation. On the contrary, at the Militant Labour congress in Morecambe in January 1996 there was an air of confidence for the battles to come. Over 250 delegates and visitors from Britain were joined by an official delegation from the striking Liverpool dockers' port stewards com-mittee as well as international visitors from Spain, Ireland, Australia and Belgium. Representatives of the CWI attended. Also present were fraternal delegates, including representatives of the USFI and from the Workers' International League (LIT). The presence of the latter two organisations – both from a Trotskyist tradition – reflect-ed the recent establishment of relations between them and the CWI. Unfortunately, no common agreement was reached in the subse-quent discussions on how to face up to the challenge presented to Marxism by the 'post-Stalinism' situation.

The main congress discussion centred on likely developments in Britain in the forthcoming period, which I introduced. I firstly emphasised the important international developments, which formed the background of British perspectives. There had been strikes in France and Belgium indicating important new develop-ments. They showed the willingness of workers to fight back. In Britain this was shown by the titanic struggle of the Liverpool dockers and Hillingdon Hospital cleaners as well as thousands of postal workers who had been out on strike. There was an accumu-lated rage and discontent in society which made it extremely unlikely that the Tories could win the general election, despite the Labour leaders' unwillingness to conduct a real campaign to drive out the Tories by offering a socialist alternative. The massive split which had developed in Tory ranks over the EU would be accentuated by an election defeat. I concluded that it was the role of a revolutionary party to feel the movement of history and to use this to win the new generation to the idea of socialist change, which was possible in Britain and throughout the world.

An indication of the roots Militant Labour had been able to sink amongst working people was shown by developments in Scotland and in the vote for Roger Bannister in the Unison election for general secretary. Liverpool dock shop stewards Billy Jenkins and Rob Ritchie received ovations when they spoke to the congress: "On every continent workers are facing the same kind of attacks." They pointed to the international support from as far afield as Australia: "It was the first time two trade unionists have ever been sent out to Australia willingly." On behalf of the 500 striking dockworkers they thanked Militant Labour for the tremendous support the party had given them. Elaine Brunskill from the North-East related how, when the multinational Siemens had announced the prospect of creating 1,800 new jobs in the area, within three hours the local Job Centre had 4,000 enquiries!

The late Bernard Roome, a member of the Communication Workers' Union (cwu) illustrated the brutal regime in the workplace. He recounted that one worker had an accident at work and endured five hours on the operating table. The next day he was visited by his boss. He hadn't come to wish him well but to fill in a form and to assess whether the worker should be disciplined. Zero hours contracts were being introduced, a harbinger of developments over the last 20 years. Bernard pointed out that BT was one of the most profitable companies and yet was demanding more and more from its workforce. However they were fighting back: "You could not judge the mood in the workplace just on the number of disputes. What about the number of strike ballots, which often bring victory without having to strike?" He went on: "In BT presently there are 30 ballots due to take place."[8]

7. Workers formulate policies 1996

There were many similar contributions to Bernard's in this vein. This was a unique feature of Militant and Militant Labour, both on the public plane and in 'internal' conferences. When policy and perspectives were being hammered out, the contributions that workers made were crucial in arriving at correct conclusions. A genuine workers' party is built not just 'for' the workers but by them as a class, at least its most politically developed layers. This is usually dismissed by some as a 'workerist deviation', supposedly not in the traditions of Lenin and Trotsky. Those who make such criticisms only display their own ignorance of revolutionary history, particularly the building of the Bolshevik party. Lenin based himself on the politically developed layers, insisting that workers' views and approaches should set the tone in internal debate and in the organisation of the party itself. Of course, this does not mean to say that workers will not sometimes be wrong and policy and orientation may need to be corrected. Nor does it mean that there should be a prejudice against 'intellectuals'. But they would acquire respect by earning this through the 'rough work' in building the party from below.

In this way Militant differed markedly from other left organisations. Firstly, because we were able to win many more workers, both industrial and white collar, then in the way we recognised the value of contributions from workers – some of them 'worker intellectuals' – and on the need for them to set the tone. In other left organisations petty-bourgeois intellectuals were to the fore but with no real experience or feel for how the working class thinks and moves. This inevitably leads to them adopting a lecturing tone which puts off workers and leads to political mistakes, some of them serious.

Even those students and intellectuals who played a role within Militant Labour were required to put themselves on the standpoint of the working class, to learn from their struggles, as a precondition for them playing a role in educating workers themselves. Of course, not all were able to meet these testing requirements, with some drifting away over time. Others, however, went on to play a leading role, participating in the struggles of the working class and developing the ideas of Militant and Militant Labour. Superficial bourgeois commentators will no doubt see this as an expression of Marxism's 'prejudice' against those coming from a non-working class background. On the contrary, some of the best leading figures have come from such a background, beginning with Marx and Engels who made huge material sacrifices in order to develop the ideas of scientific socialism while energetically participating in the workers' movement. It would be totally wrong to debar anybody who was serious about the struggle for socialism but the working class movement has every right to insist on a serious approach from all those who wish to pursue such a struggle. We have nothing in common with those carpetbaggers, careerists, place seekers and toadies who flirt with the labour movement, like Blair and his ilk, before going on to 'greater things'. This type of corrosive personality infests the ranks of New Labour and will be a factor in the eventual disillusionment of working people with this party, leading to the creation of an alternative.

A feature of all our national gatherings is also an emphasis on the international situation. Without examining world processes in the age of capitalist globalisation, it is impossible to correctly analyse the march of events in Britain. To this end, the international session of our 1996 congress was introduced by Tony Saunois and he pointed to the contradictory processes taking place: a strike wave in Europe and yet "the barbarism of counter-revolution in the killing fields of Chechnya, and the horrors of Bosnia". He pointed to the economic situation which had confirmed the prognosis put forward by Militant Labour and the CWI: "Despite three years of relative growth, capitalism has been unable to regenerate itself. Thirty percent of the world's workforce is either unemployed or underemployed... In the most developed capitalist countries of the OECD... mass unemployment is now a permanent feature... The widening gulf between rich and poor is forcing the class struggle back on the agenda." Other sessions dealt with the development of our industrial work, youth, women's issues and the progress of Socialism Today. Over £3,700 was raised for Militant Labour in the fighting fund appeal and over £17,000 was pledged in a special appeal for the donation of a week's income to fund the general election campaign, in which around 25 seats would be contested.[1]

Militant Labour did not restrict its campaigns to economic issues. We also highlighted the growing discontent, particularly amongst young people, towards the state and the government's attack on democratic rights and civil liberties. Faced with a growing revolt the Tory government had introduced the Criminal Justice Act and a whole series of measures resulting in the harassment of young black and Asian people. This was no accident, as these sections are amongst the poorest and most oppressed in society. This was an attempt to prevent them from fighting back.

Militant Labour had helped to initiate the 'justice demonstrations' which took place in October 1995. We pointed out that the last time the Tories introduced stop and search laws (the infamous 'sus' laws, short for 'suspected person') they were forced to withdraw because of an uprising against them. Over 2,000 people, overwhelmingly young, marched in Hackney on 7 October. Many were people who had been victimised by the police – like Donald Douglas whose brother Brian had been the victim of a brutal racist murder by the police in South London the previous May. Also participating in the demonstration was George Silcott, brother of Winston, who was still in prison for his false conviction for the murder of PC Keith Blakelock in the Tottenham riots. After a long imprisonment Winston was acquitted but continued to serve a sentence for another murder conviction.

At the same time, a new and successful campaign aimed at football fans and players alike, Show Racism the Red Card, was launched by members and supporters of Militant Labour. Kevin Miles and others, who have come to national prominence since then in promoting this campaign, were supporters of Militant Labour, in Kevin's case a former full-timer for Militant. This campaign was closely linked to the YRE. Militant reported that Shaka Hislop, a goalkeeper with Newcastle United, had addressed meetings in schools in support of the campaign. Project worker and YRE member Ged Grebby, also previously a full-time worker for Militant, explained: "We took our initial idea from the Kick Racism Out of Football campaign because we realised the potential for using the high profile of professional footballers to get our anti-racist message across to young people."[2]

John Reid, another Militant Labour member, had produced the first edition of his successful book Reclaim the Game, a working class perspective on the football 'industry'. Then a very effective full-time worker for Militant Labour over a number of years, he later became a London Underground worker and was eventually elected to the Council of Executives of the RMT and as its London Regional secretary. This highlights once more the distinctive working class character of Militant Labour, which differentiated it from other groups on the left. The latter were mostly impervious to working class pastimes, football and sport generally. But Trotsky had emphasised the importance of a working class paper and party being prepared to take up all of the issues affecting working people, including how workers spent the little time they have for leisure, "how they drink whiskey", etc.

Football, whether you like it or not, is an important aspect of the social life of many working class people. Therefore, it was necessary and correct for us to spearhead a campaign to drive racist ideas out of the sport. Of course, it is utopian to expect that racism will be

eliminated merely by a propaganda campaign. Struggles are necessary on social issues – for decent housing, education and social services – which, because of their inadequate provision, help breed
racism. For us, a united working class-led campaign is the key starting point in the fight against racism and the far-right. The general
climate which was created through campaigns like the YRE and
Show Racism the Red Card helped in this struggle. This was shown
by the latter's continued success and topicality, given the controversy
in 2012 surrounding alleged racist behaviour on the football field in
a number of cases, including Premier League players such as John
Terry of Chelsea, which led to fines and match suspensions.

The main campaign around which Militant Labour developed
anti-racist work was the YRE, which was international. Laurence
Coates played an important role in its work initially. However, other
issues affecting young people had also come to the fore since the
early 1990s, particularly youth unemployment, the housing crisis
and education. Lois Austin, who headed the YRE in Britain, pointed
out the changing consciousness of young people: "The reason why
young people haven't joined the traditional organisations is that they
think the traditional parties have nothing to offer." They would be
the basis for the new socialist organisation which Militant Labour
was proposing to launch: "We're trying to set up a youth organisation that is really independent. There are generational differences,
and young people are more likely to get involved in an organisation
that's representative of them, their friends, their generation," said
Naomi Byron of the YRE.[3] When the YRE was set up in 1992, it was
envisaged that, sooner or later, it would broaden out into an organisation fighting on a much wider front than just anti-racism.

Lois was later to experience first-hand the brutal heavy handed-
ness of the police when she was kettled during an anti-capitalist
demonstration in Central London and prevented from leaving to
attend to her recently born child. Consequently, the case, which
received prominent coverage in the media when legal action against
the police was taken, went through the British legal system right up
to the European Court. Also, at the end of 1993, the police attacked

a group of YRE members and anti-fascists at Earl's Court Station who were returning from a protest against the BNP. This, happening a couple of months after the second Welling demonstration, was considered as revenge by the police.

After a period of quite 'fiery' discussion and debate, a new youth organisation, Young Socialist Resistance (YSR), was formed. This played an important role over the following period as a forum for young people but also in mobilising for interventions in the student field, amongst young workers and in other demonstrations which took place. Militant had always placed a priority on work amongst young people. One of the consequences of the retreat of the labour movement – dating from the collapse of Stalinism in 1989 and the early 1990s – was the loss to socialist revolutionary politics of a whole generation. There are no easy roads, quick-fire solutions, which can guarantee that an organisation or party can escape from the consequences of a difficult objective situation. There are periods in history when the labour movement and the working class can be thrown back. Conquests gained amid big struggles appear to be under threat. For the revolutionary movement positions gained once have to be won back again and again. This particularly applies to young people. In the past, they gained an understanding of the labour movement, particularly of the trade unions, through the workplace – from the older generation of workers who passed on their knowledge and experiences of previous struggles.

However, with the massive deindustrialisation that followed Thatcher's scorched earth policies of the 1990s, young people were increasingly excluded from the big industrial workplaces, simply because they did not exist, at least on the same scale as in the past. Therefore young workers were increasingly employed in public sector white collar jobs: teachers, civil servants, etc. Of course, under the hammer blows of the crisis and the attacks of the employers and governments, an increasingly militant trade unionism would manifest itself in these fields. This was bound to rub off on the new young layers of the working class, but it would take time and experience for this to become a strong force. Moreover, many young people were in part-time jobs and unorganised workplaces where trade unionist struggle methods were a foreign land. In consequence, union membership has become older and not renewed by the entry of vital youth forces. This is where it was envisaged YSR could play a key role, promising experience gained in the battle against the Criminal Justice Act, resistance to racism and the BNP, as well as the on-going struggles in industry.

This did not mean that racism was pushed entirely into the background. The campaign continued against the BNP 'bookshop' (headquarters) situated in Bexley. A tenacious six-year campaign to close this 'vipers' nest' demanded that it be shut down. This culminated in a local planning inquiry to investigate whether the building was being used as a bookshop, as the BNP claimed, or was in effect their national headquarters. The inquiry ordered the BNP to remove all fortifications from the building within six months. On 23 August 1996 the BNP's national organiser was back in court for failure to replace the shop front and roller shutter to their premises within the specified time limit. He pleaded guilty and was fined £800. Following this successful court action the bookshop closed, a clear victory for the anti-racist and anti-fascist cause.

The Stephen Lawrence inquiry rumbled on for five years after his murder in 1993, which was followed by a police cover-up. The Lawrence family had mobilised outside the court with a banner naming the racist killers: "Dobson, Neil and Jamie Acourt, Norris and Knight – Did you kill Stephen Lawrence?" An anti-racist activist who had observed the inquiry's proceedings commented to the Socialist (which succeeded Militant in 1997): "All the five thugs' evidence was just repeating 'No, I can't remember'. When the Lawrence's lawyer held up a green T-shirt with rips in it and said evidence showed that they came from hiding large knives beneath it, Jamie Acourt just said he 'couldn't remember' how they got there."[4]

The police treated the accused with kid gloves but a different approach was adopted by the police towards DuWayne Brooks, who was Stephen Lawrence's friend and a witness to the stabbing, treating him almost as criminal. On a demonstration in 1993 protesting against the presence of the fascist BNP in Welling, they tried to prosecute him for criminal damage on the grounds, completely wrongly, that they had spotted him on video! This was not to be the last that we heard of Stephen Lawrence's murder because of the incredible persistence of his family, friends and campaigners to bring the perpetrators of this crime to justice, which eventually succeeded, as we will see later.

We recognised that to extirpate racism, its social causes must be eliminated as well. Therefore Militant Labour decided to launch a campaign against low pay. This was one of the most important issues then, as it is now, facing the trade union movement and working-class people. The years of the Thatcher and Major governments had become notorious for the rich lining their pockets at the expense of the rest. For millions of working people on benefits, just scraping through had become a weekly uphill fight. Therefore the situation demanded a national living minimum wage.

The right-wing Labour and trade union leaders told workers to wait for a Labour government. Labour had earlier committed itself to a minimum wage at the level of half the male median average. Yet as an election loomed, the likelihood of a victory meant that the Labour leaders were jettisoning all concrete promises. We launched a special pamphlet: 'The Low Pay Scandal – The Fight for the National Minimum Wage'. In the previous period, the weakening of national pay bargaining, which went together with the introduction of local pay, had tended to undermine wages. National agreements had been a safeguard for workers in small, scattered workplaces, the least organised and those, such as care workers, who were reluctant to take industrial action. The strength of the best-organised pulls up the rest. Right-wing union leaders, of course, make speeches against poverty pay but then go on to conclude agreements which perpetuate it, or fail to organise effective industrial action to improve scandalously low pay offers such as that offered to workers in the NHS.

Another vital issue that received prominence at this stage, and on which Militant Labour was a pioneer, was domestic violence.

We had launched the Campaign Against Domestic Violence (CADV) in 1991 and its second conference with 250 delegates took place in London in November 1995 with Christine Thomas playing a key role. This campaign played a pioneering role in eventually forcing the government to give priority to the issue by taking special measures, particularly in local government. However, domestic violence, sexism and violence against women continued to be important issues which we were compelled to take up again and again. A serious socialist, revolutionary force must always try and see society through the eyes of the most oppressed layers: women and young people, as well as the black and Asian population. Militant Labour sought to achieve this in the campaigns that we conducted on domestic violence, but also on the broader issues of low pay – which particularly affected women workers – and for a living wage.

8. Trade union work in the mid-1990s

For us the trade union field has always been important but was now vital to the idea of a viable mass workers' party. Leon Trotsky consistently emphasised that the key to a correct working class policy in Britain lay in a clear approach towards the unions. It was important to keep this in mind given the shift towards the right which had affected not just the Labour Party but the trade unions as well, although not to the same degree. While the Labour Party was now, in the main, a bourgeois formation, the same could not be said of the trade unions, which at their base still retained their working class character. The era of neoliberalism, together with the ideological effects of the collapse of Stalinism, had also left its mark on the tops of the trade unions. The class war had ended with victory to the bosses, therefore there was no real need for trade unions, was the unspoken suggestion of bourgeois ideologists. They would be tolerated as a relic of the past just so long so as they accepted the bosses' new mantra of industrial partnership and class compromise.

The right-wing trade union leadership, who had carried out these ideas in practice, now willingly acceded to this doctrine. Things looked entirely different, however, from below. Not just in Britain but also internationally, the bosses believed they had the whip hand in cutting wages, changing working conditions and shifting the balance of forces decisively in their favour. Because of our roots in the factories and workplaces the pages of Militant were full of accounts of the tremendous resistance to the bosses' attacks on the working class. Even at the 'best of times' – and the mid-1990s, despite the boom, was not one of those – a veiled civil war takes place between the working class and the employers. Sometimes this breaks out into open warfare but on other occasions it is largely concealed, is not evident beyond those who are immediately involved in conflict. Health workers, rail workers, train drivers and postal workers were in the frontline.

Hospitals, formerly little involved in industrial struggle, were the scenes of seemingly endless conflict because of government restrictions on pay. Hospital workers were up in arms at the insulting 1% pay offer made by Tory axe-woman Virginia Bottomley in early 1995. This was rejected by a nine to one majority and the call for industrial action, including strikes, had been passed – 97% of workers in Scotland were in favour. Even the moderate Health Visitors' Union was prepared to ballot its members for industrial action for the first time in its history. Len Hockey, at the time Unison branch secretary at Whipps Cross Hospital, Leytonstone, reported: "Our members are aware of the increased stakes in this year's pay round... It's all about smashing national pay bargaining in preparation for the total carve up and privatisation of the health service."[1] Nothing much has changed in almost 20 years, except that more and more parts of the NHS have been privatised by governments of all political hues, or are being prepared for privatisation. A climate of fear and intimidation was developing in the 1990s, which continues today in hospitals like Whipps Cross. Train drivers, with the support of London Underground workers, also came out on strike.

It is the custom today for the media to single out rail workers for being 'greedy', expecting 'privileges' which are not accorded to other workers. This theme was rehearsed in this earlier rail dispute. When workers have made concessions through productivity agreements they expect something in return: "What infuriates me is we've already given them the productivity. That's why our claim for the better increase was so justified and why the strike has been so solid. Our members recognised the justice of our case." Another rail worker commented: "The strike was as solid as a rock with a real determination, especially among the younger workers. They were the most solid even though they've got kids and mortgages. We've only had a token picket because we were confident that there would be no scabs."[2]

The strike was suspended by the left-wing leaders after an injunction was awarded to the London Underground bosses. This illustrates once more the huge obstacles in the form of anti-union legislation which is more draconian in Britain compared to others in the 'advanced' world. This legislation was consistently upheld by Blair both before he took power and in the 13 years of New Labour government! It is quite incredible, as we remarked earlier, that the trade union leaders tolerated this position and did not seek to use their power, particularly through their financial donations to the Labour Party, to demand and obtain the complete repeal of all anti-union legislation.

Indeed, some right-wing trade union leaders actually threatened to use Tory legislation for reactionary reasons in internal struggles within the trade unions themselves! For instance, the annual conference of the print union (GPMU – which was later to merge into Unite) was abandoned after the president refused delegates' demands to vacate the chair. He provoked outrage by using the Tory Trade Union Commissioner to take the union to court when the executive decided to re-run his election. That does not mean that trade unionists and socialists should not use the courts in any circumstances. Socialists need to use the legal machinery available when union bureaucracies are perceived to take undemocratic measures. This was the case when a number of candidates reported irregularities in Unison's general secretary election in 2015.

The engineers' and electricians' union (AEEU) conference was brought to a halt when delegates demanded the continuation of elections for full-time officials, something the right-wing leadership had opposed. In the NUT there was uproar and the leadership had been overturned on innumerable occasions. The conference had called for a national teachers' strike but the leadership immediately opposed the decision. In the following weeks, they spent thousands of pounds of union funds to ensure a 'No' vote from the members. At the Unison conference the leadership was also overturned on a number of occasions, particularly over their handling of the health workers' pay claim. This union's full-time officials hoped that in the upcoming general secretary election Rodney Bickerstaffe would replace the outgoing Alan Jinkinson. They were shaken by the challenge of a new left organisation the Campaign for a Fighting Democratic Unison (CFDU), which agreed to stand Militant Labour member Roger Bannister.

The civil servants unions' conferences also shook the complacency of right-wing officials. The Inland Revenue workers' union (IRSF) merged with the National Union of Civil and Public Servants (NUCPS) to form the Public Services Tax and Commerce Union (PTC). This led to the overall strengthening of the left's influence. The right wing attempted to use sectionalism to protect their own vested interests. In the CPSA, the forerunner of the current PCS, the right wing was exposed as being incapable of solving any of the problems of the members. Militant Labour members and supporters had successfully pulled together a broad left organisation to challenge the leadership. At the 1995 CWU conference, the left from the postal and telecommunications sections joined forces and were poised to play an important role within the union.

Despite the continuation of mass unemployment, which inevitably led to a drop in trade union membership, the trade unions still encompassed 8.7 million workers and 48% of workers were covered by collective agreements negotiated by them. It was true that strikes were at a historically low level, although there was a reported increase in requests for financing industrial action ballots. Moreover, there had been successful strikes for the recognition of trade unions, for instance in banking. The attacks on the health service also compelled the Royal College of Nursing and the Royal College of Midwives to abandon their rules against industrial action. This indicated that, despite previous setbacks, the mass of workers still looked towards trade union organisation to represent their interests and resist the bosses' attacks.

At the same time the trade union leaders had one foot in the camp of capitalism, as indicated by their refusal to outline a strategy to defeat the anti-union legislation. At the Unison conference a scandalous campaign was conducted against Militant Labour supporter Glenn Kelly, who moved the main motion for a campaign to defeat this legislation. The Unison leadership then put down an amendment deleting the reference to "defying the law as and when necessary". As Glenn Kelly indicated, the Unison leadership – in concert with other union leaders – had no intention of organising proper resistance to the anti-union legislation.[3] That remains as much the case today as it was in the 1990s. Of course, the hard fought-for finances and resources of the trade unions should not be risked lightly in a conflict with the government. However the union leaders were often more concerned with protecting their own cosseted conditions, including inflated salaries, than the rights of the members.

There is no doubt that a union, or more likely a number of unions together, will confront the government by defying these laws at a certain stage. The discontent with the Unison leadership was reflected in the decision of the CFDU to stand Roger Bannister in the general secretary election. Roger pledged that, if he was elected, he would take no more than the average wage of a Unison member, with the rest of his salary donated back to the trade union and labour movement. He stood for the election of all Unison officials, a minimum wage and taking privatised utilities back into the public sector. Roger, in answer to questions, also outlined his views including criticisms of the other candidates. He pointed out that one was a member of the Conservative Trade Unionists, an extreme right-winger, who had put forward a bland election address which did not give his real views. The other was Yunus Bakhsh, a member of the SWP. He pursued a scurrilous campaign, largely comprised of attempts to discredit Roger by pointing to his alleged involvement in mythical 'sell-outs'. This was despite the fact that the CFDU had approached Fight Back, the SWP's front organisation, for a united left campaign in Unison but they refused.

The vote for Roger, who came third, was a success. His call for trade union officials to live on the average wage even had an effect on the victorious candidate Bickerstaffe. After his election he announced he would not be taking the pay increase, from £57,000 to £65,000 a year! The right-wing candidate had appealed to the worst prejudices of some members. He campaigned on an anti-abortion ticket, as well as being openly homophobic. In this election, Roger addressed numerous meetings around the country. On the other hand the SWP candidate won only 4.8% of the vote compared to Roger's 18.2%. Throughout the campaign, he distorted Roger's personal record in the union. The SWP even suggested that Roger should stand down because their candidate had marginally more branch nominations. Roger commented: "However, their low vote shows that the SWP's sectarian approach to working class people cannot attract broad support."[4]

9. Fragmentation of the Tories 1996-97

1996 was the year attention turned to the upcoming general election. The Tories, the governing party, were not in great shape. The British ruling class, historically faced with the rise of a powerful working class and its organisations, the trade unions and Labour Party, had carefully built and nurtured the Tory party as its main political instrument (unlike many of its European counterparts). It was a party which, within living memory, possessed a mass base. Its membership stood nominally at over a million in the 1960s, embracing significant sections of the middle class and even some upper, skilled layers of the working class. But 17 years of Tory government had rotted these foundations. Moreover, the collapse of the Berlin Wall had decisively altered the political terrain in which the Tory party operated. The scarecrow of 'communism' abroad and the threat posed by the working class and its organisations were the glue that held together the major capitalist parties in Europe, such as the Christian Democrats in Italy. By 1996, most of these had either disintegrated or were in the process of doing so because of the removal of the 'communist' bloc and the increased bourgeoisification of former workers' parties which no longer posed a threat to capitalism.

With electoral catastrophe beckoning there was much speculation that a great schism in the most successful bourgeois party in Europe would finally take place. The rise of the eurosceptic right finally pushed the Tory 'left' to organise themselves, even threatening to form an open alliance with Labour. The pro-Europe Tory Reform Group began to organise separate offices. Some MPs even confided that they had voted Labour at the last local elections! Former Tory minister Edwina Currie openly speculated that after the general election she expected Tony Blair to be the next inhabitant of Ten Downing Street! One Tory MP was offered a knighthood to remain within the fold. His disaffection was even more noteworthy when it was revealed that he had actually delivered flowers to Number Ten on the morning after John Major's re-election in 1992. Adding to Major's woes was the electoral threat posed by the billionaire James Goldsmith's Referendum Party. It had a war chest of £20 million and, he said, in relation to Major's premiership, "I vomit on the government."[1]

This fragmentation of the Tory party was reinforced by the further 'Americanisation' of British politics, with the contest between the parties not just personalised but almost presidential. With Labour's shift towards the right Major attempted to dress himself in the garb of a champion of the poor. This was as nothing to the way in which Blair engaged in political 'cross-dressing', at one stage shamelessly seeking to imitate Major himself. Major attacked Blair as "New Labour – old school tie" in opposition to his own self-portrayal as an alleged "poor working class boy from Brixton". The transformation of the Labour Party into a bourgeois party had truly puzzling repercussions in trying to establish the dividing line between the main parties. However, the image of 'honest John' sat rather uneasily against the background of the unprecedented sleaze afflicting his government, as evidenced by the corruption of disgraced Tories Neil and Christine Hamilton. Major was increasingly reconciled to defeat but wished to limit its scale.

There was much speculation that the Tory right was pursuing a policy of 'revolutionary defeatism' – in reality, counter-revolutionary defeatism. The managers of capitalist industry also expressed their reservations about the Tory government, with 45% no longer thinking that the Tories were the natural party of business, while 56% thought it was time for the government to go. They were ready to contemplate a 'Labour' administration because they had been convinced by Blair's political evolution that he posed no danger to them or their system.

The incipient splits within the Tory party have not yet led to an open split or the formation of successful new parties of the right. Nonetheless, the growth of the United Kingdom Independence Party (UKIP) – itself a reflection of the tensions in the Tory party which it has not been able to contain – shows up the splits in Tory ranks. Ultimately this fragmentation of British politics reflects the tense underlying economic and social situation in Britain which existed even in the mid-1990s. The onset of the capitalist world crisis from 2008 accentuated this, with the economy in a much worse situation today, trapped in a death spiral.

An uneasy industrial and social peace continued throughout the 1990s. That is now likely to explode in the tense economic and social conditions existing at the time of publication. We wrote at the time that the doubling of the national debt and the constant campaign against the poorest in society would lead to a further cut in spending on welfare, along with future savage attacks on the living standards of the working class. Huge class battles loomed: "Working people will have no alternative but to take to the road of resistance to the onslaught of diseased British capitalism. Massive reaction from public sector workers is inevitable."[2] That predicted drama unfolded later.

Not content with changing Clause IV, Blair and his acolytes were determined to destroy the very notion of socialism itself. Labour MP Kim Howells hit the headlines by saying that his party should "humanely phase out" its use of the term socialism because it was allegedly outdated.[3] Howells was one of the many odious types who now infested the ranks of New Labour. He participated as a 'left' NUM official, a researcher during the miners' strike. Thereafter he hitched his wagon to Neil Kinnock and evolved rapidly to the right, in the process jettisoning his membership of the CP just before the end of the strike and becoming Labour MP for Pontypridd. A miner who was also a member of the Labour Party warned: "Watch out for him, he has more faces than Big Ben."[4]

Militant forcibly argued that socialism was as relevant as ever and 76% of people polled in 1996 believed there was a class struggle in Britain, with 43% backing 'more socialist planning'. Under the Tory government the richest 10% of the population had raised their incomes by 62% while the poorest 10% were 17% worse off. Socialism Today pointed out: "Thatcher herself reportedly told guests at a recent private dinner that Blair is 'A man who won't let Britain down'. Rupert Murdoch is convinced too." This underlined that a Blair-led government was entirely safe for capitalism. Our journal also opined: "So what difference will a New Labour government make? It will make no fundamental difference at all to the decline in living standards for the majority of working people and the continuing polarisation of income and wealth. In the short term, however, there will be some new expenditure, which will give the honeymoon government some room for manoeuvre. Although Brown will not increase tax rates, he may be able to raise some additional tax revenue. There will be a one-off windfall tax on the excessive profits of the privatised industries."[5] This was a bold claim but one which has been borne out in fundamentals. The 13 years of New Labour government did not fundamentally differ from that of the Major government, as we will see.

New Labour's own documents stated: "Fifteen million men, women and children have seen no increase in their living standards over the entire 16 years of Conservative government... One child in three is growing up in poverty." Notwithstanding this, Blair was preparing the ground for a new 'welfare to work programme', which led the Financial Times to comment that "the word is still taboo, but Labour is already tiptoeing towards workfare". On public sector pay, which was being held down, provoking a furious backlash by the workers, Blair declared at the 1995 Labour Party conference: "A Labour government... will have to say no [to public sector pay increases]... even to people in this hall."[6] Shades of Ed Balls at the 2012 TUC when he stated that public workers' pay would be held down under a Labour government and the cuts inflicted by the

ConDem coalition would not be repealed. As the French say: 'The more things change the more they remain the same'!

Tentative at first in his anti-union criticism, Blair became more and more emboldened as the election approached. Speaking to the Confederation of British Industry (CBI) he declared: "We have revolutionised our relations with the trade unions... to make clear that we offer fairness, not favours, in government." This meant, he said, that "the key elements in the trade union reforms of the 1980s will stay". Marching to the same drumbeat was the pro-capitalist New Labour leadership of the TUC through its General Secretary John Monks. He stated that "unions must shed the old 'them and us' approach in favour of partnership with employers and a new government, if they are to be part of the solution to Britain's economic problems". We asked "Partnership on whose terms?"[7] Clearly Blair would be on the side of the bosses.

Even cherished Labour history was derided by Blair and his cronies. He regretted "the division that occurred between Liberals and Labour at the end of the last [19th] century", arguing that "[Liberal politicians] Lloyd George, Keynes and Beveridge... had the same basic ideas as [Labour Cabinet ministers] Bevin and Bevan".[8] This demonstrated his complete ignorance of the history of the trade unions and Labour Party. He even claimed that the TUC had been formed by some unions which disapproved of setting up the Labour Party, yet the TUC had been formed over 30 years earlier. Blair never let a good story get in the way of the truth! In reality he wanted to blot out – particularly from the consciousness of the new generation – just how the Labour Party had been formed, manifesting as it did a working class revolt against the capitalist Liberal Party.

Blair was assisted in furthering his 'project' by the support of a phalanx of former lefts. Clare Short summed up the role of these apostates as she engaged in McCarthyite language not seen in the Labour Party for decades. She justified the exclusion of Liz Davies as a parliamentary candidate for Leeds North-East, even though she was democratically selected according to the rules of Labour's NEC. This was because Trotskyism, particularly Militant Labour, was supposedly responsible for Labour losing the last four elections since 1979! Apart from Davies not being a supporter of Militant, Short admitted, it came as a shock to us to realise that the Militant Editorial Board had 'secretly' run Labour's national election campaign and had achieved this remarkable feat while being expelled from the party as early as 1983!

It was absurd and widely recognised as such to link Davies to Trotskyism and Militant. The main charge therefore was that she had voted as a Labour councillor against the Labour whip twice in Islington: once to prevent the closure of a nursery and once against cuts. Part of Liz Davies's defence was that Neil Kinnock broke the Labour whip in parliament 77 times between 1974 and 1979 before going on to become leader. The whole procedure was straight out of Alice in Wonderland. No matter, Davies was blocked and, unfortunately, she and her supporters did not take opposition to open defiance. This would have created a certain amount of momentum for the moves already afoot for a new party. The effect was to exclude anyone on the left from standing as a Labour candidate at the next election. This would further weaken and nullify any organised left opposition, for instance the Socialist Campaign Group.

In the months running up to the 1997 general election Blair and Brown became more and more explicit over what kind of party they were in the process of creating and the kind of government over which they would preside. Although Militant Labour had argued for a number of years that New Labour was heading in the direction of the US Democrats, up to now Blair had not confirmed this. Then in January 1997 he bluntly stated: "I want a situation more like the Democrats and Republicans in the US. People don't even question for a single moment that the Democrats are a pro-business party. They should not be asking the question about New Labour." The reality was that the Democrats under Bill Clinton had taken over traditional Republican policies, such as prioritising deficit reduction and attacks on welfare.

It was debatable whether New Labour could even have been described as a 'radical' bourgeois party at this time. It was bound to come into increasing conflict with working people in the event of it taking office. There were now over 18,000 people with more than £1 million in the bank while there were 13 million officially in poverty. Around 25% of all workers had experienced unemployment under the Tories. Meanwhile, profits were allowed to surge. Peter Mandelson, now widely disparaged as a champion of the rich, infamously commented: "We are intensely relaxed about people getting filthy rich." Socialist journalist John Pilger wrote: "The real divisions between left and right are outside parliament and have never been greater. They reflect the unprecedented disparity between the poverty of the majority of humanity and the power and privilege of a tiny minority who control the world's resources."[9]

Unbelievable as it seems over 20 years later, Brown was proposing even then that child benefit would be stopped for 16 and 17 year-olds still in education. So a couple of decades before the Tory/Liberal coalition meanly withdrew the Educational Maintenance Allowance (EMA) from 16 to 19 year-olds, Brown was suggesting something similar as a policy for the Labour government! At the same time New Labour's Social Justice Report from 1994 began an ideological assault on the welfare state – carried on by the ConDem coalition and the Tory government of David Cameron, continuing under Theresa May. The fundamental idea of New Labour was that inequality is here to stay and a 'dynamic' market economy required low levels of public expenditure, especially on welfare. This, in turn, was linked to the moralising, authoritarian values of Blair setting the scene for the return to the ideas of the past, of a 'deserving' and 'undeserving' poor. There was a widening gap between those who could afford to take up private insurance against job loss, sickness and poverty in old age, and the majority of low-paid, increasingly casualised workers who were deprived of any such safety net.

Blair had been shopping around for ideas in New Zealand, which had been amongst the first to take to the road of neoliberalism in the advanced industrial countries. But the ex-leader of the New Zealand Labour Party, David Lange, admitted that his government "went too far to the right" in the 1980s. Roger Douglas, Budget

Minister in Lange's governments, went even further than Thatcher. The result was that 400 food banks had been set up handling food costing £9 million, which was handed out to the needy.[10] We were able to envisage a similar direction for British capitalism: "With a potential market of 26 million workers, it's no surprise they are eager to strip the meat from the bones of the benefits system. The Tories are planning to create a market for these fat cats by privatising the benefits system."[11] This is a policy which was tried out by the Cameron governments.

10. The national question in Scotland and Wales 1995-96

The national question, particularly affecting Scotland but also Wales, came back onto the agenda of the labour movement in the 1990s. Next to Liverpool, Scotland was a very important base for Militant and then Militant Labour. Since the 1980s we had built up a formidable position not just on Clydeside but in Edinburgh and throughout Scotland. The national question appeared to have been pushed into the background by the development of the British Empire – which allowed the Scottish upper and middle classes an outlet for their energies – together with the rise of the labour movement. However, Scotland had never been fully reconciled to incorporation into Britain by the Act of Union in 1707. Lenin, with great foresight indicated, in his brilliant book State and Revolution, almost in passing, that the national question in Scotland had not been finally 'settled'. It could come back, particularly if the position of British capitalism was severely undermined. Moreover, the Labour Party in Scotland, at its inception, inscribed 'home rule' on its banner. The rapid decline of British imperialism – which once ruled an empire 'on which the sun never set' – together with the massive deindustrialisation effected by Thatcher, particularly impacting the industrial belt of Scotland, helped to create some of the conditions which Lenin had envisaged. However, in previous decades the issue had waxed and waned, partly depending upon who was in power at Westminster at the time.

As outlined in The Rise of Militant, we consistently took the clearest position on the national question, particularly compared to any other organisation on the left. Unfortunately today even Jeremy Corbyn does not appear to recognise the importance of the national question in Scotland. He believes that anti-austerity policies will be sufficient to win Scotland back from the Scottish National Party (SNP). It will not! We recognise the national feelings of the Scottish people and defend their right to realise their national aspirations, up to and including the right to secede from the Union. However, we were not apostles of separation. We would prefer a democratic socialist confederation involving England, Scotland and Wales, and ultimately drawing in Ireland. But we would defend the wishes of the Scottish people, something which the Labour Party later, under Ed Miliband, was not prepared to do.

In the period before the mid-1990s support for independence was a minority voice. Most Scots wished some form of autonomy which would allow them to have a more direct say over how they were governed – through, for instance, the setting up of a Scottish assembly or parliament. Militant – in England, Wales and Scotland – supported the idea of an assembly but one with the teeth to intervene in the Scottish economy through extensive powers such as the nationalisation of failing industries. At the same time and in the best traditions of Marxism we opposed all forms of bourgeois nationalism, which seek to divide workers. We particularly countered any manifestation of this within the labour movement, which should always seek to integrate workers into one common organisation – of course, with autonomous powers for Scotland and Wales, in this instance. But some of the leaders of Militant Labour in Scotland did not always adhere to these general principles, very often slipping into a form of left nationalism. However, in the mid-1990s, despite the arguments which took place between the leadership in England and Wales and some Scottish leaders, there was general public agreement on the issues. Nonetheless, the tensions continued and would break out in a clash between the national leadership of Militant Labour and the Scottish organisation later in the decade.

10. The national question in Scotland and Wales

The Tories were on the ropes in Scotland and elsewhere in early 1995. Major was attacking Labour's devolution proposals: "Teenage madness... One of the most dangerous propositions ever put to the nation."[1] In Scotland the Tories were reduced to a rump, down to 12% in the opinion polls. On these figures they were destined to lose every Scottish seat. In the event of a general election Major's ploy was to appeal to English national sentiment as a means of undermining Labour. Alan McCombes, who later broke from us and succumbed to Scottish nationalism, correctly argued the programme of our Scottish organisation in the Militant: "Socialists within a Scottish Parliament would advocate the nationalisation of the major companies, not only within Scotland, but throughout Britain, and the allocation of their resources, under the democratic control and management of the working class, to the needs of society. A Scottish Parliament that does not have effective control over the economy will inevitably fail to solve Scotland's crushing economic and social problems."[2]

Support for a programme of nationalisation, within Scotland initially – outlined by Alan in that article – was not adhered to by him later. Alan McCombes would put forward arguments to the effect that it would be difficult for a Scottish Parliament to take over industries which were just one arm of the multinationals. This was bogus as, in the age of globalisation with huge cross-border investments, there is hardly a country in the world which does not have some kind of foreign investment from multinationals. According to his reasoning, this would preclude any kind of effective action involving public ownership. In Argentina even the bourgeois President Cristina Kirchner did not hesitate to take over the Spanish-owned energy giant YPF, provoking outrage from Spanish capitalism.

This was just one indication of the political backsliding of the Scottish Militant Labour (SML) leadership which, later on, produced an open schism and their decision to leave the ranks of the Committee for a Workers' International (CWI). However, even some of those who departed from our ranks did so only temporarily, while Tommy Sheridan later formed an alliance with us for a period. The same cannot be said about those like Alan McCombes or Frances Curran, both of whom had previously played an important, even substantial, role in the building of Militant but who shamefully supported Rupert Murdoch in his pernicious court cases against Tommy Sheridan.

Nevertheless, the sml leadership at this stage successfully collaborated with us in the building of the organisation. The picture that emerged was that the Tories were in headlong retreat in Scotland. In the first elections to Scotland's new 'Tory-mandered' councils, out of a total of 1,179 seats they won only 79. The election campaign had been, in effect, a referendum on the government yet nine out of ten Scots voters effectively voted for an end to Tory rule. sml had established an important presence in local councils in Scotland.[3] In this election 10,000 Scots voted for sml, although both the snp and sml lost seats. This was because the anti-Tory mood was manifested in support for Labour with the proximity of an all-Britain general election. In Glasgow three sml councillors lost their seats, although in Pollock, where Labour and sections of the media had predicted "the end of Tommy Sheridan", he held the seat, according to the Glasgow Herald, "with an impressive 1,019 votes".[4]

Other organisations on the left took one sided approaches towards the national question in Scotland. The swp initially saw it as 'a diversion from the class struggle'. Militant, however, for over 20 years – in the face of criticism from other sections of the left – supported autonomy for Scotland, with extensive economic and social powers. Now, some on the Labour left like ex-Militant and one-time leader of Edinburgh Council, Alex Wood, criticised sml for allegedly playing down the strength of national feelings in Scotland. Yet he had broken with Militant in the 1970s after vehemently opposing our supposedly unacceptable concessions to nationalism.

Others objected to our warnings against the danger of fragmentation of the trade unions along national lines. Counterposed to this was their declaration of 'internationalism'. Alan McCombes answered this very effectively when he pointed out that the left critics of SML "may be unaware of the fact that Scottish Militant Labour is part of an international socialist movement, the Committee for a Workers' International, which is organised in dozens of countries on every continent across the globe".[5] He and his supporters, however, did not stick to this concrete expression of real internationalism when they decided to end their membership of the CWI, instead of continuing the discussion and dialogue on the differences that had arisen within our ranks.

The 'Scottish question' continued to generate heated controversy in Scotland. Philip Stott, who remained with the CWI when others split away, wrote a telling piece in the Militant following a big TV debate on the monarchy, 'The Nation Decides'. He pointed out that over half of those from Scotland voted for abolition, even though all four of its main political parties were pro-monarchy. Moreover, in polls taken after the programme, 56% backed an independent republic for Scotland. This would have come as a surprise, to say the least, to the Labour leadership. The Tories seized on this, and Scottish Tory MP and Cabinet minister Michael Forsyth, who had had the ear of Thatcher on the poll tax and many other issues, warned that Labour's devolution proposals would eventually turn Scotland into "a socialist republic"![6]

But SML did not concentrate exclusively on the national question. The aftermath of the anti-poll tax struggle continued with vengeful councils seeking to use bailiffs to collect unpaid tax, even though it had been officially buried by mass opposition. In August 1995, £452 million unpaid poll tax was still being pursued by Strathclyde Council. Therefore, SML leaders were compelled to defend those usually very poor people who were being pursued by bailiffs and councils. As a consequence Tommy Sheridan and Keith Baldassara were jailed for 30 days for defending a family threatened with bailiffs seizing goods for non-payment of the poll tax, four years after it had been forced off the statute book. The sentence after the campaign was reduced to a £150 fine.

Meanwhile a steering group including trade unionists and trades councils, as well as the Scottish Socialist Movement, Scottish

Militant Labour, the Communist Party of Scotland and a raft of other organisations, was elected in preparation for the launch of the Scottish Socialist Alliance. This differed entirely from Arthur Scargill's rigid bureaucratic conception which he applied to the SLP (see earlier). Small attempts at creating socialist alliances – initiated by Militant Labour – had begun earlier in England, in London and then in Coventry. On 5 February 1996, 125 local activists turned out in Coventry to discuss the need to form a new socialist party to challenge New Labour. The meeting was called by the Coventry Socialist Alliance and Militant Labour. It was open, democratic and welcoming. A number of other initiatives throughout the country to set up socialist alliances were also under way. But the most successful was undoubtedly in Scotland where the press were forced to recognise its potential: "For the first time in living memory the Scottish left has had an idea. It isn't a complicated idea, but it is, in its quiet way, only a little short of brilliant. They call it 'open affiliation'. That means no one is obliged to surrender their loyalties to join the Alliance. It proposes an end to traditional fratricide... It says politics is as much about extra-parliamentary action as it is about elections."[7]

The same process was under way in Wales where the political landscape, according to Dave Reid in Militant, had "changed beyond recognition in the 16 years of Tory rule. One third of Welsh industry has been wiped out and the Tories have savaged the coal and steel industries – almost obliterating the coal industry... In a recent opinion poll for HTV television, 62% of Welsh people were in favour of the establishment of an assembly in Wales, with just 28% opposed." As in Scotland, working class people expressed support for devolution because they felt the Welsh Assembly, with a built-in Labour majority, would address the problems of poor housing, unemployment, health and begin to reverse the Tory attacks.

In effect, the masses were pushing to the back of their minds the declared intentions of the Labour leadership to stick rigidly to the 'tax proposals' and cuts of the Tory government. Their expectations were to be cruelly dashed when Blair and Brown took power.

Nevertheless, Wales Militant Labour critically supported the Labour Party's plans to establish a Welsh Assembly, but demanded one in which real powers could be used to benefit working people. We declared: "Wales Militant Labour supports the right for Wales to split from the rest of Britain if the Welsh people voted for it. But we oppose complete separation [at this stage] because socialists, in general, favour the maintenance of the widest possible organisation of the productive forces – science, labour and technique – where this does not violate the legitimate national rights of different peoples. It also facilitates the unity of the working class across national boundaries. We point out that a separate Wales would not be independent, but would be ruled by the major companies that already dominate our lives."[8] While there was support for greater powers for the Welsh Assembly, independence did not have great resonance amongst the Welsh people at this stage.

11. Our name change debate 1995-96

By the mid-1990s, the pro-capitalist ideological counter-revolution was in full swing. The class struggle, which the bourgeoisie imagined could somehow be magicked away, remained but perhaps at a less intense level. It was a struggle to maintain the thread of genuine Marxism in the teeth of the campaign in favour of the 'market', which appeared to be all-powerful. Capitalist ideologues touted it as the only system capable of allocating goods and services to humankind. Given this barrage, ours was a small voice which could only aim to reach small circles of workers and youth who were able to withstand the 'magnet' of capitalism. We have to remember that Britain and the world were in the midst of a boom, albeit with the colossal disparity of wealth maintained and widened.

This necessitated a change, not in fundamentals but in the public face of our organisation. Militant had a tremendous pedigree, synonymous with struggle and undoubtedly associated with militant workers. However, even at the outset of Militant's formation, it was not an ideal name, as we explained in The Rise of Militant. There were disadvantages, particularly when the bourgeois press and media used the word 'militant' as a prefix to every 'extreme' cause or campaign – including 'militant IRA terrorism' and later 'militant Islamic terrorism'. These disadvantages were aggravated while Militant was forced to swim against the stream, fighting even to be heard above the chorus of pro-capitalist voices. Therefore, our

Executive Committee (EC) proposed, in a short paper I wrote, to change the name of our paper and our organisation. Many options were explored and we had not decided on a clear alternative, but there was a majority in favour of dropping Militant.

However, quite unexpectedly to us, the suggestion provoked a big discussion and some opposition from some comrades who were opposed to what they saw as a break with our history and tradition. It was nothing of the kind. No programmatic changes were suggested. In fact, the main authors of the name change had been the most fastidious in explaining our programme and defending our method. This was a serious attempt to create the best possible means for us to enhance our intervention in the struggles of the working class and labour movement. Nonetheless, it soon became clear that we should have prepared, first through discussions and meetings and, more cautiously, with the membership and leadership before launching this discussion in a written form. This would have allowed us an opportunity to assuage the feelings of some comrades initially opposed to the idea of a name change.

The subsequent discussion assumed a drawn-out character which was so encompassing that not all the members, nor other left groups who were given the documents as part of the 'regroupment of the revolutionary left' that Militant was engaged in, understood the proposal. The Democratic Socialist Party in Australia complained to me on my visit to the country that it was impossible for them to read the voluminous documents and papers on this issue! The discussion was dragged out partly because some individuals intervened with their own agenda and sought to use it to raise other unrelated criticisms of the leadership. In the vanguard of this oppositional grouping was Phil Hearse, a refugee from the barely existing Mandelite organisation in Britain, part of the United Secretariat of the Fourth International (USFI), who had left them and applied to join Militant. We engaged in very friendly discussions, as we had done with others who had left this organisation previously, such as Murray Smith and a group around him and others in France in the Jeunesse Communiste Révolutionnaire (JCR – Revolutionary

Communist Youth). We did not arrive at complete agreement with any of these comrades but there was sufficient common ground for them to join and participate in our organisation.

This disproves the myth disseminated by some on the 'revolutionary left' that Militant was afraid of discussions with other groups, because it was sectarian. The half-understood term 'sectarian' is used against us by people who sin on this score themselves. They usually confuse a stubborn, principled defence of the fundamentals of Marxism, politically and organisationally, with their one-sidedness and political confusion. These features, alongside overweening arrogance, Hearse possessed in abundance.

The Militant Labour leadership set out its proposals to change the name in a special bulletin in May 1996. We pointed out the difficulties: "There is perhaps no issue which generates more controversy than the name of a revolutionary organisation." We emphasised that the Bolsheviks were compelled to adopt different public names in different periods. At one stage, when struggling against the tsarist autocracy and its censorship laws which outlawed 'Marxism', they assumed the mantle of 'Consistent Democrats'. Lenin correctly argued that it was necessary to utilise even the limited opportunities that existed for legal work and, accordingly, to change the name of the party in this arena at least. With this, of course, went the dangers of generating certain 'democratic' and reformist illusions. However, this was corrected internally within the Bolshevik party – which was in reality a faction of the Russian Social Democratic Labour Party at that time – and by successful legal work. Later, when conditions changed and it was necessary to draw a clear line of demarcation between genuine Marxists and the social democratic traitors of the Second International who had supported the carnage of the First World War, Lenin proposed renaming the party the Communist Party.[1]

Of course, Militant has not worked with the same difficulties that confronted the Bolsheviks. We had initially operated in a situation with less abrupt turns than those which confronted the Russian Marxists in the first two decades of the 20th century. But as Trotsky pointed out: "Even the most revolutionary parties can run the risk of lagging behind and of counter-posing the slogans and measures of struggle of yesterday to the new tasks and new exigencies."[2] These general points are relevant but the proposal to change our name had to be justified by the historical circumstances which Militant Labour faced then and later. We had already undergone a sharp change in tactics when we launched an independent organisation in the early 1990s, which allowed us to seize the opportunities that existed. However, this turn, as events demonstrated, was not enough for us to progress. A further degeneration of the Labour Party under John Smith, then Blair, also compelled us to effectively abandon any idea of transforming the Labour Party. This led us to raise publicly the idea of an alternative workers' party to Labour. We recognised that this was still a minority view, even amongst those who had retained a socialist consciousness, some of whom could be won to a revolutionary programme and organisation. This was illustrated by the singing of 'The Internationale' on mass demonstrations in France in the period following the collapse of the Soviet Union.

Taken as a whole, one of the most important tasks of the Marxists was to seek to rehabilitate the ideas of socialism more widely, if necessary in collaboration with other forces. We commented: "No mass left wing, in the sense of the Independent Labour Party in 1932, will develop in protest against the pro-capitalist policies of a Blair Labour government." This prognosis was entirely borne out when the Blair-Brown government took office. We conceded that perhaps "a parliamentary left will oppose Blair, and will probably eventually split away". This perspective was not confirmed, however, because of the political and organisational feebleness of what remained of the left within the Labour Party. They were completely incapable of organising against the right wing, either within the structures of the party or in important struggles outside. We predicted that if they did split, "they will not take a huge body of workers with them, for the simple reason that these workers no longer inhabit the Labour Party".[3] This has been completely vindicated since 1996. The forces which gathered around the Corbyn movement later were either entirely new forces or 'returnees' who had abandoned the Labour Party but were encouraged by Jeremy Corbyn's decision to stand and then by his victory.

We were looking towards a new wave amongst the working class which would raise once more the idea of socialism. In anticipation of such a development we proposed that the word 'socialist' should replace Militant in our party name. The term 'Labour' had become synonymous with Blair and the abandonment of socialism and, in the situation we faced then and in the future, this would be a barrier to us finding the ear and winning the best sections of the working class. We stated: "Militant has an honourable socialist and revolutionary pedigree. But there are many workers, advanced as well as the mass, who will awaken to political life in the future, who now have an accumulated prejudice against the term 'Militant'." We concluded therefore "that the time has arrived for a change of our name".[4] The name Militant also had negative connotations in this new period, given the fact that the media regularly referred to 'militant terrorists'. We wished to be separated from this.

We understood that the proposal to change the name generated fears, particularly among some trade union comrades, that we were now engaged on an increased electoralist road, to the detriment of union work. We reassured our ranks that this was not the intention of the leadership nor was it to be realised in action. Similar arguments were advanced at the time when we decided to organise independently of the Labour Party from 1992. We pointed out: "It would be much easier standing under the name of 'Socialist Party' to attract a wider layer of independent lefts, revolutionaries and general socialists... to work for candidates standing under this banner rather than 'Militant', which was perceived as a much narrower signboard for a new period."[5]

As expected, the proposal generated intense discussion – one of the deepest-going discussions within our ranks on strategy and tactics. Nick Wrack, a member of our EC, disagreed with the proposal to change the name and suggested instead that we call ourselves Militant Socialist Party. In reality, this proposal was an argument in favour of the status quo; workers would hear or see 'Militant' and not 'Socialist'. It did not overcome our main objection to the prominence of 'Militant' with its increasingly negative con-notations in the capitalist media.

It was not an accident that the Irish section of the CWI argued very forcefully that the term 'Militant' had become a barrier to them because of its association with terrorism and particularly paramilitary organisations. We pointed out that the political con-sciousness of the working class in the post-Stalinist period was extremely confused. The understanding which existed in the early 1970s or the period 1979-83 in Britain, particularly of the advanced layer, was ahead of the position then and today. There was a broad layer of workers who considered themselves socialists and our task was to convince them that our particular 'brand' of Marxist social-ism was most appropriate. We compared our role to the tasks that were posed at the time of the building of the Second International, helping to build a broad socialist consciousness while maintaining a clear Marxist revolutionary banner. We were not intending to build our organisation along the lines of the mass parties that existed at the time of the Second International. We did not intend to repeat their historical mistakes by recreating the Second or First International. We had the dual task of trying to recreate a broad socialist consciousness, as well as maintaining within this a social-ist revolutionary programme and perspectives.

A number of documents were produced and a full discussion took place in the following months in the ranks of our organisation. Many contributions were positive. Clive Heemskerk, playing a key role in the editing and production of our theoretical journal, Socialism Today, the Merseyside Regional Committee and the EC of the Irish organisation all added to the discussion, as did individual comrades who wrote letters which were printed in special bulletins. However, a long document by John Bulaitis, Phil Hearse and Jared Wood disa-greed vehemently with the idea of changing our name. Ironically, Hearse had spent most of his political life opposing Militant – having only joined us recently - and left our ranks shortly afterwards. In reality, their document was not concentrated on the name change alone but was a broad assault on the perspectives of our party. It only addressed the name change incidentally and in passing.

They objected to the leadership's characterisation of them as 'conservatives'. We replied: "Yet what is a 'revolutionary conservative' but one who fails to recognise profound changes when they take place and obstinately clings to a banner or an idea, or a formula, which has been overtaken by the march of events?... If our organisation was to accept their method, their approach towards perspectives, and the name change they propose [Militant Socialist Party], we would not only be unprepared for the period that is opening up we would become peripheral as far as the workers' movement was concerned."[6] In the discussion on our National Committee (NC), one comrade informed us that all the dockers and their partners – who were involved in strikes at this stage, with some joining us – supported dropping 'Militant' and, moreover, favoured the name Socialist Party. Most comrades who engaged in the discussion did so in a very positive way, even where they had doubts or disagreed with changing our name.

After a thoroughgoing, extensive discussion over six months, the party agreed at a special national congress to approve the decision to change our name to Socialist Party. This proposal received 71.4% support; the resolution to change our name to Militant Socialist Party 24.8%; and for the status quo, Militant Labour, just over 3%. However, because the debate had been conducted in a democratic and comradely way, the party moved on to implement the decision and began to campaign under our new banner. Phil Hearse and John Bulaitis, with a few others, subsequently left the party, lapsing into inactivity. Nick Wrack later joined the SWP, then left it to join George Galloway's Respect, later becoming an 'independent socialist' in the Trade Unionist and Socialist Coalition (TUSC). Nick then left TUSC and attempted to join the Labour Party and Momentum. Jared Wood, in the best traditions of the Marxist movement, forcefully argued his position but, when the conference decided against him after the open and democratic debate, he loyally accepted the decision and is currently on our NC.

No time was lost in launching the party together with the first issue of The Socialist, the new name for our paper, published on 7 February 1997. It caused significant interest with millions of TV viewers and newspaper readers, introduced to the Socialist Party through a media blitz on the 4th and 6th of that month. The Times commented: "Militant marches back as the superior socialists." The Press Gazette reported: "Militant relaunches as The Socialist as the class warriors fight on." The Daily Telegraph headline was 'Militant Returns to Haunt Blair at the Election'. The Press Association reported Dave Nellist speaking at our media launch: "After 18 years of the Tories a huge number of people want to see the back of this government, yet... Gordon Brown's big idea was to say vote Labour and there will be no change in economic policies." A spokesman for Brown, it continued, "refused to comment". There was a special report on Newsnight, including a live interview by Jeremy Paxman with myself, and a report with top political correspondent Jeremy Vine was shown four times on BBC Breakfast Time. The first phone call to the party for more information arrived 30 minutes after Newsnight ended.

Dave Nellist appeared on Norman Tebbit's Sky TV show Target. Tebbit said he would leave the country if socialists taxed more than '100 grand!' Dave retorted: "Some may regard that as a small price to pay!" As he arrived, John Prescott came out of the studio. Quizzed by Prescott, Dave explained the aims of the Socialist Party and sold the first issue of the Socialist to him for £1! We received widespread publicity in Wales, in the Western Mail, the South Wales Evening Post and The Echo. On Merseyside, there was a page in the Liverpool Echo and coverage in the rest of the regional press. Dave Murray had 30 minutes on Radio Essex and Jim Horton was interviewed live on Three Counties Radio. Elaine Brunskill, our parliamentary candidate in Tyne Bridge, was also on radio. Our newly launched Socialist Party, it was announced, would contest up to 25 seats in the forthcoming general election. Sizeable meetings and rallies took place throughout the country to launch the new party.[7]

12. General election finally called 1997

In Britain, the looming general election, which had to be held by May 1997, had dominated attention in the previous two years. When the election was announced for 1 May, we commented: "The Tories are going, after 18 years of vicious attacks on working class people. A stronger opposition would have shown Major's team of thugs the red card years ago... Millions of people will vote Labour to get rid of Major's millionaires but Blair and Co. are reaching for the yellow card. They refuse to challenge the interests of big business and the rich so little will change under a Blair government." A very accurate picture of how events panned out! We made it very clear, however, that our first priority was to begin the "fight to get rid of the Tories but if you want to send off Major and his system of greed and poverty, get involved in Socialist Party election campaigns in your area."[1] The endorsement of Blair by the Sun showed how far rightwards New Labour had travelled. Unconvinced voters remarked: "I think the two parties are much of a muchness... New Labour are just left-wing Tories."[2] Other polls indicated that 42% believed that the election result would make 'little' or 'no difference'. We urged a vote for socialists, recognising at the same time that, "had there been a joint socialist platform – which SLP leader Arthur Scargill refuses to consider – then many more people may have had a genuine socialist alternative".[3]

Incredibly, it was the stink of corruption from MPs

themselves – 'cash for questions', with brown envelopes doled out by millionaires to greedy MPs – which dominated the first week of the election campaign. Sleazeball MPs like Tim Smith, already living in a palatial six-bedroom Georgian house, representing an affluent area, were revealed as receiving money from Harrods boss Mohammed Al Fayed. We posed the question to the readers of our paper: "Who's bought your MP? 277 MPs are millionaires. They will push the dubious interests of big business to make themselves even better off. The Socialist Party is standing in 18 seats in the general election. Candidates stand on the policy of a socialist MP on a worker's wage. They would live on the same incomes as the workers they represent. Their interests would be our interests. Capitalism is a corrupt system which bullies and bribes to get its way. That's just one more reason why our party is fighting for a socialist future."[4] We compared the Tory government to a "school pupil who hides their bad end of term report, [taking] pre-emptive action by closing Parliament early".[5] This was not the first time that the corruption of MPs and big business had surfaced, nor was it the last. Neither was it restricted to the Tories. New Labour would become enmeshed with corrupt practices, which was an inevitable product of its swing to the right, its acceptance of capitalism and the ingrained inequality and corruption which goes with this.

The Socialist Party approached the election in a confident mood. Ken Loach, the famous director of films like Land and Freedom, had agreed to speak for Dave Nellist at Coventry South Socialist Party's eve of poll rally. We, of course, could not match the resources of the pro-capitalist parties, now including New Labour. Some on the left believed that Blair was correct to court the support of the Sun because the media has such power over public opinion. Ken Smith, a full-timer at our national office, answered: "Whilst the power of the press cannot be underestimated, it cannot change the economic reality that people face. All the Tory-supporting papers have not been able to undo the bitterness and disillusion directed against the Tories since the recession in 1991 and the [Exchange Rate Mechanism] fiasco in 1992."[6]

For the trade unions, particularly for rank and file trade union-ists, the election was seen as an opportunity to force the bosses back. A crippling roadblock was, of course, the Tories' anti-union laws. The Socialist showed how these laws made it easier for bosses to refuse to recognise a trade union, even when all their employees had joined. Many workplaces had organised and recognised trade unions, while 10.2 million workers maintained some form of union protection at work. However the number of workers covered by trade union representation and negotiation had fallen since 1979 from about two thirds to 47%. The decline was primarily due to deindustrialisation and was reinforced by the existence of the anti-union laws. It was obvious that it was also a product of the inability or unwillingness of the trade union leadership to effectively organ-ise the fightback against the employers' offensive.

We threw ourselves into the election with gusto. I recounted in the Socialist my own experiences of campaigning for the Socialist Party candidate in Camberwell and Peckham. On the way to can-vass, "I glanced at the Sunday Times Rich List, detailing the wealth and lives of Britain's 1,000 richest people. The distance separating these creatures of comfort from the working people I meet on this estate is greater than that between Earth and the recent comet Hale-Bopp." The area we canvassed was one of the most deprived in South London. At one door in Peckham a very young working class couple confronted me with their everyday reality. The man, with kids scampering around his feet, railed about the "shit and piss on the landings, nobody cares about us, no politician cares a toss, I'm not going to vote". The Sunday Times 500 Rich List was enough to make the blood boil when the fate of the poor, numbering one third of the population – about 17 to 20 million people – is contrasted to their lifestyles.

The Sunday Times also informed us: "For Joseph Lewis, the Bahamas-based billionaire... 1996 was a vintage year for wealth creation. With profits from his outstanding skill at playing the for-eign exchange markets, we estimate that Lewis trebled his fortune to £3 billion and it is still rising." We asked: "Does Lewis create anything? The simple answer is, no. He is a 'financier', which in simple language means that from his vast computerised dealing room, in his Bahamas villa, he makes bets. Despite the claims of 'wealth creation', he has created nothing, but gambled and won at least £1 billion from 'trading activities' on the 'money markets.'" Our opposition to the Sunday Times list did not come from the 'politics of envy'. We were fully in favour of a wealth tax but we also pointed out: "Our opposition to the rich is also because they rest on a system, the market, capitalism, which limits and holds back the full possibilities of using the productive potential of industry and of the working class... Capitalism is a system which rests on production for profit and not for social need; not to build houses, schools, and hospitals."[7]

Dave Nellist was standing for the first time in the general election as a Socialist Party candidate for Coventry South. We commented: "Twenty-five years ago Coventry was probably the richest working class city in the country. We had an engineering rate of pay called the 'Toolroom Agreement' which was the yardstick used by factory workers throughout the country to measure their own pay claims." But Coventry also summed up the catastrophic collapse of British capitalism which, in turn, had a devastating effect on cities: "Thousands of Coventry homes, even today, 1,000 days before the millennium, are without an indoor toilet, central heating, hot and cold running water. Neither of the two main parties have any intention of changing this." For over four years Coventry Socialist Party campaigned with others against the closure of Coventry and Warwickshire Hospital and its replacement with an expensive PFI hospital. The Tories did not have the time before the election to implement their plans. The Socialist Party read in the local papers that the hospital was safe. But "that night Labour dropped a bombshell – they would continue the project." Moreover, Coventry had had a Labour council since 1937 but in 1996 it "cut the sick pay of all its workers and ended holiday pay for the poorest-paid workers".

The bookies predicted a Labour victory nationally. The Socialist Party therefore said: "Sending one more Labour MP from Coventry won't affect the balance of government but will mean another MP toeing the party line. But if the Socialist Party is successful, people will have a genuinely independent voice that will take up issues like saving the hospital."[8] If a debate organised by Coventry's local churches was anything to go by, Dave Nellist was on the eve of victory, judging by the applause and laughter as the audience listened to him outline the socialist agenda. The Labour candidate, Jim Cunningham – who had narrowly beaten Dave in the 1992 general election – was anxious to say as little as possible, other than: "I agree with Dave – we need a minimum wage," though not specifying at what level.[9] Unfortunately, national elections are not decided on local issues. There was a strong feeling amongst those who wanted to get rid of the Tories that they were prepared to vote Labour. Nevertheless, the Socialist Party conducted a spirited campaign.

Blair was confronted when he made a 'surprise' visit to business people at Warwick University on the city's outskirts. Socialist Party supporters hastily improvised a few placards and jumped in a car. The first two New Labour battle buses to arrive were for the media circus. Seeing the Socialist Party banners, the Guardian reporter ran over and said: "Thank god somebody's showing some dissent. All I've heard on the coach is how wonderful Tony Blair is." The first person Blair reached told him: "I don't want to shake your hand, you're letting the students down." He was president of the Mature Students' Society.[10]

Similar campaigns took place throughout the country with big increases in the sales of our paper and many people joining the party. At the same time, there were demonstrations against the Tories and fighting for social justice. Sacked Liverpool dockers, Hillingdon Hospital cleaners, Magnet Kitchen workers from Darlington together with the strikers' families, friends and thousands of supporters, marched through Central London on 12 April. Eight hundred thousand election addresses from our candidates were distributed and hundreds of copies of the Socialist Party manifesto – 'A Real Voice for Working Class People' – were sold to bolster the case for our candidates in England and Wales. There were also 16 Scottish Socialist Alliance candidates, nine of whom were members of Scottish Militant Labour.

It was not all critical acclaim for New Labour. One pollster predicted the lowest turnout since the Second World War. We remarked: "Never has there been more discontent with what is on offer from traditional politicians. This will result in a wipe-out for Major's party in Scotland and Wales followed, probably nationally, by meltdown after the election... On Newsnight, one Labour MP was at one with the Tories and Liberals in stubbornly refusing to offer any concessions to pensioners. Contrast this to the Socialist Party's demand for a state pension for all linked to a minimum wage, as well as an immediate 50% increase to both men and women at the age of 60. Britain's pensioners should have the same rights as French lorry drivers, the right to retire at 55."[11]

These facts showed the erosion in the position of pensioners and the working class generally. Even the capitalist press commented on this decline: "We are talking about an underclass... Just under 19 million people live on the margins of poverty (on an income less than £105 per week)."[12] Things have hardly changed; if anything, they have got worse! A massive gulf was opening up in Britain which terrified the strategists of capital, including some of their more farsighted representatives like Will Hutton. They were terrified then, and even more so now, that the so-called 'underclass' would rise and shake society to its foundations. At a dockers' demonstration thousands of disenfranchised youth, kept in degrading poverty and homelessness, vented their rage against the system. We described New Labour as merely another group of managers of Great Britain Ltd, ready to take over from 'Major's team'.

The outcome of the general election was summed up by the front page headline of the Socialist: 'Tories Wiped Out'.[13] We wrote: "A huge sigh of relief has gone up all over Britain. After 18 years, the Tories have been practically wiped out in Parliament with the lowest share of the vote since 1832. Wales and Scotland are Tory-free areas, Britain's big cities very nearly match them." The election result was a landslide unprecedented in post-war political history.

The anti-Tory tide was devastating as 180 seats changed hands. Over three million voters changed allegiance, producing a 62% vote against the Tories. The Tory share was reduced from 43% in 1992 to 31% in 1997, although this massive swing against the Tories did not translate into huge votes for Labour. Labour did have a record swing of 10.5%, winning a record number of seats (419 out of 659), but its 44.5% vote share was lower than its 1945 landslide victory. It was lower even than the victory of 1966 – and lower than 1951 and 1955 when Labour lost. The overall turnout of 71% was 7% down on 1992 – and the lowest since 1945. This meant that the numbers who abstained had increased by a third on the previous election. Moreover, the lowest turnouts were in traditional Labour held seats. In addition, the swing to Labour in working class areas was lower, at 9%, than it was in middle class areas where it was 12%.

As we had warned, Labour's shift to the right had alienated many of its traditional voters. Only the burning desire to get the Tories out led people to vote for Blair's party. More than anything, on 1 May, Labour was the fortunate beneficiary of a massive and decisive rejection of the Thatcherite brutalities and inequalities of the 1980s and 1990s. The irony was that New Labour believed it had to adopt pro-Thatcherite policies to get elected when the majority of the population were overwhelmingly prepared to reject those 'values'. Samuel Brittan, the Financial Times commentator, told Britain's bosses to be grateful for the government they now had. He concluded that a Labour Party with a much more radical anti-capitalist programme of change could have been elected in the same 'landslide' proportions, such was the hatred of the Tories.

We pointed out that New Labour's biggest advantage for now was that they were not the Tory government. However, the size of the Labour victory promoted expectations and illusions that Labour was incapable of fulfilling. Ominously, on the steps of Ten Downing Street, Blair warned: "We were elected as New Labour and will govern as New Labour."[14] This meant that, despite one or two minor changes, Thatcher's counter-revolution would not be overturned. 'Economic prudence' and the firm smack of crackdowns on crime

113

and social security 'fraud' would continue to be the order of the day. Nonetheless, a new period had opened up in British politics. If the Tories were now to elect a more right-wing leader, we said it was possible they could split over Europe. Blair was flirting with proportional representation but it was put on the backburner because of the secure Labour majority. Labour's landslide majority of 1945 was overturned by the Tories six years later. This was despite popular support for Labour and its policies at the time. That was at the beginning of an unprecedented structural world economic upswing that would not be repeated during a Blair government. Blair undoubtedly benefited from the lopsided boom of the 1990s but this was nothing compared to the 1950-75 upswing in capitalism.

A new period of political volatility would open up. There were significant votes to be had outside of the three main parties. The 800,000 votes for the Referendum Party showed the tremendous disquiet that existed on Europe. Labour promised a referendum if it was to propose joining the euro. These votes, combined with a rise in the vote of the BNP and other far-right candidates, also indicated how their support could grow under the Labour government if a socialist class alternative was not offered. The 70,000 votes for socialist candidates, Socialist Party and SLP, were significant. Support at local level was also reflected by much higher percentage votes for our council candidates.

Matching the public mood, we commented: "Major's government has gone and many of the Tory Cabinet ministers have lost their seats. Good riddance."[15] There were real expressions of class vengeance in the outpourings in the immediate aftermath of the elections, even though people who voted Labour hoping for revenge against a profit-driven system would be severely disappointed. We concluded: "Never before in the history of elections has so little been promised to so many... In truth the Tories lost the election nearly five years ago on Black Wednesday... Labour modernisers' claim that it was changing the name to New Labour and the dumping of any vestiges of socialist programme or politics that won the election is bogus... Both before and after Labour's changes their vote, according to opinion polls, has stayed roughly the same."[16] French right-wing daily newspaper Le Figaro remarked: "To judge by the reverence shown by the Labour Party for the Conservative 'revolution', the great victor of 1 May poll will be neither Tony Blair nor John Major: it will be Margaret Thatcher."[17]

The Socialist Party along with others pledged that we would keep fighting for real socialist change. The three best results amongst more than 100 socialist candidates who stood in the election were for Tommy Sheridan in Glasgow Pollock with more than 10%, Dave Nellist in Coventry South with 6% and Arthur Scargill in Newport East on 5%. Our opponents predictably jeered at these results. We answered: "When Keir Hardie first stood he polled 617 votes."[18] More important than votes at that stage, our campaign resulted in new recruits to our party all over the country.

13. Liverpool dockers strike 1995-97

'Epic struggle' is sometimes an overused phrase in relation to the struggles of the working class, though not when it is applied to the magnificent fightback of the dockworkers of Liverpool against the reintroduction of casualisation of employment in their industry in the 1990s. It was a battle which began in September 1995 and unfolded over 28 months – 14 months longer than even the great miners' strike of 1984/85.They faced a brutal cabal of employers who tried to implement a lockout of the 500 dockers. This was bolstered by a near media blackout of the struggle, the aim of which was to prevent other workers coming to the dockers' assistance. This completely failed, with unprecedented international support and wide solidarity from the length and breadth of Britain, in many cases organised by members and supporters of Militant Labour and the CWI, our international organisation. However, they were not just fighting a brutal boss but also their own trade union, the Transport and General Workers' Union (TGWU or T&G) led shamefully, unfortunately, by its then General Secretary, Bill Morris. If this union leadership – and backed up by the resources of the Trades Union Congress (TUC) as a whole – would have had just an ounce of the dockers' determination they would have won in a matter of weeks. Unprecedentedly, when the dockers were forced, almost starved back to work, the Daily Mirror, a so-called 'Labour paper', claimed that they had secured a victory! The dockers themselves considered this a whitewash designed to let the trade union leaders off the hook.

The strike, which was one of the first in Britain against modern globalised capitalism, saw sustained mass picketing with a high degree of participation by the dockers themselves. For instance, it was calculated at the end of the strike that just 30 out of 500 dockers had not participated at any time on the picket line. Bill Mullins, Militant Labour's national industrial organiser, was one of the first to urge our Liverpool organisation to contact the dockers at the outset of the dispute. This came at a time when there was already friction between our EC and some of the leading Merseyside members, like Dave Cotterill and Michael Morris, on a number of issues, which subsided somewhat during the strike. However, it has to be said that these comrades, together with others like Tony Mulhearn, played a big role in the strike, as did Bill Mullins himself and many other comrades from Militant Labour throughout the country.

The employers had prepared for a long time to take on the Liverpool dockers, who had been the last to return to work after the national dock strike of 1989. That strike had been in defence of the Dock Labour Registration Scheme which for the first time had allowed dockers to either be regularly employed or, if there was no work, to receive a minimum level of wages. This had replaced the inhuman scramble for daily work in the 'pens' where employers picked out who would work for the day and who would not. As a child, and coming from a Merseyside working class family in which dockers and shipbuilding workers predominated, I had been regaled by my 'Uncle Jimmy' amongst others who had worked on the docks. The vicious dock overseers and their contemptuous treatment of the men were engraved on the consciousness of the working class of Merseyside, even amongst those who had not experienced employment in the docks first hand. For conscious socialist members of the labour movement, the dockers have a special place in their hearts, much like the miners had with the working class of Britain as a whole.

It was not an accident that this monumental dispute broke out at the time that it did. It was part of the Thatcher-inspired attempt to introduce mass casualisation of the labour force. Thatcher's heirs continue her handiwork today with a huge lowering of living standards, even for those who work, by the introduction of more and more part-time, casualised employment. The 1989 strike was lost when the T&G leadership pulled the plug and the Dock Labour Registration Scheme ended. From then on the Mersey Docks and Harbour Company (MDHC) was determined to try and break the unions. It withdrew recognition from the shop stewards, but the dockers refused to withdraw support for them. The reason why the dockers found such support, locally, nationally and even internationally, was because of their unstinting record in support of other workers in struggle. As Bill Mullins commented: "70% of the strikes were not about their own issues directly but in support of other workers outside the docks."[1]

The strike began on 28 September 1995. Right from the outset, Militant Labour pointed out: "The sacking of 500 Liverpool dockers has enormous implications for the entire working class. Liverpool is the only port not to employ casual labour... They represent the hopes and fears of millions of workers on the question of low pay, casual labour, redundancies and, above all, on intimidatory and arrogant management tactics." Through the Port Shop Stewards' Committee there had been a magnificent fightback. We warned about the possible role of the union leaders: "Unfortunately, the official position of the dockers' own union, the TGWU, has been to sit back, afraid of losing their assets if they give them official backing. The union leaders simply don't realise that the members are their one and only asset."[2] We also pointed towards the importance of the picket lines, which were organised on a daily basis, despite the difficulty in picketing a seven-mile waterfront. This often resulted in the dockers leading the police a merry dance as pickets appeared out of nowhere at this or that gate!

The conditions facing the dockworkers were described by young dockers who had been sacked: "After I became full-time for Torside [the company at the centre of the dispute], my wages were £170 top line with no pension, no sick pay, no work clothing. [The employers] can call us out to work at any time for up to 80 hours a week. You can go in at 7:45am, if there is no work in they send you home at 12 o'clock, tell you to get eight hours' sleep and come back and do the night shift."[3] Even the pro-business Liverpool Echo initially criticised the employers! Twenty years before there had been 6,000 dockers in Liverpool. This had shrunk to 500 but these moved more cargo than at any other time in history. This was an indication of the huge containerisation that was taking place in the ports. Moreover, Merseyside was one of the last ports that still had a permanent workforce and was therefore looked to by dockers all over Britain to make a stand against casualisation. From the start of the dispute Militant raised the demand for a 24-hour stoppage throughout Merseyside in support of the dockers.

Urgent steps were taken to step up mass picketing to urge MPs and councillors to maintain their political support, by putting pressure on the MDHC, by extending support groups, in particular women's support groups, and holding public rallies. Meetings and demos were held to build further public support and to extend contact and lobbying with shop stewards and workers in the Canadian and US ports; 30-40% of cargo out of Liverpool was going to Montreal. Above all, the demand went out for the leaders of the trade union movement to match the resolve of the Liverpool dockers themselves, with special attention paid to the TGWU and the TUC. The demand was for a solidarity campaign with workers refusing to handle all cargo going to Liverpool docks and organising solidarity action. The right-wing trade union leaders hid behind the Tories' anti-union legislation. They argued that the strike was technically illegal but this held no water because, in 1972, London dockers had famously defied the anti-union laws of Edward Heath's Tory government and secured the release of the imprisoned Pentonville Five.

One docker compared the past to the current scheme: "It was a step in the right direction and what we had fought for, like my father and grandfather. Everybody was employed by the National Dock Labour Board first, then you were subcontracted to an employer."[4] It was true that, through the introduction of new technology and mechanisation things became easier. However, this was not for the benefit primarily of the dockers but bolstered the profits of the employers. A ship makes no profit without its cargo. The bosses therefore wanted quick turnarounds with bigger containers. The trade unions were an obstacle to them so they wanted to do away with effective union organisation.

The international campaign in support of the dockers had the effect of increasing solidarity from co-workers worldwide, which included not just messages of support and finance but also visits to Merseyside. One such example was that of Jack Heyman from the San Francisco local of the International Longshoremen and Warehousemen's Union. He marched with the dockers on 13 January 1996 and said: "What impresses me is the militancy and unity. The support they are getting internationally is astounding; there hasn't been this sort of campaign launched in a long time." He drew parallels with their struggle in the US: "Our union has jurisdiction on the docks but the employers are attempting not to register any new longshoremen [dockers], so we are fighting the employers over casualisation. This is going to be a big fight... If dockworkers cannot organise themselves internationally unionised workforces around the world will be decimated. Three years ago we sponsored the Pacific Rim dockers' conference, which brought together all the dockers' unions in the Pacific Rim trade as a first step towards that effort."[5] Dockers in Israel, Greece, Italy and France added their support to the Australian, US, Canadian, German, Swedish and New Zealand dockers. They were prepared to take direct action against any ship that used Liverpool and the intention was to draw this altogether and coordinate it at an international conference in Liverpool.

Despite the determination of the dockers and the mass support they were receiving from ordinary workers, the leadership of the T&G, specifically Morris and his entourage, refused to use the union's resources to prosecute the dockers' struggle to the end. In words Morris 'supported' the dockers and hoped they would win a victory for the union movement. However that did not involve the vital basic principle of the reinstatement of the sacked dockers. Instead, he proposed negotiations leading to a severance deal. Morris had always been reluctant to give significant support, but this dispute was taking place at a time when the Tory government was on the rocks and would soon be defeated in the general election. A great opportunity was presented to press the dockers' case and achieve a famous victory which would have redounded to the benefit of the whole of the working class.

In practice the T&G General Executive Council (GEC) had consistently termed the Liverpool dockers' dispute as 'unofficial' and 'illegal', leaving the union with no immunity or legal protection if it declared the dispute official. It is this reason that was always invoked to explain the T&G's role over the previous 22 months. Yet the dockers said that, in effect, their dispute was not unofficial because the union had not issued any 'letters of repudiation' to the Liverpool docks shop stewards, the dockers themselves or the MDHC. The dockers were pressing for more than just limited finance and the promise of future negotiations. They were demanding the full power of the union to be used against the docks' employers.

The bosses were frank about their determination to crush the dockers, as shown by the speech of Nicholas Finney, former director of the National Association of Port Employers: "Fundamentally and long before the government repealed the scheme, we took the decision that the employers were going to abandon all national and port pay bargaining." He further revealed the viciousness and determination of the employers: "We used every political body which had influence. We also used the press and media. We constantly searched out and supplied the media with anti-docker stories... We had a Times columnist write headlines like... 'Legalised Extortion Racket'. We also encouraged radio and television to do documentary programmes on the dock scandal. We knew that confrontation would be inevitable and when at last the government announced on 5 April 1989 that they were going to repeal the dock labour scheme we knew we had won a famous victory... We had 9,221 dockers on 5 April 1989. In October 1990, there are less than 4,000 dockers left and many ports where there are no ex-registered dockers at all. But I think the greatest of our achievements is that we destroyed for the foreseeable future the power of the trade unions."[6]

The frustration of the dockworkers at the refusal of the union leadership to fully back them culminated in a ferocious clash at the TGWU's national conference in July 1997. The GEC tried to foist a statement about the Mersey docks dispute onto delegates but found themselves facing defeat. The debate was stormy, with Jimmy Nolan, chair of the Merseyside Port Shop Stewards Committee, stating that support for the executive's statement would be a knockout blow to the dockworkers. Another delegate defiantly declared: "The union is celebrating 75 years but its real establishment was in the great docks strike of 1889. The dockers are the reason we are here today."[7]

Port shop steward Bobby Morton denounced the inaction of the union leaders: "Every time they went to deliver a knockout blow internationally, the white towel flew into the ring from Bill Morris. Whilst agreeing with the protection of the fabric of the union, the reality was that the fabric is the members." Teresa Mackay, a prominent member of the Socialist Party, made a telling contribution in which she pointed to the international nature of the dockers' actions in confronting the notorious anti-trade union laws, regarded by dockers internationally as reminiscent of a dictatorship. She declared: "If the dispute was illegal, why was the union negotiating with the bosses?" Morris replied that non-compliance was against the rules of the union: "We are a law-abiding union."[8] However, the fighting contributions from the dockers and their supporters carried the day, overturning the GEC statement, despite the bureaucratic manoeuvres from the top. The dockers, however, were under no illusion about the reluctance of union leaders to ensure the success of the struggle. Attention therefore shifted towards the national and international planes with a plan of action in support of the dockers.

Militant Labour had always opposed crude 'rank and filism', a hallmark of groups like the SWP: the idea that action from below, without the involvement of the official organisations and structures of the trade unions, was enough. We have always strongly argued that action from below must be combined with consistent attempts to change the structures of the unions so that they more accurately reflect the real interests and demands of the members. It is true that Morris rubbished the dockers' struggle with his continual reference to "the 800 TGWU members still working in the port". We made searching criticisms about the structures of the union. In addition, Region 3 (Ireland) called for an official request to be made to the International Transport Federation to organise a worldwide boycott of ships going through Liverpool. Morris insisted that this would have been in breach of the law: "Now we had British anti-union laws being used by the leadership to justify inaction internationally!"[9]

Despite the setbacks the fight continued to make the union more responsive to the needs of its members. Militant Labour urged the dockers to reclaim the union, even if this particular dispute was to go down to defeat. The vindication of this position – as opposed to the direction in which some of the Merseyside Militant Labour leaders were going – was shown in the election as general secretary of left-winger Len McCluskey in 2010 and his subsequent re-election in 2013. Militant Labour gave critical support to Len McCluskey, a supporter of Militant in the Liverpool Council struggle, because of the stand taken by him in support of workers in struggle. Not one industrial dispute was repudiated by the national leadership under his stewardship up to June 2015. Nonetheless, we did not give carte blanche to him or other national union leaders. We later criticised Lenny for not going ahead with his threat to organise with other unions a one-day general strike.

Another indication of the estrangement between the national leadership of Militant Labour and some of the Merseyside comrades was that, in the whole period of the dockers' strike, our national leadership – particularly myself – was not invited to speak at any mass meeting or rally. Less prominent Militant Labour activists were. This was the first time in 30 years I had not spoken at the big meetings and rallies in the area in which Militant Labour played a prominent role. Yet the late Paul Foot was invited to speak from the balcony of the Council Chambers. He was a prominent member of the SWP which had condemned the Liverpool labour movement and Militant in its paper's headline, 'Sold Down the Mersey', following the victory of the marvellous 47 Labour councillors in the conflict with Thatcher in 1984!

This did not prevent me and other Militant Labour leaders from visiting the dockers and discussing with leaders like Jimmy Nolan. Moreover, we did not let our differences – which were not evident to the dockers at the time – stop us from energetically supporting the dockers throughout Britain and internationally. We recruited a number of dockers to our ranks. One commented: "After many years of inactivity in the movement I found myself in a dispute that has changed my life. It's difficult to put into words what the dispute has done. Sooner or later you have to make a conscious decision to fight against the attacks on the working class... I decided to join Militant Labour on the train journey from Glasgow to Liverpool. I had just finished a four-day delegation visit... I was impressed by the spirit of comrades and the issues they were addressing that affect us all on a daily basis."

Another said: "I remembered when I worked in the council in the days of the 47 Liverpool councillors, the impact that Militant Labour had on the local and national political scene and how it made me sit up and take notice of what was going on in the city. To me it was the only choice to make." Jimmy Nolan, who was also a prominent member of the Communist Party – and self-professed 'Stalinist' – commented that for the first time in a long time he was working amicably with Trotskyists! He commented in the Militant: "During the twelve months of our dispute, all Militant Labour representatives have played a highly principled role toward our reinstatement... Their organisational facilities have been put at the disposal of our organisation and their representatives have attended our mass meetings over the last twelve months."[10]

The Liverpool dockers' struggle was monumental. But after 28 months and without the backing of the national leadership of their own union or the TUC – despite the ardent support of hundreds of thousands and millions of workers – the dockers were forced to accept defeat. However, the lessons of this struggle were not lost on workers in general and particularly the dockers themselves. They participated in other battles of the Merseyside working class, including on the issue of the political alternative – a mass workers' party – that it is necessary to create in order for working class people to be victorious in the battle against the bosses.

14. The dispute with the Merseyside comrades

The 1990s involved the Socialist Party and the CWI 'swimming against the stream' internationally – both in a general sense given the ideological strengthening of capitalism in society through the continuation of the boom, and in its reflection within our ranks. In similar historical periods the labour movement and particularly its Marxist revolutionary wing was forced to confront opportunist and ultra-left theoretical backsliding. As we have remarked many times, the Bolsheviks in the aftermath of the defeat of the first Russian revolution 1905-07 faced many splits, to both the 'left' and the right. Lenin, the leader of the Bolshevik party – technically then still a faction of the Russian Social Democratic Labour Party – is usually pictured by bourgeois and petty bourgeois critics as a 'dictator' who brooked no opposition within his ranks. Yet he was defeated on crucial questions on a number of occasions.

For instance, after the defeat of the first Russian revolution, a 'boycott' of the tsarist-convened Duma (parliament) was initially carried within the Bolshevik ranks, with Lenin dissenting from this decision. This was not the only example of a mistaken ultra-left position adopted by the Bolsheviks. Lenin, however, did not resort to tantrums or the big stick to bring the ranks into line. Experience had taught the Bolsheviks that Lenin was usually correct and the decision was changed accordingly. Equally, given the defeat and isolation of the Bolsheviks, opportunist trends developed within

Bolshevik circles at this time. This was manifested in the 'liquidators' who abandoned previously held revolutionary positions, both in terms of ideas and the organisation of the party. Lenin and his collaborators came out firmly against both positions. Without Lenin engaging in this vital struggle – which used up considerable time and energy, involving numerous articles and even books – the ranks of the Bolshevik party would not have remained politically intact for the great task of the Russian revolution in October 1917. Nor would the cadres of the party have been prepared for the mighty events which developed, including the revolution itself.

Superficial, dry, academic bourgeois and petty bourgeois historians invariably picture the arguments and political clashes that took place as 'squabbles'. Marxism, on the other hand, sees the most important of them as an unavoidable and even necessary period of clarification, of polishing the theoretical weapons to be used in future battles. In the 1990s, first of all Militant Labour and then the Socialist Party, as we have seen, were engaged in serious discussions over political differences that arose, which sometimes resulted in defections from our ranks. Two of the most important developments involved the sharp political discussions that took place between our Scottish supporters and the national leadership – which we will deal with later – and a similar clash involving some former leading comrades in Merseyside.

Once the dockers' strike was over the subterranean battle between the national leadership of the Socialist Party and a number of comrades around Dave Cotterill came to the surface. He had played a prominent role, along with some of his supporters, at a certain stage in the heroic struggle in Liverpool. However, they were in the process of throwing overboard political positions which in the previous period they had supported. There was an objectively difficult situation which had developed in the city, particularly in the aftermath of the defeat brought about by the abandonment of the Liverpool councillors and the Merseyside labour movement by the treacherous Kinnock and right-wing trade union leaders.

Liverpool was a beacon of struggle and not just for Militant. We had managed to build the strongest base for the ideas and methods of Militant in the city. At our height, we had approximately 1,200 members in our Merseyside region, who effectively exercised a decisive influence both within the Labour Party and increasingly in the trade unions. We also produced a weekly supplement, Mersey Militant, to the national weekly newspaper. However, having gone much further in the city in building a base than anywhere else in Britain, the subsequent decline was also greater. Instead of politically and organisationally steeling those who were left in the ranks of Militant Labour for a difficult period, Dave Cotterill reinforced the deep scepticism and pessimism of some who were politically tired.

The differences, as is usually the case, developed first in what appeared to be secondary issues of organisation. The terrain in which we were operating in the 1990s was not favourable to a significant growth in our forces. Because of the consequent contraction in our financial base – in the regular weekly contributions from supporters and sales of the weekly paper and theoretical journal – it became necessary for us to carry through what, at times, was a very painful pruning in full-time staff and eventually selling our large premises. Some of the trade unions in Britain faced a similar situation later. They were under an onslaught from Cameron's coalition government, involving a slashing of facility time – time off from normal work for trade unionists to represent workers – as well as the undermining of the check-off system, the automatic collection of dues by the employer for the union.

Militant faced a similar situation in the 1990s and the necessary cutbacks were not enthusiastically embraced, to say the least, particularly by some of the full-time staff. Merseyside, in the past the jewel in the crown of our organisation, was treated extremely favourably by the national organisation. It received more financial help to employ more full-timers than any other area in the country, which was justified given the prominence of our position in the region. But the change in the situation in the 1990s when the Merseyside organisation had contracted – to a greater extent than in other areas – meant special treatment was no longer justified. Faced with this situation, Dave Cotterill and those around him resisted the decisions of the national organisation to cut our staff. Moreover, they increasingly linked their organisational differences on this and other issues to a political challenge.

Their organisational criticisms represented a departure from the norms of revolutionary organisation and were directed against the basic ideas of Marxism on how a revolutionary party should be organised. They were not unique in this. In the aftermath of the collapse of Stalinism and the ideological offensive of capitalism, a major target for the opponents of 'outdated Marxism' was the idea of a party, which was now to be replaced by networks and spontaneous organisation. This 'anti-party' mood is still alive and kicking today. The Occupy movement, some of the Indignados in Spain, the occupiers of the squares in Greece and most strikingly the Five-Star Movement in Italy, gave a boost to this mood. This compelled us to come out in defence of the traditional forms of organisation of revolutionary Marxism. This has relevance today. Clearly feeling that social democracy is discredited and mass revolt is developing, a campaign has been launched by the media against organisations on the 'left' who could become a rallying point for mass discontent.

Then and now we stand completely in defence of the ideas – properly explained – of democratic centralism as the best means of organising a party which seeks to change society. One of the issues raised in relation to the controversies in both Scotland and Merseyside, was that of the autonomy of regions within the structures of our organisation, and specifically how this related to finance. While we have a centralised organisation – which arises from the tasks of socialists in this era where the ruling class itself is highly centralised in its confrontation with the working class – nevertheless, the regions and branches have great autonomy. This applied in general to our party, but also in relation to issues like finance. On the other hand, our method of organisation did not merely mean linking up formally separate local groups. Even from the beginning the building of an authoritative political leadership and organisation on the national level was the key priority. On this basis, I moved to London in 1964 as the first full-timer, at least in the rebirth of our organisation in the 1960s.

There are suspicions – again, particularly in the new generation whose views have been coloured by what they interpret as the legacy of Stalinism – that power through this method of organisation will be concentrated in the hands of a 'bureaucratic leadership'. Specifically, what safeguards are there in the Socialist Party against the bureaucratic degeneration of the leadership? First of all is the requirement to convene regular meetings of the National Committee (NC), which elects and controls the Executive Committee (EC). It is the responsibility of the national leadership to convene these meetings, as well as regular congresses. There is also a provision for branches to demand an emergency conference. Nonetheless, what 'guarantee' is there that a strictly democratic regime would exist? Nobody raised these issues within our ranks, but there is an unspoken questioning in the minds of many workers and young people about inherent bureaucratic tendencies. Moreover, this is not a new question.

At one stage Leon Trotsky was asked to give "a clear and exact formula on democratic centralism, which would preclude false interpretations or bureaucratic degeneration". He replied that there is no one formula that once and for all would eliminate misunderstandings and false interpretations. "A party is an active organism that develops in the struggle with outside obstacles and inner contradictions... The regime of a party does not fall ready made from the sky but is formed gradually in struggle. A political line predominates over the regime. First of all, it is necessary to define strategic problems and tactical methods correctly in order to solve them. The organisational forms should correspond to the strategy and the tactic."[1] We commented in 1996: "Trotsky then makes a fundamental point: 'Only a correct policy can guarantee a healthy party regime.'"[2]

Of course, this does not mean that a party with a correct

programme will automatically have correct organisational methods. That is an issue for debate and discussion as to what emphasis should be given to democracy or centralism, depending on the different situations. A formula for democratic centralism must find different expression in the parties of different countries and in different stages of development of the same party. When the problem concerns political action, centralism subordinates democracy to itself. Democracy is paramount when the party considers it may need to examine critically its actions.

Many critics have aimed general and unspecified criticisms against the alleged undemocratic methods of organisation of Marxism, Bolshevism and then Militant, which stands in this tradition. However when we have set out and explained our ideas we have not received a single serious criticism of either our general approach, the theory of democratic centralism, or the concrete actions which have been taken by our party since its inception. Our critics have not responded when we pointed out that we never expelled or disciplined any individual, group or trend of opinion in the history of Militant or the Socialist Party on political grounds. In the case of the Liverpool comrades, as they described themselves – in effect ex-members of the Socialist Party – when we took action, it was because they took the collective property of the Socialist Party, including our Liverpool headquarters which Dave Cotterill and Michael Morris sold off once they left our ranks. Their organisational betrayal, however, was not an accident but was rooted in false political perspectives, which in turn arose from the very difficult objective situation which existed in the 1990s. The differences were centred on all the major questions of the era: perspectives for the world economy, the collapse of Stalinism, why it took place and its consequences.

The dockers' strike had temporarily halted the rightward political evolution of the group that was in control of the leadership of Merseyside Militant Labour. With the defeat of the strike their shift towards the right not only resumed but became, if anything, more pronounced. By 1999 this would lead to this group placing itself

131

outside the ranks of our party. The division between them and the overwhelming majority of the party was on a whole number of issues, from organisation to political perspectives. However, the central differences, as is invariably the case when divisions take place in the Marxist movement, were around politics. Dave Cotterill and Michael Morris, who were later to fall out with one another, by their own admission, produced a political 'critique' of the central ideas of Militant Labour. Unbelievably, they admitted: "There is little in this document which defines precisely where comrades on Merseyside stand on many of the issues which we are critical about in relation to the Socialist Party."[3]

We replied to this astonishing admission: "What would be said about a worker who discards his tools, without first acquiring new ones, and then proceeds to carry on working with his bare hands? He would be seen as a very inadequate worker. This, we are afraid, is how the ex-members of the Socialist Party on Merseyside will now be viewed, by those looking for an answer to the serious problems confronting the workers' movement worldwide."[4] We nevertheless traced out the political roots of this 'critique' in order to defend the stand of Militant Labour and the CWI during the whole period of the 1990s.

One of the central questions which were discussed then and since was over the role of information technology, how this related to the economic prospects of capitalism and did this signify a new structural growth of capitalism? Critics of the CWI included former member Paul Storey, who had been a leading member, in exile, of the Marxist Workers' Tendency, the CWI's South African section. On returning to South Africa in the early 1990s he dropped out of the CWI and politics altogether. Dave Cotterill clearly shared these ideas, as we will see. But he had a common position with Storey in another sense. Both rationalised their abandonment of Marxism and the labour movement with an acceptance of a new economic paradigm, a long-term growth of capitalism. However, they did not just seek to leave the ranks of our party and International but consciously sought to undermine them as their excuse for leaving our ranks.

We therefore took the opportunity in a quite lengthy pamphlet, New Technology and Globalisation: Can a Capitalist Slump be Avoided? to explain some of our views on a whole series of issues since the collapse of Stalinism. We recognised how, like the labour movement as a whole, we and Marxism in general had been pushed back. This was the starting point for the political retreat of the comrades around Cotterill. He claimed that his document was a 'collective' criticism of the Socialist Party. It wasn't! "In reality, it is written by Dave Cotterill, former regional secretary of the Socialist Party on Merseyside... The leading trade unionists in Unison [including Roger Bannister], long-standing members of the party such as Tony Aitman, who was in our ranks long before Dave Cotterill or his supporters, Tony Mulhearn who played a decisive role together with Peter Taaffe and other British EC members in the Liverpool Council battles of the 1980s, Paul Astbury, Deputy Leader of the Labour Group after Derek Hatton's expulsion from the Labour Party, Harry Smith and many other veterans of the struggle as well as the best of the new generation, remain with the Socialist Party."[5]

Moreover, we pointed out that neither Cotterill nor the others were suspended or expelled but "left when the Executive Committee of the Socialist Party asked questions about his involvement in a project on Merseyside (in effect a non-governmental organisation which arose out of the dockers' strike, which he was involved in as a paid official of the Socialist Party)."[6]

In the discussion that followed a series of organisational differences, which are mostly of historical interest today, were raised. However, as they were parting from our ranks, they naturally criticised the 'regime' of the Socialist Party which, until shortly before their document, they had defended. We pointed out: "The Merseyside socialists are a right-wing, opportunist split from the Socialist Party. Nevertheless, they were given full rights to explain their position verbally but, despite our urgings, they did not produce any substantial alternative verbal or written analysis to that of the CWI or the party leadership. Why did they wait until three weeks before the National Conference of the Socialist Party –and after Dave Cotterill had left the Socialist Party – to set their ideas down on paper?"[7]

We had answered the charge of lack of democracy within the party many times in the past, but we repeated this in relation to the new charges: "It is ludicrous for our critics, amongst whom now must be included the ex-comrades of the Socialist Party on Merseyside, to claim that debate and discussion is not the norm within our organisation. On the issues of Scotland, on France, let alone the name-change debate, we have seen an almost endless production of documents for internal discussion and debate." Moreover: "There is not a single case of any member of the party or the CWI being prohibited from putting forward a written criticism of the leadership of the party. Other organisations with access to our internal material have complained that they could not keep up with the volume of written material produced by the Socialist Party on the name debate and on Scotland."[8]

Trotsky summed up the type of opposition signified by these comrades: "Do you want to know the organisational programme of the opposition? It consists of a mad hunt for the fourth dimension of party democracy. In practice this means burying politics beneath discussion; and burying centralism beneath the anarchy of the intellectual circles."[9] In reality, these organisational criticisms were merely a sideshow. We were compelled to show to our ranks and the wider layer of workers and youth interested in us just how dishonest were the 'Merseyside ex-comrades', a sectarian fragment combining gross theoretical, opportunist blunders with ultra-left positions on issues such as the unions. On economic policy, they condemned the Socialist Party leadership as "primitive slumpists". This is a phrase that they had borrowed from the political arsenal of Militant in describing those Trotskyists, like the late Gerry Healy of the WRP, who prophesied during the boom period of 1950-75, that a slump was immediately on the agenda, alongside its corollary 'fascism'. Such a one-sided, crude position discredited organisations like this that were a caricature of genuine Marxism.

We never adopted such an approach and had fallen out with Ted Grant and Alan Woods on this issue back in 1987. In *The Rise of*

Militant we wrote: "What did the October [1987] share crash signify? The answer to this question was hotly disputed within the ranks of Militant. On the very day of the collapse Ted Grant argued that this was a precursor to a new 1929-type slump. His thinking was unfortunately reflected in the pages of Militant. In its initial comments on these developments it stated: 'A major slump in production and trade is assured, perhaps even before the summer of 1988.' Michael Roberts, who shared his view, stated that the October crash 'is a barometer predicting the impending storm that will exceed anything experienced by capitalism in the post-war period, possibly matching the great slump of the 1930s.'"[10]

However, our ex-Merseyside comrades were making the opposite – just as serious – error on the economic perspectives for capitalism in the late 1990s. They quoted Paul Storey approvingly: "The [Militant] tendency has probably made an incorrect basic appraisal of the period since 1974, relying too much on assumptions which have not been retested." Storey, when he was leaving the CWI, stated in a parting shot: "I believe, we have passed into the early stages of a new epoch in the development of the productive forces (from 'machinofacture' to 'computerfacture' for want of a better term)... we are bound to make endless mistakes unless we begin the analysis of all fundamental questions from that point."

He wanted the CWI to "pose the question of a decisive technological revolution occurring at the base of society, examine its implications and try to confirm it by careful empirical proof".[11]

Clearly, Storey and following him the Merseyside ex-comrades, subscribed to the idea that 'computer facture', married to globalisation – in effect, a decisive technological revolution – had ushered in a new, sustained period of growth for capitalism. The answer of the CWI was not to ignore the development of new technology, computers or globalisation but to soberly analyse its effects on the economy and the economic perspectives for capitalism. We pointed out that this was not a new issue: "In the 1930s, for example, many new inventions – plastics, rubber, etc. – already existed. However, they could not be fully implemented because of general stagnation in the productive forces. This only became possible as a result of the post-1945 world boom. This boom arose because of the massive demand created in the US by the onset of the war, particularly in industries which could utilise the new technologies. The destruction in Europe – the slaughter of value both of constant capital (factories, machinery) and variable capital (workers) – also cleared the ground for new productive methods and a structural upswing of capitalism."

The fundamental argument of the Socialist Party and the CWI was that new technology was an important development with particular effects in some fields. It had a decisive effect in the information technology and financial sectors, as well as in parts of industry. However, the effects of the 'technological revolution' had been misunderstood by Storey and his latter-day converts. "As opposed to the 1950-75 boom, its application had been intensive and not extensive. It had also been accompanied by cuts in the workforce, slashing of wages, etc., and the transfer of resources to a handful of countries in the underdeveloped world. Rather than avoiding crisis it has enormously aggravated it in Asia and elsewhere. The economic story of the 1990s is the limited application of technology in most industries."[12]

The Merseyside ex-comrades accused us of denying globalisation as a "concept, except in regard to financial transactions". However, we wrote: "We never denied globalisation, in the sense of an extension and development of the world division of labour, nor did we ever say that the 'Asian Tigers' were 'not important'. What we fought against were the exaggerations of those, like Paul Storey and now Dave Cotterill, of the effects of globalisation and new technology. We rejected completely that this was facilitating a 'higher stage of capitalism', of growth and stability. Globalisation, which first began to develop in the 1970s, did represent a new phase in the evolution of capitalism."

The first phase of capitalist globalisation, historically speaking, took place in the 19th century and was anticipated and described by Marx and Engels in works such as the Communist Manifesto. The post-Second World War boom of 1950-75 also witnessed an enormous extension and integration of the productive forces – science, technique and the organisation of labour – through the lowering of tariff barriers worldwide. However, this was taken to a new level following the collapse of Stalinism and the bourgeois ideological triumphalism that flowed from this, which had a material effect in weakening the labour movement, including the unions. This in turn reinforced neoliberalism by providing a plentiful supply of new, mostly cheap, labour and a massive development of globalisation. The opposite process, a trend towards 'de-globalisation', is evident today (2017) as a delayed reaction to the 2007-08 crisis, with the collapse of world trade.

We explained: "But this did not indicate the opening up of a boom period for capitalism. On the contrary, the economic crisis of 1974-75 signified a new period of 'depression'. The 1990s, seen as the 'end of history' by the bourgeoisie at the beginning of the decade, have already experienced one recession and are on the eve of another, or possibly a slump. We also showed that the Asian Tigers developed for special historical and economic reasons and did not represent the future of the countries of the underdeveloped world."[13]

Rather than showing a way out for capitalism it was precisely in those industries where new technology had been applied widely that the most devastating effects of the slump which gripped East Asia were being felt. Huge surpluses existed in the vehicle and computer chip industries, together with a classical glut, the colossal overproduction of goods. In every respect the perspectives of Storey and his belated supporters proved to be erroneous. We challenged our critics to explain why this 'revolution' in new technology and globalisation had "not led to a spectacular increase in the overall growth of the productivity of labour? Both Paul Storey and Dave Cotterill are completely silent when we point to the fact that the growth in the productivity of labour, in Britain and on a world scale, is lower in the 1990s – a period when they would argue that there has been a massive application of new technology to industry. The average growth in productivity is less than it was in the 1980s, which in turn is spectacularly less than it was during the structural upswing of world capitalism between 1950 and 1975."

Furthermore: "This was mainly because there was not the same ploughing back of the surplus extracted from the labour of the working class by the capitalists in investment in machinery and means of production as took place during the 1950-75 upswing. This technology was applied to a few industries with important results. As far as information technology and finance capital are concerned, the growth has been substantial... Moreover, the application of new technology to the 500 largest multinational corporations had seen a sevenfold growth in their sales, yet the worldwide employment of these global firms has [according to Greider] 'remained virtually flat since the early 1970s, hovering around 26 million people.'"[14]

It was true that, in the 1990s, the profits of the major monopolies in the advanced industrial countries grew significantly and in some countries approached the levels of the 1960s. This has mainly resulted not from the huge investment occasioned by new technology but by the application of neoliberal policies: increased exploitation of the working class through deregulation, privatisation, part-time working, two or three jobs, worsening of working conditions and relocation of production. Moreover, while the rate of profit had increased, the price ratio yields and dividends of shares had been very low, particularly in the us. In the 1990s shareholders' wealth came from capital gains not dividends.

Our critics tried to attack us on long-term perspectives for capitalism and especially the description of the depressionary tendencies in capitalism as far back as 1974. They said: "The Great Depression of 1873 to 1895-96 led in fact to a growth in anti-capitalist and socialist consciousness, and it led to the growth of us and German capitalism based on expanding markets and technological advance." They reinforced this point by arguing: "The 'depressionary' analysis, which really tells us very little, is taken as a sort of article of faith. It ignores the historical experience about the Great Depression at the end of the 19th century, a time of imperialist expansion, the building of trade unions, and socialist parties."

We answered: "The 'Great Depression' of 1870-1895 was termed a 'depression' because of a long-term fall in prices which, together with increased competition, cut the profits of the capitalists, especially in older capitalist countries like Britain, France and Belgium. But it was, at the same time, a period of extensive growth of world capitalism, especially in the USA and Germany, both of whom used trade protection to shelter home industries. Falling prices, while squeezing profits, raised real wages. So in many countries there was a real strengthening of the working class with offensives on wages, hours, etc."[15]

The situation of world capitalism throughout the 19th century, right up to 1914, in general followed an upward curve. As Trotsky pointed out the crises were relatively minor disturbances which did not halt this upward movement of capitalism. The partial exception was the 'depression' of the 1880s and early 1890s. There were a number of factors which led to this but the US offered an escape route for stagnating European capitalism and its millions of unemployed. This depression led to the 'boom' of 1896 to 1914.

The clear implication of their argument was that capitalism had found a new way out through new technology. These arguments were put forward just a matter of years before capitalism was to experience its most devastating crisis in history! They tried to see contradictions in our position: "Look, they say, the Socialist Party refers to a depressionary period dating from 1974-75 and, at the same time, their document speaks of a certain growth, or boom, or even a 'cyclical growth'. For Marxists there are 'cycles' and 'cycles'. The cycle in one period is entirely different in its strength, as a measure of the health of capitalism, than it is in another. In a sense it is like the heartbeat of a human being. In the full bloom of youth capitalism's heartbeat was strong, the 'booms' were greater than the occasional interruptions in production in the form of 'crises'. But the period which followed the First World War and the Russian revolution was characterised by a much more weakened 'heartbeat' of capitalism. The cycles were shorter, the crises were more often and deeper than the small ephemeral growth in production.

14. The dispute with the Merseyside comrades

"A period of 'depression' does not eliminate the cycle of growth and crisis. But a depression is marked by a general stagnation, a very feeble growth in productivity and the productive forces. Notwithstanding any 'booms', there is no structural growth, nor broad social and political stability. In the booms of the late 1970s, of the late 1980s and 1990s, the situation that has marked out capitalism since 1974-75, even in its citadels of the US and of Europe, is the stubborn existence of mass unemployment (which has lasted in the US right up until the recent period) and now beginning to affect Japan."[16]

Although Dave Cotterill and others who supported him played an important role in the dockers' strike, their advice at each stage was suspect, to say the least. As we mentioned earlier, the tendency of ultra-left groups to ignore the official structures in the trade unions was an ever-present theme of the Merseyside comrades during the docks dispute. In criticising them, we stated: "Prompted by Dave Cotterill, the Merseyside organisation, which only infrequently discussed at aggregate meetings the progress of the dispute, opposed the call for the TGWU to make the strike official. This was challenged by Roger Bannister who wrote: 'The whole discussion about the role of the TGWU bureaucracy brings into question our attitude to the trade union officialdom, how we criticise them to the rank and file and what demands we seek to have the rank and file put upon them... If no demands are placed upon them, they are off the hook and the impression is given that the leadership is irrelevant to the outcome of the struggle. It is in this light that the demand to make the dispute official has to be viewed, rather than as opening up a second front.'"[17]

If we had adopted Cotterill's position, we would have isolated ourselves in the manner of the sectarian SWP. Instead, we have not only built up a powerful position within the unions but also fought off witch-hunts, above all in Unison with the successful five-year struggle of our comrades – Glenn Kelly, Onay Kasab, Suzanne Muna and Brian Debus – who defeated the Unison leadership. We concluded: "The document of our ex-members represents a break with the ideas that built a powerful Trotskyist force on Merseyside. The purpose of their document is to supply ammunition to all the opponents of Militant, in the past, and now of the Socialist Party. No matter; we will continue along the path that we have charted out."[18]

We defended the idea of the necessity for a party, a mass party of the working class. However, we had to swim against the stream. Many of the new generation at times adopted an 'anti-party' position. This was a reaction to bureaucratic, top-down organisation of both the Stalinist and right-wing social democratic types. Even as recently as 2016, around the discussion in the Corbyn movement, we issued a timely reminder of the need for a party with a politically far-sighted leadership as the forceps which allow a revolution to be 'born': "Without the Bolshevik party – and the worker cadres assembled in its ranks who were steeled in the battle against the landlord-capitalist tsarist regime – there would not have been a successful Russian revolution. This idea is refuted today by the theoreticians of 'spontaneity', among whom Paul Mason is counted: 'You can do more with a mobile phone than a party.' This against the most ruthless ruling class in history that has concentrated unparalleled economic and state power in its hands!

"Other genuine and sincere young people in the anti-capitalist, anti-austerity movement, repelled by bureaucratic parties and their leaders, also reject political parties and naively believe that 'self-organisation' is all that is required. But the leaders of some of the new radical formations, like Podemos in Spain, while appearing to reject 'top-down' leadership and bureaucratism, in fact embrace a similar approach. Organised in a loose, virtual 'federation', real power is concentrated in the hands of the Podemos leadership with little or no opportunity on the part of others in the ranks collectively to formulate, and organise if necessary, alternatives to the leadership.

"The method of organisation of Podemos superficially puts power into the hands of the 'membership' but in reality concentrates it in an elitist fashion in the hands of the general secretary, Pablo Iglesias, and the Citizens Council. This body

141

has 81 members, consisting of the general secretary and regional secretaries, plus 62 members directly elected by a Citizens Assembly – not in a face-to-face delegate meeting but only online. Superficially, this appears to be super-democratic, but it allows the leadership to pull the strings without the challenge of face-to-face meetings.

"When the Indignados movement developed in Spain in 2011 – and was emulated in the occupation of Syntagma Square in Athens and other squares in Greece – [some] attempted to systematise spontaneity as an 'alternative' outside the 'traditional' method of organising through delegates, democratic discussion and the right of recall...

"It remains a fact that the traditional method of organisation deployed by the Bolsheviks, and emulated by the Marxist movement ever since, is the only one through which a successful socialist revolution, led by the working class, has been carried out. The highest form of this was reflected in the workers' and soldiers' councils (the soviets) – later emulated by the peasantry – in which 'direct democracy' was exemplified.

"The Bolsheviks reflected the need for control from below. They implemented the election of all officials, the right of recall, and no official to receive more than the average skilled worker's wage. In this way, careerists and opportunists were excluded and only the most devoted and self-sacrificing workers were included in their ranks."[19]

15. New Labour in government 1997

Right from the beginning the New Labour government showed that on key issues it was not likely to be even a 'reforming' government, determined as it was to carry on in the footsteps of the Tories. For instance, the Guardian revealed that the Dearing committee, set up by the previous Tory government, was considering a student voucher plan to "revolutionise the funding of universities and colleges". This would mean that free access to education would end. Parents would be encouraged to save for their children's higher education. Students whose parents did not take out special credits might, according to the Guardian, graduate owing £10,000-£20,000. Today, of course, debts of this order are considered quite small! Students finish university with twice or even three times as much debt. It is an indication of how far Blair and New Labour went in attacking students, indeed the whole of education. We wrote: "The contradictions between the promises of the government and the realities of what they will or will not do, will be borne by the working class. The continuation of Tory policies in the public sector, particularly with regard to pay cuts, means inevitable collisions. The anti-union laws of the Tories have been kept in place to be used if necessary against public sector workers who 'get out of line'."[1]

Just how far New Labour was prepared to go was illustrated by the treatment of the Prison Officers Association (POA) at the hands of Home Secretary Jack Straw. In his autobiography – modestly called Last Man Standing – he used a few choice words to describe the POA leaders: "I always worked hard for a constructive relationship with the unions, but the POA were in a category of their own... They went in for impossiblist demands, and then cried 'betrayal' when these could not be met."

For Straw anything which smacked of demanding democratic rights, let alone socialism, was 'impossiblist'. When the 'naughty children' of the POA would not listen to 'headmaster' Jack, he did not hesitate to use the anti-union laws, which he had criticised in the past. He writes: "On the morning of Wednesday 29 August 2007, I was woken at 6.30... The POA had, 15 minutes before, given notice that they were to begin a nationwide 24-hour strike there and then." This was, according to Straw, "utterly irresponsible, made worse by the paucity of their excuse for the action – that a 2.5% pay rise was going to be phased, giving ([the POA] said), a real terms increase of 1.9%." He accordingly took out an injunction against the union, requiring them to return to work.

He recounts that he was helped by the innately conservative national trade union officialdom: "Brendan Barber, TUC General Secretary, was immensely helpful in persuading the POA leadership to pull back." The same Brendan Barber was to be equally 'helpful' to David Cameron in the 2016 EU referendum, speaking on the same 'Remain' platform as the Tory prime minister. But Straw had decided to take revenge: "Since they had ambushed me, I'd return the compliment. During the autumn, I got collective agreement to add a provision imposing a comprehensive ban on industrial action by prison officers to a bill already going through the House [of Commons]. There was remarkably little dissent from Cabinet colleagues; just as remarkable was the fact that not a word about my intentions was leaked; everyone understood how high the stakes were. The ban went through with a thumping majority of 435. The POA had only themselves to blame."[2]

Could there be a clearer demonstration of just how far New Labour had moved towards the right to become the finished expression of the interests of the bosses and the capitalists as a whole? We stated earlier that in 1969, when Barbara Castle, Labour Minister in Harold Wilson's government, tried to introduce anti-union legislation which would have banned certain strikes, she was opposed root and branch by the ranks of the labour movement, particularly the trade unions. This was how fundamental the defence of union rights was to the whole movement at the time.

Straw had formerly stood on the soft left, as he recounts in his autobiography. He voted for Tony Benn in the deputy leadership contest in 1981 and had been a supporter of the left-wing journal Tribune. But this was merely a synthetic leftism. Throughout his career he was more of a politician for the main chance, anything which would benefit his climb up the greasy pole. His rapid evolution to the right involved him in attacking Liverpool city councillors, the miners and supporting the abolition of Clause iv. Therefore, his attack on the POA was not unexpected. Yet the trade union leaders in the main ignored this rapid evolution to the right as Blair, Straw and the like, converted New Labour into a completely pro-capitalist weapon for the bourgeoisie. It was no longer even the 'Second XI' for capitalism, put into bat when there was a sticky wicket, a crisis. It had sought to convince the bourgeoisie before coming to power of its total loyalty to capitalism.

In his diaries, on the eve of Labour coming to power, Tony Benn related a conversation with the secretary of Chesterfield Trades Council: "He said that some union general secretaries don't want the anti-union legislation repealed because it keeps their union under control, and I think he's absolutely right. It explains why they don't like strikes, because strikes put them under pressure, whereas, if there are no strikes and a bit of unemployment, it keeps their members quiet. I thought that was a significant comment."[3] Unfortunately, Benn, neither then nor subsequently, drew all the necessary political conclusions. Instead of boldly preparing for a new mass alternative, he dragged his feet through all the vicissitudes and attacks on working people which Blair and New Labour carried out both at home and abroad. Longer in power than any other Labour government, it was the most reactionary one. In fact, throughout the noughties it was the best possible government for the bosses and their interests.

It set out its credentials on economic policy by handing control of interest rates to the Bank of England, which met with universal praise from finance capital, in particular the City of London. This was a signal to the capitalists that it would not fundamentally interfere with the workings of the system. Control was to be in the hands of the representatives of the capitalists themselves, like Eddie George, Governor of the Bank of England, followed later by the equally conservative Mervyn King. He repaid his master Gordon Brown, Chancellor of the Exchequer after the 2010 election, by stabbing him in the back by implicitly backing the ConDem coalition and their brutal austerity policy.

However, we showed in Socialism Today that Blair had at least been consistent and open in his unvarnished courting of big business before he came to power. The trade union leaders and the left within the Labour Party should have asked questions about New Labour's pro-capitalist policies but they adopted a head in the sand position, at best, echoing Dickens's Mr Micawber, hoping that 'something would turn up'. They were to adopt this position throughout the lifetime of the New Labour government. Ken Livingstone, erstwhile champion of the left, took a 'vow of silence', declaring: "I am not going to say anything now, I don't want to be blamed if anything goes wrong." Unfortunately, Benn adopted a similar approach: "I am a soldier in the middle of a war... I wouldn't want to discuss my views of the generals."[4]

Tony Benn, nevertheless, is unsparing in his diaries in charting the rapid switch of Blair towards the right, even when it undermines his case that the Labour Party could be changed. Before the election, he commented: "The big political news today is that... Tony Blair came out in favour of the privatisation of air traffic control, of government land, Channel 4, and so on."[5] He laments: "I'm totally out of sympathy with the politics of the Labour Party."[6] The same themes developed one month after the election: "Blair read a statement saying that the difference between left and right has gone, the difference between ideologies has disappeared and we are now at the radical centre. It was all crap."[7] Moreover, the idea that the shift towards the right was merely at the top is contradicted by Benn himself when he remarked about the changing character of his own Chesterfield Labour Party: "For some time, the Chesterfield party was moving towards the right."[8]

It could not fail to be otherwise, as careerists, timeservers and place seekers, whose main attribute was contempt for the traditions of the labour movement, swarmed into and around the Labour Party. What genuine workers remained were elbowed aside by the middle class 'gilded youth'. This would be accompanied by scandals, tales of corruption and manipulation, particularly those who were gathered round the figure of Peter Mandelson.

They took their cue from the 'master' himself – Blair – who while showing contempt for working people, from his first day in office fawned at the feet of the rich and wealthy. In his autobiography *A Journey*, he states: "I hate class; but I love aspiration... When I was with a group of entrepreneurs, I felt at home." This meant concessions to the rich: "So for me, top-rate tax was not about top-rate tax. Of course you can make a perfectly good case for wealthy people paying more... but I wanted to preserve, in terms of competitive tax rates, the essential Thatcher/Howe/Lawson legacy. I wanted wealthy people to feel at home." If largesse from the table of the rich fell into his lap after he left office, who could object? "The stories of me being dazzled by the wealthy are always ludicrously exaggerated... nonetheless, I sometimes underestimated the ruthlessness and amorality that can go with moneymaking."[9] This sanctimonious hypocrisy is out of the mouth of a former prime minister who has cashed in on his reputation as a reliable supporter of the rich, amassing an estimated fortune of £80 million, some of it reward for advising dictators like President Nazarbayev of Kazakhstan! Start as you intend to go on! Blair and Brown bent the knee to big business, and Blair was certainly richly rewarded later.

If this meant challenging all the past gains of working people, the Blair government made it clear that it would do so from the outset. Frank Dobson, the newly appointed Health Minister, stated one month after the government came to power that he had "not ruled out" new charges in the NHS, for elderly people's prescriptions, state hospitals or visiting the doctor.[10] The fact that some of these measures have not yet been fully carried out, 20 years later, does not invalidate the fact that the Blair government paved the way for the attacks that are being inflicted on the NHS by the Tory government today. Flagged up were £1,000 tuition fees for higher education, again built on by the Tories in their brutal attacks on education. We commented that Brown, in his first budget, employed "mirrors, string, trapdoors and sleight of hand to disguise the budget's real content, portraying it as a budget for the people". Yet he made it clear that it remained within the Tory spending limits for everything but health and education. Rarely had a Labour Chancellor met with such a wall of praise from Labour's enemies. Ken Clarke, a former Tory Chancellor, praised the budget. We remarked in the Socialist: "And so he should because one industrialist told the Financial Times, 'It was a good Tory budget.'"

The stock market soared as did the pound. We commented: "In all the hosannas for Brown, it should be remembered that the overall effect of the budget is to increase taxes." Brown also promised a ladder of opportunity for young people with proposals for subsidies to employers for apprentices. At the same time, he made clear that he was going to introduce an element of the US system of workfare, including withdrawing benefits from people refusing to take any job offer.[11] This is precisely what the 2010 ConDem coalition government undertook. The consequence was that British capitalists can now boast a lower main rate of business tax than the US, Japan, Canada and many of its European competitors. At the same time working people, through increased costs and taxes, would pay for whatever concessions were made to the rich. The legacy of Thatcher remained: low, poverty wages, structural unemployment and inadequate resources in the public sector.

Brown then made his infamous statement, which was hung round his neck later by his opponents, as he promised to take

Britain out of the 'boom and bust cycle'. We stated bluntly that these cycles were intrinsic to the workings of capitalism and that Brown, if he remained within the framework of the capitalist system, would surely acquiesce or face colossal opposition from the 'market'. Undaunted, Labour wheeled out its privatisation programme, the centrepiece of which was the Private Finance Initiative (PFI). We gave a warning in a front page article written by Socialist Party member and Wakefield hospital worker, Mick Griffiths: "In opposition, New Labour called PFI in the NHS 'creeping privatisation'. Unison... produced thousands of posters quoting... Harriet Harman's statement: 'When the private sector is building, owning, managing and running a hospital, it has been privatised.' Now, Labour is using the PFI review to simplify, speed up and make the creeping privatisation work." In prophetic words, the article concluded: "The whole PFI is a hell on earth that will make even the current two-tier NHS seem like heaven."[12]

16. The Death of Diana
August-September
1997

Less than four months into this government came the death of Princess Diana in a car crash with her companion Dodi Fayed in Paris. Although an opinion poll only weeks before had shown support for the royal family below 50% for the first time, there was now an outpouring of public grief and soul-searching at her death. In unprecedented scenes massive crowds came onto the streets of London, in particular, and in other cities too. We posed the question: "Why did an estimated 300,000 people sign the book of condolences for someone they had never met, and who inhabited an entirely different world to theirs?"[1]

Was it just another case of mass hysteria whipped up by the press? There was undoubtedly an element of this, which provided an opportunity for us to explain and underline the class role of the monarchy today. Walter Bagehot the 19th century political journalist stated that, "The use of the Queen, in a dignified capacity, is incalculable."[2] Further: "Our royalty is to be reverenced, and if you begin to poke about it, you cannot reverence it. Where there is a select committee on the Queen, the charm of royalty will be gone. Its mystery is its life. We must not let in daylight on magic. We must not bring the Queen into the combat of politics, or she will cease to be reverenced by all combatants; she will become one combatant, among many."[3]

The public reaction to the death of Diana and her companion

revealed the complete transformation that had taken place since Bagehot's times. Deference to the upper circles of society, including the monarchy, had been shattered beyond recall. We pointed out: "In an astonishing week which followed Diana's death, the fate of the monarchy as an institution, and not just the Windsors, seemed to hang by a thread. Above all reaction to her death revealed the underlying explosive tensions in this society which came to the surface for a time." Mixed in with public grief was complete hostility to the press and the digital media. People outside Kensington Palace declared to reporters: "You killed her."[4] The appeal of Diana to sections of society who would otherwise be repelled by the monarchy was mainly due to her seeming sympathy for the 'underdog': the well-advertised visits to the homeless, accompanied by her sons; a campaign on landmines, condemned by the Tories; and a reaching out to those such as lepers, which endeared her to a broad swathe of the population.

Trained as a nursery nurse, even Diana's body language in embracing children or the disabled contrasted favourably with the dysfunctional and non-tactile Windsors. This impression was reinforced in the days following her death. As the rest of the royal family remained in their Balmoral fortress, huge crowds queued outside Kensington Palace, in effect taking over the royal parks. As the Observer put it: "Diana met the need in a lonely secular society for solidarity and warmth – and for secular saints... The past 20 years of rising inequality, decaying public institutions, the celebration of private activity and private free markets has created a new society that is more individualistic, more insecure, less anchored... A seemingly vulnerable woman appealed to millions, particularly women, who also feel vulnerable." Even bourgeois commentators remarked that Diana worship was basically anti-royal, anti-establishment: "Diana would not be thought good if the causes she had espoused were privatisation, workfare and the charity ball."[5]

One of the most striking features of these events was the rapid change in consciousness in the week following her death. The day after she died, there was complete hostility in the press and growing criticism and even hatred towards the royal family. We commented:

"This is also a reflection of the 'feminisation' of society over the last two decades. More inclined to demonstrate their feelings, women's attraction to the figure of Diana grew in inverse proportion to the growing hostility to the figure of Prince Charles. This is also an expression of the fact that even bourgeois women in class society face oppression and discrimination, not in the social and economic sense as with the working class, but personally and psychologically."

There was growing antagonism towards the Windsors and the monarchy as the Queen was contemplating a public funeral for Diana. Jolted by the barbs from the press, the royal entourage departed the Balmoral lair and descended on London. Gaffe-prone Prince Philip asked a member of the crowd outside Kensington Palace: "Have you been waiting long?" The average waiting time was over 11 hours! Blair obligingly stepped in to defend this feudal relic. In the short term he appeared to capture the public mood. This contrasted with the hapless new Tory leader William Hague, who in the days leading up to her death had attacked Diana for her anti-landmines policy. He compounded this problem by attacking Blair over his role in advising the monarchy during the events after her death. Yet polls showed that 83% of the population approved of Blair's role. These events in Britain were similar to what happened after the Dunblane massacre or the White March in Belgium following the paedophile murders of a number of children.

In the aftermath of Diana's death the media predictably took a side swipe at the left who allegedly show a lack of feeling "and even inhumanity" at the death of Diana. We pointed out that, on the contrary: "Marxism is the most humane philosophy. It is saturated with the spirit of optimism and faith in human destiny." Marx approvingly echoed the words of the poet Heinrich Heine: "Nothing which is human is foreign to me." It is possible to feel sympathy for the death of any human being (especially in horrific circumstances), including one from a privileged background and the personal loss suffered by her family.

At the same time, this does not mean that we close our eyes to the limitations of the role of an individual or the social role which she, her circle or the monarchy can play. We are opposed to any impediment or institution which prevents working people establishing a clear consciousness of its own power and strength. From a basic democratic point of view, never mind the interests of the working class and socialism, the feudal institutions of the monarchy, along with the House of Lords in all its trappings, should be abolished and put into a museum of antiquities. In the final analysis, the monarchy is a weapon for the ruling class to be used in 'emergencies'. This was shown in Australia in 1975 with the replacement of the democratically elected Labour government of Gough Whitlam by the Queen's appointed governor-general.[6]

The ruling class has not yet been forced to call upon the monarchy to play a similar role in Britain. Its more farsighted representatives can, however, envisage a huge future collision between the classes leading to a revitalised socialist labour movement. This could culminate in an election of a socialist government threatening their power and prestige. As history attests, in this situation, they would not hesitate to use extra-parliamentary methods and mobilise around the monarchy as a symbol of the 'nation'.

Following the death of Diana there was a concerted attempt to 'humanise' Prince Charles. But in 2013 we learnt that the Queen had personally intervened in a number of parliamentary bills, as had Prince Charles. This alone is an infringement of the democratic rights of the British people. The monarchy is supposed to be neutral in politics. It is not. With an intensification of the class struggle inevitable, the ruling class will gather behind all its institutions, including the monarchy, which it will try to use against attempts to move society in a socialist direction. This is why, while carefully analysing the movement that developed around the death of Diana, we never forgot the class criterion of emphasising the role of the monarchy as a weapon in the armoury of the ruling class. This issue will undoubtedly come to the fore again in future battles in Britain.

17. Fighting tuition fees
1997-98

What remained of the left clung to the wreckage of what was 'old Labour', despite the fact that the leaders of New Labour more and more defended inequality, especially when applied to themselves. Following a public outcry in September 1997 Blair was forced to review his pay rise of £41,443 (£797 per week, or £20 per hour). It was outrageous that he could even consider accepting such an increase. Meanwhile, he was asking nurses to accept "an extremely modest" pay rise of less than 3.5%, below the inflation rate. John Monks, then leader of the TUC, ever the statesman, commented: "I've always believed in paying the proper rate for the job... As far as I'm concerned, it may be a catching up exercise."

Blair moved ever closer to the Liberal Democrats and their supporters. In September 1997 we reported on what seemed to be serious considerations for a future coalition or merger. Former Labour Cabinet minister, then Lib Dem peer, Lord Roy Jenkins, who was a close adviser to Blair, stated publicly that Blair wanted to rebuild the centre-left coalition "away from the tyrannies of party politics". This was a clear attempt, even at this early stage, to ensure that Blair could carry out his pro-capitalist programme, cutting across any likely dissent that would develop within Labour, particularly from the direction of the trade unions.[1]

Ministers in the New Labour government were overjoyed with the trappings of office. Straw, ever the flunkey, wrote: "[Blair] decided that I should accompany him to Washington DC on his first official government visit to President Clinton. I've been grinding away in my 18th year in opposition. Now this – and my first ride on Concorde as well."[2] But there were no such outpourings of joy from the labour movement as the government expressed its determination to remain within the spending limits set by the previous Tory government, even if this meant limiting and cutting welfare and education. Tony Benn records that Blair justified cuts to single parents' income on the grounds that "Tory spending limits were actually too slack".[3]

He elaborated on Blair's future plans: "[Blair] listed all the achievements and said, 'Life will get harder. We are bound to anger some people. There are choices to be made. It is a test of our nerve. The Welfare State has got to be reformed. We said we would save money and modernise the Welfare State. We have got to change benefits in the right way in order to finance our education and welfare reforms. We wouldn't leave people without help... We have got to create opportunities. There are two types of criticism – constructive criticism and the sort of criticism that mouths the Tory stories that we are dismantling the welfare state. It is up to us. We listen, of course. We must deliver our pledges and remember what unites us.'"[4] This is the hymn to austerity which the Tories and Lib Dems would build on in order to carry through their savage cuts later.

Harriet Harman was given the job of implementing and explaining the cuts. The government drew on the experiences of the Clinton administration in the US – which was a model for Blair – in implementing cuts. Harman particularly pointed towards the US state of Wisconsin, which had cut its lone parent claimants from nearly 100,000 to fewer than 30,000 over ten years as benefits were withdrawn. The Wisconsin scheme, however, involved forcing people into overwhelmingly low-paid jobs. Moreover, if you refused a job and were then denied benefits, what then?

Britain already had experience of the effects of the withdrawal of income support and housing benefits from 16 and 17 year-olds. This had resulted in a dramatic rise in homelessness and poverty. Harman also spoke of encouraging lone parents of school age children to attend a JobCentre for interviews. This has a very topical ring to it today. Just remove Harman's name and replace it with Iain Duncan Smith, her successor in Cameron's governments, and the theme would be the same! This demonstrates that the attempt to cut back on the living standards of the working class, to cut their share of national income and boost the share of the capitalists, has been a process at work over decades. Moreover, Blair made sure that it was those 'left' MPs and ministers from the past, like Harman, who were called upon to do his dirty work. All the right-wing Labour ministers, including Blair, stayed away from the House of Commons while Harman was left to justify attacks on the very poorest section of the population.

Similar proposals to attack the young, cut back on education and increase tuition fees were met with the response of 50,000 students marching in twelve cities across Britain on 1 November 1997 in angry protest at the abolition of free education. These demonstrations took place despite the opposition of the National Union of Students (NUS) – a breeding ground for future New Labour MPs and careerists – because it did not want to embarrass the government. In a front page article with the headline 'Grants Not Fees' we wrote: "It will be working class students who will be most affected if the grant goes, watching student debts for fees and maintenance go up to around £20,000." Is this not what all students face today: massive debts, with the added dose of poison that few well-paid jobs are available when young people come out of university?

Education Minister David Blunkett tried to sell these proposals by writing to each MP assuring them that everything would be fine, despite the fact that applications for universities were down by 8-10%. Anger grew as students realised that they would not get any help towards paying fees. Within weeks of arriving at college in autumn 1998 students or their families would have to pay £1,000 upfront to college authorities. A student at Teesside University commented to the Socialist: "I'm disgusted. This government is making a habit of saying one thing, then backtracking. My sister hopes to go to university next year but demanding payment of

£1,000 upfront will end her university education." Another student Owen Hatherley – who subsequently became a journalist and wrote critical articles about the Socialist Party but who was, at this time, sympathetic because of his circumstances – also stated: "My mum is a single parent and this year I got a £150 maintenance grant to buy books, but they take that off her benefits."[5]

Fuelling the anger over the government's attacks on students was the spectacle of Blair sunning himself in the Seychelles over Christmas, while single parents and disabled people faced the bleak prospect of savage attacks on benefits and a further erosion of the welfare state. Benefit cuts totalling £3.2 billion had been outlined by Labour for the following two years. Moreover, like the Cameron governments, Labour conducted a smear campaign to justify these attacks. They gave the impression that the majority of those on incapacity benefit were falsely claiming and were available for work. Yet 75% of disabled people were already over retirement age.

Blair had addressed the 1997 Labour Party conference – dubbed by the Socialist 'Labour's Planet Happiness'. We commented: "What was served up, in the most duplicitous language, is a programme for attacking working class living standards." Some capitalist commentators agreed that Blair's "speech could be called in large part a Tory speech, putting words round Tory concepts like duty and ambition, except that no Conservative politician could utter them without being laughed off the stage, as they were in May".[6] Blair's buzzwords were 'reform', 'hard choices' and 'radical'. We countered: "For 'reform' read 'counter-reform'. For 'radical' read 'Thatcherism without Thatcher'." He called for 'hard choices' to be made. But it did not take a rocket scientist to work out that his hard choices would be made by working class people and not by the rich and big business. He invoked, as models for modern Labour, John Maynard Keynes and William Beveridge, who were not socialists but firm defenders of capitalism.

At Labour's conference, however, there was a spark of hope for the left, it seemed, in Ken Livingstone's defeat of the odious Mandelson in the party's NEC elections. Livingstone's share of the vote increased from 31% in previous years to 39%. He claimed that a new left coalition was taking place which stretched from the Campaign Group to Roy Hattersley! We pointed out that Hattersley "bears a major responsibility for the state the Labour Party is in today. The beginning of the Labour right's counter-revolution dates from 1985 from Kinnock's attack on Militant. Hattersley was intimately involved in the preparation and carrying out of this attack. Of course, he does not fully like the consequences of his past deeds. He has even hinted that it might be necessary for the 'moderate left' to split from the Labour Party in the future. He has drawn bolder conclusions than many left MPs who vainly hope for the left's re-emergence at next year's Labour Party conference."

We predicted that real opposition would come not from the NEC or the Parliamentary Labour Party, but from mass resistance outside of Parliament. When the poll tax was introduced, it was Militant that organised the mass resistance which defeated it and toppled Thatcher. Our summing up of the conference and the ratification of the government's programme showed just how far the Labour Party had degenerated: "In the teeth of such a programme, Labour Party conferences in the past would have been in uproar. This one had less passion than a parent-teachers' association."[7] It must be added that, since this was written, many PTAs have been in uproar over the introduction of academies and the continuation of the massive privatisation of education!

At the time of the conference and shortly afterwards there were further revelations about the closeness between Blair and the Liberal Democrats' Paddy Ashdown. Speculation in the capitalist press was rife about plans to introduce proportional representation and even the inclusion of the Lib Dems in government as a step towards coalition at a later stage. The plans included the future dissolution of the present Labour and Lib Dem parties into an Italian-style 'centre-left' party. The speculation was fed by a 'lovefest' between Blair and Ashdown. The press also revealed, according to Blair's confidantes: "Tony was a bit disappointed with Labour's 179 seat majority in the election." As we pointed out even before the election, if he had only got a small majority, Blair was prepared to offer the Lib Dems posts in a new government. Such was the size of Labour's majority, he had no excuse to include the Lib Dems as an ostensible means of maintaining Labour in office.

Blair did the next best thing, however, by setting up a Cabinet committee on constitutional reform, involving six ministers and five Lib Dem frontbenchers. This resulted in an unofficial coalition with the Liberals. Blair himself seemed at an all-time high in the polls with 83% supporting him. We remarked: "Only Stalinist dictators in Eastern Europe and North Korea have attained such popularity." We were undaunted by this because, unlike the careerists, PR men and women who infested Labour at this stage, workers and socialists were absent or drowned out by the cacophony of the Blair worshippers. We reminded the labour movement of some salient facts in relation to the political philosophy of the Liberal Democrats and their stance on key issues: "Today's Lib Dems supported Thatcher through thick and thin when she shackled the trade unions. They attacked jobs and services in Liverpool in the 1980s. Their past leader Steel has been revealed as receiving £94,000 as a parliamentary spokesman for the fox-hunting lobby." The fact that the Labour leadership could even contemplate a pact with the Liberals, with barely a murmur of opposition, showed once more that it had ceased to be a working class party.

After this dreadful conference Tony Benn argued that Labour could face a future split: "I see the Labour Party standing against the coalition government as it did during the 1930s when Independent Labour MPs stood against supporters of National governments led by Ramsay MacDonald." That, we argued, assumed that the Labour Party of the past remained intact: "Tony Benn's mistake is not to see that a 'new party' has already been created – New Labour – with overwhelmingly new, largely middle class recruits, with the unions more and more marginalised. In Guardian columnist Hugo Young's words, it is a 'capitalist' party." We added that a coalition government at that stage, "rather than leading to a split as in 1931, could be the signal for the creation of a new mass party of the working class, if one has not been created beforehand".[8] This was to become a recurring theme in the arguments we would have with what remained of the 'left' within Labour.

On Blair's honeymoon with the British people we stated that it "will not last. On tuition fees, class sizes, the catastrophic situation in the NHS, the economy and unemployment, this government will not be able to deliver. The government's present popularity will turn into its opposite particularly if, as is likely, the harsh winds of economic recession or even slump grip Britain." In view of this verdict it is possible that our critics could say that that our predictions were not borne out. Marxism does not pretend to be able to predict when processes will come to fruition. Timescale is always elastic. Sometimes it takes years, even decades, for prognoses to be borne out.

The longevity of the Blair governments does appear at first sight to have falsified our predictions. Blair won three general elections, despite presiding over real cuts in living standards, particularly of the poorer sections of the population, and accelerating the privatisation of education and the NHS. Moreover, he maintained the vicious anti-union laws fully intact – and justified this in the most brazen fashion. In addition, as with the prison officers mentioned earlier, his ministers were not reluctant to use them brutally when the occasion demanded. His government's aims and actions were entirely alien to the historic aims of the labour movement. Yet it was tolerated by the trade unions, particularly by their right-wing leaderships. Meanwhile, big sections of the population, including swathes of the working class, preferred this state of affairs if the alternative meant the return of the Tories – although without any enthusiasm.

The main reason for this is to be found in the character of the era described in our opening chapters. The collapse of Stalinism and the huge ideological boost which capitalism gained from this continued to be felt throughout the 1990s and beyond. Those making the case for socialism and class struggle policies were still swimming against the stream, particularly when it came to affecting the broad mass of working class people. At the same time, the economic recovery and the 'boom' that went with this was very one-sided, with the working class pushed back in relative terms because the leadership of the Labour movement accommodated itself to capitalism, while Blair and his counterparts worldwide went over completely to capitalism. This did not mean that the Socialist Party and Marxists could not have an effect, in spite of all the difficulties. In the main, however, this consisted of leading movements on single issues – seeking to extend and politicise them – rather than having a dramatic effect on the political consciousness of the mass of the working class. Ultimately, the consciousness of the working class is determined by the objective situation, which can only be changed by big events. In a situation where the working class is able to rub along, keeping its head above water at least, it would only be the more politically aware workers and youth who could be won to our party, to socialism and Marxism.

This is also allied to British workers' preparedness to grant time – sometimes too much time – to their leadership to show results. If you add in the fear of the return of a Tory government, it is not difficult to see how Blair could play on this to sneak back to power in two subsequent general elections after 1997. But this was achieved with greater and greater mass disenchantment with Blair himself – and a drop in turnout in elections, which undermines his alleged achievements. In his memoirs, he parades these general election victories as a great success. Nowhere does he or those like Straw ask the question of what election success and forming governments actually mean for the mass of the workers and the population as a whole. The only answer given is that it is in the 'national interest', the very same justification used by Cameron. The 'national interest' is ultimately the interests of the capitalists.

The task of Marxism in a period like this was to criticise the prevailing 'order' – which included the Blair government – to defend the analysis and programme of Marxism and seek to win more politically advanced workers and youth to our banner. We sought to be, in the concept of Marx, the movements of the future in the movements of the present. We had a dual task of seeking to rehabilitate socialism and Marxism through our analysis, while maintaining a rigorous Marxist organisation and party. Additionally, we intervened in all movements of the youth and the working class, popularising the ideas of Marxism and socialism in seeking to win the best layers.

Vital to this task was explaining the necessity for a new mass party of the working class. This in turn meant that it was necessary to seek ceaselessly to expose the real class character of New Labour. This was a precondition, particularly in the trade unions, to try to win over first of all the best workers and youth, and then the mass of the working class to the idea of a new party. In the 1930s Leon Trotsky wrote that the crisis of humankind could be reduced to a crisis of leadership. The Socialist Party concluded that, because the 'traditional' organisations of the working class, particularly their leaderships, had completely collapsed and gone over to the enemy class ideologically in the aftermath of the collapse of Stalinism, we now faced a crisis, not just of leadership but of organisation of the parties of the working class. It was therefore necessary to begin the arduous task of laying the groundwork for the emergence of new parties. In boldly taking to this new road we faced many obstacles: history, inertia, the conservatism, reluctance and, in some cases, cowardice of the trade union officialdom as they clung to outdated political concepts.

Blair declared in December 1997 at a meeting of the Parliamentary Labour Party that tuition fees "will be trouble until it happens, but then it will all be forgotten. One third of students will be exempt. It will be okay on the day. Students take out loans anyway and, if we don't have them, we will never get the money we want in education."[9] But he was profoundly mistaken if he considered that the opposition to tuition fees was just a 'little local difficulty', to paraphrase former Tory Prime Minister Harold Macmillan. Young people were furious and preparations were made for mass demonstrations to defeat this attack on basic education, rights that had been taken for granted for decades. Young members of the Socialist Party played a key role in mobilising for a mass demonstration in the first few months of 1998. The NUS leadership, allied as they were to New

Labour, dragged their feet in organising a national demonstration. Therefore Socialist Students and others organised the rank and file students in meetings and demonstrations, which culminated in a mass demonstration and shutdown of education, with almost two million students participating. One student spoke to the Socialist: "I want to go to university in September and I'm going to have to borrow a fortune. These plans are disgraceful!" Another said: "Have you noticed that the politicians who say these things [supporting tuition fees] nearly all benefited from free university education themselves? If it's good enough for them, it's good enough for us!"

With an emphasis on youth and the trade unions as the twin pillars for our party, our members played a key role in this battle. We reported on the effects of the demonstrations and education strikes throughout the country: "Thousands of students stayed away from lectures at Leicester University. Pickets, who leafleted and persuaded people not to go in, were stationed at main entrances to the university and a rally was held outside one of the university buildings... We leafleted for the shutdown, visited nearby sixth form colleges and went round the canteens."[10] Like so many others of Blair's cuts, which the Tories have subsequently built on and extended, they were never accepted and opposition has remained consistent since they were first introduced. The failure to defeat these attacks at this stage and force the Blair government to step back was entirely due to the mis-leadership of the NUS who put loyalty to the Blair government – and their future parliamentary careers, in most cases – before the real interests of students, both then and later.

18. Second year of government 1998

We did not just criticise New Labour. At the time of Brown's March 1998 budget we outlined a socialist alternative: "Unlike New Labour, we won't bow down to the wealthy minority; or worry how many of Britain's 81,000 millionaires leave the country. A socialist budget will be tough on wealth and tough on the causes of wealth." We proposed to introduce an emergency programme of job creation and poverty eradication on an unprecedented scale. Homelessness would be ended. We also pointed towards the top 500 people who had increased their wealth in one year, 1996-97, by £16.3 billion. The top 1% in Britain, around 450,000 people, owned almost a fifth of all wealth; the bottom 50% owned just 7%.

Our first measure would be a wealth tax to raise £20 billion but we couldn't just leave it at that because the capitalists would seek to avoid this tax as in the past. Therefore it would be necessary to bring the big monopolies under democratic public ownership. We proposed the democratic planning of the economy which would enable the unemployed to find work and also a national minimum wage for a 35-hour week. A shorter working week, and reduced overtime would create the need for other jobs and at the same time give working people the time to participate in the organising and running of industry and society. We also proposed a series of reforms on the NHS, housing and other public services.

We linked our day-to-day demands to the 'big idea' of changing society. We did not just deal with economic issues. We highlighted the sense of alienation and lack of control which 'modern' capitalist society meant for working people. For instance, a study in the US and Sweden established the connection between heart disease and workers' lack of participation in the desired outcome of their labour.[1] In Britain an article in the Lancet – the magazine of the British Medical Association – also highlighted that those who have little control over their jobs run higher risk of heart attacks.

Capitalism was enormously wasteful – witness the squandering of resources through unemployment, the billions spent on arms, advertising, the monarchy, the House of Lords and other feudal relics. At the same time this system shamefully wasted the talents of the British people and the peoples of the world. No party other than the Socialist Party was putting forward such a programme, either then or subsequently. In general this was still a relatively favourable period for capitalism; the boom had not yet come to an end. Yet capitalism was still failing to utilise all the productive potential. Had this been explained by a mass workers' party and linked to what was possible through socialist policies, the level of consciousness – the political outlook – of the working class and even other sectors of the population could have been raised significantly.

After all, this is what the workers' parties did in the 19th century under the banner of the Second International. They produced constant arguments against capitalism linked to the vision of a new society, socialism. The most successful parties of the Second International, like the German social democracy, grew in strength, size and even votes in elections over decades. This, it is true, brought with it some negative features: accommodation to capitalism by the leadership in a period of slow but steady growth of capitalism. This in turn meant that this leadership ultimately betrayed their own class in support of the bloody catastrophe of the First World War. The new generation would, with the help of socialists and Marxists, learn from this and, in a new party that will be created, fight to prevent its leaders degenerating in a similar fashion.

The official left within New Labour was far from drawing this conclusion, preferring to vegetate as a declining force, while Blair moved further and further towards the right. Tony Benn was an honest chronicler of the process. In March 1998 he commented on the mood of those who Blair had attempted to cosy up to, a group of pop stars: "The [New Musical Express]... had a cover with a picture of Blair saying 'Betrayed' and inside six young pop stars were denouncing New Labour on the grounds that they had been absolutely betrayed by Blair." These individuals "hated three things: Welfare to Work, which is really workfare or compulsory conscription; secondly, tuition fees; and thirdly, the failure to have an inquiry into cannabis."[2]

The alienation of the vast majority of young people from New Labour underlined the impossibility of organising a real left within the Labour Party at that stage. Tony Benn, in desperation, was reduced to seeking the company of previous enemies of the Labour movement, like Ted Heath, the hammer of the miners and the architect of the three-day week in 1974. He wrote to Heath: "I greatly appreciate the sense of your encouragement, Ted!"[3] He also commented favourably about Enoch Powell – infamous for his racism and his speech predicting "rivers of blood" in a British racial civil war – who had recently died. Benn attended his funeral and called him "a friend who made a mistake."[4] This is just one example of how even some of the best left figures can lose their bearings if their activity is centred mainly on the House of Commons. This is reinforced when they do not have an anchor outside which can act as a check and control over their activity.

The pay of MPs, as with trade union leaders, which is much higher than that of an average worker, is also a means whereby they can become out of touch and inoculated against the pressures on ordinary working class people. It is one of the reasons why the Socialist Party insists that its public representatives, both in the political and trade union fields, should be on the average wage of a worker and subject to recall by those who elevated them to Parliament or union leadership. We practice what we preach, as was shown by the example of the MPs, Terry Fields, Pat Wall and

Dave Nellist, and those comrades elected as union officials, who lived on the average wage with any income over and above this coming back to the labour movement, including to Militant.

Blair was far removed from such a concept, as was the army of careerists and place seekers who surrounded him. The machine he created in some respects mirrored that of Stalinism with its aim to control everything down to the last detail. A giant computer named Excalibur was installed at Millbank Tower, New Labour's headquarters. When Tony Benn visited he asked Tom Sawyer, then General Secretary of the Labour Party: "What have you got on it?" The reply was: "It's all published material… there is nothing secret on it." Benn then asked to see the material compiled on him and the machine duly extracted a letter that had been sent to Major: "It was a dossier, however you look at it. If ever they wanted to get me out of the Party, they would just go through the file and dig out everything damaging, highly selectively, some of which would be press reports that might not be accurate."

This was therefore sensitive territory and another apparatchik stopped Benn's visit. Then Sawyer, "who is the bloody general secretary after all", stated with some embarrassment: "I shouldn't have agreed to this. I'm sorry, you can't do it." The political character of this 'Labour' headquarters was revealed by the type of people staffing it: "They are all very young [and] didn't look particularly politically committed. They looked at me curiously, in a strange way… I got the feeling it was an organisation of an entirely managerial character, with lots of young people in shirt sleeves; it might have been a bank, an insurance company, Tory Central Office – it might have been anywhere."[5] A chasm, ideological in character and in lifestyle, separated this party from Labour in the past.

From the beginning Blair gave the impression of a man on the make. A professional New Labour fundraiser Henry Drucker remarked: "Tony has a serious weakness for rich, self-made men." His reputed wealth today illustrates this. He did not hesitate to court and accept the favours of big business, as he showed so openly in accepting large amounts of money from the likes of Bernie Ecclestone of Formula One fame. When this was revealed, he brazenly insisted that by soliciting donations from big business he had done nothing improper. Drucker set out Blair's thinking before the general election very clearly: "Basically [Blair] was saying: 'If we lose this general election. I'm going back to the Bar, I'm going to spend what I need to spend.' He was not going to lose because of money."[6]

There is a long tradition of the corruption of Labour leaders by the establishment. The Socialist pointed out that -, who betrayed Labour and formed a national government in 1931, "was given a Daimler by biscuit makers Huntley and Palmer. Wilson had connections with textile magnate Lord Kagan who was later jailed for fraud."[7] We also highlighted the selling of influence by lobbyists in the House of Commons, which has developed on a bigger scale today. Under the Tories these lobbyists even provided speeches for Tory MPs to read out in the Commons for which they were paid large fees. According to Emma Nicholson a Tory MP who had defected to the Lib Dems, the House of Commons became "a grubby, personal, cash-grabbing degeneration of the body politic, brazen in its cynicism... a procurer's delight, a den of heaving corruption". New Labour displayed all of these traits. The government was proposing a minimum wage of £3.60 an hour, yet they failed to act when people paid £50 an hour were revealed to be profiting by selling their 'insider knowledge' of Labour.

One such case was Derek Draper, who was close to Mandelson for many years. Draper's column in the Daily Express, for which he was paid £70,000, was regularly vetted by Mandelson before publication. Just after the 1997 general election a crony of Draper boasted: "Just tell me what you want, who you want to meet and Derek (Draper) and I will make the call for you." We commented: "It is not a coincidence that Draper and other former Labour Party staff that have turned to the lucrative lobbying business led the battle against Militant... in the Labour Party in the 1980s."[8] The sleaze and corruption that was primarily synonymous with the capitalist parties – the Tories and Liberals – was associated throughout Blair's period in office with New Labour and was to culminate in the MPs' expenses

scandals later. The roots of this degeneration were organically con-
nected to the time of Blair's ascendancy and domination of New
Labour. The tragedy was that the left were still trapped within the
party and therefore their criticisms were muted throughout this
period.

As we have seen, Blair had shamelessly cuddled up to Murdoch
before the general election and continued afterwards. Leaks
appeared in the press that Blair had telephoned the Italian Prime
Minister Romano Prodi on behalf of Murdoch, with the latter
rumoured to be pressing for the takeover of parts of the media
owned by Silvio Berlusconi. The symbiotic relationship between
Blair and Murdoch was also expressed by the appointment of Tim
Allan, who had been Blair's deputy press secretary since the election, as director of corporate communications for BSkyB, controlled
by Murdoch's News International. As a counterbalance to this
sleaze Foreign Secretary Robin 'ethical' Cook announced at the
previous Labour Party conference that he had suspended export
licences for the sale of armaments to the Suharto dictatorship in
Indonesia. He received a standing ovation, yet the sales ban only
affected sniper rifles and some armoured vehicles. Moreover, there
was nothing ethical when it came to the bombing and intervention
in the Balkans and the bloody consequences of the invasion of
Afghanistan and Iraq in the aftermath of 9/11.

The Labour Party conference in 1998 was a barometer of the
relationship of forces between what remained of the left in the
party and the Blairite right. Ten or fifteen years earlier the media
always described the robust clashes at conferences between rank
and file delegates and the party's right-wing leadership as 'dangerous extremism'. Such was the deadening mood of this conference
– the result of Blairite dominance – that this very same media
remarked almost appreciatively on a possible 'left-wing resurgence'. But as we pointed out: "At New Labour's Blackpool conference this week, the fires of past working class opposition will be at
best a faintly flickering ember."[9]

19. The right revolts and the Countryside Alliance 1998

The revolt against Blair's government came not only from the left, but by mid-1998 from the right, manifested in the Countryside Alliance, which we described as "a political reaction dressed up in a populist lament about rural decline".[1] The Countryside Alliance was not a spontaneous peasants' revolt but a coalition of hunting, shooting and country sporting organisations. They had spent £500,000 on a demonstration organised in London on 1 March 1998. The night before a chain of hilltop beacons rallied support and signalled the alleged threat to rural England: to "a way of life and the habit of freedom", claimed the right wing Daily Telegraph.[2] The demonstration was big, with over a quarter of a million according to the organisers, although independent monitors put it at 150,000.

The trigger was an anti-foxhunting bill, which was about to be debated in Parliament. The demonstrators completely ignored a Mori poll which showed that 63% of people who lived in rural or semi-rural areas were opposed to foxhunting. For the Alliance this was an issue of 'individual freedom' with the Daily Telegraph also saying "the rights of private property" were at stake. The Socialist Party conceded that there were many who were caught up in the protest who had genuine grievances. Small farmers, smallholders and hill farmers were scraping out a very poor living on the land, many of them barely surviving financially. In addition, farmworkers were notoriously low paid. Rural workers had much more in common with the workers in the towns and cities than with the wealthy landowners and big business. Farmers supported the protest. There were even workers on the march, who had to be there or risk losing their jobs or tied cottages. The hunting lobby were, in effect, defending the right to exploit the land as they pleased, pursuing wealth, power and pleasure without outside interference.

Farmers were squealing about the recent squeeze on farm incomes but this took no account of the increased concentration of farm ownership, with around 6% of farms with more than 500 acres accounting for around 50% of Britain's farmland. This wealthy minority of farm businesses produced a massive share of the country's agricultural output, also collecting most government subsidies. These big business farmers were behind the problems and hardships of small owner-occupiers or tenant farmers. The richest 1% of Britain's population owned more than half of all personally owned land, while the top 5% owned 74%. Moreover, many large landowners were also linked to the City of London's financial institutions and owned vast tracts of urban land. The Duke of Westminster, for instance, put £1.3 million into the Countryside Alliance's activities – collected from lucrative rents on his properties in London's Belgravia.

Hiding these embarrassing facts, the Daily Telegraph asserted: "The people who are coming to London are the backbone of the nation. They are those who have always been ready to fight for their country when required. For them 'country', in the sense of nation, is closely bound up with 'country' in the sense of green fields."[3] We concluded: "Land ownership, it seems, gives them the feudal right to lord it over the whole country." But big social changes had taken place in Britain. Such was the scale of the Tory defeat in 1997 that 15 of the 100 most rural seats fell to Labour.

This, in turn, set alarm bells ringing on the country estates. While bosses in general were at ease with Blair's victory, the rural barons were incensed by New Labour's liberal list of demands on hunting, land access and environmental protection. Many of these were even alienated from a Tory party that did not offer them much protection either. The Tory leadership of Hague was more concerned in giving their party a 'human face', aimed at winning back urban voters, than appealing to the rural backwoodsmen. Although there was little possibility at that stage of the Blair government conceding an anti-foxhunting bill – that would come later – the Countryside Alliance demonstration was a "warning for the future. It is organised and financed predominantly by one section of the property-owning ruling class. But the minute Blair ceases to serve the needs of financiers and manufacturing capitalists, they too will set the hounds on his government."[4]

New Labour's conference was asked to pay attention to focus groups rather than focus on the growing poverty and increasing unemployment that existed in Britain. The British bosses were lining up to attack the working class. In addition, Labour's officials were widely believed to have fiddled the NEC elections, "allowing 200,000 lapsed members to vote in an attempt to try and undermine the left vote".[5] What a contrast with their approach to the 2016 Labour leadership elections when they disenfranchised tens of thousands of members on the most spurious grounds, most of them believed to be Jeremy Corbyn supporters! At the same time, Blair was preparing to nullify any left resurgence by opening up his political options for the future through his relationship with Ashdown and the Liberal Democrats. The Jenkins Commission – which was to consider proportional representation (PR) – was evidently preparing for an extremely diluted form of PR, to reinforce New Labour and the Lib Dems in elections. This was a means of preparing the way for a more formal anti-worker coalition in the future.

Meanwhile, in the real world away from the conference, the job slaughter continued. We reported that over 5,000 jobs were disappearing in Britain each week. That was half the level in South Korea, which was suffering from a deep slump. What jobs were on offer? Siemens had just announced that it was to close its Tyneside factory, despite investment of £1.5 billion in semiconductors, with the loss of 1,000 jobs. This sent shockwaves throughout the region. Rover jobs were also on the line with its owners BMW attempting to bludgeon the Longbridge workforce into accepting wage cuts of 25% by eliminating all overtime and shift payments.

Bill Mullins reported that, in the previous year: "The Longbridge works committee were flown to Munich and were battered into signing a deal drastically affecting the working patterns of the workforce. This was done without Longbridge workers having any say in it." One commentator said the employers were acting in this way because "a crisis is a good time to win concessions from your workforce and force aid from the government". The right-wing unions swallowed the bosses' case hook, line and sinker. No union leader called for real opposition and the ability of workers to fight back was sapped.[6]

Alec Thraves pointed out that bosses were paying rock-bottom rates: "In the JobCentre in Swansea, you can see the poverty pay wage rates all over the vacancy boards. £2.50 an hour for a static security guard, £80 a week for a clerical assistant, £2.50 an hour for a care assistant, £2.90 an hour for a domestic. The list goes on and on. And it's the same in JobCentres across Britain." Unions demanded a national demonstration in support of a £4.61 an hour minimum wage. Sir Ross Buckland, chief executive of Unigate, had received a 43% pay rise the previous year. He took home £766,000 plus £39,000 in other payments. This was about £387 an hour![7] Reflecting this, one of our headlines in October 1998 was, 'Jobs Gloom Deepens: No Return to the 1930s'. The article pointed out: "Every day more bosses announce closures and redundancies. They don't only threaten our livelihoods, they attack pay and conditions too."[8]

In the midst of all of this Brown claimed that Britain was going to avoid capitalism's addiction to boom and bust. This was just bluster with New Labour leaders convincing themselves that all they needed to do was talk their way out of the 'boom and bust' cycle. Britain would be an exception in the teeth of the severe economic turbulence that was ravaging the world economy. This was accompanied by Brown serving up a diet of Thatcherite austerity policies which would only aggravate the continuing international economic crisis. The world recession indicated that the global economy was not bottoming out. Manufacturing industry in particular, already in recession, was so reliant on inward investment and the provision of financial services that there was no way it could remain immune from what was happening internationally.

At the Labour Party conference Blair laid heavy emphasis on New Labour's 'third way'. Trotsky once wrote that the British Labour leaders' thoughts were "far more backward than the methods of production" of backward British industry.[9] What would he have said about Blair who demonstrated in his speech a wish to return the labour movement to the ideas of the 19th century via the third way? Blair's central idea was to re-establish the Liberal-Labour coalition which preceded the formation of the Labour Party. He stated that he wished to unite "the two great streams of left of centre for democratic socialism and liberalism – whose divorce this century did so much to weaken progressive policies across the West". We later commented: "Even before this bird (the 'third way') has been able to take flight one of its wings has been severely clipped." Sweden's Prime Minister Göran Persson was forced to cancel his attendance at the New York love-in on the third way involving Clinton, Blair and Prodi. "Persson's 'third way' in Sweden resulted in savage cuts in living standards and, in the [September 1998] election, the worst performance of the Social Democrats in modern times."

During its honeymoon period the Blair government was sustained by two factors: Britain's economic bubble had not burst and the main opposition party, the Tories, was in a state of disarray bordering on complete demoralisation. The government could blow up politically at some stage but this was not at all recognised by those running it. Moreover, Blair's third way was a desperate attempt to straddle the growing chasm between the classes, reflected in the extreme polarisation of wealth and poverty, which we predicted would be accompanied by the re-emergence of class struggle at a certain stage. Even 'communists' like Eric Hobsbawm rushed to support Blair in his assertion that "ideology is gone". He wrote: "This is unquestionably true... The battle between 100% state planning and 100% free market societies is over because neither proved true." We pointed out that in fact there was never 100% state ownership in the Soviet Union, but the nationalisation of the commanding heights of the economy allowed the planning of the economy and society, albeit in a bureaucratic fashion.[10]

Fearing the re-emergence of class struggle, Blair was forced to reassess his previous support for PR. This is not an issue of principle, it must be said, either for the capitalists and their parties or for Marxists. The bourgeoisie internationally had switched electoral systems, from first past the post to PR and vice versa depending on what best strengthened their rule. Conversely, socialists and Marxists observed a very simple principle in the electoral field: we would support what best furthered the struggle of the working class and socialism at each stage. With the move to the right of the Labour Party, PR was no longer on the agenda. In the 1970s and 80s, the bourgeoisie contemplated switching from first past the post to a form of PR to bar the way to a left Labour government led by somebody like Tony Benn. Now, the Blair government was a reliable prop for capitalism. For all these reasons, we argued that the third way would very quickly be seen as a dead-end – and so it is proved to be. It has gone the way of Blair. Both have been politically nullified within the labour movement.

20. Jack Straw and General Pinochet 1998-2000

Ironically, just when the issue of Chile was raised in discussions on the third way, General Pinochet, the butcher of the Chilean people, set foot on British soil and triggered one of the most 'embarrassing' episodes of Blair's first government. As Home Secretary Jack Straw faced judicial demands from Spain for Pinochet to be extradited to stand trial for crimes that had been committed by his regime against Spanish citizens. Big demonstrations took place in London as the House of Lords pondered its verdict. Pinochet had arrived in London and almost immediately the Spanish anti-terrorist judge, Baltasar Garzón, had asked Scotland Yard to locate him and to prevent him from leaving the country.

Straw reacted with alarm. The powers to arrest Pinochet through a warrant request were vested in a judge and this was duly carried out. Pinochet's lawyers tried to cancel the provisional arrest warrant. Straw was compelled to refuse this request. After much legal wrangling there was an appeal to the law lords who surprisingly, by three to two, upheld Pinochet's extradition to Spain. Even so, Straw's past role as a 'left' came into the calculation. He had written an article for Tribune, the Labour left-wing newspaper, after a visit to Chile during his student days but this was found not to be prejudicial to Pinochet from a legal standpoint. The former bloody dictator was about to be extradited to Spain when his lawyers discovered that one of the law lords had chaired an Amnesty

International event. This allowed the original ruling on extradition to be cancelled.

The legal wrangling dragged on with the Foreign Office – still highly conservative even under a 'Labour' government – expressing the opinion to Robin Cook, Labour's Foreign Secretary, that "the sooner Straw lets [Pinochet] go, the better". Straw, in his autobiography, made it clear that Blair energetically pursued this notion, so did a slew of world leaders, including former US President George Bush senior, former Tory Chancellor Norman (now Lord) Lamont, and inevitably Thatcher herself.

The chief argument for releasing Pinochet was the 'debt Britain owed' him for his help over the Falklands. Blair wrote two letters demanding Pinochet's release. Straw rejected this, which was viewed by Blair as more or less questioning his 'manhood'. He wrote: "I am dismayed... Are you saying that it is proper for the Home Secretary to be guided by the view of private individuals but not to take into account those of the prime minister? Such a proposition is manifestly absurd. In the last resort, you are responsible for all the actions of your government."[1] But Straw was compelled to resist this pressure, not out of principle, as was subsequently demonstrated, but from a legal point of view. Pinochet's extradition was delayed for nearly twelve months.

Daily demonstrations of sometimes up to 1,000 outside the House of Lords awaited its verdict. In reality, Pinochet had very few friends and, as a consequence, the historic law lords' ruling against him was met with wild scenes of joy by the hundreds of Chileans and their supporters in Europe gathered outside the Lords and the Grovelands Priory Hospital, which was 'hosting' Pinochet at one stage. John Reid, with family connections to Chile, wrote in the Socialist that "even hundreds of lobbyists of Parliament and Tories also joined in the applause, as did drivers and passengers in cars and buses passing by, who waved and tooted their horns; showing that the vast majority of the people want the tyrant Pinochet extradited and tried." The Socialist also gave many reasons why Pinochet should stand trial for his crimes. Sixty percent of Chileans were in favour of putting Pinochet on trial. His only real supporters were the military, big business and extreme right-wingers.

Pinochet's regime pioneered the neoliberal economic policies which Thatcher introduced later. After killing thousands of workers and pauperising many more, the junta he headed brought industrial production down to the levels of 1966, with 35% unemployment, ten years after the coup in 1973. There were at least 2,700 extradition papers which had been issued. Even the CIA – which backed his seizure of power – estimated that between 2,000 and 3,000 were slaughtered in the first two months after the coup. Pinochet's junta admitted that they had 5,200 people facing the firing squad in September 1973. The slaughter of opponents of his regime took place not just within the borders of Chile. He promoted covert activities outside Chile, including the assassination of political enemies. We added: "Allende's government got 44% of the vote six months before the coup. Pinochet didn't bother with elections."[2]

The old dictator pretended that he was 'sick' but what about the old and sick who suffered in the coup? He had granted himself a permanent amnesty when he stepped down from power – he was not confident he would get away with his crimes any other way. There was enormous pressure on Straw for action, as he points out. There was "countervailing pressure from human rights groups, the left-wing press and other MPs – including, to my surprise, a vehement Peter Mandelson – calling for this 'evil war criminal' to be 'made to face a trial.'"[3] Much to Straw's relief – and the anger of all of those looking for justice – a medical panel convened at the behest of Pinochet's lawyers met to assess his fitness to stand trial.

This was a device which had been used in previous cases, for instance, with Ernest Saunders who was convicted of share trading fraud. He was originally sentenced to five years, but that was reduced because the court found he was suffering from incurable Alzheimer's disease and this led to a severely reduced sentence. When Saunders was released from jail he made a miraculous recovery! Now the medical panel found that Pinochet was not fit to stand trial. Straw writes: "The medical panel was thorough. Rather to my surprise they unanimously came to a clear view that Pinochet was indeed unfit to stand trial. The Chief Medical Officer concurred." Hiding behind this judgement, Straw wrote, quite cynically: "There was, as it were, no 'get out of jail' card for me."[4] He had to take the decision to release Pinochet to the fury of all of those looking forward to seeing this monster in a criminal court.

Straw's decision did not go without a challenge: "One of the Home Office medical experts was subsequently reported in the Observer as commenting that his panel's assessment of Pinochet's capacity to stand trial was not as conclusive as I had made out." Even one of those who participated in assessing Pinochet said later that he could not say that the decision was "unequivocal" because all "we did was list the medical facts. Whether those medical facts constitute unequivocal grounds for deciding his fitness for trial is outside our field of competence and outside our responsibilities."[5] Straw disputes this interpretation which he says was not available at the time he took his decision but the whole episode shattered the attempt of the Blair government and its ministers to pretend that they were acting in line with its much trumpeted 'ethical' foreign policy. When Pinochet landed back at Santiago de Chile airport, Straw writes, "He gave me a metaphorical 'v sign' by getting out of his wheelchair to wave at the crowds of jubilant supporters. I felt double-crossed."[6]

There was not universal celebration in Chile. In fact, the new 'centre left' government said that the general's 'triumphant arrival' damaged the image of Chile across the world. This was not the end of the Pinochet saga. In November 2006, he was charged with 36 counts of kidnapping and 23 of torture. The prosecutor sought house arrest. However, Pinochet died a few weeks later on 10 December and, as Straw comments, "aged 91, without any court, in Europe or Latin America, ever having convicted him of any criminal offence". This did not prevent Straw from commenting that he felt "privileged to have played a significant, if wholly unexpected, part in helping to make [Chile] a more civilised place"![7]

The real people who helped to ensure that Chile enjoyed a

modicum of civilisation – trade union and democratic rights in place of the dictatorship – was not the vainglorious Straw but the Chilean working class who never stopped struggling for Pinochet's overthrow. Included amongst these is Celso Calfullan, member and partisan of the CWI in Chile, who was not only arrested but tortured for his beliefs and has never stopped fighting for justice for all those who died under the iron heel of Pinochet. Celso has consistently fought for a socialist Chile and Latin America.

21. Livingstone and the left 1997-99

The sheer scale of the attacks that were being made by the Blair government produced much complaining from Labour's ranks, mostly in the corridors of Parliament and the antechambers. However a more serious revolt broke out in early 1998 when Ken Coates and Hugh Kerr, Labour Members of the European Parliament, and some of their fellow MEPs – six in all – declared in the Observer: "Our consciences say we must split with Tory Blair."[1] Coming after Ken Livingstone's election to the NEC at the Labour Party conference – beating the 'Prince of Darkness' Mandelson – and the huge parliamentary revolt over the attacks on lone parents, a major left-wing revolt seemed to be in the offing. This appeared to contradict our prognosis, set out above, and we posed the question: "Does it signify the beginning of attempts to form a new mass socialist alternative through a major split from the Labour Party?"[2]

As important: did it indicate a mass revolt of Labour Party members, led by the left, which could compel Blair to step back from his Thatcherite assault on the £100 billion welfare budget? There is no doubt that the attack on lone parents and particularly the disabled infuriated a wide cross-section of the Labour Party. We pointed out that even Gwyneth Dunwoody, arch right-winger and one of the organisers of the witch-hunt against Militant and the left in the 1980s, was in opposition, as was Roy Hattersley who had paved the way for the Blairista counter-revolution. He revealed that he had been treated "as a raving Trot" by Labour for mildly criticising the government. Other pillars of the right such as Denis Healey and Lord Jack Ashley were also threatening to organise a revolt against attacks on disablement benefits.

Labour Party membership had plunged by 17% in recent months. The Observer recounted heartrending stories about the 'plight' of government figures: "At least one minister who regularly holds a Christmas gathering at home for local party members found himself serving drinks in a half-empty house – seemingly because people would not cross the threshold of someone who had voted for benefit cuts."[3] The indignation against Blair and his poodle-like cabinets was fuelled by press reports of Blair's meeting with millionaire disc jockeys in Number Ten while the boot was put into single parents. Rubbing salt in the wound, the Independent reported that the Seychelles trip for Blair and his family over Christmas had cost £13,000! The same paper wrote: "He is a true heir of Margaret Thatcher."[4]

The MEPs who had revolted linked their decision to the attacks on the poor in Britain, as well as the completely pro-business policies of the prime minister in Europe. They pointed to the "heavy pressure from the whips in London to abandon our support for rather mild proposals (from the Christian Democrats) to protect the legal rights of employees in takeovers. Labour members were instructed by Lord Simon, late of BP, to break ranks with our fellow socialists in Strasbourg in opposing this kind of reform." The reaction against Blairism now extended beyond the usual left opponents, with Hattersley and Healey, as well as junior government ministers who would resign over the lone parents' issue, coming into opposition to Blair. However, we pointed out that the Labour right was somewhat inconsistent. They accepted capitalism, but then failed to see the crisis which was now confronting their system and the even more serious crisis that loomed in the future. This demanded that concessions that were given in the past must now be clawed back. We wrote: "The 1980s saw the piling up of debt – corporate, personal and, above all, state debt. All capitalist governments in the 1990s are compelled by the logic of the system, whether they call themselves 'Conservative', 'socialist', or 'New Labour', to seek to cut this debt."

The actions of the Blair government were not an accident. The decision to attack the very poorest had been consciously decided by Blair, Brown and their coteries. They reasoned that if lone parents, the disabled and the unemployed could be attacked so viciously, then this was a warning to teachers, civil servants, local government workers and others that they could face an even more brutal assault. As we pointed out in Socialism Today, even before Blair came to power, New Labour was entirely different to any previous 'Labour' government. At its head was a conscious bourgeois leadership which would quite deliberately transform the Labour Party from the political voice of the organised working class, the trade unions in particular, into an openly bourgeois formation. We stated: "Blair will be unmoved by appeals to alter course by heartrending accounts of the effects of his measures. His government, unlike previous Labour governments, does not have one foot in the camp of the organised working class. There was still a lingering objective of 'social democracy' but it was not sufficient to prevent Blair from pursuing his pro-business agenda. It is therefore not subject to the pressures which were brought to bear on previous Labour governments... New Labour, as Blair reminds us, is a 'new party', in which the slightest dissent will be stepped upon."[5]

Even the revolts that were taking place, we predicted, would not move Blair to alter course. Nor would the pressure from Labour backbenchers force him. He would tread in the footsteps of Persson, who in previous years had won the 'world record' for cuts in welfare in Sweden. Both Persson and Blair proceeded from the point of view of the defence of the so-called free market system. Moreover, in Sweden, the left made noises but in essence came to heel because they did not have an alternative to Persson's programme.

Unfortunately, the same applied to the Labour left in Britain. We pointed out that Livingstone, touted as a future leader of the left, was completely inconsistent in his criticisms of Blair. In the New

Statesman the previous October, he had commented: "I haven't written off Blair and I don't think the left should. There are a lot of truly ghastly people gathered around Blair, like lice on the back of a hedgehog, and they have their own agenda." But Livingstone refused to criticise the king (Blair) and concentrated on the court camarilla. He even took a side swipe at Benn, for moving too far to the left and allegedly driving Blair into the arms of the right: "Blair and others like him were lost to the cause in October 1980 when Tony Benn marched further to the left in his conference speech of that year. Benn famously called for a massive extension of public ownership and the abolition of the House of Lords within days of a Labour government coming to power."[6]

An issue which came to the fore at this stage was that of Labour's candidate for London Mayor in the first elections for the post in 2000. Livingstone was undoubtedly popular but there was only a remote possibility that he would be allowed to stand as Labour's candidate by Blair and his entourage. He was seen as far too 'risky' to Labour's pro-big business policies to be allowed to be in charge of the capital city. The Livingstone of 1999, we pointed out, was far removed from the Livingstone of his radical past. He was no longer a fighter for socialism: "If he is really interested in defending working class people and fighting for a better, socialist society, why did he praise Blair's last conference speech, which attacked teachers, or why does he generally praise Blair's leadership?"[7]

The late Paul Foot, Guardian columnist and swp member, also threw his hat into the ring. However, we did not see him as a serious opponent of Livingstone and his views. He only offered to stand if Livingstone was barred by Labour. The swp had flyposted their support for Livingstone all over London, even raising the issue in union branches and conducted a campaign for him amongst Labour Party members. We pointed out that it was correct to argue for a socialist candidate in the mayoral contest and good that the swp, after years of pouring scorn on the Socialist Party for standing in elections, had finally decided it was okay. However, we did not see Livingstone as the standard-bearer for such a campaign. It was necessary to build an alternative outside New Labour and for those policies in the interests of the working class. This could not be equated with Livingstone's stand. It was necessary to argue for a genuine socialist candidate and that is why the Socialist Party took part in an unprecedented unity slate for the European elections, the United Socialists, along with the Independent Labour Network, SWP and others.

As if to doubly emphasise his switch from left to right, Livingstone used a column in the Independent to praise "champagne socialists", a specific attack on the Socialist Party for standing election candidates and who allegedly "drone on" about their pledge to only take a worker's wage if they were elected. Dave Nellist responded to Livingstone's cynical sideswipes. We printed extracts from Dave's letter in the Socialist: "As someone who managed quite well, in nine years in Parliament, to live on the average skilled worker's wage, I enjoyed life. Including 'a glass of wine', and sometimes, Ken, even with cheese! But I enjoyed it to the same extent as the Coventry people I represented then (and again, now do) – no more, no less." He added: "I did that, not because I prefer a 'hair shirt' or because I'm 'a drone', but because living on an average wage is the best way to prevent the almost inevitable absorption of an Establishment outlook which parliamentary lifestyle is designed to produce, neutering any radical, socialist feelings MPs once might have had."[8]

Livingstone responded, not by pledging that he would accept only a worker's wage in the future; instead, he vowed to Blair to be well behaved and not to rock the boat in the event of being elected. He also echoed the pessimistic arguments of the 'modernisers' that, unless everybody toed the Blair line, there 'may never' be another Labour government in their lifetime. In so doing, he was turning his back on many Londoners who would vote for him in the expectation that he would make their lives better. He was giving a signal that he would do Blair's bidding. This provoked the Guardian in an editorial to predict that "'oppositional leftists' (i.e. the SWP) who have uncritically supported Livingstone standing for Mayor will scream that he has sold out."

This was a sure-fire prediction because the SWP had argued

without any qualification to support Livingstone. We said that it would now be difficult for the swp to avoid the inevitable political embarrassment they would suffer from arguing that, with "Livingstone... Londoners will have a socialist to vote for".[9] This was not the first or last time that the swp made political blunders by rushing after individuals and organisations who seemed to offer a quick route to building their own party, rather than taking into account the overall interests of the working class for a credible fighting candidate, even if they were outside the largely defunct New Labour.

New Labour's programme for accelerated privatisation provoked opposition from the working class and the unions in particular. The move towards privatisation came in two guises: 'best value' and the Private Finance Initiative (PFI). Best value was the government's replacement for compulsory competitive tendering whereby councils were able to undermine trade union organisation by privatising local services. Contracts were awarded to the lowest bidder, irrespective of their ability to carry out the work. This was blatantly building on the privatisations initiated by Thatcher and carried on by Major.

The other attack, which has left a lasting legacy, was the PFI. This allows private firms to build and run schools and hospitals which are then leased back, stretching payments over anything from 25 to 60 years. Its full effects were catastrophic and fully felt in the noughties and today, and were used by the Tories and Liberal Democrats to indict New Labour. A third big attack was 'single status' in local government, which claimed to 'harmonise' the conditions of blue and white collar workers. At the time this deal was proposed the Socialist Party and the Campaign for a Fighting Democratic Unison (CFDU), which organised from the base of the union, campaigned against the deal and won 46% of the vote at Unison's special conference. Single status was not centrally funded and therefore was likely to cut hours for manual workers by April 1999. That meant cutting costs locally. New Labour also planned changes in the structure of local government.

It wanted to neuter democratically elected local councils. Therefore, the unions were preparing for the battle not just against local councils, but against the policies that were being implemented by 'their' New Labour government.

In the 1980s Tony Benn had taken a stand under the pressure of a growing left wing within the constituencies and trade unions. His support for the nationalisation of the top 25 companies in Britain represented a big step forward and further enhanced the position of the leftward moving workers within the party. However, Benn was now a prisoner in the Labour Party and even criticised Ken Coates in his diaries for leaving Labour. Coates was correct to do this but mistaken in transferring to the Green group in the European Parliament – going from the frying pan into the fire. On the other hand, what remained of the left within the Labour Party, gathered around the likes of Benn and Livingstone, was extremely feeble. Previous close adherents, like Chris Mullin, a major supporter of Benn at the time of the deputy leadership contest in 1981, had enthusiastically supported Blair's candidacy for the leadership of the Labour Party. He also strongly supported Blair's welfare-to-work strategy and was hawkish on 'law and order', at the same time believing that only a 'centre left' government like Blair's could win power in the modern era. Livingstone's programme was only mildly reformist and he was not a serious socialist alternative.

This is shown by his approach towards discussions on the economy on the NEC at the time: "At the last meeting of Labour's NEC, the prime minister looked genuinely surprised when I pointed out the likelihood of a recession hitting our government in mid-term." Full marks for Livingstone for a correct observation! Yet he explained that he believed that once capitalism overcame the recession there would be a structural growth similar to the 1950s and 1960s. We consistently refuted this: "The real parallel to be drawn for British and world capitalism is not with the 1950s and 1960s but with the 1930s. A long depressionary phase of capitalism punctuated with slumps and recessions and very feeble growth is the prospect that faces the working class unless it changes society. There is no understanding on the part of the major left leaders of the real processes that are developing at the present time."

We answered Tony Benn's call for a 'refounding' of the Labour Party which, in effect, consisted of remaining inside and 'recapturing it' from the Blairites. The Labour Party was "increasingly dead as a viable political instrument for working people seeking change... Perhaps the time that Benn has been in the Labour Party explains his reluctance to take the step of founding a new mass socialist alternative. Yet Franz Mehring in Germany, faced with the betrayal of the Social Democratic Party in 1918, at the age of 72 (!) took the step of founding a new mass party, a genuine Communist Party, when there was no other alternative."

We declared that the Socialist Party was preparing for the struggle along with all genuine left forces to lay the foundation for a new mass party. The fact that this had been delayed was no argument against the idea. It was objectively posed by the situation facing the working class, but we added: "Realistically, however, we recognise that this will take time to emerge and will result from a combination of events and the experience of the working class, and tireless propaganda for the launching of such a party."[10] The emergence of the movement around Jeremy Corbyn has not falsified this perspective. The only hope for a continuation and strengthening of 'Corbynism' is to defeat the right and open up the party to the genuine forces of the left. This had not happened at the time of writing.

22. Corruption - bosses "worth fighting for"

There was a growing mood of opposition to New Labour which was fuelled by the 'Mandelson affair'. Peter Mandelson was the 'eminence grise' of New Labour, as Tony Blair pointed out, its real founder. He was forced to resign as Trade and Industry Minister on 24 December 1998 over 'financial irregularities'. We commented in Socialism Today that this was an unexpected Christmas present to all those who had been brutally trampled on or elbowed aside as Blairism had risen to dominate the Labour Party. It revealed the tensions – real abiding hatreds amongst the different cliques in the leadership – both within the party, and between it and the growing sections of disenchanted former supporters.

Mandelson was important in the sense that he personified starkly this process. He had acquired his 'legendary' abilities by allegedly managing the media. He drew some lessons – for diametrically opposed political reasons – by witnessing at first hand Militant's approach towards the media in the 1980s. We pointed out in Socialism Today that we successfully used the press to partially counter the witch-hunting manoeuvres of right-wing Labour's NEC. This involved the public discussion of 'secret' reports of right-wing party officials which detailed the behind the scenes plans to purge the left within the party, beginning with Militant and its supporters. We aimed to raise the level of understanding of Labour Party members and those workers we could reach by relating the witch-hunt to the struggle for jobs, housing, improved conditions and the broad historical struggle for socialism.

In contrast, Mandelson's 'black arts' – the US-inspired ideas of spin doctoring – had precisely the opposite intention: to deceive, mislead, misinform and denigrate opponents by falsifying their ideas and actions. One of its central aims was to dissipate the opposition, both within the Labour Party and amongst the broad mass of working people, to the policies of right-wing Labour as they rose to power. We wrote: "The events surrounding Mandelson have been given a highly personalised slant in the media. But what is highlighted here are not the personal traits and inadequacies of Mandelson, Blair and the Chancellor Gordon Brown – considerable though they are – but the failure of their policies. If tomorrow Brown replaced Blair, little would change in the policies of the government or the party regime within New Labour."[1] This, of course, was entirely borne out when Brown took over from Blair in 2007. But then Brown had to endure the odium of all the policies which Blair and he had presided over during their reign. The result was the victory of the Tory David Cameron in tandem with Nick Clegg's Lib Dems and the brutal attacks on working people which flowed from this.

Mandelson, the arch practitioner of Blairism, adopted a nauseating flunky-like attitude towards the rich and powerful. Ramsay Macdonald, even before he betrayed the labour movement in 1931, was noted for his obsequiousness towards the possessing classes. Mandelson displayed the same fawning attitude towards Prince Charles and his 'lady', Camilla Parker-Bowles (dancing with her regularly at parties). He never hesitated to bend the knee before the rich barons of capitalism. Mandelson sought to put his 'filthy rich' doctrine into practice through his friendship with the appropriately titled Paymaster General, Treasury Minister Geoffrey Robinson. This millionaire 'socialist businessman' had 'earned' part of his considerable wealth as an adviser to a Belgian millionairess named Bourgeois! He achieved notoriety when it was exposed that he held £12 million in an offshore trust located in a tax haven, along with his formal links to the corrupt ex-tycoon Robert Maxwell, not to mention his 'failure' to register his directorship of seven companies. This has a topical ring in light of the later exposure of tax evasion and corruption in the Panama Papers.

Mandelson, obviously choking with frustration in his Islington basement flat, yearned to be part of the glitterati in fashionable Notting Hill 'swanky land'. The bridge to this was a £373,000 loan from Robinson, nearly ten times his parliamentary salary. This house would be worth millions in current property prices. The most astonishing feature is that he and Blair did not see that he had done anything wrong in accepting a loan from his rich 'friend' who just happened to be a well-known candidate for future ministerial office in a New Labour government! Mandelson's only 'regret' was that he did not mention it to either Blair or to his ministerial permanent secretary. Contrast this behaviour – and the corruption that was to follow in the expenses scandal and much else besides – to the spotless record of Militant and the Socialist Party, whenever we have been elected to public positions either as MPs or trade union officials. The late Terry Fields, Dave Nellist and the late Pat Wall, when they were elected to Parliament, were selflessly devoted to the working class and lived on a worker's wage. Joe Higgins in the Irish Parliament acted likewise.

Some, even on the left, after New Labour come to power, saw the clash between the Blair-Mandelson axis and Deputy Prime Minister John Prescott and the 'Brownies' as a left-right division. It was not. It had more of the character of a struggle for influence and power within the apparatus. Sometimes, this can indirectly reflect class pressures but not in this case. So removed from reality was the discussion within New Labour that Charlie Whelan, then Brown's spin doctor press secretary, was presented in the press and by his friends, such as the Daily Mirror journalist Paul Routledge, as a 'lefty' bruiser and a 'progressive'. He was nothing of the kind. He was a fixer for the right wing in the engineering union (AEEU) before joining Brown's office. He delivered the votes of right-wing unions for the Blair 'modernisation project', including the dilution of trade union influence within the Labour Party.

This situation gave a certain space to Prescott, who called for a return to 'Labour fundamentals', thereby resurrecting the ghosts of 'old Labour', and for 'Keynesian' measures and state intervention. His very mild statements produced near panic in the capitalist press and New Labour ranks. More serious capitalist commentators were clear that this was no traditional left-right split. Blair's strength, Andrew Rawnsley in the Observer commented, lay in the fact that "there was no united body of colleagues offering a coherently argued alternative to Blairism. Is anyone calling for the nationalisation of the commanding heights of the economy and pip-squeaking hikes in income tax? Not out loud, they are not. Not in whispers either. John Prescott knows they were not elected on that programme. Gordon Brown will be at one with Mr Blair in agreeing that they would not have been elected on that programme."[2]

While all this was going on Blair had been in the Seychelles. As soon as he landed in Britain, he vindicated Rawnsley's analysis by declaring: "Labour as a party is now more ideologically united than at any time I've known it." Despite Prescott's endorsement of Brown's alleged Keynesianism, he had pursued the opposite agenda – much to the annoyance of real Keynesians, like Will Hutton of the Observer. Hutton pointed out that Brown's policies were an unhappy "mish-mash" incorporating some of the Conservatives' economic policies.

To underline the point Sir Clive Thompson, the head of Rentokil Initial, a viciously anti-union firm, declared at the CBI conference in November 1998: "Labour is now the sort of centre right party for which I would consider voting." The capitalists clearly recognised that the former social democratic leaders had abandoned socialism and were prostrating themselves before the 'market', i.e. capitalism. This was summed up at the meeting of European 'socialist' leaders. The then French finance minister Dominique Strauss-Kahn – who fell from grace after his involvement in sex scandals years later – declared: "Gone are the days when Margaret Thatcher's Britain and François Mitterrand's France were implementing almost entirely opposite policies."[3] Now the former social democrats were just implementing Thatcher's policies in a disguised fashion. The attacks on welfare recipients and the catastrophe in the NHS had all produced huge discontent faintly echoed even within Blair's sanitised New Labour. Official figures indicated a haemorrhaging of Labour Party members.

The resignation of Paddy Ashdown as leader of the Liberal Democrats, to take effect after the June 1999 European elections, meant that the proposed Blair-Ashdown 'project' – with PR at its heart – was now effectively put on ice. In December 1998, Blair had gone further than the suggestion of a Lib Dem-Labour coalition: "My vision through New Labour is to become as the Liberal Party was in the 19th century, a broad coalition of those who believe in progress and justice, not a narrow class based politics, but a party founded on clear values." He went on: "The ideological differences between me and many of the Liberal Democrats are pretty small."[4] Philip Gould New Labour's 'philosopher' in Blair's court camarilla had declared in his book The Unfinished Revolution: "The better course would be for liberalism and labourism to unite."[5]

The division between the Liberals and the Labour Party was historically rooted in the incapacity of the liberal capitalist parties to solve the problems of the working class. This was why the Labour Party was created in the first place, at the expense of the Liberal Party, particularly by winning over Lib-Lab workers. Blair had already involved the Lib Dem leadership in a government committee and was considering attaching civil servants to help them 'develop government policy'. He also proposed that they would have greater access to 'confidential government papers'. In other words the Lib Dems were already in a de facto coalition with Labour and the Tory 'wets'. Michael Heseltine and Ken Clarke were being courted with appointments to government ventures such as the Millennium Dome and 'export promotion' organisations. This virtual political fusion between the Blairites, 'liberal' Tories and the Lib Dems themselves, even if a programme of cuts in public expenditure was to take place similar to 1931, would not have provoked anything like the same response within the Labour Party at that stage. In view of this the best workers and youth were looking for a socialist alternative and the Socialist Party offered such an alternative.

Meanwhile, Brown was boasting that the economy under his supervision would be able to avoid a recession in 1999. Two days later, the official figures showed manufacturing industry was in a worse position than in 1981, a time of severe economic contraction when millions were made redundant and the unemployment level stood at over three million. Some important manufacturing companies were threatened with going to the wall. Stephen Byers, the newly appointed Trade and Industry Minister, explained that the government's role was not to "hinder entrepreneurs, but to work to ensure the market functions properly. There can be no return to the outdated interventionism of the old left... The corporate state did not work."[6] A more explicit repudiation of everything that Labour had stood for in the past was not possible. Notwithstanding Byers's lack of intervention, the economic storm clouds were gathering and threatened even industrial giants such as BMW, particularly the Rover Longbridge factory. Therefore, Byers rushed to offer government aid. Despite this, the new chairman of BMW refused to confirm that the Longbridge plant would be kept open.

The jobs of thousands of car workers were at stake. Yet the government rejected the only policy which offered some kind of solution, public ownership. We pointed out that, as the world economy was heading for a downturn, there was massive overcapacity in the global car industry, which was leading to pressure from mergers, predatory buyouts and job cutting 'rationalisations'. On the other hand, public ownership would preserve the creative skills of the Rover workforce. Managed by elected representatives of the car workers and other unions, together with the wider community, the publicly owned Rover could begin an audit of society's real transport needs. This would not be Byers's 'corporate state' but socialist nationalisation and working class control and management. The revolt against New Labour's preparedness to abandon car making at Longbridge had resulted in a revolt of Rover car workers the previous year. This pressure later forced the management to step back a savage retrenchment of jobs but it was an indication of the parlous economic situation Britain was in at this stage.

23. British economy

Signs in the economy, notwithstanding Blair and Brown's blandishments, indicated a slowdown. By October 1998 the wave of closures of factories and workplaces led to more and more redundancies being announced. Around 5,000 jobs a week were disappearing and it was the already weakened industrial sector that was being seriously affected. The closure of the National Semiconductor Company chip plant in Greenock, West of Scotland, led to the crippling axing of 600 jobs. Blairite council leaders suggested that workers in areas like this should stop looking back to traditional shipbuilding or manufacturing because hi-tech production was the future. Now that perspective had been shattered with workers asking how much money had this US-owned company received to go into areas like the West of Scotland, yet it was always the workers who were expected to pay the bill. We declared: "If the money's still there, the workplace should stay open and not one worker should be sacked. If the money's gone, we should fight to get it taken into public ownership, with minimum compensation and with workers managing and controlling production. We think that the bosses, not the workers should pay for capitalism's crisis."[1] This was a refrain which would be heard again and again from workers as the crisis of British capitalism endured and dramatically worsened in the noughties.

The slow and inexorable decline had been evident long before this. Manufacturing industry's continual contraction arose from a number of causes, not least the short-sightedness of the bosses. North Sea oil was used to cushion and prevent social upheaval, through the payment of benefits to those who were unable to work and could not find suitable employment. In particular, the criminal refusal to reinvest the surplus extracted from the labour of the working class back into production meant that British capitalism was more exposed even than its rivals with the onset of the world crisis. Also evident was the trend towards casualisation, accompanied by low pay and insecurity of employment.

It was the North, Scotland and Wales that suffered most, with a seemingly inexorable job slaughter. In October the Socialist commented: "In the past eight weeks 4,500 people have lost their jobs in North-East England. [The] Textilion garment factory in North Shields is making 230 people redundant." A worker told our reporters: "Our redundancy pay will be very small anyway, about £1,500 for 15 years' service. But because that money is due us, we won't be able to get Job Seekers Allowance! We feel we've been short changed. We've set up our own task force to ensure we get the right advice about claiming benefits."[2] This was the lament of workers in general. The avalanche of redundancies – and the seeming incapacity of the union leaderships to do their job and give a lead – produced resignation and despondency rather than a preparedness to fight. Unfortunately, this was the general picture that emerged over the next 15 years. The Socialist Party did its best, with small forces, to convince workers to resist the offensive and warned about the threat of a recession that was inevitable in the future.

Even Brown finally admitted that his forecast of 1.75% to 2.25% economic growth in the year 1998 was too optimistic. He scaled down its prediction to a measly 1% growth in 1999. Brown thereby sought to nudge the Bank of England into lowering interest rates to relieve the pressure on manufacturing industry, but the 0.25% drop which was announced did nothing to halt or even slow down the looming recession. This would mean an increase in unemployment, with fewer people paying tax, and the cost of social security rising.

Then what would happen to public spending? The 2010 ConDem coalition government wrestled with a similar problem on a much grander scale, but enormously compounded the problems by piling cuts on top of cuts. We warned about the signs in the financial sector, where banks were running hedge funds, glorified gambling schemes, despite the collapse of Long-Term Capital Management (LTCM) in 1998: "A financial system collapse would plunge the world into a depression; meaning mass unemployment, mortgages foreclosed, and even people's savings disappearing. Barclays are so big of course they'd expect to be bailed out when in trouble."[3]

Few others at this stage made such a bold prognosis as this, which was borne out in the 2007-08 crisis. Indeed, the Socialist Party was condemned by various critics, as we have seen, for being alarmist, 'primitive slumpists', incapable of understanding that 'capitalism has changed'. There was a new economic paradigm, reasoned our opponents, which makes your 'economic catastrophism' redundant. Yet not only in general have we been confirmed but, in particular, we anticipated mortgage foreclosures, that Barclays Bank would be bailed out and even that people's savings would be threatened and could disappear, as was illustrated by the 2013 crisis in Cyprus. Yet this was just the beginning. The world crisis of capitalism is not over and new convulsions loom. It took time for the recession and slump to develop, but it would have developed earlier than 2008 had it not been for the massive injection of liquidity in 2001-02 which staved off the crisis for six years, although that only meant a bigger collapse when it came. The task of Marxists was to soberly analyse the processes at work within capitalism, the inevitable economic collapse and the huge political repercussions that would flow from this.

As 1999 drew to an end, criticisms of the New Labour government multiplied. Privatisation was proving to be a disaster, highlighted by the Paddington rail crash. There was an upsurge in public anger against fat cat companies which put profits before people's lives. Ordinary people called for the railways to be renationalised and the media were forced to reflect this. They published some of the posters of the rail workers: "No protection on board. No second man with driver. Saving money is easy. Losing loved ones is hard." A West Midlands rail worker commented to the Socialist: "Drivers always get the blame. Drivers are always being blackmailed and put under pressure by the bosses because of the threat of 'disrupting' hundreds of customers."

In general, we had always supported the idea of the renationalisation of privatised industries, but then added 'compensation on the basis of proven need'. This was in order to avoid the charge that this amounted to 'confiscation' of the investments not just of the big companies, which have lined their pockets through privatisation, but also those with a handful of shares. We are in favour of compensation for the small investors. Yet the public mood was such that there was absolutely no support for compensating the fat cat shareholders and rail bosses. We went even further and suggested that "the bosses' profits should be seized and all their subsidies from public money taken back". Needless to say, New Labour rejected this. However the opposition to privatisation went beyond the railways. The government was still considering the privatisation of air traffic control and even suggested applying this to part of the London Underground. In almost every corner of the public sector privatisation was spreading its greedy tentacles, bringing more misery and potentially loss of life. We stated: "In the NHS the Private Finance Initiative (PFI) is already draining resources. In 15 years this drain will become intolerable." That has been borne out as PFI is seen as a massive failure. However, such was the outcry at its effects on the railways, that Prescott, then Transport Minister, was forced to declare that within 24 hours £1 billion would be made available for improving rail safety! He said that finding money was never a problem, which posed the question: if that was the case, why the hell hadn't he done it before and saved lives?[4]

Tony Benn recorded in his diaries: "Blair has just come back from holiday yesterday, 31 August... I feel the New Labour period is passing now; can't quite describe it. And just as all the right wingers call themselves modernisers when you want to get rid of socialist ideas, so I'm a post-moderniser. I feel the pendulum beginning to swing back."[5] Subsequent events were to show that within New Labour, despite the opposition to Blair in general and particularly from former Labour supporters, this was not expressed within the party itself. So long as Benn and what remained of the Labour left remained imprisoned within its structures, their effect was nullified.

This was indicated at the Labour Party conference, where Benn expressed deep pessimism in contrast to his recent optimism: "The conference is totally different now, they really have only tolerated any functional decision making and the media just hover around trying to find a bit of trouble. But the press may get bored with Jesus Christ, taking responsibility for all our sins... There's no question about it, the media have taken the whole thing over. As I left I was given a T-shirt and a little rubber television set (a toy) to press in my hands for stress."[6] He admitted that the left was completely ineffective: "I went down to the Tribune meeting in the Winter Gardens. I would be surprised that there were 200 people there; last year it was 1,200. It was a terribly disappointing meeting, to be truthful." Reduced to watching Blair's speech on television, he commented: "The first and overwhelming impression is of a man absolutely inflated with his own role – 'I'm doing this, I'm doing that...' It really frightened me. On the other hand, he played all the right notes about the health service, dentistry and drugs, equality of opportunity and how the class war is over. Everybody cheered him; he got a standing ovation. I thought the PM had gone right over the top."[7]

This theme – hopes for a change in the Labour Party, only to be followed by deep disappointment – was played out again and again, both in Benn's private ruminations and in the writings and speeches of the left. Occasionally there are flashes of recognition of the hopelessness of expecting Labour to change. Commenting on Livingstone's intention to stand for London Mayor, if necessary against Labour (which he subsequently did successfully) Benn commented: "I don't want to see Ken expelled from the party, which he would be immediately. On the other hand, there will have to be a break made one day, and maybe Ken standing independently in London would be the moment to break the power and reputation and standing of New Labour."[8] Moreover, the attacks of the New Labour machine on Livingstone only increased his support, as Benn conceded: "Blair launched into a violent personal attack on Livingstone, actually naming him and going back to the bad old days of old Labour, and so on; it was quite unnecessary, very stupid, because it's building a bigger sympathy vote for Livingstone."[9]

Events were to show that Tony Benn's hopes were to be dashed. Livingstone, who had evolved towards the right, was completely incapable of utilising his triumph in being elected London Mayor to then launch an initiative in favour of socialism and a new mass party. The dithering of Benn and the Labour left on this issue acted in no small measure as a brake on moves to create such a political force. There is no doubt that with the backing of leading left figures like Benn, a new party, albeit limited in the first instance, would have developed in outline at this stage. The Iraq war, the complicity of Blair and the New Labour government in this, would have given an enormous impetus to such a party as will be shown later.

24. A new millennium
2000

The New Year marked both a new century and a new millennium. Millions were out on the streets throughout the world. For a short moment the world experienced genuine human solidarity as TV carried the joyous global celebrations. Of course, the powers that be, the capitalists, used this occasion to extol the benefits of the system. The so-called free market was the best means of delivering humankind's future: "The world, in short, is becoming a better place... Capitalism is broadly accepted worldwide as the least bad way of organising economic activity." But the Observer also noted: "The gap between the incomes of the rich and the poor in the advanced democracies is widening and the disparity in wealth is extraordinary... Nor is that all. The disparity of income and wealth between countries is also becoming insupportable. More than a billion people live in abject poverty, their collective income no more than 600 of the richest men and women on earth." This did not prevent the Observer from contemptuously speaking of the "implosion of socialism as an idea".

We posed the question: why then did they draw parallels with the uncontrolled, untrammelled capitalism prior to 1914 and fearfully write: "It was the profound anger at the economic and social inequality that underpinned the growth of socialism and communism in the first 40 years of the century."[1] We also pointed to the massive share bubble which indicated that the boom was "built on a house of cards... One US firm in 1999 [has reached] a market capitalisation higher than the annual gross domestic product (GDP) of New Zealand." We also anticipated that "capitalism is heading for a fall, the timing of which and the scale upon which it will develop is unknowable precisely because it works in a blind fashion. Marxism, scientific socialism, properly understood and applied, can work out in a broad sense how events are likely to develop... This doesn't mean it's possible to work out the winner of the King George VI Chase at Kempton on Boxing Day! Marxism is the science of perspectives through understanding the broad processes which are developing economically, how they will be reflected socially and, ultimately, politically as well."[2]

In Britain a massive disparity in wealth between the rich and poor had taken shape under both Tory and 'Labour' administrations. Blair, just before the beginning of the new millennium, also extolled the virtues of capitalism's 'free market'. But the appetite for quick profits, with little care for the health and safety of the mass of consumers and transport users, was accompanied by wholesale deregulation and little accountability, as the disasters like Paddington or health scares such as the BSE or GM food scandals had shown. Labour had tried and failed to convince us that we were all middle class now. This flew in the face of the experience of working people. In 1999, 20,000 had demonstrated in Newcastle, protesting against low pay. Anti-capitalist demonstrations had taken place in Cologne and in Seattle. A BBC Online poll had installed Karl Marx as 'thinker of the millennium'.

Within days of the new millennium beginning Blair, in an interview with the TUC-sponsored magazine, Trade Unions Today, launched a bitter attack on the unions. He accused them of representing 'sectional interests', warning them to keep out of politics, especially when it came to interfering in the Labour Party. To justify his rant he said that the unions had attempted in the 1970s "to take on the government and set the agenda". He even repeated Tory myths that the reason why Labour lost in 1979 was due to the unions. Fortunately for Blair, most of the trade union leaders at this stage agreed with his analysis and were desperately trying to contain a new explosion from below. The so-called dirty strikes of 1979 happened because of the anger of working class people at the record of the 1974-79 Labour government, which had introduced wage restraint and made massive public spending cuts of £8 billion – equivalent to nearly £50 billion in 1999. This still remains the single biggest cut in public expenditure which any government has made up to now. The truth was that the union leaders in 1979 were unable to contain the working class, despite their best efforts, because of the anger of low paid workers in the health service, education and local authorities. To Blair and some of the union leaders, the strikes were 'an embarrassment'. In reality, they empowered in a real way hundreds of thousands of previously unorganised workers to act collectively and do something about the problem of wages and lousy conditions.[3]

Blair had made his attack because of the evidence of mounting discontent at the inaction of the Labour government. It had done nothing to arrest the colossal decline of British industry, which is felt sharply today in the diminished opportunities for young people in particular to get reasonable jobs and income to plan for the future. As we entered the new millennium pensioners received a miserly 75p per week rise. 'Outed' by 'their' government, one pensioner wrote to Brown, saying that the promises of cookies in the future were not much use to him as he was 77 and wanted action now. Teachers, civil servants and other public sector workers were increasingly angry at the way their wages and living standards were held down. A report at this time showed that, if teachers had access to the same kind of housing in London as they had in 1900, on average they would need a salary of £80,000 a year. Even right-wing GMB leader John Edmonds had a glimmer of understanding of the discontent that was growing in the ranks of the working class. He commented that the trade unions' 'mistake' in the winter of discontent was not to wait until after the 1979 election, when Labour would probably have been elected, before pressing demands. We commented that, in reality, they did not make a mistake as the winter of discontent arose from the colossal pressure of ordinary trade unionists from below, which then compelled the trade union leaders to 'lead' the movement.

The international mood against capitalism was also developing as the ideologists of the system were praising its achievements. The anti-World Trade Organisation demonstrations in Seattle, in the us and elsewhere indicated this. There was massive opposition to the inequality that was rooted in the system. One American economist and author David Korten commented: "The sales of the world's ten largest companies exceed the GNP of the world's 100 smallest countries. The leading 50 industrial corporations control 25% of the world's economic output. The combined assets of the world's 50 largest banks and financial companies control 60% of the world's global capital."[4] The scene was therefore set for a huge conflict which would dominate the 21st century, between the ideas of outmoded capitalism and democratic socialism, purged of the repugnant ideas and methods of Stalinism.

The onset of the New Year did not herald an end to the woes of New Labour as it approached its 1,000th day in office. Even the government's most loyal supporters were forced to admit that the "magic has started to fade". It was faced with an avalanche of bad headlines: the NHS crisis, the inability to deliver on election promises, Straw's decision on Pinochet came to a head, the government betrayal of its so-called 'ethical' foreign policy and the call for heads to roll that accompanied all these fiascos. Then the Mandelson scandal erupted. At the same time Blair faced opposition from the normally mute membership of the Labour Party. We took the opportunity to remind our readers and working people in general of what we had written in May 1997, when the government had been first elected, that "the needs of big business and finance, the drive for profit will dominate over the needs of millions of ordinary people". On the prospects for the election, we wrote: "Even if Blair were to win a general election, it will be on a massively reduced turnout and with a slashed majority."[5]

Opposition developed towards the Blair government from

within its own ranks and from the most unexpected individuals. Peter Kilfoyle was notorious, particularly in Liverpool, as a Labour bureaucratic fixer. He was particularly used by Kinnock against Militant. Before then, he had served a stint as a right-wing union bashing figure linked to the Australian Labor Party. Some writers talked about Kilfoyle rescuing Labour from Militant's 'suicide mission' in Liverpool. He had spoken about Trotskyites – that is, Militant – using 'democratic centralist' methods, but compared it to the 'control freakery' of Blair's Millbank operation.

This crude political bruiser did not have the slightest understanding of the concept of democratic centralism and, in Liverpool, had applied Stalinist bureaucratic centralist methods himself. He was playing with words – which he little understood, moreover – in order to cover up his role in Liverpool. Kilfoyle's 'success', through expulsions, led to a comeback for the Liberal Democrats in the city, mass abstention by former Labour supporters, Britain's highest council tax and massive cuts in jobs and services by successive right-wing Labour and Liberal councils. That somebody like this could come into collision with the Blair machine said everything about New Labour's right-wing character.[6] So bereft was the Parliamentary Labour Party of genuine lefts that Tony Benn seized hold of him as a genuine representative of opposition: "I saw Peter Kilfoyle... [He] is very academic, a formidable man."[7] That was not the way the Liverpool labour movement viewed him. He was a hatchet man for Kinnock and the right wing in destroying all elements of Labour Party democracy.

25. An avalanche of redundancies

In March came the bombshell of the announcement of the proposed breakup of the Rover car plants in Birmingham. Stephen Byers had offered £152 million in government subsidies. We posed the questions: "Where is the free market now? Why doesn't he go the whole hog and nationalise?" Rover had been bought by Alchemy Partners just for short-term profit, which had led to the breakup of the group. They wanted to turn Longbridge into a little workshop. We argued that the only way to defend the Longbridge plant was to occupy it. The Mini car line was still there and up and running. The technology of the plant should be protected. There was outrage at the proposals for cutbacks. Fifty thousand jobs or more were threatened in the West Midlands and an extra 25,000 in Oxford and Swindon. Previous owners BMW had already put the gun to the heads of the workers in demanding flexible arrangements or else they would close the plant. Wages had been cut and hours lengthened. Other car companies were planning cutbacks and retrenchment. Nationalisation of Rover under democratic workers' control and management was posed.

The Socialist Party intervened in the debates and discussions around the future of Rover. Dave Nellist wrote an article for the Birmingham Post in which he denounced "the disposal of the Longbridge factory in Birmingham to Alchemy Partners, a group of asset strippers, sorry, 'venture capitalists', [as] a betrayal of thousands of workers at Longbridge who've bent over backwards with concessions to a succession of owners". He pointed out that some politicians were campaigning for a strong car company to take over Rover, one with experience of the industry rather than a vulture, such as Alchemy. But "it's a forlorn hope. There's an estimated 40% overcapacity in car production worldwide." What was needed was government intervention through public ownership and control and by the involvement of Rover workers themselves. This would allow "the drawing up of a new plan of production to meet the transport needs of the whole of society".[1]

Over 100,000 working class people marched through Birmingham the weekend after the announcement against BMW's plans to shut the plant down. Furious at the betrayal of Rover workers, people were assembling by 8:30am for a march called for 11. A parade of shops was displaying 'Don't Let Rover Die' posters. One union placard portrayed the letters BMW standing for 'Betrayed Midlands Workers'. A group of young Asians holding a banner, 'George Dixon Sixth Form Support Rover', brought press attention as they jumped and cheered to drummers. TGWU official Tony Woodley appeared to boos and heckles to chair the rally at the end of the march. It was the TUC leader Monks who "recognised the efforts" of workers trying to defend their jobs. This met polite applause and comments on how much he was paid. Workers also commented that union leaders should stop defending Labour's indifference. At the well-attended Socialist Party meeting following the demonstration Dave Nellist pointed out that in 1971, Tory Prime Minister Heath took just 24 hours to nationalise Rolls-Royce and stop the breakup of the aerospace industry. He added: "There is no parliamentary obstacle for Tony Blair to do the same 30 years later. The problem is that New Labour is not a working class party. Join the fight for a programme of action to save jobs."[2]

The next day Blair, in an article in the press, bluntly stated that the government would not intervene. We commented: "Both Blair and Byers – in words and deeds – show they are the willing servants of big business."[3] The only way to solve this problem was to take ownership into the hands of the state under democratic workers' control and management. Then overcapacity could be dealt with, in some circumstances, by shifting to useful alternative production as the shop stewards at Lucas Aerospace armaments factory had proposed in the 1970s. The remorseless grip of recession and job losses in Birmingham was threatening to spread to Ford Dagenham. In addition, shipyard workers in the North-East, Scotland and Northern Ireland would also face the dole. Forty thousand textile jobs had been lost during the previous year, with 25,000 more expected to go the following year. Woodley, under pressure from workers and trade unionists, was now threatening all-out strike action to prevent the closure of production in Dagenham. It was necessary for car workers, we argued, to exert pressure on the union leaders to translate words into deeds throughout the industry.

By May the Rover bosses were stepping up the pressure by declaring that, if they did not have a suitable buyer by the end of the month, they would consider abandoning the whole Rover operation. Blair declared that he would work "night and day to save Rover jobs". This was an about-turn on his previous statement that the government was powerless to stop BMW. The proximity of a general election was undoubtedly a factor because 27 vulnerable Labour seats were close to Longbridge. However, we warned the workers not to take anything for granted and step up the pressure for the plant to be nationalised. Many workers saw the necessity for such a step.[4]

It was hoped that even union leaders may echo the call but our approach had nothing in common with the nationalisations of the past. Old-style nationalisations, while a step forward compared to private ownership, were usually dominated by a board whose directors were picked from private firms. This meant they would operate on capitalist lines – as workers in the old nationalised industries would be able to testify. The new publicly owned firm should be run under workers' control and management, which meant that the managing board should have the majority of its members drawn from the local and national labour movement. Only with the majority of industry owned and run by the working class as a whole will it be possible to democratically plan the development of society and eliminate permanently the problems which were confronting car and other workers at this time.

By the middle of 2000 the wheels were beginning to come off the Blair government. The opening of the Millennium Bridge was as much a fiasco as the opening of the Millennium Dome and London Eye. We commented that Labour's new modernisation programme, like the government itself, had "ended up wobbly, mistrusted and viewed as a failure". A seismic shift in the perception of the government was taking place. They had ignored the first law of holes: 'If you find yourself in one, stop digging!' Blair had been slow handclapped at the Women's Institute conference, which was seen as a turning point. His electoral guru, Philip Gould, described Blair's predicament in words which could have been taken out of an editorial in the Socialist from the previous period. He said that Blair was perceived as being out of touch, "of not being real. He lacks conviction; he is all spin and presentation and he says things to please people, not because he believes them." Wasn't this the philosophy of Gould himself, an arch spin doctor? Et tu Brute! Gould twisted the knife writing that Blair was "unable to hold a position... lacking guts", and that his rhetoric about traditional values was seen as "risible" by people.

Worryingly for Blair, opinion polls showed that what was until then considered a racing certainty – victory for Labour in a general election – now seemed no more than a probability. All the polls indicated that Labour's lead over the Tories was narrowing dramatically. We explained that we did not want to see the Tories returned to office and that was still not the most likely prospect. However, the return of a Labour government was also of no real benefit to working class people.[5]

The announcement in June of 10,000 job losses in one day coincided with an intensification of the infighting in Labour about when and if Britain should join the euro. The job losses at British Aerospace and steelmaker Corus deepened the problems Labour faced with the crisis in manufacturing industry, which was exacerbated by the high value of the pound. We pointed out that being part of the euro would not have averted the job losses which were taking place. The pound had devalued by 10% in the previous six weeks. So, if anything, the outlook for costs to manufacturing industry was looking slightly more promising outside the euro. These job losses had mainly occurred, as was the case with the other 200,000 manufacturing jobs lost since Labour came to power, because British manufacturing bosses could no longer compete effectively due to lack of investment. Moreover, it was easier for multinational capitalists in Britain to shed jobs here because of the Thatcher-Major anti-union laws, which were retained by Blair and meant weak labour protection which suited the bosses.

There were serious differences within the Labour Cabinet on whether or not to join the euro. Some members – Mandelson, Byers and Cook – argued that they could not protect manufacturing industry from crisis while Britain remained outside the euro. But joining the euro was practically ruled out for at least three years anyway because of the imminence of the general election and the need for a referendum. In the meantime, there was a serious haemorrhaging of jobs for which neither of the feuding wings in the Cabinet had a solution. They clung to the hope that the capitalists would come up with something. Yet the bosses were more interested in the lust for profits even if this resulted in chaos and economic anarchy. Meanwhile, on the ground, the Socialist Party was intervening and reporting about the growing angry mood of workers. In steel making areas one worker described the announcement by Corus to axe 1,500 jobs, most of them in Sheffield and Rotherham, as "all about greed. It's money, money, money, and profit." Unemployment in Rotherham was already at 17% and a Sheffield worker commented: "What else is there to do around here? The answer is nowt."[6]

Then came the shock announcement that the Peugeot management at its Coventry plant was attempting to implement new working practices involving another speed-up of production. The company was hit by two one-day strikes at the end of July and workers stood firm, maintaining a decision in a third ballot to strike against the arrogant management's plans; they had pushed workers too far.

The workers were quite conscious of the gains that had been made by the employers: "The greedy Peugeot bosses have seen their profits rise 153% to £455 million... There used to be 450 workers on trim [section], now there's just 143... The company know we're not robots... We must be united and resolute to win this battle. If we don't stop them now our lives will be made intolerable in the future." The engineering union's official completely ignored the workers' feelings, declaring that "'the company had been very reasonable', even stopping the track to explain the deal! He went on to warn that investment will be threatened [by strike action]." The workers were fuming. The press picked up his theme: "More pay for less hours – what's the problem with Peugeot?" They pictured the workers as morons who would "strike if that was really the deal". The workers expressed their appreciation to the Socialist Party: "With the help of the Socialist Party councillor Dave Nellist, we got across why we've had enough."[7]

A very successful meeting with 80 attending was held by the Coventry Socialist Party in support of the Peugeot workers. A car worker declared at the meeting: "As for the unions, their handling of this issue can only be described as a farce." Cheering broke out from the Peugeot workers. Another worker announced: "Workers rejected the union recommendation by 86%. Still, they recommended it again. Workers still voted 59% to 41% to strike. The union never articulated the workers' case, and they and New Labour then tried to silence Socialist councillors," the Peugeot workers' real voice. Then they recommended the offer again in another ballot "until they got the result they wanted".

In other words right-wing union leaders were employing the same methods that the capitalists were adopting on crucial issues for them. For instance, later in the EU referendum in Ireland they refused to accept the first ballot, which was to reject the measures proposed by the Irish government and the EU, despite the fact that this was the democratic will of the Irish people. Instead, in a new ballot, they pulled out all the stops and eventually got a majority for their proposals. This is capitalist democracy! The lessons were not lost on these Peugeot workers involved in struggle. They condemned New Labour's snub: "What's the point of having a local council that can't even verbally defend local workers against multinational companies? No wonder fewer people vote in elections."[8]

Thirty-five people including twelve Peugeot workers attended a Socialist Party branch meeting soon after this meeting. There was general dissatisfaction developing at all levels with the inactivity of the right-wing union leaders. Nigel, a TGWU member for twelve years, wrote: "The gulf between the wishes of the shop floor and the Joint Negotiating Committee has never been so apparent."[9] After the county council's refusal to discuss a Dave Nellist resolution supporting the Peugeot workers, letters appeared in the Coventry Evening Telegraph, reprinted in the Socialist under the heading, 'What about the Workers, Mr Blair?: "Throughout the dispute with the company, Mr Nellist's party has been the only one to side with the workers... If Labour is refusing to support Mr Nellist and the workers for their own electoral or petty ideological reasons, then Labour does not deserve to run the Council. Keep up the good work Dave!... We need more conviction politicians like Dave Nellist. We need fewer careerists such as those who have found their way into the Labour Party."[10]

26. Tanker revolt: seven days that shook Blair September 2000

More and more open hostility was being shown by Blair's government towards workers involved in strike action. Imitating Thatcher, Blair mobilised the forces of the state to break a fuel protest by truck drivers and farmers that broke out in September 2000. The Queen, through the Privy Council, even approved the use of emergency powers. Police were ordered to engineer a 'breakout' of tankers. Blair boasted that he solved the crisis within 24 hours. We wrote: "The dramatic 'seven days in September' of the fuel crisis and its aftermath represents the most serious challenge to the Blair government since it came to power in 1997. A handful of demonstrators (one estimate put it at no more than 2,500 nationwide), but with the mass of the British population behind them, brought the Blair government to its knees within a matter of days."[1]

Andrew Rawnsley wrote in the Observer: "The prime minister looked dazed and sounded confused. Like a man who has come within a centimetre of losing his life in a car wreck, it will take time for it all to sink in... The bleakest moment inside Number Ten, so I hear from within the bunker, was on Wednesday morning [13 September]. Tony Blair's premiership was 48 hours from meltdown. His jut-jawed pledge of the previous afternoon that the tankers would roll was not being fulfilled. One of the non-leaders of the protests gloated: 'The government is hanging by a thread.' This is what the government thought too."[2]

Predictably, David Blunkett and Margaret Beckett suggested that it was all a 'plot' organised by "people who hate the Labour government". Beckett declared that these people had "latched onto the fuel issue and were the industrial wing of the Countryside Alliance". But an Observer investigation into who was behind these events came up with the conclusion that it was "a ragbag of people, some Labour, some Tories, many apolitical, many who could trace their days of protest right back to the miners' strike. And the public, as the polls show, seems to be on their side." Equally predictably, at the TUC conference in Glasgow which was taking place at the same time, John Monks, backed up by the whole of the General Council, savaged the fuel protesters. We commented: "There is a real danger that this dispute will go down in folklore as a largely middle class protest and the lessons for the working class and labour movement as a whole will be lost... The tumultuous 'seven days in September' underline a number of vital points which the Socialist Party has consistently made."

It indicated that with the explosive social situation building up in Britain a challenge to the government could come from the most unexpected quarters. The fuel protests had been triggered by the successes of the French fishermen, farmers and lorry drivers. But few expected the British to follow that example. Even the French fishermen scornfully commented on the hostility of British tourists in Calais: "The British are cowards, they have forgotten how to strike."[3] We remarked that, while most people really smile and nod in agreement, it was an inaccurate statement of the mood developing below the surface in Britain. The wave of small but important industrial battles on which we had reported in the previous month was an indication of what was developing. The obvious point we made was that a big section of the population was now dependent on a car where there is no cheap available public transport. The immediate effect of a rise in the price of petrol was to worsen the living standards of those who depended on driving for a living, but it also indirectly impacted on the living standards of the majority of the population.

Something similar happened in France when the leaders of the main trade union confederations, the CGT and CFDT, condemned some of the lorry drivers and small farmers as 'Poujadists' (a largely small business, middle class movement of protest). We considered this was a false comparison. The Poujadists of the 1950s and 1960s had little connection with the struggles of the working class, particularly industrial workers. The movement in France and Britain in 2000 enjoyed mass support from the working class. Moreover, we pointed towards the example of the us labour movement in the 1930s, where Trotskyists played a key role in historic and successful strikes which fused different groups of drivers together, including independent owner drivers, into the powerful Teamsters union. They had established a very strong base in Minneapolis. During the Liverpool struggle we looked towards the model of Minneapolis as to what could be achieved with determined leadership.

Different branches of the Socialist Party attempted to act in a similar fashion in intervening in the tanker dispute. Dave Reid, a key organiser for us in Wales then and now, gave a first-hand account of how our Welsh organisation – particularly in Cardiff – intervened: "Two Socialist Party members drove to Cardiff Docks on 10 September to see if anything was happening there." They introduced themselves to the demonstrators and offered help for the struggle. "The core of the pickets were haulage contractors, their drivers and self-employed drivers. Some drivers worked during the day and slept in their cab on the picket line... Many pickets were owners, probably Tories at some time. During the miners' strike many haulage contractors crossed the NUM picket lines in the huge coal convoys outside the steelworks. But the fact that some of them might have crossed picket lines was no reason not to intervene. The dispute showed the power that lorry drivers have and they have to be won behind the working class."

There was no dewy-eyed romanticism: "This movement could go either to the right or the left, but was tending towards the left. We needed to try and link this struggle to the labour movement and to raise socialist ideas as far as possible. This was a strike, with unionised tanker drivers taking secondary action to support the haulage contractors. The oil companies didn't put too much pressure on the drivers – any threat of disciplinary action would have led to a complete walkout, but there was no evidence that they colluded with the protesters."[4]

The Socialist Party tried to gain support from other sections of workers. The Fire Brigades Union (FBU) and ambulance representatives came to the picket line. A very successful meeting between the FBU, the ambulance convenor and picket organisers was followed by a press conference with trade unionists confirming their support for the strike. By Wednesday, support was growing. An eight car cavalcade of ordinary working class people arrived from Pontypridd. Other visitors were arriving by the hour. A 50-strong taxi protest led by the TGWU taxi organiser (a regular buyer of the Socialist) arrived. A meeting between picket leaders and Socialist Party members discussed further action. Firstly, a Cardiff leadership committee was formed, including a Socialist Party member. They attempted to create a coordinating committee.

Despite all this evidence of mass support for the fuel protesters, Monks unbelievably compared the lorry drivers to the right-wing truckers who helped to prepare the downfall of the Allende government in Chile in the 1970s. Those truckers had been financed by Chilean big business and US imperialism. In Britain this had been a largely spontaneous revolt from below. Participating in the protests were some traditional Labour supporters who said they would never vote for Blair again. Members of the TGWU were also present on the picket lines. This movement had some features of what a general strike, or near general strike, would look like in the way it quickly paralysed society, seizing up the 'arteries of the nation', as the press put it, while at the same time placing a mighty boot on the windpipe of the Blair government.

In no way could this dispute be presented as 'reactionary'. It had the support of the majority of the population, despite the hardship which it meant. However, terrified by the newly-revealed power of important groups of workers, the government set up a task force, headed by Straw, to consider legislation that would give powers in the future to the government to make a refusal to deliver fuel a criminal offence. According to the Observer: "An essential services act would also apply to water, gas and other key public services in private hands, which would cause huge problems if they were blockaded." We drew the conclusion that this meant that "the government has now been provided with 'national' support, without a national government, to rush through emergency legislation which will be used not just against pickets of fuel stations but workers in the water, gas, electricity and other industries. Such measures are more draconian than were introduced even by the Tories."[5] Indeed, Edmonds warned that Thatcher backed off from banning industrial action in 'essential services'.

As it turned out, the Labour government did not proceed to introduce extra anti-union legislation at this stage, largely because of the electoral fallout which could have put its re-election in doubt. The mass of the population came behind the strike. It was not the same as 1984-85, when Thatcher succeeded in defeating the miners. It was more akin to 1981 when Thatcher was compelled to retreat and give concessions to them. In this crisis Blair was completely unprepared. Even the use of the army – a very risky enterprise with just 80 tankers – would have been completely ineffective. Three thousand tankers were being used to distribute oil throughout Britain. The movement had a seismic effect on the development of British politics. Some sections of the middle class, including drivers, had supported Thatcher in the conflict with the miners. But others now confessed on TV: "We were wrong. The miners were right."[6] This movement had been mainly direct action by small business people, although with widespread sympathy amongst workers. Crucially, however, it was the tanker drivers who prevented oil leaving the depots. This was a glimpse of the potential power which working class people have.

On the eve of the dispute the government was well ahead in the opinion polls and was set fair for a big majority in the election, probably to be held sometime in 2001. In the aftermath of the strike the government's self-assured image was shattered. This opened the way to increased confidence to protest on other issues. There was a massive drop in support for the government. The strength of Blair lay in the clear weakness of the Tory opposition and the feebleness of the Lib Dems. The trade union leaders had ridden to the defence of Blair. Yet in the past these union leaders had been excoriated and attacked by the Blairites. Now they had effectively propped up the Blair government. Commenting on the TUC conference and the performance of the leading right-wing figure, the Financial Times stated: "John Monks, the TUC general secretary, delivered a key-note address that (with a slight change of emphasis) could have been applauded on many points by an audience of businessmen. He warned against inter-union rivalry; described the need for economic growth, investment, training and productivity improvements; and praised the development of partnership agreements between unions and companies. By contrast, the class war battle cries of Arthur Scargill, the miners' leader, were brushed aside."[7]

After the seven days that shook Blair, we carried a front page headline: 'New Labour in Crisis: Out of Touch with Ordinary Working People, a Government for the Fat Cats.' Blair had a personal rating of minus 34, the lowest for a Labour Party leader since 1989. The columns of our paper were filled with workers complaining about the arrogance of the government: "Unless Blair pulls something out of the hat... for the first time in my life, I couldn't vote Labour... I think Blair's arrogant and he's not listening to the people he should be listening to," said a nurse at Whipps Cross Hospital, London.[8]

However, soon after the fuel dispute a terrible train crash occurred near Hatfield on the line from King's Cross to Leeds. The company responsible was GNER and the crash revealed the shocking state of the railways under privatisation. This showed eye-watering complacency on rail maintenance. The number of broken rails had increased from 750 in 1995 to 973 in 1998 and 937 in 1999. It was no accident that this coincided with a cut in the number of rail maintenance workers. We, of course, called for immediate renationalisation, a demand with mass support as all opinion polls at the time and since have demonstrated. A rail guard told the

Socialist: "Every day we see that maintenance isn't done, trains are in a bad condition. If we report a fault they don't like it, they want to run the service whatever happens. If they cancel trains, they have to pay Railtrack."[9]

Criticism mounted as the year drew to an end. Even Bill Morris, leader of the TGWU and one of the government's 'boys' against the fuel protesters, made a startling admission – for him – at the union's conference, when he described the Labour government as "a shambles". The CBI went a step further, describing Blair's Britain as being like a "Third World banana republic". Brown did his best to prettify the image of New Labour in the autumn statement in November. Kevin Parslow wrote: "If you are a Christian, the recent Pre-Budget Statement rewarded your faith – Gordon Brown reduced VAT on church repairs to 5%. If you had faith that the Chancellor would raise your living standards, you would have been disappointed." Little was proposed, outside of the concessions on pensions and fuel, which would lighten the burdens of working class people. Unlike now, the government was sitting on a cash mountain: "But rather than spending it on wage rises for low paid, public sector workers or further improvements to public services, a large part of the budget was aimed at giving bribes to big business to ensure their further support for New Labour." Furthermore: "Brown aims to make Britain the 'best place in the world for multinationals to invest' – and create the 'most modern environment for business in the world'... No wonder, with New Labour having reduced corporation tax from 33p to 30p in the pound, the lowest of all major countries and the lowest in British history."[10]

As a consequence of the battering which the government was receiving, some commentators described 2000 as Blair's 'annus horribilis' – his horrible year. Without doubt the perception of the Labour government had changed. Gone was the image of 'Teflon Tony', where no calamity could stick to him for long. During the fuel crisis he was blamed for every problem – and to some extent he was responsible. Nevertheless, we posed the question: "Why is it that a government that is presiding over such chaos, that is deeply unpopular and pursuing unwanted pro-capitalist policies like privatisation of air traffic control, privatisation of schools, health, etc., seems likely to win a general election?" The answer, of course, lay in the complete ineptitude of New Labour's rivals, the Tories and Liberal Democrats.[11] But Labour's continued patronage of big business would inevitably see growing disillusionment and anger with the government the following year, whatever the election result.

27. Opposition from the trade unions 1997

New Labour's self-imposed adherence to strict Tory economic guidelines, particularly in the field of public expenditure, meant that the Blair government was compelled to chip away at the past gains of the working class. Therefore, although there was an initial honeymoon period, there was also growing discontent, particularly from former Labour voters. The Socialist Party sought to capitalise on this through its campaigns. We concentrated particularly on the issues affecting young people as well as the ongoing industrial battles and their reflection within the trade unions.

The trade union Unison assumed great importance to us. The continuing deindustrialisation of Britain led to the collapse and virtual disappearance in some areas of well-paid manufacturing and manual jobs. Local government, the civil service and the teaching profession became alternative sources of employment for young workers who previously would have followed their parents into industry. Over time this resulted in the same combative militant traditions built up over generations in the factories being expressed in these new workplaces which, moreover, were characterised more and more by factory-like conditions: large offices, bullying management, etc. Neoliberalism in general reinforced this and was buttressed by Tony Blair and New Labour. They clearly favoured the bosses over the trade unions.

The pages of the Socialist expressed this process clearly through its reports of the bitter resistance to the employers. In 1997 we reported on the events in Waltham Forest: "Len Hockey has worked at Whipps Cross Hospital since 1989 as a porter. Within a year he became a shop steward and is now Unison's assistant branch secretary on the Whipps Cross site." Len gave a picture of the battle that was unfolding: "Being a socialist is not all one-way traffic – people receiving your arguments and instantly rallying. You often incur a bit of opposition... So initially the ideas of socialism and building a left within the union were seen to be a bit irrelevant. There used to be almost unlimited overtime so the opportunities were there for increased earnings. As the Tory cuts bit, the mood began to change and hospital workers became more receptive to the Socialist Party's ideas. During the poll tax struggle we had weekly workplace meetings, which involved 50-60 predominantly student nurses... We organised a demonstration of 400 [against privatisation] – Waltham Forest's biggest labour movement demonstration for as long as I can remember." As a result of this kind of work, "Five young porters subsequently came along to our local Socialist Party branch. This initiative spawned the joint union/community campaign, 'Health in Crisis.'"[1]

This is just one example from hundreds of the painstaking, consistent work in which Socialist Party members were involved in the workplaces and communities. In a period that was not the most favourable they still argued for the ideas of socialism.

In industry and the trade unions the Socialist Party also fought for a real alternative for working people. Yes, trade union density in Britain had dropped from 55% to just over 30% when the first Blair government came to power. In the era of neoliberalism trade unions were confronting an entirely different situation to that which existed during the post-war boom period. Then, such was the strength of the workers' organisations that in Italy, for instance, a national sliding scale of wages was won through the 'scala mobile'. Those kinds of conditions have disappeared in Italy and elsewhere as meek union leaders capitulated to the capitalists' offensive against the living standards and conditions of the working class.

There was, therefore, some similarity between what had happened to the ex-workers' parties that had become bourgeoisified and the trade unions, although the process had not gone as far in the unions.

The Socialist Party rejected the notion by some on the left that the trade unions were irredeemable and could not be changed. We wrote in Socialism Today: "The same processes [bourgeoisification] have also affected the unions although in this case there are quite clear limits to this process. Unlike the traditional workers' parties, the unions still retain their dual character; the leadership has one foot in the camp of capitalism but rests on a working class base... This role of the trade union leaders is not accidental. It is a product of their ideological capitulation, particularly reinforced by the collapse of Stalinism. The acceptance of the 'market' and the political outlook which flows from this is disastrous from the point of view of the working class. If you accept the capitalist market then the logic is to back the boss, and to see the 'point of view' of the government that supports the capitalist system. From this flows support for 'teamworking', outsourcing, privatisation."

We pointed out that in a British Airways strike, Bill Morris, General Secretary of the TGWU, "in answer to the high-handed demands of the confrontational BA management for £42 million savings, [had] declared: 'I believe in labour flexibility, but I also think that labour should have rights, dignity and security."[2] Morris offered to make the same £42 million worth of 'savings' demanded by BA management, the only difference being on method. The management wanted to cut arbitrarily; the union leadership wished the same cuts could be carried out through 'negotiations'. We explained that the standpoint of union leaders who 'see the point' of the employer not only causes confusion among the workers. It also results, for example, in the "scandalous spectacle of union leaders, in the recent Montupet strike in Northern Ireland, leading scabs across a picket line set up by members of their own union".

So far to the right had some union leaders moved that there were some similarities to the situation described by Leon Trotsky in the 1930s. He showed that there was a tendency for the union tops to fuse together with the capitalist state. Some left groups allegedly basing themselves on Trotsky's analysis concluded that the trade union leadership had gone over completely to the side of capital and were now 'the Labour lieutenants of capital', to use the phrase of the American Marxist Daniel De Leon. We rejected such conclusions and held out the perspective that the unions could be pushed in a leftward direction if Marxists and socialists, in collaboration with the rank and file, fought the right wing on a clear programme and through action, by using the method of broad lefts where this was appropriate.[3]

28. Our work in
Unison
1997

Unison was one such union in which the Socialist Party success-fully used this approach, coming up against an increasingly right-wing leadership. It takes a leap of the imagination to remember that this union once stood firmly on the left, when Alan Fisher was General Secretary of the National Union of Public Employees (NUPE), one of the constituent unions which formed Unison. Alan once wrote a front page article for Militant in the week of a big demonstration against the 1974-79 Labour government's spending cuts. It is inconceivable to imagine Dave Prentis, his successor to the leadership of Unison, doing the same thing. Those days had long gone as a succession of general secretaries more and more on the right led the union. First under Rodney Bickerstaffe and follow-ing him Dave Prentis the union moved into the embrace of New Labour. By definition this meant that it would come into collision with the ranks of the union itself.

Almost as soon as Blair was elected, opposition to his pro-capi-talist policies was expressed in the union's national conference, with a delegate declaring to wild applause: "If Labour doesn't deliver, then we will fight them just as hard as the Tories before." Another mentioned that Unison had spent £6.5 million to get Labour elected and now expected something in return. Glenn Kelly, a well-known Militant/Socialist Party member, tried to move an amendment to a motion which merely called for an 'understanding' on related matters to the Labour government. A number of branches supported his amendment which sought to include the phrase "the abolition of the anti-union laws". This caused pandemonium, with personal attacks on the proposer, but the amendment remained. Glenn was entitled to speak for seven minutes but halfway through his speech the microphone was switched off and the 'stop speaking' light came on.

An apology was made later but by then it was too late. The Socialist concluded: "This is an indication of how the union leadership will be acting in the months to come, once the direction of the Labour government becomes clearer – attacking their own members and carrying out the policies of a capitalist Labour government."[1] When arguments did not quell the opposition to the right, more forceful measures were tried, including attempting to silence and even ban left rank and file organisations like the Campaign for a Fighting and Democratic Unison (CFDU), in which the Socialist Party participated at this stage.

Bickerstaffe commented at a Unison National Executive Council (NEC) meeting a little later: "This is a defining moment for the union." Glenn, a member of the NEC, reporting this in the pages of the Socialist, commented: "Unfortunately, he wasn't talking about the need for the union to take on the Labour government over public sector spending freezes... Instead, he would argue that the NEC should ban branches from giving any backing to the CFDU. He sought to strengthen his case by using legal opinion which had advised that "no-one can use union funds to change union policy except the NEC and that the union should consider conducting an investigation with a view to disciplinary proceedings".

He was backed up by the unelected Deputy General Secretary Prentis, who said: "Some may see this as a sledgehammer to crack a nut but if we don't then the nut will become the sledgehammer and before you know it the NEC will be having to negotiate with the national committee of the CFDU." Bickerstaffe raised the alleged links between the CFDU and the Socialist Party. NEC member Jean Geldhart (not a CFDU supporter) moved an alternative motion defending the right to organise in the union. Unfortunately, 30 NEC members voted for the witch-hunt with 16 against.[2]

Despite the fact that this became the theme over the next years for the right wing, they would not be able to completely achieve their goals in significantly undermining the influence of the left. Needless to say, the wages and conditions of Unison members deteriorated under the baleful stewardship of the right wing. It was the left – particularly the intrepid band of militants gathered around the Socialist newspaper with others – which resisted the undemocratic right wing and attempted to concentrate the attentions of members on the need to improve pay and conditions.

In a sinister development in October 1997 police raided the homes of two Nottingham Unison activists. Later, the offices of the City Council branch of Unison were raided by police and computers taken away without prior approval or the council's permission. The raid was carried out because it was claimed they had been involved in "the production and distribution of 'racially inflammatory material".[3] Almost ten years later, charges of a similar character were levelled against four magnificent Socialist Party members by the same kind of people behind this attack. Both sets of charges proved to be groundless. The best answer was the victory of prominent left-wingers and Socialist Party members like Glenn Kelly and Jean Thorpe in by-elections which were held for the NEC. Their election was fought on the basis of day-to-day issues affecting Unison members, such as opposition to the public sector pay freeze and the urgent need for a decent living wage.

Blair, in his first speech to the TUC since taking office, told unions to stop fighting and join 'the real world'. His full embrace of the gravy train was not yet fully revealed. He had not yet officially entered Millionaires Row but his world had nothing in common with that of the mass of ordinary people, including Labour voters and struggling local government workers. He declared that Labour would not allow the return of "'the days of industrial warfare'... Gone were the days of 'heavy handed state intervention, nationalisation and industrial conflict." His priority was to promote "the flexibility of labour markets".[4] Just where that has led us to is revealed today in the zero-hours contracts, part-time working and mass structural unemployment. The great majority of right-wing trade union leaders were no different in their outlook. Bickerstaffe, with a left-wing past, allowed Unison to accommodate to Blair's neoliberal world while attacking the left within the unions who opposed this.

The capitalist press backed the union's right wing and Blair. Moreover, in the case of Glenn Kelly events took a very sinister turn when his employers in Bromley Council ordered a disciplinary investigation against him. There was clear collusion with the council by Unison officials. A united front between Unison officials and a right-wing Tory council was established in order to discipline and drive out someone they perceived as an important rank and file opponent of their programme of cuts. The union leadership hoped to rid themselves of this 'troublesome priest'. This and subsequent attempts to evict Glenn from the workplace failed because of a concerted and spirited campaign in his defence launched by the Socialist Party and his workmates. Bromley Council backed down over Glenn when it became clear that the workers were prepared to take action. It also emerged that the council was not going to be able to rely on the trade union officialdom to come to their assistance because of the pressure from below.

29. More battles in the unions 1997-98

A similar attempt on the part of the right wing in the civil service union, the CPSA – now the PCS following a series of mergers – also failed. The Socialist reported on an attempted "right wing seizure of power in the Civil and Public Services Association (CPSA)". National elections resulted in the defeat of Left Unity candidates. This was seen as a setback for those who were fighting the cuts, giving the green light for the policy of quiescence to these policies by right-wing CPSA General Secretary Barry Reamsbottom. The right were also helped by the defection to the Moderate camp of the ex-lefts of the Democratic Left. Reamsbottom made it abundantly clear that he was not prepared to confront the Labour government's policies, which he admitted where "unpalatable" to union members. The government had implemented a pay freeze, privatisation through the PFI and a minimum wage set at a level that would not deal with low pay. At the union's 1997 conference Socialist Party member Marion Dennison (now Marion Lloyd) condemned the right-wing steward-ship of the union and pointed out that they had no excuse now for not tackling the burning day-to-day issues facing members.[1]

Delegates to union conferences in general showed hostility to the right-wing character of the Labour government. At the National Union of Teachers (NUT) conference, for instance, the government's Education Minister, David Blunkett, was unprecedentedly heckled when he accused left-wing delegates of putting people off becoming teachers! Delegates responded by pointing to low pay and continual government attacks on teachers as the real discouragement to teacher recruitment and retention. The massive offensive against education pursued by David Cameron's ConDem coalition government from 2010 onwards was prepared by the measures introduced by New Labour, with Blunkett championing 'performance related pay' and academies, putting education in the hands of privatisation vultures.

This was the second time that a government minister had been heckled. Alan Milburn received the same treatment at Unison's health conference. The NUT backed away from action on workload following the conference but this merely stoked up the discontent. We reported the comments of a teacher at Leyton Sixth-Form College: "I have never in my life been asked to work longer for less money. No sensible person takes this lying down."[2]

The picture that emerges during Blair's first term is one of growing discontent at the union base with the refusal of the government to make any serious concessions to them. The union leadership presented a more pathetic spectacle. They were reduced to pleading with the government for some small reforms, which they hoped would mollify discontented union members. The task of Socialist Party members was to seek to cogently express the oppositional mood of the working class and reflect this inside the trade union structures, at the same time using all opportunities to mobilise as many genuine union members in a new direction. The goal was to transform the unions into fighting organisations once more.

History will record that very few concessions were achieved by the right-wing union leaders' acquiescence to Blair and Brown: a very low minimum wage, measures to avert the worst aspects of poverty though not even beginning to eradicate it. Thatcher's anti-union laws not only remained intact but were justified by Blair and Brown. Trade union leaders took refuge from the criticisms by pointing to the decline of the trade unions and the unfavourable 'political climate'. However, their argument before the election had been that this would all be changed by a Labour government. Now the brutal reality

– Blair and Brown firmly wedded to capitalism – was clear for all to see. In reality, the trade union leaders, including some on the left, saw no possibility of confronting the government or taking action to force concessions on the most important issue for the unions: lifting and defeating in action the anti-union legislation.

Huge pressure was exerted from below to force the official leaderships to act. In the NUT at the end of 1998, 172 delegates from 40 local associations met in Manchester to consider the government's recent Green Paper, 'Meeting the Challenge of Change'. The whole basis of the paper was to lay the blame for the crisis in recruiting and retaining teachers squarely at the teachers' door. Alarmingly, the NUT's national position was very muted while the more 'moderate' union, NASUWT, incredibly gave a 'guarded' welcome to the proposals. The conference called on the NUT and other unions to campaign at the earliest date for a one-day strike and further action as necessary, including a boycott of the general pay appraisal scheme.

A conference of the United Campaign to Repeal the Anti-trade Union Laws also took place with 80 delegates and visitors from many different unions present. There was much criticism of the Labour government's 'Fairness at Work' White Paper. However, the weakness of this campaign was that it made no provision for representation of union broad lefts. Heavily influenced by the Communist Party of Britain (CPB), the organisers argued that to allow broad lefts to affiliate might "not encourage trade unions to affiliate". This showed the intrinsic weakness of the small and rapidly fading CPB, which invariably turned its face towards the official structures, giving priority to union leaders – many on the right – and ignoring the growing rank-and-file revolt. The position of the Socialist Party was to put pressure on the official structures, to seek to move them in a leftward direction but at the same time trying to organise and mobilise ordinary union members. Stress on the second aspect of this approach was particularly important given the adoption of a deadening policy of 'partnership' by the right-wing Labour government.

This meant that at the TUC left-wing and socialist forces were stifled by the leadership because the left was seeking to warn delegates and the working class generally of the increasing economic problems that loomed. Echoing the government, trade union leaders dismissed all talk of recession as 'scaremongering'. Right-wing leaders like Bill Connor of shop workers' union USDAW, once a Militant supporter until he discovered the gravy train, condemned any reference to strike action as going against the spirit of 'partnership'. In Unison, however, the ordinary delegates at the national union conference, in the teeth of opposition from Bickerstaffe, passed a motion calling for a minimum wage to be submitted to the Labour Party conference. Talk of partnership between unions and the bosses was totally removed from the reality of life on the building sites, the factories or the shop floor. The Socialist was criticising the TUC for its warm embrace of partnership – symbolised by the incredible decision to invite Eddie George, Governor of the Bank of England, to the TUC conference.

At the same time we also carried a report of the case of Dave Smith, a victimised UCATT activist who had been sacked by the massive building company Costain. It subsequently emerged in 2013, that he had been a victim of the notorious blacklist, compiled by the employers and their agents, of workers considered by the bosses to be 'too dangerous' to employ. He would secure a big victory against Costain in this claim for unfair dismissal at an industrial tribunal but it took a long struggle for him and other workers to expose the vicious union-busting blacklist. How many times must it be repeated that the bosses and their political stooges do not preach class warfare because they are too busy practising it? Yet right-wing trade union leaders remain impervious to the reality facing their own members and the working class generally while ignoring the lessons of history.

Blair and the government, despite the fawning of trade union leaders like John Monks, gave few concessions. In fact, TUC leader Monks accepted the shoddy deal from New Labour for trade union recognition legislation. This meant that for unions to be legally recognised in the workplace they would have to overcome a massive hurdle of getting 40% of all eligible workers to vote 'Yes' in recognition ballots instead of achieving a simple majority of those who voted. The Socialist pointed out: "Hypocritically, Labour endorsed the result of the recent referendum for London Mayor and Assembly even though only 24.6% of the electorate voted 'Yes'."[3] In other words, one law in general for the people and another one for the trade unions. Class spite, deep and abiding fear and hatred of the unions, by New Labour as well as the Tories was highlighted in incidents like this.

Formally, some trade union leaders like Bickerstaffe and Bill Morris of the TGWU remained opposed to anything less than Labour's election commitment to a simple majority of those in the ballot for workplace union recognition. However, this opposition was passive. We urged the left within the unions to take the initiative in organising demonstrations and other protest actions. This is what was done with the Wilson government of 1968, when tens of thousands showed their anger at the prospect of a Labour government introducing anti-union legislation – the infamous 'In Place of Strife'. This opposition, which was manifested at all levels of the trade union and Labour movement, ensured the withdrawal of the White Paper before it was translated into law.

We also demanded that unions must organise industrial action to secure recognition in workplaces. One which prominently featured at the time was a small factory in Southall, West London, where 90% of the workforce were members of the GMB union. But the millionaire owner – a friend of Labour MP Keith Vaz and Lib Dem leader Paddy Ashdown – refused to recognise the union. Even the Guardian columnist Larry Elliott concluded: "The idea that 'Fairness at Work' [the government's White Paper] will unleash a tide of resurgent union militancy is fatuous. The emphasis of the White Paper is on individual not collective rights and on the main point, the threshold for recognition in a workplace ballot, the government sided with the Confederation of British Industry not the Trades Union Congress."[4]

Although the official statistics pointed to a continuation of a low level of official strikes, the mood amongst working people was one of growing opposition to the conditions which were being inflicted on them. This was again manifested amongst teachers when the NUT's national conference supported a mass boycott of appraisal schemes which were to be used to determine access to courses and training. There were also demands that ballots should be conducted on pay and conditions in schools. An indication of the rising anger of teachers was shown by the decision of the NUT to call a special conference on salaries in which a campaign for a 10% pay rise would be discussed. We reported: "Some teachers cannot live on this money, given the exorbitant cost of housing and transport. Ten percent may be three times as much as we have been awarded in recent years, but we need a 37% rise" to achieve decent living standards.[5]

The issue of deteriorating living conditions was reflected in the bitter opposition developing towards the right-wing leadership of Ken Jackson in the AEEU union, led by electricians working on the Jubilee Line tube extension in London. At one stage they invaded the national headquarters of the union. On another occasion a thousand of them gathered in a suburban park in Sidcup, most of them from the construction industry, roaring out in the best industrial language: "Jackson, Jackson, you can fuck off!"

30. Contrasting methods of work 1999-2001

Contrary to what Blair, Brown and their circle argued, the class struggle had not been conjured away by their accession to office. Indeed, the whole period of the first New Labour government from 1997 to 2001 was marked by industrial struggles, some of them extremely intense and bitter. They were also matched, at times, by ferocious clashes between left and right for support from union members. Unison, of course, was a major battleground between the left on one side, including members of the Socialist Party, and an entrenched right-wing officialdom on the other.

In early 1998 over 350 delegates attended a lay members' democracy conference in Newcastle called by the Northern and London regions of Unison. This indicated the willingness of Unison members to confront the leadership and its continual witch-hunting of the left. The attendance would have been higher but for the obstructive measures taken by right-wing officials to stop more workers attending. At this conference, while the main intention was to confront the right, tactical differences inevitably arose between us and others on the left such as the Socialist Workers' Party (SWP). This organisation, as will be seen from their record over a long period of time, tended to mix crude ultra-leftism with gross opportunism on occasions. We produced a small book Socialism and Left Unity as a criticism of the methods and programme of the SWP.

The refusal of the SWP to bloc in a principled fashion with others on the left was a continual source of division and rancour within the broad forces of the Unison left. This came to the fore during elections when they invariably sought to support others against better placed candidates particularly from the Socialist Party. This had been the case in 1995 when Roger Bannister, the only credible left candidate, was opposed by some other left-wingers supported by the SWP for the position of general secretary. Despite this he got a very good 60,000 votes. In 1998 he was the sole candidate of the left. The position had become vacant with the early retirement of Bickerstaffe. Roger explained why it was so vital to stand: "Unison members are continually under attack, with jobs and pay threatened. In the NHS and local government, there's privatisation through the extension of PFI and best value. I believe that we need to speak out strongly and organise action against these attacks, irrespective of the political complexion of the government or of the local authority."

He attacked the current policy of the union leadership which undermined democracy and was "bowing down to the fact that we have to 'co-operate' with the Labour government rather than take it on when it attacks our members". He again said he was "standing as a workers' representative on a worker's wage". This was appreciated by ordinary members and seen as a sign that they were voting for 'somebody different'. He pledged to forego much of the general secretary's £74,000 salary. He added the crucial point that the CFDU called for Unison's political fund to be used "so that, if necessary, candidates who aren't Labour Party candidates but whose policies and actions are more in line with those of Unison and its members, could be supported".

He summed up his and the Socialist Party's approach to Unison's leaders which was maintained right up to Labour's general election defeat in 2010: "I suspect [right-wing opponent] Dave Prentis's attitude, however, will be based on using pressure behind the scenes in the Labour Party to try and influence government policy. Anything that's been achieved that way, that's beneficial for Unison members, could be written on the back of a postage stamp." This was vindicated later. He answered the charge that this would isolate him: "'I'm set to fight for Unison members on jobs, pay and conditions of service' while the Blair government is 'carrying out and continuing the policies of their Tory predecessors, including attacks on public services and workers' rights.'[1] He would fight on Trotsky's advice to workers involved in the battle against capitalism and sell-out trade union leaders: "Say what needs to be said, do what needs to be done." Tony Benn, in his diaries, was coming to a similar conclusion.

It did not take long to underline the importance of the left challenge for the general secretaryship. Left activists were under attack by dictatorial management in local government but Unison's leadership did little or nothing to defend them. They have been consistent in their shameful refusal to effectively defend union members' conditions right up to the present time. While the members have been under siege in the NHS and local government rotten right-wing leaders effectively comply with management. Even minimal action, such as indicative ballots to measure the preparedness of union members to fight, has been continually blocked by Prentis and his acolytes. Only when the pressure reaches boiling point do they reluctantly sanction action.

Important industrial battles unfolded in the run-up to the general election, none more so than the bitter battle against Hackney Council, which intended to make over £22 million worth of cuts, including slashing £650,000 from education services. It was seriously considering privatising every school! This was not just an industrial battle but involved the whole of the community in what was at the time one of the poorest boroughs in London. A community conference was called in December 2000 where a strategy to fight the cuts was worked out. In a report of the conference carried in the Socialist, party stalwart Chris Newby pointed out: "Good initiatives came from this conference (many of which were raised by the Socialist Party), particularly about supporting the union's one-day strike planned for 18 December." However, because the employer, the council, was using a wrecking ball against its services, this would have both industrial and political dimensions. This would involve selecting candidates to challenge those councillors who were not prepared to oppose the cuts in the upcoming council elections.

One of the aims of the conference was precisely to bring unions and service users together in a coordinated campaign against cuts and to democratically elect a committee with representatives of all the participating organisations. This would lay the basis for a mass campaign. However, Chris pointed out: "Incredibly, some people at the conference, most notably the Socialist Workers' Party (SWP), seemed determined to undemocratically prevent this issue being discussed and to stop a vote being taken on it. They argued that the Fightback organisation initiated and dominated by the SWP should be the only community organisation to fight this campaign."[2]

This was another illustration of the sectarian policies of the SWP which sought on all occasions to promote their party over the general interests of the working class. Despite similar charges levelled against Socialist Party members for pursuing 'sectarian' policies, our opponents could not instance when we pursued this kind of policy where crucial issues for the working class were at stake. Of course, the Socialist Party sought to extend its support and strength but we linked this to strengthening the broader campaign involving others, even if this meant that we were in a minority. This approach is now generally accepted on the left even by the SWP, although they are inconsistent, and partly because of the weakening of their position through splits in their organisation. For instance, they have been compelled to participate in broader campaigns like the Trade Unionist and Socialist Coalition (TUSC), in which they were one of a number of organisations. However, before they arrived at this position their activities and policies weakened and seriously undermined the effectiveness of the left in a number of struggles.

At the Hackney conference Socialist Party members were shouted down by SWP members when they tried to raise the idea of community candidates. We pointed out that while our members in the London Socialist Alliance (LSA) – which we were part of – would obviously contest elections, it would be wrong to insist that genuine activists from tenants' associations and community groups need to stand under the LSA banner. Even the Bolsheviks at the beginning of the 1905 revolution, before Lenin had arrived back from exile and was able to correct them, incorrectly demanded that the newly created 'soviets' – workers' councils which embraced broad swathes of the working class – should dissolve and put themselves under the authority of the party! On a much smaller scale and without ever at any time enjoying mass influence, the same haughty approach was systematically adopted by the SWP and others on the petty bourgeois left. Indeed, as we will see, their activities seriously weakened for a time the urgent task of creating the basis for a new mass workers' party, the need for which had been demonstrated again and again because of New Labour's adherence to the programme of big business.

In Hackney a one-day strike was called on 20 December, with 5,000 council workers across dozens of separate workplaces coming out on strike. The councillors and council chief 'Mad Max' Caller were completely isolated, demonstrating the power of workers once they move. Grounds maintenance workers, estate workers, white collar workers in the Town Hall and other workplaces maintained pickets from the early morning with hardly anyone crossing them, apart from a handful of managers.

The Socialist Party advocated an escalation of the strike, if the council did not retreat, to five days the following January, then possibly an all-out strike. Unfortunately, the shop stewards committee amended the resolution merely to "an escalation of the action". We pointed out that the new contracts would be based on the lowest possible national terms and conditions. Local agreements would be wiped out including the Hackney low pay supplement of £40 per week. What was at stake in Hackney were workers' cherished rights and conditions and whether they would have a job or not. What followed was the biggest strike movement in 20 years for thousands of Hackney Council workers, including a three-day strike.

Caller told his staff that he was "ready to bash the unions". He seriously miscalculated the strikers' mood at mass meetings, angering workers when he bragged that, while he would be with the council for years to come, they might not! Noticeable in the strike was the issuing of 90-day redundancy notices by this "Labour, yes Labour, Council",[3] which recalled the sheer hypocrisy of Neil Kinnock and the Labour leaders in 1985. Kinnock had condemned Liverpool City Council for allegedly taking a similar measure when it issued redundancy notices as a tactical move. This had been a mistake, which we criticised at the time, but it did not result in any worker losing their job. Now the heirs of Kinnock, the Blairites to a man and woman, were carrying this out for real in Hackney and elsewhere.

This dispute dragged on for months and led at one stage to the occupation of the Town Hall by hundreds of council workers. This was in protest against the dismissal of a leading steward and chief negotiator for the workers. Management retreated on this occasion in order to continue a war of attrition against the representatives of the workforce. Singled out for special treatment were members of the Socialist Party, with Brian Debus, chairperson of the Unison branch, being told the job that had been offered to him in the council stores had been withdrawn "because of reorganisation".[4] At the same time, those affected within the local community began to fight back. This was followed by a 'mass burning' of the 90-day notices, with the Fire Brigade on standby just in case the workers took the occupation a stage further! The mood was building for more decisive strike action, involving a possible five-day strike.

At the same time others began to take action. London Underground workers had been engaged in almost continual guerrilla strikes against deteriorating health and safety standards and conditions, with management bullying rife: "If we want to go for a piss we have to put our hand up!" commented a striking electrician on the Jubilee Line extension.[5] After strikes in 2000 and 2001, we wrote: "Management now aim to smash the tube unions."[6] Just a couple of months before the election, under the headline, 'Get Organised Strike Back', the Socialist wrote: "This week tube workers brought London to a standstill and showed the power of organised labour. The courts, the press and London Underground management could not stop the first political strike against New Labour's 'privatise everything' ideology." We pointed out that a High Court judge, Lord Justice Gibbs, granted an injunction to the bosses but a 90% 'Yes' vote for strike action could not be overruled and the tube network was brought to a standstill.[7] On 29 March 2001 London Underground was brought to a halt by striking workers organised by the train drivers' union ASLEF and the RMT.

This was part of the process of workers rising to their feet and striking back: in Hackney, air traffic controllers, union members balloting against privatisation and Vauxhall workers being balloted for industrial action to defend their jobs. We warned that a new downturn in the world economy would bring further attacks from the bosses. Ingrained sceptics scoffed at warnings of the possibility of an economic crisis. Yet within a matter of months there appeared to be a real possibility of a serious crisis, with the looming collapse of the 'dotcom bubble'. Such a collapse was on the cards but, in panic, the central banks of the major capitalist powers, particularly the US Federal Reserve, managed to put off the crisis through a massive injection of 'liquidity': what was referred to later in the next crisis as 'quantitative easing'. This was only at the cost of storing up a further financial bubble which crashed in 2007-08.

Teachers were up in arms at their deteriorating conditions but the leaders of the NUT in the middle of 2000 decided to postpone the ballot for a one-day strike, which had been democratically agreed at the union's recent annual conference. There was outrage at the introduction of performance related pay for teachers. Yet the right-wing majority on the NEC came up with excuses to defer the ballot, as a means of 'helping out' the New Labour government. Distrust grew amongst the ranks. The councils were proposing a £2,000 pay rise, but only for those who showed they were performing well enough to make the grade! This was just sowing further divisions amongst teachers and Socialist Party members in the NUT predicted it would enhance the confidence of the government and their council representatives, while at the same time disheartening teachers.

The bosses' representatives, typified by Chris Woodhouse, the

Ofsted Chief Inspector, went on the offensive. He criticised Waltham Forest Local Education Authority (LEA), which he claimed had developed "an ingrained culture of failure". Linda Taaffe, who had been prominent both at a national level, as a member of the NUT's NEC and in the Waltham Forest NUT branch in the battle against the introduction of performance related pay, warned: "Once the LEA was the authority, with each school a part of an LEA. Then the Tories let schools have their own budgets (LMS), making head teachers a very powerful force, in individual competitive institutions, almost like small businesses. The LEA was undermined."

What followed was a gradual erosion of teachers' terms and conditions. We further commented: "This nonsensical situation became worse in Waltham Forest after New Labour Blairites regained a majority on the council. No-one wanted to make a decision unless it came directly from the councillors, who were so arrogant that LEA officers were left in a state of limbo... All this in an inner-city borough with huge problems such as a transitory population and a third of children being eligible for free school meals."[8] These events took place more than a decade and a half ago yet they laid the seeds for the present catastrophic situation with the systematic privatisation of schools and education as a whole.

The national trade union leaders were completely complicit in this process. Their policies of prevarication and inaction only encouraged further attacks on teachers and education generally. They had the full backing of the national press, with the Daily Mail attacking "The dinosaurs behind Britain's new class war", singling out opposition from the left from people like Christine Blower, Bob Sulatycki, Bernard Regan and others.[9] Since then, these 'dinosaurs' and NUT members have defeated the right-wing leadership, symbolised by Doug McAvoy who subsequently retired. In the next election he was replaced by Steve Sinnott, who died in 2008, followed by Christine Blower. Unfortunately, she and her supporters on the 'left', once they assumed power, reverted to the same policies of prevarication as McAvoy himself.

A series of other strikes took place in general opposition to the policies of the Labour government and the inaction of many trade union leaders. This disillusionment was summed up by Craig Johnston, at that time a Socialist Party member in Carlisle, who wrote: "A hundred years ago, rail workers were playing a key role in the establishment of the Labour Party. Now, as delegates to the conference of the biggest rail union, the National Union of Rail and Maritime Transport Workers (RMT) gather in Great Yarmouth for their AGM, the mood is very different." He pointed out that the RMT "has profoundly socialist roots. Rule 1 Clause 4 states one of the objects of the union shall be 'to work for the supercession of the capitalist system by a Socialistic order of society'." He continued: "As Labour moves more and more to the right, many RMT members have quit the party and joined other Left parties, including the Socialist Party... I was in the Labour Party for 21 years, eleven of them as a local councillor. I've campaigned for them in every election since I was 15, not any more."

This was fairly typical of an advanced layer of workers who were moving in the direction of supporting the Socialist Party and our demand for a new mass party. He explained why he had a profound change of heart: "On a recent clear out, I found some things that I would never need again – a couple of sheets of stickers proclaiming 'Stop the Sell-Off, Save Our Railways!' And then the word 'Labour' and a picture of a rose. I will not need them again because this Labour government totally supported rail privatisation, indeed they are proposing its long-term extension. [They] are currently offering rail franchises to private companies for up to 20 years – extending rail privatisation further than the Tories ever dared."[10]

A similar process was developing within Unison. The union's members in Knowsley Council on Merseyside had won a major victory in defending the 35-hour working week and extending it within the council workforce. Socialist Party member Roger Bannister was the branch secretary and led the campaign. A total of six days of strike action were taken before the council conceded the union's demands. Similar progress was recorded for Socialist Party members in the shop workers' union USDAW, where the late, heroic

Robbie Segal confounded her right-wing opponents by winning election to its NEC.

In fact, there was clear evidence that industrial action helped to radicalise council workforces. At the AGM of Hackney Unison there was a big shift towards the left. Delegates voted unanimously to refuse to pay into the union's Affiliated Political Fund (APF) as individual members, instead contributing to its General Political Fund (GPF). Unlike most unions, Unison had two political funds: the APF funded the Labour Party, while the GPF was for broad political campaigning. In this way the Unison leadership blunted the growing hostility to the link with Labour. However, the future would show that it was not possible to maintain this position indefinitely. There was a clear opposition growing to the left of Labour at this stage which was revealed in the ballot for the London Mayor selection contest. Around 80% of union members voted for Ken Livingstone, who was not in the Labour Party at this stage. Labour Party membership was dropping – from 405,000 in 1997 to 378,000 in May 2000.

31. Scotland, Wales and the devolution bills

Soon after the 1997 general election the New Labour government pushed through referendum bills for Scotland and Wales. The national question in Britain, which we have explained elsewhere[1], emerged as a key issue as the economic and political power of British imperialism waned. In the past the working class directed their gaze towards the Labour Party and the trade unions to realise their goals, which were partly satisfied by the reforms carried out by Labour governments. However, the failure of Labour governments together with the weakening of capitalism removed these factors and allowed a space for the development of nationalism furthered, ironically, by the nationalist tinge evident in the propaganda and agitation of some on the Scottish left, particularly the Communist Party.

This did not manifest itself in support for outright independence in the first instance, even in Scotland which consistently expressed stronger nationalist leanings than Wales, with demands for greater national rights, including the need for their own parliaments. Militant, even under the Labour government of the late 1970s, supported the legitimate national aspirations of the peoples of Scotland and Wales and the demand for a referendum on this issue. Others who were then on the left, such as Neil Kinnock, implacably opposed this. The defeat of the Scottish referendum in 1979 was a factor in the Scottish National Party's (SNP) decision to trigger a general election. It voted against the minority Labour government in a vote of no confidence in the House of Commons, leading to the 1979 general election being called early and a victory for the Thatcher-led Tories.

By the advent of Tony Blair's Labour government, Labour had caught up with the mood in Scotland and to some extent Wales. Soon after the 1997 general election this led quickly to the pushing through of referendum bills. Scottish Socialist Voice – the sister paper of the Socialist – backed the drive for a massive Yes vote, "but only as a stepping stone to a Scottish Parliament with real powers". Just weeks before the general election, however, 53% of the population did not believe the Scottish Parliament would be set up but the post-election mood and momentum was so strong (and the Tories had been crushed in Scotland in the election) that a referendum and a Yes vote seemed certain.[2] The Scottish working class was decisive in ensuring a Labour victory. However, we pointed out that New Labour's proposals for a Scottish Parliament "will not have any say over employment, the economy and benefits…" "This inability to tackle problems" would worsen "if New Labour initially gain a majority in the new parliament", unless real powers were given to the parliaments and decisive action undertaken which favoured working class people.[3]

In the Scottish referendum which followed there was an overwhelming Yes vote, although the turnout in Glasgow, for instance, was only 51%. Nonetheless, a total of 1.75 million people voted Yes in Scotland. The vote in favour of tax raising powers was carried by a two to one majority, reflecting the pressure for change. Not a single council area voted No to the first question, the setting up of a Scottish Parliament or Assembly. Only Orkney and Dumfries & Galloway voted against tax raising powers. Glasgow voted 83% for a Scottish Parliament.

In Wales it was not even certain that the working class would respond to the anodyne non-political campaign of Labour, 'Yes for Wales'. The Socialist reported: "Many working class people hostile to local politicians and MPs suspect that the Assembly will be just another gravy train for the politicians to climb aboard." On the other hand, there was little support for the 'Just Say No' campaign, financed by prominent bankers and Welsh tax exiles. The Welsh Socialist Alliance, in which Socialist Party members participated – as we did in the Scottish Socialist Alliance – produced leaflets calling for a Yes vote. At the same time, we called for an Assembly with real powers to fundamentally change the conditions of the Welsh working class. [4]

There was a difference between West Wales, which voted for the Assembly, and the eastern border areas which voted No. It was, however, the working class areas of the South Wales Valleys which proved to be decisive in carrying the Yes vote. Generally, working class people voted Yes although a broad layer stayed at home, unconvinced by New Labour's proposals. This knocked some of the gloss off the New Labour leaders in Wales who had been basking in the afterglow of the general election victory. They had banked on delivering a big Labour vote for the Assembly by carefully scripted appearances of Blair. But only 40% turned out, indicating a lack of enthusiasm, particularly in areas where Blair had made "high-profile appearances": Cardiff and Wrexham. The 8% majority in Cardiff against setting up an Assembly reflected the class divisions in the capital. Many of the middle class suburbs voted by 90% against devolution and it was clear there was a 50-50 split in working class areas.

The demand of Plaid Cymru (the Party of Wales) and the Socialist Party in Wales for full legislative powers for the Assembly was supported by 32% of Welsh people, compared to 19% for New Labour's proposals. Dave Reid commented: "Ironically, Scotland's decisive vote for a Parliament with tax raising powers emphasised the weaknesses of the Welsh Assembly. Had Wales had the same options to vote for as Scotland then the margin of support would have been greater." Our comrades in Wales warned that disillusionment would affect Labour and could play into the hands of Plaid Cymru which was well placed to make gains by "posing as a socialist party and offering reforms… threatening Labour in its Valleys strongholds".[5]

The nationalist parties would not have it all their own way, however. They were in competition on the left with the Socialist Party.

We challenged them in elections, particularly through the Socialist Alliances which had a strong presence in Scotland and Wales. For instance, in September 1998 the Scottish Socialist Alliance (SSA) recorded 10% of the vote in Labour's safest seat on Glasgow City Council, Possil. Overall, there was a swing towards the SNP. This was just one portent of the success of the SSA in future elections.

In Wales the manoeuvring of New Labour to ensure that the Welsh Assembly would be in a 'safe pair of hands' led to a stitch up, which saw the election of Blair's puppet Alun Michael as leader of Labour in the Assembly over Rhodri Morgan, favoured by most Labour members in Wales. Blair was forced to rely on a few right-wing trade union leaders to push through support for Michael. Even Roy Hattersley, firmly on the Labour right in the past, complained in the Times newspaper about Blair's role: "Nicolae Ceauşescu [the Romanian Stalinist dictator] did not live in vain." This played into the hands of Plaid Cymru, whose support in polls doubled to 20% compared to the election.[6]

At the same time a socialist campaign embracing a number of organisations – the Socialist Party, the Welsh Socialist Alliance (WSA), Cymru Goch (a socialist/nationalist organisation), and the SWP – was launched in preparation for the Welsh Assembly elections. Alec Thraves declared at its launch: "Plaid Cymru, despite some socialist rhetoric in certain parts of Wales, still support the market economy which is the root cause of our problems. There is a deep socialist tradition in Wales and our United Socialist-Sosialaidd candidates are giving the Welsh electorate the opportunity for a genuine socialist alternative." Unfortunately, Arthur Scargill refused to allow the Socialist Labour Party (SLP) to participate in any kind of agreement with the WSA. Incredibly, his justification for this was that the Socialist Party was elitist in supporting the European Union, ignoring our consistent opposition to the capitalist EU for 25 years.[7] It was this kind of sectarian and dishonest approach which undermined the SLP and led to its collapse – and the unfortunate demise of Scargill himself, who could have played a key role in the development of a mass workers' party in Britain.

Disillusionment with the new government led quite rapidly to a general growth of forces to the left of Labour, although not in the first instance in Wales because of the existence of Plaid Cymru, which promoted a socialist image of itself. There was a big swing to Plaid Cymru, especially in South Wales. It won three of Labour's previously safe seats in working class heartlands. Labour's share of the vote crashed to 35% from 55% at the general election, while Plaid's rose from 9% to 30%. Meanwhile, the socialist campaign was welcomed by working class people, with many workers making favourable remarks about the United Socialists' broadcast and hundreds of people showing support at the street stalls set up. This did not translate into votes because of the attraction at that stage of Plaid. Yet any new councils run by them would either have to stand up against New Labour's cuts and privatisation or, more likely carry them out and try to blame New Labour in Westminster – which is what Plaid did, as Labour councils have done since the Tories came to power.

32. Differences open in Scotland 1999-2001

In Scotland the situation was far more favourable for an electoral challenge from socialists, particularly from the Scottish Socialist Party (ssp). There were big differences between the national leadership of the Socialist Party in England and Wales and the Scottish leadership, formerly in Scottish Militant Labour (sml), then in the ssp. These disagreements were not of recent vintage. In reality, in the whole period leading up to the formation of the ssp – and we disagreed on the way this was carried out – there were differences on the national question and the approach which Marxists should adopt. It had almost been an axiom of the Socialist Party and the Committee for a Workers' International (cwi) that it was a principled position to support the right of self-determination for oppressed nationalities. Other organisations had broken their backs on this issue. For instance, the split from our organisation in 1992 led by Ted Grant and Alan Woods took a completely wrong, one-sided position to the national questions in the Balkans, Russia and Pakistan.

At the same time we are implacably opposed to all manifestations of bourgeois nationalism, which seeks to divide the working class. In fact, we stand for the greatest unification of workers, irrespective of national boundaries. This means that, while supporting the legitimate national aspirations of a subject people or nation, or even a group – the right of self-determination – we do not support demands which will reinforce divisions within the working class.

There were many occasions when we clashed with the leaders of our Scottish organisation, particularly Alan McCombes and Tommy Sheridan, when we believed they made unnecessary concessions to Scottish nationalism.

We elaborated our differences with them in Socialism Today in a critique of the book Imagine they co-authored: "If this book had been written by socialists who were evolving towards the left and a Marxist position it would deserve fulsome praise." Tony Benn, for instance, developed in this way as he started on the right but became a key figure for the left in Britain. On the evidence of their book Tommy Sheridan and Alan McCombes were evolving in the opposite direction from the Marxist-Trotskyist perspective and programme they once advocated.

On Scotland and the national question the authors wholeheartedly welcomed "the disintegration of the United Kingdom". We replied: "In general, socialists and Marxists are against Balkanisation, the splitting up and separation of multinational states." The break-up of states, even capitalist ones, while sometimes unavoidable can carry big overheads. One of these is the possible fracturing of the working class along national lines, the separation of their organisations, parties and trade unions. This can weaken the struggle against the common enemy, the capitalists, which is not restricted to the borders of one country. This is one reason why we and our comrades in Scotland opposed the bald demand of the SNP for independence for Scotland. Even then, we emphasise the right of self-determination of the Scottish people and our preparedness to defend their legitimate national aspirations. We did this at a time when significant sections of the left, as we have already pointed out, opposed any 'concessions to nationalism'. We were at one with Lenin and Trotsky in emphasising that a new socialist world could not be built with the slightest compulsion against a nation or even a grouping in society.

We had no differences when independence was linked to the demand for a socialist Scotland. However, we had profound differences about the way that the authors posed this in their book

– which they would never have done in the past when they were in our ranks. They wrote: "Socialists should be prepared to support such a step, even on a non-socialist basis as promoted by the SNP." This was a 'stageist' position supported by the Stalinists but opposed by Trotsky with his idea of the 'permanent revolution'. The bourgeois democratic revolution – including the solution of the national question – could only be carried through by the working class taking power in an alliance with the poor including small farmers. The theory of stages meant that first comes national tasks – independence for Scotland, for instance, but still on a capitalist basis. Then, separated in time, socialism would be posed. History has shown that real independence is impossible on the basis of capitalism. Only by a movement for independence and socialism combined would it be possible to satisfy legitimate national aspirations.

Indeed, they held out the hope that significant lasting reforms could be introduced which would fundamentally change the balance of power and wealth. This flew in the face of the whole historical experience of the working class, including of past Labour governments, quite apart from the bloody experience of the failure of Salvador Allende in Chile. It is one thing to put forward reforms, which the Socialist Party does consistently today. But not to warn about the limitations of such measures within capitalism stokes up illusions amongst the working class.[1]

The analysis made in Imagine has not stood the test of time. The models the SNP used for the future of Scotland on a capitalist basis were Iceland and Southern Ireland, which were steaming ahead economically at that stage. But both came crashing down in the wake of the crisis which began in 2007-08. The SSP leaders created illusions in the 'self-sufficiency' of Scotland which in a globalised world is utopian. They did not link the struggle for Scotland to the rest of Britain nor to Europe, as the Socialist Party did with the demand for a socialist confederation of Europe.

Yet these clear political deficiencies did not prevent the spectacular initial success for the SSP and particularly the victory of Tommy Sheridan who was elected as a Member of the Scottish Parliament

(MSP) in 1999. We welcomed these developments, despite the differences that we had with the SSP and their leading figures, which if anything were to widen later. The mood at the time of Tommy's election was captured by the Scottish newspaper the Herald, no friend of the left – it was, in fact, the house journal of the Blairised Labour Party in Scotland. Nonetheless, when it reported on his inauguration at the Scottish Parliament, it commented: "It took Tommy Sheridan to provoke spontaneity which he managed in style." It then quoted from his speech: "'Before making the affirmation I would like to declare that, as a democratically-elected socialist, my vision for Scotland is of a democratic socialist republic where supreme sovereignty lies with the people of Scotland and not with an unelected monarch, and I therefore take this affirmation under protest,' he proclaimed. At which point he raised a clenched fist. (Let it be noted that when this scene was replayed on television in the pubs around Edinburgh's Royal Mile, the customers cheered)."[2]

Tommy Sheridan commented in an interview with the Socialist shortly after his election: "I've had more congratulations from SNP members and even the odd Tory than I've had from the New Labour benches."[3] Little wonder because the representation of parties to the left of Labour, including the SSP, was significant. They were, of course, helped by the use of proportional representation in these elections. The combined total vote for socialists, the SSP and the SLP, together with the Greens, came to a commendable anti-establishment vote of almost 10%. It was difficult to imagine a more favourable terrain in which New Labour could fight a mid-term election; the bottom had not yet completely fallen out of the world economy and the British economy was still staggering along. Yet the Labour vote dropped by 7% compared to the UK general election. Nor were the SNP encouraged by their vote, which was the same as 25 years previously. Over 100,000 people in Scotland voted for socialists of one kind or another – the SSP, SLP, the independent socialist Dennis Canavan and the Greens. These successes were continued in the European elections later in the year and in council elections in subsequent years.

In Wales on the other hand, there was general disillusionment with the main parties and a mood of 'no confidence in any of them'.[4] The success of the SSP combined with the general disillusionment with Labour, fuelled support for Scotland to have increased powers in the Edinburgh legislature with almost 70% supporting this.

Although the Socialist Party's national leadership first proposed the idea of a new party, big differences developed between the leaders of the party and those of the Scottish organisation over how we should participate in building such a project. As will be recalled, after a period of debate throughout the British organisation, SML was launched as an autonomous part of Militant Labour's all-Britain organisation. SML achieved a number of striking successes: including the campaigns against water privatisation and opposition to the Criminal Justice Bill. As with other parts of the CWI, this arose from a clear perspective that in the aftermath of the collapse of Stalinism a bold socialist programme and tactical flexibility were necessary. We were in favour of working with others on the left, but the precondition for coming together with other organisations was the clear understanding of the need to maintain a separate political and organisational identity. Without a distinct Marxist force it is impossible to undertake this work around the idea of left unity and at the same time build the forces of Marxism and raise the level of political understanding.

At the beginning there were little differences as the comrades in Scotland adopted a similar approach with the formation of the SSA, bringing together members of SML, ex-Labour lefts and left-wing members or supporters of the SNP. However, over time the ideological differences between SML and the broad organisation of the SSA were blurred. Then, without discussion and agreement within our common organisation, SML arbitrarily changed its position. Its leadership proposed instead the setting up of the new Scottish Socialist Party (SSP). This would not, according to their proposals, be restricted to members of SML but would include all forces which were gathered under the banner of the SSA. They proposed to dissolve SML together with its full-time workers, branches, finances and fortnightly paper Scottish Socialist Voice into this new party.

Moreover, it was made clear that this party would not be affiliated to the CWI as SML was.

These proposals provoked intense discussion and opposition in Scotland, England and Wales, as well as internationally. While the majority of Scottish comrades favoured the SSP proposal, the great majority of Socialist Party members in Britain and CWI sections argued against the Scottish leadership's strategy. Such was the concern within the CWI at the proposed measures that a delegation from its International Executive Committee (IEC) visited Scotland at the end of June 1998.

The Socialist Party proposed that the best way forward for our comrades in Scotland would be to adopt one of two options. The first, was to relaunch SML as a new revolutionary Marxist SSP. This new party would continue to collaborate with other forces in a broader alliance, involving industrial work, election platforms, etc. This was the option favoured by the IEC delegation and the Socialist Party national leadership. If this was unacceptable to the Scottish organisation, then the second option would be for the SSA to be launched as a broad SSP, which would be organised on a united front basis with SML continuing its own separate identity. This would allow the participation of different political organisations, groups and trends, as well as the SML comrades. The SML Executive Committee however, rejected these options and instead proposed a 'hybrid' SSP.

There were clearly profound differences between the two camps on how to approach the problems of the labour movement and particularly the left. We are always in favour of the maximum left unity, involving an element of the united front tactic which would mean collaboration between relatively small organisations at this historical juncture. However, this could never be at the cost of diluting and eventually winding up the historical conquest of a distinct revolutionary formation. History is littered with those organisations that became infected with the 'unity bug' – unity at all costs. These 'experiments' invariably end in disappointment. The same fate awaited the leadership of SML, although this was not evident to them at that stage. We foresaw the problems that they would have on the basis of the unprincipled turn which they were carrying out.

We did not write off the whole organisation but engaged in debates and discussions with a view to keeping the majority in the CWI. A certain compromise was arrived at with the formation of a new organisation called the International Socialist Movement (ISM), open only to former members of SML and those who agreed with the programme of the CWI. We warned, however: "The formation of this section, while a step forward, does not meet the requirements of a cohesive, separate organisation of Marxists within the SSP. Members of ISM do not have the right under the draft SSP constitution to have meetings restricted to members only, which are necessary to discuss and work out ideas to fight for in the broad SSP." For these reasons, the majority of the members of the Socialist Party National Committee opposed the establishment of the SSP in the form that was being proposed. At the same time, we agreed that our comrades should engage in this endeavour which would be reviewed after one year.[5] Events showed that this compromise would not hold as the SML leadership moved further and further away from our ideas and the CWI.

This became obvious from the very beginning of the life of the SSP, at its founding conference attended by 200 people. The 16-point programme adopted, while it had some good points, was weak in a number of places: "There was no reference in the programme, or from the platform of the conference, on the need for the working class in Scotland to keep and build links with workers in England, Wales and Ireland. Unfortunately," as Hannah Sell pointed out, "it was left to a new SSP member to raise the need for links with English workers from the floor." Bill Bonner – a former Communist Party member – argued that big business would be able to unite Europe and overcome national boundaries. In his introduction, he gave the impression that real democracy could be achieved in Europe, within the framework of capitalism.

Unfortunately, the resolution was passed. However, several CWI members spoke in the discussion, among them Philip Stott from

Dundee who reiterated the long held views of the Socialist Party and the CWI: "The only way to get a people's Europe, a democratic Europe, is to get a socialist Europe."[6] It was quite obvious to those observing and listening to the arguments of the SML majority that they were well along the road to making concessions to nationalism, while watering down and even omitting to mention the programme of the CWI, which they had fully embraced in the past, particularly the emphasis on workers' unity and a socialist programme.

After a period of political sparring, the majority of the leadership of our organisation in Scotland decided at a special conference in January 2001 to leave the CWI. Prior to this, at a meeting of the IEC of the CWI, Alan McCombes had proposed an "amicable divorce" between the CWI and the Scottish organisation. We pointed out that there were very few such divorces and certainly that was the case in the political arena. We were not prepared to pass over silently the grave political mistakes that had been made in Scotland by those at the head of the SSP formerly from a CWI background.

The special conference was attended by Hannah Sell and myself from the Socialist Party and the CWI, Per Olsson from Sweden and the late Peter Hadden and Joe Higgins from Ireland. All of these spoke against the proposals to leave the CWI. In particular, I explained that we had resisted any suggestion of expelling the comrades from the CWI in Scotland who disagreed with us. They had a tremendous record of fighting for the Marxist cause and Trotskyism over many years. We differed with them on the policies they were pursuing now but we believed that over time we would win these comrades and others back politically to the CWI. In any case, I stated future events will vindicate the position of the CWI and, at the same time, politically undermine the arguments of those who propose to leave our common Marxist organisation.

A quarter of those attending – it was not a delegate conference – voted to remain within the CWI. This included some of the pioneers of our party in Scotland, including Ronnie Stevenson, Philip Stott, Eric Stevenson, Jim McFarlane, Harvey Duke and others. Moreover, the ISM majority did not have the consistent support of any other section from among the 34 sections which made up the CWI at that point. Not one of our elected representatives outside of Scotland, including Dave Nellist and Joe Higgins, supported them. They were, in fact, very vocal in arguing against their position.

33. Political differences and defections
2001

Tommy Sheridan made a wild attack on the CWI, claiming that we had slandered the SSP from "Vladivostok to Berlin". We refuted this accusation and, in the traditions of the CWI, had not attacked or criticised them outside of our ranks until the January 2001 conference. However, it was quite clear that they had distanced themselves from the CWI over the preceding period as demonstrated by a statement on 'international links'. This stated: "The (Trotskyist) model they (the CWI) have tried to apply is obsolete, if indeed it was ever a credible project."[1] This was a repudiation of the entire history of the ISM within the CWI. We pointed out that the policies and methods of the CWI made a crucial contribution to the successes of our organisation in Scotland, including defeating the poll tax. The SSP's current successes were only possible because of these past gains. Yet here the ISM was totally writing off its history, although this was not a bolt from the blue because their trajectory had been clear even before this conference. In their book, Imagine, neither Tommy Sheridan nor Alan McCombes mentioned their membership of the CWI, Militant or SML!

At a subsequent SSP conference there was a discernible move towards the right on their part, both on policy but also on internal democracy within the SSP. They proposed 'guidelines' saying organisations within the SSP could not sell their own publications. These were the same methods used by the Labour Party's right wing against us in the past. There were also many serious mistakes on programme and policy. For instance, Tommy Sheridan was quoted in the Scottish supplement of the Observer implying that the ssp would take part in a coalition government with the snp or would support such a government from the outside. This would be collaboration with what was, at this stage, clearly not a working class party but a nationalist, predominantly middle class party that would not go beyond the framework of capitalism. Tommy, unfortunately, never repudiated the statement nor did the majority of the ssp leadership, which was a factor in the eventual shipwreck of the ssp and its unprincipled adaptation to nationalism in the independence referendum a decade and a half later.

The ism leaders made similar errors on, for instance, the nature of Cuba. Tommy Sheridan had described Cuba as 'socialist' without any qualification in a prominent Scottish newspaper, the Daily Record. We made it clear that we defended the planned economy in Cuba, but that it would be wrong to describe it as 'socialist'. In fact, it was essentially a one-party regime, although at times very popular with the mass of the people. Genuine socialism could only be based on workers' democracy. Unfortunately, this position, supported throughout the cwi, was now abandoned by the leaders of the ism.

The defection of the majority of Scottish cwi members represented a blow to the Socialist Party in England and Wales and the cwi itself. Naturally, it generated a certain amount of hostility and even bitterness expressed in the days following the 'split conference' in Scotland. It led to a public disagreement between Tommy Sheridan and myself over our public reaction to the split in interviews with the press. Tommy Sheridan wrote to a newspaper and did not pull any punches in condemning my "actions and those of the cwi leadership in releasing the attached press release to the enemies of the socialist movement internationally and the working class in general... This discussion and debate [between us] were sometime heated but always took place in a democratic and comradely manner and atmosphere. It was very much a family affair. Unfortunately, you and the cwi have now committed a cardinal sin within the socialist movement. You have put our disagreements into the hands of the anti-working class, anti-democratic and anti-socialist press... I note your pathetic complaints when one of these grateful capitalist lapdogs 'distorts' what you had to say. For goodness sake, Peter, what did you expect?... This press release... will probably convince the 75% of the CWI members in Scotland who voted to leave that they were right to do so."

I replied equally robustly: "Dear Tommy, I suppose we should be grateful that you have, at last, replied to letters and statements from me and the CWI... I was contacted by the Daily Record reporter and made my remarks, some of which were misreported... in no way do I or the CWI leadership dissociate ourselves from the decision to issue the statement or its political contents. But like Shakespeare said you 'doth protest too much'. It was you and the ISM Majority who, via the net, broadcast to the world the news that you had departed from the CWI. This was done before the ISM Minority comrades issued their press statement... According to you, we have 'now committed a cardinal sin' for allowing our views to be expressed in the 'anti-democratic and anti-socialist press and media'. But, Tommy, you wrote 80 articles in your weekly column for the 'anti-socialist press and media'. Moreover, you have not hesitated on TV and in press statements to criticise other socialists such as Arthur Scargill and Dennis Canavan. You criticised the latter for his attempt to return to the Labour Party, despite earlier describing him as a 'principled socialist'... are you not guilty of double standards?"

This issue of when, where and how socialists use the bourgeois press to get some of their ideas and programme broadcast, even if it took the form of criticism of others, has come up in the past and will do so in the future as well. Marx, Engels and Lenin all, at various times, used the capitalist press to get their ideas over but this did not mean that you would use any and all news outlets. There are limits. The openly reactionary semi-fascist anti-working class newspapers and media outlets were off limits. However, we pointed out: "I am afraid, Tommy, that neither the history of the working class, socialist and Marxist movement, nor our recent experiences support you on this issue. Marx wrote regularly for the New York Tribune in the 19th century. Engels contributed a number of articles to the English capitalist press. Lenin wrote an article on Marx and Marxism for the Liberal populist publication Grannat's Encyclopaedia Dictionary. Trotsky wrote an article on Lenin in 1926 for the reactionary Encyclopaedia Britannica." He even wrote for capitalist newspapers in order to get over necessary ideas to as wide an audience as possible.

We went on: "Yet you and your supporters have consistently accused the CWI of being 'undemocratic', of 'refusing to listen'. In reality, we have listened but profoundly disagree with the political positions of yourself and your supporters. You say our disagreements were 'very much a family affair'. But, Tommy, you have walked out of the 'family'. We wanted to keep you and your supporters within the ranks of the CWI because we were confident that through debate, discussion and experience we would convince many of the comrades of the correctness of our position... One of the most astonishing, if not arrogant, statements in your letter is that 'you and the CWI stand condemned for distinctly anti-socialist and anti-labour movement actions'. So public criticism of your position and those of the ISM leadership is synonymous with 'anti-socialist and anti-labour movement actions'? Don't you think this is a wee bit intolerant and lacks a sense of proportion, Tommy?"

We concluded: "We will collaborate with all who genuinely fight to defend working class people and struggle for socialism. But at the same time, we will never hesitate to make constructive and fraternal criticisms of those ideas, policies and actions we believe will weaken the struggle for socialism. Without political clarification the working class will never be able to change society. Yours fraternally, Peter Taaffe."[2] We published lengthy aspects of this exchange of correspondence to indicate just how polarised – with charged emotions on either side – was the situation between the CWI and those like Tommy Sheridan who left. However, this did not stop us from working together with these comrades at a later stage. In particular, we energetically supported Tommy Sheridan in his conflict with what was then the ssp majority, including Alan McCombes, Frances Curran and Richard Venton, over the Murdoch press's hounding of Tommy and the shameful support given to them by this majority. We continued to work within the ssp, but in opposition to the leadership majority who quickly moved towards a politically opportunist position.

This was revealed at the ssp conference in February 2001. In the run-up to the general election, 200 ssp members discussed the manifesto of the ssp to fight the general election. Sinead Daly moved a motion which committed the ssp to refuse to participate in an snp administration at Holyrood (the site of the Scottish Parliament). Incredibly, ssp members argued that the party should keep their options open, but the resolution was overwhelmingly passed. Amendments from Dundee West, moved by the cwi opposition within the ssp, which argued for working class control of industry were also passed. This replaced phrases in the manifesto like "popular decentralised management" when referring to nationalised industries. However, former cwi member Alan McCombes, who proposed the manifesto, opposed an amendment from Kirkcaldy committing the ssp to an independent socialist Scotland as a step towards a socialist confederation of Scotland, England, Wales and Ireland. He argued that the manifesto had to be short and it was not the same as a programme. This left the ssp silent on the specific relations a socialist Scotland would have with other countries in the British Isles. By this kind of sleight of hand, the ssp leaders were moving away from the cwi's clear position.

As mentioned earlier, the ssp's new guidelines for internal discussion specifically opposed the right of platforms to sell public journals. It was Richard Venton who moved the resolution for the ssp executive. Philip Stott, in opposition, moved an alternative set of guidelines which maintained the right of platforms to publicly sell and distribute material as an organised force within the ssp. He argued that the voluntary unity of the ssp had secured its growth. Going down the road of imposing bans would repeat the mistakes of other parties including the Socialist Labour Party. He argued that it was ironic that comrades like Richard Venton, who had been expelled from the Labour Party for his association with Militant, could move such a resolution. He also pointed to the hypocrisy of the leadership platform, the ISM, who held nine out of eleven leadership positions on the executive. There was a bloc to pursue their policies, while at the same time moving guidelines that would remove the right of other platforms to do the same.

Despite his arguments, the executive motions passed by two to one – with around 60 voting against. At the same time, despite opposition disquiet, the SSP executive attempted to downgrade the annual conference by requiring that a referendum of all SSP members would be held to decide whether any conference decision to change any of the party's 'seven core objectives' would be implemented. They had to retreat from this position.[3] Bob Labi from the CWI and Joe Higgins from the Socialist Party Ireland gave fraternal greetings to the conference. While understanding the enthusiasm which the SSP's good showing in the 1999 Scottish elections had given to the party, Bob argued that the party had to learn from the experience of other left forces internationally which had once scored good votes but had failed to use them to build support for socialist ideas and then gone into decline.

We faced up squarely to the setback we had suffered in Scotland. This was primarily due to objective factors: the aftermath of the collapse of Stalinism and the ideological retreat that flowed from this. This in turn had a profound effect on all aspects of the labour movement. As history demonstrates, Marxism and the revolutionary movement in general cannot remain immune from this. Inevitably, opportunist as well as ultra-left pressures were felt within the movement.

Whether or not it is possible to withstand these pressures depends on the political resistivity of the material – the political and theoretical understanding of the cadres – to rise above temporary setbacks and see the future clearly, as well as the willpower to accompany this. Very few, particularly at the top, were capable of doing so. The leadership of the CWI in Scotland, although they had achieved a great deal in more favourable times, were incapable of keeping their political bearings in the changed situation which confronted them in the noughties. Consequently, the SSP has shrivelled and become an appendage of the SNP in the completely non-socialist referendum campaign, while the CWI in Scotland maintains an important presence, is growing and will become stronger in the future.

34. Standing in elections

During the first New Labour government the Socialist Party managed to hold its own and even put on a bit of flesh. Indeed, after the 1997 general election Dave Griffiths, the party's long-standing and intrepid Regional Secretary in the West Midlands, reported at a National Committee meeting that 500 people contacted Coventry Socialist Party during the election. Coventry has been the standard bearer of our election work outside the Labour Party. Three hundred attended a pre-election rally, which was addressed by socialist film director Ken Loach. Subsequently, over 90 people came to a members' meeting in the area.

The feeling of disillusionment with Labour emerged very quickly after the general election, as Blair and Brown dressed themselves in the same political clothes as the Tories. This necessitated preparations to begin to present a real electoral alternative to New Labour for working class people. The Socialist Party put forward Julia Leonard, a local councillor, in a parliamentary by-election in Uxbridge, West London. She was squeezed by the polarisation between the two major parties, Labour and the Tories, but came fifth out of eleven candidates, beating the far-right and neo-Nazis. At the same time, many joined the Socialist Party from the local community. Significantly, the Tories won the seat, their first by-election victory since Labour came to power only a few months before.

In Rotherham, Yorkshire, the Socialist Party's candidate in a council by-election, Paul Marshall, held onto the vote he received in the general election, capturing 7% of the poll. The turnout was low but when one worker was asked whether he voted Socialist Party, he replied: "What's the colour of my door?... Labour is not red any more."[1] The reason for standing was to build a base for the future so that more serious challenges could be made.

This was typified by the experience in Lewisham, South London. In 1998 Ian Page challenged New Labour, achieving 13% of the vote. This was seen as a step forward by Socialist Party members in the area but, predictably, was met with derision from our opponents. Nevertheless, it was an important stepping stone for the eventual success for Ian and the Socialist Party later. In the following election he received 38%, coming second behind Labour. In the May 1999 local election he was victorious in the Pepys ward receiving 40% of the vote. His victory was all the sweeter given that he had been expelled from the Labour Party when he was a councillor for the crime of fighting against cuts in jobs and services. This was an important milestone in the electoral success of the Socialist Party at this stage, as well as being a measure of the discontent that was growing with New Labour.

In the initial period of the 1960s London was not the strongest area for us, but was where our national centre and leadership were located and based. Over time and through the considerable efforts of self-sacrificing comrades, particularly the full-time workers on our paper and later the party, we established a very strong base which endures to this day. Many comrades contributed to this but the work of Paula Mitchell, London Regional Secretary since 1998 – with a short break for domestic reasons – has been tireless and very effective in building our influence. Also, full-timers like Jim Horton and Chris Newby, part-timer Chris Moore and others have made considerable contributions to building our influence.

Ironically, the Liberal Democrat leader Paddy Ashdown wrote in the Guardian, just one day after the election in Lewisham, that "socialism is dead". This was a refrain that we had heard many times before and since. However, Samantha Dias became the second Socialist Party councillor in Lewisham shortly afterwards. This came after a very successful campaign effectively led by the Socialist Party against the handing over of council housing to housing associations.

There were also good results for the Lancashire Socialist Alliance candidate in Preston (over 5%), and the Scottish Socialist Party (SSP) candidate in Glasgow (over 7%). In the Euro-elections in the West Midlands, the Socialist Alliance stood with commendable results. This was despite the fact that there was a complete press blackout of the campaign. Even rallies involving Tommy Sheridan, MSP, alongside well-known comedians such as Mark Steel, Mark Thomas and Jeremy Hardy, received scant attention from the capitalist media outlets. Nevertheless, the Socialist Alliance candidates received more than the SLP which had the advantage of a national election broadcast.

In Coventry there was electoral success with Karen McKay (in 1999) and Rob Windsor (2000) joining Dave Nellist on the council – three Socialist Party representatives to fight for working people. This was reflected on the national plane with evidence that the establishment was becoming worried about the favourable electoral prospects for those challenging the deadening unanimity of the three major parties.

Labour introduced a Register of Political Parties which was used to try to prevent socialists standing in elections. The Socialist Party was told that its name would not be registered. The chairperson of the parliamentary advisory committee which took that decision was none other than Labour MP Gwyneth Dunwoody. She had been prominent on Labour's NEC with others in expelling Militant supporters in Liverpool, including leading councillors. Now her committee sought to ban us from using our own name, even though we were the only political party using the word 'socialist' which was refused registration. We roundly condemned this: "New Labour are using dictatorial methods to prevent socialist views being heard." We pointed out that the "majority of the [Labour] MPs on the parliamentary committee that took this decision also voted to expel supporters of the Militant newspaper..."[2]

We had changed our name to the Socialist Party in 1996 after a yearlong debate. Since then, we have spent our time building our forces and, in the process, trying to popularise our name. The alleged reason for the introduction of the register had been to prevent parties from deliberately setting out to cause confusion. To give an example, a Home Office spokesman said: "There was confusion between the Literal Democrat and the Liberal Democrat."[3] We explained that such an accusation could not apply to the Socialist Party. Firstly, because we always try to avoid standing against other left-wing parties whatever their name. Secondly, the very fact that the three political parties represented on the committee for registration have the power to ban the use of a name freely chosen by other parties was inherently undemocratic. We would never set out deliberately to mimic the name of any other party so as not to cause confusion where it can be avoided. This ban remains to this day and has compelled us to stand as Socialist Alternative and other titles in elections, which could undermine our 'brand' in the perception of the electorate.

This betokened further incursions on democratic rights during the reign of New Labour which have been continued by the Tories. The revelations of mass surveillance by governments, even snooping on one another – like former US President Barack Obama listening into the German Chancellor Angela Merkel's phone calls – has outraged the world. There are enough restrictions on working class activity, such as the limitations on the right to strike and other undemocratic measures worthy of a police state. Indeed, if a dictatorship was to take power in Britain, it would not need to introduce many new laws but could use those which are already on the statute book!

All this did not deter the Socialist Party, however, which stood 48 candidates in the May 1999 elections. Only a few weeks previously the Socialist Party had been barred from using our own name and it was feared that the enforced change to Socialist

Alternative might confuse voters. Yet, despite the ban, Karen McKay achieved an outstanding victory in Coventry, winning just under 50% of the vote. Karen's victory was recognised by the Coventry Evening Telegraph: "Socialists in Coventry were celebrating today... supporters sang the revolutionary socialist hymn the 'Internationale' as Karen McKay won St Michael's Ward for the new party... Mum of two and part-time librarian Karen... added: 'Labour isn't a socialist party anymore.'"[4]

The disillusionment with Blair's government was Britain-wide. Voters saw little difference between the pro-big business, pro-capitalist market policies of the three larger parties and voted with their feet by not turning out. These elections and other developments marked the end of the extended honeymoon for Blair. There was a particularly low turnout of just 29% in England's local elections and just over one third of those voted Labour. The Lib Dems took some key urban councils. This was in marked contrast to the success of the ssp and left candidates in Scotland, which threatened to make the Tories an exclusively English national party. Other socialists consistently saw results around 3% to as high as 20%. This would have been higher had it been possible to reach an agreement with Arthur Scargill's Socialist Labour Party (slp). Unfortunately, the slp once more decided to go it alone. One of the key distinguishing features of these elections, however, was the refusal to vote by a significant number of the electorate. This highlighted the crucial task undertaken by the Socialist Alliances, which were united in one national organisation at this stage, to create the basis of a bigger force.

35. Ken Livingstone again 1999-2001

Ken Livingstone first emerged as a major figure in the battles of Labour councillors and councils against the Thatcher government in the 1980s. His base was in the Greater London Council (GLC), which became Labour-controlled in May 1981, following four years of job losses and cutbacks under the previous Tory administration. Its programme of reforms meant that it became a focal point of opposition to Thatcherism. However, when it came to a serious defence of the flagship GLC policy, cheap fares for public transport, as well as a campaign against cuts in government grants to local authorities and the abolition of the GLC itself, Livingstone was found wanting.

Workers enthusiastically greeted the implementation of the GLC's manifesto commitment to cut fares by 32%. However, the law lords, the highest court of appeal, ruled that London Transport (LT) – should be run on 'business principles'. This reactionary decision threatened further increases of 200% and the loss of a quarter of LT's workforce. Militant called for all-out strike action by LT's 40,000 workers supported by a 24-hour regional general strike. Unfortunately, this was rejected in favour of the 'Keep Fares Fair' propaganda campaign. At the time, Livingstone admitted that the mood existed to build a mass campaign led by LT unions but he failed to take up the cudgels. An opportunity to inflict a major defeat on the Tories was missed.

35. Ken Livingstone again

The weakness of the GLC left was rewarded with a move by the Tory government, after its re-election in 1983, to abolish the GLC. Confronted with a Tory majority of 140 seats, Livingstone declared: "There was no chance of defeating the abolition proposals... There seemed to be no chance of industrial action by the trade unions at County Hall."[1] However while Livingstone was ruling out the idea of struggle in London, Liverpool City Council, under the influence of Militant, mobilised a mass campaign for more money and against rate-capping, which limited the maximum level of local property tax that could be levied by councils and cut their government grants.

The mood amongst workers in London was no different. In November 1984, 100,000 workers came out on strike in the boroughs threatened by ratecapping and in opposition to the abolition of the GLC. Thirty thousand marched in the capital. Opinion polls showed up to 70% opposed GLC abolition. Yet, rather than mobilising this enormous latent support into a mass campaign, Livingstone launched the 'GLC Roadshow', as it became known, involving celebrities, fun days and festivals.

Livingstone preferred a slick campaign to the serious mobilisation of working people. In 1984 Liverpool City Council had already compelled the Thatcher government to retreat and make concessions through strike action and mass demonstrations.[2] Moreover, in 1985, 25 Labour councils faced ratecapping. Liverpool councillors argued for the tactic of setting a deficit budget and had already shown the potential for the mass mobilisation of workers demanding the return of the money stolen by the Tory government. Livingstone and other left-wing council leaders opposed this, arguing that they should not set rates at all until the Tories made concessions. While this appeared to be a more dramatic gesture, it actually obscured the issues involved. In reality the Labour left had no intention of not setting a rate. It was merely a gesture of defiance. In February 1985 the Tories on the GLC (in a manoeuvre to wrong-foot Livingstone) unexpectedly announced they would vote against the government's rate-capping limit. It became clear that even with the Labour right-wing voting against illegality the left would have a majority not to set a rate.

With astounding frankness Livingstone later explained how this presented difficulties for the GLC left: "Suddenly, for the first time we faced the possibility that the GLC might really refuse to set a rate. This presented several problems, not least of which was that, as everyone had assumed that behind all the rhetoric there was no real possibility of this happening, none of us had even begun to explore the question of how to run a bankrupt council. Certainly, no one had given any thought to how staff would react to no pay or how we would provide essential services to the public."[3] We commented: "Not preparing for such an eventuality was at best irresponsible. At worst, it exposed not only the falsity of the 'no rate' tactic but also the political bankruptcy of left reformism in general and Livingstone in particular: verbal, symbolic opposition until the commencement of battle, and then capitulation."[4] Of the 25 councils which promised to defy the Tories, the GLC was the first council to cave in.

In a section drafted by Militant supporters and approved by a London Labour Party conference, Labour's 1981 GLC election manifesto said it would seek to build "mass opposition" to the cuts, appeal "to the Labour and trade union movement to take action, including industrial action" which "could become the focal point of a national campaign... against the cuts".[5] Livingstone had no intention of even trying to carry out such a campaign. Towards the end of 1984, Livingstone was already preparing the way to back down. He organised the splitting of the broad left in the Greater London Labour Party in order to remove from its executive those who would oppose the retreat, including Militant supporters.

When the Blair government announced the establishment in 2000 of a Mayor for London, Livingstone threw his hat into the ring as an independent. He was pitted against the hapless Frank Dobson, who had been selected as the Labour candidate after defeating Livingstone in the selection vote. This transformed a contest which was lacklustre into an acrimonious squabble for the crown. For many workers Livingstone still retained a radical reputation and was seen as an alternative to Blair and New Labour's openly Thatcherite policies, even though he stated that he would work with the government. He admitted his ideological retreat from a left-wing firebrand into a staunch defender of capitalism: "Twenty years ago I would have said a central planned economy could be made to work better than the Western capitalist economy; I don't believe that anymore."[6]

The illusion that he represented something different was indicated in a letter to the Independent: "With the Labour Party having lost its way and facing a meltdown in its heartlands, it would seem a great opportunity for the formation of a socialist party in time for the next general election. After becoming Mayor of London perhaps Ken Livingstone should consider this possibility."[7] Livingstone's reply was to the point: "I am not setting up another rival party, I am just giving Londoners the right to choose who they want as mayor."[8] Despite this, by March 2000, 61% of those intending to vote indicated support for Livingstone, while Dobson notched up just 16%, and the Tory candidate, Stephen Norris, 13%. He was ahead amongst all groups of the population: men and women, young and old, middle class and working class voters. The Evening Standard reported that, incredibly, "he has now overtaken Mr Norris among Conservatives, and is miles ahead of Susan Kramer among Liberal Democrats".[9]

The Standard's resident psephologist, Peter Kellner, a former Maoist who reinvented himself as an election 'expert' in the service of the Blairites, could scarcely contain himself: "Today, astonishingly, he would win easily even if every Labour supporter stayed at home." We commented: "Support for Livingstone has many different and seemingly contradictory strands. The sense of disillusionment with the government is so wide and deep that an inchoate 'stuff Blair' sentiment has lined up behind him... This is itself a comment on the character of Livingstone's appeal. It is entirely different to the wide support for Tony Benn when he stood for the deputy leadership of the Labour Party in 1981. Benn's campaign was of a pronounced left and socialist character. Traditional Tory and Liberal voters would not have supported Benn in the way they have lined up behind Livingstone."

We went on to draw an analogy between similar figures in the

US, where there was no party of the working class, and in parts of the neo-colonial world: "The result has been that dissent has often expressed itself in support for radical figures without a party, or against parties in general. If Livingstone is cast in the mode of 'populism' over the last three years, it has been of a pronounced moderate variety." While quietly whispering 'socialism', his campaign was predominantly moderate, claiming to represent 'all the people'. Notwithstanding this, the impression was that he stood on the left and would be a counterweight to Blair.[10]

Unfortunately, support for Livingstone did not advance the cause of those like the Socialist Party who were for the clear demand of the need for a new mass workers' party. In London we recognised the working class had not yet moved decisively into action. Moreover, in the capital the weight of the middle class 'intelligentsia' is generally of greater significance than outside of London. Consequently, the influence of sectarian, largely middle class grouplets was more of a problem and the genuine voice of the working class tended to be crowded out. Like the SWP, they were inclined to gather around Livingstone but failed to give his campaign a socialist content. Notwithstanding this, we recognised that a victory for Livingstone would represent a defeat for Blair, although not a decisive one. Ultimately, they were cut from the same ideological material.

This was made clear even before he was formerly sworn in as the new Mayor. Just before election day he had denounced the Reclaim the Streets anti-capitalist May Day demonstrators. He refused to support the London Socialist Alliance, calling instead for a Labour vote in the London Assembly constituencies and the all-London top-up list. The Independent wrote that he had "wisely dropped much of his old rhetoric and alliances and now stands as a vaguely leftish Keynesian: hardly the stuff of tabloid nightmares".[11] He energetically courted big business, touting his business friendly agenda, increased transport spending, investment, and a skills plan geared to employers' needs: "I will build a strong partnership with every section of London business, the city, large employers and small firms."

Paradoxically, Livingstone's victory had features of Blair's in the previous general election yet he had prospered because of the disillusionment with Blair. Certainly, there was no advance for the left, as those who had uncritically supported Livingstone expected. And he made his position clear: "I really want to make the system work."[12] Concessions, therefore, would be very small, particularly as far the working class was concerned. Blair indicated he was prepared to work with the new Mayor and Livingstone, on a salary of £76,000, appointed a New Labour deputy. Other appointees followed a similar pattern. In reality, Livingstone took Blair's coalition policies much further with Liberal Democrats, Labour and Greens staffing a pro-business administration. Kellner gloated: "He no longer behaves like a doctrinaire socialist. For the most part, he now works in an inclusive, consensus-seeking manner."[13]

After his first year in office, he reapplied to rejoin the Labour Party just as workers were moving in the opposite direction. His application was rejected by the party's NEC, but this was a mere interlude as he was readmitted later – after a 'decent interval' had elapsed. He smoothed the way by acting like a typical Blairite, refusing to speak to demonstrations of public sector workers in a rally outside the offices of the Greater London Assembly (GLA), and distancing himself from anti-capitalist demonstrators. A sign of the change that had taken place was that Labour officials hinted that they would not expel Labour Party members who had supported Livingstone in the elections, so long as it was not done too openly! This was one indication of the growing weakness of Blair and his Labour machine.

There was growing hostility from the unions, such as the RMT, CWU communication workers and the GMB. Not yet prepared to completely break from Labour, they nevertheless cut back their funding to the party, reflecting the increasing anger and opposition from their members towards the government. Despite some radical phrases at different times, including opposition to the Iraq war, Livingstone never played again the role he had in the 1980s. Back then people like him could become a pole of attraction for workers and young people who were looking towards a struggle against capitalism and for a new socialist world. Because Livingstone remained within Blairised Labour's ideological prison, his mayoral reign proved to be a big disappointment – and paved the way for the victory of the unspeakable Tory Boris Johnson later.

Other opportunities existed in London. The Socialist Party played a pivotal role in Socialist Alliance work from the very beginning, in London and nationally, setting up the London Socialist Alliance in 1995 and helping its development politically and organisationally. This was at a time when the SWP and other left groups were pursuing a policy of 'ourselves alone'.

36. The Socialist Alliances 1998-2000

On 5 September 1998 a meeting had been organised in Rugby to set up a national network of Socialist Alliances in England. Over 120 attended, including three Labour MEPs – Hugh Kerr, Ken Coates and Michael Hindley – who all spoke. Dave Nellist also addressed the conference: "Our task is to explain and popularise the ideas of socialism." Jean Thorpe, on the NEC of the public sector union Unison, led a session on fighting against low pay. A campaign was launched to get a million signatures supporting a £6 an hour national minimum wage.[1] This shows how little broad swathes of the working class have advanced in almost 20 years. There are still millions receiving the minimum wage, which will reach only £7.50 an hour in April 2017. It also shows the kind of political and industrial 'Sherpa' work undertaken by members of the Socialist Party and others on the left who heroically led struggles for a new political alternative for working class people. Our proposal to lay the basis for a new party provoked some resistance from those who wanted to remain in the calm of the New Labour bay. At another meeting in Doncaster Ken Coates stated: "We do not seek to create a new party, but we are anxious to compel the Labour government to return to its roots."[2]

Many who were still members of the Labour Party and politically opposed to us were prepared, nonetheless, to work and discuss with us in left alliances. In some areas there were even votes taken as to what such a body should be called: Socialist Alliance, Socialist Alternative or Alternative Labour List. This reflected the way in which the British working class movement has tended to move: in a rather ponderous and protracted fashion particularly before big historical changes were posed. This is underlined when we examine the way that the trade unions moved very slowly to disengage from the Liberal Party, a process extending over 20 to 30 years at the end of the 19th and the beginning of the 20th centuries. It took a further period of time – encompassing the increasing crisis of British capitalism, the First World War and the Russian Revolution – before the Labour Party adopted a socialist clause in its constitution. In reality, having thrown the Labour Party up onto its shoulders the British working class, particularly its upper echelons, was reluctant to let it go.

Support grew, however, for left-wing candidates prepared to challenge New Labour after the experience of three or four years of Blair's government. This involved a minority, but a quite determined layer of workers and youth who were prepared to work energetically to provide a real alternative to the discredited 'Blair project'. Attempts at creating networks developed at this period but began to take on flesh in the run-up to the London Assembly elections. The Socialist Party had the only socialist councillor in the capital, Ian Page. There were two other socialist councillors elsewhere, Dave Nellist and Karen McKay in Coventry. We had been participating for five years in the London Socialist Alliance (LSA).

Belatedly, the SWP decided to throw its weight behind the LSA. Previously, like in the hokey cokey, it had been neither in nor out but, in effect, was actually opposed in the past to alliance work and denounced socialists who stood in elections. Its turn towards the LSA was because it believed it could now benefit doing so and not as part of a process to build a new mass working class party. Unfortunately, alongside this came the methods of the SWP with the compliance of other left groups. They turned away from the previous democratic joint decision-making which was a feature of the alliances up to then. In Wales the SWP got involved in the Welsh Socialist Alliance (WSA) and only participated in the Assembly elections under the temporary moniker United Socialists. The SWP maintained its sectarian approach in the trade unions, consistently working outside of or even against broad left formations. The SWP had stood recently against Socialist Party candidates in union elections, winning fewer votes.

Outrageously, it attempted to expel us from the LSA notwithstanding the fact that we had been one of the founding members. Once in the LSA, SWP leaders arrogated to themselves the right to make public statements in the LSA's name on issues as yet undecided by the Alliance. For instance, in an Evening Standard article, Paul Foot said that LSA London Assembly candidates backed Ken Livingstone for Mayor. This had not been agreed by us or others.

The Socialist Party remained committed to building the alliances even though collaboration with the SWP was extremely difficult given its approach. For instance, on the night of a Waltham Forest Socialist Alliance public meeting, a Socialist Party member and local health worker was told that he could not speak from the platform. The SWP later admitted that they banned him in case he criticised the LSA's decision to stand candidates against the Campaign Against Tube Privatisation (CATP), which was supported by leading figures in the RMT, the rail, maritime and transport workers' union. The Socialist Party was actively participating in both the CATP and the LSA, campaigning for a joint slate in the party list section of the Greater London Assembly elections. When co-operation failed to materialise we urged the LSA to withdraw its list in favour of the CATP and just concentrate on the constituency elections.

Most politically developed workers instinctively seek the widest possible unity in struggle and are dismayed that there is not often a united workers' list to vote for. We blamed the leadership of the LSA and CATP for this situation. However, we decided that we would recommend a vote for the LSA in the Assembly elections, where we had Ian Page and others standing. In the party list section we also recommended a vote for the LSA – reluctantly and with reservations. This was because the CATP was restricting their campaign to one issue, rail privatisation, when workers were looking for a broader challenge, particularly to Labour. Moreover, the LSA would be seen by many as offering such a challenge. We also declared: "For the LSA to be a socialist alliance in any real sense, it is a prerequisite that it is open and democratic. Unfortunately, this is no longer true of the LSA under the control of the SWP. The SWP has used force of numbers to push through decisions beneficial to its own narrow interests."[3]

This was linked to a completely false perspective for Britain in general, but particularly in relation to the Labour Party. The SWP opposed the demand for a new party. It falsely compared developments around the LSA with the setting up of the Labour Representation Committee 100 years previously, which led to the formation of the Labour Party. However, the SWP failed to draw the obvious conclusions from that experience: the Labour Party was formed from the coming together not only of socialist groups but, more importantly, workers' struggles and the new trade unions formed at the end of the 19th century. It was the position of the Socialist Party that it would take struggles of a similar scale to forge a new mass party, which was then and is now even more so desperately needed by working people.

For the SWP, the LSA represented the only left electoral alternative to New Labour at that stage. While opposing the SWP's sectarian methods, the Socialist Party engaged in debate, hoping to lay the basis for the emergence of a bigger socialist force which could lead to a mass party. The different methods and approach were to some extent put to the test in the 2000 elections for the London Mayor and the GLA. The turnout was not great at less than 34% and the Labour vote plummeted, although there was no great rise in support for the Tories. Instead, left and Green candidates attracted 3-4%. A Green Party member was elected to the 25-member Assembly and the total left vote in the constituencies was 47,000, with the majority going to the LSA, Independent candidates or one of Ken Livingstone's supporters. Unfortunately, matters were complicated for the party list section with four left-wing groups competing against one another. Between them, they won over 66,000 votes (3.9%). In other regions, the Socialist Party did well – for instance in Coventry and also in Carlisle where we won 24.5% of the vote.

The battle between left-wing organisations continued after the elections, primarily between the Socialist Party and the SWP and its fellow travellers. This became evident because of the likelihood of a general election in 2000 or 2001. The SWP manoeuvred frantically to ensure that its candidates got priority on the Socialist Alliances' lists. It proposed that the officers of the Socialist Alliance should form a small election committee which would have the power to formally endorse local candidates, agents and material. We opposed this, pointing out that the LSA could suffer the same fate as the SLP which was in the process of disintegration. After some delay, this prognosis was borne out. The sectarian methods used by the SWP in the Socialist Alliances and later in Respect led to the disintegration of these organisations – and a significant weakening of the SWP following big splits.

An uneasy truce held, nonetheless, inside the Socialist Alliance in the run-up to the 2001 general election but political hostilities did not completely evaporate. In January 2001 at a Socialist Alliance liaison committee, the SWP launched an attack on the Socialist Party, demanding that our general election candidates should submit themselves to 'selection conferences' and have their campaigns vetted by local or regional alliances. We pointed out that we had never been afraid of putting our ideas before broad audiences. We had also stood in elections much more successfully than anyone else in the Alliance and in the selection of activists in trade union broad lefts. However, compulsory selection meetings would mean ceding control of our candidates and campaigns – and the finances to pay for them – to the SWP and its allies. This was not acceptable in an alliance which was a federation.

The SWP backed away at that stage. We also made compromises promising, for instance, to stand in two of the London seats as Socialist Alternative and not as the Socialist Alliance. This was because the SWP and its allies, regardless of the strength of socialist forces on the ground and the potential for the election campaign to build up that strength, were not prepared to mount a challenge in seats held by 'Labour left-wingers'.

A mass meeting of 400 Hackney Council workers agreed to continue the campaign against the council's attacks on wages and conditions, and 27 shop stewards, branch officers and convenors agreed to support Glenn Kelly as an anti-cuts, anti-corruption candidate in the by-election on 7 June 2001. The SWP-dominated Hackney Socialist Alliance decided to stand against him in the selection contest. It continued to oppose Glenn even when John Page, Hackney Unison branch secretary, tried to persuade it not to go ahead with the original proposal. The 27 convenors and stewards maintained their support of Glenn in the by-election.

37. 2001: economic storm clouds

2001 was an election year when the record of all parties, particularly the governing party, would be examined and tested. As was usual, The Socialist opened it with a perspectives article for Britain and the world. We wrote: "Eighteen months ago, George W Bush was told by an economic adviser that the US was heading for a 'painful adjustment' (read recession or slump). Bush's reaction was: 'If you're right, I'm not sure I want this job [the US presidency!]'." In the event, Bush did stand for office – and stole it from Al Gore, the inept Democratic Party candidate, through blatant electoral fraud worthy of a banana republic and a legal coup d'état by the Supreme Court. The only issue in doubt in relation to the US economy was whether it would collapse in a 'hard' or 'soft' landing. We summed up the choices he faced "Like the Duke of Wellington after the Battle of Waterloo, Bush may well ruminate that 'nothing except a battle lost can be half so melancholy as a battle won.'"[1]

We expected that the effects of the US meltdown would wreak havoc on the world and particularly the exposed British economy. Already, significant groups faced redundancy, including workers at General Motors (GM) in Luton, and Corus steelworkers in the North-East and South Wales. The working class seethed with anger at the capitalists who were shutting factories as easily as matchboxes. Economic worries combined with horrendous floods seemed to conjure up the biblical spectacle of the Four Horsemen of the

Apocalypse. At one stage, an area the size of the county of Lancashire was under water. The natural disasters were compounded by the capitalist disaster of a severe lack of infrastructure investment.

As the election approached, New Labour remained in the driving seat although it was the memory of the greater devastation when the Tories were in office which boosted its prospects. Moreover, New Labour was fortunate in that it had not faced a serious economic crisis in its first period in office. Gordon Brown put this down to his economic 'prudence'. However, the British economy had benefited from the upswing of capitalism in the previous eight years. At the same time, Tony Blair admitted that by continuing with Tory restrictions on state spending he had starved the NHS of funds. The journal of the British Medical Association said that doctors were "clinically depressed" at the state of the NHS. Britain's Housebuilding Federation declared: "Britain has had the lowest level of housing investment as a percentage of gross domestic product of any developed country for decades."

Accumulated anger was breaking out and not just in Britain. In Spain there had been a massive strike of 2.2 million public sector workers – the first there since 1996. A similar general strike took place in Greece and a huge industrial wave in Southern Ireland. On matters big or small, New Labour was a mouthpiece for big business. The government had known about proposed redundancies of car workers in Luton, but never informed the trade unions or the workforce. Blair even promised the bosses the previous November that the minimal rights for those unfairly sacked would be weakened. Employment tribunals, he promised, would be given new powers to strike out "ill-founded claims" that allegedly "had no real chance of success". These are the very proposals which the ConDem coalition government later implemented.

An avalanche of proposed job losses was announced in the New Year. "Britain is working again," boasted Education and Employment Secretary David Blunkett. Yet this was against the background of 2,000 Vauxhall workers in Luton, 2,600 Ford workers in Dagenham, 2,000 at British Aerospace (BAE) and a massive 30,000 Corus steel workers facing the dole queue. Even the TUC claimed that 10,000 manufacturing jobs per month would be lost in the next year. Drunk on his own hype, Blunkett said that New Labour was likely to achieve full employment. We wrote: "What tosh! The dot.coms of the 'New Economy' have turned into dot.bombs as the speculative stock market shares bubble has burst."[2] The betrayal of New Labour was matched by the acquiescence of the right-wing trade union leadership to the pro-big business agenda. This was best summed up by Roger Lyons, the discredited General Secretary of the MSF finance workers' union. He had led officials and some NEC members, complete with a priest and candles, outside the Bank of England to plea for a reduction in interest rates to "help manufacturing industry". The only policy these trade union leaders had was literally a hope and a prayer!

Luton car workers showed that the mood was now changing, however. The new generation were not prepared to allow themselves to be driven back into poverty and deprivation. This new mood had already been reflected within the civil service union PCS with the victory of Mark Serwotka, the left-wing candidate for General Secretary, who was supported by Socialist Party members in Left Unity. We ended our perspectives article by pointing to the reality which lay behind the myth of capitalist triumphalism: "The claims made for this system as the bearer of culture, of new technology for all, of rising living standards, and a future of undreamed of plenty for the mass of the peoples of the world will be further undermined in the next year."[3]

Car workers at GM in Luton showed this in a magnificent 10,000 strong march. This clearly reflected the anger of people against the multinational companies which were threatening to close down whole towns at the first nervous twitch of their shareholders. However, there was no real strategy to effectively resist them on the part of union leaders. They had promised a European-wide day of action in late January and, even though there was an expectation that something would happen in Luton and perhaps Ellesmere Port, very little was proposed from the platform of the march. The

Socialist reported: "It was left to a local radio DJ who was chairing the rally to say everyone should go sick on the day! Tony Woodley, the chief transport union negotiator for the car industry, talked about the traumatic year for the industry with the closure plans for Dagenham, the threats still hanging over Longbridge and now Vauxhall. He complained how the Luton closure demonstrated the role of a multinational like GM".

The strategy seemed to consist solely of holding out for mass pressure to change GM's collective mind. The Socialist demanded "a call to arms, including strike action, if the pressure is to have any effect... [Trade unions and the workers] should be campaigning for the nationalisation of all GM plants under threat of closure, whether in Britain or any European country." The union leaders merely challenged GM over figures for overcapacity with Ken Jackson of the AEEU pleading for the protection of the manufacturing base of the UK economy. John Monks, TUC General Secretary, suggested a national campaign for proper corporate standards of behaviour![4]

While these workers were fighting for their jobs, the lives of New Labour luminaries faced upheavals. The resignation of Peter Mandelson once more revealed the rottenness arising from their pro-big business policies and the patronage that went along with it. Mandelson's fall from grace was generally greeted with enthusiasm in labour movement circles because he personified New Labour's arrogance and subservience to the bosses. He was seen as the arch-Blairite and a big business stooge. He was also a lightning conductor for all the anger building up against the government. When his resignation was announced, his erstwhile colleagues in the Parliamentary Labour Party greeted it with cheers!

There were desperate attempts to shore up New Labour but the backbiting could not be contained. Clare Short briefed that "Mandelson went... because he's got problems with telling the truth." His ally's departure left Blair vulnerable, not on his character judgements alone but also on wider political issues. A major reason why the Murdoch papers went for Mandelson and Keith Vaz with such abandon was because of their advocacy of the EU and joining the euro. The Socialist made the point: "The main factor in the [Millennium] Dome, [Formula One and Hinduja brothers] fiascos is that when you ask big business for donations they expect bigger favours in return."[5] Vaz's financial dealings were subsequently raised in the exposé run in the media in 2016. So desperate were they to appease big business, they had stepped in where even the Tories feared to tread and gave passports against government agency advice to big business pals.

The rottenness was exposed in Servants of the People, a book by Andrew Rawnsley, political editor of the Observer. He showed that from the beginning Blair and Brown had set up two camps like a 'dual monarchy'. Rawnsley described the way Mandelson had "swanked around the salons of the wealthy, the powerful and the right wing". Rawnsley also revealed what the Socialist had maintained all along: that Blair and Brown were conscious of the kind of policies that were necessary for capitalism: "Brown told Harman that, to remain within her budget limits, she would have to choose between two Tory cuts, both of which Labour had bitterly attacked when in Opposition". He pointed out that 'cabinet government' was a myth because "the people who make the decisions and effectively run the show [are] Blair himself, Brown the Chancellor, Alistair Campbell (Blair's press secretary) and, until [he was removed], Peter Mandelson."[6]

Meanwhile, pressure was mounting on the government for action to stop the haemorrhaging of jobs. Most of the unions, such as the ISTC steel union, had no strategy other than proposing that different groups of capitalists should buy out the owners of bankrupted firms – in the case of steel, the whole industry. We commented: "This will not provide a solution, but Corus rejected this from the outset saying it would hardly allow its most productive plant to be set up in competition with its remaining plants." There was widespread support for the renationalisation of steel – of course, with no compensation. The shareholders had received a £750 million pay out when the company was formed in 1998 and their share values had jumped by 10%, but there was not a whisper of a real solution by New Labour. Blair went out of his way to introduce 'state capitalist' measures of which Thatcher would have been proud. He stated: "The purpose of this government has been not to turn the clock back on the enterprise agenda; but to deepen it and then to correct the instability and under-investment."

The problem for Blair and New Labour was that this pro-capitalist ideology was not working anywhere. Moreover, there had been a shift in public opinion towards public ownership. We remarked: "Compare the crisis-ridden privatised utilities in Britain with their state-owned counterparts in Europe, where for example train travel is cheaper, faster and safer because of massive public investment." The Socialist argued for "socialist nationalisation with workers' control and management and a proper plan of production based on need not profit. This would guarantee sufficient investment to protect jobs and ensure modern working conditions. That is the only way working class people can end the 'instability and under-investment' of the capitalist market."[7] Yet the steel unions refused to even countenance this, the only measure that could save jobs. What mattered to the shareholders was not the need to retain this vital industry but the maintenance of their share price.

The foot and mouth disease epidemic that broke out illustrated how a minor crisis turned into a disaster for the government. A virtual state of emergency was called over a relatively mild animal disease, although one which produced big concerns largely for the profits of the farming industry, public health and animal welfare. The farming industry was and is dominated by finance capital, agribusiness and big landowners. Each year £30 billion was handed out in subsidies by the EU's Common Agricultural Policy (CAP), 80% of which went to the richest 20% of EU farmers. The Economist estimated that the foot and mouth disease fiasco cost £9 billion. We asked: "Who'll pay the price for this chaos? Not government ministers or big business. It will be workers in agriculture, tourism and small farmers."[8] One million animals were slaughtered in the UK when only 5% had the disease. Nevertheless, this crisis illustrated the deficiencies of food production in Britain on a capitalist basis.

In March Brown's budget was tailored towards a forthcoming general election. Labour was so far ahead in the polls that Hugo Young commented: "This was not a budget to win an election, but a budget for an election that is already won. Its handouts were slight, its promises distant, its perspectives closer to five years than five weeks."[9] The budget did little for ordinary people, although Brown made some attempt to buy off lorry drivers hit by the fuel crisis. From the Treasury's huge surplus, he chose to repay £34 billion of the national debt. Kevin Parslow pointed out in the Socialist: "It was reported that, last year, five million people were living in conditions of absolute poverty in Britain."[10]

The Financial Times commented: "An economist from Mars examining the public finances under Tony Blair's Labour government might conclude that it came to power early in 1999. His first glance at the figures would suggest that in 1997 and 1998 Britain's public finances were being managed by someone who out-Thatchered Margaret Thatcher for restraint."[11] Even Polly Toynbee, the usually steadfast friend of New Labour, wrote: "This has been a deeply conservative government, dogmatically attached to private finance and privatisation."[12]

New Labour's plans for a second term were outlined with a focus primarily on education. These were so outrageously right wing that the Tories' then education spokesperson, Theresa May, said indignantly that Labour had adopted Tory education rhetoric! Labour promised to introduce selection in schools, more religious-based schools and a massive expansion of private provision in primary, secondary and higher education. All of this amounted to a massive boost for privileged education for a small elite. Moreover, New Labour was still under pressure from vice-chancellors of the elite universities to introduce top-up fees. We promised to organise resistance to New Labour's education attacks, through mass union-led campaigns of teachers, parents and students.

38. 2001
general election

Unsurprisingly, reports appeared in the media which indicated that Tory candidates were in a state of panic: "At the party HQ officials [were] reaching for the Prozac in a situation of 'descending depression.'"[1] Only 17% expected that William Hague, the Tory leader, would remain in situ after the election. Yet the paradox of 2001 was that New Labour, above all Blair, was not at all popular. Even in 1997 people had voted negatively – more against the Tories than for New Labour. Now a Gallup Poll in the Daily Telegraph indicated that two thirds of people said that Blair was out of touch with ordinary people; 50% thought that he showed poor judgement and spent too much time with the rich and powerful. This was before the horrors to come, particularly the Iraq war.

The problem was – and remains unfortunately – that there was no political channel through which mass discontent could be expressed. This, we concluded, would lead to many working class people not bothering to vote for either of the two 'evils', or for any other established party. The number of people who indicated that they were 'certain' or 'very likely' to vote was 10% lower than in 1997. The Socialist Party indicated that we would stand 13 candidates – eleven in England (ten as part of the Socialist Alliance), and two in Wales under the banner of the WSA. We advised workers to vote for this socialist alternative.

Another key question for the left was what to propose where

socialist candidates were not standing. The SWP's answer came through John Rees – then one of its leaders who later departed its ranks – in its magazine Socialist Review: "The choice for those who do not have a socialist candidate to vote for will be this--either they vote for the open, unashamed representatives of big business... Or they vote for a party which is certainly pro-capitalist, but is funded and supported by working class people, including the majority of class conscious workers."[2] We pointed out, however, that New Labour was not just another right-wing reformist government following in the footsteps of the previous Labour governments of Wilson and Callaghan but had some policies decidedly further to the right.

Although Blair had been fairly successful in persuading millionaires to part with some of their cash, New Labour still relied on the trade unions for a third of its income. Despite the fact that Blair had rubbed union leaders' noses in the dirt, they still coughed up when the tin came round. Trade unions no longer had any say in the selection of parliamentary candidates. Decision making had been removed from the delegate-based annual conference in favour of toothless policy forums.

The comparison with the Democratic Party and the way it treated the unions was obvious. The US trade unions are not affiliated to the Democratic Party yet they still contribute millions of dollars to its war chest. We pointed out that in 2000, "Six of the ten biggest donors were unions... The AFL-CIO trade union federation pledged $48 million in union resources to support Al Gore while every major union, except the Teamsters, backed his presidential election campaign."[3] Occasionally, under pressure, the Democrats would make radical sounding pro-worker speeches at election time, as Gore was forced to do in response to Ralph Nader's challenge from the left in 2000.

We recognised that there would be some sections of workers who maintained an electoral allegiance to the Labour Party. There was still, in a sense, a very small element of social democracy within Labour, particularly amongst older layers of trade union activists who hoped against hope that 'this time', if New Labour was elected, it could be pushed towards the left. Yet even the editorial board of Labour Left Briefing pointed out that "the left in the Labour Party remains small and isolated".[4] Contrary to everything our critics from the left had argued against the idea of campaigning for a new workers' party, the experience of a Labour government had not resulted in workers moving into the party to reclaim it. Nationally, firefighters, rail workers and communication workers would all discuss the question of disaffiliation from New Labour.

On the eve of the June 2001 general election we hoped that the deepening crisis of capitalism would intensify this opposition and lead to a new party. Essentially, the Socialist Party's role was to speed up a process that was objectively lodged in the situation. However, the crisis did not break out with full intensity in the next couple of years. A certain breathing space was found for capitalism, at the cost of storing up even greater problems which finally exploded in the financial and economic collapse of 2007-08.

New Labour was re-elected and on the surface the election seemed to signify no change of the political landscape. In reality, it indicated a huge shift in the attitudes of millions of people. The Tories did not advance from the electoral disaster of 1997, indeed they fell back slightly. The Liberal Democrats benefited from their opportunist stance, situating themselves to the left of New Labour. Yet the most decisive development was the massive drop in turnout, by 12.5%. Four out of ten electors – 17 million people – refused to vote. This was the lowest turnout since the general election of 1918, when electoral administration had been disrupted by the First World War. Just over 26 million people voted, compared to almost 29 million in 1950 when the population was much smaller and 18-21 year-olds did not have a vote. Even as recently as 1992, 34 million voted. We concluded: "Tony Blair is the first prime minister since 1923 to discover the day after his election victory that those who voted for him were outnumbered by those who did not vote. Moreover, turnout was far lower amongst the young – only 38% voted – while 79% of the older voters turned out."[5]

The lowest turnout was registered in Liverpool Riverside at a mere

34%! Not far behind was the neighbouring Walton on 43%. This seat was won by Labour candidate Peter Kilfoyle who wailed: "Britain was in danger of emulating the United States where less than half the voters participated in the presidential elections."[6] We remarked: "What an annihilating condemnation of the policies of Labour's right wing, nationally and in the city! Kilfoyle is one of the architects of the low turnout." We reminded the movement of the electoral achievements for Labour when Militants played a key role in the city. At that time the right wing claimed that we were "an electoral albatross", yet never before or since has there been a greater involvement of the people of Liverpool as when socialist, Marxist and Militant ideas held sway.

In the May 1983 council elections, for instance, Labour's vote increased by an astonishing 40%. In the general election a month later there was a swing to the Tories nationally, although in Liverpool there was a 2% swing to Labour. The only notional or actual 'Tory seat' (after big boundary changes) won by Labour was in Broad Green, where Militant supporter Terry Fields was elected on a 72% turnout. We have recorded elsewhere – in The Rise of Militant and Liverpool: A City that Dared to Fight – that it was those like Kilfoyle and the right wing of the Labour Party who destroyed this by witch-hunting Marxists and socialists. The pitiful turnouts in the city in 2001 represented a rejection of the alternatives of the three major capitalist parties. Liverpool Council was now in the firm grip of right-wing reactionary Liberal Democrats. We wrote: "This is the epitaph of right wing New Labour in Liverpool."[7]

The general election in Scotland was a non-event for many people with the turnout falling just as dramatically. Despite the differences we had with the leadership of the SSP, CWI comrades in Scotland continued to work within it. Our organisation, the International Socialists (CWI Scotland) made up eight of the SSP candidates. Excellent results were achieved by Ronnie Stevenson in Glasgow Cathcart (1,730 votes) and Jim McFarlane in Dundee West (over 4%), while Jim Halfpenny in Paisley North scored almost 1,000 votes (3.6%) and Harvey Duke in Dundee East polled 2.7%.

The SSP made a very creditable electoral intervention winning over 3% across Scotland, nearly 73,000 votes in total. In nine out of the ten Glasgow seats the SSP held its deposits, the best being Glasgow Pollok with 2,522. The other encouraging sign for the SSP was the vote in rural and island areas, such as the tremendous 4.6% in Orkney and Shetland. Throughout Scotland there was only one change of seat. The SNP lost Galloway, which was the sum total of the Tory revival in Scotland where they had been wiped out at the previous general election. The Lib Dems held onto their ten seats but made no other inroads.

Labour was the big winner in Scotland and on the surface emerged strengthened. It won 56 out of 72 seats with nearly 44% of the vote. Nonetheless, this disguised the steady erosion of its base with mass disillusionment on working class housing schemes over the issue of benefits, poverty and crumbling public services. In an article in Socialism Today Jim McFarlane and Harvey Duke concluded: "The CWI in Scotland has proven its ability to campaign and build the SSP while at the same time building a Marxist organisation within it."[8]

The Tories had tried to play the asylum card, a variant of the race card, in a desperate attempt to split the working class. Hague promised to lock up all asylum seekers pending acceptance of their request or instant deportation, labelling them all as 'bogus'. Retiring MP John Townend denounced the creation of a "mongrel society". He referred to Britain becoming a "foreign land". Prominent amongst the Tories' election strategists was Andrew Lansley, later the butcher of the NHS, who openly boasted to the Observer that the Tories' anti-immigrant propaganda in the 1992 election had "played particularly well in the tabloids and has more potential to hurt" Labour.

This campaign took place despite the fact that official figures showed that the big majority of asylum seekers to Britain came from countries ruled by dictators, torn by civil war or subject to ethnic or religious persecution. Yet New Labour had not combated the Tory offensive. Indeed, at times, it appeared to be competing to scapegoat asylum seekers. The Sun, quoting 'inside sources' in Number Ten, announced that David Blunkett would be Home Secretary after the election. It concluded: "He'll blitz asylum cheats."[9] Many of the themes the Tories are putting forward today were played out during this election – although then with little success.

The election campaign was, as the Socialist Party described it, a battle between "the lesser of two evils", which was no choice at all.[10] The bookmakers put Labour's odds at 40 to 1 to win. What we called for was a vote for those who stood under the banner of a socialist alternative. The campaign was effective and the results established a good platform upon which to go forward. Overall, the Socialist Alliance pulled over 50,000 votes in England and Wales, with 31 candidates winning over 1,000 votes each. The Green Party doubled its votes compared to 1997, scoring 166,000 in 144 seats. The SLP stood with some important results as did independents.

Labour spokespersons like Jack Straw sought to explain the fact that millions turned away from the electoral process as an expression of the "politics of contentment". Yet this election took place against the backdrop of strikes amongst postal workers, the threat of strike action by rail workers, riots in Oldham and Leeds, and big clashes in Aylesbury. It represented a significant deepening of the Americanisation of British politics. Poll expert John Curtice wrote that Labour "is no longer clearly the party of the working class or of those on the left in Britain. Its support fell by four percentage points in the most predominantly working class seats, while the party held its own in middle class seats. Some of those votes appear to be lost on an unprecedented scale to parties of the far left."[11]

The 10.5 million votes for New Labour were actually lower than the number that Labour got when it was defeated under Neil Kinnock in 1992. Strikingly, there was a 6,000 drop in those who voted for Blair in his own constituency in comparison with 1997 – a 10% fall in turnout. We commented that voters took revenge on the aristocrats of New Labour in areas where the Millbank machine imposed its favourite sons or daughters on local Labour parties. For instance, Tory defector Shaun Woodward, who ran the anti-Labour propaganda for the Tories in the 1992 election, managed to reduce New Labour's majority in the St Helen's constituency by 50%.

In contrast, and highly significantly, was a radical fighting campaign conducted in the constituency of Wyre Forest where the candidate was a retired doctor. He defeated a Labour minister on the issue of the closure of Kidderminster Hospital and the removal of its services 80 miles away from where most people lived! Here, the turnout was significantly higher than the national average. This and the votes for socialists were indications of the new possibilities opening up. In fact, it was a symptom of a massive revolt against the privatisations carried out assiduously by New Labour. Faced with this mounting criticism they switched their approach slightly. In place of the mammoth manifesto promise to privatise everything not nailed down, they launched the slogan: 'Education and Hospitals First.' We commented: "If they were honest, they would have added at the end of the phrase, 'to be privatised.'"

This is precisely what happened under subsequent Labour governments, with education seeing the widespread introduction of academies, the further privatisation of the NHS and the dismantling of local government. At this stage polls showed 72% were opposed to privatisation and demanded the immediate renationalisation of Railtrack. Even sections of the capitalists, such as writers in the Financial Times and the Independent had made the case for rail renationalisation. The Daily Mail joined in, advocating that the railways should be taken back into public ownership. In an opinion poll 42% of those questioned suggested that even British Telecom should be renationalised. Yet it was clear that Blair, Brown and the New Labour cabal would take no notice, wedded as they were to a further programme of neo-liberal measures which had been at the core of the government's previous four years in office.

Meanwhile, the Tory party was traumatised having been at the receiving end of its worst results since the 1830s. Its so-called 'left', led by Ken Clarke and former 'wets' like Michael Heseltine, pursued a policy of what we called 'counter-revolutionary defeatism' of their own party. They clearly recognised that they were going to be defeated under Hague but wanted the biggest possible defeat in order to "bring the Tory party to its senses". They dreamt of the recreation of 'One Nation' Toryism but the soil for this to take root had disappeared through the ongoing and organic crisis of capitalism.

It was this that forced subsequent Tory leaders to lurch from 'one nationism' to right-wing flirtations with Thatcherism. This is illuminated by the political evolution of David Cameron, who later became prime minster. Originally, he flirted with so-called 'compassionate conservatism' only to move towards the right with his Chancellor George Osborne under the whip of the economic crisis. We commented just after the 2001 general election: "It is possible that the Tory party will be effectively marginalised and defeated in a third general election, so out of tune are they with modern Britain. In this election, the vote for the far-right, neo-fascist British National Party in Oldham was significant, where they came third in two constituencies with a combined total of 11,000 votes. This was a warning to the Labour movement and socialists."[12]

This time there would not even be a semblance of the euphoria which greeted Blair's first victory. His second term, we predicted, would be "more turbulent than the first". So it proved to be. Belatedly, union leaders warned Blair of this. Even Dave Prentis of Unison and Ken Livingstone came out and said that private companies would not run public services more effectively. Unlike in 1997, public sector workers in particular had not greeted Labour's re-election with any enthusiasm. There was a recognition that it was going to be four or five years of more of the same. Incredibly, one of Blair's chief cheerleaders, Sir Ken Jackson of the AEEU, echoed the idea raised by Cabinet ministers that strikes should be outlawed in essential services! Time magazine wrote that, despite a seemingly unassailable position, "Britain's real problems could crush [Blair] after election day". They cited trains, schools, hospitals, race, crime and the euro as just some of the big immediate headaches he would face. Others would include the underlying economic situation, growing unemployment and sleaze, as well as strikes. The German magazine Stern warned that Blair's much vaunted claim for economic progress was for a country that had a "Third World infrastructure".[13]

Many of the policies he intended to pursue had been flagged up before the election. Blair reaffirmed his commitment to big business, telling Forbes magazine he wanted to make Britain "the number one place to do business in the world". He boasted of Britain's "flexible labour market", and said: "I want to see far more emphasis on entrepreneurship in schools, far closer links between universities and business." The Sun, still supporting Labour because it still supported Murdoch, called Brown "a socialist chancellor". Nothing was further from the truth as Brown spent less in his first two years than the Tories would have spent had they remained in office after 1997. Public spending was cut by 0.6% in Labour's first two years. The Tories spent more on the NHS.[14]

39. The CWI's history and work in Ireland 1995-2005

Ireland, posing sharply the approach of socialists towards the national question, occupied a key position from the inception of Militant. This was the first country in which we acquired forces outside our original base in Britain. We formulated our political position in the late 1960s when Ireland burst into a prominent position. This has stood the test of time, even with the many twists and turns in the situation.

This arose from a visit I made in 1969 to the city of Derry/Londonderry at the invitation of Paul Jones, who had previously lived in London and had joined our ranks. Discussions were held with individuals like Eamon McCann, who we had also known in London but who later became a member of the SWP. I was introduced to other figures on the side of the workers and youth then gathered in the Northern Ireland Labour Party, resisting Loyalist attacks on the Catholic/nationalist population. Through this initial discussion many others were won to our ranks including the late Cathy Harkin. I also went to Dublin but drew a blank in gaining support for our ideas in terms of potential contacts and sympathisers.

Beginning with work in the North – added to later with the winning of others such as Peter Hadden who was to play an important role in the development of our Irish section – we established over time a very strong base in Southern Ireland as well. This has been reflected in the great success of our comrades over a number of years, which resulted in winning key people like Joe Higgins. Following him came others like Kevin McLoughlin and, from Northern Ireland, Niall Mulholland who became an important part of the leadership of our Irish section, and his brother Ciaran, together with Stephen Boyd. Niall subsequently moved to London and is now a member of the CWI's International Secretariat. Kevin is the national organiser of the Socialist Party Ireland. Joe and the Socialist Party had the distinction of winning a seat in the Irish Parliament (the Dáil) in the 1990s on a socialist, Marxist revolutionary programme. This was all the more remarkable given that it was achieved before the complete exhaustion of the greatest economic boom which the country had ever faced – the so-called 'Celtic Tiger'. Capitalist 'experts' believed it would mean that workers would be impervious to a radical socialist message.

We opposed the terrorist campaign in Northern Ireland of the Irish Republican Army (IRA) from the outset, explaining that an armed guerrilla tactic, located primarily in urban areas and based on a minority, the Catholic population, could not succeed in defeating British imperialism. Nor could it overcome the opposition of the Protestant population, who then constituted two thirds of the population of Northern Ireland, to force Irish unification on a capitalist basis. We counterposed the need to unify the workers of the North on a class and socialist basis.

In the third edition of the Militant International Review, we wrote: "The only way to undermine the power of British Imperialism and their capitalist allies North and South of the border, as the only way of bringing about real unity, is through class unity." This was shown by the election of Bernadette Devlin on the basis of an astounding 92% turnout and the vote of 6,000 Protestant farmers and workers, demonstrating the way forward for the working class. But for it to be guaranteed of long-term success, it had to be channelled through the organised labour movement.[1]

This was a precondition if the whole of Ireland was to be unified – if, indeed, that was the choice of the peoples of Ireland. This was possible on a socialist basis but impossible through the methods and programme of capitalism and its parties – or by terroristic methods. This meant serious work would have to be pursued through the trade unions, the factories and workplaces in order to cement unity amongst the working class. The achievements of the cwi's Irish section – both North and South – over decades in defending this approach have stood out. We have had comrades killed, intimidated and threatened by sectarian paramilitaries for sticking doggedly to the tasks they set themselves and had significant results on occasions.

Our original stand and consistent work were dramatically confirmed when the IRA leadership, after a long period of behind the scenes negotiations, called a ceasefire in August 1994. Our Northern Ireland comrades declared: "The British and Irish establishments have co-operated to produce a re-echo of the 1973-74 Sunningdale Agreement. Then, the IRA opposed that deal as a sell-out to Unionism while the Protestant working class reaction in the form of the 1974 [Ulster Workers' Council] strike swept it away as a sell-out to Dublin."[2]

From the negotiations came the Framework Document on Northern Ireland in 1995. We pointed out that it was an 'agreement at the top' amongst essentially pro-capitalist politicians. This would not solve the underlying problems which bred sectarianism: high unemployment, inadequate housing, the segregated education system. The agreement did not contain anything about jobs, decent wages, properly funded public services or opposition to privatisation. We commented: "How could it? It was produced by two governments – the Irish and British governments – who stand for privatisation, low wages and exploitation."[3]

Following a brief resumption of fighting after the breakdown of the 1994 ceasefire, the IRA declared a further ceasefire in July 1997, which reflected the dramatic shift of Sinn Féin and the abandonment of two decades of armed struggle. It was the Republican leadership and not the British ruling class which had shifted ground. Gone were pledges to self-determination for all the people of Ireland, as well as British action to persuade the Protestants to accept a united Ireland. There were references in the agreement to cross-border bodies but this was a sop to allow the Republican leadership to sell this deal to their rank and file as a stepping stone to a united Ireland. However, Unionists insisted that the institutions set up be accountable to the Northern Ireland Assembly as well as the Dáil.

Over the following years leaders on both sides were engaged in a process of trying to condition Catholics and Protestants to accept this arrangement as 'power sharing'. The negotiations were punctuated by the resurrection of sectarian outrages and it appeared sometimes as though any agreement hung by a thread and would break down, possibly resulting in sectarian civil war. However, after decades of conflict there was a pronounced 'war weariness' on both sides of the divide. The mood in the mid-1990s was entirely different to 1974. This time, middle class Protestants seemed to acquiesce and the local organisation of the employers' body, the CBI, welcomed it. Even in Protestant working class areas the predominant mood was that it was time for talking, not fighting. Paramilitaries and ex-paramilitaries were reluctant to be the unthinking foot soldiers again for warlike middle class politicians.

Our sister party in Northern Ireland, Militant Labour, gave critical support to the referendum on the Good Friday Agreement, concluded at Easter 1998 by Blair's New Labour government, the Irish government and the Northern Ireland parties, including Sinn Féin. Our comrades welcomed the situation because a new space had opened up which could hopefully see the re-emergence of class politics. As on all occasions like this it was necessary to invoke, particularly for the new generation, past examples of working class unity which could be taken up by working people in the period opening up. To this end, Militant Labour sought to convince workers from both sides of the divide – and neither – to apply these lessons.

Predictably, the attempt to open up a dialogue between workers, leading to class unity between Catholics and Protestants, was attacked in Ireland, Britain and internationally. Our comrades were denounced for even talking to the Progressive Unionist Party (PUP), the political wing of the Protestant paramilitary Ulster Volunteer Force (UVF). In the eyes of hidebound political sectarians this represented a sell-out to Unionism and British imperialism. The fact that the two giants of the Irish Labour movement, James Connolly and James Larkin, had endeavoured to do the same thing was a book sealed with seven seals to such critics. In 1907 Larkin had organised workers to march together in support of strikes, even going to the lengths of organising Orange and Green bands. Connolly did the same in 1911. Moreover, in 1932, at the time of the 'unemployed riots' – protests against the slashing of unemployment pay (outdoor relief) – workers came together in Belfast from the mainly Protestant Shankill Road and the predominantly Catholic Falls Road. A real opportunity was presented to cement class unity. Unfortunately, there was then no organisation or party able to build a non-sectarian movement on firm political foundations.

As we predicted, events showed that the 'peace agreement' in 1998 did not eliminate sectarianism. In fact, the increasing number of 'peace walls' separating communities meant that Northern Ireland was more divided, in a sense, than before the Good Friday Agreement. At times, subsequently, it has appeared as though Northern Ireland was once more on the verge of sectarian civil war: after the Omagh bombing, the aftermath of the Warrington bombs, during the stand-off at Drumcree, or the many clashes which ensued over parades. What helped to prevent this nightmare, above all, was the intervention of the organised working class through the trade unions, with Militant Labour playing a key role in this process.

For instance, when sectarian attacks began again in 1996, not just in Northern Ireland but in London, working class demonstrations involving 100,000 people took to the streets in towns and cities across Northern Ireland on Sunday 25 February. Massive crowds assembled, with 50,000 in Belfast, 20,000 in Derry and 7,000 in

Coleraine. This was preceded by two weeks of rallies and protests with hundreds of thousands participating in peace phone-ins and letter-writing protests to the paramilitaries and politicians. The Provisional IRA leadership of Gerry Adams and Martin McGuinness, in particular, managed to sell the agreement to IRA members because of a number of important changes that had taken place, particularly within the besieged Catholic population of the North. Kevin McLoughlin had summed up the situation following the Canary Wharf bombing in London in 1996: "In the South of Ireland the vast majority have never supported the Provos' campaign and opposed this bombing outright."[4]

Previously, Protestant paramilitaries had decided to pursue a brutal and ruthless 'counter-terrorist' campaign in answer to the IRA. This involved the indiscriminate murder of entirely innocent Catholics, exerting pressure on the Catholic community through sheer terror, the fear of indiscriminate murder and violence. This is detailed in the book Loyalist by Peter Taylor.[5] It compelled the IRA to tone down and eventually abandon its campaign which, in turn, led to the Loyalist paramilitaries also declaring ceasefires. This uneasy situation threatened to fall apart at times but held largely because of the overwhelming desire for peace and the pressure of the labour movement to ensure that this would be the case. This was on display after one of the biggest terrorist outrages, the Omagh bombing by dissident Republicans in 1998.

A huge wave of anger swept across Northern Ireland. The trade union movement stepped into the situation with shop stewards approaching management in the factories. This resulted in a number of enterprises closing for a period, reflecting the revulsion at this outrage (probably committed by a split from the Provisional IRA). Stalls set up by members of the Socialist Party (the new name of the CWI in Northern Ireland) were inundated with people who wanted to sign petitions calling for a one-day general strike. Many considered this the minimum that was required. The mood was generally non-sectarian – Catholics and Protestants were similarly outraged – with even demands that the bombers should be 'bombed'.

The Real IRA, the organisation from which the bombers came, was besieged and its leaders forced to flee their homes. Other Republican paramilitaries, like the Irish National Liberation Army (INLA), were forced to consider a ceasefire.

From 1996 onwards, the history of Northern Ireland has been marked by endless proposals for lasting peace from the British government and its Irish counterparts. This then inevitably breaks down, resulting in upheavals and splits within the paramilitary organisations, followed by a revival of peace negotiations. In all this, none of the major issues confronting working class people – jobs, housing and education – have been solved. Neither the IRA or its civilian face, Sinn Féin, nor any of its Loyalist counterparts could solve any of the social problems confronting the working class of Northern Ireland. Inevitably, in this situation, and without any concrete gains accruing to the paramilitaries, ceasefires broke down. Sinn Féin, on the other hand, having turned to the political front, increased its vote to 15.5% in the 'Forum Elections' of 1996, its biggest share since the 1950s. Yet fearing a split it initially hesitated to enter the Forum, an institution set up to enshrine the peace process.

However, Sinn Féin was eventually forced to bite the bullet and enter these institutions – including the Assembly at Stormont later, taking responsibility for policing and security. The net result of the peace process, as we pointed out, was to harden the sectarian divide. Marxists had no illusions in the process but were not prepared to just stand aside when a serious conflict could easily spill over into sectarian fighting or worse, a civil war. Merely proclaiming against sectarianism was not enough. Nor was it sufficient to issue general propaganda in favour of unity between different religions on a socialist and class basis. It was necessary to give answers, to provide possible solutions in a very polarised situation.

One of the thorniest questions was the issue of parades. What should the solution be when communities demand the right to organise traditional parades? Sometimes parades by the Orange Order were construed by Catholics as intimidatory, especially as the Royal Ulster Constabulary (RUC) was considered a paramilitary force biased towards the Protestants and without authority in the Catholic population. When parades took place, the police were perceived as hemming in local residents who consequently felt threatened. Similarly, Protestants, when denied access to a traditional route, believed that their rights were being taken away.

The response of Militant Labour in Northern Ireland to these conflicts was to recognise that equal rights could only be settled by negotiation. During the parade stand-offs in the late 1990s, Militant Labour recognised the right of the Apprentice Boys to march through the city "except for the section of the walls overlooking [the Catholic area of] the Bogside". This was seen as reasonable and fair in the circumstances. Our comrades declared that they were "opposed to sectarian organisations such as the Orange Order and its equivalents on the Catholic side. However, we respect the right of these organisations to march and to do so freely... Local agreements acceptable to all could be worked out... Where there are agreements over parades, there should be no police presence, rather the stewarding... should be left in the hands of the community representatives."[6]

While our comrades were swimming against the stream to some extent in the North this was not the case in the South of Ireland. Even while the Celtic Tiger was in full swing, Joe Higgins, representing Militant Labour, almost won the Dublin West by-election for the Dáil in early 1996. Joe has a long history of struggle for the ideas of the CWI within the ranks of the Irish labour movement. He had been a leading member of the Labour Party, until it became corrupted and transformed into a bourgeois party. He then became a Militant Labour councillor, prominent activist and leader in the anti-water charges campaign in the 1990s. He and Militant Labour campaigned to enter the Dáil, but linked this with the fight against the government's new water charges which would hit Dublin's poorest areas severely. They called for an organised mass non-payment campaign similar to the anti-poll tax struggle in Britain. As with the renewed water charges campaign from 2014 onwards, the Labour Party in 1996 was participating in a coalition government, then led by Fianna Fáil, the main capitalist party. Joe came within a whisker of winning the by-election, losing by only 370 votes on the final count.

The Socialist Party, as it was now called in Ireland, stood five candidates, all in the Dublin area and closely associated with the anti-water charges campaign. Candidates also stood in Tipperary and Cork. Despite the extensive boom, the economic situation was not what it seemed. The cream was being skimmed off by the elite. A recent poll had shown that 62% said they had not experienced the feel-good factor. The figure for skilled workers rose to 75%. Socialist Party candidates stood on the platform of only taking the average worker's wage and donating the rest to the Socialist Party and the labour movement. Opposition to water charges was the centrepiece of the campaign. Other issues which came up included a huge drug problem which was plaguing Dublin. The failure of the state in this field resulted in a massive community-based movement to tackle drug dealing and provide help for addicts. The Socialist Party played a leading role on this issue in a number of areas. Joe Higgins's campaign was a triumph for genuine socialist ideas. Once in the Dáil, he became a model representative of the wider labour movement in opposition to Irish freebooter capitalism.

Many Southern Irish workers felt as though they had not been invited to the Celtic Tiger party. As the rich and powerful gorged themselves Joe Higgins and the Socialist Party helped to organise the working class and poor in the mass campaign which defeated the attempt to introduce water charges. In 2002 he stood in the election and was once more triumphant. His re-election confirmed that the shine was beginning to be taken off the economic upswing; more a stooping tiger than a crouching one now!

One beneficial effect of the boom was the huge changes in the Irish working class. It had assumed a more dynamic and concentrated character, with significant sections of women absorbed into the workforce. Much of the population lived in the Dublin area, which was experiencing increasing health, traffic, housing and education chaos. This in turn led to a greater determination to challenge the capitalist establishment with many workers looking for a real alternative. Joe and the Socialist Party were able to tap into this mood. Parties which were seen to stand outside the capitalist establishment – also, to some extent, the Greens and Sinn Féin, along with independents – saw a big increase in their vote. Joe was re-elected as a TD (MP) in Dublin West, coming second out of the constituency's three elected candidates, increasing his vote.

However, the overall results showed that it was business as usual. Bertie Ahern's ruling Fianna Fáil emerged as the biggest party. On the basis of this election, Sinn Féin was regarded, at least by its own voters, as being in opposition to the Irish political establishment and picked up five TDs. It distributed an abundance of glossy material and organised expensive stunts, including hiring planes with huge display banners over Dublin West two days before the vote. The press predictably played up Sinn Féin and the Green Party, while virtually ignoring the Socialist Party. While there was disappointment that the Socialist Party had not been able to elect another TD, there was a confidence that Joe's experience of winning after losing first time out would be repeated in the future. Even with one TD the media played down the significance of Joe's re-election, referring to the Socialist Party as 'independents', while building up the success of Sinn Féin.

But it was not long before the Socialist Party was in the thick of the resistance to government attacks. Joe Higgins and Clare Daly were arrested and sentenced to a month in prison in Mountjoy jail for their part in the campaign against the imposition of bin charges. These events became front page news and a major talking point with Socialist Party representatives debating against government ministers and other establishment figures on national TV and radio. The jailings were clearly an attempt to deal a crushing blow to the Socialist Party which had become a constant thorn in the side of the government. Prime Minister Bertie Ahern, who had been mercilessly subjected to attacks by Joe Higgins in the Dáil, personally defended the jailings. Asked why he had previously objected when another TD was jailed for protesting in defence of Dublin traders, he tried to draw a distinction by saying that the other TD was "a nice man"!

The bin charges attack on the working class was a symptom of the mounting economic problems for Southern Irish capitalism, with growth slowing dramatically to close to zero. The gap between rich and poor was the second highest in the advanced industrial countries. The real legacy of the Celtic Tiger was that 40% of Irish children were living on or below the poverty line. During the 'economic miracle', the super-rich managed to avoid paying taxes and Joe Higgins had exposed the corrupt practices of politicians, receiving bribes in 'brown envelopes'. Councils reacted to the bin tax non-payment campaign by declaring that they would no longer collect the rubbish off non-payers. This was met with mass leafleting by the anti-bin tax campaigners suggesting blockades to stop bin lorries if collections were stopped. The centre of the protest was in the Fingal area, with Joe Higgins and Ruth Coppinger playing a role in the resistance, and in Dublin North.

The right-wing General Secretary of the Irish Congress of Trade Unions (ICTU), David Begg, attacked the campaign and accused Joe and Clare Daly of leading people into "imprisonment in pursuit of a political objective". Joe roundly condemned this "stab in the back" in the first public statement he was able to make from his prison cell.[7] The campaign spread to the Greater Dublin area with the bin service effectively shut down in October by pickets of bin depots organised by the four anti-bin tax campaigns throughout the city. The action had been called in response to the jailing of 13 other people, most of them residents of Fingal and other parts of Dublin. Eventually, Joe and Clare were released declaring themselves "proud, unrepentant, defiant and more determined".[8]

The esteem amongst working people that Joe Higgins and the Socialist Party had built up was reinforced when he and Socialist Party councillor Mick Murphy lifted the lid in 2005 on the ruthless exploitation of foreign, mainly Turkish, workers in Dublin employed by the infamous GAMA construction company. It was revealed that this firm, with major government and local authority contracts in Ireland, had for years been working its migrant work-force excessively: up to twelve hours a day, seven days a week. "What we have is mass fraud, a grand larceny of workers' wages," said Joe.[9]

GAMA then claimed that it had deposited the rest of the workers' wages in accounts with the Dutch-based Finansbank. The workers knew nothing about these accounts so Joe and Mick took four former employees of GAMA to Amsterdam, walked into the Dutch bank and spoke to stunned officials, demanding the workers' access to their accounts! One worker had €24,000 yet had known nothing about the account's existence! It was estimated that as much as €40 million of the workers' money had been deposited in this bank. These revelations led to demonstrations of 300 workers from GAMA sites in Dublin in an unofficial protest against the company's below minimum wage payments. They were joined by Joe and other workers on a march to the Dáil and Liberty Hall, the headquarters of the country's largest trade union, SIPTU. This action eventually brought some recompense to the workers but it also highlighted the systematic actions of the bosses to cheat very low-paid workers out of even the minimal pittance that was due to them.[10]

Workers and parents marched as part of the successful campaign in 2007 to save school dinners in Waltham Forest, east London.
Photo: Paul Mattsson

Linda Taaffe (right) on the steps of Waltham Forest Town Hall and Nancy Taaffe, with then Labour leader Clyde Loakes looking, on following his announcement of the council's u-turn on scrapping the school dinner subsidy.
Photo: Paul Mattsson

School students in Hackney, east London, protest against academisation in 2006.
Photo: Paul Mattsson

Left: Young members of the Socialist Party played a key role in mobilising for a mass demonstration in 1998. Right: The late Socialist Party councillor Rob Windsor campaigning with the call for a movement of mass non-payment to make tuition fees unworkable.
Photos: Socialist Party

Over 200 of the workers out of the 240 Unison branch members joined the picket over the two-day strike at Whipps Cross hospital in East London in 2006 led by Len Hockey.
Photo: Molly Cooper

Health cuts was the issue around which a successful campaign was conducted to have Socialist Party member and GP Jackie Grunsell (holding megaphone) elected as a councillor in 2006
Photos: Socialist Party

Left: The mass demo on 15 February 2003 against war in Iraq. Photo: Molly Cooper
Right: ISR and the Socialist Party called for school students strikes which first took place on 7 March (pictured in Lewisham, South London) and the day war started. Photo: S Sachs

Socialist Students and ISR's 'Red Bloc' on the March 2005 anti-war demo. 'No to war and terrorism. No to racism'
Photo: Alison Hill

315

Launch of the book, Liverpool: a city that dared to fight, with l-r Peter Taaffe, Ken Smith and Tony Mulhearn.
Photo: Militant

Terry Fields, Jeremy Corbyn and Dave Nellist, left Labour MPs on a demo against the witch-hunt.
Photo: Militant

Joe Higgins TD celebrates the victory of Turkish workers who won back stolen wages from ruthless exploiter Gama in 2005.
Photo: Socialist Party Ireland

With a bold approach, Socialism 2005, the party's main annual public event saw attendance double on the previous year. L-R: Sascha Stanicic, Joe Higgins, Sarah Sachs-Eldridge, Hannah Sell, Jane James and Peter Taaffe.
Photo: Paul Mattsson

317

Siri Jayasuria and Peter Taaffe at the conference of the United Socialist Party, the CWI affiliate in Sri Lanka.
Photo: Paul Mattsson

CWI contingent on a march in Belgium with Bill Mullins marching alongside members of the CWI in Belgium.
Photo: Paul Mattsson

250,000 marched on the biggest demonstration Edinburgh had ever seen to Make Poverty History in 2005. The CWI contingent – with comrades from England and Wales, Scotland, Belgium, France, Sweden, Germany and elsewhere staying in a camp near Edinburgh – made a magnificent socialist intervention in this demonstration. Photo: Paul Mattsson

A great sea of red filled the meeting hall after the march, with about 160 packed in and half that number again listening outside. Left: Peter Taaffe addresses the meeting. Above right: the audience. Below right: The energy on the CWI bloc. Photos: Paul Mattsson

The CWI on the anti-capitalist march in Genoa, 2001. We declared that the time was ripe to move beyond the mood of "anti-the system" to a specifically socialist approach. The hundreds of thousands of protesters faced tear gas and police violence.
Photos: Socialist Party

The connection between the policies of Thatcher and the privatisation drive of the Blairites was increasingly understood by working class people - even the kids could see it!
Photo: Socialist Party

In the May 1999 local election Ian Page was victorious in the Pepys ward, Lewisham, South London, receiving 40% of the vote. His victory was all the sweeter given that he had been expelled from the Labour Party when he was a councillor for the crime of fighting against cuts in jobs and services. Photos: Socialist Party

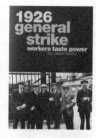

Left: a book signing event for The Rise of Militant and right: some of the books produced during this period
Photos: Socialist Party

In 2001 we were unaware that a police spy had been deployed within our ranks. Known to us as 'Carlo Neri', here he is present at meeting in Italy with Peter Taaffe.
Photo: Socialist Party

We had launched the Campaign Against Domestic Violence (CADV) in 1991 and its second conference with 250 delegates took place in London in November 1995 with Christine Thomas playing a key role.
Photo: Socialist Party

The main campaign around which Militant Labour developed anti-racist work was the Youth Against Racism in Europe (YRE), which was international. Pictured, Hugo Pierre.
Photo: Socialist Party

International Socialist Resistance organised protests against the racist asylum policy of Blair's governments. Socialist Party members were involved in many defence campaigns against deportations.
Photo: Socialist Party

Karen McKay: "We stand for the possibility of alternatives to privatised services and for change... we argue to fight for more."

Top: left, Councillor Karen McKay; secomd from left, Councillor Rob Windsor; centre, Martin Reynolds; right, Councillor Dave Nellist. Bottom: Councillors Chris Flood and Ian Page. Inset: Councillor Sam Dias

Photos: Socialist Party

Alan Hardman provided cartoons that summed up the essence of Blairism.

Bromley Council ordered a disciplinary investigation against Glenn Kelly (right). There was clear collusion with the council by Unison officials.
Photo: Socialist Party

Second from left, Chris Baugh PCS assistant general secretary, second from right, Janice Godrich, PCS president, right, Mark Serwotka, PCS general secretary.
Photo: Socialist Party

The late Bob Crow, general secretary of the RMT, at the union's conference on political representation. Photo: Paul Mattsson

Left, Roger Bannister; Above, Martin Powell-Davies.
Photos: Socialist Party

During this period members and observers of the Executive Committee included: Judy Beishon, Clive Heemskirk, Lois Austin, Bill Mullins, Hannah Sell, Paula Mitchell, Ken Smith, Jane James, Lynn Walsh, Sarah Sachs-Eldridge, Chris Thomas and Peter Taaffe

Many of the regional organisers during this time: Steve Score, Elaine Brunskill, Dave Griffiths, Hugh Caffrey, Alistair Tice, Alec Thraves, Robin Clapp, Dave Reid, Nick Chaffey, Chris Moore, Jim Horton, Jackie Grunsell, Chris Newby. Editorial staff included: Roger Shrives, Alison Hill, Dave Carr. Printshop staff included: Keith Pattenden, Mick Cotter, the late John Sharpe, Mark Pickersgill

Photos: various

CWI organisers: Tony Saunois, Clare Doyle, Bob Labi, Niall Mulholland, TU Senan, Philip Stott (Scotland).
Party organisers and staff included: Kevin Parslow, Manny Thain, Ken Douglas, John Reid, Keith Dickinson, Pete Mason, Matt Dobson, Ben Robinson, Neil Cafferky, Bob Severn, Rob Williams, Naomi Byron, Kieran Roberts, Clare James
Photos: various

40. The effects of setbacks 1997-2001

The world capitalist economy sets the scene for our perspectives, our programme and, ultimately, how we intervene in the labour movement. We fully recognise, as we have explained throughout this book, that economic prospects are decisive in shaping events – although not necessarily directly or immediately. As we have explained previously, the formulation of our programme and analysis was the product of a collective discussion and debate throughout our organisation. We are proud of the fact that our economic analysis made at each stage stood the test of time and events. The leading bodies of our organisation, the Executive and National Committees, as well as the International Secretariat and International Executive Committee were closely involved in this task. But of course, individuals made significant contributions to this analysis: Lynn Walsh, myself and others, including individual comrades like Robin Clapp, the long-time Regional Secretary in the South-West. Accordingly, on the basis of the political victory for capitalism as a consequence of the collapse of Stalinism and the planned economy, we envisaged that the 1990s would be difficult for us and the labour movement. We expected that a certain economic growth, though it would be uneven, was likely to take place in the foreseeable future.

However, this did not prevent us from assiduously analysing at each stage the peculiar one-sided character of this boom: the piling up of debt, the underlying 'depressionary' features inherited from the 1980s: low growth, rising inequality, low and stagnant wages, the disappearance of high-paid full-time jobs and their replacement with part-time, precarious employment. In short, this saw the emergence of the 'precariat' in low paid and insecure jobs, which is now almost a fixed feature of neo-liberal capitalism. It was also necessary to combat the propaganda of the capitalists, summed up in the phrase of Francis Fukuyama, that "history had ended". From this flowed the political capitulation of the summits of the labour movement, the Blairites and their right-wing counterparts in the trade unions. There were also some 'Marxists' who were in danger of succumbing to the colossal pressure which bore down on those who still adhered to a socialist perspective.

Not for the first time, Marxism had been thrown back. In the 19th century, the boom that followed the revolutions of 1848-51 led to the complete collapse of Chartism and the political isolation of Karl Marx and Friedrich Engels. The workers' movement revived somewhat in the 1860s, which led to the creation of the First International, through the efforts of Marx and Engels. Then the defeat of the Paris Commune of 1871 set back the workers' movement once again. The boom of 1896-1914 saw the building of the workers' movement but led to a reformist softening of the leadership of the mass social democratic parties, culminating in their siding with their own national bourgeoisie – social patriotism – in the First World War. Equally, Lenin and Trotsky were isolated following the defeat of the first Russian revolution of 1905-07. They nevertheless patiently prepared for the future by soberly analysing all the factors which led to the consolidation and strengthening of capitalism, but also those processes which would inevitably undermine it – and would lead to a revival of the workers' movement.

In the pages of the Socialist and Socialism Today, together with all the journals of the Committee for a Workers' International, a very rich analysis of economic processes had helped to sustain and breed confidence in the ranks of our party and International. We had been reduced in numbers it is true, but we were still capable of making a significant contribution to the theoretical arsenal of

Marxism and the labour movement. In article after article we countered with facts, figures and arguments the myth sedulously fos-
tered by the capitalists and their echoes within the labour movement like Brown, that a new economic paradigm had been created,
that 'modern' capitalism had overcome its contradictions and that
the boom-bust cycle had been abolished.

Confirmation was not long in coming as the first eruptions
developed in the 1997 economic crisis – beginning in Southeast
Asia but reflected throughout the world. Then in the 1998 economic
meltdown in Russia, followed by the bursting of the dot.com bubble at the turn of the 21st century. These were the precursors for the
devastating slump of 2007-08. Even before this, the signs of an
impending crisis were clear. A massive speculative bubble had
fuelled the growth of the world economy with share prices reaching
dizzying heights as the stock exchange sharks sought to cash in on
growing company profits, which had risen to peak levels. George
Soros symbolised the world of the spivs and speculators who Marx
had described as "the pleasant company of swindlers". Soros had
accumulated a fortune through currency manipulation.

This reflected the domination of finance capital in the modern
era, sometimes described as financialisation. Speculation is a parasitic tendency of capitalism on the back of the banking system but
it had reached epidemic proportions. Moreover, the banks and
major industrial companies like carmakers were (and are) also
involved in speculation. Then there were junk bonds, which developed in the 1980s and enhanced the power of the speculators. James
Carville, one of Bill Clinton's aides, stated that if there was reincar-
nation, he would come back as the bond market because you could
intimidate everybody! In effect, the financial markets have more
power than governments. This was highlighted in this crisis.

Any real growth in the economy had been achieved mainly
through the intensified exploitation of the working class. The
underlying growth had been feeble, as had productivity. Ironically,
it was the Asian 'tigers', formerly growing at a faster rate than the
developed economies, that were now plunged into crisis. In early

1997 Blair had pointed towards the Asian economies as examples for British workers to emulate. But this 'model' of flexibility and deregulation meant cheap sweated labour – more perspiration than inspiration as far as workers were concerned. At the first signs of crisis we pointed out: "It will be the working class and the poor peasants of Southeast Asia who will pay the terrible price... Economic crises are inevitable [on the basis of capitalism] and will have a greater effect on the lives of working people than the worst volcanoes, earthquakes or hurricanes."[1]

A financial meltdown loomed in Asia. Speculative funds, so-called hot money, that had previously poured into the region now sought to flee to the 'safe haven' of the dollar. Some of the local capitalists like Prime Minister Mahathir Mohamad of Malaysia sought to prevent this outflow with capital controls. He had spooked the world financial markets by declaring: "The free-market system has failed." The crisis produced convulsions in Malaysia, a country that would become the third largest economy in Southeast Asia, reflecting the gains spilling over from China's growth. Now it had been thrown into reverse, generating more and more discontent. It was suffering from over-borrowing and overcapacity. The next day, Mahathir removed Anwar Ibrahim, identified as an apostle of 'free market' economics, as Finance and Deputy Prime Minister.

Anwar condemned this political conspiracy which included obviously trumped-up sexual charges. He launched the Reformasi campaign which chimed with the growing opposition of the masses as the crisis deepened. Mass rallies of upwards of 100,000 took place. In his youth, Anwar had been associated with campaigns to protect the people. He now invoked his past and sought alliances with opposition parties, such as the Islamic PAS and the socialist PSM, who later had connections with the CWI and had discussions with myself when I visited Malaysia a few years later.

Mahathir's stand on capital controls provoked opposition from Lee Kuan Yew, Prime Minister of Singapore, who feared that this could herald a backing away from globalised finance. Soros and the supporters of globalisation were also opposed because of the threat

335

this represented to world trade which had expanded massively in the previous period. This had been helped by the dismantling of national economic controls – the imposition of the 'free trade' loved by neo-liberals. The financial crash meant that the global flow of credit was sharply reduced to the area. This resulted in a vicious downward spiral of closures of businesses and rising unemployment. The International Monetary Fund (IMF), which was originally designed as a post-1945 Keynesian instrument to boost spending and help governments facing economic distress, now intervened to impose ruthless austerity. We predicted the inevitability of mass revolts. Workers carried banners in mass demonstrations which read: 'IMF – I aM Fired.'

The biggest capitalist powers, the US, Japan and Germany, were terrified at the prospect of South Korea's collapse and piled in help through an IMF bailout, but with 'bone carving' conditions. The intention of the dominant imperialist powers was to open up the Korean market to foreign competition. This neo-colonial stance outraged the national sensitivities of the Korean people given the occupation of the country and the national humiliations inflicted on them in the past. This in turn had compelled the Korean Confederation of Trade Unions (KCTU) to organise general strike action.

The newly elected Kim-Dae-Jung administration inevitably came into collision with the workers' organisations. The militant KCTU federation was accused of frightening investors off with its threat of renewed strike action because of the violent clashes that took place at the May Day demonstration in 1998, when 120,000 of its members protested in the first round of a campaign over job security and the right to life. The union was demanding the renegotiation of the IMF deal and an end to what it called 'illegal' redundancies that the giant conglomerates (chaebols) had imposed with the backing of the IMF. Thousands of Korean workers were thrown out of work, with no prospect of an income to maintain them and their families.

The 1997 crisis came ten years after the 1987 economic crisis.

These economic eruptions were never explained by the soothsayers of capitalism. No analysis was made as to why their system was periodically convulsed in this fashion. It was as if economic crises were an act, if not of god, then of nature's headwinds but all of them left in their wake massive economic damage and the wrecking of the lives and hopes of millions of workers. They produced revolutions of the downtrodden, exploited masses. Huge sections of the Indonesian population rose against Suharto and forced him from office. He was in Egypt when the major cities of Indonesia were engulfed by angry crowds who took vengeance for the new round of price rises.

The end of his regime, however, would not by itself guarantee a lifeline for the masses. A period of instability developed with the Indonesian people trying out one party after another only to find them wanting. Banned organisations like the People's Democratic Party held out the possibility of change. However, this organisation and its leaders such as Megawati, who came to power, were not prepared to go outside the framework of capitalism and carry through a socialist revolution in this nation of 17,000 islands. This would have sent shockwaves not just throughout the region but the world. Even the Financial Times characterised the post-Suharto regime as "an unfinished revolution".

The Asian crisis deepened in the following year and reverberated worldwide with gyrations on the world's stock exchanges starkly reflected in the plunge in share values in Russia. Capitalist commentators endlessly repeated that the 'fundamentals' of the system were sound and yet we witnessed the meltdown in Russia, another link in the chain of crises that was developing. Russia had been reduced to a smaller economy due to the restoration of capitalism which resulted in a world record drop in production of about 50%. Japan, which had bad debts of at least $1 trillion, was locked into what would become 'two lost decades'. This was an anticipation of what would happen to the whole global economy later.

The Asian crisis had triggered a sharp drop in world prices of oil, gas and metals, all vital Russian exports. This meant a dramatic drop in its national income. Some economists dismissed Russia's economy as being "too small" to exercise a big effect on the world economy but it had borrowed colossal sums in the world markets and faced a huge increase in the cost of imported goods. Moreover, Russia was the world's largest gas producer and supplied a large proportion of the world's oil, metals, gold and diamonds.

However, the 1998 economic collapse in Russia marked a new turn. It shattered the perspective, peddled by the oligarchic Russian capitalists, that Russia was on the road to rising living standards, if not of America then at least of West Germany. Our Russian comrades posed the question: "Who lost Russia?" Rob Jones wrote: "The new capitalist Russia has achieved in just eight years what the Soviet Union failed to do in 70 – threaten to bring down the whole capitalist system."[2]

The consequences of the jump in prices and falling production were felt in a dramatic increase in the non-payment of wages and actual layoffs. Western companies were withdrawing investment. Any company that relied on imported materials faced dramatically increased costs. At the same time the economy was being criminalised, a direct consequence of the restoration of capitalism, including the privatisation of state assets with huge industrial complexes transferred into private hands. Industrial production fell as a consequence from a 67% share of the economy in 1991 to 43% in 1998. So bad was the situation that the state was forced to step in and renationalise some sections of industry. In reality, the clock could not be turned back completely. The result was the existence of a form of state capitalism, a comfort blanket for the oligarchs and the gangster capitalists to plunder the assets of the peoples of Russia.

Despite the foregoing analysis, the picture presented by capitalist commentators of the period from 1998 onwards is one of steady recovery of the system. In reality, the world capitalist economy remained blighted. None of the problems had been solved. This was indicated by the insolvency and near collapse of Long-Term Capital Management (LTCM), a premier hedge fund. This brought the world financial system to the edge of meltdown. Only a rapid $3.6 billion rescue organised by the US Federal Reserve averted catastrophe. For the big financiers, LTCM was 'too big to fail', the very same reason used almost nine years later for bailing out the big banks. If LTCM had been allowed to collapse, then arguably the whole unstable financial house of cards would have gone down with it. Yet the financial 'authorities' were incapable of learning or doing anything to avert such potential catastrophes. Like the Bourbons, the capitalists and their representatives learned nothing and forgot nothing. By January 2001, Time magazine was once more warning: "Here comes the slump."

Some alleged Marxists have accused the Socialist Party of exaggeration, forecasting the dangers of 'imminent economic collapse'. Some even accused us of being 'primitive slumpists'. Our 'mistake' has been to warn the working class that the underlying trends in the economy result in a collapse and only the timing is unforeseeable. Yet we see that the more farsighted capitalist economists then and now seem to fall into the same 'trap' as the Socialist Party in issuing such warnings.

Time magazine went on to agree with much of the analysis of Marx: "Karl Marx theorised that capitalism was condemned to repeat depressions because of 'cycles of overproduction.'" It said that he got some details wrong but that, had he seen the US economy in the first week of January 2001, "he would no doubt have felt vindicated".[3] Similarly the Economist, in a special report on the world economy, stated: "One by one, economies around the world are stumbling. By cutting interest rates... the Federal Reserve hopes it can keep America out of recession. But in an increasing number of economies... GDP is already shrinking. Global industrial production fell at an annual rate of 6% in the first half of 2001."[4]

The dot.com 'revolution' had been hailed as a new saviour, a new field of investment and production, which would banish the prospects of a recession or slump. We showed earlier in our answer to the arguments of some of our former comrades in South Africa and Liverpool that we rejected this perspective. Microprocessors, even if applied on a wide scale, could not avert economic collapse. They were mostly used to improve accountancy in the retail sector, but new technology did not represent a massive new field of investment which would lead to growth in the productive forces and a new boom. This was confirmed in the collapse of the dot.com bubble, which looked as though it was going to initiate a widespread economic crisis and collapse. Indeed, this was only cut across by a huge injection of liquidity by the central banks which act as a backstop for the world economy, but only for a time. Ultimately, capitalism ran out of palliative measures. Throughout the globe, working class anger was growing. Even fervent advocates of capitalism like Bill Gates of Microsoft and investment guru George Soros realised that global capitalism was increasingly being questioned. Then in 2007-08 the scenario which we had sketched out and which was an integral part of our analysis came to pass.

41. The Dotcom Bubble bursts 2001-05

As commented previously, an ongoing analysis of trends in the world economy at each stage was a feature of the work both of the CWI and the Socialist Party. The change in the economic sphere of world capitalism in the early part of the 21st century led to a considerable amount of additional space given over to this question in our publications. This was necessary in order to prepare our comrades and workers we could reach for future developments. However, in approaching economic perspectives we are always conditional. Capitalism is a blind system, with economic developments unfolding behind the backs of society. Therefore, the real processes can only be fully revealed when statistics, facts and figures can be assembled afterwards, as Friedrich Engels commented in the 19th century.

This does not mean that it is impossible to analyse and predict the general character of processes in the contemporary economy as they are developing. The failure to do so would be a negation of the very essence of Marxism itself, substituting empiricism for an understanding of the laws of capitalism as worked out by Marx and Engels. Perspectives, we would emphasise, are only a rough approximation of developments. Nevertheless Marxism is the science of perspectives, which applies to the economic as well as to the political field. This necessitates the drawing of general conclusions at each stage, which can be added to and corrected as events develop.

However, the charge made by the capitalists, and their very small echoes on the outskirts of the labour movement, that Marxists in general, the CWI and Socialist Party in particular, were predicting a slump virtually every year is crude and childish. An examination of our written economic prognoses disproves this.

In the period prior to 2001, the capitalist economic pundits were upbeat for the prospects of their system, seemingly reinforced by the development of 'new technology', which offered a further boost to the system, they believed. We challenged this at each stage. In September 2000 the FTSE 100 fell to its lowest level for three years and prompted one fund manager to comment: "There is panic in the market and about what consumers will do. It is feeding on itself." Another described the situation as "very hairy and very scary". Manufacturing in Britain experienced its fourth recession in 10 years with one economist commenting "There is as yet not even a hint of a let-up in the pace of decline".

A symptom of the situation was the crisis of the former manufacturing giant Marconi. Faced with colossal overcapacity, in one year its share value plummeted from £30 billion to £800 million. Losses of £5 billion were expected in 2001 – one of the biggest collapses in corporate history. The company's creditworthiness was now junk status. This was accompanied by a bigger than expected rise in unemployment in the US, which in turn sent US share prices tumbling. Commentators who forecast a recovery just around the corner were now admitting that a recession seemed 'unavoidable'.

The interconnection between the different sectors of capitalism was demonstrated as a banker warned: "The main fear is that deteriorating job prospects will finally start to undermine consumer confidence, which is the only thing standing between the US and recession." The US Federal Reserve had already cut interest rates seven times within the previous year, to little effect. Moreover, the rest of the world was in no position to bail out the US economy. Argentina and Mexico were already in recession, Japan was on the brink after 10 years of virtually stagnant growth and output was slowing much faster than expected in Germany and the eurozone. According to the Economist, "The most striking aspect of the current slowdown is that it is more widespread than in previous world slumps in 1975, 1982, and 1991."[1]

The US economy, at that stage the Atlas of world capitalism as it sustained the rest of the world, faced its worst economic contraction since 1945. The Socialist pointed out that in the previous three months, the US's "gross domestic product (GDP) was shrinking at a 0.4% annual rate while consumer spending fell at its steepest rate for 14 years." Japan faced a deepening crisis and unemployment was on the increase in Europe. The World Bank reported: "The global economy is slipping precariously towards recession." The growth in world trade volume was slowing down to 2% or less a year from a record 12.5%, the sharpest drop in decades. We remarked: "This points to a serious crisis of global capitalism which could last for years. The world now has no major engine of growth."[2]

We concluded that the whole of 2001 was truly an 'annus horribilis' following the terrorist attack on the Twin Towers. An especially poignant moment was subsequently revealed: as the Twin Towers began to disintegrate, a spaceship with an international crew had passed over New York, which witnessed and photographed the full carnage below. We commented: "In that incident alone is encapsulated the choice which confronts the peoples of the world. Together, we can harness and develop science, technique, and the organisation of labour on a gigantic scale which would eliminate the poverty and oppression which created the conditions for 11 September. Or the products of the genius of humankind can be misused to create a world of horror without end.

"The choice is not between 'evil' or 'good' as George Bush or Tony Blair pretend. It is between outmoded rotten capitalism – which will be a world 'war without end' according to US Vice-President Dick Cheney – or a determination to share the resources of the planet for the benefit of all. This can only be fully achieved through world democratic socialism."

However, the current reality was a "'vicious circle of downward adjustment"' rippling out from the battered US economy to the rest of the world." The Guardian reported that the drop in US output in December 2001 was "almost three times faster than earlier estimates." But could Europe and Japan take up the slack created by the downturn in the US? In Japan, unemployment climbed to 5.4% of the workforce, the highest level ever recorded up to then. The eurozone was expecting that unemployment would rise by 700,000 to 12.5 million in the next year and 9 million were expected to be unemployed in 2002 in the US.

What were the causes of this looming crisis? We sought to explain this through Marxist perspectives: "There are many factors which can lead to or trigger a crisis in capitalism - such as the tendency for the rate of profit to fall and a sudden drop in profits."

This incidentally gives the lie to assorted dogmatic critics in the recent period that the Socialist Party had rejected Karl Marx's ideas on this issue. We accept his explanation of a tendency, over an extended period, for the rate of profits to decline. We also accept his explanation of the countervailing factors as well.[3] However, we went on to explain: "The ultimate contradiction of this system is that the working class cannot buy back the full value of what they produce. What Marx called 'surplus value' – profits – is that part which is appropriated by the capitalists. However, this contradiction – the working class not being able to buy back the full value of their product – is temporarily overcome by the capitalists reinvesting back into production.

"For a time, the economic cycle once more goes forward but then reaches a saturation point – a market glut of unsaleable goods – which Marx described as 'overproduction'. This is accompanied today by 'overcapacity'.

"Part of industry lies idle because the working class and the middle class, with stagnant or even contracting incomes, cannot buy back the goods which they produce. Hence the cycle of boom and bust, which like poverty, national oppression and the other ills which beset humanity, are organic to capitalism and cannot be 'reformed' away."

"The economic day of reckoning can sometimes be postponed on the basis of an injection of what Marx called 'fictitious capital' – massive borrowing which was a feature of the 1990s. The result is a huge piling up of debt; national debt as the case of Japan shows, corporate debt and personal debt."

This statement, while answering the dogmatists, explains how capitalism was able to postpone the looming crisis for a temporary period, evident in 2001 by a massive injection of what they called 'liquidity'. This postponed the 'day of reckoning' for a few years that nevertheless materialised in the 'Great Recession'. Indeed, we pointed out that short-term palliatives at this time had "even led to a renewed capitalist 'confidence' – in the teeth of the evidence to the contrary in the real economy – that the 'worst is over' and the revival of world capitalism is under way."[4]

This was an accurate description of the approach of capitalism in general at this stage. We correctly foretold how they can manage to put off a major crisis, which was in place even as early as 2001, only to reap the whirlwind later. Rates were slashed, with the base rate in the US dropping from 6.5% in 2001 to 0.75% in 2002. This was the explanation for the unusual resilience in consumer spending in what was still a recessionary phase in the business cycle, with abundant cheap credit for mortgages – which in turn led to the massive sub-prime crisis of 2006 – and consumer credit. This created a short-term spiral effect. An additional factor in this 'growth' was the running down of manufacturers and retailers' stocks. The growth of consumer spending alarmed even capitalist economists because 1.4 million workers had lost their jobs in the previous period, indicating the boom was built on credit. Investment was falling, one of the reasons being huge overcapacity in the US and the world.

At the same time, the parasitic and predatory character of 'modern' capitalism was exposed in the Enron scandal of 2002. This was one of the biggest companies and therefore one of the biggest scandals in the history of US capitalism. In the top ten of Fortune 500 companies, Enron fell from a "successful business model" to bankruptcy in less than a year. In this process was

revealed the involvement of the Bush regime. In return for millions of dollars of support for Bush, a climate of favouritism was
created, a sleazy, unregulated environment in which Enron
thrived. It had made fabulous profits gambling on future energy
deliveries, while at the same time rewarding its political collaborators, mostly the Republicans in the Bush White House. From a
total of $5.8 million spent in the previous 12 years of federal elec-
tions, 73% went to Republicans. Bush himself received almost $1
million, until the scandal broke, jovially referring to Kenneth Lay
– his Enron Godfather –– as 'Kenny boy'.

On 1 December 2001, "America's greatest company" filed for
bankruptcy with pensions completely worthless. "The upper-level
executives got their money," said one Enron worker. "I was let go by
voicemail... I don't think I'll ever trust another company."[5] This was
a scandal which exposed both the economic skulduggery at the
heart of capitalism and the close involvement of the political elite in
both the Republican and Democratic parties. There was public outrage at the overwhelming corruption of elections by business
money. It enhanced the case for a mass radical workers' party in the
US. We predicted that it would be the poor and working class who
would be called upon to foot the bill.

The basic laws of capitalism, as analysed by Marx, remain valid,
but the specific features which confronted us then were examined
thoroughly in the pages of The Socialist and our theoretical magazine Socialism Today in 2001-02.

However, the collapse of one company after another – Enron,
Global Crossing, WorldCom, Xerox – and the modern 'financiers'
behind them, Kenneth Lay of Enron and Bernard Ebbers of
WorldCom, made the "swindlers of Marx's day appear like house
burglars compared to bank robbers". Even the Daily Mirror commented: "How Karl Marx must be rubbing his hands with glee and
saying I told you so."[6] When the Asian crisis broke in 1997, US economic commentators growled about 'crony capitalism'; now the
much vaunted neo-liberal Anglo-Saxon model of capitalism was
revealed as an even more blatant example of crony capitalism.

The parasitical character of this model – decisions on the basis of shareholder value, the colossal processes of mergers and acquisitions, which amounted to at least $1 trillion in Europe and the US alone in 1997 – was clear. It had now produced the world's largest bankruptcy (Enron) and the world's greatest accounting fraud (WorldCom). Will Hutton, former editor of the Observer, and defender of 'European capitalism' against the US model, remarked acidly at the time: "The majority of mergers and takeovers in this stock market-dominated economy have proved destructive: few add any value and most lower it. Between 1993 and 2000, Wall Street had brought 3,500 small hi-tech companies to the stock market; even before the dotcom bubble had burst, more than half were trading below their initial offer price or had gone bust. While dividend distributions have doubled as a proportion of profits, investment in the core of American business was troublingly low; the US has less invested capital per employee than France or Germany."[7]

Many capitalist commentators comforted themselves with the notion that all booms bring with them 'overheads'. "Yet, never has financial chicanery, fraud and 'crony capitalism' taken place on such a scale as during the 1990s boom. The late 1990s were... a time when many turned a blind eye and levels of corporate governance and auditing clearly became, in many cases, lax." This was a polite way of saying that the system was rotten from top to bottom. This kind of situation led to the covering up of a 'black hole' of $4 billion in the case of WorldCom as shares were boosted to unprecedented levels 30, 40 or even 50 times the real value of assets!

This in turn led to a position where Chief Executive Officers (CEOs) in the US made $42 for every $1 made by one of his or her blue-collar workers. By 1990 that had stretched to $85 and by 2000, CEOs were earning $531 for every dollar taken home by an ordinary worker! The average industrial worker has been impoverished, relatively speaking, and many in real terms. Most voters in US elections had lost from the shares collapse; 50% of those who voted in the previous US elections had admitted that they owned stocks and shares!

What these events underlined was the completely false picture of the 1990s boom presented by the capitalist economists at the time, which we argued against at every stage. Profits were shown to be artificially inflated in the balance sheets of companies. The much vaunted productivity miracle, touted widely at the time, was accepted as a fact; the CWI and the Socialist Party argued strongly against this in written material.

Nevertheless, this did not stop some capitalist economists from claiming that they had gone through the "recession that never was". Comparing the world economy to an aeroplane, they argued, rather than landing in recession, it merely experienced "touchdown" on the runway and was poised once more to soar into the heavens. We flatly declared: "This is entirely false". The period ahead was likely to be a continuation of insecurity and uncertainty. Capitalist economists were consulting the equivalent of "tea leaves, totally unaware of what was coming down the line". Our conclusion was that "lodged in the situation today is the possibility of another devastating slump like 1929".

An example of the 'primitive slumpist' analysis of which our critics accuse us? On the contrary, the more farsighted capitalists were making the same points and, moreover, this disaster came to fruition in the economic meltdown of 2007-08. They avoided this temporarily once more through the massive bail out of the banks and the financial system. This meant that a highly unstable situation persisted which clearly in the future could produce another 1929 economic scenario and one that capitalism would not be able to so easily avoid. We also sketched out the likely economic scenarios to follow: "A period of stagnation, of deflation, of an extended period of economic depression with only small anaemic growth in production and a growth in the social malignancy associated with this, of poverty, rising unemployment, increased class conflict... is possible."[8] We drew all the necessary political and social conclusions from this, which would be manifested in increased conflict between the classes.

Naturally, the defenders of the system, notwithstanding all the evident drawbacks of capitalism, still clung to the alleged efficacy of the system over all others. Polly Toynbee, a fervent Blairite and 'liberal' columnist of the Guardian, wrote in the system's defence: "Capitalism is the only system that works."[9] This despite reports, factual comments and information in her own newspaper that the system she supported was working very badly. We wrote at the time: "Potentially, it is on the verge of a catastrophic breakdown. An economic tsunami on a world scale could follow the disaster in Asia." The wealth of the super-rich had doubled since Toynbee's hero Blair had come to power!

It certainly was working for some: inequality rose in Britain by 40% between 1979 and 2001. The number of dollar millionaires in Britain rose by 28,000 to a staggering 383,000 in 2003. We wrote that any economic and social system is "ultimately judged on the basis of whether it can develop, maintain and increase the productive forces – science, technique and the organisation of labour, and with it the living standards of the majority." The reality was the colossal polarisation between the rich and poor, as the representatives of the rich ruthlessly applied neoliberal policies. This in turn generated incipient revolts amongst the young and growing numbers of working-class people, which would turn into outright revolt later.

The US economy which, we argued, had held up the international system, "was mainly sustained after the economic shock of 1997 by huge inward investment by foreign capitalists, particularly from Asia, with the governments of Japan and China in particular also plugging the US federal deficit by buying Treasury Bonds." Moreover, Bush had colluded in the devaluation of the dollar, which in turn cheapened US exports against the major competitors of Europe and Asia. In effect, the US would put European capitalism on reduced 'rations', driving up the euro to an exchange rate of almost $2, which acted to savagely undermine the stagnant eurozone economies.

However, Asian governments were also terrified of jumping off this speeding economic merry-go-round for fear of the collapse of the whole financial house of cards. A former US treasury secretary described this as "a balance of financial terror". Significantly, we wrote, not ex post facto but in 2005: "When and just how the system could implode is unpredictable but as the British economist Wynne Godley comments: 'The crunch may be at hand.'"[10] The crunch did indeed come just a few years later in 2007-08!

One of Polly Toynbee's colleagues at the Guardian, Martin Kettle, had sought to reinforce the message by proclaiming the previous year: "Socialism is dead. Long live liberalism and social justice."[11] We answered: "Yet the past year has shown that his claim is false. Capitalism, even 'liberal' capitalism, and 'social justice' are not twins but polar opposites. What is 'liberal' or democratic about Blair's capitalist Britain? Lord Butler[12] has revealed that Blair and a handful of cronies take all the decisions, with little or no reference to the rest of the government. The Cabinet meets for the same length of time as the TV programme Ready, Steady, Cook!"[13]

This was reinforced by the comments of one capitalist commentator in the US who wrote that politicians were "servants of the economic cycle and second to the Federal Reserve. 'The candidates might have some impact on jobs in the margins but Greenspan is more important than the President and the economic cycle is more important than Greenspan.'"[14]

We also pointed to the inevitable revolt of the working class, with the continued worsening of the situation. National opinion polls had revealed that 73% of respondents were in favour of increasing the top rate of income tax on incomes of greater than £100,000 from 40p in the pound to 50p. Only 22% were opposed and even 68% of those in the top AB social grade were in favour. This was against the background of massive stagnation in wages, with big falls in real incomes recorded in some countries. Globalisation, according to economist Stephen Roach, was accelerating at hyper-speed and corporations were thinking "long and hard about giving rewards to workers at home". Internationally, trade soared to 28% of global GDP, compared with 19% in 1991. Moreover, "a whole range of services that were once considered 'untradeable' can easily be provided on the other side of the globe: anything from accounting and legal services to software programming, engineering and financial analysis."

But there was another side to the piling up of profit by big business. By cutting the share that the working class received, ultimately this cuts the 'market'. The ability of working people to buy back the goods that they produce is therefore undermined by the threat of an economic recession or slump: "If you want to milk the cow you need to feed it," stated one capitalist. The reaction to all this was shown in the big social explosions that were developing in Europe, the first signs of which were in France with mighty workers and students' demonstrations in 2005.[15]

42. Anti-Capitalist Movements 1999-2001

The anti-capitalist movement burst onto the scene at the end of the 1990s, indicating the general discontent against globalised capital and the conclusions that youth and working people were beginning to draw from their new experiences of the economic crises analysed earlier. The movement in Chiapas, Mexico from 1994 represented the first stirrings against the seemingly unstoppable forward march of globalised capitalism.

William Greider, in his book One World, Ready or Not, summed up the mood that capitalist globalisation was unstoppable: "Imagine a wondrous new machine, strong and supple, a machine that reaps as it destroys. It is huge and mobile, something like the machines of modern agriculture but vastly more complicated and powerful. Think of this awesome machine running over open terrain and ignoring familiar boundaries. It plows across fields and fencerows with a fierce momentum that is exhilarating to behold and also frightening. As it goes, the machine throws off enormous mows of wealth and bounty while it leaves behind great furrows of wreckage.

"Now imagine that there are skilful hands on board, but no one is at the wheel. In fact, the machine has no wheel nor any internal governor to control the speed and direction. It is sustained by its own forward motion, guided mainly by its own appetites. And it is accelerating."[1]

This view, which prevailed in the late 1990s amongst the

capitalists, was shattered by the huge demonstrations against this machine of uncontrolled capitalism and globalisation. The first movement came from the heartland of capitalism itself, the us. As the high priests of global big business met in Seattle in 1999 at the World Trade Organisation (wto) summit, 100,000 marchers showed their opposition. The Port of Seattle was shut down. The International Longshore Workers Union (dockers) closed all the ports on the us West Coast. Unionised construction workers walked off downtown building sites as Seattle was effectively closed down. The crowd were demonstrating their anger at the 300 multi-nationals that dominated world trade while a quarter of the world's population lived on 60p a day, together with a colossal growth in the gap between rich and poor. Even us President Clinton was compelled to say "globalisation must have a human face".[2]

In Seattle itself police used armoured personnel carriers and teargas against the demonstrators. The capitalist press tended to write off the anti-capitalist/globalisation movement as the work of students and other "marginal groups". Yet 20,000 demonstrators were brought to Seattle by the main trade union federation, the AFL-CIO. At this demonstration there were large contingents of steel workers, construction workers, dockworkers, public employees, farmers, truck drivers, teachers, machinists and every type of union-ised worker in the us. There was a glaring and obvious contradiction in the fact that they were brought to Seattle by the AFL-CIO and yet this union had recently endorsed the Democratic Party and its free trade supporter, Al Gore, for the presidency in 2000.

This demonstration was the biggest mass protest and police crackdown in the us since the anti-Vietnam war demonstrations and civil rights marches of the 1960s. Arguments to the effect that the students and demonstrators were prone to instigate violence, because of a few smashed shopfronts, were answered by one Filipino leader: "They are worried about a few windows being smashed. They should come and see the violence being done to our communities in the name of liberalisation of trade."[3] Seattle was a disaster for Clinton. He was shaken, like the capitalists as a whole, by the strength of the anti-WTO demonstrations and especially by the fact that the protests were unmistakably directed against corporate capitalism.

Clinton already had an atrocious record on workers' rights. As with his 'buddy' Blair, anti-union measures, introduced under Reagan, had not been reversed, while casual, low-paid employment and prison labour had spread enormously under his administration. Union leaders who were present in Seattle were not there to oppose the WTO, let alone its neo-liberal, free trade philosophy. They fully endorsed this but wanted a 'place at the table'. Yes, some of them were swayed by the strength of feeling of the demonstrators. Seattle showed that beneath the surface of prosperity, there was a huge growth of class anger at the conditions that workers were facing.

The consciousness that was emerging through these first anti-capitalist demonstrations was not yet fully formed and did not draw clear class conclusions. However, big attention was being focused on Karl Marx, including by wealthy investment bankers: "The longer I spend on Wall Street, the more convinced I am that Marx was right... Marx's approach is the best way to look at capitalism."[4] Statements like this became quite common, even in capitalist circles from then on and particularly following the crisis of 2007-08. The violent eruptions of the system demanded an explanation, which even the capitalists themselves found in the writings of Marx. They could accept some of the diagnosis of the maladies of the system but it was another thing entirely to draw the same revolutionary conclusions as Marx. Nevertheless this favourable publicity for his works widened the possibility of extending the number of supporters for the ideas of the genuine Marxists.

The year 2000 saw further widespread anti-capitalist demonstrations: 10,000 protested in Washington against the World Bank and IMF's exploitation of the Third World. Again, there were arrests – 1,300, including six members of Socialist Alternative, the US co-thinkers of the CWI. In London on May Day a very significant and impressive 10,000 strong anti-capitalist demonstration took place which saw the participation, for the first time in a long time, of a new generation prepared to confront the system.

This represented a break from the consciousness of the 1990s, which was dominated by triumphalist capitalism. Then, single issues tended to dominate the outlook of young people, making it difficult to generalise and pose the need for the socialist alternative. The 'apathy' of young people towards 'politics', constantly played up and exaggerated by the press and the rest of the media, was in fact an expression of the rejection of capitalist politics.

Taken aback at the scale of the May Day demonstration at first, the outbreak of clashes generated a campaign of vitriol from press and politicians who attacked the participants. New Labour, as well as the press, seized on the trashing of a McDonald's and graffiti sprayed on the Cenotaph to justify their venom. They also used the term 'riots' to describe the events on May Day in an attempt to smear the anti-capitalists.

We countered this: "Of course, the painting on the Cenotaph will understandably have upset many ordinary working-class people, particularly the generation who fought or lived through World War Two."[5] However, as a protester was defacing Churchill's statue, a former soldier said: "Churchill was an exponent of capitalism... The Cenotaph is a monument to ordinary soldiers and I'm an ordinary soldier."[6] The Prime Minister, Tony Blair, predictably expressed outrage at this 'violence'. Yet he still had blood on his hands from the cowardly bombing campaign in the Balkans, with worse to come in the obscenity of the invasion of Iraq.

The real violence came from the police and the state on that day. Members of the Socialist Party were illegally corralled and detained, denied the right to go to the toilet for hours in a police cordon. Lois Austin, a prominent Socialist Party member and active in its ranks since she was a teenager, was amongst those who were prevented by the police from collecting her child from nursery. As a result of this police harassment, she took legal action in the British courts and right up to the European Court of Human Rights. She and the Socialist Party did not get justice from the inherently biased capitalist legal system, which was used to justify the vicious methods of the police on this day. However, the publicity generated helped to make people, particularly the labour movement, more aware at the encroachment on civil liberties presided over by Blair and his Cabinet.

In other cities and on other continents, the anti-capitalist demonstrators dogged the footsteps of the leaders of capitalism wherever they met. A three-day protest against the capitalist World Economic Forum in Melbourne, Australia took place in what was one of the biggest anti-capitalist demonstrations in Australia's history. Ten thousand, mainly building and manufacturing workers, came out on strike for the day to march in solidarity with young people. Socialist Party members rose to the occasion, resisting the political pressure from government and media and the beatings from the police. This represented a big change in Australian politics. Thousands of workers and even more young people came out onto the streets for 72 hours of continual action against capitalism.

The meeting of the World Economic Forum at the Crown Towers Hotel, which was blockaded, saw 1,000 of the world's richest chief executive officers meet to discuss furthering their neoliberal agenda. 'S11', coordinating the protest within which the Socialist Party operated, independently visited 60 schools to build support. This prompted the police to visit schools warning of "left-wing terrorists" in S11, singling out in particular the Socialist Party. Australia's highest-selling paper said about the Committee for a Workers' International: "This international linking of extremist groups is a true threat to globalisation."[7] Within S11, it was only the Socialist Party who had members in the unions and was therefore able to lobby them to strike and march with the students: "The school student strike was brilliant with 500 students jogging down in formation at 9am to join the blockade that had begun two hours earlier". Ten thousand unionists downed tools and marched in four separate rallies to the blockade, with divisions opening up between the more militant workers and unions and the conservative official leadership.[8]

Later in the year, a massive demonstration of up to 100,000 trade unionists and young people, socialists, anti-capitalists and environmentalists marched in Nice, France, demanding a "different agenda for Europe". There were big trade union contingents plus youth and organisations from across Europe, including Poland, Slovenia, Norway, Sweden, Macedonia and Turkey, indicating how the movement had spread on a European and world level. 10,000 protested in Washington against the World Bank and the IMF's exploitation of the Third World. At the same time, stock markets lost £2 trillion in share value worldwide in what the financial press wrote off as "jitters". In fact, the stock market falls showed that the bubble of the world share boom was bursting.

In early January, nearly 5,000 delegates from 117 countries gathered in Porto Alegre, Brazil– most of them however, from Brazil itself – to attend the World Social Forum and debate the issue of globalisation and an alternative. For many at the forums, their alternative consisted of 'humanising globalisation' or 'democratising the international institutions'. On the principle 'if you can't beat them join them', the French government sent a minister to the gathering, who argued that Porto Alegre was not in opposition to Davos – where the billionaires of capitalism met regularly – but was complementary! This was answered by supporters of the CWI, particularly at the Intercontinental youth camp, where socialist ideas dominated and attracted more than 2,000 who camped out, discussed and debated. This camp agreed a manifesto: "A different world, a socialist one, is possible."[9] This indicated the divisions taking place within the anti-globalisation movement between those who wished to confine its role to just criticising 'unacceptable' aspects of capitalism but not the system as a whole and those with a class analysis who wished to go much further.

We welcomed the development of this movement which, as we have seen, was international in character with demonstrations and movements reverberating from one continent to another. We saw it as an opportunity to develop a more rounded-out class consciousness, although in the first period in particular it included large sections of idealistic young people with some participation of workers.

However, the working class did not dominate this movement, partly because the trade union leaderships largely stood aside allowing muddled radical intellectuals to set the tone. There was no question that the working class was open to the ideas that were raised by this movement and in some cases did participate in the demonstrations in large numbers, as was seen in France and later in Genoa. Despite this, it was those like Susan George and Walden Bello whose ideas were to the fore in the first stage of the movement.

Walden Bello had at least been an activist in the struggle to oust the Marcos dictatorship in the Philippines as well as a commentator. He predicted the Asian financial crisis of 1997-98, which he described as the "Stalingrad of the IMF", the implication being this was that organisation's 'beginning of the end'. Unfortunately, this is still not the case decades later. Like all the institutions of capitalism their demise is linked to the struggle against the system as a whole. Walden Bello also made trenchant criticisms of the WTO and correctly pointed out that the founding of this organisation in 1994-95 was "the apogee of capitalism in the era of globalisation". He was clearly pessimistic: "Socialism had collapsed and the Washington consensus seemed to carry all before it."

Susan George, Naomi Klein and Walden Bello made valuable contributions in denouncing neoliberal policies. However, Susan George was wrong to suggest in a speech at Porto Alegre that neoliberalism and its policies – the application of new technology, privatisation, depression of wages and part-time working – was a "totally artificial construct". We pointed out that these policies had grown out of the largely unconscious economic developments in capitalism itself, dating from the late 1970s. They began to be implemented in a big way in the early 1980s and particularly in the 1990s.

A huge boost to the capitalists' ability to implement these policies was furnished by the collapse of Eastern Europe and the former Soviet Union. This made possible the ideological commitment to 'the dictatorship of the market' made by ex-social democratic, ex-'communist' leaders of mass workers' organisations. A more serious deficiency of Susan George and others who sought to lead the anti-capitalist movement was the lack of a viable alternative from these writers and thinkers. She declared in her Porto Alegre speech: "Let's

make clear that we are 'pro-globalisation', we are in favour of sharing friendship, culture, cuisine, travel, solidarity, wealth and
resources worldwide. We are above all 'pro-democracy' and 'pro-
planet', which our adversaries most clearly are not."

Yet their alternative did not go beyond the system itself. She was
a member of 'ATTAC'[10], which originated in France and was among
the most prominent proponents of the Tobin tax. This suggested a
levy on certain currency transactions, which we supported as a step
forward, but recognising it would not seriously undermine capitalism, even if it was implemented. In Porto Alegre however ATTAC, if
anything, stood on the right of the conference. It was they who
were invited to the event with the French 'socialist' ministers and
past ministers, who were roundly booed by the participants. Susan
George also declared: "I'm sorry to admit it but I haven't the slightest idea what 'overthrowing capitalism' means in the early 21st century. Maybe we will witness what the philosopher Paul Virilio has
called the 'global accident' but it would surely be accompanied by
enormous human suffering. If all the financial and stock markets
suddenly collapsed, millions would be thrown out onto the pave-
ment as large and small firms failed, bank closures would far out-
strip the capacity of governments to prevent catastrophe, insecurity
and crime would run rampant and we would find ourselves living
in the Hobbesian hell of the war against all. Call me reformist if you
like – I want to avoid such a future."

This "hell" actually came to pass later in the wake of the 2007-08
crash. We, the Marxists, prepared for this and warned the working
class in broad outline that this was the likely outcome of a continuation of capitalism. We support all reforms which benefit working
people, contrary to what Susan George implied but we recognised
then and now that the struggle for such improvements in the lives
of the working class is inextricably bound up with the need to
change society in a socialist direction. Susan George and those who
led the anti-capitalist movement at this stage were blind to the ruinous economic and social trends within capitalism, which were to
explode later. The anti-capitalist movement posed indirectly the

question of world socialism. The global struggle for this was and remains the real answer to globalised, rapacious capitalism. This is the message that we sought to drive home in our intervention in this important movement.

The working class was then, and even more so today after the tumultuous events of recent years, evidently the main force in society which can bring about change. It was not perhaps as clear when the anti-capitalist movement first developed, but it is striking today the way the working class, when it asserts its power, is the strongest force in society. Witness the number of general strikes and near general strikes in Europe – over 30 in Greece alone – the mass revolutionary demonstrations in Egypt, Brazil and elsewhere.

Naomi Klein wrote: "Direct action is all that is left between Exxon and the Alaskan wildlife reserves." The highest form of 'direct action' – as opposed to 'directionless action' – is the mass mobilisation of the working class in struggle: the strike, mass demonstrations, the general strike and the taking power out of the hands of the tiny band of billionaires and placing it in the hands of working-class people.[11]

Before May Day 2001, the traditional international Labour Day, Mark Seddon, editor of the left-wing Tribune newspaper, writing in the Independent pointed out: "The TUC will be elsewhere. No official demonstration is planned. With the honourable exceptions of the rail unions and their supporters, the streets may echo to smashing glass and raucous tones... this may be the shape of things to come."[12] In other words, the absence of the organised trade union movement, orchestrated by the right-wing, for movements like this meant that others could steer it in a false direction. We declared that the time was ripe to move beyond the mood of "anti-the system" to a specifically socialist approach. Mass demonstrations followed in 2001 in London again, in Québec, Canada, in Gothenburg in Sweden and above all in Genoa. The latter stood out, firstly, because it signified the huge opposition against capitalism involving big sections of workers as well as young people and secondly, unfortunately, because of the death of a young worker, Carlo Giuliani, which had enormous political repercussions in Italy and beyond.

Millions protested on May Day worldwide against capitalism. Yet Blair said this was because they wanted to confront the police in unsupported "spurious causes". The Socialist answered this slander by pointing to the attacks that were being made against working people: "20% of the world's six billion people to live on less than $2 a day; ten million children under-five each year to die from preventable diseases; half a million mothers to die in childbirth from complications that can be prevented with proper healthcare; 113 million children globally get no chance to go to school; 100,000 IT workers across the world to be sacked in the space of ten days. The combined wealth of the world's seven richest people (according to the UN) to be worth more than the poorest 48 countries."[13]

As mentioned earlier, on May Day itself hundreds of Socialist Party members joined thousands in defiance of over-the-top policing, with threats to use rubber bullets, to demonstrate against capitalism in London and other cities in Britain. However, the thousands who turned out were not intimidated. At all the demos there were many young people who had never been to a protest before and over 10,000 people demonstrated. All day police tactics hemmed in people in protest gatherings around the capital, using a technique known as 'kettling' (because it builds up pressure). One line of riot police would block the road while others drove protesters back, trapping people in between. Nevertheless, over 400 copies of The Socialist were sold with over 50 people filling in forms to join the Socialist Party. Shamefully, women were forced to go to the toilet on the streets; the singer Billy Bragg was compelled to argue with police officers to get one woman out. Sympathetic barristers mobilised pressure for the release of demonstrators.

At the mass rally on May Day in the Hackney Empire, workers gathered to hear the only Labour councillor to support the borough's workers in their recent struggle. He condemned his Labour Council leaders as "'political whores' who had an 'odious coalition with Tory crooks'".[14]

Next was the turn of Québec, with 34 leaders from North, Central and South America and the Caribbean convening in

Québec to establish a new 'Free Trade Area of the Americas' (FTAA). This free trade zone generated huge anger and created one of the most radical movements in recent Canadian history, with over 50,000 young people, workers and environmentalists converging on Québec City to oppose it. Some union leaders said they wanted to reform this body but most demonstrators wanted it abolished. Québec City was turned into a battlefield with confrontations engulfing the city and police carrying out 400 arrests. A huge barricade, the 'wall of shame', to protect 'America's leaders' was torn down by youths while tear gas floated above the city. Unbelievably, the labour leaders in the city refused to march to the area of the summit. Instead, they marched out to the suburbs, leaving the militant youth on their own to confront the police.

Socialist Alternative was critical of the organisers, who did not have proper stewarding for the demonstration. Clare Doyle on behalf of the CWI reported: "Quebec was indeed an event that none of the residents of that historic French-speaking city will quickly forget. Eye-witnesses were shocked at the ferocity of the police attacks on predominately young and peaceful demonstrators. They looked on, full of admiration for the courageous demonstrators making a stand against what they believe to be an unfair society."

She reported the comments of a former federal government minister who observed the events: "To my horror, the police... fired teargas canisters directly at those sitting or standing on the road... (We) felt our eyes sting and our throats bake." Clare observed: "Many protesters saw themselves as socialists, even if they were not sure what socialism was and exactly what was needed in order to achieve it. This must, to some extent, reflect the fighting, revolutionary history of France, as well as of the French-speaking people of Québec. Québec has all the militant traditions of the French, without the negative experience of Jospin – the [then] 'Socialist Party' Prime Minister of France – who has carried through more privatisation and anti-working-class policies than the previous Conservative regime. Canada too, as a whole, has strong traditions of struggle and powerful trade union organisations. All these traditions will be revived as the economy moves into recession". The New Democratic Party (NDP) – once a party of labour – made a point of being on the streets of Québec, although they failed to put forward a socialist alternative. Only Brazilian President Cardoso and Hugo Chavez from Venezuela dissented from the final communiqué.[15]

George Bush, the illegitimate occupier of the White House because of the fiddling of the 'hanging chads' in Florida following the presidential election, went to the European Union leaders meeting before their Gothenburg summit to sell 'Son of Star Wars' to them. At the same time, in a calculated insult to anti-capitalist demonstrators, he made it clear that his government did not care about the Kyoto Protocol on climate change. The response was 15,000 participating in a demonstration, making it clear that "Bush was not welcome." On 14 June, the day after Bush left, 20,000 took to the streets to protest against the EU and the European Monetary Union. This mainly peaceful demonstration was the biggest held in Sweden for many years. Yet the police shot three people and then utilised this to unleash a propaganda barrage against the growing anti-capitalist movement in general and socialists in particular.

Per Olsson, on behalf of our sister organisation Rättvisepartiet Socialisterna (RS – Socialist Justice Party), reported: "One quarter of Sweden's total police force were in Gothenburg to protect Bush and politicians attending the summit – the biggest police mobilisation ever in Sweden". The establishment used the riot that erupted on Friday, 15 June, the destruction and the vandalism that followed in its wake, to attack the anti-capitalist movement in general and the socialist left in particular. Nearly 1,000 demonstrators were arrested and held by police for six hours during these three days. Three people were shot by the police, one critically injured and more than 60 were taken to hospital. The 'democratic' Swedish media reported that the police simply said the demonstrators were to blame!

We made it quite clear that socialists do not advocate smashing shop windows as a means of political protest, as some of the left-anarchist type of organisations do. These events came as a shock and there were even people from the main protest organisation

'Gothenburg 200', who argued that the following day's demonstration should be cancelled. Despite this, members of RS were instrumental in convincing others that the demonstration should go ahead.[16]

Joe Higgins, Irish Socialist Party TD, spoke at the demonstration, to applause. He denounced police brutality. This 'police riot' went down in Sweden's history as 'Black Friday'. The violent clashes that took place shocked Swedish society with its tradition of social peace and pacifism. These events had made a mockery of the claim of the Swedish ruling class that they wished for 'dialogue' with the anti-capitalists. A campaign of denigration ensued with Blair, predictably, joining in and attempting to criminalise the anti-capitalists.

These events produced a split within the anti-capitalist movement itself. The CWI issued a statement condemning the state violence against demonstrators and its attempt to use the events "to unleash a propaganda barrage against the growing anti-capitalist movement in general and socialists in particular".[17] On the other hand, one of the organisations behind the demonstrations, ATTAC, split on the issue. Many condemned the provocations of the Gothenburg police. Others condemned the demonstrators and defended the police who "fired – in self-defence – at violent hooligans". Susan George, who was at the Gothenburg protest, claimed that the police were provoked by "acts of violence". She did not condemn clearly the Swedish police, even though she had explained the day before that the rioting was in response to the police breaking prior agreements on the demonstration. The effect of George's statement was to aid the campaign to criminalise the more radical anti-capitalist campaigners.[18]

The more serious strategists of capitalism, however, were beginning to recognise the strength of the movements and the damage it had inflicted on their global institutions. George Soros, the notorious speculator, admitted that there was "considerable justification" for criticism of global capitalism's "present arrangements". The anti-globalisation movement, he said, "may have a violent fringe, but there's some very serious forces and movements involved."[19] This indicated that they were losing the argument as more and more workers and poor peasants worldwide were losers and victims of capitalist globalisation.

After the violence of Gothenburg there was enormous tension in Italy and beyond as a major demonstration loomed in Genoa. This proved to be the high point of the movement as a 300,000 strong demonstration mobilised in the city on 21 July and the days following. The main organisers of the week-long protests, the Genoa Social Forum, had not expected more than 120,000 for the international march. In the event, there was a massive show of solidarity and protest in the face of an aroused bloody-minded Italian police force. Huge contingents marched under the red banners of Rifondazione Comunista (PRC) and the Young Communists, and there were massive contingents from the trade unions: CGIL, metal workers (FIOM), the independent union COBAS and many other workers' groups.

Lined up along the seafront, before the private bathing beaches of the Italian Riviera, were seemingly endless ranks of young people and trade union activists from all over Italy and different parts of Europe and the world. They were met with teargas, with many demonstrators choking and fearing that the violence of Gothenburg would be repeated by the police or worse. Some groups were cornered by the Genoa cops and forced to walk past them, their hands raised in the air. Some were chased from the streets onto the beaches with a cloud of crippling fumes engulfing them. Others were forced to flee through the narrow streets of Genoa. Every time they tried to regroup and find the main body of the march, they were forced against the steep sides of Genoa's mountains.

Clare Doyle, who participated in this demonstration with many other members of the CWI, commented: "Luckily, it was in this part of the town that most Genoese workers live. Few of them had the luxury of leaving town. In spite of all that had gone on the day before, the local population gave enormous material and moral support to the demonstrators. Berlusconi had called on all local residents to make sure there was no underwear hanging on their washing lines when the important people of the world came to town (an edict unheard of since Mussolini's time)."[20] In fact, the population did the opposite, just as they did when Mussolini invited Hitler to Genoa. There was massive violence by the forces of the state, particularly the police. Medical organisers said that 150 medics had been called out 500 times. One young demonstrator, Carlo Giuliani, was murdered by the riot police and the perpetrators of this crime are still walking free today.

We were unaware at the time that a police spy had been deployed within our ranks. He was known to us as 'Carlo Neri'. He accompanied Clare Doyle and me when we later visited Italy to discuss with co-thinkers! He was present in Genoa, ostensibly in our 'camp' but gathering intelligence for the state and police. The full scope of underhand and anti-democratic methods by the police was only revealed in 2016.

Protests were organised outside the Italian Embassy in London against the police attacks. Hannah Sell, who had just arrived back from Genoa, was interviewed by BBC regional news and commented: "If the world's capitalist leaders are so keen to hear our socialist views on ending world poverty and the anti-capitalist alternative, why did they send in police to smash our demonstration?"[21]

The repercussions of Genoa were felt throughout Italy, Europe and the world. Metalworkers held a half-day strike. Demonstrations took place in Milan, Turin and Bologna, with thousands participating, against the Italian state violence. In Genoa, the memory of past fascist-inspired violence immediately provoked more opposition. In reality, the Italian trade union leaders should have called for a general strike, first in Genoa and then preparing similar action on a national scale. This was not just an attack on Carlo Giuliani, but an attempt to intimidate the working class and labour movement as a whole. There was also a savage attack on the Genoa Social Forum's media centre and the illegal detention and torture of protesters by clearly fascist members of the security services.

On 24 July, there were protest demonstrations in many Italian cities. Robert Bechert pointed out in the Socialist: "Many remember that in the 15 years up to 1960, 94 Italians were killed during strikes or protests. Then, as the workers' movement gathered strength in the late 1960s and 1970s, the fascists and their police supporters started their 'strategy of tension' that led up to the August 1980 fascist bombing of Bologna railway station that killed 85 people." Fini, the 'post-fascist' Deputy Prime Minister to Berlusconi, suddenly took command of security operations. There were reports that some of those illegally arrested in the media centre raid were forced to salute pictures of Mussolini and sing the fascist song Faccetta Nera!

An important factor involved in these events was the role of the PRC, the workers' party that many looked towards. However, the PRC had supported the 'Olive Tree' government, formed from ex-communists, socialists and Christian Democrats, that attacked living standards. In its paper Liberazione, it admitted: "We have voted for cuts amounting to 100,000 billion lira". Little wonder then that in the previous May elections, its vote collapsed. There existed at one stage great potential for this party. Moreover, its supporters were predominant in the huge contingent of Italian workers who attended the great Genoa demonstration.[22] However, moving towards the right, supporting different bourgeois coalitions, combined with a failure to work out a clear revolutionary programme, has meant that this party has now (effectively) disappeared from the Italian political scene.

It is a warning of what could happen elsewhere, especially when new parties of the working class are formed then fail to work out a rounded-out socialist perspective and programme. The anti-capitalist movement was not completely crushed by the events of Genoa, but the writing was on the wall. However, the experience in this movement was an important, even a necessary prelude, in preparing for the important workers' movements that developed in the course of the next decade. It was also a training ground for the development of a new generation who went on to intervene and play a key role later in the workers' movement.

43. Socialist Alliance splits 2001-02

In the aftermath of the 2001 general election, it was obvious that the Socialist Alliance was heading for the rocks. The organisation had made some modest steps in the general election. In England the Socialist Alliance received an average of 1.7% of the vote in the 92 seats where it stood. This included some very good votes, such as Dave Nellist in Coventry with 7.08% and Neil Thompson in St Helens, 6.88%. While the overall vote was a step forward, it was nevertheless an extremely modest step at that stage, particularly when compared to the mass abstentions.

One of the crucial issues upon which the Socialist Alliance broke its back was how to relate to the many community and trade union-initiated campaigns which were independent from the Socialist Alliance. It was not just the SWP who were guilty of sectarianism. An independent left, Mike Marqusee, from Hackney Socialist Alliance, justified opposition to Glenn Kelly standing with the backing of council stewards, on the grounds that Marqusee's organisation was a much broader forum and had a much larger base than the Hackney Stewards Committee, which had organised seven days of strike action by thousands of council workers! Needless to say, Marqusee did not stay the course in the Socialist Alliance, leaving when his partner, Liz Davies resigned in October 2002.

Looking towards the future, we pointed out: "If we are to

maximise the number of campaigns and organisations that are prepared to join the Socialist Alliance, it is crucial that we have a federal approach. This means that we unite the participating forces on the basis of a common socialist platform, while allowing organisations, groups and individuals, to uphold their own political positions."

We drew on the experience of the British labour movement. At the founding conference of the Labour Representation Committee in 1900, Keir Hardie argued that the structures of this new organisation should ensure that "each of the affiliated organisations would be left free to select its own candidates without let or hindrance, the one condition being that, when returned to Parliament, the candidate should agree to be one of the Labour Group there, and act in harmony with its decisions. In this way, it would avoid the scandal... of seeing trade unionists opposing socialists and vice versa."[1]

This very good advice from the founder of the Labour Party himself was completely ignored by the SWP. Moreover, Hardie was speaking to an audience which represented almost 400,000 people, a much larger number than in the ranks of the Socialist Alliance. This put the tentative beginnings of the Socialist Alliance in England, when measured against the Labour Party's progression, into a proper historical context. These arguments, however, were swept aside by the SWP and their allies who emphasised a rigid centralisation, in opposition to a federal approach, which was to ultimately wreck the Socialist Alliance. We, on the other hand, argued that the local Socialist Alliances were the key units where campaigning and electoral decisions should be taken. We were flexible but the SWP and their allies were unbelievably centralist, which was totally at variance with the needs of the movement at that stage.

We also saw the political diversity within the Socialist Alliance not as a hindrance but a big positive. Indeed, an examination of the experience of other parties and formations which developed after the demise of the Socialist Alliance in Britain – in Italy, Greece or Spain – revealed a form of federal organisation with the prevalence for internal discussion and debate. The PRC in Italy allowed platforms which were able to campaign openly against the position of the leadership when necessary. Syriza in Greece was extremely open and friendly in its first period, when it grew rapidly in popular support from 4% to 25% of the vote. This demonstrated that internal discussion and debate in a broad mass workers' party can be a big help in building support for such a party. Only when a large part of the bureaucratic apparatus of PASOK collapsed into Syriza was the party leadership able to clamp down on freedom to organise and discuss within the party.

All the signs pointed to the SWP and their allies mobilising to bulldoze their proposals through against all opposition at the national conference scheduled for December. We warned that this would lead to a split in the Socialist Alliance because the Socialist Party was not prepared to effectively allow the SWP to impose their candidates in local Socialist Alliances. We had put in a great amount of work when the SWP were decrying the very idea of attempts to unify the left electorally.

This meeting was preceded by an organised debate between the SWP and the Socialist Party at 'Socialism', our national event, in November 2001. Chris Nineham represented the SWP. Nineham criticised the Socialist Party's proposals, saying they amounted to a "democratic deficit" by allowing small groups to have a veto. Having quotas, he said, would put off people joining by "institutionalising" the power of minorities. Steve Score, from the East Midlands, made the point, "As soon as one party imposes itself on others then that Alliance will break down."[2]

Individual members of the Socialist Alliance, not subscribing to either the SWP or the Socialist Party, could see the dangers in the SWP's proposed constitution. One of these, Mark Edwards, wrote to us: "I believe that in practice this will lead to the domination of the Alliance by the largest member organisation... It seems to me that the Socialist Party's proposed constitution would ensure that the rights of member organisations and the majority of individual members to have their views taken into account are safeguarded."[3]

To no avail. With a narrow overall majority, the Socialist Workers

Party and a handful of allies pushed through the new constitution that effectively transformed the Socialist Alliance from a federal, inclusive organisation, into another Anti-Nazi League type SWP 'front'. Clive Heemskerk had submitted our proposals for a constitution which was consensus-based and enshrined the federal principle. One of our most experienced comrades, Judy Beishon – who has been both National Treasurer of the party and editor of our weekly paper – spoke for us. Her short speech was to the point: "The advocates of having 'one person, one vote' throughout the alliance are portraying it as the only fair and democratic basis for the constitution. Of course in some circumstances this method is appropriate, but it's necessary to say firstly that there's no principle involved in it as some have argued – after all, it was a tool of the Labour Party right wing in consolidating their position – and secondly, in this alliance, right now, it's a disastrous proposal because it means trying to force organisations that have worked separately and have a history of mistrust towards each other, into unity purely on the basis of the voting power of the strongest organisation numerically – in this case the SWP.

"The Socialist Party has been accused of demanding a veto but it's important to recognise that our constitution gives the right of veto at local level to all the main participants, including a majority of the individual members; whereas the SWP constitution gives a veto to one organisation only – their own."[4]

We declared that we could no longer participate in such an organisation. This, we concluded, meant that the Socialist Alliance would be a repeat of history. Like Arthur Scargill's ill-fated Socialist Labour Party, it would end up in an historical cul-de-sac and would eventually disappear. This is what happened later, when the SWP unilaterally wound up the Socialist Alliance, in order to join George Galloway's Respect organisation. Disappointing though it was, this would not be the end of attempts by the Socialist Party to create the basis of a new independent working-class force capable of offering an electoral alternative.

The Socialist Alliance desperately attempted to secure for itself a trade union base with 'trade union conferences'. They were nothing of the kind, with the overwhelming majority attending from the SWP itself. We continued to press for trade unions, particularly the left trade union leaders like Mark Serwotka of the PCS and Bob Crow of the RMT, as well as Matt Wrack, who held a prominent position in the firefighters' union, the FBU, to put forward an alternative.

Matt, an ex-member of the Socialist Party and future general secretary of the FBU, attached himself to the Socialist Alliance, which allowed the SWP to give the false impression that the trade unions were moving in their direction. This mutual support reinforced the false position both had in relation to the Labour Party. The SWP were not prepared to break completely from the Labour Party and Matt Wrack shared a similar position. He was the author of a Socialist Alliance pamphlet on democratising the political funds. When still a member of the Socialist Party he did not secure a single vote when he put forward his position of fighting for policies within the Labour Party at the Socialist Party's 2002 conference.

As we have seen earlier, developments on the left in answer to the swing further towards the right of New Labour were contradictory. On the one hand, big opportunities were presented at least to begin to establish an electoral alternative to the left of New Labour. This was expressed in the attempts through the Socialist Alliances to bring together organisations and trends of opinion, some with serious programmatic differences with one another, in order to establish a common approach. This in turn held out the prospect of swinging over many workers who had no political 'home' to a new pole of attraction.

However, for this to succeed there had to be a certain political and organisational give-and-take, which was unfortunately foreign to the Socialist Workers Party in particular. They pursued a policy of 'rule or ruin', clearly demonstrated in their refusal to accept a federal form of alliance, which in turn led to the forcing out of the Socialist Party of England and Wales from the Socialist Alliance. This was in spite of the fact that we had been pioneers of the project. Prior to entering the Socialist Alliance, the SWP were still pursuing a sectarian policy, including their historical virulent opposition to supporting the Labour Party in elections. This was at a time when the Labour Party still retained the features of a bourgeois workers' party, a leadership that was pro-bourgeois but which rested on a worker base. Therefore it was correct to give a critical vote in elections for a Labour government. This approach allowed Militant, as we have seen, to successfully work within the Labour Party in alliance with the other genuine left forces in successfully pushing the Labour Party towards a more radical socialist position.

The emergence of Corbyn later did not invalidate our approach at this time towards a new party. While building our own independent party, our pressure for a new mass party prepared the ground for the Corbyn phenomenon, which came primarily from outside the party.

Unfortunately the swp, while abandoning formally its previous sectarian approach, in effect carried on with the same methods in the Socialist Alliance, which in turn led to the split first in England and then in Wales. Shortly after our exit Liz Davies, one of the Socialist Alliance's most prominent members, resigned from its executive and the position of national chairperson, which only served to confirm our analysis that the swp's domination made the Socialist Alliance little more than an electoral front for their organisation. In a resignation letter, she declared: "The premise of the Socialist Alliance was that individuals and groups from differing political backgrounds and perspectives could work together on a common political project. It was always clear that trust among the elements of the Socialist Alliance, and in particular trust among members of the executive and national officers, was essential to this endeavour. As a result of recent events, I feel that trust no longer exists."[5]

Events in the Welsh Socialist Alliance (wsa) took a similar course. At a special all-Wales meeting in October 2002, Socialist Party Wales members unanimously agreed to withdraw from the wsa. Originally, all socialist organisations were invited to join the alliance in Wales but the swp declined because of their "principled opposition to standing in elections". When the swp changed their position, and decided to stand in the 1999 assembly elections, they still refused to join the WSA. The Socialist Party and the majority of other members in the WSA subsequently did stand in elections with the SWP under the banner of the 'United Socialists'. Eventually, attempts to work with the SWP became difficult as they sought to gain complete control of the organisation. They packed meetings and blocked Socialist Party candidates who would have a better position than them to make an electoral impact. The exit of the Socialist Party, following the disaffiliation of left nationalists Cymru Goch, led to the collapse of the whole project, for which the SWP were entirely responsible.[6]

44. Al-Qa'ida and 9/11
2001

September 11, 2001 and the two wars that flowed from 9/11 – first Afghanistan and then Iraq – were the defining moments on an international plane for Blair and his government. The carnage in New York and Washington DC, resulting from the suicide air attacks on the World Trade Center and the Pentagon, was a world event like few before.

It is said that everyone who lived through this can remember where they were when the news of this event came through, as with the assassination of US President John Kennedy. I was busy packing a suitcase, in expectation of flying the next day to visit Costa Rica via Miami, to discuss with a group of Trotskyists who appeared to be open to the analysis and ideas of the CWI. I had one eye on the television because Blair was due to speak at the TUC that day. The news that the New York World Trade Center had been hit was stunning but as we witnessed – live on television – the second attack, it was even more so. Blair was forced to change his agenda. He cancelled his prepared speech to the TUC, apart from a few perfunctory remarks, and immediately returned to London. I continued packing, naively expecting that I would be able to proceed with the arranged visits, if not on September 12, then a few days later. The trip was eventually cancelled, with few flights out of London for weeks and even for a month to some destinations.

The CWI rushed out a lengthy statement a few days after

September 11, in which we condemned the slaughter and sought to draw some immediate conclusions. We wrote: "New technology and the speed of modern communication allowed millions of people on every continent to follow the horrific events as they unfolded. This resulted in an outpouring of emotion, a deep sense of concern and revulsion throughout the whole of the planet. In the neo-colonial world, particularly in the Middle East, there are also expressions of open regret that innocents have had to suffer but this combines with the feeling that this is the result of the crimes of US imperialism in the countries of Africa, Asia and Latin America.

"These events have colossal repercussions for the US and its after-effects are still reverberating globally. Thousands of people have been killed and countless others maimed on the bloodiest day of violence on US soil since the battle of Antietam in the civil war in the 19th century. More than 300 firefighters, who heroically rushed into the World Trade Center (WTC) to rescue victims, were killed. Many emergency service workers perished. It is not possible to remain unmoved by the scenes of devastation and death."[1]

The attacks on the World Trade Center and the airliners revealed a terrible human tragedy in all its dimensions. The firefighters were heroic with one survivor commenting that as he was frantically rushing down the stairs to escape, they were going up to rescue those trapped above. They subsequently perished when the World Trade Center collapsed. The scenes of people jumping from windows – with one couple holding hands as they did so – in a desperate attempt to cling to life, were etched into the consciousness of the world. The remarkable story of a man who fell 83 floors and survived is another example. There was also the tragic case of a firefighter rushing to save people who were killed by somebody who jumped out of the World Trade Center windows.

This added to the basic human feeling of the horror at these events. These sentiments are shared by Marxists who in no way turn their eyes away from the terrible conditions which motivated the suicide bombers and who refused to line up with the hysterical hypocrites of Bush, Blair and the capitalist rulers of the world, who banged the war drums in preparation for military action, not just against the perpetrators of these actions but many innocents as well.

The bombing attacks were completely indiscriminate. Ironically, included amongst many of the thousands of us workers killed at the World Trade Center were those of many ethnic and national backgrounds from the neo-colonial world. The cwi condemned these and similar bombings. They were reprehensible and played into the hands of the ruling class in the us and internationally and the consequences rebounded on the masses particularly in the neo-colonial world.

The repercussions from a 'security', economic, social and political standpoint were greatest immediately in the us. This was a worldwide event which left no part of the world untouched by its repercussions. This was the biggest attack on the us ever. Comparisons were drawn with the Japanese attack on Pearl Harbour in 1941 but even that paled before the suicide attacks of the World Trade Center and the Pentagon. Just over two thousand were killed in the Pearl Harbour attack but the estimated numbers who perished in the World Trade Center were greater. Moreover, the Pearl Harbour attack took place on a Pacific island. This was the first attack on the us 'mainland' since the 1812-14 war with Britain. The us had not experienced this type of attack before (leaving aside the failed attack on the World Trade Center in 1993), despite the fact that it went through the Second World War, the Cold War, including the Cuban missile crisis, and the Gulf War.

"A handful of suicide attackers armed with knives managed successfully to devastate the financial centre of the us and, therefore, of the world – the wtc, downtown Manhattan and, indirectly, Wall Street – and the military power of us imperialism concentrated in the Pentagon. At the same time, the crashed airliner in Pittsburgh, presidential spokesmen claimed, was possibly targeting the White House, Camp David or even Airforce One, with Bush on it at the time. New York City, which was paralysed for days in the aftermath of the bombing, was one of the richest cities on the globe independently 'raking in more annually than all of the world's most advanced states. In 1998, the city's budget exceeded that of some major countries, including Russia."[2]

New York was more than just a wealthy city of eight million people. It was the financial capital of the world's largest economy. As the significance of what happened in New York sank in across the country, America's smaller exchanges closed down one by one. But it was the New York stock exchange that moved global financial events. This was the first time since the Second World War that the New York financial markets were closed for two consecutive working days.

Even before the full effects of this tragedy were digested, the questioning and divisions within the US ruling class and worldwide had already opened up. Questions were being posed, such as, how was it possible for US imperialism and its 'security agencies', with its battery of the latest hi-tech equipment, with an army of 'counter-spies' to seemingly have no warning of these events? This is despite the fact that Osama bin Laden, the main culprit, according to US spokesmen, and the author of these events, "warned as recently as three months ago of retribution against the US for the 'crimes against the peoples of the Middle East and Islam as a whole."[3]

Moreover, other states, such as France, had received recent warnings and had taken action against attacks from Islamic militants. We commented at the time:

"Mixed in with the bewilderment and anger at the bombings and their perpetrators is a growing realisation and a perplexity that the US is not perceived as the 'defender of liberty' internationally but is hated by significant sections of the world's population for its role as an oppressor, particularly in the neo-colonial world. It is the foremost power and champion of untrammelled global capitalism...

"Gone like the snows of yesteryear is the concept now of 'Fortress America'. The effect on the consciousness of the US people, and foremost among them the US working class, will be felt in the medium and long term. Paradoxically, the idea that the fate of the majority of the US population is tied to that of the peoples in Africa, Asia, Latin America, never mind in Europe and Japan, will grow. But in the first instance, a patriotic and maybe even a xenophobic mood will develop and be whipped up by the US ruling class."[4]

The world bourgeoisie, beginning with the US, sought to use these events to vilify the anti-capitalist, anti-globalisation protesters and, at the same time, bolster the repressive apparatus of the state. In the aftermath of the Oklahoma bombing, measures were used to tighten up 'security'. However, it was not just in the US or in air travel, either internally in the US or internationally, that the capitalist states sought to strengthen their role. Serious attempts were made to undermine individual and personal liberties including the freedom to travel. For example in Germany, the then opposition Christian Social Union suggested that the German army should be deployed in an internal security role, a prohibition eventually lifted in 2012. The National Guard and army were deployed in New York and Washington DC with their panoply of tanks and armoured cars.

While we issued a warning against the war preparations of the bourgeoisie – which were evident almost immediately after 9/11 – at the same time, we unreservedly attacked the terrorist methods used by the perpetrators. We wrote of the event:

"This underlines the argument that Marxism has always made against terrorist methods carried out by conspiratorial groups, which, no matter what the underlying causes – oppression, discrimination, poverty... – always has the opposite and reactionary effects to that which its perpetrators anticipate.

"In the past, Marxists, who base themselves on mass action, had to oppose 'individual terrorism', usually action by individuals or small groups to assassinate individual representatives of the ruling class, who would simply be replaced by new leaders. The attacks in the US, however, are a form of mass terrorism carried out by a conspiratorial group, not only striking a blow at the symbols of US wealth and power but also indiscriminately claiming the lives of thousands of ordinary people.

"The denunciation of 'terrorists' in the mouths of Tony Blair, Bush, Ariel Sharon, Vladimir Putin and the rest of them is pure hypocrisy. They are the greatest perpetrators of mass terror, usually against mostly defenceless peoples...

"The veteran expert on the Middle East, Robert Fisk, commented in the British daily, The Independent: 'Ask an Arab how he responds to 20,000 or 30,000 innocent deaths and he or she will respond as decent people should, that it is an unspeakable crime. But they will ask why we did not use such words about the sanctions that have destroyed the lives of perhaps half a million children in Iraq [a Palestinian journalist in The Guardian has put the figure as one million children who have died from the effects of depleted uranium and starvation]... [12 September]

"Leaders of the G7 sat down for talks with Putin in Genoa, Russia's prime minister at the time of the final Russian assault on Grozny, Chechnya, in 1999 which resulted in the slaughter of thousands of people.

"We oppose 'terrorism' but we use this term in a different sense to the pejorative fashion in which the bourgeoisie uses it. For Blair, Sharon and Bush it does not apply to them when they use mass terrorist methods. However, they argue it is legitimate to use this term, when a subject people, take up arms to defend themselves against an oppressive regime. By this reasoning, the South African masses had no right to resist the apartheid regime armed to the teeth. The Palestinian masses are expected to lie down and meekly accept the unspeakable social conditions, the denial of legitimate democratic and national rights, the torture, and the daily bombardments and killings including of women and children...

"Similarly, no matter what the motivation of the suicide bombers was, the net result, as is already evident in the few days following these events, has been to create the conditions to allow the ruling classes of the world to begin to strengthen and justify repressive measures aimed not just against 'terrorists' but against working-class movements, radicals and those who intend to protest against the inequality and injustice of the capitalist system."[5]

Bin Laden was a creature of US imperialism's intervention, particularly through the medium of the CIA (who financed him), in the proxy war they organised through the Mujahideen against the

Soviet Union's presence in Afghanistan. The sins of the past of US imperialism were being revisited on the heads of innocent American men, women and children today. We stressed that we should also remember that Bin Laden and al-Qa'ida are not in any way progressive forces and are even to the right of the theocratic regime in Saudi Arabia.

War hysteria was whipped up in the US and to some extent worldwide. One New Yorker on the day of the attacks declared: "I feel like going to war again. No mercy. We have to come together like '41, go after them."[6] Rather than countering such sentiments, if anything, the 'sober' spokespersons for US capitalism appeared to be stoking this mood. The Washington Post declared: "The nation must prepare itself to fight its first war of the new century— one that will begin with identifying and punishing the authors of yesterday's mass murder, but one that must continue until the sources of support for the terrorists have been eliminated and the country's defenses against such unconventional warfare decisively strengthened." Speaking of the new "enemy", it went on to state that the US "must seek to assemble an international alliance to identify and eliminate all sources of support for the terrorist networks that would wage war on the United States. If necessary, it must act alone."[7]

Kissinger, with the blood of thousands of Chilean workers on his hands from the coup which he inspired and helped organise against the democratically elected government of Salvador Allende in September 1973, jumped on the bandwagon to denounce 'terrorism'. He demanded US forces and their allies should be prepared for an invasion of offending states: "Any government that shelters groups capable of this kind of attack, whether or not they can be shown to have been involved in this attack, must pay an exorbitant price."[8]

Through Britain a NATO coalition, similar to that assembled at the time of the intervention in and bombing of Serbia during the Kosova war, was prepared for action. Indeed, US imperialism was trying to go even further. Just days after the attacks, they attempted to assemble an even wider coalition, similar to that established at the time of the Gulf War.

Gerhard Schröder the German chancellor, who criticised us imperialism at the time of the Gulf War, fell into line and sent troops to serve with NATO in Afghanistan, as he had done in Kosova. Blair had no need to change his position as traditionally he acted, as had all representatives of British imperialism since 1945, as the poodle of American capitalism. Even Russian capitalism, in the form of Putin, fell in solidly behind us imperialism on this issue. Even if the 'coalition' would not hold in the mid- and long term, it nevertheless, at this time, enormously strengthened us imperialism's hand to use whatever measures it deemed necessary to strike back.

As we wrote, this provided the chance to prepare for "at the very least some kind of military intervention, possibly not just air strikes but the use of ground troops, will be deployed against bin Laden's 'bases' in Afghanistan... This would have repercussions not just in Afghanistan but also in Pakistan, with the rise of Islamic fundamentalism, which the Musharraf government is impotent to combat. The Pakistani regime is armed with nuclear devices, as is India, and it has been an enduring concern of American imperialism that conflict in this theatre could spiral out of control and result in a limited nuclear exchange."

We could point to the retrogressive effects of terrorism:

"In Britain, for instance, Blair faced a revolt of the trade unions at the September TUC congress on privatisation. It was widely canvassed beforehand, that he would face the most hostile audience since coming to power four years [previously]. However, just before he was due to speak, the attacks took place in the us and he promptly cancelled his speech. There was no debate, therefore, at the TUC congress on privatisation.

"Thus this key issue facing the British working class and labour movement was not even aired properly at the TUC. Moreover, the conference was wound up early for the first time since 1939 (when the Second World War was declared), adding to the 'war atmosphere' which the British ruling class along with the ruling classes worldwide want to create. One of the by-products of this 'non-class' or 'all-classes-together' attitude will be the capitalists' intention to carry through with the minimum of opposition fundamental attacks on the living standards and the rights of the working class. The Bush administration is being pressed to immediately cut 'capital gains' tax."

In Germany the slogan used for the rally at the Brandenburg Gate was: "No power to terror – solidarity with the USA." It was interesting that the bourgeoisie and the social democratic leaders had to borrow some of the language of the working class – 'solidarity' – in order to justify the expression of unity with the employers and with their system which, of course, is responsible for spawning the conditions which have given rise to terrorism in the Middle East and elsewhere.

The only reason why the British TUC did not call a similar demonstration was probably the fear of setting a precedent, as well as their lack of influence in general in society and amongst their members. If a demonstration had been called, it would undoubtedly be invoked in the future as an example of what could be done on burning social issues such as cuts and privatisation.

The atmosphere of hatred and intimidation whipped up against the seven million Muslims in the US and in other countries is typified by what was reported from Chicago. Many taxi drivers came from Muslim countries and one fleet ordered drivers to go home on Tuesday following a proliferation of abusive comments from passengers. Moreover, many Muslim colleges and mosques remained under guard. In Europe there were examples of verbal abuse directed against Asian people. It remained an important task for 'Socialist Alternative' (the US co-thinkers of the CWI) where possible to seek to defend verbally and in action this minority which could be witch-hunted and persecuted in the next days, weeks and months.

On what bearing these events would have on perspectives, we conceded that it was possible that the anti-globalisation movement would be temporarily thrown off balance; some people who had participated in the movement or joined in demonstrations may be discouraged and drop away. "But the objective situation which led to these movements will not go away; on the contrary, it could worsen with the overall position of capitalism undermined."

However, the general situation, at least in the short term, would not be now as favourable as we anticipated, perhaps particularly in the US. "In the medium and long term the fundamental weaknesses of US and world capitalism will be compounded by these events. For instance, if as expected US imperialism explodes in a military interventionist fashion, with the thousands of victims that will result from this, that will in turn have a powerful effect on the consciousness of the already worldwide anti-globalisation movement. The issue of war and peace will come much more to the fore with the possibility of powerful peace movements coalescing with the anti-corporate, anti-global capitalism movement. It should be remembered that, notwithstanding the military might of US imperialism, while it can pursue military-police operations including invasions and temporary occupations of countries or parts of countries, it cannot, as Napoleon discovered, sit on bayonets to hold whole nations in chains."

Everything depended on whether US imperialism would be able to establish a military 'victory'. International military incursions, even if they were carefully calibrated, would only compound the problems in the Middle East and, particularly, Israel/Palestine which remained a powder keg. Under cover of these events, the Israeli ruling class temporarily moved in and occupied two Palestinian towns and then subsequently withdrew. Sharon, the Israeli prime minister at the time, announced the intention to establish a buffer zone between the West Bank, Gaza and Israel proper.

This conflict was given a further twist by the involvement for the first time ever of an Israeli Arab in a suicide bomb attack, which heightened the conflict within Israel itself. It also reinforced the tendency of a section of the Israeli ruling class to contemplate the doomsday scenario of a repartition of the area, involving the driving out of the million Arabs in Israel, the consolidation of a number of the Israeli settlements already in the West Bank into Israel, and the erection of a cordon sanitaire around Israel. The exclusion of all Palestinians from Israel, we argued, would enormously compound the social and economic problems of the West Bank and Gaza and provide a festering source for another round of vicious terrorism, from which America, with the rest of the capitalist world, would once again suffer. This running sore would be a guarantee of a further round of terrorist attacks, including on the US, and counter-measures.

Therefore, no matter which route US and world imperialism was to choose, it would find no solution to its problems. Temporarily, class and social issues could be pushed to the background by these events. We emphasised that there would be a minority, and a significant minority at that, who would look for explanations and could eagerly embrace the analysis and programme that we put forward.

We stated bluntly that: "This period will be a testing time for our US collaborators in particular, and for the CWI as a whole. But we must not be blown off course."[9] We would remain firm in the face of what could be another vicious round of bourgeois ideological warfare which aimed to demonise all who stand against their system as 'terrorists'. However, the relationship of class forces would not be fundamentally altered by these events. The economic situation and its political repercussions would be felt in the political arena ultimately. The CWI had established very important points of support and could grow substantially, especially in the medium and long term, if we ideologically came to terms with this new situation. This was a very important turning point in US and world history. How we faced up to this position would be an important test of socialists and CWI members and supporters.

Blair and Bush seized on the attack on the World Trade Center and the Pentagon to prepare, within days, a war in Afghanistan. In his book Blair writes: "In the Arab world, condemnation was nearly universal, only Saddam ensuring that Iraqi state television played a partisan song, 'Down with America', calling the attacks 'the fruits of American crimes against humanity.'"[10] By dragging in

Saddam, he indicates that he and Bush already saw military action in Afghanistan merely as a preliminary foray for the real war in Iraq later.

However, ruminating later on the war, he writes: "If I had known then that a decade later we would still be fighting in Afghanistan, I would have been profoundly perturbed and alarmed."[11] Amen, say the peoples of Afghanistan, Iraq, the Middle East as a whole and the majority of the world's population. The truth is that the attack on the World Trade Center was a pretext for military intervention, which Blair and Bush thought would involve a quick military action and then a victorious withdrawal. They were to learn a very harsh lesson, one that all invaders of Afghanistan have experienced: Alexander the Great, the British Empire and Russian Stalinism. The mountainous terrain and the scattered population were ideal for a protracted guerrilla war, making outright military victory well nigh impossible. Blair admits later: "I knew little about Afghanistan, but I did know it was a country that over the centuries had been invaded, occupied and plundered yet always seemed eventually to swallow and spit out the invaders."[12]

Yet despite this, he committed himself with Bush to "remove the Taliban, and a reconstruction plan for Afghanistan".[13] The world is still waiting for the achievements of these two 'war aims'. In the meantime, Afghanistan has been laid waste, as has Iraq and the Middle East as a whole. The population of Iraq are now so besieged by uncontrollable terrorist attacks that they look back wistfully to the regime of Saddam Hussein.

Blair also comments: "I left the stage of the TUC – ironically given a better reception than any I ever enjoyed..."[14] This completely bears out our warning that terrorist methods in general would not strengthen but weaken the working class. Blair details the war preparations: "The next weeks were spent in a frantic but essentially well-organised process to put together the military operation to remove the Taliban."[15] Yet despite the colossal expenditure in lives, as well as the treasure of the British and the American people, that task remains as yet to be completed. When the invasion took place, the Taliban just melted away, regrouped and prepared for a protracted struggle. US imperialism has now largely withdrawn, as have the British, although huge military bases like Bagram were retained to ensure a continued presence in the country and allow swift intervention if necessary.

Even before the war in Afghanistan began, a polarisation was taking place with undoubted support from perhaps the majority of the us population, but with a significant minority opposing the rush to war. Socialist Alternative intervened in the growing anti-war movement.

In Britain, 63% indicated in a poll that they were prepared to see British troops, ships and planes take part in action, but there was also significant unease about Britain being plunged into a prolonged war.

45. War in Afghanistan
2001

Blair indicated just how unprepared and light-minded he and Bush were in rushing to war in Afghanistan. Even Pakistan's President Musharraf, although publicly supporting Blair and Bush and condemning the actions of the Taliban, nevertheless warned Blair in private of actions by leaders which can have unintended consequences: "He told me something I reflected upon a good deal in later years: in the 1970s, General Zia had made the fatal error of linking Pakistani nationalism to devout Islam, in the course of which he had adopted the manner of a religious as well as a political and military leader, proudly showing the mark on his forehead from being pressed to the ground in prayer. The connection between the two, Musharraf explained, had furthered radicalism [right-wing political Islam] in the country, heightened the issue of Kashmir and made reconciliation with India harder."[1]

Blair claimed: "The Taliban had collapsed by the end of 2001, remnants melting back into the Pushtun populace in southern Afghanistan and the Pakistani tribal areas."[2] Yet he concedes after the fact: "Many who were not extremists nevertheless shared a sense that they were justified in fighting us; that this was a battle between the West and the people of Afghanistan."[3] So to eradicate the Afghan people's 'false consciousness', they had to be bombed back into the Stone Age! This did not work, as he in effect concedes: "I certainly misjudged the depth of the failure of the Afghan state and the ability of the Taliban to immerse themselves into local communities, particularly in the south, and to call upon reinforcements from across the border in the mountainous highlands that seemed a law unto themselves."[4] He certainly would have 'understood' if beforehand he had studied the history of Afghanistan, particularly the fate of invaders of the country, or if he had perused the publications of the CWI!

Incredibly, Blair claims that, in his partnership with Bush, invading Afghanistan and then Iraq, he "had become a revolutionary"![5] He has missed out one little word: "counter"! Imperialist intervention in the region perpetuated its age-old poverty, with the added aim of securing their strategic interests, including the defence of their oil interests. The invasion of Afghanistan was christened 'Operation Enduring Freedom'. A more apt description for the peoples of this blighted country and region would be "enduring misery, poverty, war and backwardness".

The US ruling class and its allies launched a massive ideological offensive to prepare the ground for the physical offensive against 'terrorism'. We stated that this offensive would not just be aimed at those Middle Eastern groups attacking US imperialism but could also be used to attack anyone challenging the capitalist system. The journals of capitalism began to claim that this was a battle between the 'civilised' and the 'uncivilised', with Bush in his usual simplistic fashion, arguing that the choice was between 'good' – represented by him and Blair – and 'evil': not just bin Laden, but anyone who stood in the way of the aims of the US and imperialism as a whole. We reminded our readers that the roots of the developing conflict were found in the wars conducted 10 years previously in the Gulf and the horrific sanctions against Iraq which killed an estimated half a million children.

Bush and Blair played on the feelings of outrage at 9/11 and initially got significant support, especially in the US where 84% said that they supported military retaliation. Yet we argued that despite the bombing of Iraq, through the 'no-fly zone', Saddam was still "in place. It was not the bombings during the war in Kosova that removed Milosevic, but mass action by ordinary Serbs, including the organised working class."[6] Bill Clinton had also bombed targets in Iraq with B-52 bombers armed with up to 300 cruise missiles in 1998. We had argued that the US wanted "Saddam out of the way, by military strike, coup or assassination."[7] Just weeks after his inauguration, George W Bush had flexed his country's muscles by bombing Iraq, with the intention of demonstrating his 'decisiveness'. As usual, Tony Blair applauded his actions, playing the role of US imperialism's lapdog.

The New Labour government's ministers for defence, John Speller and Geoff Hoon, with their usual breathtaking hypocrisy, supported this action, claiming that it was necessary to cage Saddam Hussein and thereby protect the Kurds of the north and the Shia Marsh Arabs in southern Iraq. While there was majority support for Bush's stance, certainly in America, with the opinion polls initially at over 90% approval, the highest ever for the US president, we argued that there would be significant opposition and this would grow, especially in the event of an invasion.

After 9/11 the anti-war movement began to develop. In London 2,000 people assembled on 21 September to condemn Bush and Blair's plans for war. So crammed was the room where the meeting was taking place that an overspill room was organised, which heard speakers outside. These included Tariq Ali, Socialist Alliance member Liz Davies and others. But Socialist Party member and Socialist Alliance chairperson Dave Nellist was prevented from speaking – another example of the exclusive and sectarian position of our left opponents. Apart from the fact that Dave Nellist had been consistently elected as a councillor and was part of the same broad Socialist Alliance as the organisers, the SWP made sure that he was not given a platform. John Rees – in the SWP at this time – attempted to offer some 'analysis' in distinction to other speakers but he was the only one not to condemn the atrocities in the US – merely concluding that if we stopped the war now, there would be a "better life for decent, ordinary people everywhere".

This was an example of the SWP's avoidance of any criticism of right-wing 'political Islam', which caused divisions then and later in the anti-war movement. We opposed their stance as well as that of other organisations on the left on this issue, which amounted to giving 'critical' support to what they perceived were "anti-imperialist" forces in the Middle East and elsewhere. We set out our differences in a lengthy document, 'Afghanistan, Islam and the revolutionary left'. [2002, full document on Marxist.net] We pointed out:

"War is an acid test for the programme, perspectives, strategy and tactics of all political formations, particularly those that stand on the left. Everything which is positive, which in action shows a way forward for the working class, is revealed. Conversely, everything that is rotten, which is false, is also laid bare. So it was in the Gulf war, in the conflict in Kosova/Kosovo and now also in the war in Afghanistan...

"Compare the positions taken by the CWI and its sections with those of other organisations, particularly those who claim to stand on the revolutionary left... Most of [them] erred, and sometimes quite grossly, during the war. Some were opportunist; mostly however they were ultra-left and sometimes managed to combine both opportunism and ultra-leftism."

We stated:

"To call baldly and crudely for the 'defeat of US imperialism' and its coalition allies as an agitational slogan is wrong. When Lenin used the term 'revolutionary defeatism', as Trotsky subsequently explained, it was in order to clearly delineate revolutionary Marxism from opportunism following the betrayal of the German social democracy and their opportunist international co-thinkers at the beginning of the First World War. It was primarily a policy for the cadres to draw a clear line of separation between the revolutionaries and the opportunists. It was not a policy that could have won the masses to the banner of Bolshevism or to the revolution. It was the programme of the Bolsheviks and everything that flowed from this, including the taking of power by the working class in alliance with the peasantry, which guaranteed the success of the Russian Revolution."[8]

What is required today is not a simple repetition of ideas which fitted the conditions of 60 years ago or even 20 years ago. The development of independent states and national bourgeois regimes is a big change compared to when Trotsky wrote on these issues. Some of them, like that of Saddam Hussein, had the most hideous and repulsive features of dictatorship. They suppressed the working class and denied national and ethnic rights. This changed the circumstances in which Marxists work today. It means that we cannot simply imitate the approach of Trotsky at the time of the Chinese/Japanese war in the 1930s or in Ethiopia in 1935, or base ourselves upon the hypothetical situation sketched out by Trotsky in relation to Brazil.

Internationally, the anti-war movement developed rapidly with 10,000 demonstrating in Bellingham, Washington State, us, in September. The cwi's German section, sav, intervened in mass demonstrations with the slogan "No more victims, stop the war!" In Britain in October, the Socialist carried the slogan "War is no solution". We pointed out that "Blair and George Bush will declare war on the dirt poor country of Afghanistan – a third of whose population (8 million) are dependent upon United Nations food handouts to survive... even if this war succeeds in dislodging the medieval rule of the Taliban, it's extremely unlikely the opposition Northern Alliance will restore democratic rights to the Afghan people."[9]

From the beginning we pointed out that the real solution lay in the hands of ordinary Afghans who must fight for a government of working people and the rural poor as part of a socialist confederation of the Middle East. At the same time, we demanded that the working class should not pay the price for capitalism's war. In its approach towards the war, the us faced confused 'war aims'. Colin Powell, Secretary of State, defined the limits of us capacity: "We do deserts, we don't do mountains."

By early November, the systematic bombing of Afghanistan had begun. There was plenty of talk of conducting this war in a 'humanitarian' fashion. We pointed out that it was likely that us imperialism would succeed in overthrowing the Taliban, which by this time was extremely unpopular in Afghanistan, by using a combination of bombing, limited ground troops, funding the Northern Alliance and attempting to split the Taliban itself. Robert Fisk in the Independent accurately described the Northern Alliance as "a confederacy of warlords... rapists and torturers." He described how, when they took control of the capital in 1992, they "looted and raped their way through the suburbs of Kabul".[10] At one stage previously, the Mujahideen as a whole were receiving around $1 million a day from the US.

Terrorism, we argued, far from being defeated, had increased. At the same time, the working class in the West would be expected to foot the bill for the war in the form of job cuts, attacks on public spending and tax increases. Moreover, the ruling class in the US and elsewhere used the attacks to justify a serious undermining of democratic rights. The Prevention of Terrorism Act in Britain was introduced as a knee-jerk reaction to the IRA bombings in Britain in the early 1970s. It did not defeat the IRA but it was responsible for miscarriages of justice such as in the cases of the Guildford Four and the Birmingham Six. Any repressive laws introduced would undoubtedly generate a climate whereby racist attacks on Arabs and Muslims around the world could take place. In the immediate aftermath of 9/11, people had been shot in racist attacks. In Britain an Afghan taxi driver was paralysed after an assault.

In the US opinion polls at first showed overwhelming support for military action but in Britain the majority said they would oppose military strikes if they harmed civilians. The economic fall-out was considerable as well. Not surprisingly, the attacks brought the biggest stock exchange fall since 1929 – inevitably echoed by similar falls in stock exchanges around the world. The most immediate impact of the attack was on airlines, which faced devastating losses and even bankruptcy. Before 9/11, US airlines had been forecast to make a combined loss of up to $3.5 billion in 2001. The airline bosses had no hesitation in going to the President and Congress demanding a $24 billion rescue package in the form of tax relief and guaranteed loans. The price of oil rose immediately after 9/11, but big oil producers like Saudi Arabia and the United Arab Emirates rushed to help their friend, the US, promising they would increase production in order to meet demand. However, the price of oil had already tripled since the slump in prices following the Asian crisis of 1997-98.

Just a month after the attacks, we drew a balance sheet of the repercussions for the changed era we were likely to pass through. Even the popular press were pessimistic: "We are looking at civil war, revolution, international conflict. We are facing uprisings by fundamentalist fanatics against America and its allies."[11] We commented: "It is a measure of how much the world has changed, and 'changed utterly', when the British 'popular' (gutter) press speaks in such apocalyptic tones about the future, in the aftermath of the terrorist attacks on New York and Washington."[12]

A US Army strategic planner stated that the US "may be embarking on an endless war of attrition against a faceless enemy – think of a global Vietcong."[13] A lawyer in Washington commented: "No one wants to hear about American policies or how they might have influenced or caused what has happened."[14] For the time being, this will be the case, we wrote. Yet the shattering of 'Fortress USA' would ultimately force the population to confront the reality of the 'country's standing in the world'.

Thousands died in the terrorist attacks. Yet terrible as this was, it was outstripped by the number of children who died in Iraq every month through lack of medicine and food because of the US government's sanctions policy. Author Martin Amis wrote: "It will also be horribly difficult and painful for Americans to absorb the fact that they are hated, and hated intelligibly. How many of them know, for example, that their government has destroyed at least 5% of the Iraqi population? How many of them then transfer that figure to America (and come up with 14m)?"[15]

There was worldwide condemnation of the attacks. Even Iran, Hezbollah guerrillas in Lebanon, and Syria, together with Gaddafi's Libyan regime condemned the attacks without overtly signing up to the 'coalition' organised against Al-Qa'ida. We foresaw future developments when we wrote: "The capture or killing of bin Laden would not shatter the terrorist network which exists. His organisation acts as an umbrella organisation, a 'think tank', a kind of 'Ford Foundation for terrorism' which, it is alleged, has a presence in at least 60 countries."[16] Prophetic words in view of the later killing of bin Laden under Obama and the increase in terrorism in the Middle East, Africa and Asia.

Even before the invasion of Afghanistan, the country was in a terrible position and was already firmly located in the Stone Age. "Life expectancy... has fallen to the age of 42 for women and 44 for men."[17] Out of 26 million people, at least five million had fled the country. With the economy in ruins, drought and famine faced those who were left behind. The US was preparing to bomb the country. Ferocious pressure was exerted on Pakistan to force the Taliban to hand over bin Laden and provide facilities for operations against Afghanistan. Pakistani officials complained to the Financial Times: "The US told us: 'you are either with us or against us'... Under the circumstances we had no option but to sign up."[18] In this sense, the Gulf War was being repeated, with huge financial subsidies dangled before those who would sign up and sanctions against those who wouldn't.

In Pakistan itself right-wing Islamism at this stage derived its strength from state patronage rather than popular support. The ascendancy of religious fundamentalism was the legacy of the previous military dictator, General Zia al Haq, who had received backing from Washington during his 11 years in power. As president he created a network of madrassas (religious boarding schools) which were funded by the Saudi Arabian regime. We pointed out that religious zealotry alone would not have guaranteed victory for the Taliban. It was the Pakistani army, through the medium of 'volunteers', that guaranteed its success. Moreover, this was the only foreign 'victory' of the Pakistani army, hence its tenacious support for the Taliban.

Fuelled by the rottenness and corruption of successive Pakistani regimes, as well as the worsening of the conditions of the already impoverished masses, political Islam began to sink roots in Pakistan itself and was now like a giant octopus threatening to completely strangle the country. The intervention of the US and Pakistan in Afghanistan provoked complaints, with the former head of the intelligence service protesting: "America has shown breathtaking arrogance in asking Pakistan to once again demonstrate that it is a friend. We gave everything in the 1980s to help America drive the Soviet Union out of Afghanistan, and when it no longer suited their interests, the Americans simply abandoned us." This source went on to point out that bin Laden was part of an anti-Soviet Mujahideen group that received at least $10 million from the US during the 1980s. "The Taliban regime of Afghanistan grew directly out of the generous funding that the US gave to Islamic Mujaheddin groups in the 1980s."[19] Another general spat out: "Pakistan was the condom the Americans needed to enter Afghanistan. We served our purpose and they think we can be flushed down the toilet."[20]

In the US we anticipated that opposition would grow despite the fact that Bush had been given greater support in Congress than any president since the Gulf of Tonkin resolution in 1964 (opposed by only two Senators), which led the US to immerse itself in the Vietnam disaster. This time round, only one congresswoman, representing the district covering Berkeley University and Oakland, California, voted against giving Bush unlimited powers. We wrote: "This unanimity will not hold in the teeth of the increased problems which will confront the prosecution of this 'war'. But at the same time, a different kind of 'war' will eventually unfold in the US and throughout the capitalist world, in parallel with the military efforts of US imperialism and its allies: a class war. This will result from the inevitable resistance of working class people to the capitalists' attempt to use the cover of this conflict to carry thorough wholesale attacks on workers' living standards."[21] It took a long time for the working out of this perspective, but it is revealed in the huge changes taking place in the US today, symbolised by the victory of Kshama Sawant in Seattle in November 2013.

In the immediate days after 9/11, we reaffirmed our opposition to terrorism. It is the responsibility of the capitalist class who are incapable of solving the problems of the world: poverty, unemployment and deprivation. As shocking as the events of the World Trade Centre were, out of this carnage we predicted a layer would ask questions as to why these horrific events took place, while large parts of the world were already submerged in poverty and barbarism. We expected that they would ultimately discover that the system was incapable of satisfying the needs of the majority on the planet and that they would turn towards the ideas of socialism and Marxism.

46. Preparations for the Iraq invasion

The bombings by the US and Britain of Afghanistan, commencing on 7 October 2001, met with protests in the Middle East, Asia, Europe, the US, indeed throughout the world. We intervened in Britain in the protests in London and elsewhere. At the London demonstration, there were comrades from the US and Austria who also spoke at an impromptu rally. They were in London for an international meeting of the CWI to discuss the prospects of war and the plans of the CWI to oppose it. In the following period, practically every section of the CWI – then in 35 countries throughout the world – was involved in protest, which indicated that the opposition to this war was greater than at the equivalent stage before the first Gulf War.

On the actual bombing itself, Robert Fisk remarked in the Independent newspaper: "There are no Saudi Arabian or Kuwaiti pilots in the night skies over Afghanistan. This is not a Western-Muslim coalition. This is the West on its own, bombing a Muslim country that has a standard of living close to the Middle Ages."[1] What was at stake, however, was the prestige of the US ruling class, severely dented by 9/11. Crushing military measures were perceived as the only way to re-establish its power but rather than eradicating terrorism from the skies, we said that this would only create even greater terrorism below. Then, in an ominous development within days of the 9/11 attack, the US Republican right raised the prospect of completing what was started in 1992 but not carried through, namely the overthrow of Saddam Hussein. This was even before the invasion of Afghanistan. David Owen, former British Foreign Secretary, Donald Rumsfeld, the US Defence Secretary, and Tony Blair, in a debate in the British Parliament, all either stated explicitly or implied that after the Taliban was 'dealt with', Iraq could be the next target!

Blair fully committed himself and his government to supporting Bush when visiting the latter's ranch in Crawford, Texas in April 2002. He effectively misinformed the House of Commons one week later when he stated: "I repeat, however, that no decisions on action have been taken. Our way of proceeding should be and will be measured, calm and thought through. When judgments are made, I shall ensure that the House has a full opportunity to debate them."[2] Everything that was necessary to justify the war flowed from this, including the completely false 'dodgy dossier' which indicated that Iraq had substantial stockpiles of weapons of mass destruction (WMD). This was subsequently found to be completely false by every reputable source including Hans Blix, UN chief of weapons inspectors and Dr David Kelly, British government specialist (who was later found dead in mysterious circumstances) and, especially, by the majority of the population. Blair later tried to pretend that "the intelligence was wrong and we should have, and I have, apologised for it".[3] But he steadfastly refused to apologise for the war and justifies it at every turn. As a result, Blair is widely considered to be a war criminal, as is George Bush.

Undoubtedly, bin Laden and his supporters were grist to the mill of imperialism and their plans to intervene in Iraq and the Middle East. Shortly after 9/11, he made a video which was carefully constructed to appeal to the downtrodden and oppressed throughout the Arab and Muslim world. The contrast between his video, shot in the caves of Afghanistan, and the broadcasts of Saddam Hussein during the Gulf War, dressed in a western suit, could not have been greater. Moreover, he appealed not just to the Arab world, but to all 'Muslim people'. This immediately resonated with the oppressed, like the Palestinians in Gaza who came out onto the streets in a mass demonstration of support. In Pakistan 10,000 demonstrated in Quetta in Baluchistan, which borders Afghanistan itself.

This signified, we believed, that the world was at the beginning of what the strategists of imperialism/capitalism said would probably be a 'long war'. In effect, the capitalists used the term 'Muslim fundamentalist terrorism', as they had previously used 'Stalinism', as a scarecrow to frighten the masses in the West. They hoped this would bolster support for building up the military apparatus, attacks on civil liberties (symbolised by the obscenity of Guantanamo Bay), torture, the national security state and infringements of civil liberties. Step by step there were attempts to condition the population in western countries to tolerate new repressive measures. This was especially the case in the US, Britain and Germany where new security measures were either rushed into law or preparations were made to do so. The authorities were unapologetic about an estimated 1,000 people arrested immediately after 9/11.

Measures taken against anti-war activists were part of a process to roll back the growing opposition to war and capitalist globalisation. The issue boiled down starkly to "Those who are not with us are against us." Hilary Armstrong, Labour chief whip in the House of Commons, told a Labour MP who had dared to question the war policy and asked for a free vote, that he must follow Blair's line as "war is not a matter of conscience... It is government policy that we are at war!... I am not going to have a dialogue with you about that. It was people like you who appeased Hitler in 1938."[4]

However, it took time for Blair and Bush to assemble their 'coalition' in preparation for the invasion of Iraq. The counter-pressure began to build as the anti-war movement, with the recent experience of Afghanistan, began to amass its forces. The demonstrations that took place in an effort to prevent the war were some of the biggest in history. And the US did not always get its own way. Lesser rivals to the US, such as France, Germany, Russia and China, who had already agreed oil and trade deals with Iraq, were opposed to

US unilateral action against Saddam. There was an intense debate within US ruling circles as well. Such was the opposition, Bush was compelled by the pressure of his own side, particularly the likes of Secretary of State Colin Powell, to seek legitimacy for the war through a resolution of the United Nations. Therefore, despite allowing weapons inspectors back into Iraq, an eventual US-led war seemed extremely likely.

The anti-war movement in Britain prepared to mobilise mass pressure to prevent war. In January 2003, 800 attended the Stop the War Coalition's national conference. Tony Benn, in a rousing speech, said, "We speak for humanity. This is an argument between the people of the world and the rulers of the world." The former president of Algeria, Ahmed Ben Bella, received a standing ovation when he declared: "There is terror in the world – the terror of George Bush... The world system keeps 85% of the population in poverty and dependency." He called on the British anti-war movement to "take the smile off Tony Blair's face". The conference cheered when George Galloway MP paid tribute to the train drivers in Motherwell who refused to drive trains loaded with ammunition intended for use against Iraq. The conference agreed to campaign with the trade unions for such decisive action on a mass scale to stop the war.

Dave Nellist, Socialist Party councillor, called on the recently elected left union leaders to plough at least some of the money they were giving to New Labour into the anti-war movement and to drive on this campaign. Later in the day, an announcement that soldiers in the north of the country were refusing to go to Iraq was met with huge applause. The conference agreed that the immediate priority was to aim for an unprecedented turn-out on the national demo called for 15 February. The British demonstration was to be synchronised with demos in most European capitals and many other countries. Plans were laid for the day war broke out, including proposals for mass occupations, walkouts, strikes at schools, colleges and workplaces all over the country. On behalf of the Socialist Party, Dave argued that "demonstrations alone won't shift a capitalist government like New Labour". But referring to the political and economic interests of the US, "Only sustained, organised mass civil disobedience can stop a war in progress and force a government to retreat."

He gave the example of the poll tax, led by Militant, which was rooted in the estates, schools, colleges and workplaces and was organised through democratic structures locally, regionally and nationally. To great applause he also stressed that as well as fighting against the war, "we have to raise an alternative, and be just as determined to build a new world... a socialist world."

The anti-war coalition was a broad-based campaign built around support for three minimal demands: stop the war, no to a racist backlash and defend civil and democratic liberties. The Muslim Association of Britain agreed to these demands and, via the mosques, mobilised tens of thousands for anti-war demonstrations. This strengthened the anti-war movement and also gave an opportunity to reach a wide layer of Muslims with socialist ideas. We supported a resolution that "unreservedly condemns terrorist attacks", which was opposed by the Socialist Workers Party and was defeated at the conference. We made it clear that we thought this was a serious mistake for the coalition to take this position. It was further proof of how out of touch some of the groups involved in the anti-war movement, without real connections with working class people, really were.[5]

The US and British-led coalition gained a relatively easy victory in Afghanistan over the Taliban government. The Taliban were not equivalent to the National Liberation Front (Vietcong) in Vietnam, who appealed to the peasant masses in particular with a social programme of land to the peasants and unification of the country. Moreover, the rule of the Taliban was a nightmare for the people of Afghanistan. During the previous 23 years more than one and a half million Afghans had been killed as a direct result of the wars that had taken place on Afghan soil. Most of those who had been killed were civilians, including children who were out on the street playing or in the mountains shepherding their animals. Much of Afghanistan was like a scene from 'Mad Max' or some futurist, brutal war movie. Present everywhere was the debris of war. When the Taliban entered Kabul in 1996 they dragged the former President Najibullah from the United Nations compound, tortured him to death and hung him from a lamp-post. This set the scene for Taliban rule.

Lacking any real political alternatives after the invasion of the country, the US desperately cast around for a government. They even flirted with the return of the previous deposed king, or his nephew, who had deposed him. Various brutal warlords, who dominated the country, were courted and then discarded before Karzai was installed as a puppet of the coalition.

Bolstered by the 'victory' in Afghanistan – hollow as it proved to be in the long term – Bush and Blair turned to preparations for the invasion of Iraq. Intense discussion took place within the labour movement and outside as to whether or not the war would actually go ahead. There was a certain incredulity that Blair, still nominally considered by some working people as 'Labour', would actually proceed. After all, Harold Wilson could not support US President Lyndon Johnson in the prosecution of the Vietnam War. Even the Blairite Labour Party was forced to reflect, however feebly, the unprecedented anti-war mood.

There was a public division between Foreign Secretary Jack Straw and Defence Secretary Geoff Hoon. In fact, in his biography, Straw, with his usual touching modesty, writes: "I could have prevented the United Kingdom's involvement in the Iraq war."[6] Yet his contribution amounted to a few squeaks before the actual war began, then full support for Blair and the war, and thereby his complicity in this war crime. More seriously, a survey of local Labour Party officials indicated mass resignations of rank-and-file members were threatened if Blair was to go ahead with backing the US-led war, particularly without UN approval. We warned that, despite this and other negative repercussions, "Bush could still, with the support of Blair, push ahead with war in the next couple of months."[7]

The price of oil was climbing in anticipation of an attack on Iraq in early 2003. Moreover, the build-up of troops and weapons had a momentum of its own. Sustaining public opinion, let alone financing and maintaining the morale of 100,000 troops in the desert, or bringing them back, would have been extremely difficult, if war were to be delayed. Anti-war protests exploded before the war began in many US cities and across the world. Two hundred thousand people marched in Washington and 100,000 in San Francisco, with tens of thousands in other cities around the country. In Washington, the march was so vast that as the front completed encircling the White House, the last quarter of the march had not even begun moving! There were also big demonstrations in many European cities. In Germany the Schröder government's anti-war rhetoric slightly lessened the degree of opposition as compared to the massive opposition in Britain to Blair's sycophantic support of the US. In Stockholm and Gothenburg thousands marched, as they did in Barcelona, Copenhagen, Madrid, Rome, Mexico City and Seoul.

Although there was opposition within the Labour Party from the likes of Tony Benn, it did not have much effect on Blair's drive towards war. The whole character of the Labour Party had changed decisively. When the war was at its height and when the bodies of those killed and maimed were piling high, the Labour Party conference endorsed Blair's support for the war! Even the constituency Labour parties, who were firmly on the left in the past, were decisively pro-war this time. It was a measure of just how far the Labour Party had been purged of fighting oppositional left activists.

Tony Benn, in his diaries, recorded his disgust at Blair's bellicose approach: "On the radio I heard Tony Blair had warned the Afghanistan government, the Taliban, that if they didn't give up Osama bin Laden they would face the consequences. The man has absolutely no capacity to deliver on his promise. He's just the voice of President Bush."[8]

Tony Benn's policy for opposing the war amounted to appealing to world leaders, the UN, even former Tory leader Ted Heath. His conversation with the latter is revealing both about his lack of a real class alternative on the war and the desperation felt by what remained of the Labour left. He wrote: "I rang Ted Heath again.

'Who is it?' 'Tony Benn. Ted, you got my letter? What advice can you give me? What should I say at the Conference today?' 'Oh I don't know, I can't advise you.' 'Well what do you think?' He said, 'I think Blair should pipe down! He's pretending he's the leader of the whole world. It annoys the Europeans and the Americans; he should pipe down!' He was very candid, and actually just about got it right."[9]

The appeal to the United Nations to stop the war, to oppose Bush, was the equivalent of appealing to Beelzebub against Satan! The United Nations, reflected in its name, represents the ruling class and elites of the world. It can sometimes be a forum for the solution of secondary problems. Some of the work of the UN agencies, on food relief for instance, can play a certain humanitarian role but when the fundamental interests of nations, of the ruling classes in these nations to be more precise, are at stake then the UN will be bypassed. This has been the case in previous wars, such as the Korean War. Commenting on Blair's speech to the conference, Benn wrote that it had been reported all over the world: "This Churchillian figure warning the Taliban to give up Bin Laden or surrender power in only a few days. It's absolutely pathetic! We haven't got enough forces in Britain to recapture the Isle of Wight."[10]

The drive towards war flew in the face of the overwhelming majority opinion in Britain and throughout the world, with the mood hardening in early 2003 against the war. January 27 was set as a deadline for the first weapons inspectors' report to be presented to the UN. The hundreds of site inspections in Iraq finally produced 12 empty rocket shells!

Blair committed 34,000 UK troops to the war, joining 150,000 US troops. Spokespersons for US imperialism like Colin Powell attempted to refute the idea that war with Iraq was all about oil: "The oil of Iraq belongs to the Iraqi people..." he claimed, "It will not be exploited for the United States' own purpose."[11] Few people believed him then or since. It was true that the oil was not the only reason why the US wished to crush Iraq. The prestige of US imperialism – as the world's policeman – and its geopolitical interests worldwide were at stake. The calculation was that if the war against

Iraq was successful this would be enough to make any other 'upstart' in the Middle East and elsewhere contemplating opposition to the US think again. Iraq had at that stage the world's second largest proven oil reserves. The US and world capitalism was dependent on this. An amazing 20% of all US military war spending at that stage went on defending oil installations.

Due to these factors, the US and Britain, through Bush and Blair, were determined to brush aside all objections, including any evidence from the weapons inspectors that proved that Saddam did not have weapons of mass destruction, which was the only real argument to justify going to war. Hans Blix had commented that he "told the Security Council many times he had found no weapons of mass destruction." However, many today, like Dr Jafar Dhia Jafar, criticise him for not screaming louder: "You could have stopped the war. You should have still stood up and said there were no weapons." Blix replied: "I could not prove a negative... we would have lost all credibility if we had claimed the evidence was conclusive."

This is just a lame excuse by Blix. As with the case of David Kelly, which had all the features of a frame-up by the establishment over the so-called 'dirty dossier', it indicated the iron determination of imperialism, particularly the US and Britain, to go to war come what may. It is true that even if Blix had stood up and said there was no evidence of weapons, it would have been brushed aside and the war launched on some other pretext. Today, Blix admits that "I do weep over the results of the mad rush to war by Bush and Blair. Tragically, the US and UK trusted their own faulty intelligence more than the inspection reports we gave."[12]

Even before the war began, it conjured up one of the greatest mass movements in history, which the CWI and the Socialist Party in England and Wales fully participated in. We conceded before it began that, because of its overwhelming military supremacy, the 'coalition' would win any war with Iraq, but at what cost in humanitarian terms for the world economy and in the instability and unrest worldwide?

The anti-war mood infected the trade unions that were coming into opposition to the Blair government on other issues. The fire-fighters, for instance, took action at the end of January 2003, with widespread public support. Labour minister Nicholas Raynsford, responsible for the fire service, complained that the FBU was "no longer credible" because they would not come to heel! According to press reports, Blair was compelled to reduce the number of troops covering the dispute and make those deployed work longer shifts because of the thousands of troops they were sending to the Gulf. John Prescott announced in Parliament that he would consider reactivating the 1947 Fire Services Act, repealed in 1959, to take control of the fire service and impose a pay settlement on the fire-fighters. Many firefighters thought that it would be necessary for an all-out strike to take place which would compel the government to retreat and at the same time give confidence to other workers involved in, or contemplating, industrial action.[13]

47. Massive worldwide resistance to Iraq War 2003

At the end of January 2003 we reported on "Global resistance to the war – massive protest in Bush's backyard". Comrades from the US reported "a number of trade unions and labour councils have taken a strong stand against the war. One hundred delegates representing over two million organised workers formed US Labor Against the War at a meeting in Chicago."[1] But as in Britain, while attacking Bush, not a word of criticism was made at many of the meetings of the Democratic Party, who were tied to big business as much as the Republicans and were firm supporters of imperialist wars and military intervention. In Britain preparations were in full swing for the national mobilisation on 15 February.

This emphasis on the need for democratic forms of organisation was paramount for the success of this movement. As the organisations that had been established were ad hoc, not having the traditional structures of the organised trade union and labour movement, it was therefore even more necessary to arrive at a consensus by having an approach which embraced all forces involved but at the same time striving for a clear programme. A clear class programme was an issue under dispute on occasions, even in the Stop the War national coordinating body.

The Socialist Party came into collision once more with the SWP and their allies over the inclusion of the Liberal Democrats on the platform of the 15 February demonstration. We argued that nobody should be debarred from participating in the demonstration, including Liberal Democrats. Many were very sincerely opposed to the war. For the leaders, however, the anti-war movement represented an opportunity to gain support for their political 'project' and that did not challenge the roots of this war, which was to be found in the nature of capitalist society and its imperialist manifestation. Unfortunately, the SWP, in collusion with others, gave a platform to Liberal Democrats leader Charles Kennedy. We predicted in advance that he would use this platform to burnish his anti-war credentials but once war began would distance himself from the Stop the War Coalition and any consistent opposition to the war. This was what happened.

Ahead of Hans Blix's report, divisions opened up between the US administration – backed by Tony Blair – and France and Germany, backed by Russia. The press in Britain savaged the US administration's 'evidence' to justify an invasion of Iraq. The Daily Mirror declared: "Dodgy tapes, grainy videos, great rhetoric, but where's the PROOF Colin [Powell]?" After his infamous appearance at the UN, where he supplied the "information" justifying intervention, The Daily Mirror's retort was simply "not enough".[2] On the other hand, some leaders of trade unions were increasingly demanding action to oppose the war. An array of trade union leaders demanded a recall TUC Congress, including the leader of the lecturers' union, Paul Mackney, the communication workers' Billy Hayes, Bob Crow of the RMT, Mark Serwotka of PCS and Mick Rix of ASLEF.

In the preparation for the demonstration, we pointed out that this invasion was just the latest example of the many wars that had taken place since 1945. Since then, there had been a war every year with the US using its superpower status to increasingly sweep aside any objections. Since 1945 it had bombed or invaded 23 other countries.

"Millions march against war" was the headline of The Socialist following the colossal 15 February demonstration. "Britain has never seen anything like it. Up to two million people flooding the streets of central London in a massive sea of anti-war protest.

Hundreds of thousands were on their first ever demonstration and it was a day that nobody will forget. As demonstrators converged on London they were strengthened by knowing that they were part of a worldwide movement with millions more making their voices heard across the globe."[3] A placard featured in this issue read: "War on Iraq could kill this many", referring to the size of the demonstration! And this was not far wrong in its estimation!

The Socialist received an enthusiastic welcome from the demonstrators. Of course, compared to the massive number of marchers, Socialist Party members were spread very thinly throughout the demonstration. Hannah Sell, national organiser, coordinating our intervention, reported that we sold 4,500 papers and 140 people applied to join the Socialist Party. All along the route of the demonstration we sold papers. Four members of the Lambeth branch sold 250 copies at Waterloo Station in a shift that lasted from 8.15 in the morning to 2pm. Over 100 were sold at Euston, 211 papers were sold by one comrade on the Embankment. The march set off early and a seller from Wales reported: "As we approached Parliament Square, Wales Socialist Party members formed a line of sellers across the road, selling to everyone. By the end of the march Swansea Socialist Party had sold 72, with 40 plus from Port Talbot, 50 from Pontypridd, and Cardiff sold 70. People were grasping our leaflets and using them as mini-placards."

Reports showed the resourcefulness of Socialist Party members when faced with police harassment: "In the morning the police were stopping the 'usual suspects' from putting up their stalls in the park - including the Socialist Party. So we put up our hoardings on Park Lane. The police then barricaded us off from the march, so we ferreted our papers into the park as the demo arrived. The march streamed into the park from every entrance. We sold 250 papers at the Queen Elizabeth entrance, and London West Central branch sold 153 from the Hyde Park Corner entrance. People held up our paper and leaflets as placards as they entered the park. Groups of anti-Saddam, anti-war Iraqis came up to our stall buying papers and taking our material."[4]

Opposition to the invasion was not at all universal, particularly from Iraqi groups in exile, many of whom welcomed any military action to remove Saddam. We had many a debate with them and the few bands of Blair supporters, which revolved around how best to remove Saddam Hussein. We had common ground that he was a bloodthirsty dictator, presiding over an unacceptable regime. We argued that the task of removing Saddam Hussein was primarily that of the Iraqi people, with the support of the labour movement internationally. Our opponents said this was hopelessly utopian; Saddam and his regime possessed all the guns and means of repression, therefore resistance and struggle were futile, doomed to endless defeat.

Blair later unbelievably argued the 'Arab Spring' justifies the decision to intervene against Saddam! It proves exactly the opposite of what he argued to justify the invasion of Iraq. The Arab Spring of 2011 was a mass uprising of the Tunisian and Egyptian masses which overthrew Presidents Ben Ali and Mubarak, not outside military intervention. In fact, when military intervention was used by imperialism – the bombing of Libya and the foreign intervention of Saudi Arabia in Bahrain – the end result prepared the ground for counter-revolution. Our opponents could argue, "Well Egypt has ended up with a new 'popular' dictator, Sisi". On the contrary, that was not the situation in the immediate aftermath of Mubarak's downfall when power resided with the masses in the streets, factories and squares. What was lacking in Egypt was a mass revolutionary party, resting on democratic committees capable of consolidating the power of the working class and the poor peasants by carrying through an expropriation of landlordism and capitalism.

Blair has also invoked the example of Syria and the Assad regime to justify the criminal invasion of Iraq. This also proves exactly the opposite. The opposition to the Syrian regime perhaps began as a genuine movement for democracy but it was skewed through the intervention of outside forces, particularly right-wing political Islam backed by the reactionary oil sheiks. This resulted in a bloody stalemate in Syria itself with the conflict spilling over to the region

411

as a whole and a sectarian nightmare. The only way to cut across this is by the development of an independent workers' movement, resting on the cardinal principle of relying on its own forces to effect change, through real workers' democracy and socialism in Syria and throughout the Middle East.

Highly significant, was the political message of 15 February. The most positive feature was, of course, the size of the demonstration, together with some of the speeches made in Hyde Park that became the scene of one of history's biggest ever open-air meetings. Millions marched, but hundreds of thousands gathered together in Hyde Park "to make a human central heating system that kept out the biting cold." The best received speeches were those which were not only anti-war but anti-capitalist and anti-imperialist: "We want regime change in Britain. Bring down Blair!" said Tariq Ali. Tony Benn got a huge response, saying that the march was the foundation of a new political movement, the first-ever simultaneous global demonstration. Unfortunately, he never followed through with "a new political movement" in Britain, remaining tied to the discredited 'Labour' party to the end. This movement could have laid the foundations for a new workers' party.

In fact Dave Nellist and I, on behalf of the Socialist Party, had a quite detailed discussion with George Galloway in the run-up to this demonstration on the possibility of using his speech as a launching pad for such a venture. However, George veered away from this – putting misplaced faith in the Labour left to restore him back into the ranks of the Labour Party. When he realised the futility of this, he set up Respect with the SWP, which represented, as we pointed out in advance, another cul-de-sac.

Bob Crow got loud cheers for his call for "workers to take action on Day X, the day the war starts." This speech and others and the way they were received showed that there was a big constituency for the launch of a new anti-war, anti-capitalist formation.

Former Labour Cabinet minister Mo Mowlam and Charles Kennedy were initially warmly applauded but by the time they concluded their speeches, applause was polite and muted. When Mo

Mowlam concluded her speech using New Labour's old campaign slogan, "things can only get better", there was derisory laughter. Kennedy proposed going through the UN, but Jeremy Corbyn, Labour MP for Islington North, made it clear that even if the US were to "corruptly cobble together support for a second UN resolution, this war would still be wrong and we would still oppose it".

All the speakers from the left spoke passionately and carried the crowd with them. Billy Hayes warned New Labour that the unions were fed up with being ignored and if Blair persisted with his drive towards war, the unions would fight to get the government to end it. Again, unfortunately, this was not transformed into action by actually proceeding to form a new trade union-based party. The same could be said of George Galloway, who concluded his remarks by stating: "If he takes Britain over the cliff and into war, he will break the Labour Party he is supposed to lead. Some of us are prepared to pick it up and rebuild it out of the wreckage as a real Labour Party."[5]

This promissory note was not redeemed despite Blair actually going to war and big opportunities were lost for launching a new party in the years since the Iraq war began. In fact, the experience of 15 February revealed the positive and negative features lodged in the underlying explosive situation that had developed in Britain, which were brought to the surface by the war. The demonstration and its immense power were enormously encouraging. However, the fact that politicians like Charles Kennedy could appear on a platform demagogically opposing the war and not be answered forcefully by others, like the SWP and the left speakers who were present, only served to build up their 'radical' credentials. This, in turn, bolstered their electoral appeal amongst youth in particular, which was only finally punctured after they entered the coalition with the Tories in 2010.

Up to 30 million people in 72 countries, according to American broadcaster CNN, poured onto the streets of cities, towns and villages around the world on 15 February in protest against the war plans. We reported: "This simultaneous action was the biggest anti-war protest in history, as the following reports from CWI members testify... The global tidal wave of humanity began in New Zealand and Australia and over the next few days spread like wildfire from one end of the world to the other. A magnificent expression of solidarity was witnessed across Latin America, Europe, Africa and Asia ... The largest demonstration was in Rome, where an incredible three million people marched against Bush and the right wing Italian prime minister and fervent war supporter, Silvio Berlusconi." Barcelona and Madrid also saw millions protest.

In the US, the foremost imperialist power, a magnificent half a million marched in New York – despite Mayor Bloomberg's draconian restrictions – and hundreds of thousands across the country. Up to 150,000 marched in Dublin, 80,000 in Glasgow and 70,000 in Amsterdam. 3,000 Israeli Jews and Arabs demonstrated in Tel Aviv. Some Israeli Arabs addressed the demonstration, speaking in Arabic, something not often heard in mixed demonstrations in Israel. Members of the Israeli section of the CWI, Socialist Struggle Movement, participated in the demonstration, selling 150 copies of their newspaper. Given the scale of the protests, it was not surprising that they were varied in character and embraced a wide number of political ideas. These included pacifist ideas and illusions over the role of the United Nations.[6]

Despite the massive protests over the war, the US unleashed its war machine against Iraq in a stupendous 'shock and awe' campaign. An air force general declared it "such a shock on the system that the Iraqi regime would have to assume early on that the end is inevitable."[7] Once war began this represented a new challenge to the anti-war movement. The first thing that became clear was that the US and British troops met with determined resistance and far fewer Iraqi soldiers defected than was expected. One Iraqi returning from Baghdad explained: "I'm not fighting for Saddam, I am fighting for Iraq".[8] A US opinion poll taken just after the war started found that 41% expected US casualties would be no more than 100. Two days after war broke out an anti-war demonstration of between a quarter and a half million took place in New York; a similar number protested in London.

The bombing of Baghdad horrified world public opinion. Ordinary Iraqis suffered with widespread deaths and terrible injuries. We commented: "Left union leaders like Bob Crow of the RMT are opposed to war with Iraq and have pledged to support any workers who take action against it. They now have to be more proactive. They should immediately organise an anti-war conference of rank-and-file union members, union reps, executive committee members and general secretaries who support the Stop the War Coalition. Such a conference could discuss taking action against the war, including naming the date for a one-day strike."[9]

There had already been a tremendous response from young people who marched out of their schools and colleges on Day X. For instance we reported: "The London Borough of Waltham Forest has never seen anything like it. At the peak of the protest 3,000 school and sixth form students took over the streets. It all started at 8.45 when 200 school students from Kelmscott School walked out and marched to the town square... Terrified teachers rushed to lock the gates and stop students from joining the march, although a few managed to escape... ISR/Youth Against the War spent weeks leafleting for the strike. On the day so many wanted to join ISR/Youth Against the War that we couldn't keep up." Thousands also marched to Parliament from Tower Hamlets and Hackney, with many other towns and cities throughout Britain also seeing anti-war demonstrations.[10]

48. After Iraq, who next?
2003

Shortly after the war began we drew a balance sheet in The Socialist. We wrote that in the bloody equation of war, how it would unfold was unknowable but it did not take a military genius to conclude that the US would 'win' the war. Yet at what price? Even before a shot had been fired, all the hallowed institutions which underpinned the power of world capitalism lay in ruins. The UN was now an 'irrelevancy', according to Bush, because it did not acquiesce to the wishes of the representatives of the new 'Empire'. The military alliance of European and US capitalism, NATO – already weakened by the demise of its 'enemy', the Stalinist states of Eastern Europe and the former Soviet Union – then appeared to be completely redundant.

The new so-called 'democratic imperialists', who dominated the Bush administration – Richard Perle, Paul Wolfowiz and Donald Rumsfeld – claimed the use of Iraq's oil resources would achieve a new democratic flowering of Iraq and the rest of the Middle East. Instead, "we see the unseemly scramble by US firms to grab the lion's share of these resources and use them for their own benefit." Iraq's nationalised oil industry, it was envisaged, would be "privatised" for the benefit primarily of the US, with even Bush's allies being pushed aside.

The real fruits of the war had already been portioned out as the Bush administration awarded contracts worth $900m (£560 million) to American companies to undertake the profitable aspects of 'reconstruction'. We concluded: "This is a war for the re-colonisation of Iraq, not a war of 'liberation' and 'democracy'." We pointed out that the US had been drawn into the "quagmire of a possible civil war between the Sunnis and Shia, and a similar conflict between the Kurds and the Turks in the North. The Kurdish leaders, once more foolishly ensnared into supporting the US, will be betrayed again... A successful war against Saddam... would still have huge consequences. After Afghanistan, the impression will have been reinforced amongst the more than one billion Muslims that the 'Christian West' is bent on another crusade to crush them. In reality, this war is not being conducted against Muslims alone but to enhance the economic power of US imperialism through the acquisition of Iraq's oil and, at the same time, to reinforce the role of US imperialism as the world's policeman."

We concluded: "The adventure in Iraq is projected by the 'hawks' to lead to similar action, possibly against Iran, Syria, Libya and any other 'evil' or 'failed' state. 'Diplomacy' will be used for the time being against North Korea but as both Bush and Blair have admitted in recent months, action to 'disarm' North Korea will also be posed. The conflict between the US and Europe, as well as the divergences which have emerged over Iraq with Russia, China and other powers, symbolise a return to the same kind of inter-imperialist rivalries which marked out world capitalism in the decades prior to 1914."

These perspectives have been generally borne out in the bloody inferno which the Middle East is today. The writer Gore Vidal commented that the US's policy was one of "permanent war for permanent peace". Such an approach would inevitably come up against the resistance of the peoples of the world. We concluded that the mass demonstrations, particularly on 15 February, and the strikes which followed were not enough to stop the war. Nevertheless, they were sufficient to temporarily stay the hand of Bush and Blair and this mood had not gone away.

The fallout from the war, we predicted, would be huge and it would be measured over months and years. Not least of the effects would be a revival of the anti-capitalist movement itself, combined with a mass anti-war feeling. We wrote: "In Britain, even if he wins, Blair will ultimately lose as a result of his backing of this obscene war. Even the sanitised Labour Party is split from top to bottom and big defections from its ranks are taking place." All of this was laying the basis for a profound radicalisation in Britain and throughout the world.[1]

"You're next" was the message that Bush's adviser Richard Perle said he wanted to send to any country that opposed US imperialism's interest internationally. Before the war had even started, the US administration was accusing Syria of "hostile acts". Syria had also been attacked for giving refuge to leading figures from Saddam Hussein's regime, supporting terrorism and having chemical weapons. According to the Guardian, US Defence Secretary Rumsfeld ordered a review of contingency plans for a war against Syria after the fall in Baghdad. We posed the question: "So will the Syrian people be next in line after Iraq to suffer the consequences of the US's overwhelming military might?" We answered our own question by saying that they would not proceed to invade Syria at that stage.[2]

Any attack then would have had even less international support than the war in Iraq. Nevertheless, the leaders of the major capitalist powers were absolutely relentless in the pursuit of the long-term goal that they had set themselves. With the help of the counter-revolution in general in the Middle East that followed the North African revolution – the Arab Spring – imperialism returned to the task of unseating the Syrian regime. We oppose this undemocratic blood-soaked government and we stand for its removal. We believe that is a task primarily of the Syrian people and above all of the working class in an alliance with the poor peasants, supported by the workers' movement internationally, fighting against all manifestations of capitalism and for a new socialist future for Syria and in the Middle East as a whole.

There was some persecution of civilians from the fallout of the Iraq war in Britain. The young people who walked out on Day X, when the war started, were harassed, some of them prosecuted and some who took action in the workplace were disciplined. In the north-east 100 school students were suspended at one school while at another, students were expelled. In Lewisham, South-East London, the police had used considerable numbers to try to prevent school students from participating in the Parliament Square protests on Day X. In so doing, they arrested ISR coordinator at the time Karl Debbaut and charged him with an assault on a police officer, which he denied. After a number of court appearances, with the police producing slanted video evidence and after consistent lobbying by the ISR in conjunction with the Socialist Party and others he was found not guilty. The Lewisham police gained a reputation amongst young people for persecuting protesting school students, often seeing them as mindless truants 'manipulated' by older anti-war protesters.

In East London Nancy Taaffe and another library worker were threatened by Waltham Forest Council for walking out on Day X. The council originally said it would have a flexible attitude to workers wanting to protest on the day but it reneged on this and instigated disciplinary action. It was no accident that library workers in Waltham Forest were fighting cuts in their working conditions as the council was preparing for privatisation. Nancy was the Unison co-convenor for the libraries. This attack was defeated but she ultimately lost her job in the savage cuts eight years later, when a nominally 'Labour' Council passed on the cuts of the ConDem government.

In the first few days after the 'victory' over Iraq, Bush and Blair were celebrating but within a matter of hours it became clear that piecing Iraq back together again would prove much more difficult than the war itself. The rapid fall of the Saddam regime left a vacuum that had been filled by looting and chaos. Many Iraqi people, while relieved to be rid of Saddam Hussein, blamed the US and Britain for the turmoil that the war had unleashed. It had been conducted under the signboard of 'democracy' but instead the Iraqi people faced occupation by US and British troops with, at best, the installation of a stooge regime in power at the behest of US imperialism. As with all military incursions – like Northern Ireland or later on Israel's occupation of South Lebanon – some Iraqis initially welcomed the troops. However, the troops rapidly came into bitter conflict with the very communities that had first greeted them.

The US's attempts to rely on elements of Saddam's old state apparatus to maintain law and order met with opposition, particularly from the Shias, with the mosques organising to fill the vacuum of power. A massive crowd of 20,000 people demonstrated in Nasiriya outside a meeting called to discuss the future of Iraq and in protest at the inclusion of the US in the talks. They chanted: "Yes to freedom, Yes to Islam, No to America, No to Saddam."[3] The Pentagon's choice as the first proconsul of Iraq, Chalabi – a figurehead for the future pro-US government – was totally rejected. The tensions between the different national groups developed into a sectarian civil war between the Shia and the Sunni within a very short period following the US occupation.

Within the anti-war forces in Britain a debate – sometimes fierce – unfolded within the Stop the War Coalition on "Where next in the aftermath of war?" This was also reflected within the trade union movement. Some left trade union leaders like Paul Mackney, general secretary of the lecturers' union NATFHE, tended to think that by taking an anti-war position they were somehow insulated from criticism when it came to domestic issues in Britain. The late Andrew Price, a long-standing supporter of Militant and then the Socialist Party, as well as a fine orator, criticised Mackney in our paper for not being sufficiently "forthcoming on strike action in support of members' pay and conditions".[4] Paul Mackney exercised his right of reply: "I don't usually rise to Andrew's attacks and I welcome robust debates on our industrial policy. But you may wish to consider whether it is appropriate at this time to carry articles attacking trade union leaders because they have been in the forefront of organising the resistance to this imperialist war."[5]

This summed up the approach of some union leaders, even those who nominally stood on the left, like Paul Mackney, which amounted in our opinion to a 'love of the distant'. International issues were separated by them from what was done in the day-to-day struggle in Britain. We, on the contrary, believed that foreign policy was a continuation of home policy, not just for the bourgeoisie but also, above all, for the working class and its leadership. There had been a tradition in Britain for some of the left leaders to attempt to screen themselves from criticism by the members by taking up radical positions on foreign policy, which Paul Mackney's letter signified.

Similar discussions took place in the Stop the War Coalition soon after the occupation of Iraq had begun. Ken Smith was the Socialist Party's representative on this body's committee. The Socialist Party laid heavy emphasis on the need to organise a meeting of workplace representatives, union executive committee members and general secretaries to mobilise for the next phase of the resistance. While on Day X there were lots of protests and workers taking time off, actual industrial action was, unfortunately, limited because many union leaders did not back up their calls for action with concrete plans. The swp placed heavy reliance on further national demonstrations, arguing that they could create a crisis for the government similar to the one which developed around the 15 February demonstration. And while everyone supported some form of national demonstration, merely rehashing the same kind of demonstration would not stop the war. In particular, the decision was taken to popularise the idea of workplace action in different forms – on May Day in particular – including through the production of leaflets and to build a network of union anti-war organisers.

Opposition to the occupation of Iraq rumbled on throughout 2003. We recognised that the war had entered an end-stage – at least in terms of set-piece battles and conflicts – within a few months of the invasion. It appeared as though overwhelming military might had broken the back of the Iraqi military resistance on the ground despite determined resistance from a number of Iraqi militias and armed forces. Nevertheless, the us and Britain were shocked by Iraqi hostility towards the invading forces and the degree of armed resistance. They believed their own propaganda when they claimed their troops would be welcomed as liberators. While the Iraqi people had not welcomed the US and British troops as liberators, most were not prepared to fight and defend Saddam Hussein's dictatorship. There was chaos for all to see in Iraq as the old regime collapsed and the US struggled to create a new leadership and apparatus. Nationalist conflict broke out between Kurds, Shia and Sunni. US imperialism was undoubtedly crowing behind-the-scenes because of their 'fourth military' victory in a row. Yet we predicted they would reap an unwelcome reward through the global mass indignation and increased opposition within Iraq that would inevitably follow.

Meanwhile, while most of the population were preoccupied with the news from Iraq, the British government sought to bury 'bad news', as they had done with 9/11. John Prescott dropped his threat of big council tax rises and then announced a new bill to impose terms and conditions on the firefighters. Home Secretary David Blunkett widened police powers to let them take fingerprints and swabs from anyone arrested. The Lord Chancellor's Department also agreed to allow bailiffs the right of forcible entry into people's homes. The last piece of hidden news was that New Labour 'fat cat' Lord Sainsbury was giving £2.5 million to the Labour Party, taking his contribution to £8.5 million! The 'really good news' from the point of view of working people was the massive 24-hour general strike called by the unions in France against the right-wing government of Raffarin.

By mid-May the issue of the absence of weapons of mass destruction (WMD) in Iraq took centre stage. Blair declared to Parliament on 30 April: "I am absolutely convinced and confident about the case on weapons of mass destruction." He continued that those who doubted the presence of WMD "will be eating some of your words".[6] In fact, it was Blair who was forced to eat his words as divisions began at the top between the intelligence agencies and the government on this issue. As no weapons were found, the decision to go to war against Iraq lacked any credibility. Some of the higher echelons of the American 'intelligence community' began to confirm this. CIA director George Tenet admitted that he was wrong to let part of an 'intelligence dossier' compiled by Blair's government be included in Bush's State of the Union speech in January 2003. This was the much criticised 'dodgy dossier' of September 2002. The claim that Saddam Hussein had a new source of uranium from the African state of Niger to reactivate a nuclear weapons programme was investigated by the International Atomic Energy Agency and was found to be based on forged documents.

Then in July came the bombshell of the death of the scientist Dr David Kelly. Before his suicide, he had written an email about "dark actors playing games". In reality he had become a tragic pawn in New Labour's cynical game-plan to divert attention from the lies and distortions they had resorted to in order to go to war. They had also claimed that WMD could be launched within 45 minutes of an order from Saddam. Yet three months after the invasion, no WMD had been discovered, while the body count of soldiers and ordinary Iraqis rose. An opinion poll carried out prior to Dr Kelly's death, found that 66% of people in Britain thought Blair had misled them about going to war.

The Socialist Party demanded not another fake inquiry, but a genuine inquiry made up of workers and community representatives, which would look not just at the immediate issues surrounding Dr Kelly's death, but the wider question of Blair's reasons for going to war. A YouGov poll for the Daily Telegraph found that 39% of people thought that "Blair should go now". This once again underlined the character of the Labour Party now as a lying machine in the interests of big business.[7]

The same month, the annual international school of the CWI was convened in Belgium with over 300 primarily young people attending the event. Most of the CWI's sections had grown as a result of the intervention in the anti-war movement. The confidence of CWI members at this event was shown by the collection of well over £11,000 in the financial appeal.

Another inquiry was convened – this time by Lord Hutton – to examine the background to the Iraq war. We wrote of this event: "A shoddy string of Pontius Pilates roll out before the inquiry, trying to absolve themselves of any responsibility for the events leading to David Kelly's suicide, desperately trying to point the finger of blame elsewhere." The stark reality was that the occupying forces had now spent longer inside Iraq by August than the UN weapons inspectors were given before the conflict began, yet still they had found no evidence of WMD. Indeed, Blair had now changed his tune to say that they were looking for evidence of programmes for WMD, rather than the WMD themselves. We concluded: "The real force that will hold Blair and his cronies accountable is not sitting inside Court 73 of the Royal Courts of Justice. It is residing in Britain's factories, offices, shops, schools, colleges and streets – the people who opposed the war and will never believe another word Blair or his government says."[8]

Finally, in 2009 the Gordon Brown government commissioned the Chilcot Inquiry into Britain's role in the Iraq War. The subsequent report took seven years to write, ran to 2.6 million words and condemned the war. It effectively tried to exonerate Blair, made no recommendations for prosecutions and said that Blair did not "deliberately" mislead people. Nevertheless, many of the families of soldiers killed and maimed in Iraq branded Blair a "bloody murderer" and the real "terrorist". He was effectively condemned in the court of public opinion.

As a result of the commotion around the death of Kelly, Alistair Campbell, Blair's liar-in-chief, was forced to quit the government. The calculation was that by leaving then he would lessen the harm to Blair. Campbell's exit was expected to make it easier for Blair to make a 'fresh start' at the upcoming Labour Party conference. However, Blair has never escaped, not even today, his mantle as a war criminal in the Iraq catastrophe.

Moreover, the domestic front was littered with minefields, which could explode at any one time. The economy was in an uncertain state. Brown could see a budget deficit of £10 billion in the current year. He was already warning that the next public spending round could be the 'toughest' since Labour came to power, with spending frozen or cut. Industrial action from firefighters and postal workers loomed, and huge anger was building up on the issues of foundation hospitals, PFI and tuition fees.

One of the effects of the Iraq war was a renewed interest in past wars, particularly the Vietnam War. Therefore, I decided to write a book, 'Empire Defeated', which gave an historical analysis of the Vietnam War – called the 'American War' by the Vietnamese themselves – drawing out the lessons for today's generation.

As the year drew to an end, the anti-war mood remained intense. This was reflected in over 200,000 people marching at the end of November in Central London in protest at Bush's visit to Britain. The massive turnout, the biggest ever for a midweek demonstration, showed the endurance of the anti-war movement and the active layer who sustained it. Particularly evident was the number of school, college and university students, as well as many working-class people turning out on a demonstration for the first time. Unfortunately, not as many trade unionists were able to go on the day because of the difficulties of getting time off work. Also there were fewer Muslims than on the previous demonstrations. It also felt like a carnival, but one of outrage at the actions of Bush and Blair and the anger at Bush's state visit.

In December came the news of the capture of Saddam Hussein. We argued that this was not the "beginning of the end" of the Iraq quagmire. Saddam had been found but not WMD – the reason given for conducting the war. Moreover, any benefits from Saddam's capture, and the propaganda value that flowed from this, was likely to be short lived. Within two hours of Saddam's capture, two car bombs exploded outside Iraqi police stations, killing nine people and injuring many others. Bush had consistently tried to blame suicide bombings and the 20 or so attacks each day against US forces on 'remnants' of the Saddam regime. Serious analysis identified between 15 and 30 resistance groups active in Iraq, yet most of them had no links with Saddam. While Saddam had been captured, we posed the question, "What about justice for the prisoners

425

languishing for years in Guantánamo Bay? What about a trial of us imperialism and its role in financing and arming Saddam's brutal rule?" We also demanded that Saddam should be put on trial by a democratic tribunal of elected representatives of the working people who suffered at his hands, not by the imperialist countries who backed him when it suited their own interests.[9]

49. The War at Home
2001-02

There were two wars being conducted at this stage in Britain and worldwide. One was in Iraq and the other was the continuous social war of capitalism against the working class, its past gains and organisations. This second war was orchestrated in Britain by New Labour, with Tony Blair the general of the capitalist 'army'. We made the point in Socialism Today: "In all capitalist wars the government of the day invariably bangs the drum of 'national unity' as a means of mobilising the population for its war aims. Sure enough, Britain's official parliamentary 'opposition', the Tories, have fallen in behind the Blair government with almost military precision, appropriate for a party now led by an ex-army junior officer [Iain Duncan Smith (IDS)]."[1] The late Hugo Young commented in the Guardian: "Never, perhaps, has the official 'opposition' been more timid or supine than now: "Far from giving himself elbow room, IDS's shoulder was thrusting to push ahead of TB's [Tony Blair's] in mutual bondage."[2]

Moreover, Blair had achieved the compliance of right-wing national trade union leaders for the short term, who waved the white flag over issues such as privatisation at the truncated 2001 Labour Party conference, as well as at the TUC. We pointed to the serious world economic and financial situation, with a looming default in Argentina, which took place subsequently. The seriousness of the situation compelled even the most orthodox capitalist economists to reassess and change their position. The Economist, previously the ideological bulwark of monetarist policies, now stated that "Keynes is back in fashion."[3] This meant that the rosy future painted by Blair for the British economy had been savagely darkened, reducing his room for manoeuvre, and some bourgeois economists were urging a change from cuts to a 'looser' regime involving Keynesian measures.

The trickle of redundancies was now threatening to turn into a flood and this exerted pressure on the government to take measures to ameliorate the conditions of the working class. There was rising discontent on tuition fees and even a partial retreat from the government, where there were suggestions that it would introduce a 'graduate's tax', a kind of deferred fees. These issues, together with the growing revolt against privatisation, were partially pushed into the background for a time in 2001-02 in the aftermath of 9/11.

Within months of its election victory, the government had performed more somersaults and body swerves than a circus acrobat. It was busy jettisoning every unpopular policy introduced in its first term of office. It carried through the renationalisation of Railtrack by the back door, which earned the scorn of the city for this 'confiscatory' measure. We pointed out that this was a 'state capitalist' rather than a socialist measure. Moreover, we said that the government was compelled to rescue an industry ruined by the capitalists and would then seek to renovate and sell it back to the private owners at a later stage.

A revolt was brewing against New Labour. The comments of Roy Gladden, secretary and convenor of the GMB's 413 branch on Merseyside, were highly significant. Although he was one of the 47 councillors who had defied Thatcher and the right-wing Labour leadership by carrying through an 'illegal' budget In Liverpool, he ended up supporting the right wing, and Neil Kinnock in particular, against the socialists and Marxists around Militant. He declared in 2001 though: "For the first time in my recollection I have activists who supported Labour all their lives openly discussing whether the unions should continue to give their political levy or any other financial support to the party, locally or nationally."

The Liberal Democrats were manoeuvring at this stage in order to benefit from the split which had developed within the Tory party and inevitable disenchantment with Labour. All they needed to do was to stand still and they would appear to be to the 'left' of Labour. We concluded: "The seeming tranquillity of the 1990s is over once and forever. The broad consciousness of the mass of the people has not yet caught up with objective reality. But that it will do so, and in convulsive leaps, is certain."[4]

The issue of privatisation, specifically the privatisation programme ruthlessly carried out by New Labour, was one of the dominant features of this period. Nothing was sacred: education, the NHS, social services were all subjected to the remorseless pressure of Blair to outdo Thatcher through privatisation. Linda Taaffe, in a front-page article in the Socialist, recorded the comments of teachers: "Once the fat cats get a foot in the door it will soon be individual schools that are handed over to private companies for profit." "They will be charging teachers to rent their classrooms next!"[5]

Such sentiments were forcing teachers and support staff to take action against the privatisation of education services in the London Borough of Waltham Forest. Teachers there were balloting against this proposal, the first of its kind in the country. It was difficult to find anyone in favour of private shareholders making money out of education. Teachers and support workers opposed it. Parents organised a lively campaign against it. Yet the government continued with its programme. Shortly afterwards, "A mass of angry parents, teachers and education workers made a last ditch attempt to persuade Labour councillors to stand up to government blackmail and refuse to hand over Waltham Forest education services to EduAction." The Secretary of State, of a 'Labour' government remember, had promised to privatise anyway if the councillors did not vote for it themselves. The last time there were stormy scenes like this at Waltham Forest Town Hall, activists recalled, was during the introduction of the poll tax.

The campaign culminated in a one-day strike by about 100 workers in the NUT, Unison and the Transport and General Workers'

Union in protest at their jobs transferring to a private company. On the two large and lively picket lines, strikers had little difficulty in persuading other workers not to cross them. The Education Centre was almost empty and the Education Department severely depleted. In the evening the campaign reassembled for the full council meeting. Only the Liberal Democrat councillors, now placing themselves to the left of Labour, decided to vote against, even though they had taken no part in the campaign over the previous year. Every other councillor was given a severe ear-bashing by the demonstrators. To add insult to injury, a couple of directors of private education companies suddenly turned up for the council meeting. This was a red rag to the bull. They had a hard time getting in and had to be escorted out by police.

Earlier in the year at the annual general meeting of Nord Anglia the chairman of the company had stated, referring to the Waltham Forest privatisation, that they believed they could fulfil their promise to shareholders with "these new market opportunities." He then added: "I am confident we are on course to meet our profit expectations." Our report concluded: "No doubt they will be giving thanks to Labour... As the two directors left the building they were again berated by strikers. There is no mood just to accept this decision. This is not the privatisation of ten years ago. The mood has changed. The campaign will reconvene in September to decide what next, but borough-wide and national action must be on the cards."[6]

This battle was typical of those that were taking place in other areas, usually with Socialist Party members providing leadership but workers at local level were invariably left to fight alone. National and regional trade union officials rapidly disowned any local leaflets and other propaganda produced by local union branches that implied that industrial action had anything to do with privatisation. The excuse was that the courts had deemed these as 'political' strikes and were therefore 'illegal'. This meant that workers were forced to oppose the effects of privatisation, rather than the privatisation itself. This in turn meant that the real position of right-wing union leaders, aired just behind the scenes, was that it did not matter who runs the service or industry as long as their members' conditions were protected. The essence of the matter was, however, that privatisation was an essential part of neoliberal policies, with the ultimate end being to drive down wages, which had been the overwhelming experience of the working class since these policies were introduced.

This position led to a campaign orchestrated by a number of union broad lefts to coordinate action against privatisation. Left Unity in the PCS, United Left in Unison, the Socialist Teachers' Alliance and Campaign for a Democratic Fighting Union in the NUT, the CWU Broad Left and NATFHE Rank and File banded together to call an anti-privatisation conference for 24 November 2001. On this date, 100 delegates from more than 13 different trade unions attended with the six national trade union broad lefts represented as well.

Mark Serwotka, recently elected general secretary of PCS, explained the determined mood to fight back and win. Since his election in January, there had been 147 separate submissions in the PCS for strike action. Brian Debus from Hackney came straight from the picket line to speak to the conference. He pointed out that 96% of library workers voted for strike action over the issue of Saturday payments for their work. Representatives from Brighton GMB and the Northern Ireland Public Sector Alliance (NIPSA) also spoke, as did Linda Taaffe. Speaking in a personal capacity, although a member of the NUT's National Executive Committee, she pointed out that while some privatisation ventures, such as Education Action Zones, were falling by the wayside, others were going ahead and planned for the future: "The union leadership doesn't inspire confidence. But we can fill that gap. Rank-and-file teachers organised a campaign against performance related pay."[7]

Members of the London Underground Regional Executive Committee of the RMT said it was just a matter of time before the Paddington or Hatfield rail disasters were repeated on the Underground. Under the Public-Private Partnership (PPP), profits would come before safety. Such was the feeling growing against privatisation alongside hostility to the already privatised industries that the government was compelled at the end of 2001 to announce the renationalisation of Railtrack. Stephen Byers, then the Transport Secretary but later to be sacked himself, admitted "Railtrack is finished".

Only two months before this New Labour had said it couldn't possibly take back control of Railtrack because it would be "too expensive" and contravene the Human Rights Act! But they were now forced to call in the administrators and take the company out of private hands. As Christine Thomas commented: "At last New Labour have had to admit what everyone else already knew; privatisation on the railways has been a total disaster... 'Profit before safety' seems to have been Railtrack's slogan. Seven people died in the Southall train crash, 31 at Paddington and four at Hatfield. Cost-cutting and mismanagement linked to privatisation were implicated in all three disasters."[8] However, while giving this decision a qualified welcome we also called it "Nationalisation – but not as we know it... New Labour are desperate to avoid being accused of 're-nationalisation' but for the 'shocked' City investors this is what it is. The financial pages of the Independent (10 October 2001) called it 'confiscation.'"

This did not represent a wild swing to the left. They were only acting in the same way as previous Tory and Labour governments had both done. When faced with a major crisis of a key part of the British economy which, if allowed to collapse, would cause major damage to the profits of other companies, they implemented state capitalist measures – top-down nationalisation in order to benefit the capitalists themselves, invariably with lavish overcompensation.

We took this opportunity to explain our alternative of democratic public ownership. Rail workers were and are the real experts in the industry. We therefore demanded that "The rail unions must have a major say in the running of the industry. That means direct representation on the board of a wholly publicly owned rail industry."[9] They should represent roughly one third of the positions on the boards running the industry at every level. Another third should come from representatives of the trade unions as a whole and, if it was deemed necessary, one third from the government itself. All representatives to be subject to recall and having the average wage of the people that they represent, rail workers and workers generally.

There were further retreats by the government at this stage. The New Labour government made a big U-turn on higher education on 3 October, by announcing it would restore student grants and review its position on tuition fees. Yet despite the furore, as we explained, this was not a return to free education on the part of New Labour's education secretary, Estelle Morris, but the introduction of a gradu-ate tax. The reasons why she proposed the change were because "'many low-income families find fear of debt is a real worry' and that this could act as a barrier to higher education".[10] How much more so is that the case today when tuition fees are at a far higher level than was the case then? And New Labour's measures prepared the way for the 'ConDem' coalition government to introduce their draconian attacks on young people, with massive increases in tuition fees, which has crippled the educational ambitions of young people today.

As we entered 2002, thousands of workers went on strike to defend their conditions and fight for a living wage. 60,000 PCS union members working in the Department for Work and Pensions (DWP) took two days of strike action towards the end of 2001 and threatened further action in benefit offices and Jobcentres. They were encouraged by the election of new left leaders in the Public and Commercial Services Union (PCS), the National Union of Rail, Maritime and Transport Workers (RMT) and the Communication Workers Union (CWU).

This was followed by RMT members on South West Trains strik-ing in protest at an inadequate increase of pay of 7.65% over 18 months. This was followed by management's threat to sack striking train workers orchestrated by the infamous Brian Souter, the bil-lionaire owner of Stagecoach, who also owned this company. He had jumped on the bandwagon of many anti-working class and reactionary social issues in the previous few years. Mick Rix, then general secretary of ASLEF, waded in to support the RMT. As was the norm at this stage, the TUC was playing a despicable role, holding secret meetings involving government ministers with the intention of backing the bosses. We advocated: "The RMT should go over the heads of the TUC and make a direct appeal to trade union members to come to the aid of the rail workers. The stage is being set for a mighty struggle. Perhaps not yet on the lines of the 1970s, but the issues are the same – solidarity with those in struggle and the need for a bold union leadership."[11]

In the midst of the strike wave Blair, at New Labour's local government conference, attacked as "wreckers" anyone who opposed his privatisation plans and compared them to "the Militant Tendency". On behalf of the Socialist Party, I publicly replied to him: "At the time of our expulsion from the Labour Party, we predicted that the campaign against the Militant Tendency would be the thin end of the wedge. Militant ferociously defended public services against Tory cuts... We warned that the right wing's attacks on the left would not end with the expulsion of the Militant Tendency, but that socialist policies and even the defence of the living standards of the working class would be next in the Blairites' sights... the right-wing trade union leaders did not heed our warnings; on the contrary they backed our expulsion... [Then GMB leader] John Edmonds has correctly compared New Labour's privatisation programme to Thatcher's poll tax. However, the poll tax was not defeated simply because it was unpopular. It was defeated because our party took the initiative to launch what became an 18 million strong, organised campaign of non-payment... We appeal to trade unionists to fight for a new party, a party that represents the working class instead of the fat cats, a mass workers' party that campaigns for socialist policies."[12]

50. Opposition on all fronts 2002-03

Candidates standing on a socialist basis received significant support in England, for instance in Coventry, where there were three councillors at one stage, and in Lewisham, South London. They exercised a significant effect by opposing cuts and privatisation which were introduced in the main by New Labour. Karen McKay, who stood for re-election in 2003, spoke about what it meant to be a Socialist Party councillor: "In the council meetings we are mainly a voice of opposition to the coalition of Labour and Tory councillors who vote the same way on all major policy. We are the only ones who consistently oppose their privatisation and cuts in services. We've opposed the sell-off of the council housing, Private Finance deals for our hospital and schools, school closures, tuition fees and attacks on the pay and conditions of council workers."[1] This could almost be written today, with the difference that it is not New Labour which presides over this but the present Tory government. The pro-capitalist parties are head and tail of the same capitalist coin.

Making the breakthrough on the electoral plane is extremely difficult for a new, as yet untested force or party. "We're out six nights a week now canvassing for Dave Nellist," wrote Martin Reynolds, sales organiser for the Socialist in Coventry before the 2002 elections. "We visit people who... voted Labour – and now buy the Socialist, or want more information on what we are about."[2] This indicates the tenacity of Socialist Party members fighting to lay the basis for a new mass formation. A measure of the respect which the Socialist Party has built up in areas like Coventry is shown by the comments of a spokesperson for the homeless: "On behalf of the residents of the Manor Guild House, Bell Green [Coventry], we would like to express our thanks for the extreme effort displayed by Councillor Rob Windsor and Socialist Party candidate Martin Reynolds in our fight to keep our hostel for the homeless open. We couldn't have done it without their total support and it has been a great morale boost", said Derek Shaw, residents' chairperson.[3]

Ian Page and Sam Dias stood for the Socialist Party in Lewisham: "Everywhere we go, people say how they know Ian and Sam".[4] Ian Page was re-elected but unfortunately Sam just missed out by 43 votes. Overall, as the Socialist commented, "The Socialist Party scored two brilliant victories in the local elections in England. Dave Nellist and Ian Page were both re-elected as councillors, Dave in Coventry and Ian in Lewisham."[5] In Coventry, the party had contested eight out of eighteen wards and received 14.9% of the votes cast in those wards. There were also remarkable achievements for other candidates who were not elected but got significant results. Eighteen months later, Chris Flood was elected in a by-election in Telegraph Hill Ward in Lewisham, before which he had declared: "There's a lot of disillusionment amongst Labour's former voters, over the war with Iraq and the occupation that has followed it, and on subjects such as education and housing."[6] Additionally, Karen McKay scored an excellent victory in St Michaels Ward in 2003, and it was telling given the fact that Labour lost five seats, despite the big teams they had out in an attempt to stop her election!

Labour increasingly at local level resorted to the same lying methods as the bourgeois parties in election campaigns. If you embrace capitalist politics, then you then adopt the same campaigning methods of lies and deception that goes with them, summed up by New Labour's use of 'spin doctors' – a fancy name for gutter politics à la the Sun! In shameful leaflets, Labour claimed that the Socialist Party "supported terrorism". This was because we were opposed to the curtailing of democratic rights under the draconian Terrorist Act and, bizarrely, we supported the "evil regime of Robert Mugabe in Zimbabwe", which we have always opposed!

While council elections are not usually history-making, the results in 2002, 2003 and particularly the by-election in which Chris Flood was elected, were pointers to what was possible. For the first time ever, no Labour representation existed in Telegraph Hill Ward. The opposition had gone to the left and not, for example, to the Lib Dems. Moreover, it was only by the Socialist Party immersing itself in local campaigns, particularly in relation to a new school, that it was possible to forge an alliance and therefore an electoral agreement with activists involved in this campaign. It would have been wrong for socialists to have stepped down but the leaders of the new school campaign turned down our offer of a joint candidate and, partially under the influence of local SWP members, argued that the socialist candidate was less likely to win. This left us with no alternative but to contest alone with a friendly approach to the campaign.

Chris Flood joined seven other elected SP councillors nationally. This showed that an election challenge by a new party in the 'first past the post' system could result in success, although subsequent events demonstrated that it was no easy task to put together an effective alliance of the left to contest elections. Individual and therefore isolated contests in general council elections were not sufficient. Based on these experiences, the Trade Unionist and Socialist Coalition (TUSC), formed in 2010, concluded that it was necessary to seek to stand in most if not all of the wards in a local authority. This was put to the test in 2014 and 2015 local and general elections in England.

These successes stimulated the discussion and the search for how to begin to create the basis of a new party in the situation in which New Labour was becoming increasingly discredited on the Iraq war abroad and on the war at home by the Blair government against the working class and the poor. This was undoubtedly a major theme in and around the build-up to the historic 15 February march of the millions against the drumbeat of war. We commented at the time:

"February 15 was a day when the world was on the march, when it was turned upside down, when the 'dissenting minority' became the majority. The Bush junta, the Blair cabal, the crooked circle of Berlusconi, and the rotten court camarilla of Aznar, cowered in their bunkers... One thing is clear: such numbers could not come out onto the streets without the latent colossal support of the mass of the population behind them. Aznar's argument that the 'silent majority' were opposed to the demonstrators is like a multi-storey building resting on flea's legs!"

The demonstrations in Britain and worldwide indicated that the mass of the people believed that they must act themselves because bourgeois leaders and their parties in all their hues and disguises could not and would not prevent the world from sliding into war and the suffering, degradation and poverty that war brought, the consequences of which are with us today. It was clear to us that the mood behind the demonstration would not die down, but represented the political reawakening of a generation characterised by generosity, even the naivety, which characterises the 'spring' of all mass movements. The question was how could this be sustained? There was a huge vacuum to the left. The list of betrayals and broken pledges of New Labour was endless. On the issue of top-up student tuition fees, a 'mainstream' Labour MP Eric Guisley declared in the Commons: "This is a betrayal of working people in my constituency. It will be the equivalent of taking out an extra mortgage and it will mean university is not for people like my family." We commented: "If the children of MPs are denied a chance at university, what hopes are there for the working class?"

Additionally, the vicious attitude adopted towards the firefighters at this stage was bringing to a head the discontent with the government. John Prescott's threat to bring back the 1947 Fire Services Act earned him a stinging rebuke from the Daily Mirror, which characterised him as "a working-class zero". Its political editor, Paul Routledge, who had sung his praises in the past, wrote bitterly: "John Prescott is a child of the unions. He was educated by his union; sent to Ruskin College, Oxford, by his union – the National Union of Seamen. He got to parliament as a union man. He lived in a union flat." This sense of betrayal by Labour-inclined journalists was powerful, but it was nothing compared to how the working class as a whole felt. Routledge furiously added: "The Labour Party is finished." We replied: "Not quite yet, Paul, we would add but the forces that could significantly break the influence of bourgeoisified New Labour over the British working class and the organised trade union movement are rapidly maturing."

Labour Party membership was collapsing and, officially at 180,000, only half the number when Blair assumed the leadership. Labour was also at its lowest point in polls since the fuel protests of September 2000 and on a par with Labour support in the 1992 general election, which it lost. In reality, bitter anger existed in Britain and the world that could find no political expression. The anti-war movement provided such an outlet but this required a political alternative.

Even John Monks, the right-wing TUC general secretary, in the pocket of New Labour, warned: "It was virtually impossible for anyone [at that stage] to win a union contest standing on a Blairite ticket". The election of the so-called 'awkward squad': Mick Rix and Bob Crow in the rail workers' unions, Mark Serwotka in PCS, Andy Gilchrist in the Fire Brigades Union and Derek Simpson in Amicus all signified the rank-and-file revolt against New Labour stooges in the unions. We predicted that "the TGWU is likely to join the growing 'awkward squad' with the prospect of Tony Woodley winning the general secretary's election to replace the discredited [Bill] Morris." We nevertheless added: "General Secretaries (in the aforementioned unions) have raised the need for change, some of them suggesting or hinting at an alternative outside the Labour Party. However, their public statements have indicated a certain inconsistency."[7] In the FBU for instance, probably 80% had already contracted out of the political levy paid to the Labour Party or intended to.

51. George Galloway and Respect 2003-04

Bob Crow had not yet come out clearly for a new political alternative. Despite the friendly discussions that we had with him, he and other union leaders had burnt their fingers in Arthur Scargill's ill-fated Socialist Labour Party. Bob was a workers' leader who clearly resonated with the rank-and-file of the unions and the wider working class but at this stage he was reluctant to make a bold call, probably because he could not see a ready-made constituency for a new mass party existing at that time. Brown was no real alternative, as was indicated in his consistent support for capitalism, the market, which went together with berating the 'old left' for its 'fetish' in supporting the public sector. We warned: "The election of Brown as New Labour's leader after Blair's resignation or overthrow would mean a continuation of the 'project' ... with all that would mean for the working class of Britain."[1] This was borne out to the letter in the reign of 'Gordon the brief', which led to the disaster of the 'ConDem' coalition government following the 2010 election.

After the huge anti-war movement, a meeting did take place in London under the signboard 'Where is New Labour going?' Over 500 predominantly left activists attended, including prominent speakers like Mark Serwotka and George Galloway. The latter welcomed the discussion but stated that a decision on the issues under debate was coming closer with indignation rising at the spectacle of trade unions' money going to New Labour, which was helping to pay for the war. He declared: "This cannot go on. Enough will eventually be enough. The rail union NUR, predecessor of the RMT, founded the Labour Party 103 years ago. They were told it was premature and divisive... But the vast majority came to see that independent political representation was necessary. 103 years later Blair, on the other hand, thinks the foundation of his own party was a historic mistake." The speaker from the Fire Brigades Union, Linda Smith, explained how the left in the FBU had argued for the democratisation of the funds going to the Labour Party but the recent strike meant that the FBU had moved on. She reported that the London FBU voted 15-0 to suspend all payments to the Labour Party until the FBU conference discussion on this issue.

John Rees, then of the SWP, also spoke on behalf of the Socialist Alliance. In the past, the SWP had argued that New Labour was no different from the Labour Party of the past. However, reality now forced them to abandon this untenable position. He stated: "We cannot watch history rolled back 100 years to a time when there is no party to represent the trade union movement. We are on the cusp of that happening." This was yet another example of the flip-flop approach of the SWP.[2]

Later in 2003 Galloway, MP for Glasgow Kelvin at the time, was expelled from the Labour Party for sticking to his principled opposition to Blair's war in Iraq. This decision was taken by Labour's National Constitutional Committee. Galloway declared afterwards: "This was a politically motivated kangaroo court whose verdict had been written in advance, in the best tradition of political show trials. It was a travesty of justice." We concluded once more: "There is no room for socialists and principled fighters in today's pro-big business Labour Party. Energies should now be channelled into building a new mass trade union based party that could be a focus for all those looking for a left alternative to New Labour."[3] Following this, Galloway spoke at the Socialist Party national rally in November 2003, where he denounced his expulsion and hinted – but didn't clearly call for – an alternative to the left of Labour.

In the midst of the hectic anti-war movement, Channel 4

produced the TV programme 'The Deal', which as well as providing a convenient diversion, apparently purported to show that the origins of New Labour were all Dave Nellist's fault! He was responsible for the alliance formed between Tony Blair and Gordon Brown! Dave, as a new MP in 1983, shared a small office with Tony Blair for three weeks. This was enough; they were chalk and cheese, and destined to separate. The programme confirmed that, not unsurprisingly, Blair could not stand the presence of Dave and requested John Smith move him into Gordon Brown's office: "Can he share with you? He can't get on with Dave Nellist... It's because of dinosaurs like [Dave] that we lost the election." It was the right of the Labour Party, typified by Smith and the new man on the make, Blair, who were responsible for the 1983 defeat. Back then there was also a reference to Dave Nellist wearing a 'crimplene' suit.[4] Shades of Cameron's criticism of the dress sense of Jeremy Corbyn!

The search for the establishment of a new mass party to replace the increasingly discredited New Labour dominated the work of the Socialist Party in 2004-05, a period running up to a general election. Galloway and others took an initiative by establishing 'Respect – the Unity Coalition' (RUC) that drew in the SWP. It was initially centred on standing in the June 2004 European and Greater London Authority elections. However the establishment of Respect was supported by the SWP by means of a pronunciamento, with no discussion and no democratic debate either within their ranks or with their other 'partners' still left in the Socialist Alliance. This completely confirmed everything that we had said about the methods of the SWP when we were compelled earlier to leave the Socialist Alliance. Nevertheless it came as a shock to those who remained after we were forced out.

Galloway made a mistake by placing exaggerated expectations in the strength of the 'Labour left' – Tony Benn and others – to prevent his expulsion from the Labour Party. We pointed out to him that the right wing was hell bent on purging those who offered the slightest resistance to the Iraq War and its neo-liberal programme, never mind someone like himself. Despite any other drawbacks he may have, he nevertheless courageously opposed New Labour, Blair and Bush in the US, including Congress, on the Iraq War.

Even then we engaged in a discussion over the programme and policies of Respect, with a view to participating in this venture if agreements could be arrived at. Unfortunately, as with the Socialist Alliance, the same approach was adopted by both the SWP and Galloway for an exclusive not inclusive party. We explained: "On December 17, 2003 the Socialist Party wrote to the signatories of the [Respect Unity Coalition's] founding declaration (George Galloway MP, Salma Yaqoob, Lindsey German, John Rees, Linda Smith, Ken Loach, and George Monbiot) asking to discuss the RUC initiative... At this stage there is no evidence of a genuinely open discussion on how to build RUC."[5]

A meeting did take place between Socialist Party representatives and Respect at which they appeared to be keen for us to join and take places on its executive. However, we explained that we did not feel that Respect represented a genuine step towards the formation of a new workers' party at that stage. From the beginning, Respect had a 'communalist' character. In the lexicon of Marxism this describes parties that base themselves primarily upon one ethnic group, particularly in a multi-ethnic society or region. London was already that and is, even more so today, one of the most culturally and ethnically diverse cities in the world. As the history of the labour movement demonstrates, great care has to be exercised in appealing to one section of society so as not to alienate the rest. This approach has marked out the CWI in ongoing situations of racial or national conflict, such as in Northern Ireland or Sri Lanka. In all countries our organisation has sought consistently to unite workers on a class basis.

However this was not even the declared intention of Respect. In fact prior to this, the SWP and Galloway had already moved to a position of uncritical support not just for 'oppressed Muslims' in general but also the 'leaders' of 'Muslim organisations'. This was an integral part of their entirely one-sided analysis of the world situation, particularly since George W Bush came to power. Initially the swp was opposed to any criticism of Al-Qa'ida, as explained above, at the time of the 2001 attack on the World Trade Centre. Previously, the swp had not gone quite as far as this in their one-sided approach to movements in the neo-colonial world but having thrown in their lot with George Galloway in the formation of Respect, they were compelled to follow his 'pro-Muslim' evolution.

Our response was to point out that if this strategy was pursued, it could foster dangerous divisions within the working class between Muslims and other communities. If Respect made gains by being seen as a Muslim party that would not address the needs of other sections of the working class, it could push them away and reinforce racist and divisive ideas. We also pointed out that what was striking about their position, implicitly endorsed by the swp because they never criticised it at the time, was the emphasis on Muslims as a community. Mohammed Sarwar, who may have been 'Britain's first Muslim MP', was nevertheless still tied to New Labour. Moreover no distinction was made between poor, working-class Muslims and the estimated 5,400 Muslim millionaires in Britain at the time who were hostile to the interests of working-class Muslims and the ideas of socialism.

The New Labour government was carrying out the vicious war against the Muslim workers and peasants of Iraq and Afghanistan. We commented: "Imagine if the pioneers of the labour movement had acted like this in Liverpool or Glasgow, appealing to 'Catholics' as a 'community', and likewise to Protestants."[6] This has been the hallmark of ethnically and religiously-based parties. In the case of Northern Ireland, the 'nationalist' organisation the Social Democratic and Labour Party (SDLP), despite the inclusion of 'social democratic' in its name, was a religiously-based party. It remains the case even when these parties are tinged with an element of 'radicalism'. The same applies to Sinn Féin, which was not averse to occasionally mentioning 'socialism' in the past but nevertheless was and is a sectarian organisation rooted in one section of the 'community'. The maxim 'show me who your friends are and I'll show you who you are' is applicable in politics.

After he was expelled from the Labour Party Galloway wrote a book I'm not the only one, which was reviewed in Socialism Today by Jim Horton. This book offered an interesting insight into one of the founders of Respect. Of course, there is a searing indictment of the war and the continued occupation of Iraq as well as a scathing analysis of all those New Labour MPs who sheepishly voted for the conflict. However, what the book also revealed was that the setting up of Respect was not an accident but was rooted in Galloway's long-held political opinions, which showed that he "at various times described himself as a socialist, but in his book is hardly a scintilla of a socialist programme".

During the 1980s Iran-Iraq war Galloway "supported Iran, as did Syria, the Arab country to which I was then closest".[7] His support for Iran went beyond the war issue: "In the absence of a powerful socialist or secular opposition in Iran, my perspective led me to support the Islamic revolution of Khomeini as a people's movement that promised the end to an oppressive dictatorship."[8] There is no suggestion of supporting an independent movement of the working class, which was the main issue that should have been raised and was raised during the Iranian revolution. In fact, Khomeini brutally suppressed the main workers' party at the time the Tudeh party and the rest of the left. This was only possible because this party had failed to build a politically independent working-class movement. In that sense it had the same false perspective as Galloway, looking towards a 'progressive' movement to oppose the Shah while offering Khomeini a "popular and united front" against the monarchy. In other words, this party soaped the hangman's rope of the regime of Khomeini, which destroyed Tudeh.

Galloway offered for this country a "British democratic revolution", a completely outmoded concept, linked as it was to a capitalist democratic revolution that had taken place in Britain four centuries previously. At the same time, he attacked those socialists like Militant who led mass movements against capitalism and Thatcher. He cited the Liverpool city councillors who between 1983 and 1987, as we have explained, mobilised in a major battle to defeat

445

the Thatcher government for more resources for the city. Galloway accused them of being "ultra-left", pursuing "gesture politics" and "not averse to kamikaze acts, such as refusing to set a municipal rate, or otherwise breaking the law". He specifically referred to the "Militant group of Trotskyist entrists working parasitically within the Labour Party", and mocked the "starry-eyed, far-out, far-left fantasies of the fanatics".[9] This is straight from the book of Neil Kinnock together with the worst witch-hunters in the Labour Party. Tony Benn never criticised the heroes of the Liverpool struggle in this way.

Galloway also argued that MPs should be paid twice as much as their existing salaries – then £47,000 per year – plus expenses! This was massively more than what ordinary workers received at this stage. He opposed the Socialist Party's call for all labour movement officials to receive no more than the average wage of a skilled worker. Nevertheless while we sharply disagreed with him on these and other issues, we were still willing to take part in an electoral formation with him and Respect so long as it was based on appealing to broad layers of trade unionists, anti-capitalists and the anti-war movement. Such a movement would need a democratic structure which would allow open and honest discussion and the freedom for the Socialist Party and others to argue for their own programme within the framework of such an organisation.[10]

Despite his political deficiencies Galloway, standing for Respect in Bethnal Green and Bow, won a high-profile victory in the May 2005 general election. He was to remain a figure on the left but never succeeded in breaking out from a very narrow political approach which could not appeal to the mass of the working class.

52. European Union and the euro 1996-97

The European Union (EU) arose from the attempt of European capitalism to overcome the contradiction between the growth of the productive forces – science, technique and the organisation of labour – and the existence of separate national states which hemmed in these productive forces. The giant monopolies, transnational companies, looked not just towards the national sphere but the markets of whole continents and even the world. Yet the attempt to unify Europe on a capitalist basis – a 'United States of Europe' – was doomed to fail because capitalism could not overcome fully the limits of the nation state.

Even a common currency was unlikely to succeed in the long run, although the capitalists over the next two or three decades made Herculean efforts to achieve this. A European Exchange Rate Mechanism (ERM) was constructed before the common currency, which Britain joined for a short period before crashing out of it in 1992. We predicted – in the teeth of much opposition, even from some Marxists – that even limited measures towards unity would clash against the reality of the interests of the different national capitalist classes of Europe. Yet without a unified Europe, capitalism would be incapable of standing up to its rivals internationally: the US, China and Japan.

During a boom it is possible for significant collaboration between the different national capitalist classes to take place. This can even appear to go very far and be 'irreversible'. It seemed at such moments in history that it had become possible to create a unified 'European bourgeoisie'. Indeed, the cwi at international meetings sought to argue that this was not possible; for instance, at an International Executive Committee of the United Secretariat of the Fourth International (usfi) in 1997, Lynn Walsh, who argued this for the cwi, was virtually laughed down by 'fellow Trotskyists'. For many Marxists and Trotskyists, the unification of Europe seemed obvious and could be carried out on a capitalist basis.

The eu's proposals to introduce a common currency, the euro, generated intense discussion within the ranks of the cwi. Some, such as our Swedish and Greek comrades, argued that the euro could be introduced. Others, the leadership in Britain, for instance, were sceptical. This was linked to economic perspectives. We reasoned that if the European and world economy continued to expand – as proved to be the case – the European bourgeoisie could succeed in introducing the euro. If the crisis struck immediately, then the euro would not be introduced. With the onset of the crisis in 2007-08 and a looming repetition of this in the next period, it is possible that the euro in its present form can collapse.

The irony is that rather than banishing nationalism – which the eu amongst its aims was supposed to have achieved – exactly the opposite has taken place. We fought against illusions on this score. Even in the 1990s, we warned: "The social upheavals, largely against the Maastricht criteria, show the limitations of the process of European union. The very policies needed to fulfil the criteria for economic and monetary union threaten to provoke upheavals which put the whole process in jeopardy. Germany alone could drag Europe into a recession." Is this not what has happened in a somewhat different form in Greece and, in the future, may happen in Spain, Portugal, Ireland, Italy and even in Britain itself? We also pointed out: "It is no accident that there has been a resurgence of Euro-scepticism in France and devaluation of the franc is a possibility."[1]

However, these problems and difficulties standing in the way of a unified monetary system were very real from the outset of the eurozone but the European capitalists, led by the French and the Germans, were able to proceed, mainly because they were still rising on the crest of the 1990s boom. It was this factor which allowed the bourgeoisie to drive through the European 'project'. It was also the inevitable collapse of this boom at a certain stage that allowed us to predict the undermining of the euro and the placing of a huge question mark over the very future of the currency and the eurozone as a whole.

The majority of the bourgeoisie and their 'social democratic' echoes did not just entertain illusions on Europe but also on the prospects for the world economy. We consistently argued against the illusions generated by the 1990s boom that capitalism had managed to overcome the normal cycle of boom and bust. Gordon Brown – British Chancellor of the Exchequer following the 1997 general election – predicted that he and his bourgeois counterparts in Europe, the US and Japan had indeed abolished 'boom and bust'. This in turn generated certain illusions, even in the labour movement. The capitalist media were full of references to the 'economic paradigm' which capitalism had now firmly established. We subjected these ideas to a rigorous analysis in the pages of The Socialist and Socialism Today.

On the occasion of the downfall of the long-standing British bank Barings in 1995, we took the opportunity to remind our readers of the realities of capitalism which lay behind the boom. Without the check provided by the labour movement, capitalism was running riot, engaging in all kinds of speculation of a parasitic character, piling up a mountain of debt – which the Barings scandal laid bare – thus preparing the way for a massive crash. This was indicated by the development of 'junk bonds'. George Bush senior had to act in 1989, in effect nationalising the savings and loans industry. It was the American 'consumer' who paid the bill for this.

Despite the fact that the ruling class faced no real challenge from the labour movement – held in chains by right-wing leaders – they nevertheless enjoyed only very low and feeble growth. Speculation on financial markets, always a feature of capitalism, assumed a frenzied character. New and dangerous 'financial instruments' such as derivatives developed on a huge scale. This involved gambling on future price increases where derivatives were contracted by currency or interest rate swaps purchased relatively cheaply, with the sole intention of selling them on at a higher price. This ultimately led to the crash a decade or so later. The Barings shock – involving as it did a relatively small merchant bank – nevertheless was one of the first tremors indicating the earthquake to come. We compared the trillions of dollars moving around the money markets to unsecured cargo on a ship that could result in opening up a huge hole in the hull which could sink the ship itself.

While capitalism, in the wake of the collapse of the Berlin Wall and the liquidation of the planned economy, seemed to have 'won', as the Wall Street Journal expressed it in 1990, nevertheless, the whole period was characterised by insecurity on the part of the majority of the population and dissatisfaction with the deterioration in the 'quality of life'. Particularly heinous crimes could provoke mass outrage, as shown in the scandal in Belgium involving the kidnapping and death of at least four young girls. A vast world of criminal activities and corruption involving police, judges and politicians, including a paedophile ring led by Mark Dutroux, was revealed. In the process, large-scale crime in the 1990s came to light, also involving the murder of Belgian Socialist Party ex-minister Andre Cools. These revelations led to a mass demonstration, the 'White March', involving a third of a million people and highlighting opposition to the police's handling of the issues. Brussels workers carried the slogan: "Clean up the state". Factory workers walked off the job to "occupy motorways". The tempo of the class struggle increased, with the CWI's Belgian organisation Militant Links (Militant Left) intervening.[2] But a combination of the state cracking down and the refusal of the trade union leaders to give a clear lead resulted in the movement ebbing away.[3]

As mentioned earlier, our Irish comrades had been involved in a number of mass campaigns. In 1996 an epic battle was taking place in Ireland against the introduction of water charges, whose leading spokesman was Joe Higgins. There were 20,000 signed up members of the anti-water charges campaign in the south of Ireland. Moreover, in Dublin North constituency, the Socialist Party in Ireland was at the head of a campaign against heroin on the estates, against drug pushers and for a socialist approach to the problems of addiction. Mass meetings took place, including one of 1,500 parents and youth on the estates, which was overflowing and where speakers outside had to relay what was being said inside. Joe Higgins was a candidate in a by-election for the Dáil, the Irish Parliament. He came within 370 votes of winning – a tremendous achievement for a small party with limited resources.

We were encouraged when Joe and the Socialist Party achieved a magnificent victory and became a TD (MP) in the Dáil in June 1997. This was on the back of the great victory in the anti-water charges campaign, which had successfully defeated the Irish government and was led by the Socialist Party.

This was followed by a tremendous intervention in the 50,000 strong European March for Jobs on 14 June 1997. This was probably the first major international intervention of the CWI under its own banner. Alongside the Italian unions and others, the CWI had its clear international political colours on the demo. The German section of the CWI, Sozialistische Alternative, organised over 600 people to go on the march. As well as these campaigns on specific issues, the CWI was involved at this stage in organising discussions with other socialists – and particularly those from a Trotskyist tradition – to see whether we could arrive at common action and from this to explore and discuss how to build the socialist movement and a new international.

Despite the collapse of Stalinism, the basic organisations of the working class – the trade unions – although weakened, remained intact. The historic goal of the labour movement, the realisation of a socialist society, seemed to have receded in the consciousness of the working class, following the collapse of Stalinism in Russia and Eastern Europe and the ensuing dismemberment of the planned economy. But the working class retained its instinctive resilience in

451

the face of newly emboldened capitalism's onslaught against their rights and conditions. Although significant sections of the top trade union leaders moved towards the right, this was not necessarily the case for the mass of working people.

53. Building Socialism in the US 1994-2004

The 1992 split with the Grant and Woods minority was international in character and not just restricted to Britain. This necessitated an increased number of international visits by me, but mostly by those comrades who worked primarily for the cwi at this time. Tony Saunois, Bob Labi, Clare Doyle and Simon Kaplan carried most of the burden of this work. However, Lynn Walsh and I also played an increased role following the split as a means of consolidating our international support. Some of this initially involved working with small forces.

This was the case when I visited the us in 1994 for the first time. For decades, a small band of dedicated Marxists has worked to lay the basis for the victory in Seattle in 2013 of Kshama Sawant and the party to which she belonged, Socialist Alternative.

The 1994 visit took place in one of the most difficult periods ever to find an echo for socialist and Marxist ideas, particularly for a small group, coming as it did just a few years after the collapse of Stalinism, when capitalist triumphalism was at its height. The attendances at meetings, as well as the broad response, were meagre to say the least! One of the purposes of my visit was to speak at the National Committee of the us organisation sympathetic to the ideas of the cwi – called Labor Militant at the time – which was well attended and was very useful for me in assessing their strengths and weaknesses. Moreover, travelling round this vast 'country' on a continental scale allowed me to form a picture of the conditions of the US working class, which proved to be useful in drawing some conclusions as to their consciousness and the state of the broad labour movement.

In the month I was in the US and Canada, I spoke at about ten public meetings, which meant criss-crossing North America. I travelled from New York to Philadelphia, then to Boston, from there to Toronto, back to New York – for the National Committee – then to Chicago, Oakland in California and on to Seattle, where I addressed a very small meeting. It was difficult to imagine then that in this quite attractive city the biggest breakthrough for US socialists would come 20 years later! I was then driven up the West Coast to Vancouver before returning via Seattle back to London.

Labor Militant, which was in solidarity with the CWI, had been raising the issue of a Labor party for many years and was actively involved in Labor Party Advocates. It had 20 delegates at the National Convention of this body and also when the Labor Party was set up at the conference of 6-9 June 1996 in Cleveland Ohio. They were able to make a significant intervention. The hope was that this meeting would be the most historic for the US working class since the building of the mass industrial unions in the 1930s. 1,400 delegates were at the founding convention of the new Labor Party. A worker from the Oil, Chemical and Atomic Workers Union told this convention: "We regard the Democrats and Republicans as so similar that the two candidates Clinton and Dole are like a toothache and a headache, both painful in ways that makes no real difference to the sufferers – working Americans."[1]

As soon as Ralph Nader indicated his intentions to stand as an independent in the 2000 Presidential elections we gave critical support to this campaign, before the rest of the left had taken a position. It immediately gained an echo, rising on the high tide of anti-globalisation sentiment with a host of progressive celebrities jumping onto the bandwagon. Subsequently Nader was blamed, even by formerly supportive radicals, for allegedly allowing Bush to win by standing in Florida. In fact, the Democrats represented by

Al Gore had a weak, ultra-cautious approach in the election campaign, even losing Gore's home state of Tennessee. Moreover, when it was clear that George W Bush and his cronies – particularly his brother Jeb who was the governor of Florida – had in effect corruptly fixed the election by debarring the infamous 'hanging chads' (incompletely punched holes in electronic ballot papers) in Florida, the Democrats refused to organise a mass movement to dispute this and demand that the decision be revoked.

After much prevarication and under the pressure of Socialist Alternative amongst others, Nader again decided to run in 2004. The appeal of John Kerry was so weak that the Democrats lost ground in their core constituencies. In contrast to the 2000 elections, Nader's 2004 run was built on the back of the anti-war movement and with most middle-class progressives feeling scarred after the lies and four years of Bush's assaults. However they were successfully bullied into the comforts of 'unity' behind Kerry.

We were confident that out of the anti-capitalist, anti-globalisation and anti-war movements, a new consciousness would develop. This was not yet of a broad socialist character but an important layer of workers and youth had begun to draw socialist and revolutionary conclusions. Even in the US elections, the underlying situation reflected a polarisation which could take a more conscious form in the period that followed. We stated that "Socialism and Marxism are now going with the grain of history after the difficult struggles of the 1990s to maintain a revolutionary pole of attraction."[2] The predictions made here were borne out, with some delay, but borne out they were in the election of Kshama and the new radical, socialist period which is opening up in the US and worldwide.

54. Visiting Russia
1998

I visited Russia for the first time in 1998, after the collapse of Stalinism and the planned economy which accompanied this. I was there to speak at the all-CIS conference of the section of the CWI. In both Russia and Ukraine, I witnessed at first hand the degradation, which had come suddenly, to whole layers of the population, the old and the most vulnerable literally begging on the streets, drunkenness born of despair, which was visible and could not be hidden from public view. Life expectancy was generally recognised to have dramatically dropped to about 58 for men, mostly through alcoholism.

The CWI had the great advantage of receiving first hand reports from the end of the 1980s from our comrades in Russia. At the cost of great personal self-sacrifice by comrades like the indefatigable Clare Doyle and Rob Jones, and against the backdrop of a social counter-revolution, we had maintained an organised presence in Russia and other countries of the former 'Soviet Union'. They had to swim not just against the stream but against the big wave of pro-capitalist sentiment while the living standards of the people seemed to be on a sharply downward trajectory. Therefore it was incumbent on those members of the CWI who did not work in the same desperate conditions as these comrades to assist their work with visits.

A number of comrades had already visited Russia – Tony Saunois and Lynn Walsh, both members of the International Secretariat of the cwi, amongst them– in the first period after the collapse of Stalinism. They recorded their impressions in the pages of The Socialist on their return. When I followed them in 1998 I first travelled to Kiev in Ukraine where we had a small but active group. Kiev at the end of winter appeared to me at first a grim place but looking around the city, in particular visiting some buildings, the Orthodox churches, I could see the beauty and attractiveness of the city. I was interviewed by journalists and appeared on local TV, with my comments on the political situation reported in a relatively unbiased fashion. Discussions took place with a small group of Ukrainians who supported the cwi, held in very tiny 'Khrushchev flats' in the massive, soulless blocks of concrete which passed for workers' dwellings. Indeed, I was informed that when these were built in the 1960s, they were looked on as a desirable improvement over previous housing.

On this visit to Ukraine and the Russian cities of St Petersburg and Moscow, I spoke to quite large meetings – particularly in Ukraine – explaining the perspectives of the cwi internationally and in the former Soviet Union. When I travelled to Moscow in the company of Rob Jones, I met the first secretary of the regional committee of the Communist Party in Bishkek, the capital of Kyrgyzstan, which had a population of 800,000. He told me: "We have pure dictatorship here with 16 parties officially registered, 15 of these are pro-presidential, that is they support the ruling power. Approximately 90% of the workforce is unemployed... Most people manage to at least exist by becoming 'shuttlers', they travel from one country to another, buying and selling goods through primitive barter, now the norm for most of the population."

I asked him if he could date the time of decline in the country, and he replied: "It roughly began from 1991. Privatisation only really began in earnest about two or three years ago. There were a lot of clashes in the ruling elite, struggling for the spoils of privatisation and the return of the 'free market'." Most of the countries of Central Asia were like this, having swapped the Stalinist state for a capitalist dictatorship, the only difference being in the markedly rapid decline of the conditions of the masses. This comrade attended the conference in Moscow of 'Left Vanguard', the section of the CWI in the Commonwealth of Independent States (CIS). I asked him why he was attending the conference and he replied: "We were enormously impressed with the campaign you launched in defence of Kazakhstan comrades. We said to ourselves why is an organisation which seems to have existed for such a short period of time so effective when others with seemingly huge memberships are incapable of defending workers in the CIS? Our organisation sent me to meet you and discuss common action in the CIS and throughout the world." The terrible conditions in Kazakhstan were outlined to me by workers from that country. The Workers Movement of Kazakhstan adhered to the CWI as a sympathising section for a period.

At this stage most of the small Marxist groups had abandoned the country in despair, openly declaring that it was not possible to build in such unfavourable terrain. Some, like a small group who temporarily supported Alan Woods (who had split from the CWI in 1992) could only be described as a motley collection of misfits and cranks. Such weird and wonderful organisations were not at all uncommon in Russia. Some would think nothing of attempting to combine neo-fascist ideas and wearing military fatigues alongside quasi-'Bolshevik' symbols.

One such organisation which still exists today is the National Bolsheviks headed by Eduard Limonov. When I spoke at a public meeting in Moscow in 1998, I was verbally attacked by Woods, who was in the city at the time, over the split in the CWI in Scotland mentioned earlier. He prophesied, as he had done before and would do again, the imminent collapse of the CWI. He attacked our alleged 'nationalist degeneration' in Scotland – because we recognised the right of self-determination for the Scottish people, including the right to secede from Britain if they so desired. He was supported by supporters of Limonov, who I naturally answered, both at the meeting and in a subsequent public statement that indicted Woods for his unofficial political bloc with the neo-fascists, which he formed at this meeting to attack me and the CWI.

Later, in the company of Rob Jones and a young comrade in Moscow we were attacked on the Metro by a group of Russian fascists and some who had come to support them from East Germany. This attack was reported in the Guardian: 'Veteran Marxist Attacked in Moscow.'[1] This indicates just how complex the task has been in assembling a Marxist cadre in a situation like this.

55. Latin America 1996-2004

Latin America presented special difficulties for an organisation like ours, rooted as we were in Britain and with cadres coming from a working class background, with a smattering of intellectuals and students familiar with languages other than English. Other Trotskyist organisations, who began with intellectuals and students, with most not progressing beyond a narrow circle, initially possessed a greater capacity to intervene through the languages of Latin America, principally Spanish and Portuguese.

Nevertheless, through the diligent work of pioneers, such as Tony Saunois, Tom Nerney, Paulina Ramirez and her brother Matias, we eventually were able to build an important base in Chile and Brazil in particular. The original group that we had established in Argentina allied itself to the Grant-Woods split of 1992 and did not play any further role in the CWI. Our work brought us valuable comrades in Chile, such as comrade Celso, with a long history in the workers' movement including fighting the Pinochet regime in the underground, suffering in the process terrible torture and imprisonment. Another valuable addition was a young 19-year-old Andre Ferrari, a founder of the Brazilian section. In both countries the CWI now has flourishing organisations which are growing and attracting the best of the workers and the youth.

Tony Saunois visited Mexico following the uprising of the Zapatista guerrilla movement (EZLN) whose main spokesperson was 'Subcomandante Marcos'. The country had been hailed by international bankers as a model of 'neo-liberalism'. In the 1990s, however, the Zapatistas organised a revolt of the Mexican people against this 'model'.

Tony Saunois attended the Zapatistas' gathering on behalf of the CWI in 1996. He commented: "In 1996, the first Encuentro Internacional (International Assembly) was called by the EZLN in the rain forests of Chiapas. This meeting was attended by a few thousand youth and academics from all over the world. This was historically a very important meeting in that it was the birthplace of many of the ideas of the anti-capitalist movement which emerged later on a world scale.

"Rejecting the 'centralised planning' and Stalinist forms of organisation, most of those present supported the building of 'horizontal networks' as an alternative to political parties. While neo-liberal capitalism was rejected and opposed, socialism was viewed as a relic of the past. It was a reaction to the Stalinist forms of organisation and ideas which became discredited with the collapse of Stalinism. In practice, Marcos and the EZLN leaders demonstrated in Mexico what such ideas would mean."

In Chile there had been initial rejoicing at the arrest of Pinochet in London in October 1998. The population had become accustomed to the idea that he was immune from such actions. The right, infuriated by Pinochet's arrest, abandoned the mask of the 'democratic far right' and returned to death threats against victims' families, left-wing intellectuals and former political prisoners. On demonstrations they carried effigies of left leaders, particularly the leadership of the Communist Party. Moreover, when student federations, who were the first to celebrate, organised demonstrations the police were unleashed against them. Nevertheless, the arrest of Pinochet – despite his subsequent release – indicated that the winds of change would affect Chile after the long rule of the dictator and his authoritarian state.

As the new decade broke, the crisis that was affecting the West quickly manifested itself in many countries of Latin America, particularly Argentina, in a catastrophic economic situation that led to political turmoil and working-class protest. Argentina was not a 'typical' Latin American country. At the beginning of the 20th century it had higher living standards than Spain, Italy and even Germany at one stage. By 1933 it was the tenth richest economy in the world and a decade later was ninth. In 1945 it was even richer than France – then suffering the effects of the Second World War – and posted at one stage higher living standards than Canada. It was up until this point enjoying perhaps the highest living standards of Latin America.

A severe social crisis in Brazil led to a new movement for a new workers' socialist party launched by former Workers' Party (PT) activists, trade unionists and socialists. This came only one year after the presidential election victory of Luíz Inácio da Silva ('Lula') who, despite his promise before the election to take a different road, carried through a pro-capitalist programme. As a result, on 19 January 2004, in Rio de Janeiro, representatives of various left-wing socialist organisations, including the Brazilian section of the CWI, Socialismo Revolutionario, together with trade union leaders, intellectuals and former PT MPs, met to launch a "left democratic socialist movement".

I visited Brazil to attend the first conference of the new party that was taking shape, Partido Socialismo e Libertade (Socialism and Freedom Party, 'P-SoL'). This conference met in the capital Brasilia and was attended by about 1,000 workers and representatives of different left organisations, most of them from a Trotskyist background. Subsequently one of the MPs that were expelled from the PT, Joao Batista (Baba), visited London to speak at our annual 'Socialism' event. In an interview in Socialism Today with me, he commented on the factors that led to the development of P-SoL: "Instead of satisfying the aroused political and social expectations of the masses, Lula has moved in the opposite direction. He has surrounded himself with the pillars of international capitalism. The president of the Brazilian bank is the former head of the Bank of Boston, and is now the right-hand man of Lula." He had accepted completely the dictates of the IMF, allocating more than 50% of the budget to repay debts and interest charges: "Not even Cardoso spent so much on this. And this is at a time when President Kirchner in Argentina carried out a partial repudiation of debt in 2003."[1]

Venezuela, after the coming to power of Hugo Chávez in 1999, was the Latin American country in which the battle between contending social forces, revolution and counter-revolution, assumed its sharpest expression over the subsequent decade or so. Imperialism remained suspicious and afraid of the contagious effects of Chávez and the Venezuelan revolution. His government had given popular expression to the anger felt by the masses against the elite and neo-liberalism, as well as their desire for big changes. But the majority of the workers had neither drawn clear class conclusions nor embraced the idea of the need for an alternative revolutionary programme.

Chávez evinced a form of radical Venezuelan nationalism with concern for the poor, partly rooted in his own peasant background. His stress on this found a reflection within the armed forces, which contained radical nationalist elements linked to concern for the 'people' and the need to modernise and develop Venezuelan society. He invoked, particularly in the first stages, the powerful tradition of Simón Bolívar, the early 19th century fighter for liberation from Spain, during his ascent to power. After his election, he took the mantle of Bolivar and paraded through the streets to jubilant cries from the mass demonstrations that greeted him. This was widely interpreted as a step towards a struggle against imperialism and capital. This terrified the ruling class in Venezuela and aroused the opposition of the US in particular; its representatives denounced the 'dictatorial' methods and powers of Chávez. He used the colossal income from oil – Venezuela has one of the largest oil reserves in the world – in order to introduce substantial reforms, which benefited the poor. Despite the continual attempts of reaction – with the support from imperialism outside especially during the coup of 2002 – Chávez managed to win election after election.

We gave critical support to the progressive measures which were introduced but we never went to the lengths of others, like

Alan Woods and the International Marxist Tendency, who tried to compensate for their small forces with shrill, noisy and largely uncritical praise for Chávez and his regime. The fact that Hugo Chávez expressed an interest at one stage in the ideas of Leon Trotsky, mentioning on occasion the 'permanent revolution', did not mean that he was about to be transformed into a rounded-out Marxist or Trotskyist.

Significantly, at the World Social Forum in Brazil in January 2005, Chávez spoke for the first time of the need for socialism. He declared: "It is necessary to transcend capitalism. But capitalism can't be transcended from within capitalism itself, but through socialism, true socialism, with equality and justice." We welcomed this step forward, at least in words, but pointed out that it was not enough just to support the ideas of socialism. A programme was necessary to achieve this. Unfortunately, he was not putting forward a clear programme for the working class to overthrow capitalism and establish a socialist planned economy. In fact, when he announced the nationalisation of one firm, he declared that this was "an exception, not a political measure".

At this stage his nationalisation programme was restricted to abandoned factories and land. While welcoming such measures, we said this was not enough: "Why only take the bankrupt companies leaving those still functioning and making a profit in the hands of the ruling class?"[2] We drew on the experience of Chile under the Allende government, which went a lot further than Chávez was proposing. Partial measures in Chile merely gave reaction the chance to organise and strike back.

With the death of Chávez, Venezuela has now entered a very uncertain period. His successor Nicolás Maduro has confronted a far more determined opposition, which has resorted to street demonstrations and forms of civil disobedience in order to force the new president – who scraped home in the first elections after Chávez's death – to once more subject himself to the verdict of the electorate. They hoped that would lead them back to power and the whole Venezuelan 'experiment' would be defeated. The isolation of

Cuba and the concessions which are being made to the 'market' by the Cuban regime following Chávez's death have further strengthened the pro-capitalist forces in Venezuela and Cuba itself.

However, events in Venezuela are taking place against an entirely different background to when Chávez first came to power. There is not one stable capitalist regime throughout Latin America. The pages of The Socialist recorded the almost constant upheavals in countries like Ecuador, Bolivia and Mexico, even while the continent on the surface appeared to be progressing, at least economically.

My 2004 visit to Latin America, primarily to Brazil, also took in Chile. This country, let us remind ourselves, was held up as a shining example of the neo-liberal model which was capable of lifting the continent out of its age-old poverty. We analysed the real content of the 'Chilean experiment', which consisted of a colossal impoverishment of the masses when it was under the heel of the Pinochet dictatorship. This allowed Chile to develop in a one-sided fashion, benefiting as well from the so-called super-cycle commodities boom – through massive increases in copper exports. This was fuelled by the growth of world capitalism, and particularly of China, throughout the 1990s and the early 2000s.

That has now come to an end with the increasing economic slowdown confronting China. This will be reflected in a contraction of income for a swathe of countries in the neo-colonial world that linked their fate with the seemingly endless economic progress of China. It is not an accident that Chile saw increased strikes and social struggle erupt in 2013, beginning with the youth in the mass uprisings of the students. This in turn has impacted on the working class as a whole. The discontent was reflected in the mass abstentions, which took place in the November 2013 general election, in which just 42% of the registered electorate voted.

In Brazil, the left political organisations that began to coordinate the task of building an alternative to the PT included a number from the PT, many of them from the Morenoite tradition,[3] and the Brazilian section of the CWI, Socialismo Revolucionário (SR). Outside of the PT there was the United Socialist Workers Party

(PSTU) which had split from the PT in 1992-93. They remained aloof from the process of creating a new movement. Heloisa Helena, a PT deputy, unlike the leadership of her own organisation Socialist Democracy (DS) – the Mandelite group – stated that she would vote against the pension bill in the Senate. This led to her expulsion from the PT, joined by others, including some deputies. They formed the core of the new party P-SoL at its founding conference, which I attended with our Brazilian comrades.

An early indication of the favourable prospects for P-SoL was shown at the anti-globalisation World Social Forum (WSF) of early 2005 in Porto Alegre. This was attended by our Brazilian comrades and a very enthusiastic, largely youth, international contingent from the CWI. This gathering was notable for the attendance of Hugo Chávez, who spoke at an enthusiastic main rally. Kevin Simpson, part of the CWI contingent, reported: "From four hours before the rally, young people in their thousands streamed towards the Gigantinho ('little giant') stadium in the sweltering summer heat... The queue snaked as far as the eye could see... These thousands had come to hear Hugo Chávez... speak of the rebellion against 'neoliberalism' and US imperialism... Unlike the Lula... meeting earlier in the week, where his supporters were bussed in, all expenses paid, all those here came of their own volition and were overwhelmingly youth... Many of these young people were Brazil's (and Latin America's) new generation of fighters for social change in the making. They have broken with any illusions in Lula and capitalism; they are anti-capitalist and anti-war – as are many of their generation in other continents – but there is an important difference: they have come through the experience of what has been a continental-wide rebellion in the last few years against neo-liberalism."

This just gives a flavour of the effect of the revolutionary events in Latin America, particularly of young people worldwide. The report goes on: "By the time the auditorium was full, huge red flags were being waved in the air – a large P-SoL contingent took up the left bank of the stadium and led the way chanting anti-Lula and anti-imperialist slogans." When a small group of the youth section of the Brazilian Communist Party, which was participating in Lula's government, started chanting pro-Lula slogans and waving their party flags, "In literally seconds a seething anger and a bitter hostility filled the air as thousands of people shouted for them to be kicked out." The chant went up 'pelego', which is a cushioned blanket put on horses' backs underneath the saddle to allow the animal to be controlled. In contrast, "A wall of sound greeted Chávez's arrival on the stage". The right-wing trade union leaders who tried to introduce Chávez were booed.

The mood changed again completely when Chávez began to speak: "I am not here as the president of Venezuela. I do not feel like the president. I am only president because of particular circumstances. I am Hugo Chávez and I am an activist as well as a revolutionary. Because to break the hegemony of capitalism and that of the oligarchs, the only way is revolution", to which the crowd roared their approval. He emphasised the fight of the southern continents against the 'rich north'; however, he did not raise this in the context of the struggle between social classes internationally and quoted, favourably, the work of the 'non-aligned group of nations' in the 1960s and 1970s as an example of what could be organised amongst Latin American nations today. Significantly, he moved on to quote Leon Trotsky, commenting that the coup against him in 2002 illustrated the point made by this leader of the Russian revolution that "every revolution needs the whip of the counter-revolution".

He had faced a least three serious attempts to overthrow him. These had been defeated by the mass movement but as we explained in the meetings of the WSF, unless the revolution was taken forward and capitalism overthrown, the counter-revolution will strike again until it succeeds. In answer to this he stated: "There are people within my country. Good people... who say I don't go fast enough or that I am not sufficiently radical. But these comrades have to realise that this is a process, a process with phases and rhythms. Remember, we are taking on a world system which is a big task. I know that I am at risk of being booed but Lula is a good man and a friend of ours." The report continues: "And Chávez was booed but this was partially drowned out by the applause he received as he ended his speech."[4] At this stage P-SoL was scoring 3% to 5% of the vote in opinion polls. The candidature of Heloise for the presidency in 2006 was floated at this meeting and received much support.

The cwi sections in Latin America have continued to advance, as demonstrated by the highly successful annual Latin American School, which brings together workers and youth from many of the countries throughout the continent. The cwi now possesses a very strong section in Brazil, a growing force in Chile and possibilities in other countries. Latin America is a crucial arena of the class struggle and therefore it is vital that the cwi not only continues to advance, but acts as a catalyst for bringing together into a common organisation the genuine forces who are willing and able to build a tenacious revolutionary party, leading to mass organisations of the working class. The road to mass revolutionary parties lies in the first instance through the likely formation of transitional formations, broad parties, in which the Trotskyists and Marxists can play a key role, leading at a certain stage to mass revolutionary parties. In order to achieve this, we must avoid the pitfalls of sectarianism and opportunism.

56. Socialist Party activities 2002-05

The national congresses of the Socialist Party always played a key role in both assessing the general situation in which the party would act and discussing the organisational targets for building the party. Our 2002 conference heard many of the delegates comment on the shift towards the left that was taking place, the result of attacks on workplace conditions and wages. One London Underground worker spoke on the breakthrough for the left represented by Bob Crow's election as leader of the RMT. London Underground workers now wanted more action to defeat Blair's privatisation scheme, he said. Ninety-five percent of the money for the scheme would come from the government yet the private companies involved will own the infrastructure for 30 years. Strike action extracted the promise of no compulsory redundancies. Socialist Party members on London Underground would keep fighting in the unions for a public campaign against privatisation, including demonstrations, and for the renationalisation of the whole railway network. The Underground worker also said that many RMT members had concluded that the union should disaffiliate altogether from the Labour Party.

As previously mentioned, Matt Wrack attended this congress as a visitor. He argued that it was premature to campaign for trade union disaffiliation from the Labour Party. Instead, we should campaign to democratise the political funds, demanding union leaders put pressure on New Labour. He also said that we should not have left the Socialist Alliance as some workers may still look towards it, including FBU members. Glenn Kelly, then a National Executive Committee member of Unison, replied to Matt, pointing out that our principled position was for disaffiliation from the Labour Party now that it is a big business party but he explained that the tactics of the campaign would develop differently in each union. Many council workers hated New Labour locally but on a national basis could not see an alternative. That is why we call for the formation of a new mass workers' party, at the same time supporting all steps towards such a party, such as campaigning in Unison for the formation of a third political fund.

Dave Nellist, leader of the Socialist group on Coventry City Council, stressed that a genuine alliance needs more than just a name to mean anything to workers. Amongst other things it must have a democratic approach. He believed that the forces for a new workers' party would come from the trade unions and community campaigns, and workers will demand open and inclusive organisations to fight for their demands. These debates and exchanges give the lie to the myth sedulously disseminated by our opponents that the decisions on policy, programme and organisation are decided by one or two individuals, a small cabal in the leadership of the Socialist Party.

In fact, before we launched the Socialist Party, when we worked in the Labour Party as Militant, we were scrupulously democratic in the way we discussed, formulated and agreed policies. We had local and national meetings in which all views were aired and, only after full discussion, arrived at decisions. Matt Wrack was listened to, the debate took place, and he was in a minority on this issue. He subsequently left our ranks because of growing political differences – not least on the need to develop broad lefts in the unions, which he opposed, preferring a highly individualistic approach. However, the Socialist Party has always sought to maintain a friendly approach, even where we will on occasions differ politically, sometimes quite sharply with those like Matt, as well as other left leaders.

The 2004 national congress of the Socialist Party was held in

Skegness which recorded a significant increase in the influence and the membership of the Socialist Party. Half of our new members in 2003 were under the age of 26. The previous year had seen two socialist councillors re-elected in Coventry, Lincoln socialists take 16% of the votes in the same council elections and, repeating the pattern of previous years, the best results for the left on Merseyside were in wards where the Socialist Party stood. In Deptford in London, in a normally solid Labour-voting ward, we gained 13% of the votes. Labour had panicked as it appeared that Socialist Party candidate Jess Leech was picking up support.

The sp conference also discussed the rise of the far right, manifested at that stage by the development of the British National Party (BNP). In fact, the emergence of the BNP as a threat led to Labour benefiting temporarily in places like Stoke-on-Trent, but it did not stop the BNP gaining more than 6,000 votes in the city. Some other left organisations merely hurled insults at the BNP but the Socialist Party, particularly in one ward, put forward an alternative designed to appeal to working people and prevent them going into the BNP's camp. The result was that the Socialist Party campaign and candidate greatly improved its votes from a by-election only a few months previously! This was just one example of the decisive contribution made by the Socialist Party in the struggle against the far right and the fascists.

Our congress was followed by an equally successful weekend of discussion and debate at Socialism 2004, in which the Brazilian MP Joao Batista ('Baba') participated. One young worker commented on the speeches at Socialism: "What I found most inspiring were the international comrades. Despite the difficulties in other countries which dwarf what we face, those comrades' dedication to socialism is an inspiration to us all."

Socialism 2004 heard an important contribution from Chris Baugh, a long-standing member of the Socialist Party, and newly elected Assistant General Secretary of the PCS. Chris showed how "workers will join the trade unions if they're motivated to do so by policies which fight for ordinary union members." Joe Higgins

471

spoke on the battle against the hated bin tax for which he and other Socialist Party members in Ireland were jailed. The sp had consequently built up enormous respect during this struggle, which led to 14 candidates standing in the local elections of June 2004.[1]

In September Hannah Sell, speaking on behalf of the Executive Committee at a special National Council of the Socialist Party, spelt out the plans for building in 2005. She reported that in the previous year substantial progress had been made with most regions of the party having a significant layer of new young members who transformed the branches or, in some cases, founded new ones in towns where the Socialist Party had never existed before. This was laying the basis for success on a bigger scale at a later stage. Vital in this regard was the work of Socialist Students, which had had its most successful ever freshers' fayres campaign in 2003, with 800 joining up. Hannah reported that this was the only national anti-capitalist organisation which was run democratically by, and for, young people and students.

2004 was also the 40th anniversary of the founding of Militant itself. A special feature, alongside meetings in London and elsewhere held by our party commemorated these events. We wrote: "The Independent newspaper, recently commenting on the life of a deceased Olympic athlete, wrote that his critics described him as 'the sport's Militant Tendency'. David Beckham was accused of leading a 'millionaire Militant Tendency' – a contradiction in terms – after England's football team refused to speak to the press following a recent international match because of what they considered unfair criticism of their previous performances."

These are just two out of thousands of examples of how the terms 'Militant' and 'Militant Tendency' had permeated everyday language in Britain over the last 40 years. Like 'bolshie' or 'commie' in the past, they were now general terms for all those prepared to stand up for the poor, the weak and the exploited against the bosses and authoritarian forces of all kinds.

This was also recognition of our effect on the political landscape in Britain over decades. We took the opportunity to remind workers of our political antecedents. We pointed to the first issue of our paper, commenting on the role of the Labour leadership in 1964, when we wrote: "By showing themselves as 'safe and responsible' leaders, not fundamentally different from the Tories, the Labour leaders have played into the hands of the Tories."[2] We were a very small force when we made these comments, producing a four-page monthly paper in black-and-white only, subject to the whims of a small printer in West London as to whether the paper was even produced or not. Many doubted whether this new 'baby', ill clad and lacking in substance, would even survive its first few months. We were able to do so because of our youthful, boundless faith in the socialist future of the working class and humankind. We also had enormously committed supporters, although in 1964 only numbering around 40 nationally.

We had had many successes in the previous 40 years, not least in the trade unions. For instance, John Macreadie, in the Civil and Public Services Association, which later merged into the PCS, won the general secretaryship of that union fair and square. However, he was debarred from taking this leadership post by blatant manoeuvres, undemocratic and dictatorial measures from the right wing, backed by the capitalists and their courts, with the blessing of Thatcher, as revealed in recently released papers. However, the real bitter hostility of the capitalists was reserved for Militant when its influence was sharply expressed in the epic Liverpool battle. The Liverpool working class and labour movement, with Militant in its leadership, managed to inflict a serious defeat on Thatcher in 1984.

An indication of the growth of support for Marxist ideas was the vote in 2005 for Karl Marx as the greatest philosopher of all time by BBC Radio Four listeners, much to the chagrin of Melvyn Bragg, presenter of the programme In Our Time. Marx won with 28% of the vote compared to his nearest rival, the free trade supporter of a contemporary of Adam Smith, David Hume, who received only just over 12%. This undoubtedly represented an ideological blow to capitalism and its supporters in the media.

57. Looking forward: Labour government 2003-04

"In the past year, Britain entered a period of upheaval and turbulence. There were huge anti-war demonstrations which convulsed Britain and the world – compelling the New York Times to comment on the emergence of a "new superpower" – together with the rise in militancy and strikes in industry." We pointed out in our 2004 New Year message to our readers that if the trade union leaders possessed one tenth of the determination of the working class, then the anti-union laws would have already been a dead letter. Instead, they – including, unfortunately, some of the so-called 'awkward squad' – acted like Rabbie Burns's 'wee timorous beastie' in shamefully acquiescing to these laws.

There was boiling anger amongst trade unionists at the virtual reign of terror – in effect, a semi-dictatorship of capital – in the workplace. Some trade union leaders like Tony Woodley reflected this when he stated: "The only thing that talks louder than money is the united voice of mobilised people." Unfortunately, he went on to argue that the government's tax and economic aid policy should do more to "reward the good investor and punish the bad".[1] The implication was that a solution must be sought to the pressing problems of working-class people from the 'good capitalists' rather than the 'bad' ones. Capitalism is a system based upon production for profit and not social need, and it is this which drives on all wings of the boss class. Gordon Brown was asserting that Britain faced a relatively 'benign' economic situation, with unemployment officially at a 28-year low.

However, the statistics did not take account of hidden unemployment. Like the Tories before them, New Labour had massaged the figures and concocted a whole series of 'make-work' measures to remove the long-term unemployed from the register. Millions had been shifted to the 'disabled' category. Under the ConDem government, these disabled workers would be cruelly punished. In reality, by 2004 the UK had amongst the worst poverty in the European Union, the longest working hours and the lowest 'social spending'. Three times more UK children had fallen below the poverty line than in 1970. A tenth of the population received pay rises averaging 7.3% in the previous year, while the bottom tenth got 4.5%. The comfort blanket of the growth in services to replace manufacturing had been snatched away. Big business also 'relocated' jobs in the service sector to Asia and Eastern Europe, with 50,000 call centre jobs going in the previous two-year period and an estimated two million banking and insurance jobs destined to follow. The "sucking sounds of jobs disappearing" in Britain had even alarmed the CBI and produced panic in the government.

Workers in the countries where these jobs were going received one tenth of the wages of the workers they had replaced. Even if capitalism was capable in the medium and long term of plugging the 'gaps' left by the outsourcing of hundreds of thousands of jobs abroad, the net result was that British workers, particularly the low paid, would have fewer job opportunities and in general a lowering of wages and conditions. Today a certain 're-shoring' is taking place with an estimated 100,000-200,000 predicted to be relocated from abroad to Britain in the next ten years. In the US tens of thousands of manufacturing jobs were re-shored in 2014 alone. This has arisen not because of some 'benevolence' of 'good' capitalists, but entirely for reasons of greater profit. The wages in some neo-colonial areas – China for instance – had risen and the capitalists were relocating not just to Britain but also to cheaper areas for them, such as South-East Asia and within China to even poorer areas.

For the capitalists, as always, it is a question of 'follow the money'; their loot is invested wherever they can make a bigger profit, while the social consequences are secondary or non-existent. We said in 2004: "Like the US, the British workforce is in danger of becoming 'hamburger flippers' on the basis of diseased capitalism. High-paid, high technology employment is to be replaced by low-paid, sweated labour. " This is the reality in Britain and many other countries today. We also pointed out that "in desperation, the British capitalists, led by Blair and Brown, of course, have a half-formed idea that the continued prominence of the City of London in finance can now be linked to the expansion of the education and health sectors." We predicted that tuition fees would be driven up to establish an elite system similar to the US 'Ivy League'.

This process provoked ferocious opposition not just from the working class, but from increasing numbers of the middle classes. Reflecting this, over 100 Labour MPs threatened to vote against the government on Blair's top-up fee proposals. It was clear to us that the social democratic dream of a 'ladder of opportunity' provided by education had been snatched away. The working class, particularly the youth, was being given a harsh lesson in the realities of capitalism as well as the class character of New Labour, as with the Tories before. We also anticipated that "it is destined to become worse under the baton of Brown".

The key to the situation, then as now, lay in the labour movement and its ability to mobilise against these policies and the dead-end prospectus of the right-wing trade union and Labour leaders. The election of the left-wing 'awkward squad' represented a step forward for the movement compared to the right-wing leaders who preceded them. However, "The industrial and political limitations of many of this 'awkward squad' have been recently highlighted." They were hesitant about leading workers into action partly because of "an almost fatalistic attitude" that privatisation cannot be defeated. We asserted that it could be defeated by a mobilised working class.

The lack of confidence they displayed on industrial issues was mirrored on the political terrain. Some still clung to the false notion that Labour could be 'reclaimed'. Yet 63% of the delegates at the Labour Party conference did not even want to discuss the Gulf War! George Galloway had been expelled, despite the opposition of Tony Woodley, Tony Benn and even Michael Foot! Bob Crow supported the disaffiliation of the rail workers from the Labour Party in Scotland and their affiliation to the Scottish Socialist Party, which we recognised was a big step forward. But at the same time, we stressed that the RMT "still remains affiliated" to the Labour Party elsewhere. We commented: "Why? New Labour is no different in England and Wales than in Scotland."

It was to the great merit of Bob Crow and the RMT that, later, they were one of the very few unions who moved decisively in the direction of creating the basis for a new party, in Bob's case by helping to form the Trade Unionist and Socialist Coalition (TUSC). We forecast: "British society is at a crossroads. If Blair is replaced by Brown this could foster illusions that Labour is in the process of being 'reclaimed' by the social-democratic 'sleepers', who will allegedly come out into the open. In reality, however, the character of the Labour Party will not be changed by this. Nor will illusions in Brown last for any length of time."[2] This is what happened when Gordon Brown took over the helm of government from Blair in 2007.

Yet even in 2004, Tony Blair's position was extremely shaky. This was revealed over the issue of top-up fees in January of that year. Blair himself admitted subsequently that the closest he came to being removed from office, in a re-run of what happened to his heroine Thatcher, arose not over the Iraq war, where clearly he was in a small minority amongst the British people, but over top-up fees. Our headline in The Socialist read: "Top-up fees and Blair's future in the balance". As the vote approached in the House of Commons, one anonymous Labour MP told the Daily Telegraph: "Even if Tony Blair offers £20,000 a year and free flights to the Bahamas to every poor student, I'll still vote against him. We've got to get the bastard out." In polls, 60% were firmly opposed to top-up fees, including 51% of Labour voters. 85% believed that the proposal would lead to fewer people going to university. Also two thirds of people thought that Blair should resign if the Hutton report showed that he had lied over the leaking of Doctor Kelly's name. Nearly 50% believed that he did lie!

Blair narrowly survived the vote on top-up fees. He saw a massive majority of 161 evaporate to just five, over what he himself called this "flagship" policy. At the eleventh hour, some spineless New Labour MPs bottled it – bullied and bribed into submission by Blair, Brown and their 'muscle', Education Secretary Charles Clarke. Blair had faced significant rebellions over Iraq, foundation hospitals and now, most damagingly, over top-up fees. At least 200 New Labour MPs voted against the government at some point during that Parliament. Gwyneth Dunwoody, a leading light in the witch-hunt against Militant in the 1980s, boasted to her Constituency Labour Party that she had rebelled against Blair's government 27 times!

Blair was so worried about losing the whole policy he even had to rely on Gordon Brown to try and bail him out. But this served to further undermine the myth that Brown in some way was 'secretly' different from Blair. This was the man who was pushing PFI in public services, supported the war in Iraq and was on record as admiring the US economic system at the same time as being "whole heartedly" in support of top-up fees. We posed the question: "What more evidence do trade union leaders and others who back him as a 'left' alternative to Blair need to prove that Brown is fundamentally no different to Blair in his support for big business and attacks on working people?"

This was underlined not just by his vote in the House of Commons but also by the revelation of a 'think in' he had hosted with top business people, including the world's richest man, 'Sir' Bill Gates of Microsoft. These fat cats told Brown he must stop taking money out of their pockets – and Brown listened attentively to them. Another participant, Jean-Paul Garnier of drugs giant GlaxoSmithKline, had been paid £22 million in a pay and perks package the previous year.

Despite this, there were attempts to build up the reputation of Brown, in anticipation that Blair would be forced to resign in the foreseeable future. Some, including a number of left-wing trade union leaders, believed that this would result in a progressive, 'Old Labour' government and a chance to reclaim the Labour Party for the left. A new book was also published by the noted Keynesian economist William Keegan – The Prudence of Mr Gordon Brown – who wrote then and still writes today a weekly column for the Observer newspaper.

In order to counter this quite widespread view, at least in academic circles and a petty bourgeois layer within the Labour Party, we produced an analysis of its contents. Keegan attempted to show that Brown had not sold out but that his economic 'prudence' was part of a 'longer' plan. We wrote that ultimately, Keegan hoped, "Brown's radical reforming zeal, in the best traditions of 'Old Labour' if not socialism, will be revealed." In reality, Keegan showed Brown and his youthful (at the time) 'guru' Ed Balls to be deeply conservative, having accepted the agenda of Labour's traditional enemies, the capitalists and the Tories. Indeed, we wrote that "this book should be obligatory reading" for all those who entertained the hope that Brown would be different to Blair and the Labour Party could be 'reclaimed'.

Keegan hinted at his own traditional right-wing social democratic views while attacking the 'extreme left', the supporters of Tony Benn in the 1980s. Predictably, he attacked "the so-called Militant Tendency extreme left group, whose antics were especially prominent in Liverpool". He repeated the myth that "in the long run, Labour gained from the tough stand taken against the anti-democratic and potentially revolutionary Militant Tendency." Like most bourgeois writers, the word "anti-democratic" is never substantiated. As we have pointed out, the biggest electoral victories for Labour in the history of Liverpool occurred during the time the City Council was under the leadership of this 'anti-democratic' group. In the 1980s, Keegan accidentally met some of the Militant leaders – including myself – at the BBC, where we were all appearing on the Radio 4 'Today' programme. He subsequently wrote in his Observer column that the Labour leaders should not be concerned about Militant because their leaders were "old". Most of us were considerably younger than Keegan at the time!

Keegan comments about the role of the trade union leaders in propping up Blair and Brown: "Gordon Brown and his colleagues were lucky that there was then also a 'moderniser' at the TUC in the shape of John Monks, at the time Assistant General Secretary." Monks told Blair, then shadow secretary for employment, "that the TUC would not insist on the return of the closed shop, against which Mrs Thatcher had legislated". Keegan also quotes the words of Balls prior to New Labour coming to power: "In order to do what a Labour government should do, you've got to earn credibility first." Not with the working class, but with the bosses!

Balls himself had studied under the "guidance of Lawrence (Larry) Summers, who left Harvard to become a deputy secretary to the US Treasury in the Clinton administration." One British Treasury official joked later: "Gordon Brown and Ed Balls are eclectic. They imported ideas to try out here which North American economists could not get through Congress." They had adapted to the market and big business so completely that when Balls, probably in an unguarded moment, dared to suggest that a Labour government could still responsibly raise the top rate of tax to 50%, Blair replied, "Wash your mouth out."

As bad as this was, the pre-election stance of New Labour was, if anything, mild compared to its actual practice when it came to power. The 'landslide' of New Labour in 1997 was achieved with a share of the vote slightly smaller than what Harold Wilson received when Labour won a four-seat majority in 1964! Nevertheless, such was the revulsion at and rejection of Thatcherism in Britain at that stage, New Labour's massive parliamentary majority would have allowed it, if it so wished, to carry through radical measures. Keegan correctly points out in relation to the public sector: "Britain was and is a brutal example of what JK Galbraith described as 'private affluence and public squalor.'" Within days of the election victory, the Bank of England was effectively denationalised. Yet a well-known columnist, not at all a socialist, James Meade, said "We nationalised the Bank of England in 1946 to prevent another 1931."

In this book Keegan cannot disguise his disappointment with

the performance of New Labour, even by his own social democratic yardstick: "There was precious little sign of any narrowing of the gap between rich and poor – a gap that had always been the traditional focus of Labour governments... this continued to widen". He further writes: "When Brown's ally, Harriet Harman, introduced cuts in the benefits of lone parents, a former Conservative cabinet minister observed to me at the time: 'On security, welfare-to-work, they are daring what we dared not do'. The same was true of the so-called Private Finance Initiative (PFI) and the Public-Private Partnerships (PPP) championed by Balls and Geoffrey Robinson, which Brown accepted." He also quotes Tony Blair when faced with meltdown on the railways: "You can do anything you like as long as you don't call it renationalisation."

Yet despite the long catalogue of retreats, abandonment of previous positions, ingrained conservatism towards even minimal reforms, Keegan still held out the prospect that the "cautious approach" to fiscal and monetary policy by Brown and Balls, "prudent" in the short-term, was all designed for a long-term "purpose". We commented: "Yet, the author clearly understands the parlous industrial and economic situation facing British capitalism, contributed to in no small measure by the New Labour government. New Labour has now been in power for seven years! Truly the mountain has laboured and produced a very small mouse."[3]

In fact, the outcome of their policies was much worse than this. They paved the way for the Cameron-Clegg coalition government and then the Cameron-led Tory one with its vicious and cruel attacks on the poor and the working class. However Keegan could not help hoping against hope for improvements in the future. He concedes that the government Blair and Brown presided over was "a Labour government elected with an enormous majority [but] was pusillanimous in its approach."[4] Yet despite this he hoped, perhaps, that Brown would display his 'real' radical, if not socialist, soul in a third Labour government.

But those hopes, as we know, were completely dashed. This arose because the Brown government, as with the Blair government, was bourgeois to its marrow, remained within the framework of capitalism, did the bidding of big business and continued to disappoint, alienate and infuriate working-class people. It was quite clear from everything that had gone before that New Labour, 15 years after Thatcher had been overthrown and driven from office, was proposing measures more Thatcherite than anything the Iron Lady herself had implemented. Even the Liberal Democrats, who previously portrayed themselves slightly to the left of New Labour, pledged to privatise anything they could still find in public hands, including the Royal Mint and a wholesale sell-off of the prison service. Tories on the other hand were in reality proposing virtually the complete privatisation of what remained of the public sector, in particular education and health. We warned that with an election looming, and "Looking at the nightmare prospect of a new Tory government, many working-class people will feel they have no choice but to go out and vote for New Labour... It is this fear of the long, dark night of a new Tory government... Despite deep-seated disillusionment with New Labour, they are most likely to win a third term."[5]

However, the question was posed in this period: would New Labour go into the election with Blair or would he be unseated before then? There was much speculation as to whether he would become a casualty of the war in Iraq: "It's like an elephant in Tony's sitting room," said one cabinet minister, "It doesn't matter which way he looks it's always there."[6] The Daily Mirror went further, calling Iraq "An ice splinter in the Prime Minister's heart."[7] The press and media generally were full of reports and rumour of intrigue about if and when Blair would go. The bookies, often a good barometer of which way the wind is blowing, shortened the odds on him being Prime Minister at the next election. A YouGov poll showed that 46% of people thought he should go before then. But the Tories coming back to power would be a disaster. The Liberal Democrats opportunistically made a play for the anti-war vote but they had supported the troops when they went into Iraq and never called for them to come out.[8]

The mass disillusionment with the government was reflected in the June 'Super Thursday' elections, which combined the local elections with the European elections. They were a disaster for Tony Blair. Once more, there were threats, particularly from the left unions, to withhold or withdraw funds from New Labour. The Tories picked up an extra 283 council seats. But their 38% share of the vote in the local elections was no greater than under William Hague's leadership, five years before and 13 months before their 2001 general election debacle. In other words, there was no real comeback for the Tories, even from their 'traditional' base. Another significant development, which was to become subsequently a semi-permanent fixture of politics in Britain, was the UKIP vote, 16% (2.6 million votes). Ken Livingstone, in London, who had been readmitted to the Labour Party in January, was re-elected as mayor, but with a smaller share of the vote than his first victory standing as an independent against Labour in 2000.

The election showed that while the Tories were not seen as a credible alternative there had been a massive shift away from New Labour. The overall effect of the election, therefore, was to fuel even greater speculation as to who would inherit Blair's crown if he departed the scene. We commented: "Political commentators... are like the Kremlinologists of old, who tried to discern who were the winners and losers in power struggles in Stalinist Russia by observing who was next to the 'leader' on the plinth in Red Square during parades." The super-Blairite Alan Milburn was seen as having 'won out' over Brown and the 'Brownies'.

We concluded that this was of little consequence to working class people as "both wings of the leadership of this capitalist party want to take the axe to what remains of the public sector, to brutally slash the numbers receiving disability benefits (2.7 million at present) and to support the bosses in worsening hours, undermining conditions and cutting back on wages." Only the mood music was different from the two camps. Blair and Milburn wanted to use a New Labour victory at the next general election to carry out "'substantial reforms' (read savage attacks) on welfare spending."

Brown was a little nervous of working-class people's reaction if a frontal offensive was launched. He supported Blair's programme but on an instalment plan! One Labour MP, Andrew Smith, resigned as Secretary of State for Work and Pensions, partly because he was one of the few Labour MPs who still lived on a council estate (in Oxford). Some of his neighbours were, he said, "Chronically sick and disabled," which would have been very uncomfortable for him when the proposed measures went through. We can see from this that all the draconian plans enacted by the 'ConDem' coalition government between 2010 and 2015 were flagged up by the rotten Blair-Brown government.

The objective basis which necessitated cuts for capitalism was ultimately the dire situation of the British economy, which today is in a lot worse state under the Tory government. We postulated: "British and world capitalism could face an economic storm comparable to Hurricane Ivan that recently wreaked havoc in the Caribbean." While house prices were escalating rapidly, household debt exceeded £1 trillion. Some capitalist commentators believed in an indefinite 'golden' future for British capitalism. They were in denial, as they were in the late 1980s when an economist wrote: "There are good reasons for arguing that this historic norm (the widening of the ratio of house prices to income) may no longer be applicable in today's economy." That was in early 1989, a few months before the biggest property crash in 40 years.

These were heat lightning flashes of the coming storm, totally unexpected by the economic 'experts' of the system, which crashed over them in 2007-08. We linked this gathering economic storm to the desperate situation which would face the government elected after the next election: "Whoever is elected as the next government intends, as... Brown made clear, to further cut public sector expenditure... Brown's plan to reduce public-sector jobs by 100,000 is the biggest attack on a single workforce since the Tories' assault on the miners."[9] This also anticipated the role that was taken by the Coalition government later.

58. Balance sheet of trade unions 2004-05

In the latter stages of the New Labour government of 2001 to 2005, the trade unions occupied a central place in developments and particularly for the activity of the Socialist Party. In the NUT, Unison, PCS and a number of other unions we had a presence and in some of them quite a decisive one. The election of a new generation of 'awkward squad' union leaders raised expectations amongst workers that the unions could once again start to effectively represent their members.

This was partly reflected in the rise in strike statistics, although they were contradictory. Until 2003 there had been a relatively upward curve of industrial action. In 2002, 1.3 million days were lost to strikes. But in 2003 this dropped to just under half a million and the number of workers taking action also declined. However, in the first three months of 2004 –before the civil service strikes developed – 172,000 working days were lost in strikes as 135,000 workers were involved in 40 stoppages.

Simultaneously at the top level of the trade unions, an intense debate was raging about their future. An oppositional movement to the government's plans was evident amongst trade unions. There was intense discussion throughout the union movement, particularly amongst the leading rank-and-file layer who were concerned about stagnation in union membership and the strategy and tactics for taking on the employers and even the government itself. Their leaders were conscious of the fact that if they did not deliver some-thing against flint-faced managers, then they would suffer the same fate as their right-wing predecessors. This had already happened to Mick Rix of ASLEF, who had been voted out and replaced with a right-wing maverick, Shaun Brady. It was claimed that New Labour and the rail companies funded Brady's campaign. Brady and other ASLEF officers were later removed following a fight at a barbecue in the union's headquarters!

A new summer of discontent began to take shape. Prison offic-ers took strike action as well as nursery nurses in Scotland. Even the TUC had been forced, under pressure, to organise its first national demo for decades, on 19 June, on the issue of pensions. In this situation, the Socialist Party was undergoing quite rapid growth within the unions, both in numbers and in our specific weight. This was reflected in Socialist Party members challenging for national positions within the unions. We have always fought for positions, both at local level and nationally, including the national executives of unions. We have pursued a united front policy, through demo-cratic broad lefts, which saw us sometimes supporting others for national positions who had better chances to win, even when they were not always in complete agreement with us. As our influence grew, however, and the calibre of our comrades stood out as the best standard-bearers of the left in general, they were nominated by the rank and file for leadership positions. This was always done in such a way as to avoid splitting the left vote as far as possible.

However, history does not stand still, either with individuals or events. The history of the labour movement provides numerous examples of figures elected on a left ticket who eventually moved to the right under pressure. The danger of this happening was enhanced if candidates were just individual lefts and not subject to the discipline of the rank and file through democratic broad lefts. 'Democratic' is the operative word in this respect because many so-called 'broad lefts' were really undemocratic caucuses, not repre-sentative of the rank-and-file advanced workers. They were, moreo-ver, selective in whom they invited and whom they did not, to participate in their deliberations.

For instance, this was true in some of the unions that coalesced into the present Unite. But these practices were also prevalent in a number of other 'broad lefts' in other unions. Some of them – such as the United Left in Unite – are now more open and therefore tend to be more democratic than in the past. There are no fixed organisational forms, as far as Marxists are concerned, for organising the struggle of the working class. Regimes and parties can atrophy and decline under the pressure of unfavourable objective developments, sometimes becoming the opposite of what they were when they were founded. This is what happened with the physical liquidation of the Bolshevik party, including murders by Stalin and Stalinism. The same could be said about the destruction of the Labour Party as a workers' party at bottom through Blair's 'New' Labour.

On a much smaller scale, even ad hoc organisations that are thrown up, such as broad lefts, can turn into the opposite, particularly when they smell success or actually are successful in gaining a majority and becoming the leadership of the union. Therefore the Socialist Party has pursued flexible tactics, which involve striving to arrive at agreement within the broad lefts. But when the situation required – if a candidate of the 'broad left' was so 'broad' as to not really stand on the left any more – our comrades have not hesitated to stand and offer a militant challenge in order to give the ranks of the unions a real choice.

Such a situation arose in the NUT in 2004. Up to this time, we had striven to work constructively within the Socialist Teachers Alliance (STA) but the refusal to consistently challenge the leadership effectively led to the decision of Martin Powell Davies to stand for union general secretary following the resignation of right-winger Doug McAvoy. This evoked charges from some that by standing Martin would split the left vote and allow the right-wing standard bearer, Steve Sinnott, to win. Yet the 'left' candidate had previously been defeated in the national officer's election, indicating that there was no guarantee of success in the upcoming election. He had effectively imposed himself as a candidate on the rest of the left having failed to be selected at a meeting in Nottingham the previous year. Many teachers expressed doubts about his programme and how accountable he would be if elected! In his election address he claimed that he was "not controlled by any party or faction", code for "not accountable to the left as a whole". [1]

Martin Powell Davies presented a very clear programme: "For a general secretary in touch with teachers; defend members against management bullying; for NUT action to oppose excessive workload and enforce a real 'work-life balance'; for teacher unity in action – a campaign to persuade all unions to withdraw from the 'workforce agreement'... no to the private profiteers." He wasn't hesitant to comment on wider issues which thousands of teachers were also concerned about: "Like thousands of teachers, I was opposed to a war for oil in Iraq which has wasted thousands of lives and billions of pounds that could have been spent on schools and other public services. Yet the current NUT leaders refused to even allow the national union banner on the demonstrations. I would make sure that the NUT took a full part in the wider campaigns of the trade union movement while seeking trade unionists' support for our campaigns."

During the election campaign he emphasised: "For too many years, successive governments have piled the pressure on teachers... The NUT leadership – including John Bangs and Steve Sinnott – have to share much of the responsibility for failing to stand up to the relentless attacks on teachers and education."[2] Martin received over 6,000 votes. This did not stop the Socialist Workers Party from arguing that by standing, Martin had split the left vote and allowed Sinnott to win. Close scrutiny of the voting figures refuted these arguments – the vote for the left candidates was not enough to overhaul the votes of Steve Sinnott and John Bangs in second place. Moreover, because the STA refused to nominate a left candidate, some teachers voted for right-wing candidates like John Bangs.

Martin's campaign allowed a sharpening of the left's programme as well as pushing the election debate to the left. The behaviour of the STA – which in 2007-08 shipwrecked the campaign of Socialist Party member Linda Taaffe for re-election to the NUT's National

Executive Committee (NEC) – showed that it was not acting as a fighting organisation to mobilise the left, preferring manoeuvres and intrigues rather than principled political struggle. Moreover, the SWP were supporting them after spending more than a decade vilifying the 'soft left' in the union.

A similar situation arose in 2005 in Unison when Roger Bannister challenged Dave Prentis again for the general secretaryship of Unison. He had also demonstrated at local level how a fighting union branch could achieve results for its membership. The Socialist reported in April 2004: "Over 1,200 local authority employees of Merseyside's Knowsley council are moving this month from a 37 to a 36-hour week, with no loss of pay, in the first of a two-part move which will result in a 35-hour week across the council workforce." Roger, as branch secretary in Knowsley and a member of Unison's NEC, provided the leadership which gained this big advance. It meant that, in the main, workers would reduce their hours for no loss of pay. This was a major improvement on the national 'Single Status Agreement' in which working hours remained at 37. Knowsley Unison negotiated with the council – one of New Labour's 'one-party states' in the North – for over two years. When victory was achieved, "The mood of the pickets was high, organising line dancing in the main street of Kirkby."[3]

Roger also moved the resolution at the 2003 Unison Local Government Conference to ballot for industrial action to defend pensions. Moreover, he was the only candidate who was opposed to the union's ties to the Labour Party and pledged that if he was elected, he would ballot members to allow them to have their say on continued affiliation to Labour. The outcome of the election resulted in Dave Prentis winning, as expected, but Roger polled 41,000 votes – 16.9% of those who voted.

Significantly the other left candidate, Jon Rogers, received less than half of Roger Bannister's votes at just over 7%. Roger had been informed before the election that Jon Rogers represented the 'organised united left forces' in the union. This boast was completely undermined by the outcome. In reality, Jon Rogers's support base represented in practice no more than the forces of the SWP and relatively few independent individual lefts. What clinched support for Roger Bannister was his explanation of the role of the Labour Party and how the union's leadership was too close to the Labour government. His call for a complete break with Labour went down a storm amongst council workers in particular. In reality, for the majority of the more than 1.4 million people entitled to vote in this election, the first they knew that there was a general secretary contest was when the ballot envelope dropped onto their doormats. After the poor showing of its candidate, the SWP referred in its weekly paper to "left-wing challengers for the leadership, Jon Rogers and Roger Bannister who gained 8% and 17% respectively" – giving no indication that it had promoted and backed Jon Rogers![4]

RMT rail union members working at London Underground stations also won a 35-hour week. However, concessions wrested from brutal capitalist managements are temporary so long as capitalism continues to exist. Even with this deal some strings were accepted by the RMT. There was reluctant acceptance that 200 ticket offices would close. This was the same issue that provoked the bitter London Underground strikes later in 2014 and 2015.

The PCS civil service trade union also became involved in a protracted struggle over an 18-month period, including six days of national action, unofficial action, non-cooperation with performance development systems, suspensions, work to rule and an overtime ban. Following this, PCS activists and members in the Department for Work and Pensions (DWP) were entitled to feel a sense of achievement over the pay offer that they received, which was recommended for acceptance by the Group Executive Committee (GEC). The PCS, through this action, had broken big obstacles which management placed in the way of a reasonable deal. The agreements also broke the Treasury pay limit of 3.5% for 2004 settlements, a real achievement in not very favourable circumstances. This was recognition of the strength of the union's campaign. The deal, planned to last for three years, in overall terms was worth 4.6% in the first year and 4.1% in the following years.

This was a solid testament to the determination of members to stand up to arrogant and ambitious management. Moreover it vindicated the strategy of a fighting left leadership at both group and national level. They were prepared to lead the members in standing up to the most anti-union management in the civil service. It is important to mention the future achievements of the PCS in the teeth of the coalition and Tory governments from 2010 that slashed wages, resulting in an average drop of £1,600 per year for every worker in Britain. It was clearly recognised that while 15% in total over three years was a step forward, particularly for those on the minimum wage it did not go far enough. Nevertheless general secretary Mark Serwotka endorsed the actions of the DWP group executive, which he said reflected the PCS "at its best".

This is in stark contrast to what was happening in unions dominated by the right wing. These leaders had allowed New Labour to attack their members' interests with impunity. This led to the election of new leaders in some unions, which was a direct response to the inertia of the previous right-wing incumbents. The militancy of the PCS, in contrast, was revealed clearly at its 2004 conference. This was the first year in which the union was led by Left Unity and the conference backed the executive on all the key issues confronting the civil service and PCS members. However, Mark Serwotka still warned: "If the government says there will be 20,000 jobs cut in this or that department regardless, we will vigorously protect those services and jobs... including the very last resort of industrial action. It was a disgraceful sight seeing a Labour Chancellor, cheered on by ministers, announcing 40,000 job cuts. Real people with real lives doing real jobs."[5]

At the PCS conference itself the discredited 'Moderate Group' had nothing to say apart from announcing on the last day the formation of a 'new group', comprising two right-wing factions on the NEC. But it didn't even have a name, which went together with no policies and reflected the discrediting of the right within the union. The Socialist Party, on the other hand, demonstrated its growing support at the conference with a very well attended lunchtime fringe meeting, at which I spoke, with eight party members then on the executive (one additional NEC member was recruited at the conference).

A magnificent strike by Scotland's nursery nurses lasted for 14 weeks, the longest since the miners' strike, culminating in them winning important concessions. A parent support group was set up, which was then widened to include other trade unions. Five weeks into the all-out strike, the Convention of Scottish Local Authorities (Cosla) was forced into talks. This was significant as all along it had said it was up to local councils to reach negotiated deals. Shamefully on 20 April Unison effectively abandoned its strategy for a national agreement without consultation with the vast majority of strikers, who were outraged. Nevertheless, the strikers forced the local employers into conceding deals they would not have given without an all-out strike.

The role of New Labour angered strikers and completely changed the outlook of many involved in the strike. One nursery nurse commented: "I voted Labour all my life. I really did believe that they were the working people's party... I thought that socialists were a group of people who were a little mad fighting for things they had no chance of winning... I now know they are not mad but are fighting for the rights of ordinary people." She continued: "The 'big men' in Unison who... left us with no option but to accept the local deal should be held accountable for their actions! I've volunteered to become a shop steward now along with a number of colleagues who were not active in the union before the strike. Some of the 'big men' at the top had better watch out. I hope nursery nurses can stay strong and united and build a union that respects and listens to its members."[6]

"Strike against jobs carnage". This headline[7] summed up the mood, particularly amongst PCS members. Mark Serwotka described the government proposals precisely as "carnage" for public sector workers as a whole. Gordon Brown had announced 140,000 job losses in the civil service. New Labour ministers were now insultingly referring to ordinary civil servants as 'bureaucrats'. Brown received his answer with thousands of civil servants striking in the DWP at the end of July over this issue linked to privatisation. The ideologues of New Labour wanted to reduce the public sector to little more than a core workforce, which would oversee the £120 billion a year spent by the government to provide services to its citizens. Clearly Labour, in its higher echelons at least, wanted to smash public sector workers like Thatcher did with the miners. There was a plan by them to obviously and quite consciously seek to isolate the most left-wing unions, like the PCS and the Fire Brigades Union (FBU). One councillor even told the Financial Times: "A lot of councillors and the government want to smash the FBU. Why don't they want to be honest about it?"[8]

We emphasised that this could only be met by action. A public sector workers' united front was necessary, around the demand for a 24-hour public sector strike. This came to a head at the TUC conference with Tony Blair attempting to persuade delegates that he had not lost touch with the concerns of "hard-working families". Glenn Kelly, the branch secretary of Bromley Unison and a member of the Socialist Party, commented: "In his speech, Blair said it was time to come home, recognising he'd been on a seven-year holiday from dealing with the difficulties facing working people in Britain. He at last recognised that there were people who were sick and disabled who needed help and are struggling. But behind that we know his government is planning cuts in incapacity benefit... This is a government that has sat back while poverty has destroyed the lives of millions."[9]

Hundreds packed into a fringe meeting organised by the PCS and including 12 union general secretaries. Even TUC general secretary Brendan Barber appeared but only in his capacity as a giant brake on the many workers wanting to take action. He supported the PCS but said they "should not act without the other civil service unions". Mark Serwotka, in an interview with The Socialist, expressed his delight "with the unanimous passing of the composite resolution". He also declared: "I need to make clear that the

PCS isn't affiliated to the Labour Party. But, on a personal level I've been on record for a long time that there needs to be an alternative to Labour because an industrial response alone is not enough... My message to people who are working on an alternative, whether it's people in the Socialist Party or people in Respect is that we need to work together. We need to ensure that there is a legitimate alternative voice."[10]

Mark was correct and is even more correct today when the objective position facing working people is much worse than in 2004. Principled left unity is essential in maximising the potential within the unions and on a political plane. But it involves a willing- ness to collaborate in pushing the interests of the left to the fore without being obliged to dismantle the different left organisations. The Socialist Party has always argued for unity and, moreover, has demonstrated it in action within the PCS with the formation of Left Unity, for which the Socialist Party was mainly responsible and which also led to Mark's victory against the right within the union.

This has not been the case historically with the SWP as we have seen already. This was now manifested in Unison, where Socialist Party members were compelled to withdraw from the Unison United Left (UUL), which gathered independent lefts with members of the Socialist Party and the SWP. The main reason for this was that under the political influence of its largest component, the SWP, the United Left was drifting towards the right. This was at a time when attacks by the New Labour government on the working class in general and on public sector workers in particular was leading to increased militancy and radicalisation amongst the grassroots.

The right-wing evolution of the UUL was expressed over the dif- ferences on the political fund and the Labour Party. In the forth- coming year, Unison members would be voting on the continuation or not of the political fund. This was against the background of the decision of the RMT to support non-Labour candidates and parties, leading to the union's expulsion from the Labour Party. At the same time, a similar debate was taking place in unions like the FBU. This was, we argued, clearly an issue of fundamental importance for the working class. The UUL, under SWP influence, was arguing for continued support for affiliation.

This meant that £3 million of union members' money had been handed over to the Labour Party in the previous year. Moreover, there had been no attempt to seriously implement the United Left's position of opening up the funds to allow support for other candidates, as well as New Labour. Socialist Party members had advanced the idea of a 'third fund', a tactical way of progressing the debate within the union. This was opposed by the SWP and therefore by the United Left, which placed it outside the debate at Unison conferences.

Given the conference decision to support the status quo, the Socialist Party was now calling for a second, parallel vote to be conducted along with the statutory political fund ballot to give ordinary members the opportunity to express their views on how the political fund should be spent. This too was opposed by the SWP, who seemed more concerned not to alienate the handful of Labour 'lefts' in the UUL. These 'lefts' had advocated a somewhat disingenuous strategy for the political fund ballot, arguing in the Greater London region that the Labour Party link should be played down for fear of losing the vote!

Moreover, Socialist Party members were concerned about the increased sectarian manoeuvrings against them within the UUL by the SWP, which was clearly a rerun of what happened in the Socialist Alliance, resulting in the splitting and later inevitable dissolution of that organisation. They voted for the removal of Socialist Party member Glenn Kelly from the UUL slate for the Regional Committee, despite his obvious support amongst lefts in the region. Other action was taken against members of the Socialist Party with the obvious intention of neutering our comrades within the union as an effective force. We took the decision to leave the UUL but with the hope that a change of approach on behalf of the SWP and other lefts would make it possible to reunite in a democratic and open broad left within Unison capable of winning support from the members.

Meanwhile, the new 'Agenda for Change' (AfC) was proposed in the NHS, which supposedly tackled issues like job progression. The Unison leadership declared this was a great "step forward" and "historic" but Socialist Party members and many on the left disagreed. "Members are being conned," the Socialist declared. Under this scheme, the lowest paid would still be on £5.69 an hour. This deal arose because the union leadership was desperate not to upset the Labour government in the run-up to the general election. This in turn was due to the link with the Labour Party. We called for rejection of the scheme.[11]

The central issue confronting the unions at this stage and later was the attack on pension rights. Millions of public sector workers were faced with huge cuts to their pensions – some from as early as April 2005. This led to the unions threatening strike action because thousands of pounds would be robbed on an annual basis from many of the lowest-paid local government workers, many of whom were facing retirement in just a few years' time. Entrants into teaching in 2006 would face 'career average' salaries as the basis of their pensions. Linked to this was the likely ending of the allowance to retire at 64. This was extended further by the ConDem government later. Finally, the government wanted to take more from workers by compulsory increasing their level of contributions. This while employer contributions decreased, effectively carrying through a pay cut.

Trade unions like the GMB, Amicus and the TGWU were already facing massive pension crises amongst members in the private sector. Similar pressure was now exerted on those in the public sector, with Kevin Curran, GMB general secretary, admitting that he faced an outcry from his members in the private sector who were phoning the national office in their thousands demanding action. A few unions, like the NUJ, NUT and FBU, already had conference decisions committing them to industrial action if their pension schemes were changed. The local government section of Unison had lodged a request to hold a ballot on industrial action over pensions. The government announced months previously that they were introducing legislation to cut council workers' pension rights.

French workers had been striking in their millions against the government's plans to cut back the welfare state, including pension rights. Strikes in Britain were planned for Wednesday, 23 March, the first time for years that the unions had come together in action. This was not thanks to the TUC leadership, who constantly blocked any moves to unite unions in defence of the public sector. This included trying to stop the PCS putting a motion on the TUC agenda. The call followed days of action during working time against the pensions' tax.

We pointed out that 200,000 civil servants went on strike in the previous November, for the first time in over 10 years. The government's clear intention was to completely undermine effective trade unionism in the public sector. Over 60% of the 6 million workers in the public sector remained in unions. The Socialist demanded: "All out to defend pensions." Roger Bannister reported: "Unison's national Industrial Action Committee has decided to conduct a strike ballot of local government members. The meeting, which I chaired, voted to ballot for strike action against the proposed changes in the local government superannuation scheme. This is a major step forward in the campaign to defend public sector pensions."[12]

A titanic struggle loomed with the prospect of millions of workers being on strike on 23 March, in protest at the government's plans to rob over £100 billion from the pension entitlements of workers. Linda Taaffe reported: "The goal of those of us on the left in the National Union of Teachers (NUT) fighting to save teachers' pensions was to get a national ballot of teachers to join in with a one-day public sector strike... After much hard campaigning, the NUT... is organising a consultative survey." It was ridiculous for the union's national officers to merely conduct a survey when there was a mood for action.[13]

Fortunately, this was not the last chance to take action because the pensions crisis was not going away. This was illustrated by the fact that the government was compelled to beat a retreat. The threat of coordinated strike action forced them into a major step back. Even the Financial Times commented: "The retreat is a huge climb-down." The prospect of a million workers coming out panicked Blair into instructing Alan Johnson, the DWP Secretary of State to sort out the problem. However, we warned that the government, any government, when faced with mass pressure could retreat, as the 'Iron Lady' Thatcher herself did in the face of threatened national strike action by the miners in 1981. She came back later to crush the miners in 1984-85.

Predictably, union leaders like Dave Prentis drew entirely the wrong conclusions. He claimed that the outcome "shows social partnership at its best." The bosses' organisation, the CBI, more realistically accused the government of "backing down in the face of political pressure" and argued that it was "sending the wrong signal". We drew the opposite conclusion: "Workers will draw confidence from this initial skirmish. The prospect of workers striking together has raised the sights of many in the workplace that the years of retreat – by the union leaders – can be reversed."[14]

59. Workers fight back
2004-05

The temper of the working class in Britain in 2004 was indicated by the series of strikes or threat of strikes in the previous year. The firefighters inflicted a partial defeat on the government's attempt to renege on the agreement which ended their dispute. Local government workers had been in action, embittered by what they were forced to accept in reduced wages and conditions. One indication of the situation developing in Europe and on a world scale, to some extent, at this stage was an opinion poll in East Germany where 51% opted for 'socialism' as a better system. Germany was suffering at this stage from a calamitous economic and social situation.

This was the atmosphere in which the Labour Party conference took place in September where violent jockeying for positions ensued. This had nothing to do with fighting for the interests of working people but was an opportunity to enhance the careerist credentials of different factions of the Labour leadership. So far to the right had New Labour travelled that even the witch-hunter Peter Kilfoyle, who viciously attacked Liverpool District Labour Party on behalf of Neil Kinnock, found himself part of the anti-Blair 'rabble'. He advised that "Labour members should gaze around the room at your next meeting. Consider yourself lucky if the branch or constituency still meets... The party seems on its last legs in many areas." Kevin Curran, general secretary of the GMB union, said: "Just imagine if a disaffected, disengaged trade union movement decided to identify independent candidates... to concentrate on 300 seats... The difference we could make in national politics would be enormous."[1] Yet to the intense frustration of thousands of GMB members and millions in the trade union movement as a whole neither Curran nor other leaders were prepared to take this step.

During this conference Blair announced that he intended to serve out a third term as prime minister. It became quite clear that the leaders of the 'big four' unions (TGWU, GMB, Unison and Amicus) had all been mollified by Blair and Brown's vague promises of more 'worker-friendly' policies to keep their members in check in the run-up to the election. An indication of this was the evaporation of the threatened revolt on the Iraq war by the unions at the conference. Blair himself had a 30-minute meeting with the Amicus delegation. A member of the Iraqi Federation of Trade Unions – a stooge organisation at this stage – met the Transport and General Workers Union delegation to warn them that if troops were "pulled out too soon, trade unionists in Iraq could die in a civil war". This individual also warned of the "'Balkanisation' of Iraq in urging British trade unions to allow the troops to stay".[2] Foreign policy is always a continuation of home policy.

New Labour was reactionary abroad and anti-democratic at home. The anti-terror bill scraped through the Commons by just 14 votes. This was a deeply draconian piece of legislation introduced under the guise of fighting terrorism. The same excuses were used about the 1974 legislation in the wake of the Birmingham pub bombings, which led to many innocent Irish people, including trade unionists, being harassed and imprisoned. Home Secretary Charles Clarke had been an opponent of Militant in the student field and, ineffectually, in the Labour Party Young Socialists as well. He was Neil Kinnock's right-hand man when Liverpool Labour Party was completely undemocratically purged of socialists and therefore was well fitted for his role of trampling on long-held democratic rights. Until New Labour came to power, 'Innocent until proven guilty' remained the letter of the law.

The bill that was proposed by Clarke was designed specifically to be used to lock up people without even producing any evidence against them, never mind proving them guilty. Even the Labour peer Helena Kennedy expressed opposition: "Sugar-coating the unpalatable by suggesting all will be well if a judge makes the order is to forget that it may not feel significantly different if it is Mr Justice Floggem or the Home Secretary who issues an order if you still don't know the nature of the allegation or the evidence on which it is based."[3] We called on all socialists to campaign for the repeal of this legislation and previous authoritarian legislation such as the Criminal Justice Act.

The idea of a new mass workers' party came back forcefully onto the agenda, following a special conference of the RMT. This gathering voted by 42 votes to 8 to reject Labour Party intimidation and reconfirmed its decision to support political organisations other than Labour. This included affiliation to the Scottish Socialist Party. Even before the debate had taken place, the Labour Party held a gun to the head of the union, saying that if the conference took a decision to confirm their position on disaffiliation in Scotland, it would face automatic expulsion.

At this conference the total disillusionment with New Labour was quite evident. Opening the debate, union general secretary Bob Crow said that the only part of New Labour's programme he agreed with were the bits that said 'The' and 'End'! Steve Hedley, a delegate from Area 20, argued that if Labour was a new party coming to the RMT for support on the basis of its current programme, "there would be no way the union would consider affiliating to the party". Craig Johnston, a Socialist Party member at the time, delegate from Area 5 and a conductor on Arriva Trains Northern, made a devastating case for the union breaking from Labour. He pointed out how this debate really started in 1997. He was then still a Labour Party member but soon realised it was no longer delivering for working-class people. Pete Skelly from Area 16 in South Wales said that the political fund issue had been debated in a well-attended special meeting. He said workers questioned why the RMT – like other unions – gave Labour a distinct advantage over other political parties when New Labour had shown such contempt for the unions.[4]

The issue was also raised and debated at Unison conference with Socialist Party members playing a leading role. A similar discussion took place at the FBU conference where Tony Maguire from the Northern Ireland Fire Brigade moved at its conference in Southport an historic proposal for the union to disaffiliate from the Labour Party. He declared: "Our choice is whether to stay in the Labour Party, docile and tame, or leave and fight like tigers for what these class traitors have denied us... The future starts here and the future starts now... You have the power – you can do it."[5] The composite motion proposing complete disaffiliation was passed by more than two to one.

The GMB and the TGWU announced they were withholding millions of pounds from Labour's general election fund. Derek Simpson, general secretary of Amicus, claimed at the TUC pensions demo in 2004 that trade unionists had a duty to fight to retain Labour at the next election. However, within a week he admitted in a Guardian article that he had been deluged with mail, questioning his judgement and saying how rotten Labour was. This then forced him to openly call for Blair's removal.

Unfortunately, the communications union CWU, its general secretary Billy Hayes and the union's broad left argued for staying in the Labour Party. An emergency resolution from the postal side of CWU warned that if Labour didn't make a manifesto commitment to retain Royal Mail as a public enterprise then the union should immediately disaffiliate. This was just used to screen the retreat of the leadership.

Tony Maguire of the FBU also stated at this time: "The FBU has not rejected the ideas of political trade unionism but we do believe we should be supporting a political party that represents the interests of unions, communities and young people not a party that has clearly been hijacked by big business." Furthermore and significantly, Kevin Curran of the GMB stated in the Guardian: "We now spend a lot of effort in trying to persuade our members not only that the Labour Party is worth fighting for but that we should not contemplate a relationship with any other political organisation."[6] These lines were written more than 10 years ago! They are an indication once more of how the right-wing trade union leaders have held back the political evolution of organised workers and, through them, the mass of the working class.

It compelled us at this stage to go once more over the early history of the Labour Party and to draw comparisons with the current situation. There were many similarities of both an economic and political character. We pointed out that the Liberals at the turn of the twentieth century, as the party of so-called laissez faire capitalism, were much like New Labour. Trade unionists and workers came up against Liberal employers, particularly in the industrial centres, in the struggles for a living wage and improving rights and conditions. This fuelled the opposition to the Liberal Party in the movements for the creation of an independent party of the trade unions and the working class.

The pioneers for this demand battled over two decades for the realisation of this goal. The struggle did not proceed in a straight line but was full of zigzags, steps forward and sometimes two steps back. Keir Hardie, the miners' leader from Scotland and the 'father of the Labour Party', was originally a Liberal who tried to 'reform' the party but concluded that it was impossible. He first of all established the Scottish Labour Party and in 1893 founded the Independent Labour Party when 120 delegates met in Bradford. The ILP incorporated a number of different trends, including the Fabians and representatives of Engels himself, the continuator of Marx's ideas in this period. Five delegates from the Social Democratic Federation (SDF) also attended; this organisation was nominally Marxist but neither Marx in his lifetime or Engels supported its politics and methods.

Some trade unionists also attended but Hardie and the ILP conducted a protracted battle to break the trade unions from the Liberal Party's coat-tails. He was elected by South Wales miners in Merthyr as an MP in 1900 after his defeat in his previous seat of

West Ham. However, the South Wales miners as a whole were not free from illusions in the Liberal Party, even when they set up their own political fund in 1899. Yet Hardie and others hammered away each year at the Trade Union Congress for 'independent Labour representation'. This was eventually successful at the conference to form the Labour Representation Committee (LRC) in 1900, attended by trade union delegates, the Cooperative Movement and socialists of various kinds. The miners' union, however, abstained due to their connections with local Liberal associations.

This lasted almost a decade. In fact, there was limited trade union membership of the LRC at the beginning with only 353,000 out of nearly 2,000,000 trade unionists in all affiliated to this body. The 'new unions' joined but the longer-established skilled workers' unions initially stayed aloof. The turning point was the Taff Vale judgement, which awarded heavy financial damages against the Amalgamated Society of Railway Servants for alleged loss of profits to the Taff Vale Railway Company during a strike.

By 1903 the affiliated membership of the LRC had risen to 873,000 but the LRC, known as the 'Labour Party' from 1906, was still a long way from constituting a party. It didn't even have a programme – only an affirmation of willingness "to co-operate with any party which, for the time being, may be engaged in promoting legislation in the direct interest of Labour'". Nor was there much organisation under the party's control. Although local Labour representation committees and Labour parties existed in a number of areas, they were not admitted to affiliation to the national party or represented at its conferences. One of the reasons for this was the trade union leadership fearing that "local LRCs would more easily pass on to socialist control". Only during the First World War did Arthur Henderson, who was originally a Liberal Party agent, as Labour Party treasurer reorganise the party. Formal recognition was granted to local Labour parties as an integral part of the party's constitution. We commented: "This step forward for independent political representation of the working class was not at all ideal, was not neat and tidy but reflected the reality of the situation at the time."

It would be a mistake to base the programme and structures of a new party on an identical 'repetition' of what happened over a century ago. However, the method of moving forward cautiously at the beginning with the creation of broad structures is something to learn from. We commented: "It is one of the reasons why the Socialist Party supports in the initial period a loose federation in which genuine forces can collaborate, by gradually building confidence between the constituent parts possibly leading later to a rounded-out party. Absolutely essential in this era is that it should be open and democratic, with the right of platforms." The Socialist Party, together with other forces such as in the RMT, have consistently argued, in the same way as the pioneers, that this could produce similar results in the development of a new mass party at a later stage.[7]

60. Split in the Scottish Socialist Party 2003-05

The split in the CWI in Scotland, dealt with earlier, meant that there were now two distinct political trends with their political antecedence in the CWI within the Scottish Socialist Party (SSP).The International Socialist Movement (ISM) in the majority within the party, was represented by Tommy Sheridan and Alan McCombes. The International Socialists, the minority, whose main spokesperson was Philip Stott, had remained within the CWI alongside pioneers like Ronnie Stevenson and others. The debate which had taken place within the CWI, and in which we clearly differentiated from the political trajectory of the majority of the SSP, now developed on a wider scale to a battle of ideas for a socialist programme in the party.

This was a crucial issue as elections to the Scottish Parliament loomed in 2003 in which the SSP was expected to make gains. However, its draft manifesto reflected the qualitative shift away from a socialist internationalist position, which Tommy Sheridan and others in the majority had supported in the past. Philip Stott, in the CWI's criticisms of the manifesto, quoted from an article from Tommy Sheridan in the SSP's journal Scottish Socialist Voice: "[The SSP] stands for an Independent Scotland and that the people of Scotland, with whom sovereignty would ultimately lie, can then determine for themselves whether it will go down the socialist road or not."

CWI delegates to the SSP conference drafted amendments, including on the wider issue of socialism and the national question, which challenged this position of the SSP's leadership. There was no reference in the manifesto to the need to link the struggle in Scotland to the workers in England, Wales, Ireland and internationally. As Philip Stott pointed out: "Instead, there was a tendency to see the achievement of independence for Scotland as a necessary first step before socialism could be built."

In a motion from one of the SSP branches supporting the leadership it was argued: "Independence will provide the Scottish people with the democratic machinery to support their struggle for socialism." It was pointed out by CWI members that it would not be possible for "an independent Scotland, on a capitalist basis, to stand up to a globalised economy and tackle poverty, low pay and inequality without breaking with capitalism and linking up with workers internationally". On this basis the CWI opposed this motion, but it was supported by the SSP leadership. The CWI argued and sought to persuade the SSP to include public ownership under democratic working class control of the economy as the only means of carrying through lasting reforms.

The SWP in Scotland were also part of the SSP at this stage but in a completely opportunist fashion supported the leadership on all these issues. Moreover, they also helped to defeat an amendment from the Glasgow Cathcart branch which put the position of the CWI: "We stand for an independent socialist Scotland that would seek to work with a socialist England, Wales and Ireland in a free and democratic socialist confederation or alliance... While standing for an independent socialist Scotland we advocate the maximum possible unity of the working class in Scotland with workers throughout the rest of Britain."

They also took an incorrect approach on international issues. The SSP executive did support a motion from the CWI that put forward the need for a socialist alternative to the war. The SWP moved an amendment during this debate which called on the SSP to "ensure our anti-war slogans and propaganda emphasise that the main enemy is at home and the violence of the oppressed is not equivalent to the violence of the oppressors." These were nevertheless methods and reactionary ideologies which socialists would definitely oppose.

Their amendment was heavily defeated. At the previous conference in 2001, the ssp's position, drafted by the swp, for a single secular Palestinian state to replace Israel was passed. This year, however, its position was defeated but the motion passed in its place was confused and wrong. It called for support for the Palestinian struggle and argued for a socialist state in the future on the land that was Palestine pre-1948. In the meantime, it supported a step in that direction by calling for a Palestinian state in the West Bank and Gaza. This motion came from the ism grouping of ex-members of the cwi.

One leading member of this group was the ssp's international officer, Frances Curran, who argued that it was not our job to put forward solutions to the Middle East conflict from Scotland but to offer support to the Palestinians' struggle. cwi member Jim McFarlane answered her by pointing out that a socialist Israel and a socialist Palestine as part of the socialist solution to the Middle East crisis was the way forward. He explained that "this is not a programme written from thousands of miles away. But one that has been fought for by socialists and members of the cwi, day-in and day-out in Israel and the region." Despite the differences that our former Scottish comrades had with the leadership of the ssp, which they would continue to put forward, we nevertheless concluded that the ssp was likely to make important advances in the forthcoming May elections. cwi members in Scotland would be campaigning for a big ssp vote.[1]

"Spectacular gains for the Scottish Socialist Party" was indeed the headline in The Socialist reporting on the election's outcome. There were big advances for the ssp and the Greens, who between them won 13 seats, an increase of 11. Moreover, four independents were elected, including left ex-Labour mp Dennis Canavan in Falkirk with the biggest majority in the Scottish Parliament. This was in contrast to the massive rejection of New Labour and the SNP. Turnout fell below 50%, while Labour's vote fell by 4% on the first poll – their lowest vote since 1931 – and 5% on the second proportional representation based party list vote!

It was the SSP and the Greens which captured the imagination, winning between them 250,000 second votes. The SSP stood in 70 out of 73 first past the post constituencies, winning 6.2% of the first vote. The party polled over 5% in 43 seats with Tommy Sheridan winning 28% of the vote in Pollok. Well over 100,000 people voted SSP on the first vote and 130,000 people voted SSP on the second vote – trebling the SSP's vote compared to 1999. Independent left and anti-establishment candidates, the Greens and the SSP, took an incredible 20% of the second vote and 10% of the first vote. While welcoming the great success of the SSP, we warned that it was essential that the party should fight for public ownership of the major sectors of the economy under the democratic control of the working class. This was the solution to poverty and inequality which scarred Scotland then and is even more so today.[2]

The CWI within the SSP continued to dissect the policies of the party and warn about the inadequacies of its programme. For instance, Norway and Denmark were held up as models for Scotland. Tommy Sheridan indicated this in a BBC interview before the election: "A number of countries... have a successful mix of public ownership and high-taxation... like Norway and Denmark they manage to combine high levels of public ownership with high taxation for the wealthy." It has long been a hallmark of the SWP and others on the 'revolutionary left' that they baldly call for such a measure but do not link this up with other demands, such as nationalisation of the banks, democratic state control of all imports and exports and nationalisation of the major monopolies to stop the rich from fleeing abroad with their ill-gotten gains.

Tommy Sheridan, as the main Parliamentary spokesman for the SSP, put forward a programme which made significant concessions to this idea of left reformism. In an interview with The Herald[3] he was asked what role the market would play if he was in power. His answer: "We very much believe in a mixed economy." Reporter: "It doesn't sound like it, Tommy." His reply to this comment was, "Well, our mix is different from New Labour's mix. Labour would like to add a wee drop of whisky to the Atlantic Ocean and say that's a mixed economy. We think that's wrong. We think there's a larger role for the public sector to play."

The idea of a mixed economy was precisely the way that the right wing of the Labour Party in the past had described capitalism. When 80% is in the hands of big business and 20% is in the hands of the state (it is much less than this today) the 80% will dictate to the 20% and not vice versa. This position had been adopted by Militant almost from its beginnings and was an idea that Tommy Sheridan and Alan McCombes had consistently argued for over decades. Now they were clearly adopting a reformist approach, which we predicted would be the inevitable outcome of their rupture with the CWI. It did not stop us working with these comrades, but we consistently argued against their mistaken approach. It ultimately led to the shipwrecking of the SSP and the squandering of another golden opportunity to establish a real mass socialist alternative in Scotland.

Tommy unfortunately compounded his error in the above interview when he was asked: "Would you nationalise Tesco?" He answered: "I don't think there's a need to nationalise Tesco right now. What I think there's a need for is to impose on Tesco proper wages and employment conditions. What we would be doing is regulating business. You don't have to own it, you just regulate it." Our Scottish comrades pointed out in answer to this: "Tommy Sheridan's statement about not nationalising Tesco flows from the idea that you can't deal with multinational companies in a Scottish context, other than by "regulating" them. It is a recognition that within the limits of an isolated Scotland there would be limits on what could be achieved. But it is wrong to view it in that way. If the socialist transformation of society takes place in Scotland first, which is by no means certain, the long-term survival of a socialist Scotland would depend on the spreading of a socialist revolution internationally."[4]

Any differences with Tommy Sheridan, however, did not prevent us from defending him when he came under sustained attack from the Murdoch press later, which was unfortunately supported by former comrades like Alan McCombes and Frances Curran.

The Scottish Socialist Party attracted 400 delegates and visitors to its 2004 conference in late March. This was the fifth and largest SSP conference and the first since the party's election success the previous May when six SSP members were elected to the Scottish Parliament. Moreover, the Scottish Regional Council of the RMT had affiliated to the party. The Edinburgh Number Two branch of the Communication Workers Union had also agreed to affiliate. The SSP's membership stood at this stage at around 3,000, an indication not just of growth but also the potential for the party.

Contrary to the myth that the CWI opposed the formation of this party, we participated and took a leading part in the debates at the conference itself, counterposing the policies of the CWI to those of the leadership of the SSP. They had previously supported CWI policies but were now distancing themselves from them. Alan McCombes introduced the draft manifesto for the upcoming European elections, which he described as "red-blooded socialist" in character. However, CWI supporters pointed out that it marked a big shift away from the clear socialist policies supported by him and other former members of the CWI in the past. It entirely avoided calls for the public ownership of big business and the multinational corporations that control the Scottish and European economies. Instead, the SSP pledged itself to build a "social Europe" rather than a socialist one.

We had predicted at the time of their split from the CWI that these comrades, having abandoned a distinct Marxist policy and organisation, would evolve in an opportunist right-wing direction. This conclusion was entirely justified by their contributions at this conference. Sinead Daly, from Dundee SSP and a CWI member, explained that "the term 'a social Europe' is even used by some capitalists in Europe, by the right-wing trade union bureaucracy and by governments to justify their policies. We have to be clear that it is another form of capitalism." She was supported by Ian Fitzpatrick, a delegate from Motherwell ssp who explained, pointing to the cuts carried out by the Brown government, that the ssp had the "responsibility to explain that socialism is the only answer to the attacks on the working class". Alan McCombes replied: "We need a manifesto for the long term and the short term. These amendments are arguing that nothing can be done until we have socialism. We can't let the rich off the hook in the short term."

This attempt by Alan McCombes to separate so-called "short-term" demands from "long-term" solutions was precisely the way classical social democracy put forward the 'maximum' demands for the long term and the 'minimum' policies for the short term. This represented, in effect, the going over of the ssp leadership to a social-democratic position, precisely at a time when the basis for social democracy was being undermined because capitalism is no longer capable of accepting lasting reforms.

The cwi amendment was supported by 50 of the delegates but there was a verbal commitment by the ssp executive to redraft the manifesto with some reference to public ownership before the election. There was also a debate on the national question, in which the ssp had proposed a convention that would "help to build support and confidence in an independent Scotland". The cwi, while defending the programme of an independent socialist Scotland, opposed this move. We explained that there would be little support in the working class at that stage for a campaign to fight for an independent Scotland. Moreover, there was a danger that the ssp leadership would be seen arguing for an independent, capitalist Scotland as a route to ending poverty and inequality. The cwi resolution opposing the launching of the convention and defending the programme of an independent socialist Scotland which would voluntarily link up with a socialist England, Wales and Ireland was defeated but with 40 to 50 delegates again voting for the cwi position.[5]

Notwithstanding this, the ssp faced the possibility of a substantial growth of influence and members, particularly if it could be persuaded to develop a clearer, more rounded out socialist programme and perspective. But that was before the bombshell of Tommy Sheridan's resignation as SSP convenor in November 2004. SSP members were stunned when he announced he was stepping back from frontline politics in order to be "a hands-on father", as his partner was expecting their first child the following year. The catalyst for his resignation was a meeting of the SSP executive the day before, which discussed allegations about Tommy's private life that were expected to appear in Rupert Murdoch's rag, the News of the World, the following Sunday. Tommy had insisted that he intended to deny the allegations and seek legal action. This prompted the SSP's Executive Committee to pass a motion threatening to remove him as national convenor unless he abandoned this strategy by the following Saturday. He therefore resigned the next day and, following publication of the article in the News of the World, he announced his pursuit of a libel action.

We opposed the measures of the SSP Executive Committee. The CWI, despite its openly expressed differences with the SSP leadership including Tommy, had welcomed the impact that the party had made, which was attracting a new layer of workers prepared to fight for the ideas of socialism. We condemned anything which undermined this as a block to the socialist movement in general. Moreover, our Scottish comrades stated that if the EC had not given the ultimatum to Tommy to drop his denial and then made it clear publicly that the right-wing tabloid's allegations were an attempt to undermine the SSP and Tommy Sheridan, the whole situation could have been avoided.

Incredibly, the SSP EC acted even before seeing the Murdoch hirelings' claims. We did not deny that, on occasions, the personal conduct of a leading member of a political party can damage, sometimes fatally, the reputation of a party. But these tabloid allegations against Tommy Sheridan, which were completely unproven, did not fall into this category. The CWI recognised that Tommy had significant authority amongst working-class people in Scotland, which these allegations, if answered properly, would not substantially alter. It is difficult not to draw the conclusion from this event that there were people in the leadership of the ssp with a personal axe to grind against Tommy. They took the opportunity to remove him from positions of influence without any recognition that this would strengthen the Murdoch press and the bitter opponents of all those who fight for socialism.[6] Subsequent events demonstrated that this was the case as the ssp went into a spiral of decline, which was quickly reflected at its 2005 conference.

This conference was entirely different from previous ssp events, with the authority of the leadership considerably undermined by the events surrounding Tommy's effective removal as the party convenor. A veiled dogfight took place over the vacant crown with Colin Fox attempting to distance himself from the majority of the leadership, standing against Alan McCombes. He had the support of Tommy Sheridan and won by a large margin of 252 votes (62%) to 154. The poll for the chair of the conference was topped by Rosemary Byrne, ssp member of the Scottish Parliament. She had openly criticised the ec's action in calling on Tommy Sheridan to stand down. Tommy Sheridan topped the poll for the male list to the ec.

Delegates from the cwi platform played a leading, at times decisive role in the debates. The issue of Iraq was taken first with a motion to the conference inspired by the Socialist Worker platform, which called for uncritical support to the Iraqi 'popular resistance'. The only amendment to challenge this came from Dundee West ssp from cwi members. The amendment called for the removal of all occupying troops and support for mass resistance to the occupation, through the building of workers and farmers' militias that sought to unite all the different ethnic and religious groups in Iraq. It also called on the ssp to oppose the reactionary anti-working class forces that made up part of the 'resistance' in Iraq. Sinead Daly declared: "We cannot as socialists give our support to those forces in Iraq whose ideas and methods are anti-working class, anti-women and who, in some cases, are intent on trying to provoke a civil and sectarian war in Iraq. We should support a movement to unite the working class and the poor based on a struggle for a living wage, healthcare, education, and basic services, as well as opposition to the imperialist occupation."

This amendment was opposed by a long succession of swp members, who claimed that "the working class are not able to struggle just now" and that the "trade unions are too weak and strikes in the public sector are banned". They also opposed and tried to remove the reference in another motion that called on the ssp to "support the organised working-class and trade union movement as the most important part of the resistance". The ssp leadership adopted an abstentionist position. Philip Stott's report of the conference said: "Without doubt the cwi's amendment went a long way to saving the ssp from a storm of media and political attacks had the swp motion been passed unamended."[7]

What followed was the slow decline of the ssp, which was a gift to the Scottish National Party (snp), who had been in difficulties at this time. In the 2004 European elections, the snp's share of the vote fell to 19%, its worst since the 1987 general election. Its previous electoral highpoint was in 1994 when it polled 33%, followed by a 28% score at the inaugural election for the Scottish Parliament. However, in the 2003 Scottish elections the snp lost one fifth of their msps as their vote fell to 23%. The claimed membership of the party also fell significantly to just over 8,000 members from more than 15,000 in the 1990s. This was a consequence of the move to the right by the snp leadership of the previous few years, which involved embracing a business tax and pro-market ideas modelled on the 'Celtic Tiger' in Ireland. This had been shown to fail in building a mass base.

61. Outcome of the 2005 general election

A general election took place in May 2005. In its run-up we warned those workers we could reach not to expect significant benefits from New Labour. There was not much hope for the likely third term for Blair and Brown. In the election, only a relatively small number of seats would have socialists contesting them. In Scotland the ssp contested every seat. In England the Socialist Party stood 15 candidates as part of an electoral alliance, the Socialist Green Unity Coalition, which provided workers in 30 seats with the chance to vote for candidates with socialist ideas. Respect, led by George Galloway and the Socialist Workers Party, stood in 28 seats. However Galloway, it should be recalled, had missed the opportunity in 2003 to launch an open, democratic formation – standing on an explicitly socialist programme – which would have had the possibility of drawing in other forces. Without any serious challenge from the left, it was not surprising that the central social and economic issues did not dominate the election campaign. Although the Socialist Party sought to draw attention to the underlying explosive situation, which would form the background to the next government, the trade union movement, particularly at leadership level, adopted a wait-and-see policy until after the election.

The outcome of the election was almost preordained, with Blair and New Labour returned for a 'record' third Labour term. Margaret Thatcher had also won three elections but was now so discredited that even Tory leader Michael Howard distanced himself from her regime early on in the campaign. The outcome of this contest was hardly a ringing endorsement of the New Labour 'project'. The government's majority collapsed from 166 to 66, with its percentage of the popular vote (36%) the lowest of any governing party in history – the most unpopular party to form a government since the 1832 Reform Act. Labour's vote was lower than Harold Wilson's Labour government of 1974, which scored 39%. The Tories on the other hand flat-lined, gaining seats but with 32.4% of the vote this was just a 0.7% increase on their disastrous showing in 2001. The Tory leader quickly said he would resign; he already had "something of the good night about him".[1] The only age group in which the Tories led was the over-65s with 42% voting for the Tories.

The British National Party recorded its best vote at a general election. In Barking in East London, it achieved its highest share of the vote in any Parliamentary constituency (17%) beating the Liberal Democrats into third place, and only losing out to the second placed Tories by just 27 votes. In neighbouring Dagenham it notched up 9%.

On the left, the Respect party of George Galloway was successful in Tower Hamlets in beating the Blairite apologist Oona King. Galloway's election campaign undoubtedly tapped into the mood of radicalisation and anger at New Labour – particularly amongst the poorest sections of Muslims. Around 40% of the electorate in the constituency were Muslim, with many of them having broken with New Labour as a result of the Afghanistan and Iraq wars, as well as their increased repression in Britain. We called for a vote for Respect and welcomed Galloway's victory but he did not draw the obvious conclusion from his victory that a new party was needed. In fact, he mistakenly raised the idea that Respect could play a part in the process of "reclaiming" the Labour Party that had only recently expelled him!

John Curtice in the Independent, in a one-sided way, described it as "the best performance by a far-left party in British electoral history". We commented that if this had been the case, it would be a cause for celebration for all of those on the left looking for an alternative. Unfortunately, despite the electoral success of Respect, as we pointed out many times, it was too narrowly based, gaining support from Muslims but not from the non-Muslim sections of the working class, even in Tower Hamlets itself. Respect continued to be narrowly based and focused on one section of the working class, which led to its eventual demise as a serious force on the left.

Galloway wasn't the only 'independent' who received significant votes at this election. Anti-war campaigners Reg Keys and Rose Gentle, both of who had lost sons serving in the armed forces in Iraq, stood as independent candidates in the election. Reg Keys received 10.3% of the vote and Rose Gentle 3.1% where they stood. Moreover, Wales Assembly Member Peter Law was dumped by the Labour Party nationally who then imposed a Blairite candidate on his Blaenau Gwent constituency party. He then won the seat as an independent with a massive majority of 9,121!

Most importantly, the estimated 1.1 million votes lost by Labour between 2001 and 2005 arose from disillusionment at the Iraq war. Nevertheless, the relentless pounding away on the theme of 'don't allow [Tory leader] Howard in by the back door' had an effect on certain sections of the working class and others who otherwise would have been prepared to desert Labour and look for a more radical left option. The election had shown that there was no longer a stable core for Labour, as New Labour imagined. For the three main established parties (New Labour, Liberal Democrats and the Tories) it was a 'non-ideological' contest between different management teams for control of 'Great Britain plc'.

All pretence of collective leadership during the campaign was brushed aside by the leaders of the parties as the election became a contest between virtual 'presidential' candidates. This was personified by Blair, who adopted a more 'humble' posture. But even after that electoral setback, the day after the election in Downing Street he still uttered the phrase: "I, we, the government..."

The majority of the capitalists – reflected in the stance of the media – were prepared to extend their support to Blair in this election. Not just The Sun, but The Times, the Economist reluctantly – "No alternative, alas" – and, most importantly, the Financial Times lined up behind Blair. The Financial Times declared that Britain no longer had a "business party" and an "anti-business party". They pointed out that the gap between Michael Howard's Conservatives and Tony Blair's Labour Party was smaller than that in the previous US presidential election between Republicans and Democrats. This brutal assessment, we said, demonstrated beyond doubt that New Labour was unremittingly a pro-business party, in sharp contrast to the forlorn hankering of sections of the Labour left for Labour to return to its roots as a working class party at its base.

It was not just the performance of the right within Labour but also the so-called 'left' which repelled working people. For instance, Neil Gerrard, erstwhile left MP for Walthamstow, astonished teachers in a hustings debate in his constituency, also involving the local Socialist Party candidate, when he approved PFI specifically for the local hospital, Whipps Cross, and the setting up of educational academies. An academy had been previously defeated in a successful campaign involving the Socialist Party. Even left-wing MP Jeremy Corbyn, in his constituency manifesto, praised the government for investment in his seat and particularly singled out Trade and Industry Secretary Patricia Hewitt! We commented: "Tell that to the Rover workers who were made redundant while she stood aside like Pontius Pilate and did nothing!" The demoralisation of the left was indicated by the defection to the Lib Dems of Brian Sedgemore, previously a member of the left Campaign Group of MPs and Parliamentary Private Secretary to Tony Benn from 1978 to 1979 in the Labour government.

It was no accident that capitalist commentators drew the comparison with this election and the 1992 election, which was "an election to lose"; 'Black Wednesday' followed with devastating consequences for the Major government. Blair was now clearly a lame-duck Prime Minister who threatened to become a 'dead duck'. The same fate also awaited Gordon Brown because of the earth-shaking economic events that were to unfold.[2]

62. Climate Change and 'Natural Disasters' 2004-05

Marxism – scientific socialism – proceeds from an analysis of objective reality. One of the most important realities which it has had to face, along with the whole of humankind, is the danger to the environment posed by the very existence of capitalism itself through the growth of carbon emissions and the seemingly inexorable rise of global warming. The idea perpetrated by opponents of scientific socialism that Marx and Engels had little to say about this problem is false. Indeed they were, as in so many things, ahead of their time. In Volume 3 of his monumental and major work Capital, Marx makes the following point: "From the standpoint of a higher economic form of society, private ownership of the globe by single individuals will appear quite as absurd as private ownership of one man by another. Even a whole society, a nation, or even all simultaneously existing societies taken together, are not the owners of the globe. They are only its possessors... they must hand it down to succeeding generations in an improved condition."[1]

The starting point of any contemporary discussion on climate change is the incapacity of the 'economic arrangements' of the world created by capitalism to solve these problems. Just take the demand for growth in the neo-colonial world – necessary in order to eliminate hunger and lack of shelter – against environmental damage, which inevitably flows from this. In my book, Marxism in Today's World, I commented: "We face an unprecedented situation today.

The kind of development of the productive forces under capitalism in an unplanned way, even if you do not have a new economic crisis, means that the majority of humankind will have to challenge this system on the question of the environment alone in order to prevent an unstoppable decline. The leading Chinese environmentalist... has said that for China to reach the living standards of the US will need the resources of four worlds! Do we conclude from this that the Chinese people will never reach the living standards of the American people today and that they are condemned forever to [underdevelopment]? I think it would be wrong to say this. We can have sustainable growth and we can avoid the crimes that have been committed against the environment by capitalism and Stalinism."[2]

This general approach was brought to bear in wrestling with the issues that came up in the environmental movement. The new generation is particularly motivated to take action and have the most to lose if destructive climate change proves to be irreversible. The capitalists themselves cannot appear to be impervious to this. This led to the world environmental summit in Kyoto in 1997. The debate there concentrated on what to do about carbon dioxide emissions. The Rio summit in 1992 had agreed to stabilise the release of emissions at 1990 levels by the year 2000. Leaving the capitalists to carry out this task and to decide on environmental issues for the future of the planet was, we said, "like appointing a Formula One magnate to take charge of health care – profits always come first."

We concluded that "The biggest threat to the environment and the job security of workers on this planet is the capitalist system".[3] Of course, we supported all measures to curb emissions, to prevent waste in the energy industry – costing in 1997 $300 billion per year. The summit, predictably, failed to agree measures which would slow down the process of global warming. Yet each year demonstrated that the danger posed from global warming was growing.

This was illustrated in a series of articles, books and pamphlets by Socialist Party comrades who specialised in this field. However, this was not an issue for specialists alone. The working masses were profoundly affected. I came across whole villages in Malaysia on a visit in 2005 that had experienced life changing effects from environmental pollution.

This applies not just to the environment in general but also to planning for unforeseen events: 'natural disasters' like earthquakes, tsunamis, etc. Indeed, such events can be the trigger for major upheavals in society itself, provoking a profound crisis in a regime. It is not for nothing that such events have often been the midwives of revolution. Such was the profound effect of the Nicaraguan earthquake in 1972 that after the dictator Somoza embezzled funds meant for the victims, it provoked his overthrow.

The 150,000 deaths as a result of the Indian Ocean tsunami that broke on 26 December 2004 provoked a similar reaction. Countries affected included India, Sri Lanka, Thailand, Indonesia and many others, leading the Financial Times to comment that this event was unique in the sense that "the number of foreign holidaymakers caught in the tsunami... ensured the rest of the world paid attention to a disaster that... encompassed such a large area and so many countries."[4]

The fact that many from the 'rich' countries were affected led to unprecedented coverage throughout the world. Alongside the terrible sadness there was also anger at the tens of thousands who had died needlessly, as experts pointed out. Jon Dale, writing with the authority of a doctor, commented in the Socialist: "Despite the biblical scale of floods and destruction, the death along the Indian Ocean coastline was no 'Act of God.'" He pointed out: "The Pacific Tsunami Warning Center was set up in 1949, based in Hawaii. Despite its existence, destructive tsunamis have continued. But technological improvements in recent years have enormously improved the ability of scientists to detect them and issue warnings to coastal areas of their approach."

Yet despite this, so many lost their lives. Was this avoidable? A Canadian tsunami specialist was in no doubt: "The waves are totally predictable. We have travel-time charts for the whole of the Indian Ocean. From where this earthquake hit, the travel time for waves to hit the tip of India was four hours. That's enough time for a warning." But "The instruments are very expensive and we don't have the money to buy them," said an Indonesian meteorological expert.[5] The harrowing scenes carried on television led to massive and unprecedented generosity, solidarity and internationalism. In Britain individual donations piled up at £1 million an hour, with more than £70 million collected in total.

Our comrades in key countries such as India and Sri Lanka were affected by the tsunami. However, the CWI centre was able to report "with great relief that, after heroic efforts to establish the whereabouts of all its members, the United Socialist Party (USP – the CWI's section in Sri Lanka) has found that it has sustained no direct loss of life." This was despite the fact that many USP members and their families lived and worked near where the tsunami crashed into Sri Lanka: "One national committee member in Galle... was severely injured and hospitalised but has now returned to his home to recover fully. More than 25 USP members and their families in the south and east of the island are homeless, most living in makeshift camps and in urgent need of water, food, clothes and medicine."

We called upon supporters and members of the CWI to rush finance and resources to help stricken comrades. Clare Doyle, who co-ordinated the international efforts to assist our Sri Lankan comrades, reported: "We will be sending goods to Sri Lanka by container in the next two days and again next week. If you can spare tents or plastic sheeting, light clothes (including underwear) or light bedding please email us." In Sri Lanka itself, the USP demanded that reconstruction needed to be "controlled by elected committees of workers and poor people to ensure maximum assistance to those who most need it, regardless of nationality, religion and political affiliation... They can have no faith in capitalist politicians. Outbreaks of communal conflict must be prevented as the struggle for scarce resources continues."[6]

This was in the best traditions of the USP which, often at the risk of their own lives, has stood for the unity of the working class and the right to self-determination of the oppressed Tamil-speaking people. They were the only organisation that produced a paper in both the Tamil and Sinhala languages. Aceh in Indonesia was also profoundly affected but there was suspicion and resentment that they would not get help from the Jakarta government, which continually drained the province of its rich oil and gas resources.

Similar suspicions of the ruling parties in Sri Lanka were witnessed by Jim Hensman, a long-standing Socialist Party member from Coventry, whose family came to Britain from Sri Lanka. He was visiting family and friends there when the tsunami struck. Shortly afterwards, at a National Council of the Socialist Party, he described what happened: "'We all have to put aside our differences', 'we all have to pull together'... This was the case in Sri Lanka initially. But within days the crass inefficiency and the failure of the weak capitalist class, tied in with world capitalism, to carry out even the basic tasks of relief became apparent."

He then recounted an amusing story going round the villages of Sri Lanka, which highlighted this point. The Hawaii Tsunami Reporting Centre contacted a senior government minister in Sri Lanka. They told him there was a tsunami in Indonesia arriving in about two hours. "Can you take the necessary action?" they asked. The government minister springs to life and two hours later he is at Colombo airport with a placard which reads "Sri Lanka welcomes Mr Tsunami from Indonesia."[7]

A few months later I visited Sri Lanka on behalf of the CWI and witnessed some of the areas most devastated by the tsunami. I wrote afterwards: "The tsunami and its terrible aftermath is the overarching issue that still dominates every aspect of Sri Lankan society... The 'fortunate' few are living in 'temporary' accommodation – one-room wooden boxes with wafer-thin roofs – while many are arbitrarily removed kilometres from the sites of their original houses."

I reported the following: "We stop at a spot near Galle where the remnants of the Colombo to Galle express was lifted by the great wave and thrown hundreds of metres inland... speak to a woman sitting outside her new 'home', a shack, albeit of new wood ... Before 26 December, there were six members of their family... Three of her children were killed on the day of the tsunami: her only daughter and two sons." This was just a little glimpse of the heartbreak which many Sri Lankans suffered. This woman survived the tsunami by clinging to a tree; her husband, meanwhile, was swept many kilometres away from the seashore.

The government had given £25 to every household whose home was destroyed. The tsunami victims received just over £2 a week for the three people left in this household. The members of the USP, particularly Siritunga Jayasuriya (Siri) who accompanied me, had played a key role in the launch and success of the newspaper Voice of the Tsunami People. They asked the young man "if they have taken any collective action or if a committee exists to represent them and air their grievances. He says no, but he would be prepared to organise structures like this, such is the anger now felt by the tsunami people." The organiser of the meeting that we addressed, the key person in the village, was the ex-head of the local Sri Lanka Freedom Party (SLFP) – the governing party. Following our meeting he was visited by SLFP thugs and beaten up.

President Chandrika Kumaratunga complained bitterly that the Sri Lankan government had so far "not received even five cents" from the money collected internationally. We declared: "It is buried in the vaults of foreign governments and of some international agencies and charities." Apparently, 40% of all monies collected by charities for disasters like this are swallowed up by administration costs, which are caused by the fat salaries of those who head these organisations. We asked, "Why weren't the resources of the Sri Lankan state and society put into emergency mode and placed at the disposal of the people of these regions?" who had suffered terribly. After all, 40,000 people lost their lives in Sri Lanka, with an estimated 800,000 people made refugees.[8]

Senan, a CWI member originally from Jaffna but now living in London, condemned the way the government was dealing with the situation: "[The] people have reacted far quicker to the tsunami disaster than their government. Unexpectedly, it has provided an opportunity for the Tamil and Sinhalese masses to work together...

and to experience it. Unfortunately, the authorities are not using this opportunity to forge unity on the divided island, but the opposite." The USP had condemned the government for its treatment of the disaster victims and called for aid operations to be under the control of left committees and workers of all peoples, without any discrimination on the basis of nationality, religion or caste.

Unfortunately, ethnically based armed groups undermined this attempt to bring working people together on a class basis. This applied equally to the Tamil Tigers (LTTE) and the People's Liberation Front (JVP). The USP called upon the LTTE to responsibly "ensure that all aid is distributed without discrimination". This was particularly important in the East of Sri Lanka, which contains Tamil-speaking people who were also Muslims. The USP, which had members in this area with many displaced in 11 counties, fought against any manifestation of discrimination with regard to nationality or religion.

The scale of the destruction caused by the tsunami was monumental, an estimated cost of $1 billion in the first year alone. Without democratic control misappropriation of money in these circumstances by corrupt bureaucrats compounded the suffering of the ordinary working people and poor. US imperialism intervened not in order to relieve the suffering but to immensely enhance its own position. Colin Powell, Bush's proconsul, visited Thailand, Sri Lanka and, most importantly, Jakarta in Indonesia, the world's most populous Islamic country. The Muslims there had, along with the rest of the world, "an opportunity to see American generosity, American values in action". He went on: "I hope as a result of our efforts... that value system of ours will be reinforced." The US relief work, he added, should also "dry up pools of dissatisfaction which might give rise to terrorist activity"![9]

India, a rising imperialist power in its own region, sought to profit from the disaster by sending in its own troops under the cover of aid to Sri Lanka, the Maldives and Indonesia. They were pursuing their own regional ambitions, aiming to rival China and Japan in Asia. The suffering of the masses in this region through the tsunami was of secondary importance to these contending powers. After all, every week 150,000 people were dying of preventable illnesses associated with shortages of food, clean water and sanitation. This arose from the inadequacies of landlordism and capitalism and represented the equivalent of the death toll of the Indian Ocean tsunami every seven or eight days!

The suffering was not restricted to the neo-colonial world. As Offensiv, the paper of the CWI's Swedish section reported, the country appeared to have suffered the "worst disaster for Sweden since World War One" with initial fears of a thousand dead tourists, although that figure proved overly pessimistic. The Swedish Foreign Minister was targeted for much criticism because she did not cut short her holiday until 31 hours after the tsunami, and was reported to have gone to the theatre after she had heard that it had struck.[10]

The effect of the tsunami was to emphasise the number of natural disasters which were occurring throughout the world – estimated to have risen from 100 a year in the early 1960s to around 500 a year by the early 2000s – and the neglect of capitalist states' reactions to this. There was a wide variation between where these events took place and the response of governments to them. One thing emerged clearly: the corrupt capitalist politicians and bureaucrats invariably diverted disaster relief and money into their own pockets. The sections of the CWI in disaster areas always emphasised that workers and poor farmers were the only force which could direct relief and reconstruction in the interests of the people in general. This should be channelled through workers' committees without any discrimination between different ethnic, religious, caste and other groups. Similarly, reconstruction should be under the democratic control of the left and workers' committees to guard against corruption and ensure that rebuilding met the needs of workers and other toilers.

Many of the countries affected were burdened with massive foreign debt; five Indian Ocean countries affected by the tsunami collectively owed $300 billion. We demanded cancellation of this debt and the nationalisation of the banks, under democratic workers' control and management. However, the tsunami brought out the best amongst the world's population, particularly the aid that was rushed by working people and the poor to their brothers and sisters in the affected areas. It was a manifestation of the instinctive internationalism of the masses. This can only really be fully harnessed for the world by the working class and labour movement in the struggle for socialism.

In contrast, this disaster highlighted the murderous incompetence of the representatives of the landlords and capitalists throughout the affected regions. Jagadish Chandra slammed the Indian bourgeoisie: "It is criminal on the part of the Indian government not to be a member of the Pacific Tsunami Warning Centre. This would have warned the devastated people at least four hours in advance... The avoidable scale of the death and destruction of the Bhuj earthquake in Gujarat, India, in 2001 and the 2004 tsunami disaster are a warning about the horrific consequences of poverty and neglect in countries exploited by capitalism and imperialism."[11]

The clear stand of the Sri Lankan USP during the tsunami and the work done after this paid off when presidential elections were called a year later in 2005. As expected, the Prime Minister, Mahinda Rajapaksa and his party the SLFP won the election narrowly. Siri, the candidate of the USP, came third with the highest vote for a left candidate. Just after the new president made his acceptance speech, Siri declared on camera to Rajapaksa's face: "This is the first time in Sri Lanka that a president has been elected on the votes of the Sinhala (majority) population. The Sinhala Buddhist zealots have dominated your election platforms. As president, you have a duty to control these forces which you have encouraged. Their hatred of the Tamil-speaking people, including the Muslims, poses a huge danger in this country... You have made a lorry-load of promises to this country. If they are not implemented, the United Socialist Party... will go to the streets. We will mobilise behind the demand that they be implemented or that you step down."

Some of the main TV stations and newspapers had been so careful not to mention the name of our party or its candidate. Siri continued: "The USP will continue its work with trade unionists, with the Tsunami-affected people still fighting for justice, with the Tamil-speaking minority, and with the young people whose future hangs in the balance as long as capitalist forces rule."[12]

Clare Doyle, for the CWI, reported that the "government had been in league in this election with two arch-chauvinist, anti-Tamil parties – the JVP and the JHU." Already in the East a number of dead and injured resulted from this.[13] The determined resistance of the USP was in the best traditions of the labour movement, particularly of the Lanka Sama Samaja Party (LSSP) in the past. The work that was done then is preparing the ground for the emergence of the future socialist Marxist forces in Sri Lanka.

I visited Pakistan in 2005 and witnessed the conditions of the masses there: "Nothing can prepare you for leaving the quite modern Karachi Airport to confront for the first time the living hell of the sprawling conurbation of Karachi... I was taken to a 'two-star' hotel, which at first glance I took to be another of the slum dwellings I saw on the journey from the airport. This residence, whose poorly-paid staff were extremely polite and helpful, would certainly not make it onto the guest house list of a British seaside resort!" These were the opening lines of the report of my visit.

Lenin once described capitalism as "horror without end" for the working class and the poor. Pakistan is a living example of this. Yet, when I was there, it was relatively tranquil compared to the recent situation, with Pakistan's main industrial city Karachi divided into spheres controlled by nationalist or different armed groups with the nightmare of sectarian civil war ever present. We wrote: "Pakistan is a powder keg ready to explode at any time." That was largely because of the social situation pertaining then and its political reflections in a split in the ruling class against the background of a rising tide of mass discontent.

Pakistan is a byword for poverty, disease and suffering. I reported: "Recently, outside Lahore Press Club, 20 kiln workers lifted their shirts to display savage scars on their bodies. This was the result of their 'donation' of a kidney for money to pay off crippling loans to their kiln bosses. In one Punjabi village, 3,000 people donated their kidneys. Most of these 'donations' don't go to rich Westerners but to rich Pakistanis." If anything, the conditions have got much worse since then. The army still exercises not just military but colossal economic power as well, with direct stakes in industrial conglomerates. The Islamic fundamentalist parties like Jamaat-e-Islami are a dead end, "with 34 of its Central Committee members millionaires or billionaires."[14]

It was not just the neo-colonial world that was struck by 'natural' disasters. The richest country on the planet, the US, was hit by the devastating Hurricane Katrina as it struck the Gulf Coast, affecting thousands in New Orleans and throughout the region who died from drowning, dehydration, starvation and, in some cases, a lack of medical care. The city, which was once known for its culture, art, food and hospitality, now provided no secure shelter or food for its residents. As the incompetence and lack of preparedness of the Bush regime became more and more evident so mass anger rose. The working class and poor, overwhelmingly Afro-American, including the elderly and sick, residents of hospitals and care homes, were abandoned without water, food, medicines, electricity or clear information about effective relief.

This contrasted to the truly heroic efforts, not witnessed on television, of the working class in New Orleans; for example, the maintenance man who used forklifts to carry the sick and disabled or the engineers who nurtured and kept the generators running. Even before the hurricane, 20% of the city's residents lived below the poverty line. Bryan Koulouris, from Socialist Alternative, sympathisers of the CWI, commented: "Just like thousands of homes on the Gulf Coast, the roof has been torn off of US society for all to see the rotten underbelly of the world's biggest economic and military power."[15]

The biased US media betrayed, vilified and portrayed as criminals the overwhelmingly poor Afro-American residents left behind in squalor because they were taking food, water, clothing and other things to survive. However, it was the Bush regime and big business that were not prepared for this calamity who were really responsible for the situation. In New Orleans and other places throughout

Louisiana, Mississippi and Alabama working class and poor people resorted to desperate measures to get hold of food, water and clothing. Bush claimed that nobody could have "anticipated the breach of the levees" in New Orleans. Yet experts had warned in 2001 that unless a large-scale engineering project called 'Coast 2001' – first developed by engineers and scientists in 1998 – was put in place, something like this calamity was possible.

Incredibly Bush praised Michael Brown, head of the Federal Emergency Management Agency (FEMA) which openly displayed its bureaucratic incompetence in the first few hours of Katrina: "Brownie, you're doing a heckuva job!"[16] There were over 6,000 National Guardsmen from Louisiana and Mississippi – who were supposed to deal with domestic emergencies, although they were often used to break strikes – in Iraq helping the US attempt to occupy the country for the benefit of Haliburton, Texaco and other US corporations.

The Bush regime was rattled as anger mounted against inaction at the top. We commented: "The last few weeks have been the worst of the 248 in which [Bush] has been in office." The Katrina catastrophe was linked to the corruption charges levelled against top Republicans in the cronyism at the heart of the regime. The 'legal profession' was up in arms because his nominee for the Supreme Court had worked for Bush as a 'Commissioner for the Texas Lottery'. Bush's personal ratings in opinion polls were now lower than even Ronald Reagan's during the Iran-Contra scandal.

The deadly combination of the unwinnable war in Iraq, a web of intrigue and corruption in Washington and Hurricane Katrina – which lifted the lid on the poverty and racism in the US – meant that this was a generalised crisis, not just for Bush's presidency but for the system itself. It was directly linked to the extreme polarisation of wealth in the US, exacerbated by the policies pursued by both major parties since the 1970s and continued by Bush.[17]

American workers and youth drew widespread conclusions from this event, helping to fuel the anti-capitalist movement which in the 'noughties' became almost a permanent feature of the US.

This helped to prepare the ground for the 'Occupy Movement', which in turn was a big factor in the election of the socialist, Kshama Sawant in Seattle, and which can lead to a renaissance of the labour movement in the US on a national scale.

63. Mass movement against world poverty
2005

While capitalism was experiencing an underlying crisis in the economic sphere, it was also facing an immediate and increasing challenge from the new generation of workers and youth against the rise of poverty worldwide. This was reflected in the massive demonstrations in July 2005 coinciding with the meeting of the G8 – the leaders of the most important capitalist powers – in Edinburgh, Scotland. The slogan of the Socialist for the demonstration read: "Down with the G8 – Make poverty history – Fight for a socialist future!"[1]

To this end we sought to explain how ending the plight of the masses in the neo-colonial world in particular was organically linked to the idea of socialism. More than 20,000 people were dying each day in the neo-colonial world because of 'extreme poverty'. In sub-Saharan Africa – the immediate object of the mass campaign to 'Make Poverty History' – were 4.8 million children who died before the age of five every year, according to the United Nations. That's nine deaths every minute! Africa, Asia and Latin America were scarred by unspeakable poverty, which meant a brutish, half-human existence for billions. For instance in India, supposedly still 'shining', in the state of Andhra Pradesh 4,000 farmers, crushed by debt and despair, committed suicide between 1998 and 2005. The majority of the Indian population are compelled to defecate in the open. This is a reflection of the poverty which persists in the neo-colonial world.

It was outrage at these conditions that propelled the youth in particular to take to the streets in the G8 protests in Edinburgh in their hundreds of thousands, which was matched by massive demonstrations elsewhere. In our intervention in this kind of demonstration we seek to echo the anger with fighting slogans. At the same time it is necessary to draw out general conclusions from this and to explain the alternative. In the Edinburgh protests we began with the plight of the masses in the neo-colonial world: "The poverty of Africa is not an act of god but the product of a system, capitalism, which is based upon production for profit for the benefit of a few at the expense of the social needs of billions on this planet. Just over 500 rich individuals, overwhelmingly men, the owners of the large transnational companies, have as much income as three billion people, half the world's population." We went on to explain that gross inequality was reason enough to oppose the system but the owners of this wealth were also incapable of taking society forward. It had become obsolete and therefore should be removed: "This is a failed system... corporate profits soar, 89 countries are worse off than in the early 1990s." This arose from the unequal terms of trade between the rich capitalist and imperialist West – the US, Japan and the EU – and the neo-colonial world itself.

The way to change the situation was neither by wringing hands nor by seeking to butter up capitalist dignitaries which, unfortunately, was the method adopted by some of the official organisers of the G8 protests like celebrities Bob Geldof and Bono. They had a tendency to greet uncritically small, exceedingly small promises for increased debt relief to 18 countries in Africa. The same governments that promised this aid, such as Blair's in Britain, also presided over a system which was stripping English-speaking sub-Saharan Africa of its doctors and nurses. An estimated 60% of doctors trained in Ghana in the 1980s had left the country. There were more Ghanaian doctors in New York than in Ghana itself! The same analogies could be drawn with any of the advanced industrial countries.

Jeffrey Sachs, former neo-liberal guru and now a repentant

"friend of the poor", said that debt relief proposals are new "weapons of mass salvation". We declared that they were nothing of the kind. All the debt relief and aid taken together was like taking a thimble to empty an ocean. One example of this was the agreement to lift the debts of 18 countries, which did not take account of the monumental amounts that were still owed to private banks. Moreover, the poorest third of developing countries had seen their share of world trade fall by a quarter. At the same time, it was estimated that the cost of money-laundering amounted to $2.5 trillion, approaching 10% of the world's GDP! We declared: "There is no way we can begin to eradicate this gangsterism without nationalising the banks and finance houses and establishing a state monopoly of trade."

This was the reality of 'modern' capitalism, which Tony Blair and George Bush were offering in Edinburgh as a 'model' for the world. They may 'regret' some features of their system which produces poverty but ultimately they defend it lock, stock and barrel, by force if necessary. Hence the Iraq invasion whose real purpose was not to root out terrorism but to grab the country's vast oil reserves. Capitalism by its very nature is an unplanned system, based as it is on private ownership of the means of production, distribution and exchange by a few oligarchs. It is the reason why any mention of 'planning' society or even partially in one industry is denounced almost as the work of the devil! Yet there is a high degree of planning internally in the great transnational corporations. If there is a surplus of one component or a scarcity then it is an administrative decision within a factory or a company to move resources so there is 'equilibrium'. In this way a certain harmony in production is established, which ends once the produced goods are thrown onto the market. There anarchy reigns and chaos is king. With a 'surplus' of unsold goods, 'equilibrium' is ultimately established once more by the closure of some industries, the eviction of workers from the factories and in time, in theory at least, their absorption back into 'growth industries'.

Capitalism is also an inefficient and wasteful system. This has been demonstrated again and again under the present phase of venal and aggressive imperialism. This was indicated by the US's attempt in the period following its seeming military triumph in Iraq to completely dominate the world militarily – 'full spectrum domination' – full control, by the use of military power, of the world and its resources. We posed the question: "Imagine what would be possible if the wasteful expenditure of capitalism was utilised for useful production for the benefit of all."

The rejoinder of the bosses to this is usually: "You cannot allow unskilled (meaning ignorant) workers to manage complex industries; that is the role of specialists." Firstly, those close to production, the producers, usually have a better idea of how to improve efficiency and the running of industry than the so-called experts. Vodafone conducted a poll, reported by the Daily Mirror in June 2005, in which 70% of workers felt that "their brainwaves were unrewarded" and 24% "never even bothered to tell anyone about their ideas". One of the reasons for this was that suggestions to increase efficiency and thereby boost productivity under capitalism can result in workers being sacked. Why, therefore, should working people cut their own throats by helping the bosses to boost profitability and then emptying them out of the factories? Also, the idea that workers are 'too selfish' and uneducated to run and control industry is false.

An example of this selfishness was the alleged refusal of French workers to work an extra 'Solidarity Day' during the heat wave of 2003 when some of the elderly in France died in the torrid conditions. The French workers refused to do this not because they were 'selfish' or didn't sympathise with the elderly but because it was a cynical ploy by the right-wing Raffarin government to demand 'sacrifices' while attacking pensions, thereby the old, and also trying to eliminate the 35-hour week. On the basis of a democratic, socialist planned economy with ownership in the hands of the majority instead of a handful of parasites the working class would respond to a genuine call for 'all' to make sacrifices.[2]

These were the ideas that we took onto the streets of Edinburgh and in the meetings which we organised around the G8 protests. A colossal 250,000 demonstrators filled the Scottish capital, the biggest demonstration Edinburgh had ever seen. The CWI contingent -- with comrades from England and Wales, Scotland, Belgium, France, Sweden, Germany and elsewhere staying in a camp near Edinburgh – made a magnificent intervention in this demonstration. Paula Mitchell, London Regional Secretary, recorded: "Impossible not to be moved by the... CWI rally on Saturday after the main demo. I heard the comment, 'That was fantastic' again and again. A great sea of red filled the hall. About 160 had packed in, and easily half that number again [was] listening outside, nearly all wearing the brilliant red CWI/ISR T-shirts."[3] Leading speakers– Philip Stott and Sinead Daly from Scotland, comrades Titi from Nigeria and Joe Higgins, Socialist Party TD from Ireland, and myself for the CWI's International Secretariat – addressed this memorable meeting.

It was just one example of the growing influence of the CWI, particularly in attracting some of the best layers of the youth moving into struggle at this stage. Needless to say, the G8 leaders – eight men – after meeting in a hotel protected by 10,000 police who made 358 arrests, never in any way proposed policies or programmes to alter the burgeoning poverty of the Third World, which in 2017 still gets worse by the day and year! The mood generated by this magnificent demonstration of youth and the working class for unity in the task of eradicating poverty and for change was a necessary reminder of the potential for radical socialist ideas.

64. London and Madrid Bombings 2005

The splendid demonstration in Edinburgh showed the enormous potential for a powerful youth and workers' movement to confront the bosses. However, the consistent failure of the right-wing trade union leaders and New Labour to utilise the situation to advance workers' interests was once more transparent. The inevitable mood of disappointment was added to by the London bombings which took place within days of the mass mobilisation at the G8. In its wake it conjured up the possibility of ruinous ethnic strife in London and elsewhere. However, when similar methods had been deployed by al-Qa'ida terrorists in Madrid a year earlier, it had the opposite effect by reinforcing mass opposition to the wars in Iraq and Afghanistan and class unity.

Al-Qa'ida and such terrorists have a warped sense that they are acting on behalf of the 'oppressed masses'. But nothing could be further from the truth. It is the poor masses and working class who reap the bloody harvest of their work, above all in those countries where the majority of the population is Muslim. The bombings in Madrid inflicted the greatest suffering against those who opposed the war: the working class and the youth. The largest number of deaths took place on a double-decker train in a working-class sub-urb of Madrid. Large numbers of migrant workers from Latin America and Eastern Europe lived there. Among the dead were many trade union activists, students and workers.

Like many others these victims had marched against the war in Iraq; 92% of Spaniards had opposed the war, which had been enthusiastically backed by the right-wing People's Party (Partido Popular – PP) government of José Maria Aznar. This government tried to exploit the bombings by blaming them on the Basque nationalist forces, with a history of terrorism. The masses angrily refused to buy this tale; rage swelled up against the government. This attack took place in the week before a general election. Consequently the PP share of the vote fell from 44.52% in 2000 to 37.08%; they lost over 690,000 votes. The beneficiary of this angry mood was the so-called 'Socialist Party' (Partido Socialista Obrero Español – PSOE) which was by this time a staunch supporter of Spanish capitalism, 'socialist' only in name. Nevertheless, the defeat of the PP was seen as a big victory by the workers and the youth. Unfortunately, the alternative of the United Left (Izquierda Unida – IU, dominated by the Spanish 'Communist' Party) signalled that it was 'loyal' to the new government and did not offer any real alternative to the 'market-friendly government'. The leader of PSOE, José Luis Zapatero, was able to rule for a fairly lengthy period on the basis of an artificial boom in the 2000s, which eventually spectacularly collapsed resulting in mass unemployment and poverty.

However, the London bombings of 7 July 2005 (7/7) did not have the same political repercussions by toppling Tony Blair, the dual architect with Bush of the Iraq disaster. When it took place there was a huge wellspring of sympathy and solidarity for the victims of the London Underground and bus bombings. We pointed out: "The unspeakable horrors that have been visited on the innocent have produced a deep sense of outrage in London, throughout the country, and even internationally." Those who carried out this heinous act deserved the unqualified condemnation of working people everywhere. We also pointed out that "So do those who have created the conditions for the growth of terrorism." Eager to shift blame, Blair rushed out a statement arguing the "Iraq war had nothing to do with the events of 7/7". Incredibly, Ken Livingstone, who had now re-joined the 'war party' of New Labour, together with 'eminent Islamic scholars', all agreed with Blair in an article in the Independent!

However, this was not the view of the government's own Joint Intelligence Committee, which warned before the war that the terrorist threat "to Western interests... would be heightened by military action against Iraq". The year before this bombing a former Australian Foreign Minister said: "The net result of the war on terror is more war and more terror. Look at Iraq; the least plausible reason for going to war – terrorism – has been its most harrowing consequence."[1]

Jack Straw, in an unreal intervention, stated that the bombings had "come out of the blue". He must have been the only person in Britain who held this view, as police and intelligence chiefs had warned relentlessly that it was not a question of 'if' but 'when' such an attack would be made. This bombing was a direct result of the terrible war in Iraq and the subsequent occupation.[2]

Its effects on working people in the capital were reflected in the pages of The Socialist. Hugo Pierre, local government worker and Socialist Party member, commented on the effects on workers: "I contacted shop stewards in the Town Hall, opposite Kings Cross station. It had been evacuated because of further bomb threats and staff were moved to a neighbouring building. Everyone was told to stay in their workplace and not to travel until they were given further advice. Eventually a message was sent to tell people that buses and tubes were shut down and they could walk home."[3]

A London bus driver also wrote: "One Muslim driver at my garage told me he'd got abuse from some passengers after the bombings. Working-class Muslims in Iraq are victims of both the invading armies and the terrorists. In London they face the anger of a mindless minority... I don't see how Blair can ever stop the threat of terrorism. He's the one who's fanned the flames. He can't eliminate the causes."[4]

The effects of the cuts on the fire service were illustrated by a fireman writing: "Only a month before the bombings, one of the two fire engines based at Bethnal Green Fire Station was removed, as part of a 'reorganisation' by the London Fire Authority. Altogether 10 fire engines were taken from fire stations in inner London and transferred to outer London stations along with a number of firefighters."[5]

The Socialist Party, particularly our comrades on the Stop the War Coalition steering committee, pressed for demonstrations within days to show that the anti-war movement was opposed to terrorism as well as to the war and occupation in Iraq. In particular, they were concerned about any racist backlash or an erosion of civil liberties in the aftermath of these bombings. This initiative, however, was not taken up. Meanwhile, the Guardian reported Blair at a Cabinet meeting, "likening Islamic extremism to the Trotskyist Militant Tendency".[6] As SP general secretary, I wrote an immediate protest letter to the newspaper: "Blair's remarks are an outrageous slur. Militant Tendency, now the Socialist Party, has always condemned terrorism; both the terrorism of individuals and groups both in Britain, Ireland and internationally, and the state terrorism of the US and British governments that is estimated to have resulted in the death of 100,000 civilians in Iraq."[7]

The effects of the bombing radiated beyond London. Mike Foster, Unison representative in Kirklees in Yorkshire, knew the mother of one of the alleged 7/7 bombers. He wrote in the Socialist: "When I read newspaper stories of the arrests in West Yorkshire, I realised that the Dewsbury bomber was the son-in-law of... a Unison member I visited only three weeks ago. I knew that she'd be devastated... I rang the school and spoke to the steward. Word had already got out. I explained the need for discipline, things would get tough in the workplace. I also rang the head teacher and offered the union's help in dealing with any difficulties. Later [the Unison member] rang me, distraught... She had been forced to flee her house... She was terrified of the BNP who live up the road from her. She wanted to clear her name – could the union help?"[8] This is just an example of how the trade union movement is able to step in, as in Northern Ireland over many years, to defend those subjected to or threatened with attack from bigots, which in the process can help to create class unity.

Fear was sweeping through Muslim communities that more bomb attacks would lead to a racist backlash and that the government was trying to exploit the bombings for the purpose of proposing measures against Muslims. In particular, as with previous bombings of Britain by the IRA, there was an attempt to push through emergency measures that would massively restrict civil liberties. Along with others we energetically campaigned against this attack and participated in the protests at the killing of an innocent man on the London Underground, Jean Charles de Menezes. To this day, the culprits have not been brought to justice. We also demanded a genuine public inquiry under the democratic control of trade union and community organisations into these events, as well as police heavy-handedness when it was reported that the driver of a tube train in Stockwell station was held at gunpoint. We also drew a connection with what had happened in the US in the aftermath of the 9/11 attacks, with the introduction of draconian laws and internment in Guantánamo Bay under the guise of taking measures against 'terrorists'.

Britain already had the most sweeping anti-terrorist legislation in Western Europe. This did not stop Blair from declaring at a press conference: "The rules of the game have changed."[9] The fact that such a serious issue as terrorism and the gnawing fear which this engendered were referred to as a 'game' earned Blair the scorn of even capitalist commentators. Proposals for the setting up of a special secret anti-terrorist court, the granting of punitive powers to investigating magistrates – along the pattern of the French judicial system – and the right to detain people without charge in terror cases for up to three months had even the judges up in arms. In effect, these proposals ratified internment without trial, unprecedented in peacetime outside of Northern Ireland.

We pointed out that when such measures were introduced by the Tories in Northern Ireland in 1971, it acted as a huge recruiting sergeant for the Provisional IRA. Another half-baked measure was the threat by the government to reactivate treason laws, last used against the British Nazi collaborator, William Joyce (Lord

Haw Haw) in 1945. This was hastily dropped when it was realised that they could charge the most unlikely of people. For instance, James Hewitt could have been indicted on treason charges for having 'relations' with Diana, Princess of Wales, the wife of the future monarch!

There were also proposals to ban 'dangerous' Muslim organisations. This would only serve to drive some Muslim youth into the arms of such organisations. All of this confirmed that capitalism, which alienates the youth and reinforces poverty and discrimination, was incapable of effectively countering the ideas of right-wing Islamic fundamentalism. It was not an accident that the 7/7 bombers were representative of disconnected, alienated Muslim youth in Yorkshire towns blighted by poverty and unemployment. They saw no hope in the blind alley of British society and therefore took some refuge in the reactionary utopia of a return to a 7th century caliphate! Their inchoate anger was expressed in one poll which showed that 5% of Muslims – 7% under 35 years old – 'justified' the suicide bombings in Britain. Two thirds of Muslims expressed the wish to leave Britain following the atmosphere created by 7/7.

The anti-terror legislation introduced in the aftermath of the bombings only served to widen the discontent and alienate Muslims young and old. We made it clear that the Socialist Party, while opposing such undemocratic actions, did not condone the bombers or oppose effective class measures which defended innocent Londoners. There was real fear of venturing onto the Underground or taking a bus, signified by a 30% drop in tube travel and a big increase in the number of cyclists. We reiterate: the only way to counter this danger is to first of all understand the roots of terrorism. The fear of Londoners was real but the government was using this as a means of strengthening its own wrong undemocratic policies, to deflect responsibility from itself and vilify anybody who sought to explain the roots of modern terrorism.

These arguments had little effect, as expected, on New Labour or its Home Secretary, Charles Clarke. With over 200 'anti-terrorism' legal measures already in existence, Blair's government was subject to widespread criticism from civil rights campaigners and others for planning more. Yet Clarke, with Blair's support, introduced a whole slew of such measures. The police themselves admitted that the government had already introduced more than sufficient powers to arrest and prosecute suspects where there was evidence of terrorism.

65. "Labour a sham": Steps towards a new party 2005-07

Friedrich Engels commented about the distinctive characteristics of the British working class and its organisations: "One cannot drum theory into them beforehand but their own experience and their own blunders and the resulting evil consequences will blunt their noses up against theory and then all right. Independent peoples go their own way, and the English and their offspring are surely the most independent of them all. Insular, stiff-necked obstinacy annoys one often enough, but it also guarantees that what is begun will be carried out once things get started."[1]

Since Engels wrote these lines the British working class has been renewed many times. Yet his acute observation still retains all its force today. When a fundamentally new departure is called for, involving the abandonment of one outmoded, used-up political party and its replacement by a new one, these characteristics are on display. The idea of a new mass workers' party was first posed by the Socialist Party in the early 1990s well in advance, as we have shown, of the ill-fated launch of Arthur Scargill's Socialist Labour Party.

Other countries had witnessed earlier the birth of new political formations. The best-known of these were Rifondazione Comunista in Italy, Die Linke (the Left Party) in Germany, P-SoL in Brazil and, since then, Syriza in Greece and Podemos in Spain. Yet the British labour movement, with its empirical, almost ponderous traditions,

545

has not as yet followed this path despite big efforts on the part of Socialist Party members and trade unions like the RMT to persuade the more politically advanced British workers to take even the first steps along this path. Nevertheless, they will proceed in this direction as the election to the Labour leadership of Jeremy Corbyn has shown. This phenomenon – which took everybody by surprise, including Corbyn himself – developed as a mass anti-austerity mood initially outside the Labour Party. As we write, Labour is now composed of two parties locked in a civil war. It is to be hoped that Corbyn and the new forces will predominate, which could create, in effect, a new party.

The Brown and Blair government, with their blatant pro-capitalist bias, helped us considerably to make the case for a new party. Christopher Beale, chairperson of the Institute of Directors, declared in 2006: "So far, so good. Within reason, we have a business friendly government." So demoralised were Labour's ranks that only a third of constituency Labour parties bothered to spend the £500 to attend the 2006 Party conference in Brighton, presided over by Blair and Brown "wielding a neo-liberal club to crush any lingering hopes for a genuine swing towards the left within the party."

The total disconnect of the Labour Party tops from the working class was highlighted by the disgraceful ejection of the 82-year-old refugee from Nazi Germany, Walter Wolfgang, for daring to shout out "Nonsense!" at Jack Straw's claim that those who opposed the Iraq war were "pro-Nazi sympathisers". Walter was held and questioned by police under Section 44 of the Prevention of Terrorism Act! We commented: "Twenty years to the month, the Daily Mirror [which objected in an editorial to the treatment of Walter Wolfgang] cheered on Neil Kinnock in his infamous denunciation of Militant (now the Socialist Party). Paraphrasing the words used by Kinnock, who is now a multi-millionaire: 'You start by expelling Militants for fighting for socialism and you end up with the grotesque chaos of manhandling and ejecting an 82-year-old protester.'"[2]

Walter stated that the party had been "taken over by a gang of political adventurers".[3] Then somewhat despairingly but ironically, he remarked: "I will remain a member [of the Labour Party] for the simple reason that we can outlive them." We remarked: "The courageous Walter deserves full marks for his perspectives on his own longevity but not for the Labour Party itself."[4] We had warned in advance that the expulsion of Militant supporters could end up with the destruction of the Labour Party as a genuine working class party. In the disgraceful scenes played out in Brighton this was confirmed.

Even worse was the brutal restatement in Brighton by the New Labour leadership of the neo-liberal mantra of no concessions to trade unions, despite persistent demands for the abolition of Thatcher's law preventing 'secondary solidarity action' by fellow trade unionists. Further privatisation, particularly of the NHS and schools, would be the calamitous consequences of a continuation of this government's programme, we said. There was no action proposed to alleviate the desperate housing problem. Support for big business in general was affirmed but particularly the paving of the way for the bosses to get children's education into their clutches with a massive introduction of academies.

All of this was spelt out in Brighton. In other words, more of the same, only worse, was promised for working class people. Those who hoped that Gordon Brown would be like a 'socialist' St George, slaying the New Labour Dragon once he was prime minister, were disappointed by his interviews and speeches at the conference. He restated his enthusiastic support for the New Labour project.

Even Guardian writer Polly Toynbee, once of the right-wing split from the Labour Party, the Social Democratic Party, wrote: "Brighton has exposed Labour as a shell, deserted by members... Labour is in danger of becoming a phantom party – a self-perpetuating oligarchy given absolute power by only 25% of the electorate through a perverted voting system that will, with a swing of the pendulum, deliver the same power to an equally unrepresentative Tory clique."[5] Brian Reade went further: "The Labour Party conference is about as pointless as a surfboard in an ice rink... How to stop collapsing in hysterics when they sing the Red Flag. From mass-produced prompt cards."[6]

Yet what remained of the left stubbornly refused to draw the obvious conclusion that Labour as a vehicle for the working class was dead in the water. They pointed to the conference decisions against further privatisation of the NHS and other issues. The reality was, as we pointed out, that there was "less chance today of Blair or Brown repudiating this and the... pernicious anti-union laws introduced by Thatcher than the Liberals... in 1906."[7]

That Liberal government, under pressure from the newly created Labour Party, did repudiate the House of Lords anti-union Taff Vale judgement, which awarded heavy damages against unions taking industrial action. Yet the equivalent of Taff Vale today was precisely the prohibition of 'secondary action', which seeks to effectively neuter workers from taking industrial action in support of their brothers and sisters fighting against pernicious bosses and slave-like conditions and wages.

A similar well-known example is the austerity programme proposed by Ramsay Macdonald in 1931 which came up against the rock of working class and organised trade union resistance. Macdonald could not push his programme through and therefore broke with the Labour Party and established the 'National Government'. The Blair government did not need to do that for two reasons. Firstly, this was, to all intents and purposes, a 'national government', the best that the British capitalists could expect at that stage. Secondly, the trade unions were effectively politically neutered while the Blairite iron grip was exercised over the party at all levels.

Politically superficial commentators smugly point to the history of the labour movement with examples of where the Labour leadership ignored conference decisions, at a time when it was a genuine working-class party at the base. However on decisive issues, particularly those which directly affected the working class, the specific weight of the trade unions was sufficient to force the leadership either to back away or be broken, as mentioned earlier over Labour's own anti-union proposals, 'In Place of Strife', in 1969.

The Tribunite left demonstrated in article after article that the

New Labour project was unreconstructed Thatcherism. This applied not just to Blair but to Brown also. He had declared before the conference: "The programme of reform [read counter-reform – PT] and modernisation will continue when Tony steps down."[8] Brown wanted "more home ownership, more asset ownership. He wants – some claim – to be more Thatcherite than Blair," commented Jackie Ashley.[9] It began to dawn on more and more of those genuine socialists who remained in the Labour Party that there was little possibility of arresting this pro-capitalist development.

This was underlined by, amongst many, Colin McCabe, a representative of the artistic intelligentsia who had gone along with New Labour up to then. He announced his resignation from the Labour Party following the conference after 41 years of membership. He simply wrote of Blair: "You lie as you breathe."[10] He was 'answered' by Denis McShane, the Blairite former minister, later jailed for fiddling his expenses: "Please think again comrades." McShane defended Blair: "I was in France and Germany. Both countries would die to have a Tony Blair leading them out of high unemployment." We commented that only a matter of months previous to this, the French and Dutch working class showed in EU constitution referenda what they thought of 'Blairism'! The massive 'No' votes were as much a vote against Anglo-Saxon neo-liberalism, symbolised above all by Blair, as against even the EU constitution itself. The German working class at this stage had also seen what Thatcher and Blair had inflicted on the British workers and wanted none of it.[11]

The Campaign Group of MPs also held the forlorn hope that the Labour Party could be transformed. It had been suggested that they would put up a 'stalking horse' against Blair that could trigger an electoral contest for the Labour leadership in 2006. Even if this had succeeded, the victorious candidate that emerged would likely be Brown, "the replacement of Tweedledum by Tweedledee". We also warned: "The disappointment of the last eight years of Blairism will be compounded by an epoch of Brownism. It could pave the way for the return of the hated Tories, perhaps given a facelift by some kind of Cameron-Clarke duumvirate." This prognosis was born out to the letter, although 'Brownism' lasted much shorter than we anticipated, and also Cameron initially shared power with the Liberal Democrat Nick Clegg – which amounted to the same thing! We also pointed out: "The daily drip feed of attacks on the working class, which can be enormously aggravated by a new world economic recession or slump, will continue apace."

At the same time we supported Bob Crow's suggestion that we could call a conference in early 2006 of organisations and parties to discuss the idea of a new party. Naturally the Socialist Party welcomed this because it gave some industrial and trade union basis for the first steps towards a new party. However, we warned against a repetition of Respect which "was unlikely to make a significant breakthrough amongst broader layers of the working class". We also pointed to the recent success of the left alliance in Germany which became Die Linke winning 8% of the vote and 50 MPs in the 2005 federal election. The repercussions of this development would be felt throughout Europe and not least in Britain. It is true that the Left Party did not develop in a straight line but a start had been made towards a genuine left party (not yet fulfilled).[12]

The crucial difference between the two countries was that in Britain there was no major left figure or trade union leader apart from Bob Crow who had called for action to create the conditions for a real new mass party, as Oskar Lafontaine had in Germany. We therefore pressed the leaders of the left, particularly the left trade union leaders, to come out boldly for such a party. There appeared to be every chance, given the disillusionment with the Blair government, that this was likely to develop at this time. Those who still clung to the Labour Party in the hope that it could be 'reformed' were just recycling the arguments of those adherents to the 'Lib-Lab' philosophy who tried to capture the Liberal Party for the working class in the latter part of the 19th century.

When the RMT's political conference was held, despite expectations and a large attendance, it became quite clear that while Bob was in favour of taking the initiative, in his opinion the RMT was not yet quite ready. He therefore proposed that in preparation for such a party a conference should take the initiative of establishing a shop stewards network. The result was the founding of the National Shop Stewards Network (NSSN) which was destined to play a crucial role in the industrial battles that developed under both New Labour and Conservative-led governments from 2007 onwards.

There was undoubtedly disappointment, once more, that the first step towards a new mass party was further delayed. This necessitated us launching the Campaign for a New Workers' Party (CNWP). At its conference in March 2006 Socialist Party councillor Dave Nellist reported that more than 1,300 people had signed its 'Declaration for a New Workers' Party' from 25 different trade unions and a whole range of community campaigns. Mark Serwotka, general secretary of the civil servants' union PCS, congratulated the organisers of the event on a "magnificent turnout". He pointed out that in the previous six months 14 unions gave more than £1.6 million to New Labour yet "many of those unions are having to take strike action to defend their members against the government's attacks on their pension rights".

Claus Ludwig, a councillor for the new party in Germany 'Election Alternative for Work and Justice' (Arbeit und soziale Gerechtigkeit – Die Wahlalternative – WASG) reported on its success and the discussion about a possible merger with Die Linke, which had been in the Berlin regional government and had carried out neo-liberal attacks on the working class. The CWI in Germany opposed this and he commented: "Talking about socialism on Sunday and carrying out cuts during the week was no way forward." There was some debate at this gathering on what would be the character of a new party, an ongoing issue in Britain, the Socialist Party favouring the development of a party which is federal in character with the affiliation of trade unions, socialist parties and groups.[13]

Shortly afterwards it was reported that the number signed up in support of a new workers' party had reached more than 2,000. The character of this campaign was largely propagandistic at this stage, preparing the ground for developments later, particularly in the trade unions. A second successful conference took place in 2007 and subsequently other gatherings maintained the momentum for a new party. However, it met with resistance from those such as the Labour Representation Committee (LRC) and Respect. Labour MP John McDonnell was the only leading figure behind the LRC. He had considerable influence and respect beyond the Labour Party's ranks, particularly with trade union leaders. However, there was no clear strategy by him or the LRC beyond calling for trade unionists to become party members. At its conference in 2006 one delegate pleaded: "I'm not asking you to be happy about joining the Labour Party; it pains me every time I write out a cheque for my subscription." John argued that it was wrong to found a new party and instead the aim should be to "re-found" Labour. He said he would like to see the RMT and the FBU back in the party. Ironically, as Bob Crow pointed out, none of the unions backing the LRC at this stage was affiliated to Labour. On the other hand, none of them was taking the necessary step of giving union backing to the idea of forming a new party either.[14]

Despite this, John McDonnell threw his hat in the ring for the leadership of the Labour Party but he did not even get the backing of the 45 Labour MPs necessary to get on the ballot paper. Bob Crow also stated that his members and many other trade unionists did not see New Labour "in any sense as 'their party' and would not join". This was vindicated by the fact that wherever workers had taken strike action, it had tended to increase demands for unions to disaffiliate from the Labour Party. Nowhere had strikes led to an influx of workers joining New Labour to change it, as was the case when the Labour Party was a workers' party. Despite our differences with John McDonnell, we nevertheless gave critical support to his leadership campaign. In the course of the debates and discussions around his candidature we hoped to be able to get our message through to a wider audience.[15]

A new volume of Tony Benn's diaries appeared in 2007: More Time for Politics, Diaries 2001-2007. In them, he took a pop at the Socialist Party and others on the left: "The setting up of a new Socialist Party is a waste of time."[16] In our review of the diaries, we posed the question "What is his alternative to the Socialist Party's idea of a new mass workers' party?" Tony Benn's answer was: "There is a vacuum and that's what the Labour conference has to do, fill the vacuum, because you cannot have a democratic system without a serious alternative, and people want a Labour government."[17] This was naive to say the least; Labour, as Tony freely admitted throughout his diaries, was now mainly stuffed with Blair and Brown's toadies, right-wing councillors who carried through cuts and sheep-like MPs who trotted into the division lobbies of the House of Commons to back them up.

Then there was what actually happened at the conference where Tony expected there to be an alternative: "New Labour is more violently anti-union and anti-left than for many, many years... Constituencies are no longer on the left, because all the decent socialists have left, so it's a Blairite romp."[18] As if to put the concluding arguments for a new party, unconsciously it might be added, Tony wrote: "What Blair is doing is privatising the Labour Party. He wants to get rid of the trade unions. After all, 7 million trade unionists give £7 million, and 10 million people contributed nearly £14 million and some end up in the Lords. My dad left the Liberal Party because Lloyd George was so corrupt in his use of patronage."[19] Very good advice which, unfortunately, the late stalwart of the left did not follow with actions. We concluded: "Sadly, Tony Benn rejects this path. It will not stop the march of history, which will see in Britain, as in other countries, new political formations of the working class."[20]

Mark Serwotka wrote an article at this stage for The Socialist indicating his support for a new party: "We need to do more than mount an effective industrial campaign. We need to consider what can be done in the political arena to challenge the new pro-business, anti-welfare state consensus between all three main parties... This has led to a growing debate within the trade unions about political representation. When this debate takes place, the question quickly turns to the existing political choices that we have." This was the reason why, he explained, the PCS was using its political fund on 'Make Your Vote

Count' to further the campaign for new political representation.

He pointed to the recent successes of the ssp in Scotland and George Galloway, elected as a Respect MP, despite the difficulties of the electoral system for new parties. We recognised that these represented limited advances. He also pointed towards what he called the "split nature of the left... On 17 November last year, I found myself speaking to three competing left events in London – the Labour Representation Committee, the Socialist Party and the Respect conference." He also argued in favour of incorporating "the left in the Labour Party", which he claimed had an important role. He recognised the positive role played by John McDonnell, as the chair of the PCS Parliamentary group, in assisting his union amongst others.[21]

This contribution of Mark led to a debate in the Socialist. I answered some of Mark's points: "Unfortunately, Mark, while making some useful suggestions, has not set out a strategy to create such a force [a new party] in Britain. The Socialist Party, and particularly Socialist Party members in the PCS who have a considerable influence, support the union's initiative 'Make Your Vote Count.'" Moreover, Mark recognised by implication that the idea of a new mass workers' party was popular: "I am in no doubt that the 2005 PCS ballot on setting up a political fund was won, in part, because we would not donate to, or affiliate to any political party – including Labour." We posed the question to Mark: "Why not then suggest that those unions still tied to Labour should immediately disaffiliate and join in the campaign for a new party?"

He made a plea that we should accept the "important role" of the left in the Labour Party. We recognised that Labour MPs such as John McDonnell and ex-MPs like Tony Benn "still have political authority but one that can diminish in the stormy events that impend in Britain if they insist on clinging to the battered wreckage of the Labour Party. We are prepared to work with the Labour left on resisting attacks, the need to repeal anti-union legislation, etc. But we will also criticise them." We also recognised that the PCS was correct to utilise left MPs to support and enhance its campaign and its position in Parliament. Before the formation of the Labour Party, the unions utilised sections of the Lib-Lab MPs in a similar role. But this did not prevent the pioneers of the Labour Party from criticising these very same MPs for propping up the Liberal Party, a bulwark of capitalism. Left MPs "imprisoned in New Labour, [are] reduced to smuggling out protest notes through the bars".[22]

We followed this up with discussions with others on the left, like Respect and the Socialist Workers Party, despite our differences with them. We have set out our differences with the SWP in our book Socialism and Left Unity which is both of an historical and contemporary character. Our criticisms of Respect were mentioned previously.

66. Party activity 2005-07

The period before the 2005 general election and afterwards were successful years in terms of membership and the growth of our resources. In 2005 the Socialist Party raised over £100,000 for its fighting fund. The National Committee therefore proposed increasing the fighting fund quarterly target to £25,000 and increasing membership dues by £3,000 a month. It was also agreed that a drive to increase paper sales should be a priority. The 2006 Party Congress agreed after discussion a target for the year of 700 new members. It also received a report from our Youth Department about the success of Socialist Students, which had been set up in 49 universities with over a thousand students signed up during the freshers' fairs. The Campaign for a New Workers' Party (CNWP) was receiving an echo within the labour movement. It received a warm response at that year's RMT conference on political representation.

2006 also saw an important milestone for Socialism Today, which celebrated the production of its hundredth issue (prior to this, we produced Militant International Review, intermittently however). Socialism Today, in contrast, maintained 10 issues per year. Moreover, "Events since Issue Number 1 have, in our view, confirmed the key importance of the issues we raised and validated our approach." This was in the teeth of a continuous ideological barrage in favour of the 'triumph of capitalism', the European Parliament... adopted a resolution condemning "the crimes of totalitarian communist regimes."

The ideological offensive was not a genuine attempt to clarify the character of the former Stalinist regimes of the Soviet Union and Eastern Europe. It was yet another attempt to use the record of Stalinism to discredit genuine socialism. There were still people on the left, of course, who continued to act as apologists for Stalinism. Seamus Milne, who later became Jeremy Corbyn's press officer after his election to the leadership, rightly asked why the European Parliament was taking no steps to publicise and repudiate the bloody history of European colonialism and imperialism. While referring to the social gains achieved by the workers in the former Soviet Union, however, Milne sidestepped the issue of totalitarian repression and an absence of workers' democracy under Stalinism, writing "No major political tradition is without blood on its hands." Jeremy Corbyn, on the other hand, supported a motion in 1988 from Terry Fields, 'Militant' and Labour MP, calling on Russian President Gorbachev to rehabilitate Leon Trotsky, which Gorbachev never did!

The impression given by Milne of the former Soviet Union was of an authentic, if imperfect, model for socialism. This meant that socialist publications, particularly The Socialist and Socialism Today, needed to explain the Soviet Union's contradictory nature: the positive of the planned economy; and the negative of bureaucratic dictatorship. This was vital for Marxists in differentiating between Stalinism and the genuine democratic socialism of Marxism. One of the authors of the resolution in the European Parliament gave the game away when he said that it was not just to remember the victims of communism but to combat "communist nostalgia" for public ownership, the class struggle and "elements of communist ideology, such as equality or social justice [which] still seduce many". The MEPs voted 99 to 42 with 12 abstentions for the possessing classes' message: that there is no alternative to capitalism and any attempt to change the system will lead to violent totalitarianism.

We argued the case for genuine socialism and Marxism against the background of many left organisations that had in reality capitulated to the notion that there was no alternative to the capitalist market. George Monbiot, a prominent figure in the anti-globalisation and anti-capitalist movement of the streets, complained: "Whenever anyone announced that capitalism in all its forms should be overthrown, everyone cheered. But is this what we really want? And, if so, with what do we hope to replace it? And could that other system be established without violent repression?"[1] In other words, "No, there is no alternative to capitalism." We replied that a genuine socialist transformation, a socialist revolution, could only be carried through with the overwhelming support of the majority of the population. The working class today is immeasurably stronger and on a much higher cultural level than the working class in Russia in 1917. It would never therefore allow a greedy, totalitarian bureaucratic regime to usurp power from a democratic workers' state, in which the voice and actions of working people would dominate.[2]

Many who were unwilling to take to the difficult road of electing just one or two councillors in the beginning, with the intention of becoming the majority later, dismissed our attempts at gaining representation on councils. "It was ineffective; a handful of councillors could achieve very little." In fact, the record of Socialist councillors in a number of areas such as Coventry or Lewisham in South London showed that a great deal could be achieved. Chris Flood and Ian Page, councillors for Telegraph Hill Ward, pointed out in The Socialist: "We played a leading part in forcing Lewisham's Labour administration to build a new school to replace one that was knocked down – Labour had always argued against a new school," said Chris. He went on: "So this is an on-going campaign. Importantly, we are the only councillors in the borough arguing consistently against cuts and closures and privatisation. We are leading an anti-housing sell-off campaign at present." This struggle was linked by us to socialist change and an alternative to the parties of big business. It also showed that socialist methods and ideas were still very popular: "In that sense it's about raising and maintaining the banner of socialism. It gives a profile to the Socialist Party."

Karen McKay, Socialist councillor in Coventry, commented

that she and her fellow councillors Dave Nellist and Rob Windsor had won many battles for local residents: "We stand for the possibility of alternatives to privatised services and for change. Most councillors don't know what that feels like, as they have to toe a party line which is not in people's best interests. They accept the limitations that the government puts on local budgets and services, while we argue to fight for more."

Chris Flood explained: "Just look at how discredited Labour are currently! Lewisham Labour are straight out of this New Labour mould. In fact they are ultra-Blairite. We are the only principled opposition party in the council chamber. In our ward, Telegraph Hill, the contest is literally a vote between us and Labour. A vote for anyone else is a waste. Would-be Greens and Liberals need to vote for us! But we will obviously be calling on our core support as well."

Ian Page added: "All the other parties are the same. They all vote for cuts in the council chamber. The Lib Dems, Conservatives and the Greens in Lewisham have all supported Labour's policies on education and housing and even voted against our motion to call on the government to fund the budget deficit at Lewisham Hospital."[3]

In Yorkshire the health service had been under continuous attack and was the issue around which a successful campaign was conducted to have Socialist Party member and GP Jackie Grunsell elected as a councillor. This was just part of an ongoing campaign to save the NHS from the privateers, a battle which is all the more intense today. The campaign began when the hospital trust and local primary care trusts announced plans to centralise services. They wanted to move maternity, children's and surgical services from Huddersfield to Halifax and also close a local hospital, St. Luke's. The councillors were lobbied but they refused to join the campaign. Only then did the Socialist Party decide to stand a candidate with massive local support. Jackie won with 2,176 votes, a majority of 807 in the Crossland Moor and Netherton Ward, hammering the main establishment parties and the BNP. She was then inundated with phone calls with offers to help join the campaign, particularly from people in the Asian community saying, "We voted for you... We're really pleased you've won... It's the first time I've ever voted."[4]

The 'Save Huddersfield NHS campaign' sent shockwaves around the local political establishment. Jackie's victory was similar to the success of Dr Richard Taylor in 2001, when he was elected as MP for Wyre Forest, following a similar 'Save our Hospital' campaign. Mike Forster, who played a big role in the election victory, commented: "In an atmosphere where people do not appear to be participating in politics, in pubs, churches, mosques, school playgrounds and shops across this ward, people were talking about the election and discussing who they would be voting for."[5]

In 2006, Ted Grant, one of the founders of Militant, the Socialist Party's forerunner, died at the age of 93 in London. Although he had long departed from the ranks of the Socialist Party, we recognised that he had made a major contribution to the arsenal of important theoretical and political issues of Trotskyism. His followers, such as Alan Woods, ascribed to him almost political infallibility, despite the fact that he made an increasing number of serious errors in his estimation of the Labour Party and the 'mass organisations' which, he dogmatically claimed, the working class would return to "again and again". His disciples repeated this ad nauseam after his death only to repudiate this idea when they were hit in the face by reality. They completely rejected the Labour Party after the Scottish referendum. Moreover, Pasok in Greece, to which both Grant and Woods also maintained the Greek working class would turn, has also been reduced to an insignificant rump.

Incredibly, Woods in his obituary of Grant claimed: "In 1964, we [!] decided to launch a new paper called Militant. We held our first meeting in a small room in a pub in Brighton." This was a complete fabrication. Alan Woods was not involved in any Labour Party Young Socialist activity on a national scale until after 1964. Militant was founded that year but it certainly was not established "in a pub in Brighton", where Woods was a student. The reality was that the founding of Militant was mainly a product of discussions in

Liverpool and London. Woods's farcical attempt to rewrite history did no justice either to the memory of Grant or the contribution that he made. We wrote at the time: "It is a self-serving attempt to enhance Alan Woods' own 'historic' profile." Despite all his attempts to burnish his credentials as a 'pioneer' of Militant he did not play any major role in Britain. So much so that a journalist who closely followed Militant's development, Andy McSmith, in his book Faces of Labour mistakenly called him Andy Woods – mixing him up with Andy Bevan, a fellow Welshman who had dropped away from our ranks in the past.[6]

As Militant grew to become the most effective and largest Trotskyist movement in Britain and most of Europe, it was necessary to present our ideas in the most popular and accessible form. Ted Grant was no longer capable of fulfilling this role. He was incapable, like Woods himself, of adapting to changing situations, particularly after the collapse of the 'Soviet Union'. They gave 'critical support' to the organisers of the 1991 coup in the Soviet Union. They justified this on the basis that Trotsky had the position of 'critical support' for a section of the bureaucracy that would maintain the planned economy. However, the bureaucracy had long since degenerated and was no longer capable of ensuring the development of the planned economy. There was no wing in 1991 which still adhered to the planned economy. Grant stuck to a wrong, dogmatic perspective, which held that the social counter-revolution in the former Stalinist states had not 'yet' been carried out. It was only in the late 1990s that he came to the conclusion that capitalism had indeed returned in Russia. Before he split from the Socialist Party, he only received 7% of the vote at a national congress of Militant supporters against launching the 'Scottish Turn'. After this, his followers remained on the margins of the labour movement, without any real roots in Britain.[7]

The Socialist Party is of course affiliated to the CWI. It is one of the reasons why The Socialist carries so many informed articles, in depth, on international themes, as does Socialism Today and the CWI website. We encourage the exchange of opinions and discussions on important topical international issues. One such debate took place at Socialism 2006 on the important question of Cuba between myself and Bernard Regan of the National Union of Teachers, representing the Cuba Solidarity Campaign. I had written a book 'Cuba: Socialism and Democracy' which featured in this debate.

The Socialist Party was now a factor in events, particularly in the industrial field. The 2007 Socialist Party Congress addressed one of our main tasks, building a base amongst young people, starting in the universities and colleges. Matt Dobson, national coordinator of Socialist Students, explained that the Campaign to Defeat Fees was taking off, with the NUS forced to back the launch day of action. Around half joining our party were young people now involved in launching new branches.

The world economic crisis had not yet fully struck and this affected our work, particularly on the electoral field. In Coventry, which was one of our strongest bases, our local council vote held up quite well. After a hard-fought battle in St Michael's Ward, the Socialist Party narrowly lost by a majority of 84 and we now held two seats on the Council. Most of the remaining major factories in the city had declined, the main Royal Mail sorting office with 600 jobs was threatened and in the week before the election closure of the main Post Office was announced. Three years before this the Tories had gained control of the council because of anger at Labour's cuts and Blair's decision to go to war in Iraq.

Despite this setback, Coventry socialists prepared assiduously for the next round, which met with great success in 2008, the re-election of Dave Nellist.

At this stage, no matter where you turned, it was Socialist Party members and their allies who were to the fore in campaigning on the streets and in workplaces against the cuts that the New Labour government was imposing with many carried through by Labour councils. In the past, it would have been Labour and other left activists who organised and conducted this opposition but the uninterrupted, steady shift of the Labour Party towards the right led to disillusionment and a consequent unwillingness and inability to lead working people in struggle. It was Socialist Party members who were prominent in campaigns.

This was magnificently demonstrated on the issue of school meals in the London Borough of Waltham Forest. The council announced their decision to remove the subsidy to school meals and get rid of the borough's catering services, which not only financed and organised school meals but also provided 'meals on wheels' for the elderly. In just three weeks of campaigning by the local trade unions, parents and socialists, councillors were seriously rattled.

This was followed by a noisy 'pots and pans' march by around 250 angry dinner ladies, teachers, parents, supporters and children, marching from the town square to the Town Hall. A representative of the bin workers promised that if the campaign continued, "Next time he would bring the bin trucks out to block the roads." Demonstrators chanted: "If you want to keep school dinners – bang a pan". A young education worker with an Asian drum and people with pans, wooden spoons, tin lids, rattles and whistles joined in. Passers-by and shop-keepers took leaflets, offered donations and cheered the demonstration. As part of their campaign, the organisers of the demonstration contacted Jamie Oliver, the famous TV chef, who had a keen interest in making sure that the nation's children were properly fed. As a consequence he gave support to the campaign.

Waltham Forest's council leaders were forced to extend the school meal subsidy at least until 2009 – an unequivocal victory for the campaign! They capitulated but words were not enough; the demonstrators insisted that they put in writing a pledge to maintain school dinners. They promised a 12-month reprieve but one dinner lady declared: "Now we've got to fight to keep it forever. We must keep lobbying, collecting petitions and keeping ahead of what's going on." Nancy Taaffe, a key organiser of the campaign and a prominent member of the local Socialist Party branch, said: "We are not standing down the campaign. We will monitor the situation and hold all [council leader] Councillor Loakes' promises to account." Seventy copies of the Socialist were sold on the day and signatures were gathered on a petition for the CNWP declaration. When one dinner lady was asked who she would vote for in the next election, given the council's attitude towards vital services, she said: "I don't trust any of them. They're all the same now. We need a new party in there, don't we? A complete new party. Put me in there!"[8]

This was just one of a number of local campaigns which were scoring victories. The Socialist reported: "The campaign against closure of the Maudsley hospital emergency mental health clinic in south London won a concession when it was announced that the clinic would stay open for information purposes." In Southampton a four-year campaign saved St Mary's Leisure Centre and a £250,000 refurbishment was planned, while a strike by Southampton care workers fought off plans to cut pay for current staff on the council. The Unison branch balloted its members for strike action against privatisation of 800 jobs, redundancies and other cuts. More often than not it was Socialist Party members who were to the fore in these and many other campaigns. Many were lost because of ineffective trade union leadership. Nancy Taaffe remarked of the victory in Waltham Forest: "At a time when it feels like the working class does nothing but lose, this small victory feels like we've won the World Cup."

Brighton tenants also at this time dealt a massive blow to their council by voting against its privatisation plans. Greenwich Unison members, through mass meetings, forced the council into concessions on pay and a reduction in hours. Socialist Party members brought to the battle confidence in the capacity of the newly active workers to struggle and to play a role, individually and collectively. "Now give us a wage rise!" was the cry when the council leader in Waltham Forest backed down on the school meals cuts in front of an angry demonstration.

The Socialist commented: "Contrast this approach with that of most of the national trade union leaders, who often refuse to even acknowledge the massive anger that exists over attacks on the health service and on other issues, never mind taking a lead in campaigning against them. They play the role of attempting to prevent struggle, rather than helping it. If the union leaders gave a real lead against NHS cuts, devising a campaign strategy – through democratic discussion with rank and file union members – for a programme of industrial action, demonstrations and other events, the government could be stopped dead in its tracks."[9]

However, the evolution of the Socialist Party did not proceed in a straight line. This was also true of the CWI. There were periods when we made important gains, sometimes spectacularly so, and other periods when we either stood still or were even compelled to take a step or two back.

67. Post-2005 general election

Barely six months after the election that gave Blair a third term, the knives were out for him. Steve Richards wrote: "A Prime Minister re-elected six months ago faces the prospect of humiliating defeats on the pivotal elements of his entire domestic agenda ... defeat in relation to NHS policies, education, welfare reform, the introduction of ID cards, smoking bans... The leader of a parish council will have a bigger influence on events in the coming months."[1] There was talk in the Guardian of the Parliamentary Labour Party (PLP) "disintegrating". More than a fifth of the PLP did not support the government's so-called 'anti-terror' Bill, resulting in defeat by 31 votes in the Commons. We wrote: "Blair, in every speech he now makes, shows he is an unalloyed capitalist politician, refusing to make even the slightest genuflexion in words, as he did earlier, on the need for a state sector. There is not even the smallest concession to social democratic ideas, the 'mixed economy.'"[2]

He was the high priest of unreconstructed neo-liberalism. Some of his supporters took this to its logical conclusion and ended up supporting the right-wing US neo-conservatives. Jonathan Freedland wrote in the Guardian that a New Labour MP had actually supported George Bush in the previous US presidential election! Brown, in the expectation that he would soon replace Blair, defended and extolled the neo-liberal mantra.

At the annual Trade Union Congress, Blair was faced with a

rebellion of the trade union leaders, as he opposed the TUC's demand for the EU limit of a 48-hours maximum working week to be applied in Britain. This came after the government had been compelled to partially retreat over its proposals to increase the retirement age for public sector workers. The reaction of the capitalist press, however, from the Daily Telegraph to the Guardian reflected the explosion of anger of the capitalists over the pensions' agreement: "government surrender", "loss of nerve".

They were even posing the question of the usefulness of the government itself. Martin Wolf, prominent Financial Times columnist, expressed this: "Let me be frank; the public-sector unions have used their monopoly power to demand money with menaces from the taxpaying public."[3] We commented: "This is the language of war; the mere threat of strike action from the working class results in them being compared to robbers and thugs! Similar noises were made by German capitalist commentators before the 2005 general election. [Chancellor Gerhard] Schröder [leader of the 'Social Democrats'] had done the bidding of the capitalists but it was not enough; they demanded even more of their pound of flesh and concluded that only an openly capitalist government led by the CDU could carry out their wishes. However, they miscalculated and ended up with a weak, unstable coalition."

The government put forward education proposals which would clearly worsen the lot of the most disadvantaged. This signified a complete somersault from Labour's historic goals – when it was at bottom a workers' party – of education being one of the tools to end inequality in society. We never believed that without altering the economic and social foundations of inequality in society as a whole, that is by abolishing capitalism, that these goals could be achieved. Nevertheless, we generally supported comprehensive education and opposed selection. But now Blair and his Education Secretary Ruth Kelly, who left parliament and politics later, wanted to remove the 'historical consensus' which underpinned Labour's previous education aims. We predicted: "Schools will be run by businesses, middle-class schools will expand and those in working-class areas will become even more sink schools." Is this not what is taking place in 2017 with academies and free schools, and the alienation of teachers, parents and pupils alike?

Health Secretary Patricia Hewitt wanted to 'privatise' 250,000 nurses and other medical staff in one 'big bang'. Even Blairite MPs, it seemed, were alarmed at the details, which emerged when Hewitt was 'roughed up' in a meeting of the PLP. She was then compelled to withdraw this proposal. The class character of New Labour, now completely in thrall to the propertied classes, was revealed in Hewitt's interview with the Independent. She drew on historical parallels to put a case for the privatisation of healthcare. She described the defeat of Harold Wilson's anti-union proposals 'In Place of Strife' in 1969 as an 'historic mistake", as was Labour's opposition to Thatcher's policy on council house sales! As we pointed out earlier, Wilson was defeated by a mass revolt of the trade unions and Labour's rank and file but the Tories capitalised on his efforts in the vicious anti-union legislation which Thatcher introduced. Now Labour was carrying out Thatcher's 'legacy' and the fact that it had been able to get away with it said everything about the character of the Labour Party, then and now.

As to our arguments and those of others about the need to create a new mass party, Tony Benn wrote in the Guardian at this time that he witnessed, as a child, the betrayal of Ramsay MacDonald. However, he wrote that the Labour Party then recovered... in 1945! It took 14 years to overcome this betrayal! There was, however, a fundamental difference between the Labour Party of 1931 and now. Labour then was still a workers' party at bottom, even after the defection of MacDonald, although it had been reduced to 52 MPs. It remained a viable instrument within which workers could work and have an effect.

We said that even if Brown replaced Blair, as was likely, it would not make a fundamental difference to its political character. We also gave a very clear warning to the labour movement for the next election: "Although he is dismissed as a lightweight, [David] Cameron could yet lead the Tory party to an electoral victory...

Labour's victory was down to just three points." We were more correct than New Labour supporters and our critics in charting the decline of Labour, which prepared the way for Cameron's victory in 2010, albeit leading to the coalition with the Liberal Democrats. We wrote just after the 2005 election: "The proponents of the 'Orange Book' in the Liberal Democrats – which enshrines their neo-liberal programme – like Vincent Cable, their treasury spokesman and a former top oil executive, could easily sit in a Liberal Democrat/ Tory cabinet."[4]

Rumblings came from the direction of the trade unions soon after New Labour won its third term. Derek Simpson, leader of one of Britain's biggest unions Amicus (now part of Unite), told his conference after the election that it was increasingly difficult to get his members to "keep faith with the Labour government". Many Amicus members, he added, voted Labour against their better judgement. But they hoped that the delivery of 'Warwick', a reference to the previous year's agreement on 57 issues between the government and the unions, would be implemented. We pointed out: "Naively, the union leaders believe that – with Blair's reduced majority and their 'negotiating' skills – they can force a third-term Labour government to drop its neo-liberal privatisation mania."[5]

There was the fond hope that it would return to a more traditional social-democratic programme. This was linked to the expectation of an early replacement of Blair by Brown. The union leadership grossly underestimated the effort that would be needed to defeat Labour's pro-capitalist agenda. On pensions, the unions had forced the temporary retreat of the government with the threat of coordinated strike action in March 2005. However, the new minister responsible for pensions, David Blunkett, declared that nothing was ruled out after the report of the Turner Commission on pensions to be published the following autumn. Most unions therefore adopted a wait-and-see passive position. The exceptions were unions like the pcs and the rmt– both led by militant left-wing leaders – who had conducted successful strikes and consequently had increased their membership by tens of thousands.

There was a growing angry mood amongst trade unionists on a range of issues from 'fat cat' pay to pensions, to changes in working practices, lengthening working hours and worsening working conditions. Trade union leaders had become aware of the weakness of union organisation, particularly in the private sector after decades of Thatcherite attacks carried out under both Tory and Labour governments. Their answer to this was to propose 'super-union' mergers and hire teams of union organisers, many on temporary contracts with little say in how the union could develop. We urged the leaders of left unions to consider calling a council of union members, going beyond the current narrow layer of activists, to discuss a programme of action to defend working class people, strengthen the unions and link their struggles together more effectively.

A clear sign of growing militancy and anger was the success of the Socialist Party in Unison, where we increased our representation on the national executive to five. Our existing NEC members – Roger Bannister, Raph Parkinson and Jean Thorpe – all held their seats and were joined by Glenn Kelly and Diane Shepherd, who sadly passed away during her term of office. Glenn's victory was particularly welcomed by activists because he defeated Nigel Flanagan, someone they had seen shifting from the SWP to the right-wing. The overall left presence on the NEC would have been greater but for the divisive tactics, once more, by the Unison United Left (UUL) with a heavy presence of the SWP who split the left vote. The SWP had seen two of their members knocked off the NEC. Despite the antics of the UUL, Socialist Party members pledged to work effectively with all on the left to defeat the right wing in the union.

An important strike was that of the catering workers at Gate Gourmet at Heathrow Airport. Commenting to the Socialist, workers stated: "I was treated like a slave." Over the previous few years British Airways (BA) had been taking on workers at lower rates of pay than those of existing workers. The workers' union, the Transport and General Workers Union (TGWU), had a total of 30,000 members in Heathrow and amongst airport suppliers. By using its industrial muscle, it could have compelled the brutal Gate Gourmet bosses to reinstate sacked workers immediately. They had arrogantly assumed that the workers would be left in isolation after they were sacked and they had prepared the ground for months before to provoke workers into action. Gate Gourmet's British operation was just one fifth of the total worldwide workforce of 21,400 of this US-owned company. The Heathrow workers' action was 'illegal' not only because they did not ballot beforehand but also because the anti-union laws in Britain say workers in one company cannot go on strike in sympathy with workers in another.[6]

BA still had control over Gate Gourmet as its main supplier for airline meals. It had consistently squeezed suppliers over the years to reduce their costs and had cut the cash given to Gate Gourmet for the contracts to supply meals. This was common practice whether in a hospital that had put out cleaning to the lowest bidder or anywhere else where the scourge of privatisation was happening. So blatant and brutal were the employers that Tony Woodley threatened to bring out almost 20,000 members of the TGWU at Heathrow if Gate Gourmet workers were victimised. Unfortunately, he did not stick to this promise as the strike went on.

The High Court was then used to scandalously declare in a judgement that the pickets were not even allowed to speak to scabs when the latter tried to cross picket lines. We commented at the time: "Heathrow is one of Britain's strongest trade union-organised workplaces. The TGWU has thousands more members across the hinterland of suppliers and services around the airport."[7] Those other workers from the union should have been called on to win this battle; anything less was an abdication of leadership. Unfortunately, the union did let down the Gate Gourmet workers who grudgingly accepted a deal cobbled together between the union leadership and management. It was a bad deal, which meant that 144 of the original workers sacked were made compulsorily redundant. It was, moreover, a warning of the way the bosses would behave in the new industrial climate in Britain. They were using unorganised migrant workers to divide the working class and drive down wages. If the TGWU had organised proper solidarity action it would have brought these bosses to their knees.

At the T&G's 2007 Biennial Delegate Conference, Socialist Party member Rob Williams, who was the convenor of the former Ford plant in Swansea which was later sold to Linamar, moved a resolution attacking the anti-trade union laws and specifically calling on Tony Woodley not to write any more 'repudiation letters' to workers taking unofficial industrial action. Woodley spent 20 minutes explaining why the union could not support this motion, citing sequestration of its funds. The motion was defeated two to one. Yet Woodley's successor Len McCluskey has refused to write any repudiation letters during his term of office without any threats to the union as a result! The trade union leaders should be much bolder in taking on the anti-union laws and defeating them, as happened in the 1970s.

The cowardly approach of most of the union leaders was growing as industrial militants were picked on and sacked; those who stood against these policies within the union were victimised. Three Amicus members of staff were suspended from their jobs, one of them while still on holiday and not knowing anything of his suspension until he returned to work. The other two were escorted off the head office premises without any explanation but were told they would be given reasons for this action in "due course". This was in preparation, it was suspected by militants, for a possible merger with the TGWU, which was being bulldozed through Amicus by its general secretary Derek Simpson.

The TGWU was involved in other important struggles at this time. Andy Beadle, a TGWU shop steward at Peckham bus garage in South London and a longstanding member of the Socialist Party, was summarily dismissed by his employers, the 'Go Ahead' bus company running privatised services. This was symptomatic of the dictatorship of the bosses increasingly exercised in the workplaces. He had, it seems, produced an "unauthorised notice" calling on his members to vote against the pay deal being proposed by the local union official. His members had already voted against the deal once; this was the second ballot on the issue. Andy's determination to oppose the deal obviously annoyed the bosses and the local union officialdom. Ordinary workers were outraged, began to organise themselves and formed a committee to campaign for Andy's reinstatement.

The breakup of London bus workers into separate companies had led to huge differences in the earnings of drivers from one part of London to another and nationally. The incompetent right-wing officials had signed a deal which would have still left £50 per week difference with other London bus workers. After a very well-organised campaign, Andy Beadle won his job back with full back pay! However, the company ensured that he should be transferred to a neighbouring garage, which meant he could no longer be shop steward at Peckham. TGWU officials were compliant in this scandalous concession to the bosses but Andy declared: "Even if I am no longer rep, I will continue to be an active member of the TGWU and help build the organised strength of bus workers."[8]

It was against this background that the annual TUC conference took place. One of the major issues debated was the need to defend workers' pension rights. Congress passed a resolution which would not have happened if the PCS had not campaigned amongst other public sector unions for united action. It had actually delivered strike ballots within the unions. This, in turn, forced the government to back down. Janice Godrich, Socialist Party member and president of PCS, explained in an interview with The Socialist: "The TUC has a potentially major role to play in ensuring that all the unions whose members are threatened by these proposals stay united."

At Congress the PCS organised a fringe meeting on this issue attended by 13 general secretaries. Adair Turner, former chairman of the CBI, had been invited, quite scandalously, to address the TUC. Linda Taaffe, a delegate from the NUT, explained Turner had been made responsible for drawing up recommendations for the government on the future of pensions, arguing that pensioners' benefits should be cut. Linda called for the government to cut the tax-avoiding scams of the super-rich amounting to £100bn a year. She also exposed the fact that the European average of GDP spent on pensions was 10%, whilst the figure for the UK was only 5.4%. All that

Turner could say was "it was outside his remit". Janice Godrich made the point that it "amazes me that our employer announced live on national television the cutting of over 100,000 jobs when the chancellor made his pre-budget speech last year. Since then PCS has worked hard to dispel the myth of civil servants as bowler-hatted bureaucrats". These cuts, we have to remember, were proposed under a Labour government. The 'ConDem' coalition merely built on Labour's work in cutting the public sector through their massive retrenchment programme. However, because of the left leadership given by the PCS, the union had "grown in membership".[9]

These attacks provoked a mood within the unions for a TUC-led initiative culminating in coordinated strike action. This was despite the government's partial retreat. This merely disguised their determination to still proceed with the introduction of a two-tier pension system throughout the public sector, with new entrants working until they were 65. Unison, the largest local government union, also took a decision to ballot for strike action. The pensions' battle intensified in late 2005, with the government forced to concede its second major retreat over this issue within six months, by agreeing to maintain existing workers' conditions.

The reaction of the capitalist commentators was universal condemnation of the Labour government for bowing down to the pressure of the unions. The Financial Times called it "abject surrender". Digby Jones, head of the CBI, was apoplectic when debating with PCS general secretary Mark Serwotka on Channel 4 News. He declared: "We're going back to the 1970s with the unions calling the shots." The PCS was compared to the NUM of the past, suggesting the government would never concede on arrangements for all existing staff and would move to crush the unions. Yet ballots in a number of public sector unions defending pension rights came out in favour of strike action. Other unions made noises about possible strike action. We strongly urged the unions, particularly the PCS in which we had a certain weight, to recommend strike action amongst their members. Over 90,000 PCS members in the Department for Work and Pensions were mobilised for the ballot in December against the cuts in the

Department, with a projected loss of 30,000 jobs.[10]

The pension struggle dominated everything. For the best part of two decades big business had slashed and burnt its way through the pension funds and entitlements of working people. This climb down forced on the British government over public sector occupational pensions began to swing the pendulum away from the bosses. The Socialist warned that a battle had been won but further struggle still loomed. CBI members were never reconciled to this – furious, on behalf of the bosses, that workers were still allowed to retire at 60! In reality, many workers were not retiring at 60 in the public sector at this stage.

An almighty tussle took place over a prolonged period on this issue between the working class and its organisations with the bosses and their government. Yet in the end the government, first of all Labour and then the coalition, were actually successful in pushing back the working class and establishing retirement ages of 67 and 68. This result was entirely down to the role of the leaders of the unions, particularly the right wing, who prevaricated and never called action in time on a vital issue – a past gain for the working class. This, in turn, prepared the ground for a revolt against these leaders and a shift towards the left.

68. Demise of Blair
2006-07

"I went over to the conference, and I heard that the resolution to renationalise the railways had passed through quite substantially, with the unions voting in favour and 72% of the constituency delegates voting against, which shows what's happened to the Party," wrote Tony Benn.[1] It said everything about the 'rank and file' of New Labour. Whereas in the past, the constituency party delegates were always to the left of predominantly right-wing led trade unions, the reverse was now the case. The unions had voted in favour of this radical resolution but the ranks of New Labour were filled out with careerists, local councillors who were carrying through cuts and every type of backslider.

Within the trade unions there was an unmistakable shift towards the left. This was reflected in the victory of Matt Wrack in the ballot for the general secretary of the Fire Brigades Union (FBU). We expected that "Matt's election should see the FBU take a firmer stand on vital issues like pensions and pay than it has done in the last year, where the majority of the union leadership have preferred to attack and witch-hunt their own members, rather than preparing a fight on these issues." The Socialist Party welcomed his election while at the same time hoping that this would lead to a rebuilding of the confidence of the membership after the setbacks following their dispute in 2003 and the misrule of the previous general secretary Andy Gilchrist.[2]

Blair pushed on with his privatisation agenda, trying to extract every ounce of benefit for big business out of his remaining time in office. He promoted 'free schools' and 'academies', which were freed from local authority control and oversight. Blair had to rely on Tory MPs to pass the Education Bill through its second parliamentary reading. Labour 'rebels' who voted against it called him 'Ramsay McBlair', after the first Labour Prime Minister Ramsay Macdonald who formed the National Government with the Tories in 1931.

This, together with corruption scandals that were breaking out, led to reports of 'civil war' in New Labour, fuelled by the fear of what would happen to its vote in the 2006 local elections. In capitalist circles there was concern on how discredited Blair had become, and how this was adding to a level of disgust with capitalist politicians in general. A poll revealed that the Blair government was seen by 70% as more sleazy than John Major's Tory government. The headline in the Socialist read: "The stench of rotten Labour – time for a new workers' party".[3] The Guardian echoed the first part of our demand telling Blair to go and adding that "the office degrades all its holders".[4] We pointed out that this may apply to capitalist politicians, with many sinking their snouts into the parliamentary pig trough while carrying out attacks on workers' living standards. A new workers' party would be different; all elected officials would be fully accountable to the party and live, as the 'Militant MPs' (Dave Nellist, Terry Fields and Pat Wall) had done, on the average wage of the workers they represented.

The Labour Party itself was becoming increasingly empty and, at the same time, intolerant of any dissent or even discussion. Tony Benn once more records that "At Party meetings people are barracked if they say unpopular things... Quite a number of people said to Blair, 'Look, the problem stems from you and Gordon Brown'... One MP said, 'The Party has just disappeared. There are no local parties. There's nothing to campaign with. It's all top-down and instructed from Party headquarters; all the experienced regional organisers have gone, and there are people on short-term contracts." He then added: "The nature of the crisis in the Party must be becoming apparent to people."[5] Unfortunately, Tony Benn himself failed to see the full extent of the decline of the Labour Party, because of the death grip exercised by Blairism on it.

Tony Benn gave an interesting insight into the approach of the media and how it reports on the working class and its organisations, like the trade unions. Channel 4 News anchored by Jon Snow, while in no way consistently left-wing, usually attempted to give a relatively objective analysis of events. Yet even Snow, Tony Benn wrote, could not conceal his hostility to the labour movement and its representatives: "I said [to Jon Snow], 'Why don't you invite trade unions? 'Well, they don't matter anymore. In the old days trade unions mattered, but they don't anymore!' Jon's the son of a bishop. I asked, 'Have you ever been convinced by anybody, or persuaded by anybody, you've listened to?' 'Yes,' he said, "every time I go to Number 10, I think the Prime Minister is right."' Tony Benn then asked: "'To whom are you accountable?'... When I said that people he interviewed wanted to say something: 'Oh, they're not there to say something. They are there to answer my questions!'"[6]

If this media outlet, usually viewed as 'fair' and 'to the left' can display such bias, through its main news anchorman, what hope is there for the rest of the media? It shows that only mass campaigns, mobilising the working people from the bottom up, will get the labour movement's message across. This is the lesson of all great battles of the labour movement: Liverpool 1983-87, the miners' strike 1984-85, and the poll tax struggle, where a mass campaign was able to overcome a poisonous media barrage seeking to distort, lie and undemocratically mould public opinion to the benefit of the boss class that they represent. Blair was the capitalists' creature as he effectively destroyed the Labour Party as a workers' party and carried on Thatcher's work through a ruthless implementation of neo-liberal policies.

But he came a cropper in the May elections. New Labour lost over 300 council seats with the main beneficiary being the Tories. Parties and independents on the left also gained, but so did the far-right BNP. The BNP won 32 seats, an increase of 27 on its pre-election position. The Greens won 130, an increase of 21. The Socialist Party increased its positions to seven councillors. Yet Blair acolytes skulking in 10 Downing Street displayed the same air of unreality as Margaret Thatcher did in her last days in office. The Observer reported the conclusion of Blair's fans: "They basically said people were angry with Tony because they love him so much and are angry because they think he might go."[7]

The BNP had picked up some 'Old Labour' clothes, discarded by Blair, calling demagogically for the railways to be taken back into public ownership as a single company. It also declared in relation to Iraq: "It's time to take our soldiers home from America's Iraq war." It even farcically claimed to stand "for strong trade unions... to protect the workers from exploitation." Of course, the far-right, fascistic or neo-fascist organisations, beginning with Mussolini and Hitler, had always relied on 'socialistic' phraseology, calculated to appeal to the working class and sections of the disillusioned middle-class. This did not alter their character as a largely middle-class mobilised force to attack the working class. They were used to smash and atomise the working class and its organisations.

Now, this election showed that the BNP had established a significant foothold in places like Barking and Dagenham, parts of the West Midlands, Lancashire and Yorkshire. The BNP was far from repeating the success of Hitler and Mussolini in Britain but there was no room for complacency. Labour minister Margaret Hodge was blamed after the disaster of the local elections because she blurted out that eight out of ten voters in her constituency in Barking considered voting BNP. While she had exaggerated, this warning was confirmed when 11 BNP councillors were elected in the borough.[8]

Respect, led by George Galloway with the SWP in tow, was successful in getting sixteen councillors elected, twelve in Tower Hamlets, three in Newham and one in Birmingham. However, their appeal was mainly to Muslims. It is a necessary task for the labour movement to win significant support amongst 'immigrant communities' but the approach of Respect, we pointed out, could lead to a certain polarisation. The white working class BNP voters of Barking and Dagenham could only be won away from the BNP by a left party that puts forward a class-based alternative. We pointed out that "It is not so much a question of what Respect's election material says, but of what it doesn't say." While it put across opposition to NHS cuts, council house privatisation, the war in Iraq and other welcome positions, it did not consistently include a class-based appeal to all sections of the working class.[9] This is one of the reasons why, despite early success, its support subsequently diminished and it was now playing a marginal role.

In the wake of the local election disaster, even the majority of New Labour MPs, who up to then had clung to the coat-tails of Blair as a 'vote winner', began to stir. They could be compared to the 'plain', the broad mass of 'neutral' assemblymen during the French Revolution who supported the dominant force in power at any one time, so long as their interests were defended and enhanced. However, once their position was in danger, they turned on the incumbent! Blair had once brazenly boasted: "'I have taken from my party everything they thought they believed in. I have stripped them of their core beliefs,' Blair confided. 'What keeps it together is success and power.'"[10] Brown's intense struggle for the throne was not primarily ideological but personal. He was, as Blair himself admitted, "New Labour to his fingertips."

The catastrophe of privatisation and particularly the Private Finance Initiative (PFI) reached volcanic proportions. House of Commons investigations revealed how financial sharks were bleeding the NHS through 'overpayments'. Patricia Hewitt, the Health Secretary, got a whiff of this when she addressed the Royal College of Nursing (RCN) conference. There was an outcry when she tried to big up Labour's recent record on the NHS. This ranked alongside the treatment of Blair himself at the Women's Institute conference a few years before. Like Blair, Hewitt was also forced to leave the stage to jeers. Mass opposition was growing to the social and economic decline of Britain. Brown was not an alternative to Blair but New Labour's twin pillar. This meant that there was already suspicion of him from workers, even before he took over from Blair.

An interesting side issue was the discussion which broke out over the performance of Respect in the elections. The SWP had taken up, not publicly but in internal 'notes', the Socialist Party's criticisms of them and Respect in the local elections. We posed the question: "Are the criticisms of Respect and, by definition, the SWP made by the Socialist Party and Bob Crow [who also criticised Respect] inaccurate and unfair?... [If] Respect represented a turning away from Labour, now a capitalist party, by Asian workers towards a more developed class consciousness, this would indeed be a positive step. But, unfortunately, under the leadership of George Galloway and the SWP, Respect has so far not acted as this bridge to a new workers' party, but reinforced the idea of 'Muslim interests' completely separate from those of other sections of the working class."[11]

Throughout 2006 and 2007 the Socialist Party analysed the death agony of Blair, although Blairism continued to dominate the Labour Party. We sought to patiently explain the case for a new mass socialist alternative. However, the leadership of the trade unions still harboured illusions that if Brown was to take over from Blair then a new 'radical' period would open up. This was despite the fact that even opinion polls in the capitalist press suggested that a Brown-led Labour Party would only gain at most two points in the opinion polls. We commented: "The New Labour machine is making a mistake if it believes that ditching Blair will simply solve their problems. It is not only Blair, but Blairism, which people are fed up with... There will be some workers who are hoping against hope that Brown is only pretending to be a Blairite, and will reveal his 'true socialist' colours once elected." Their illusions were unfounded, as Brown had consistently pursued an anti-working class, pro-big business agenda as Chancellor.

At the Labour Party conference in 2006, Blair emphasised in his speech the continuity between New Labour and the Labour governments of the past – pointing out, for example, that in 1969 Labour Prime Minister, Harold Wilson, tried to introduce anti-trade union legislation in the form of the misnamed In Place of Strife White Paper. Blair argued that the difference then was that

Wilson did not dare to go ahead. Blair was right. The tops of the Labour Party had always acted in the interests of big business. Nevertheless, Labour governments in the past were forced to respond to the pressure of the working class. In 1969 a series of strikes put the government under such pressure that it threatened to split. Wilson was forced to retreat.

We pointed out in 2006: "Today is a very different situation within the Labour Party - where the Blairites have completely insulated themselves from the pressure of the organised working class in the form of the trade unions. While the trade union vote still has power at conference, the conference itself has no decision-making power at all!... According to the Labour Representation Committee [a remnant of the once powerful left] resolutions have been ruled out of order on: Iraq, Trident replacement, the council housing 'fourth option', nuclear energy, trade union laws, Venezuela, incapacity benefit, school admissions policy, party political funding, and Thames Water!"

Yet the majority of trade union leaders still mistakenly argued that New Labour could be changed. If they were sincere in this, why didn't all those affiliated trade unions support John McDonnell MP's campaign for the leadership, as the only candidate who stood on a programme in the interests of trade union members: opposition to cuts, low pay and privatisation? A survey of the incredibly conservative approach of the union leadership towards New Labour then gives a picture of complete abdication of political leadership towards the interests of their members.[12]

The 2007 local elections were every bit as disastrous as the previous year's. Labour lost control of the Scottish parliament with its lowest vote since 1955, had its worst result since 1918 in Wales and lost almost 500 council seats in England. There were now almost 90 councils where Labour had been totally wiped out. The Tories, however, had not enjoyed a groundswell of popular support but were seen in the main as the 'lesser evil'.

Blair resigned shortly after these elections. The reactions of working people to his departure were predictable: "For Jamie Oliver's dinner ladies in Greenwich, Blair's legacy is more work, more hours and if you're lucky a £2 a week pay increase and gardeners here face a £111 a week pay cut! It's an absolute disgrace!" said Onay Kasab, then of Greenwich Unison. A Durham socialist student commented. "For me Blair's legacy is leaving university with about £15,000 worth of debt."[13] The Socialist simply stated: "Curtain falls on disastrous reign." A fitting political obituary from the Financial Times read: "The New Labour project looks increasingly like Margaret Thatcher's final triumph." Kenneth Clarke appeared on BBC Question Time and praised Blair for "finishing off socialism" in the Labour Party. Election 'guru' John Curtice wrote in the Independent: "The party that was originally founded to provide working-class representation in Parliament is no longer regarded as a working-class party. In 1987, the British Election Study found that 46% of the electorate thought the Labour Party looked after the interests of the working class 'very closely'. By the time of the last election, only 11% did."[14]

Brown was crowned leader with no contest, a spectacular case of Labour MPs "tobogganing towards disaster with their eyes closed". He had actually pretended to want a contest but when left-wing challenger John McDonnell struggled to reach the required 45 nominations, Brown refused to ask some of his own supporters to nominate McDonnell. Could he have done a 'Corbyn' and been elected Labour leader at this stage if right-wing MPs had lent their votes to get him on the ballot paper? Highly unlikely. A crucial difference between then and Corbyn's victory lay in giving the right to vote to forces outside the Labour Party – the £3 'associate supporters' – who massively opted for Jeremy Corbyn. This in turn was only made possible by a change of rules, following the Collins Review, that was originally a device by the right wing to nullify the collective organised voice of the trade unions but which backfired on them!

The candidate supported by the major trade unions for deputy leader, John Cruddas, opposed higher tuition fees but he also nominated Gordon Brown for the leadership. Hilary Benn, firmly in the Blairite camp, only managed to get on the ballot paper for the deputy leadership contest through getting some final nominations from members of the parliamentary Campaign Group whose 'socialist' conscience amounted to only nominating him out of sympathy for his father, Tony Benn.

Tariq Ali wrote later about the strained political relations between Tony Benn and his son Hilary. He commented on the latter's shameful support for the bombing of Syria in 2015 and his parliamentary "disingenuous speech – Hitler, with the Spanish Civil War thrown in for good measure – [which] was loudly cheered by Tory and hardcore Blairite MPs. (What a pity that the two-hour row between Hilary Benn and his father over the Iraq War, of which Hilary was an ardent supporter, was never taped and transcribed in Tony Benn's printed diaries – though he did talk about it to friends.)"[15]

We concluded that the departure of Tony Blair after 10 years in power did actually represent a turning point in political developments in Britain. Gordon Brown, however, represented a continuation of the 'ancien regime', the substitution of 'New Labour' by 'New, New Labour'! We commented: "It also represents a psychological break in a changed British and world situation. Shakespeare's Malcolm declared of the Thane of Cawdor in Macbeth: 'Nothing in his life became him like the leaving of it.'"[16]

Yet Blair's political death would not lead to an enhancement of his reputation. The manner of his exit, after remaining in the political departure lounge for a seemingly interminable period, summed up his disastrous reign. Certainly for the labour movement, rather than the crowd 'asking for more', as suggested by his small coterie, he was met with derision and catcalls from almost all sides. The 'uber-Blairites' were undoubtedly correct when they claimed that he was forced out by a Brown-inspired 'coup' at the 2006 Labour Party conference. However, we pointed out that his government began to the strains of "Things can only get better" but ended with a mere 22% of the population believing that he had done "a good job". Five million voters had deserted Labour since 1997. We reminded working people that the so-called Blair landslide of that year was achieved by New Labour polling just 30.8% of the electorate, 13.5 million voters. Since then, the numbers voting for New Labour had progressively declined in subsequent general elections to 24.2% in 2001 and 21.6% in 2005. Labour Party membership in this period officially dropped by 50% but in reality this underestimated those who had deserted its ranks.

Labour was now virtually indistinguishable from the other two capitalist parties. It was similar to former social-democratic parties which had gone over to a defence of the system and abandoned the claims of the working class. Some of them did retain an element of 'social democracy', which allowed significant sections of the masses to see them for a period as the 'lesser evil'. This allowed some workers to support New Labour candidates in the vain hope that they would prevent 'slash and burn' policies, the destruction of elements of the welfare state, by the Tories. Peter Mandelson stated after Blair's departure that his control of the Labour Party had resulted in Labour becoming a "'normal social democratic party' on the pattern of the rest of Europe." Nothing could have been further from the truth. In words and deeds, New Labour had broken with the ideas of social democracy: defence of the welfare state, reforms and gradual improvements in living standards, state intervention as a lever to increase the share of the working class at the expense of the rich and powerful. New Labour and the former social-democratic parties had gone over hook, line and sinker to the anti-state 'greed is good' philosophy of neo-liberalism.

An indication of this was shown by the Financial Times, approvingly quoting comments made by Jim Murphy, then a government minister for welfare reform. He had declared that "Britain's welfare state 'will never' pay benefits high enough to lift people out of poverty, adding that he didn't think it should." He went on further: "Work, he declared, was now 'the only route out of poverty in the UK." The Financial Times commented: "A decade ago, such remarks from a Labour MP would have caused a riot."[17] The pitifully low wages on offer in Britain for unskilled jobs would not provide an escape route out of poverty. Unemployment began to inexorably rise, which completely falsified Murphy's contentions.

Brown's election was a 'Stalinist' exercise in machine politics and arm-twisting. Taken together with John McDonnell's failure to even get on the ballot for the leadership contest, it reinforced our arguments that New Labour represented a decisive rupture with the Labour Party of the past. We had also argued though that the mass of the working class, in particular trade unionists, could at a certain stage move to 'reclaim' the party from the right-wing. Brown's coronation irrefutably demonstrated that this was going to be difficult, if not impossible. While not on the scale of Stalin's triumphs in elections (who once received 101% of the vote) Brown nevertheless received the 313 nominations to ensure a single candidate election. His henchmen achieved this by suggesting to the PLP, behind the scenes of course, that a vote for McDonnell would be construed as a "career ending" step!

Despite opposition to the proposition of John McDonnell and others on the left that new life could be breathed into a moribund Labour Party, we nevertheless supported the idea that if it came to a vote he should have been supported, particularly by the unions. But the trade union leaders were at this stage terrified of such a struggle because even though McDonnell would not have won, in the course of the battle a left could have emerged. But 'hope springs eternal'. The trade union leaders refused to fight for the 'crown' – a leadership of Labour beholden to them – but instead concentrated on the position of the 'dauphin', the mostly meaningless position of deputy leader, which had given the hapless John Prescott the semblance of power. The stance of Tony Woodley, general secretary of the TGWU, and other trade union leaders amounted to lining up behind Brown and hoping for concessions via the deputy leader, which, in the main, would never materialise.

In reality, New Labour bent the knee consistently to the CBI, the bosses' union but it never listened to or retreated before trade union pressure, unless it was confronted with the threat of actual strike action. On the issue of perspectives, we stated: "Brown may even cut and run for an early general election." But what would be the choice before the British people in such an election? All the three main parties were, in effect, three wings of the same capitalist party.[18]

Conclusion

In the last chapter of The Rise of Militant we pointed out that at that time (1995) "bourgeois commentators have already drawn the conclusion that Marxism is historically obsolete". We hope that we have shown in this book that this claim has not been borne out.

True, the collapse of Stalinism, coming after the phase of neo-liberalism and the capitulation of the official leaderships of the labour movement to this, has weakened genuine Marxism and socialism. But it did not obliterate completely its ideological and practical attraction for an important layer of the more developed workers and young people, as we hope we have demonstrated.

We showed in advance the reasons for this: "The very idea of socialism came out of the life experiences of the working class. The insoluble contradictions of capitalism, its incapacity to provide even the minimum requirements of employment, shelter and food on a world scale drove the working class to seek an alternative system. Unless the defenders of the capitalist system can now show that late 20th-century capitalism has overcome these contradictions... Marxism... remains as relevant as ever. This... despite the fact that the understanding of the working class of the underlying reality lags far behind the objective situation."

As we moved into the 21st-century this conclusion was vindicated. We also wrote in 1995 "capitalism is demonstrating its incapacity to furnish the basic requirements of humankind". We then detailed the deleterious effects inflicted on the British and the world working class with rising poverty, mass unemployment and "a general offensive against welfare and those workers employed in the public sector"; all of which came to pass to a degree that even we underestimated at the time. For instance, on the issue of inequality which has grown enormously, as numerous studies and media stories together with the work of authors like Thomas Piketty have demonstrated. The chasm between the classes – between rich and poor – has grown and is now wider than the Grand Canyon.

The Guardian in March 2017, reporting on the colossal development of new technology warned: "Robots could displace 10 million British workers." Thirty percent of jobs in Britain are potentially under threat from breakthroughs in artificial intelligence; 2.5 million jobs were at high risk in wholesaling and retailing alone.

The capitalists themselves are half-conscious that the development of technology cannot be fully harnessed by them without precipitating a further rise in mass unemployment and an economic and social crisis. A halfway house is therefore suggested by some – e.g. in Finland and Sweden – involving "special measures" a programme for "lifelong learning and job matching to ensure the potential gains from automation are not concentrated in too few hands". Proposals such as the need for a "living basic income", which are already being tested in Finland, indirectly confirm our analysis of capitalism and the impossibility of fully satisfying the demands of the working class within the framework of this system.

In the past the workers' movement – drawing on the international experience of the working class in periods of mass unemployment – demanded from the bosses 'work or full maintenance' i.e. work or full pay.

The capitalists invariably reply, particularly today, that with swollen and rising state debts it is impossible to meet this demand fully. They may under pressure – i.e. a mass movement of the working class – introduce partial measures but they cannot provide the means by which you can guarantee a really human existence with enough money for everyone to enjoy a house, food and the basics.

The reply of the working class should be: "If you can't afford this then we can't afford your system!" Evacuate the scene of history and make way for a new democratic socialist society that can provide food and shelter at least for everyone, not just in one country but worldwide.

In this sense the next book – which will cover the period from 2007, including the beginning of the world economic crisis – until today will show how Marxism, the Socialist Party today, held to the vision of a new socialist society in the face of triumphant capitalism. This was in preparation for the economic and political convulsions which we were sure were coming.

We concluded the last chapter in our previous book by stating: "One thing is clear: the ground has been prepared for colossal social and political upheavals in Britain and throughout world capitalism... Marxism will once more arise with such force that it will astound bourgeois sceptics and socialist 'fainthearts' alike."

In our next book, which is already largely written, we will show how our predictions worked out as the crisis of capitalism itself deepened.

Abbreviations

AEEU   **Amalgamated Engineering and Electrical Union,** trade union in Britain and Ireland which merged with MSF in 2001 to form Amicus and is now part of Unite.

AFL-CIO   **American Federation of Labor and Congress of Industrial Organizations,** major trade union federation in the US.

ASLEF   **Associated Society of Locomotive Engineers and Firemen,** trade union mainly organising drivers on the railways.

BNP   **British National Party,** far-right political organisation that won council and European Parliament seats for a short while before breaking up after internal squabbles.

CADV   **Campaign Against Domestic Violence,** organisation formed to defend women victims of abuse and those imprisoned for defending themselves against violence.

CATP   **Campaign Against Tube Privatisation,** group backed by railway workers and others formed to oppose privatisation on London Underground and which stood in the 2000 Greater London Assembly elections.

CBI   **Confederation of British Industry**, the major
            employers' organisation in Britain.

CFDU   **Campaign for a Fighting Democratic Unison**,
            former left organisation in Unison fighting for a
            democratic union.

CIA   **Central Intelligence Agency**, spying organisation
            of the US government.

CLP   **Constituency Labour Party**, Organising body of the
            Labour Party in each parliamentary constituency.

CNWP   **Campaign for a New Workers' Party**, campaign set up
            to fight for a political alternative to New Labour.

CPB   **Communist Party of Britain**, left organisation formed
            after the break-up of the former Communist Party of
            Great Britain.

CWI   **Committee for a Workers' International**, the
            International organisation to which the SP is affiliated.

CWU   **Communication Workers' Union**, major union in UK
            for postal and telecommunications workers.

EC   **Executive Committee,** body of the Socialist Party
            elected by its National Committee to deal with the
            day-to-day business of the party.

EZLN   **Ejército Zapatista de Liberación Nacional** (Zapatista
            Army of National Liberation) radical leftist group based
            in Chiapas, Mexico that led an uprising in 1994.

FBU   **Fire Brigades Union**, the firefighters trade union in the
            UK.

GEC   **General Executive Council**, leading elected body of the
            TGWU. Also **Group Executive Committee**, sector
            committee within the PCS union.

GMB   Originally standing for **General, Municipal and Boilermakers,** one of the larger trade unions in the UK.

GPMU   **Graphical, Paper and Media Union,** trade union in Britain and Ireland for print and associated workers. Merged into Amicus and now part of Unite.

IEC   **International Executive Committee,** leadership body of the CWI elected at its world Congress.

ISM   **International Socialist Movement,** name by which the Scottish section of the CWI was known for several years following the dissolution of SML.

ISR   **International Socialist Resistance,** youth organisation formed throughout Europe to give a socialist programme in the anti-capitalist protests at the turn of the century.

IST   **International Socialist Tendency,** international organisation of the SWP.

ISTC   **Iron and Steel Trades Confederation,** steel workers' union, now part of Community trade union.

IU   **Izquierda Unida** (United Left) major left-wing formation in Spain for many years, dominated by the Communist Party.

LIT   **Workers' International League,** Trotskyist International with its major sections in Latin America led for many years by Nahuel Moreno.

LRC   **Labour Representation Committee,** a federation of workers and socialist organisations formed in 1900 to increase political representation for the working class. Became generally known as the Labour Party. Also the name of the left-wing organisation in the current Labour Party closely linked to John McDonnell.

LSA **London Socialist Alliance**, regional body of the Socialist Alliance in England.

MDHC **Mersey Docks and Harbour Company**, overall owner and proprietor of the Merseyside docks, involved in the dockers' dispute in the 1990s.

NASUWT **National Association of Schoolmasters Union of Women Teachers**, teachers' union in UK.

NC **National Committee**, the leading body of the Socialist Party, elected at its Congress.

NATFHE **National Association of Teachers in Further and Higher Education**, union now part of the University and College Union (UCU).

NEC **National Executive Committee** (or **Council**), the leading elected body of the Labour Party and some trade unions.

NSSN **National Shop Stewards Network**, organisation established in 2007 by the RMT union under Bob Crow as an umbrella group for all trade union workplace reps.

NUM **National Union of Mineworkers**, miners' union which organised the year-long strike in 1984-85 against pit closures.

NUPE **National Union of Public Employees**, public sector union that merged with NALGO (National and Local Government Officers' Association) and COHSE (Confederation of Health Service Employees) to form Unison.

NUS **National Union of Students**, body representing Further and Higher Education students in Britain.

NUT **National Union of Teachers**, major teachers' union in England and Wales.

PCI   **Partito Comunista Italiano** (Italian Communist Party), former left-wing party in Italy dissolved into the PDS.

PDS   **Partito Democratico della Sinistra** (Democratic Party of the left), party in Italy formed by right-wing of the PCI and various pro-capitalist formations.

PFI   **Private Finance Initiative,** method of funding public sector projects by borrowing from the private sector, normally at exorbitant and crippling interest rates.

PLP   **Parliamentary Labour Party,** the body of Labour MPs in the House of Commons.

POA   **Prison Officers Association,** trade union organising prison workers.

PRC   **Partito della Rifondazione Comunista** (Communist Refoundation), a left-wing split from the PCI after its dissolution, it has itself dwindled in significance due to its rightward moving policies.

P-SoL   **Partido Socialismo e Libertade** (Socialism and Freedom Party), left-wing party in Brazil formed in opposition to the rightward moving policies of the PT government of President Lula.

PSOE   **Partido Socialista Obrero Español** (Spanish Socialist Workers' Party), ex-socialist party in Spain now firmly pro-capitalist.

PSTU   **Partido Socialista dos Trabalhadores Unificado** (United Socialist Workers' Party), left-wing party in Brazil and largest section of the LIT.

PT   **Partido dos Trabalhadores** (Workers' Party), a once left party in Brazil formed by ex-President Lula.

RCP   **Revolutionary Communist Party,** the organisation of Trotskyists in Britain from 1944-49.

RMT   **National Union of Rail, Maritime and Transport Workers,** union formed from merger of National Union of Railwaymen and National Union of Seamen in 1990.

RUC   **Respect – the Unity Coalition,** left organisation formed by George Galloway and the SWP which mainly appealed to Muslims.

SAV   **Sozialistische Alternative** (Socialist Alternative) Section of the CWI in Germany.

SLP   **Socialist Labour Party,** party founded in 1995 by Arthur Scargill and others as left split from the Labour Party.

SML   **Scottish Militant Labour,** formed in 1992 following the 'open turn' in Scotland.

SNP   **Scottish National Party,** major pro-capitalist party in Scotland with a pro-independence position.

SP   **Socialist Party** (in England and Wales), formerly Militant Labour.

SSA   **Scottish Socialist Alliance,** federal organisation that put forward left ideas in Scotland in the 1990s against New Labour which included SML. Dissolved when SSP was formed.

SWP   **Socialist Workers' Party.**

SSP   **Scottish Socialist Party,** broad socialist party set up as successor to SSA, which at its height won 6 Members of the Scottish Parliament but broke up over allegations concerning Tommy Sheridan.

STA   **Socialist Teachers Alliance,** organisation of the left in the NUT.

TD   **Teachta Dála,** member of the Irish Parliament (Dáil).

TGWU (also T&G) **Transport and General Workers Union**, Major trade union in Britain and Ireland which merged with Amicus to form Unite.

TUC **Trades Union Congress**, federation of trade unions in Britain.

TUSC **Trade Unionist and Socialist Coalition**, an electoral coalition including the SP with the RMT union formed to pose a anti-austerity alternative to New Labour.

USDAW **Union of Shop, Distributive and Allied Workers**, the major union for retail and similar workers in the UK.

UCATT **Union of Construction, Allied Trades and Technicians**, building workers' union in Britain and Ireland, now merged into Unite.

UKIP **United Kingdom Independence Party**, right-wing party formed to oppose the EU.

USFI **United Secretariat of the Fourth International**, a Trotskyist International led for many years by Ernest Mandel.

USP **United Socialist Party**, Sri Lankan section of the CWI.

UUL **Unison United Left**, former organisation of the left in Unison.

WRP **Workers Revolutionary Party**, organisation led by Gerry Healy which broke apart in the 1980s.

WSA **Welsh Socialist Alliance**, counterpart to the Socialist Alliance in England but including left nationalist parties.

YRE **Youth against Racism in Europe**, youth organisation throughout Europe fighting racism and the far right.

YSR **Young Socialist Resistance**, youth organisation formed in 1990s.

Bibliography

Tariq Ali, **The Clash of Fundamentalisms: Crusades, Jihads and Modernity**, Verso, London 2003

Walter Bagehot, **The English Constitution**, Chapman & Hall, London, 1867

Tony Benn, **Free At Last, Diaries, 1991-2001**, Hutchinson, London, 2002

Tony Benn, **Diaries 2001-2007; More Time for Politics**, Hutchinson, London, 2007

Tony Blair, **A Journey**, Hutchinson, London, 2010

D Butler and D Kavanagh, **The British General Election of 1992**, MacMillan Press, October 1992

GDH Cole, **The Second International 1889-1914**, Palgrave Macmillan, London, 1969

Michael Crick, **Militant**, Biteback, London, 2016 edition

George Galloway, **I'm Not the Only One**, Allen Lane, London, 2004

William Greider, **One World Ready or Not**, Simon & Schuster, New York, 1997

William Keegan, **The Prudence of Mr Gordon Brown**, John Wiley & Sons, Chichester, 2003

Bibliography

Ken Livingstone, **If Voting Changed Anything, They'd Abolish It**, HarperCollins, London, 1987

Alan McCombes & Tommy Sheridan, **Imagine**, Rebel Inc., Edinburgh, 2000

Andy McSmith, **Faces of Labour: the Inside Story**, Verso Books, 1996

Karl Marx, **Capital**, 3 volumes, Lawrence & Wishart, London, 1959

Karl Marx & Friedrich Engels, **The Communist Manifesto**, Penguin Classics, London, 2005

John Pilger, **Hidden Agendas**, Vintage, London, 1998

Andrew Rawnsley, **Servants of the People: The Inside Story of New Labour**, Penguin, London, 2001

Ken Smith, **A Civil War without Guns**, Socialist Publications, London, 2004

Hannah Sell, **Socialism in the 21st Century**, Socialist Publications, London, 2002

Jack Straw, **Last Man Standing: Memoirs of a Political Survivor**, Pan MacMillan, London, 2012

Peter Taaffe, **Afghanistan, Islam and the Revolutionary Left**, CWI, http://www.socialistworld.net/pubs/afghanistan/00.html , 2001

Peter Taaffe, **Empire Defeated**, Socialist Publications, London, 2004

Peter Taaffe, **Marxism in Today's World**, CWI, London, 2006

Peter Taaffe, **New Technology and Globalisation: Can a Capitalist Slump be Avoided?** Socialist Publications, London 1999

Peter Taaffe, **Socialism and Left Unity**, Socialist Publications, London, 2008

Peter Taaffe, **The Real History of Militant**, Socialist Publications, London, 2002

Peter Taaffe, **The Rise of Militant**, Socialist Publications, London, 1995

Peter Taaffe & Tony Mulhearn, **Liverpool, The City that Dared to Fight**, Fortress, London, 1988

Leon Trotsky, **Collected Works 1929-40**, Pathfinder, New York, various editions, 1969-78

Leon Trotsky, **In Defence of Marxism**, New Park, London, 1974

Leon Trotsky, **My Life**, Dover Publications, Mineola NY, 1996

Leon Trotsky, **The Third International after Lenin**, Pathfinder, New York, 1996

Leon Trotsky, **Where is Britain going?** In **Leon Trotsky on Britain**, Pathfinder, New York, 1998

Journals
Australian Herald • Coventry Evening Telegraph • Daily Mirror • Daily Record • The Daily Telegraph • The Economist • Evening Standard • Financial Times • The Guardian • Hansard • The Herald • Independent • Independent on Sunday • International Herald Tribune • International Socialist (Scotland) • London Review of Books • Mail on Sunday • Militant • Militant international Review • Morning Star • New Statesman • New York Times • Observer • Scottish Socialist Voice • Socialism Today • The Socialist • Socialist Review • Sunday Business Post • Wall Street Journal • Washington Post

Endnotes

INTRODUCTION

1. *See: Liverpool, The City that Dared to Fight*

2. *Trotsky, Trotskyism and Trotskyites, The Briefing Room,* BBC Radio 4, September 2016

3. *Into the Red Nineties: Decade of Revolution, Militant 974,* 19 January 1990

4. *See: The Rise of Militant and Militant's Real History for a full explanation - socialistparty.org.uk*

1. END OF THE TORY GOVERNMENT

1. *Editorial Comment, Militant 1249,* 20 October 1995

2. *Leveson Inquiry: John Major Reveals Murdoch's EU Demand,* BBC website, 12 June 2012

3. *Join our Fight in '95, Militant 1210,* 6 January 1995

4. *This Far and No Further, Militant 1214,* 3 February 1995

5. *Anger, Anxiety & Dissent, Militant 1223,* 31 March 1995

6. *The Day the Tories Dived, Militant 1229,* 12 May 1995

7. *The Tories' Civil War, Militant 1236,* 30 June 1995

2. BLAIR'S COUNTER-REVOLUTION IN THE LABOUR PARTY

1. *Guardian,* 1 January 1996

2. *1996: The year the Tories died?, Militant 1258,* 12 January 1996

3. *A Journey, Tony Blair, p.xlix,* Random House, 2011

4. *Ibid, p.xlix*

5. *Ibid, p13*

6. *Ibid, p26*

7. *Ibid, p36*

8. *Ibid, pp75-76*

9. *Ibid, p43*

10. *Ibid, p84*

11. *Quoted in Labour after Clause Four, Militant 1228,* 5 May 1995

12. *Ibid*

13. *Ibid*

14. *Clause Four: Opposition to Blair grows, Militant 1211,* 13 January 1995

15. *Backstage at the Rolling Rose Rally, Militant 1227,* 28 April 1995

16. *Sunday Times,* 23 April 1995

17. *A Meeting of Minds with Maggie?, Militant 1227, 28 April 1995*

18. *Blair Widens the Gap between Labour and the Unions, Militant 1238, 14 July 1995*

19. *Militant 35, March 1968*

20. *Blair, op cit, p85*

21. *Winning Hearts and Minds, Militant 1221, 17 March 1995*

22. *Blair's 'Modernisers' Turn Back the Clock, Militant 1228, 5 May 1995*

23. *Blair, op cit, p87*

3. BLAIR ENCOURAGES THE TORIES

1. *Labour off Tracks on Rail Privatisation, Militant 1212, 20 January 1995*

2. *Blair, op cit, p94*

3. *Ibid, p96*

4. *Ibid, p97*

5. *Dear Mr Blair, Militant 1239, 21 July 1995*

6. *Blair, op cit, p46*

7. *Free At Last: Diaries 1991-2001, Tony Benn, Random House, 2009, p274*

8. *Ibid, p272*

9. *Ibid, p288*

10. *See The Rise of Militant*

11. *Tony Blair's Unfinished Counter-Revolution, Militant 1244, 15 September 1995*

4. TIME FOR A NEW PARTY

1. *Time for a Socialist Labour Party?, Militant 1252, 10 November 1995*

2. *Can the Labour Party be Reclaimed?, Socialism Today 68, September 2002*

3. *Labour after Clause Four, Militant 1228, 5 May 1995*

4. *Time for a Socialist Labour Party?*

5. *All quotes from Future Strategy for the Left, A Discussion Paper, Arthur Scargill, 4 November 1995*

6. *Virtual Unreality: Where has Blair taken Labour? Militant 1248, 13 October 1995*

7. *Time for a Socialist Labour Party?*

8. *Militant's Real History*

9. *Time for a Socialist Labour Party?*

10. *Scargill Calls for Socialist Alternative, Militant 1253, 17 November 1995*

11. *Scargill, op cit*

12. *Editorial Comment, Militant 1253, 17 November 1995*

13. *The British General Election of 1992, D Butler and D Kavanagh, MacMillan Press, October 1992*

14. *Scargill, op cit*

15. *Editorial Comment, Militant 1253*

16. *Quoted in Ibid*

17. *Morning Star, quoted in Is the Time Right for a Socialist Party?, Militant 1256, 8 December 1995*

18. *What Now for the Left? Militant 1254, 24 November 1995*

19. *SLP Threatened by Exclusive Approach, Militant 1257, 15 December 1995*

20. *Ibid*

5. NEW PARTY, NEW FORMS OF ORGANISATION

1. *Success for New Party Depends on Openness and Democracy, Militant 1257, 15 December 1995*

2. *Editorial Comment, Militant 1262, 9 February 1996*

3. *A Workers' MP on a Worker's Wage, Militant 1262, 9 February 1996*

4. *SLP Conference: Socialism Endorsed but Policies Confused, Militant 1275, 10 May 1996*

5. *Scargill Says No Alliances, Militant 1273, 26 April 1996*

6. *Scargill Rejects Appeal for Unity, Militant 1280, 14 June 1996*

7. *Letter to Arthur Scargill, Militant 1304, 13 December 1996*

6. MILITANT LABOUR CAMPAIGNS

1. *Police Take Blame for Riot, Militant 1212, 20 January 1995*

2. *Labour Councillor Expelled for Supporting Socialism, Militant 1232, 2 June 1995*

3. *Campaign Puts Militant Labour on the Map, Militant 1219, 3 March 1995*

4. *Quoted in Blowing the Whistle on BNP Bullies, Militant 1219, 3 March 1995*

5. *Southampton Militant bring Council Back to Earth, Militant 1243, 8 September 1995*

6. *Results Show Support for Socialism, Militant 1275, 10 May 1996*

7. *Labour Haunted by the Ghost of Nellist, Coventry Evening Telegraph, 21 December 1994, quoted in 'Rottweiler' Dave Dogs Labour, Militant 1215, 3 February 1995*

8. *Militant Labour Conference 96, Militant 1260, 26 January 1996*

7. WORKERS FORMULATE POLICIES

1. *The Worldwide Struggle for Socialism, Militant 1261, 2 February 1996*

2. *Show Racism the Red Card, Militant 1269, 29 March 1996*

3. *Really Radical?, Socialism Today 8, May 1996*

4. *Stephen Lawrence Inquiry: Corruption and Racism, Socialist 71, 10 July 1998*

8. TRADE UNION WORK IN THE MID-1990S

1. *Health Workers Vote for Action: Strike Now! Militant 1231, 26 May 1995*

2. *Reject this Rotten Deal: Railworkers Talk to the Militant, Militant 1240, 28 July 1995*

3. *A Small Taste of Things to Come, Militant 1237, 7 July 1995*

4. *A Great Vote for the Left, Militant 1252, 10 November 1995*

9. FRAGMENTATION OF THE TORIES

1. *Tories: Is the Party Over?, Socialism Today 13, November 1996*

2. *Ibid*

3. *Who Needs Socialism? We Do, Militant 1292, 20 September 1996*

4. *The Changing Faces of Labour, Militant 1292, 20 September 1996*

5. *What Will Happen... in New Labour Britain?, Socialism Today 17, April 1997*

6. *Virtual Unreality: Where has Blair taken Labour?, Militant 1248, 13 October 1995*

7. *What Will Happen... in New Labour Britain? Ibid*

8. *New Labour or New Liberals?,*
Militant 1292, 20 September 1996

9. *Hidden Agendas, John Pilger,*
p538

10. *The State They're In, Militant*
1277, 24 May 1996

11. *Job Seekers' Allowance: Who*
Benefits?, Militant 1290, 6
September 1996

10. THE NATIONAL QUESTION
IN SCOTLAND AND WALES

1. *John Major, New Year's Message*
1995

2. *Tories Play the Union Card,*
Militant 1213, 20 January 1995

3. *See The Rise of Militant*

4. *Tories Routed: 10,000 Votes for*
SML, Scottish Militant 1224, 7 April
1995

5. *Scotland: The National*
Question and the Struggle for
Socialism, Militant 1242, 25 August
1995

6. *Will Britain Break Up?, The*
Socialist 3, 21 February 1997

7. *Ian Bell, The Scotsman, quoted*
in Scottish Socialist Alliance
Launched, Militant 1263, 16
February 1996

8. *Tory Wreckers Boost Support*
for Devolution, Militant 1217, 17
February 1995

11. OUR NAME CHANGE
DEBATE

1. *Statement on the Name of the*
Organisation, Members Bulletin 17,
19 May 1996

2. *The Third International after*
Lenin, Leon Trotsky

3. *Statement on the Name of the*
Organisation

4. *Ibid*

5. *Ibid*

6. *For the Socialist Party Proposal,*
Members Bulletin Name Change
Debate III, September 1996

7. *Socialists Make the Headlines,*
Socialist 2, 14 February 1997

12. GENERAL ELECTION
FINALLY CALLED

1. *Give Tories the Red Card,*
Socialist 7, 21 March 1997

2. *FCB opinion poll, 12 February*
1997, quoted in Vote Socialist,
Socialist 7, 21 March 1997

3. *Vote Socialist, Ibid*

4. *Who Owns Your MP?, Socialist*
8, 28 March 1997

5. *Sleazy Tories, Socialist 8, 28*
March 1997

6. *Media Bias, Socialist 8, 28*
March 1997

7. *The Rich: Kick 'Em into Orbit,*
Socialist 10, 11 April 1997

8. *Coventry's Socialist Agenda,*
Socialist 10, 11 April 1997

9. *Widespread Support for*
Socialist Ideas, Socialist 10, 11 April
1997

10. *Coventry: New Labour, New*
Tories, Socialist 11, 18 April 1997

11. *Why You Should Vote Socialist,*
Socialist 12, 25 April 1997

12. *Observer, quoted in Why You*
Should Vote Socialist

13. *Tories Wiped Out, Socialist 13,*
2 May 1997

14. *May Day Massacre for Tories,*
Socialist 14, 9 May 1997

15. *Tories Wiped Out, Ibid*

16. *Tory Collapse, Socialist 13, 2*
May 1997

17. *Radical Change is Not On*
Offer, Socialist 13, 2 May 1997

18. *Standing for Socialism, Socialist 13, 2 May 1997*

13. LIVERPOOL DOCKERS STRIKE

1. *Liverpool: Dockers Defiant to the End, Socialism Today 26, March 1998*

2. *Editorial Comment, Militant 1250, 27 October 1995*

3. *Somebody has to Make a Stand, Militant 1250, 27 October 1995*

4. *No Going Back to the Dark Ages, Militant 1255, 24 November 1995*

5. *Fighting for a Future, Militant 1260, 26 January 1996*

6. *Speech to the right-wing HR Nicholls Society, Melbourne Australia, 15 September 1990, quoted in Abolition of the Docks Labour Scheme: Straight from the Horse's Mouth, Socialist 16, 23 May 1997*

7. *TGWU Conference: Dockers Achieve Breakthrough, Socialist 23, 11 July 1997*

8. *Union Ranks Secure Dockers' Vote, Socialist 24, 18 July 1997*

9. *Liverpool: Dockers Defiant to the End*

10. *United in Struggle, Militant 1293, 27 September 1996*

14. THE DISPUTE WITH THE MERSEYSIDE COMRADES

1. *On Democratic Centralism and the Regime, Leon Trotsky, 1937*

2. *Democratic Centralism, Peter Taaffe, Published in Militant Labour Members Bulletin No.16, 18 March 1996*

3. *The Political Evolution of the Militant/Socialist Party in the 1990s: Merseyside's View, p1 para2*

4. *New Technology and Globalisation: Can a Capitalist Slump be Avoided?, Peter Taaffe 1999, p2*

5. *Ibid p4*

6. *Ibid pp4-5*

7. *Ibid p5*

8. *Ibid p5*

9. *In Defence of Marxism, Leon Trotsky, p92, Pioneer Publishers*

10. *The Rise of Militant, pp447-448*

11. *Addendum on Some Points of Theory, Paul Storey, 1992, p4*

12. *New Technology and Globalisation, p8*

13. *Ibid, p8*

14. *One World Ready or Not, William Greider, quoted in New Technology and Globalisation*

15. *New Technology and Globalisation, p15*

16. *Ibid, p16*

17. *Militant Labour Members Bulletin 25, December 1997*

18. *New Technology and Globalisation, p38*

19. *Leon Trotsky's Living Legacy, Socialism Today 201, October 2016*

15. NEW LABOUR IN GOVERNMENT

1. *Blair's First Month, Socialism Today 19, June 1997*

2. *Last Man Standing, Jack Straw, pp504-506*

3. *Free At Last, Tony Benn, p408*

4. *The Independent, 25 April 1997, quoted in Tony & Bill, Socialism Today, 19 June 1997*

5. *Ibid, p402*

6. *Ibid, p403*

7. Ibid, p417

8. Ibid, p421

9. Blair, op cit, pp115-116

10. Did You Vote for This? Socialist 20, 20 June 1997

11. Brown's Sleight of Hand, Socialist 23, 11 July 1997

12. Labour Privatises the NHS, Socialist 27, 8 August 1997

16. THE DEATH OF DIANA

1. Diana Outpouring: Virtual Protest?, Socialism Today 22, October 1997

2. The English Constitution, Walter Bagehot, 1867 edition p58

3. Ibid pp85-86

4. Diana Outpouring: Virtual Protest?

5. Observer, 7 September 1997

6. Diana Outpouring: Virtual Protest?

17. FIGHTING TUITION FEES

1. Labour and Liberals Coalition in the Air?, Socialist 32, 26 September 1997

2. Last Man Standing, p227

3. Benn, op cit, p450

4. Ibid, p454

5. Let Down and Disgusted but... Fighting Back, Socialist 41, 28 November 1997

6. The late Hugo Young, Guardian, quoted in Labour's 'Planet Happiness'! Socialist 35, 10 October 1997

7. Labour's 'Planet Happiness'!

8. The Blair-Ashdown 'Lovefest', Socialist 33, 3 October 1997

9. Benn op cit p450

10. A Show of Strength, Socialist 54, 13 March 1998

18. SECOND YEAR OF GOVERNMENT

1. Our Socialist Budget: For Need Not Profit, Socialist 54, 13 March 1998

2. Benn, op cit, p469

3. Ibid, p466

4. Ibid, p469

5. Ibid, pp482-483

6. Quoted in Blair's Fatal Weakness, Socialist 40, 21 November 1997

7. Friends in Low Places, Socialist 40, 21 November 1997

8. New Labour New Sleaze, Socialist 72, 17 July 1998

9. Who's Left in Labour?, Socialist 80, 25 September 1998

19. THE RIGHT REVOLTS AND THE COUNTRYSIDE ALLIANCE

1. Rural Reaction, Socialism Today 27, April 1998

2. Daily Telegraph, 28 February 1998

3. Ibid

4. Rural Reaction

5. Who's Left in Labour?, Socialist 80, 25 September 1998

6. Rover: Jobs on the Line, Socialist 85, 30 October 1998

7. Exposed! Slave Labour Bosses, Socialist 73, 24 July 1998

8. Jobs Gloom Deepens: No Return to the 1930s, Socialist 85, 30 October 1998

9. My Life, Leon Trotsky, Chapter 45

10. The Third Way Meets Reality, Socialism Today 33, November 1998

20. Jack Straw and general Pinochet

1. Last Man Standing, pp258-259
2. A Criminal Claiming Innocence, Socialist 92, 18 February 1998
3. Last Man Standing, p253
4. Ibid, pp261-262
5. Ibid, pp265
6. Ibid, pp264
7. Ibid, pp267

21. Livingstone and the left

1. Observer, 28 December 1997
2. Labour Left: Heading for a Split?, Socialism Today 25, February 1998
3. Observer, op cit
4. Quoted in Labour Left: Heading for a Split?
5. Ibid
6. Steve Richards interview with Ken Livingstone, New Statesman, 10 October 1997
7. Champagne Socialists or Campaign Socialists?, Socialist 96, 29 January 1999
8. Ken's Cheesy Remarks: The Worker 'Drones' Reply, Socialist 96, 29 January 1999
9. Giving Londoners a Choice, Socialist 97, 29 February 1999
10. Labour Left: Heading for a Split?, Socialism Today 25, February 1998

22. Corruption - bosses "worth fighting for"

1. The Mandelson Affair, Socialism Today 35, February 1999
2. Ibid
3. Ibid
4. Financial Times, 11 January 1999
5. Quoted in The Mandelson Affair
6. New Labour, Rover and the Market, Socialist 98, 12 February 1999

23. British economy

1. Stop the Jobs Slaughter, Socialist 82, 9 October 1998
2. Turn Anger into Action, Socialist 83, 16 October 1998
3. Why Not Bail Out Jobs?, Socialist 83, 16 October 1998
4. Privatisation: The Route to disaster, Socialist 131, 15 October 1999
5. Free At Last! Tony Benn, p554
6. Ibid, p558
7. Ibid, p559
8. Ibid, p561
9. Ibid, p568-9

24. A new millennium

1. Observer, 2 January 2000
2. 21st Century Socialism, Socialist 141, 14 January 2000
3. New Century, Old Attacks, Socialist 141, 14 January 2000
4. 21st Century Socialism
5. Labour's Troubles Are only just Beginning, Socialist 143, 28 January 2000
6. Kinnock's Poodle Bites Blair, Socialist 145, 11 February 2000
7. Free At Last, p610

25. An avalanche of redundancies

1. Nationalise Rover, Socialist 151, 31 March 2000
2. There is an Alternative, Socialist 152, 7 April 2000

2. See Liverpool: the City that Dared to Fight and The Rise of Militant

3. Ibid, pp313-314

4. Can Ken Deliver? Socialism Today 46, April 2000

5. Quoted in Why the GLC Caved In, Militant 741, 22 March 1985

6. Evening Standard, 19 October 1999

7. Independent, 7 March 2000

8. Guardian, 8 March 2000

9. Quoted in Ken Livingstone and a New Workers' Party, Socialism Today 46, April 2000

10. Ken Livingstone and a New Workers Party

11. Independent on Sunday, 7 May 2000

12. Livingstone after the Elections, Socialism Today 48, June 2000

13. Evening Standard, quoted in Livingstone Fails End of Year Report, Socialist 215, 20 July 2001

36. THE SOCIALIST ALLIANCES

1. Socialist Alliances Build for the Future, Socialist 78, 11 September 1998

2. Preparing a Socialist Alternative, Socialist 91, 11 December 1998

3. The Choice for Socialists in the London Elections, Socialist 153, 14 April 2000

37. 2001: ECONOMIC STORM CLOUDS

1. 2001: A Year of Workers' Reawakening, Socialist 187, 5 January 2001

2. Stop the Bosses' Jobs Slaughter, Socialist 189, 19 January 2001

3. 2001: A Year of Workers' Reawakening

4. Car Workers: Turn Pressure into Strike Action, Socialist 190, 26 January 2001

5. When Flunkies Fall Out, Socialist 191, 2 February 2001

6. Servants of Big Business, Socialist 191, 2 February 2001

7. The Case for Socialist Nationalisation, Socialist 192, 9 February 2001

8. It's their Crisis: Make the Bosses Pay, Socialist 200, 6 April 2001

9. A Cautious but Cunning Budget, Guardian, 9 March 2001

10. After the Drought, a Few Drops of Rain, Socialist 197, 16 March 2001

11. Quoted in After the Drought, a Few Drops of Rain

12. Well, Did Things get Better? Guardian, 20 February 2001

38. 2001 GENERAL ELECTION

1. Plain Sailing for Blair? Socialist 195, 2 March 2001

2. The Opposition to New Labour, Socialist Review 250, March 2001

3. Socialists and the Election, Socialism Today 55, April 2001

4. Resolution to Labour Left Briefing 2001 AGM

5. Britain's Growing Discontent, Socialism Today 57, June 2001

6. Independent, 9 June 2001

7. New Labour Turns Away Liverpool Voters, Socialist 210, 15 June 2001

8. Scotland's Election, Socialism Today 57, June 2001

9. All quoted in Asylum: Tories

and Labour Play the Race Card, Socialist 208, 1 June 2001

10. An Alternative to the Lesser of Two Evils, Socialist 205, 11 May 2001

11. Independent, quoted in Britain's Growing Discontent, Socialism Today 57, June 2001

12. Britain's Growing Discontent

13. Both quoted in Labour's 'Just in Time' Election, Socialist 209, 9 June 2001

14. Both quoted in New Labour's 'Ten Year' Plan, Socialist 206, 18 May 2001

39. THE CWI'S HISTORY AND WORK IN IRELAND

1. Crisis in Northern Ireland, Militant International Review, Autumn 1970

2. A Framework for What? Militant 1220, 10 March 1995

3. Workers' Unity the Key to Peace, Militant 1220, 10 March 1995

4. No Return to the Troubles, Militant 1263, 16 February 1996

5. The Loyalist Psyche, review in Socialism Today 40, July/August 1999

6. Should Marches be Banned? Militant 1285, 19 July 1997

7. Joe Higgins and Clare Daly: Jailed over the Bin Tax, Socialist 317, 4 October 2003

8. Joe and Clare after their Release from Mountjoy Prison, Socialist 320, 25 October 2003

9. All that's left? A Profile of Joe Higgins TD, Sunday Business Post, 17 April 2005

10. Bosses Low Pay Racket Exposed: Socialist Party Action

Uncovers Massive Wage Fraud, Socialist 387, 7 April 2005

40. THE EFFECTS OF SETBACKS

1. Asia's Financial Whirlwind, Socialist 29, 5 September 1997

2. Who Lost Russia? Socialism Today 32, October 1998

3. Time, 8 January 2001

4. Economist, 23 August 2001

41. THE DOTCOM BUBBLE BURSTS

1. World Recession Looms, Socialist 221, 14 September 2001

2. World Economy: Deepest Downturn since the 1930s? Socialist 229, 9 November 2001

3. See our documents on the Tendency of the Rate of Profit to Fall

4. 2002: Capitalist Crisis – Workers' Struggles, Socialist 235, 4 January 2002

5. Enron's Collapse: Workers Feel Pain of Layoffs and Added Sting of Betrayal, New York Times, 21 January 2002

6. Daily Mirror, 29 June 2002

7. Bye Bye American Pie, Observer, 30 June 2002

8. Behind the Financial Scandals, Socialist 263, 19 July 2002

9. The Naked Kleptocracy that Leads Britain's Private Sector, Guardian, 8 December 2004

10. Fighting a Failing System, Socialist 375, 8 January 2005

11. Guardian, 26 October 2004

12. Cabinet Secretary under Thatcher, Major and, briefly, Blair

13. Fighting a Failing System

14. It's the economy, dammit, Observer, 24 October 2004

15. Profits Soar, Wages Fall in the Globalised Economy, Socialist 389, 21-27 April 2005

42. ANTI-CAPITALIST MOVEMENTS

1. One World, Ready Or Not: The Manic Logic of Global Capitalism, William Greider, Penguin Books, 1998

2. Activists Trigger Security Scare, Guardian, 30 November 1999

3. Real Battle for Seattle, Observer, 4 December 1999

4. The Return of Karl Marx, New Yorker, October 20, 1997

5. Bosses Threaten all Protesters, Socialist 157, 12 May 2000

6. Ex-Soldier Admits Defacing Statue of Churchill, Guardian, 8 May 2000

7. Australian Herald, 28 August 2000

8. Australian Anti-Capitalist Action, Socialism Today 51, October 2000

9. World Social Forum, Socialist 194, 23 February 2001

10. Association pour la Taxation des Transactions financières et pour l'Action Citoyenne (Association for the Taxation of financial Transactions and Citizens Action)

11. The politics of anti-capitalism, Socialism Today 56, May 2001

12. Independent, 23 April 2001

13. Global Capitalism: A System Under Siege, Socialist 204, 4 May 2001

14. Hackney Workers Strike on May Day, Socialist 204, 4 May 2001

15. Storm in Quebec, Socialism Today 57, June 2001

16. Gothenburg's Police State, Socialist 211, 22 June 2001

17. After Gothenburg... Anti-Capitalist Resistance Continues, Socialist 211, 22 June 2001

18. ATTAC! Socialism Today 58, July/August 2001

19. Soros: May Day Protesters do have a Point, Observer 6 May 2001

20. Genoa and the Future of the Anti-Capitalist Movement, Socialism Today 59, September 2001

21. Summit for Nothing, Socialist 216, 27 July 2001

22. The Aftermath of Genoa, Socialist 217, 10 August 2001

43. SOCIALIST ALLIANCE SPLITS

1. The Future of the Socialist Alliance, Socialist 217, 10 August 2001

2. What Future for the Socialist Alliance? Socialist 229, 9 November 2001

3. A Critical Conference for the Socialist Alliance, Socialist 230, 16 November 2001

4. From Judy Beishon's own notes

5. Liz Davies, 21 October 2002

6. Open Letter from Socialist Party Wales to the Welsh Socialist Alliance National Council, October 2002

44. AL QA'IDA AND 9/11

1. Attacks on the US – Aftershocks Rock the Globe, Socialist 222, 21 September 2001

2. Stratfor (strategic forecasters) website, 11 September 2001

3. *Attacks on the US – Aftershocks Rock the Globe*

4. *September 11 – Political and Economic Aftershocks, a Socialist Analysis, CWI statement, 14 September 2001*

5. *Ibid*

6. *American Muslims Fear Reprisals amid Calls for Swift Revenge, Guardian, 12 September, 2001*

7. *September 11, 2001, Washington Post, 12 September 2001*

8. *Attack System of Terrorism, International Herald Tribune, 13 September 2001*

9. *September 11 – Political and Economic Aftershocks, a Socialist Analysis*

10. *A Journey: My Political Life, Tony Blair, p342*

11. *Ibid, p347*

12. *Ibid, p355*

13. *Ibid, p358*

14. *Ibid, p351*

15. *Ibid, p358*

45. WAR IN AFGHANISTAN

1. *A Journey, Blair p360*

2. *Ibid, p361*

3. *Ibid, p364*

4. *Ibid, p362*

5. *Ibid, p369*

6. *Military Action No Solution, Socialist 222, 21 September 2001*

7. *Iraq: Clinton's Deadly Endgame, Socialist 88, 20 November 1998*

8. *Afghanistan, Islam and the Revolutionary Left, socialistworld. net*

9. *War is No Solution, Socialist 224, 5 October 2001*

10. *Just who are our Allies in Afghanistan? Independent, 2 October 2001*

11. *Mirror, 18 September, 2001*

12. *A New World for the Last Superpower, Socialism Today 60, October 2001*

13. *Images of Past Wars may not Fit Present Foe, Washington Post, 16 September 2001*

14. *Better to be Silent than Out of Step when Bush Bangs the Drum, Independent, 18 September 2001*

15. *Fear and Loathing, Guardian, 19 September 2001*

16. *A New World for the Last Superpower*

17. *New York Times service, quoted in International Herald Tribune, 14 September 2001*

18. *Quoted in A New World for the Last Superpower*

19. *Financial Times, 18 September 2001*

20. *The Clash of Fundamentalisms: Crusades, Jihads and Modernity, Tariq Ali, Verso 2003, p197*

21. *A New World for the Last Superpower*

46. PREPARATIONS FOR THE IRAQ INVASION

1. *War Disturbs the Most Dangerous Political Tectonic Plate in the World, Independent, 7 October 2001*

2. *Hansard, 10 April 2002*

3. *Blair, op cit, p463*

4. *Mail on Sunday, 21 October 2001*

5. *Building a Mass Anti-War Movement, Socialist 283, 17 January 2003*

6. *Last Man Standing: Memoirs of a Political Survivor, Jack Straw, Pan MacMillan 2012, p361*

7. *War on Iraq: The Pressures Grow, Socialist 283, 17 January 2003*

8. *Benn, Diaries 2001-2007; More Time for Politics, p8*

9. *Ibid, p10*

10. *Ibid, p12*

11. *US Begins Secret Talks to Secure Iraq's Oilfields, Guardian, 23 January 2003*

12. *Hans Blix: From the Hell of Iraq, Hope for an Era of Peace, Independent on Sunday, 16 February 2014*

13. *Build solidarity action with the firefighters, Socialist 285, 31 January 2003*

47. MASSIVE WORLDWIDE RESISTANCE TO IRAQ WAR

1. *Global Resistance to the War – Massive Protest in Bush's Backyard. Socialist 284, 24 January 2003*

2. *Daily Mirror, 6 February 2003*

3. *Anti-War Demonstration, February 15 2003: The Day that Made History, Socialist 288, 21 February 2003*

4. *Socialism on the March, Socialist 288, 21 February 2003*

5. *Cheers for System Change, Socialist 288, 21 February 2003*

6. *The World Turned Upside Down, Socialist 288, 21 February 2003*

7. *A Top General's Thoughts on Iraq, Christian Science Monitor, 5 March 2003*

8. *Financial Times, 25 March 2003*

9. *Step Up Action against this*

Bloody War, Socialist 293, 28 March 2003

10. *The Rising of the Youth, Socialist 293, 28 March 2003*

48. AFTER IRAQ, WHO NEXT?

1. *War and the 'New World Disorder', Socialist 293, 28 March 2003*

2. *The Chaotic Aftermath of War, Socialist 296, 19 April 2003*

3. *Ibid*

4. *FE lecturers: Vote 'No' to Miserable Pay Offer, Socialist 291, 14 March 2003*

5. *Paul Mackney Replies, Socialist 293, 28 March 2003*

6. *Hansard, 30 April 2003*

7. *Kelly Death Deepens Blair's Crisis, Socialist 320, 26 July 2003*

8. *Hutton Inquiry: a Can of Worms for Blair, Socialist 23 August 2003*

9. *Saddam's Capture – Not the 'Beginning of the End' in Iraq, Socialist 328, 20 December 2003*

49. THE WAR AT HOME

1. *War on the Home Front, Socialism Today 61, November 2001*

2. *Guardian, 11 October 2001*

3. *'A Stimulating Debate, Economist, 25 October 2001*

4. *War on the Home Front*

5. *Strike Back at School Sell-Offs, Socialist 213, 6 July 2001*

6. *Workers Strike as Labour does the Dirty Deed, Socialist 216, 27 July 2001*

7. *Anti-Privatisation Conference: 'We're Determined to Fight Back and Win', Socialist 232, 30 November 2001*

8. *Railtrack – New Labour's U-Turn*, Socialist 225, 12 October 2001

9. *Son of Railtrack: Nationalisation – But not as we Know it*, Socialist 227, 26 October 2001

10. *Why Labour Climbed Down on Tuition Fees*, Socialist 225, 26 October 2001

11. *Solidarity and a Bold Leadership Needed*, Socialist 239, 1 February 2002

12. *Militant Tendency Shows the Way*, Socialist 240, 8 February 2002

50. Opposition on all fronts

1. *Coventry Socialist Party Councillor making a Difference*, Socialist 295, 12 April 2003

2. *Coventry Socialists Launch Election Drive*, Socialist 245, 15 March 2002

3. *Politics is Dull and Boring*, Socialist 249, 12 April 2002

4. *Winning Benefits for Local People*, Socialist 250, 19 April 2002

5. *Step up the Fight for Socialism*, Socialist 253, 10 May 2002

6. *Vote for Real Change: Vote Socialist*, Socialist 323, 15 November 2003

7. *A New Movement Emerging*, Socialism Today 73, March 2003

51. George Galloway and respect

1. *A New Movement Emerging*, Socialism Today 73, March 2003

2. *A New Alternative to New Labour?*, Socialist 290, 7 March 2003

3. *Where Now After Galloway's Expulsion?* Socialist 321, 1 November 2003

4. *Apparently it's all my Fault...*, Socialist 319, 18 October 2003

5. *Respect Unity Coalition – What we Think*, Socialist 330, 17 January 2004

6. *Socialism and Left Unity*, Peter Taaffe, p46

7. *I'm Not the Only One*, George Galloway, Allen Lane, 2004, p41

8. *Ibid*, p40

9. *Ibid*, pp135-137

10. *Respect and the June Elections*, Socialist 353, 26 June 2004

52. European Union and the euro

1. *The Europe of the Workers*, Militant 1303, 6 December 1996

2. The CWI's Belgian comrades became Linkse Socialistiche Partij in 2001. The Francophone comrades were organised as *Mouvement pour une Alternative Socialiste* (MAS) from 1999 and they became the *Parti Socialiste de Lutte* (PSL) in 2009

3. *The Anger Behind the 'March in White'*, Militant 1296, 25 October 1996

53. Building Socialism in the US

1. *Union Fighters Form Labor Party*, Militant 1281, 21 June 1996

2. *More War Years?* Socialism Today 88, December/January 2004-05

54. Visiting Russia

1. Referred to in Socialist 63, 15 May 1998

14. *Pakistan – A Powder Keg Ready to Explode, Socialist 387, 7 April 2005*

15. *Hurricane Katrina: A Disaster Made Worse by Capitalism, Socialist 406, 25 August 2005*

16. *Class, Race and Katrina, Socialism Today 95, October 2005*

17. *Bush Presidency Goes into Freefall, Socialist 414, 3 November 2005*

63. Mass movement against world poverty

1. *Front cover of Special G8 issue of the Socialist and International Socialist (Scotland), 30 June 2005*

2. *Fight for a Socialist Plan, Socialist 399, 30 June 2005*

3. *'Fantastic' CWI meeting, Socialist 400, 7 July 2005*

64. London and Madrid Bombings

1. *Quoted in Blair's Blowback, Guardian, 11 July 2005*

2. *London Bombings and Iraq, Socialist 401, 14 July 2005*

3. *Horror on our Doorstep, Socialist 401, 14 July 2005*

4. *A London Bus Driver's View, Socialist 401, 14 July 2005*

5. *Stop Fire Service Cuts, Socialist 401, 14 July 2005*

6. *Blair Plea to Muslim Leaders at No 10 Meeting, Guardian, 20 July 2005*

7. *No to Terror, Guardian Letters, 22 July 2005*

8. *Workers Maintain Class Unity, Socialist 402, 21 July 2005*

9. *'Blair Vows to Root out Extremism', Guardian 6 August 2005*

65. "Labour a sham": Steps towards a new party

1. *Engels to H Schlüter, 11 January, 1890*

2. *Towards a New Workers' Party, Socialism Today 96, November 2005*

3. *Daily Mirror, 29 September 2005*

4. *New Mass Workers' Party: Conference for Action Needed, Socialist 413, 27 October 2005*

5. *This Strangulation of Dreams is Creating a Phantom Party, Guardian, 30 September 2005*

6. *New Labour? More like Neutered Labour, Daily Mirror, 29 September 2005*

7. *New Mass Workers' Party: Conference for Action Needed*

8. *Sunday Times, 25 September 2005*

9. *Labour Will Spend this Week Avoiding the Key Questions, Guardian, 26 September 2005*

10. *Why I'm Tearing up my Labour Party Card, Observer, 2 October 2005*

11. *Towards a New Workers' Party*

12. *New Mass Workers' Party: Conference for Action Needed*

13. *Successful Launch Conference, Socialist 432, 23 March 2006*

14. *Hope and Desperation, Socialist 450, 27 July 2006*

15. *John McDonnell's Leadership Bid, Socialist 450, 27 July 2006*

16. *More Time for Politics, Diaries 2001-2007, Tony Benn, p143*

17. *Ibid, p141*

18. *Ibid p145*

19. *Ibid p299*

20. *More Time for Politics Review, Socialist 516, 17 January 2008*

21. *How can an Alternative to the Main Political Parties be Developed? Socialist 519, 6 February 2008*

22. *Socialist Party Welcomes Debate, Socialist 519, 6 February 2008*

66. PARTY ACTIVITY

1. *Rattling the Bars, Guardian 18 November 2003*

2. *Fighting for Socialism, Socialism Today 100, April-May2006*

3. *Socialist Party Councillors Make a Difference, Socialist 434, 6 April 2006*

4. *Victory for NHS Campaign, Socialist 439, 11 May 2006*

5. *'Kidderminster Factor' Visits Huddersfield, Socialist 439, 11 May 2006*

6. *Faces of Labour: the Inside Story, Andy McSmith, Verso Books 1996, p116. The error was corrected in a later edition.*

7. *Militant Pioneer Dies, Socialist 450, 27 July 2006*

8. *Campaign Brings Victory Against Cuts, Socialist 489, 31 May 2007*

9. *Local Campaign Successes Show Effective Leadership in Action, Socialist 489, 31 May 2007*

67. POST-2005 GENERAL ELECTION

1. *Amid all the Doom and Gloom, There are Signs of a Way Out of this Mess, Independent 15 November 2005*

2. *Blair's Reign Unravels, Socialism Today 97, Dec-Jan 2005-06*

3. *Fatal Loss of UK Nerve on Pensions, Financial Times, October 20, 2005*

4. *Blair's Reign Unravels*

5. *Growing Class Struggles will Increase Tensions, Socialist 396, 9-15 June 2005*

6. *Defend Workers' Rights, Socialist 405, 25 August 2005*

7. *Gate Gourmet – Solidarity Action is Vital, Socialist 405, 25 August 2005*

8. *Victory for Andy Beadle as he Wins his Job Back, Socialist 419, 8 December 2005*

9. *Hands Off our Pensions, Socialist 408, 22 September 2005*

10. *Pensions Battle Not Over – but Labour in Retreat, Socialist 413, 27 October 2005*

68. DEMISE OF BLAIR

1. *Tony Benn, More Time for Politics: Diaries 2001-2007, p203*

2. *Left Victory in Firefighters' Union, Socialist 392, 12 May 2005*

3. *The Socialist 432, 23 March 2006*

4. *Nine Years is Long Enough, Guardian 20 March 2006*

5. *Benn, op cit, pp304-305*

6. *Ibid, p309*

7. *The Last Throw of the Dice, Observer, 7 May 2006*

8. *Blair's Election Defeat, Socialism Today 101, June 2006*

9. *Dangers in Respect's Development, Socialist 439, 11 May 2006*

10. *Servants of the People: The Inside Story of New Labour, Andrew Rawnsley, Penguin UK, 2001*

11. *Dangers in Respect's Development*

12. *Blair's Long Goodbye, Socialist 456, 28 September 2006*

13. *Good Riddance to Blair! Socialist 487, 17 May 2007*

14. *Blair's Departure: Curtain Falls on Disastrous Reign, Socialist 486, 15 May 2007*

15. *Corbyn's Progress, Tariq Ali, London Review of Books, 3 March 2016*

16. *The Coronation of Gordon Brown, Socialism Today 110, June 2007*

17. *Financial Times, 2 May 2007*

18. *The Coronation of Gordon Brown*

Index

626

LAFONTAINE, *Oskar* 58, 550

LAMONT, *Norman* 177

LANGE, *David* 90

LANSLEY, *Andrew* 295

LARKIN, *James* 62, 304

LAW, *Peter* 518

LAWRENCE, *Stephen* 61, 75, 76

LAY, *Kenneth* 346

LEECH, *Jess* 471

LEFT UNITY (CPSA) 229

LEFT UNITY (PCS) 431, 491, 494

LENIN, *Vladimir* 3, 69, 92, 101,
126, 127, 239, 251, 261,
262, 333, 529

LEONARD, *Julia* 63, 64, 266

LIBERAL DEMOCRATS 14, 154,
155, 158, 159, 168, 172,
186, 190, 193, 205, 218,
220, 233, 267, 269, 274,
276, 293, 294, 295, 408,
409, 429, 430, 437, 482,
517, 518, 519, 550, 559,
569

LILLEY, *Peter* 15

LIMONOV, *Eduard* 458

LINKE - *The Left Party (Germany)*
58, 59, 545, 550, 551

LIT - *Workers' International
League* 67

LIVINGSTONE, *Ken* ix, 157, 181,
183, 184, 185, 186, 187,
199, 200, 244, 271, 272,
273, 274, 275, 276, 277,
280, 281, 298, 483, 539

LLOYD *George, David* 88

LLOYD, *Marion* 229

LOACH, *Ken* 108, 266, 443

LSSP - *Lanka Sama Samaja Party
(Sri Lanka)* 529

LTTE - *Liberation Tigers of Tamil
Eelam* 526

LUDWIG, *Claus* 551

LULA - *Luíz Inácio da Silva* 462,
466, 467, 468

LUTTE OUVRIÈRE 42

LYONS, *Roger* 286

M5S - *Five Star Movement (Italy)*
129

MAB - *Muslim Association of
Britain* 402

MACDONALD, *Ramsay* 159, 168,
190, 548, 568, 577

MACKAY, *Teresa* 122

MACKNEY, *Paul* 409, 420, 421

MACMILLAN, *Harold* 162

MACREADIE, *John* 50, 473

MADURO, *Nicolás* 464

MAGUIRE, *Tony* 502

MAHMOOD, *Lesley* 54

MAJOR, *John* 11, 12, 15, 17, 33,
76, 85, 87, 94, 107, 112,
114, 115, 167, 519,

MANDELSON, *Peter* 36, 90, 157,
168, 178, 181, 189, 190,
191, 204, 210, 287, 288,
585

MARQUSEE, *Mike* 368

MARSHALL, *Paul* 267

MARXIST WORKERS' TENDENCY
(South Africa) 132

MARX, *Karl* 3, 11, 22, 25, 70, 136,
261, 262, 333, 334, 339,
341, 344, 345, 346, 354,
473, 503, 520

MASON, *Paul* 141

MAXWELL, *Robert* 190

MAY, *Theresa* 90, 290

631